AUTOMOTIVE BODY REPAIR AND REFINISHING

SECOND EDITION

WILLIAM H. CROUSE
and
DONALD L. ANGLIN

GREGG DIVISION
McGRAW-HILL BOOK COMPANY

New York   Atlanta   Dallas   St. Louis   San Francisco
Auckland   Bogotá   Guatemala   Hamburg   Lisbon
London   Madrid   Mexico   Montreal   New Delhi   Panama   Paris
San Juan   São Paulo   Singapore   Sydney   Tokyo   Toronto

Sponsoring Editor: D. Eugene Gilmore
Editing Supervisor: James Fields
Design and Art Supervisor/Cover Designer: Frances Conte Saracco
Production Supervisor: Priscilla Taguer

Text Designer: Gene Garone
Cover Illustrator: David R. Archambault
Technical Illustration: Fine Line Illustrations, Inc., and Bob Beane

ABOUT THE AUTHORS

William H. Crouse

Behind William H. Crouse's clear technical writing is a background of sound mechanical engineering training as well as a variety of practical industrial experience. After finishing high school, he spent a year working in a tinplate mill. Summers, while still in school, he worked in General Motors plants, and for three years he worked in the Delco-Remy Division shops. Later he became Director of Field Education in the Delco-Remy Division of General Motors Corporation, for which he prepared service bulletins and educational literature.

Mr. Crouse has contributed numerous articles to automotive and engineering magazines, and has written many books about science and technology. He was the first Editor-in-Chief of the 15-volume *McGraw-Hill Encyclopedia of Science and Technology*. In addition, he has authored more than 50 technical books, including *Automotive Mechanics*, which has sold over a million copies. His books have been widely translated and used in automotive mechanics training throughout the world.

William H. Crouse's outstanding work in the automotive field has earned for him membership in the Society of Automotive Engineers and in the American Society of Engineering Education.

Donald L. Anglin

Trained in the automotive and diesel service field, Donald L. Anglin has worked both as a mechanic and as a service manager. He has taught automotive courses in high school, trade schools, community colleges, and universities. He has also worked as curriculum supervisor and school administrator for an automotive trade school. Interested in all types of vehicle performance, he has served as a racing-car mechanic and as a consultant to truck fleets on maintenance problems.

Currently, he devotes full time to technical writing, teaching, and visiting automotive instructors and service shops. Together with William H. Crouse, he has coauthored a number of magazine articles on automotive education, as well as several books in the McGraw-Hill Automotive Technology Series.

Donald L. Anglin is a Certified General Automotive Mechanic, a Certified General Truck Mechanic, and he holds many other licenses and certificates in automotive education, service, and related areas. His extensive work in the automotive service field has been recognized by membership in the American Society of Mechanical Engineers and the Society of Automotive Engineers.

Library of Congress Cataloging in Publication Data

Crouse, William Harry, date
    Automotive body repair and refinishing.

    Includes index.
    1. Automobiles—Bodies—Maintenance and repair.
I. Anglin, Donald L. II. Title.
TL255.C69   1986   629.2′6   84-25097
ISBN 0-07-014867-8

ISBN 0-07-014867-8

CONTENTS

PREFACE

Much has happened since the publication of the first edition of *Automotive Body Repair and Refinishing*. At the time the first edition appeared, almost 95 percent of new cars had a separate frame with the body mounted on it. This is called body-and-frame construction. And only 5 percent were of the unitized body, or unibody, type of construction. Now, the percentages are reversed. That is, 95 percent of all new cars are unibody construction!

Also, since 1975, the use of high-strength, low-alloy (HSLA) steel for body panels and structural parts has increased by 150 percent. The HSLA steels have a very high tensile strength ranging from 80,000 to 150,000 pounds per square inch (psi). This contrasts with 50,000 psi for the cold-rolled, low-carbon steels that have been used for body panels and structural parts. Thus, using HSLA steel means a great savings in weight. Thinner, lighter-weight panels of HSLA steel have the same strength as the low-carbon steels formerly used. In 1975, the average car weighed 3800 pounds. In 1985, the average was 2700 pounds. This weight savings was not entirely due to using HSLA steel, however. Cars were downsized, and weight was saved in engines, transmissions, brakes, cooling systems —even the spare tire!

The use of HSLA steel has required a new approach to collision repair. To retain the strength of this steel, the heating of areas surrounding a collision repair must be minimized. For this reason, the metal inert-gas (MIG) welding process is now recommended for repairing HSLA steel panels.

The swing to unibody construction has also necessitated the use of special straightening equipment, such as the bench system of body alignment. New straightening techniques are also required to retain component strength.

Also, in recent years, the front-wheel-drive car has become very popular, with most new cars using a front-wheel-drive arrangement. Front-wheel drive has introduced a whole new dimension to body repair. Now, auto body technicians have to handle not only sheet-metal and structural repair, but also steering, suspension, and front-drive elements.

In recognition of so many new developments, *Automotive Body Repair and Refinishing* has been completely rewritten, and much new material has been added to cover these advances. The book maintains its original objective—to supply complete and current coverage of the practices used in the more than 60,000 body and paint shops in the United States. All aspects of body repair and repainting are covered, with emphasis on the most up-to-date methods.

Automotive Body Repair and Refinishing, Second Edition, covers the subjects included in the National Institute for Automotive Service Excellence (ASE) certification tests: *Body Repair* and *Painting and Refinishing.* These ASE tests are used for certifying specialists under the ASE voluntary testing and certification program.

A *Workbook for Automotive Body Repair and Refinishing,* Second Edition, is available for use in the shop. This workbook has been especially developed to provide the student with specific instructions in the most commonly performed shop jobs. These are the jobs considered basic to the profession of body repair and refinishing.

Also available, to instructors only, is the second edition of the *Instructor's Planning Guide for Automotive Body Repair and Refinishing.* It includes articles that will help the instructor gain new insight into the field.

These materials add up to an instructional program that will fit any type of teaching situation whose purpose is to train automotive body repair and refinishing technicians.

The authors are grateful to the many people, both in the industry and in education, whose contributions and suggestions have helped to shape this new edition of the book.

WILLIAM H. CROUSE
DONALD L. ANGLIN

ACKNOWLEDGMENTS

During the preparation of *Automotive Body Repair and Refinishing*, the authors were given invaluable aid and inspiration by many, many people in the automotive industry and in the field of education. The authors gratefully acknowledge their indebtedness and offer their sincere thanks to these people. All cooperated by providing accurate, complete information that is useful in training automotive technicians.

Special thanks are owed to the following organizations for having supplied information and illustrations: American Motors Corporation; Applied Power, Inc.; ATW; Badger Air-Brush Company; Binks Manufacturing Company; The Black & Decker Manufacturing Company; Buick Motor Division of General Motors Corporation; Cadillac Motor Car Division of General Motors Corporation; Channellock, Inc.; Chevrolet Motor Division of General Motors Corporation; Chicago Pneumatic Tool Company; Chrysler Corporation; Dana Corporation; DeVilbiss Company; Ditzler Automotive Finisher Division of PPG Industries, Inc.; Du Pont; Fisher Body Division of General Motors Corporation; Ford Motor Company; General Motors Corporation; Guy Chart Tools Limited; Harris Calorific; Hunter Engineering Company; Kamweld Products Company, Inc.; Lenco, Inc.; The Lincoln Electric Company; Lincoln St. Louis Division of McNeil Corporation; 3M Company; Metalflake, Inc.; Nicator, Inc.; Oatley Corporation; Oldsmobile Division of General Motors Corporation; Pontiac Motor Division of General Motors Corporation; Rego Company; Reynolds & Reynolds, Inc.; Rinshed-Mason Company; Rockwell International Corporation; Sherwin-Williams Company; Snap-on Tools Corporation; Society of Automotive Engineers, Inc.; Stanley Tool Company; Toyota Motor Sales Company, Ltd.; Union Carbide Corporation; and Volkswagen of America, Inc. To all these organizations and the people who represent them, sincere thanks.

TO THE STUDENT

As you study, you should be getting practical experience in the shop. That is, you should handle automotive parts, automotive tools, and automotive servicing equipment. You should perform actual servicing jobs. To assist you in your shop work, there is the *Workbook for Automotive Body Repair and Refinishing*, Second Edition, that includes 33 jobs covering basic servicing procedures required in the body and paint shop. If you do every job covered in the workbook, you will have had "hands-on" experience that will provide you with skill and confidence.

If you are taking a regular course in a school, you have an instructor to guide you in your classroom and shop activities. But even if you are not taking a regular course, the workbook can act as an instructor. It tells you, step by step, how to do the various jobs. Perhaps you can meet others who are taking a regular school course in automotive body repair and refinishing. You can talk over any problems you have with them. A local body and paint shop is a good source of practical information. If you can get acquainted with the automotive technicians there, you will find that they have a large amount of practical information. Watch them at their work if you can. Make notes of important points and file them in your notebook.

Service Publications

While you are in a shop, study the various publications they receive. Automobile manufacturers and suppliers publish shop manuals, service bulletins, and parts catalogs. They are published to help service technicians do a better job. In addition, automotive magazines deal with the problems and methods of automotive service. Paint manufacturers have excellent magazines on automotive and truck refinishing. These publications will be of great value to you. Study them carefully.

Such activities will help you get practical experience. Sooner or later, this experience plus the knowledge you gain in studying *Automotive Body Repair and Refinishing* will permit you to step into the automotive shop on a fulltime basis. Or, if you are already in the shop, they will equip you for a better and a more responsible job.

Checking up on Yourself

At the end of each chapter, you will have the chance to check your progress by answering a series of questions. Each prog- ress quiz should be taken just after you have completed the pages preceding it. The quizzes allow you to check yourself. Because they are review tests, you should review the entire chapter by rereading it, or at least checking the important points, before trying a test. If a question stumps you, reread the section indicated at the end of the question to find the answer. This type of review is valuable because it helps you remember the information you will need when you go out into the automotive shop.

Keeping a Notebook

Keeping a notebook is a valuable part of your training. Start it now, at the beginning of your studies. Your notebook will help you in many ways. It will be a record of your progress. It will become a storehouse of valuable information that you will refer to time after time. It will help you learn. It will help you organize your training program in a way that will do you the most good.

When you study a lesson in the book, have your notebook open before you. Start with a fresh notebook page at the beginning of each lesson. Write the lesson title or textbook page number at the top of the page, along with the date. As you read through your lesson, jot down the important points.

In the shop, make your notes on a small scratch pad or on cards. Transfer these notes to your notebook as soon as possible.

Make sketches in your notebook. Save articles and illustrations from technical and hot-rod magazines. File them in your notebook. Also, save the instruction sheets that come with new parts. Paste or tape these to sheets of paper, and file them in your notebook.

Your notebook will become one of your most valuable possessions. It will be a permanent record of how you learned about automotive body repair and refinishing.

Glossary and Index

There is a glossary (a list of definitions) of automotive body repair and refinishing terms in the back of the book. If you are not sure about the meaning of a term, or the purpose of a part, refer to the glossary. There is also an index at the back of the book. This index will guide you to the page in the book where you can find the information you need.

PART 1
THE AUTOMOTIVE BODY SHOP

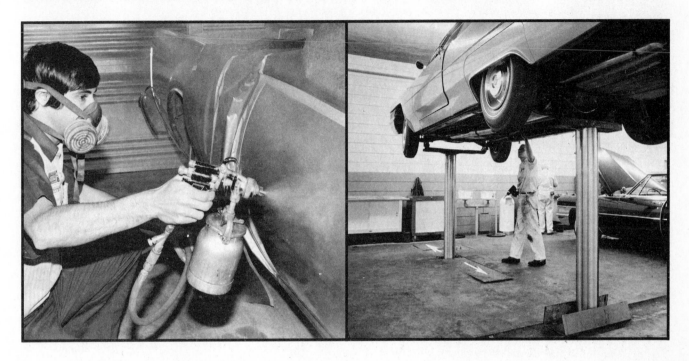

In this part, we discuss opportunities in the automotive body-repair business. Then we introduce you to a typical automobile body, describe its component parts and accessories, and explain how everything is put together. This is important information, because the body-repair technician must know the car body inside and out to work successfully on it. The body includes not only the panels that you can see but also the underbody and the frame. In addition, the glass (called the *glazing*), grills, trim, molding, bumpers, doors, door latches and locks, windows and window controls, upholstery, seats and seat controls, and safety equipment such as seat belts and air bags are all considered part of the body and are included in this book.

Part 1 of this book also includes discussions of the tools and materials used in the body shop. In addition, Part 1 covers safe operating practices that will help prevent anyone getting hurt in the shop. There are eight chapters in Part 1, as follows:

Chapter 1 Opportunities in Automotive Body Repair
Chapter 2 Automobile Body Construction
Chapter 3 Safety in the Shop
Chapter 4 Fasteners, Gaskets, Sealants, and Adhesives
Chapter 5 Hand Tools
Chapter 6 Body-Shop Electric Power Tools
Chapter 7 Pneumatic Tools
Chapter 8 Hydraulic Body Tools

CHAPTER 1
OPPORTUNITIES IN AUTOMOTIVE BODY REPAIR

After studying this chapter, you should be able to:

1. Discuss opportunities in automotive body repair.
2. Explain why more auto body technicians are needed.
3. Discuss the various jobs in the automotive body shop.
4. Explain what it takes to have a successful body shop.

≡ 1-1 WHY MORE AUTO BODY TECHNICIANS ARE NEEDED

Estimates show that more than 30 million paint and body jobs go through body shops every year. The total bill for all this work runs into many billions of dollars. This means that it takes hundreds of thousands of men and women working in body-repair shops to handle all this business.

There are about 63,000 auto body and paint shops and about 200,000 body and paint technicians working in these shops. But this is not enough. Walk down the street in any city and look at the cars passing and parked at the curb. You will see many cars in need of body and paint work. Many of the owners of these cars would like to have this work done. However, the owners are often put off by being told to come back to the shop in a few days or weeks. The shops they check with may be booked up a long time in advance.

There is a great deal of body work to be done. However, body shops and body-repair technicians are not always available to do the work when the car owner wants it done. This means that there are opportunities in the auto-body-repair field for anyone who wants to work on automobiles. Body-repair work is more than simply removing and replacing parts, using hand tools. The auto body technician gets great personal satisfaction from taking a car that has been damaged and restoring it to its original condition.

≡ 1-2 JOBS IN THE AUTO BODY SHOP

Many people think in terms of two jobs when they talk about auto body repair. These are metalwork and painting. But there are many more jobs than these performed in the auto body shop. In the body shop (Fig. 1-1) which handles complete vehicle rebuilding, you might see the following:

1. Manager (who may be the owner)
2. Foreman
3. Estimator
4. Body-repair technicians
5. Power-equipment operators (such as frame and alignment specialists)

Fig. 1-1 A typical automotive body shop.

6. Painting and refinishing technicians
7. Upholsterers
8. Glass technicians
9. Office Staff

In smaller shops, some of these separate jobs are combined. For example, the manager or owner may also be the foreman and the estimator. Body-repair technicians, who repair or replace body panels, may also operate the power equipment. The painter may also work on the sheet metal, sanding and filling in preparation for painting. Some shops may not have an upholsterer or glass technician. These jobs may be sent out, or sublet, to other shops specializing in this work. The office staff may be one person who handles all the paperwork, such as billing insurance companies, ordering parts and materials, answering the phone, and paying the bills. This job also may include writing the paychecks. Now, let's look at each of these jobs.

≡ 1-3 MANAGER

Usually the body-shop manager or owner (Fig. 1-2) started out as an apprentice metalworker, working for someone else. Gradually, he or she learned all aspects of the job and moved up to become foreman, estimator, or body-shop manager. Later, this person decided to open an auto-body-repair shop. Today, about one out of every eight body-repair technicians is self-employed. In many of these small shops, the owner does it all.

The manager is responsible for everything that the shop does or does not do. During the day-to-day operation of the shop, the manager hires, trains, and fires workers, as required. Also, it is the job of the manager to

Fig. 1-2 The job of the body-shop manager may include preparing estimates.

Fig. 1-3 The estimator prepares an estimate of front-end damage to a car.

see that a steady flow of body repair and paint work is coming into the shop. Once a job is in the shop, the manager makes sure that the parts needed are received by the body technician within a reasonable time. In addition, the manager checks that each worker is skilled and productive. Those who are slow or find certain jobs difficult receive instruction or are sent to school for training. Some managers try to personally meet each customer who brings in a car for repair.

This description does not cover all the things that a manager has to do. But in the body shop, the manager is "the boss."

≡ 1-4 FOREMAN

The foreman runs the shop. Duties include assigning jobs to the workers, checking on when jobs will be completed, making sure materials and parts are available, determining that all workers are productive, and observing that quality jobs are being turned out. In the smaller shops, the manager is also the foreman. Larger shops have a separate foreman. In other shops, the estimator may share some of these responsibilities with the manager.

≡ 1-5 ESTIMATOR

The estimator (Fig. 1-3) gets the repair jobs for the body shop. In the smaller shop, the manager or owner is also the estimator. Larger body shops have one or more specialists to handle this essential job. Estimating requires a knowledge of automobile construction. Personal experience in body repair is an asset for the estimator.

When a car is damaged or wrecked, the estimator looks over the car—inside and out, top, sides, and bottom. Then it is the estimator's job to prepare a written estimate of the cost of repair. A good estimate must cover the shop expenses in doing the job, plus a profit for the shop. This is especially difficult on cars that have had considerable damage, particularly to the underbody or frame. On these cars, additional serious damage may not be obvious. However, the experienced estimator knows what to look for.

As the cost of repairing a wrecked car goes up, the chances that the car will be repaired decrease. If the repair costs are too high, the car may be declared a "total." This means that the car is damaged so much that it is not worth repairing. The cost of making the repairs would be higher than the value of the car. For example, insurance companies and most owners would not want to spend $1000 to repair a wrecked car that was worth only $500 on the used car market. This makes the car a total loss. Such a car usually is sold to an automobile junkyard, salvage dealer, or dismantler. Useful and undamaged parts then can be removed for installation on other cars of the same model.

The estimator must walk a narrow path between making too low an estimate and making too high an estimate. If the estimate is too low, the shop loses money on the job. If the estimate is too high, the shop can lose the job to another shop that offers to do it cheaper. Chapter 38 covers estimating in detail.

≡ 1-6 BODY-REPAIR TECHNICIAN

The sheet-metal worker or body-repair technician (Fig. 1-4) straightens or replaces the various sheet-metal, plastic, and fiberglass parts on the car. If a part is not too badly damaged, it can be straightened or repaired

Fig. 1-4 The body-repair technician straightens a damaged quarter panel.

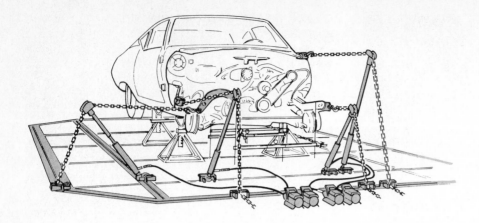

Fig. 1-5 Hydraulic body-and-frame straightener making pulls on a car to straighten the frame and body. (*Applied Power, Inc.*)

satisfactorily. Usually, this means restoring the original contour and filling the low spots with plastic body filler or solder. Then the repair is smoothed by filing and sanding so it will be ready to accept the primer and final paint coats.

If a metal panel or part is too badly damaged to straighten, it is cut out. A new part is welded or riveted in its place. The welds or rivets are pounded down below the contour and the low spots filled and finished in preparation for painting.

≡ 1-7 POWER-EQUIPMENT OPERATOR

Power equipment uses compressed air, chains, clamps, and fasteners to pull or push on bent parts so they are brought back to their original shape. Figure 1-5 shows a car with power equipment attached. When the technician operates the air switch or switches, the power cylinders expand or telescope. This applies force (a push or a pull) that will straighten the bent parts. In many shops, the front-end technician operates the frame-straightening equipment.

≡ 1-8 PAINTING AND REFINISHING TECHNICIAN

After the body panels, doors, roof, hood, and trunk lid — whatever parts were damaged — have been restored to their original contours, the sheet-metal surfaces are smoothed by sanding. This job is started with coarse sandpaper and finished with very fine sandpaper. Then the painter applies a coat of primer, followed by the final coats of paint (Fig. 1-6). Painting is an exacting job and takes some time to learn. The paint must be mixed in the right proportions to match the color of the original paint. If this is not done, the paint patch will dry to a different color. Then the customer will not be happy with the job.

Before the paint job is started, all parts that are not to be painted must be covered with paper and tape. You can see these protected areas in Fig. 1-6. Often the painter has a helper who does this job. It is called *masking*. The car is then ready for painting. This is often done in a special paint booth. It is very important to keep dust out of the air in the painting area. Dust on the freshly painted car will show up, and the job may have to be done over. After the fresh paint is on, heat may be applied by heat lamps to speed the drying process.

≡ 1-9 UPHOLSTERER

The upholsterer removes worn upholstery from the seats and replaces it with new material to restore the original look to the interior of the car (Fig. 1-7). The upholsterer also installs new headliner (the lining above the passengers' heads that is the inside "roof" of the car) and new carpet. In other words, the upholsterer's job is to maintain and repair the car interior. Some customers may want a custom interior. This means that the upholsterer will use special materials and patterns for the seats, headliner, and carpet.

≡ 1-10 GLASS TECHNICIAN

The glass technician installs new glass in the car. This may require two people, as, for example, when installing a new windshield (Fig. 1-8). Some shops specialize

Fig. 1-6 A painter spraying a door. A respirator is worn to prevent the inhaling of dangerous fumes.

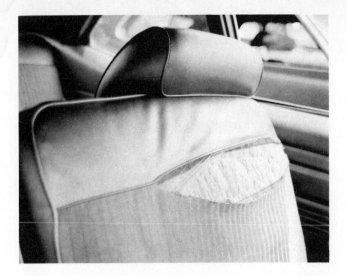

Fig. 1-7 A car with a seat in need of new upholstery.

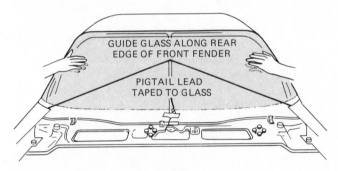

GUIDE GLASS ALONG REAR
EDGE OF FRONT FENDER

PIGTAIL LEAD
TAPED TO GLASS

Fig. 1-8 Installing a windshield. *(Copyright by Fisher Body Division of General Motors Corporation)*

in this work, because it is easy to chip or crack the new glass during installation. Many body shops send, or sublet, their glasswork to a local glass shop.

≡ **1-11 OFFICE STAFF**

The size of the body shop determines the size of the office staff. Except for writing the estimate and the re-pair order, the office staff handles all paperwork in the shop. This includes billing, paying bills, and keeping records. In some shops, it also includes ordering parts, checking parts when they are received, and charging the parts to the job being worked on. In larger shops, all of this paperwork is handled by a separate individual (Fig. 1-9). It is a full-time job.

≡ **1-12 THE SUCCESSFUL BODY SHOP**

Success in a body shop starts with good management. A steady flow of repair jobs must come in. Then they must go out finished on time. The manager must see that all sections of the body shop operate as they should. The shop must be kept clean, both inside and out. There must be spaces where customers can park, a drive-in area where customers can get an estimate, and a clean customer lounge or waiting room.

In particular, records must be properly kept so that the manager will know at all times how the shop is doing financially. More business failures are caused by poor record keeping than by any other single problem.

Fig. 1-9 Billing, paying bills, and keeping records are the job of the bookkeeper, or office staff.

REVIEW QUESTIONS

Select the *one* correct, best, or most probable answer to each question. You can find the answer in the section indicated at the end of each question.

1. The auto body includes the   (≡1-6, 1-7)
   a. wheels, trunk, tires, and brakes
   b. hood, engine, and battery
   c. body panels and frame
   d. fuel, ignition, and exhaust systems

2. Each year paint and body-repair jobs are performed on more than   (≡1-1)
   a. 30 billion vehicles
   b. 30 million vehicles
   c. 3 million vehicles
   d. 3 thousand vehicles

3. The "boss" in a big body shop is the   (≡1-3)
   a. manager
   b. glass technician
   c. painter
   d. upholsterer

5

4. Checking on the quality of work produced by the shop is one duty of the   (≡1-4)
   a. foreman
   b. office staff
   c. front-end technician
   d. painter

5. Figuring out how much it will cost to profitably repair a wrecked car is the job of the   (≡1-5)
   a. metalworker
   b. painter
   c. estimator
   d. foreman

6. Filling in low spots with plastic body filler is done by the   (≡1-6)
   a. office staff
   b. manager
   c. foreman
   d. body-repair technician

7. Masking the car for painting may be done by the painter or by the   (≡1-8)
   a. painter's helper
   b. foreman
   c. estimator
   d. glass technician

8. Repairing a torn seat is the job of the   (≡1-9)
   a. glass technician
   b. metalworker
   c. upholsterer
   d. foreman

9. Figuring the amount due in each employee's paycheck is the job of   (≡1-11)
   a. each employee
   b. the office staff
   c. the estimator
   d. the foreman

10. Most businesses such as body shops that fail do so because of   (≡1-12)
   a. high parts prices
   b. poor record keeping
   c. low labor rates
   d. poor location

CHAPTER 2
AUTOMOBILE BODY CONSTRUCTION

After studying this chapter, you should be able to:

1. Describe the two main types of automotive body construction.
2. Explain what is meant by "body sheet metal."
3. Discuss unitized-body construction.
4. Describe the properties of sheet metal and what happens to it when it is stamped.
5. Explain how body and frame parts are put together.
6. Describe the special construction features of vans, pickup trucks, and convertibles.
7. Discuss doors, hoods, trunk lids, sun roofs, seats, and other components of the car body.

≡ 2-1 TYPES OF AUTOMOTIVE BODY CONSTRUCTION

There are two main types of automotive body construction:

    1. Body-and-frame construction
    2. Unitized-body construction; also called *unibody* and *unit* construction.

The body-and-frame construction was the most common arrangement until a few years ago. Then smaller fuel-efficient cars came along, using front-wheel drive. Most of these have unibody construction. Figure 2-1 shows the two basic types of cars—rear-wheel drive, and front-wheel drive with a transaxle. The *transaxle* is a combined transmission and differential, attached directly to the engine. The assembly mounts on the front of the car and drives the front wheels.

≡ 2-2 BODY-AND-FRAME CONSTRUCTION

The body-and-frame construction uses a separate frame such as shown in Fig. 2-2. The frame supports all body and engine parts and is, in turn, supported by the front- and rear-wheel springs. The frame is made of channel or U-shaped steel members that are riveted or welded together. Note, in Fig. 2-2, how the frame members are shaped to take the various parts that are attached to it. Figure 2-3 shows a frame on which the wheels and springs, engine, brakes, steering system, and body have been mounted. This assembly is the complete automobile.

≡ 2-3 BODY

The body for the body-and-frame construction includes the body panels, doors with their window-operating mechanisms, seats and their adjusting devices, floor carpet, headliner (lining overhead), trim, lights, bumpers, windshield washers and wipers, grills, instrument panel with instruments, trunk and trunk lid, and other parts described later. The body includes about everything except the running gear (engine,

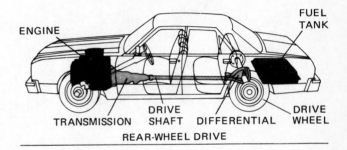

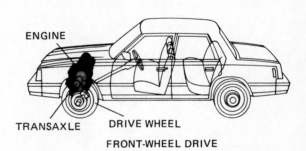

Fig. 2-1 Power train for a front-engine rear-wheel-drive car compared with the power train for a front-engine front-wheel-drive car.

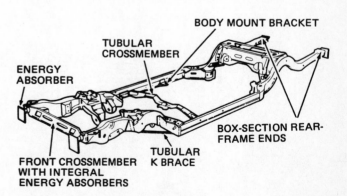

Fig. 2-2 Typical automobile frame. The frame curves upward at the rear (to the right) to provide room for the rear springs. The frame narrows at the front (to the left) to permit the front wheels to turn from side to side for steering. *(Ford Motor Company)*

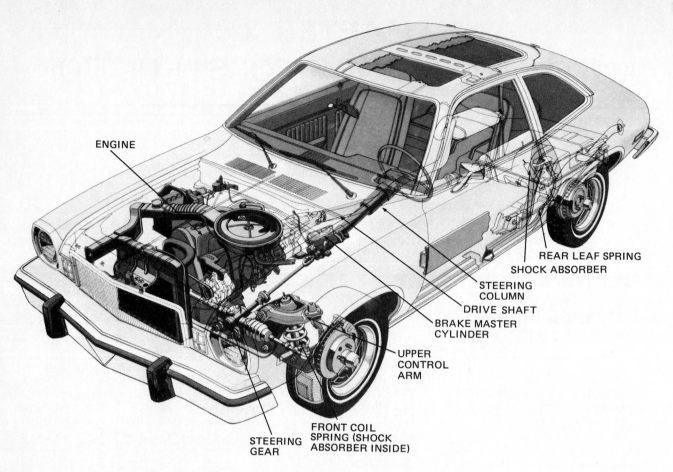

ENGINE

REAR LEAF SPRING
SHOCK ABSORBER

STEERING
COLUMN

DRIVE SHAFT

BRAKE MASTER
CYLINDER

UPPER
CONTROL
ARM

FRONT COIL
SPRING (SHOCK
ABSORBER INSIDE)

STEERING
GEAR

Fig. 2-3 Phantom view of an automobile, showing the suspension and steering systems. This is a front-engine, rear-wheel-drive car. It uses coil springs at the front and leaf springs at the rear. *(Ford Motor Company)*

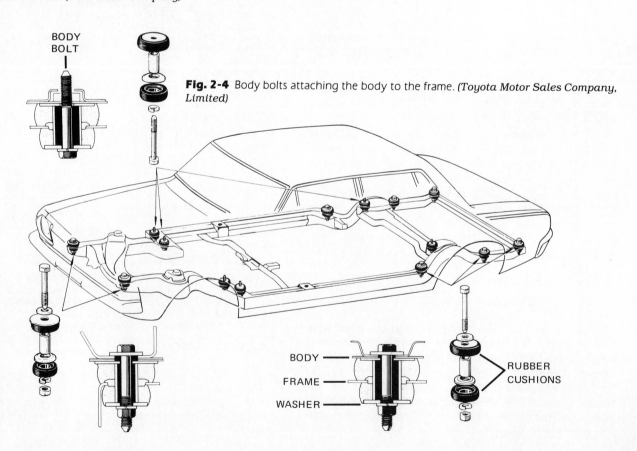

BODY
BOLT

Fig. 2-4 Body bolts attaching the body to the frame. *(Toyota Motor Sales Company, Limited)*

BODY

FRAME

WASHER

RUBBER
CUSHIONS

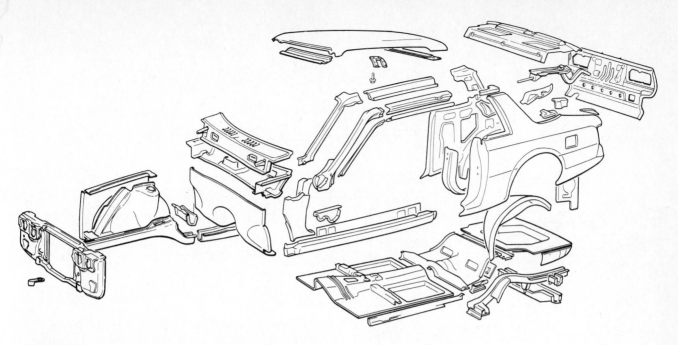

Fig. 2-5 Separate steel stampings which are welded together to make the unitized body. *(Chrysler Corporation)*

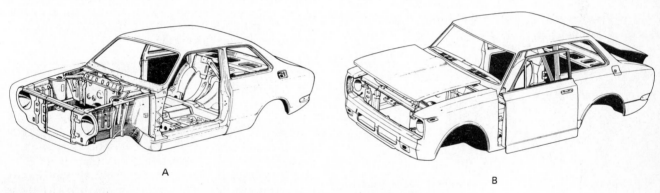

A   B

Fig. 2-6 Construction of a unitized body. (A) The body is welded together to make the basic body. (B) Body with the hood, trunk lid, and doors added. *(Toyota Motor Sales Company, Limited)*

wheels, power train, etc.) that is required to make the complete automobile.

Figure 2-4 shows a body ready to be attached to the frame. In the body-and-frame construction, the body is attached to the frame by a series of body bolts. These bolts use rubber washers or body mounts to isolate the body from the metal of the frame. This prevents the transfer of noise and vibration from the frame to the body. Figure 2-4 shows how the body bolts fasten the body to the frame while isolating vibration in the frame from the body.

≡ 2-4 UNITIZED-BODY CONSTRUCTION

This type of body does not have a separate one-piece frame, such as shown in Fig. 2-2. Instead, the floor pan serves as the center part of the frame. All body panels (shown in Fig. 2-5) are welded together to form the body, as shown in Fig. 2-6A. Figure 2-6B shows this same basic body with the front fenders, doors, hood, and trunk lid added.

The unitized construction requires partial frames, called *stub frames* or *cradles,* as shown in Fig. 2-7. The cradle supports the transaxle and is, in turn, supported by the front-suspension system. The cradle is attached

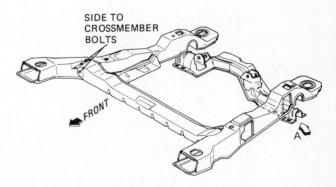

SIDE TO CROSSMEMBER BOLTS

FRONT

A

Fig. 2-7 Unitized-body construction requires the use of a partial frame, such as this stub frame or cradle. *(Buick Motor Division of General Motors Corporation)*

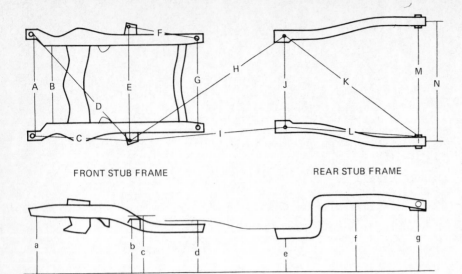

FRONT STUB FRAME   REAR STUB FRAME

Fig. 2-8 Horizontal and vertical checking dimensions on stub frames on a vehicle with unitized construction. *(Copyright by Fisher Body Division of General Motors Corporation)*

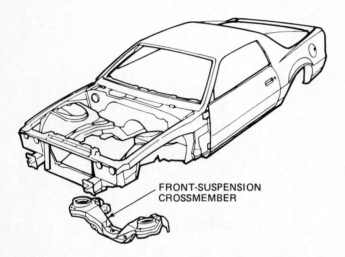

FRONT-SUSPENSION CROSSMEMBER

Fig. 2-9 The front-suspension cross member is the only major bolt-on structural component of a car with full integral construction. *(Chevrolet Motor Division of General Motors Corporation)*

to the unitized body. Figure 2-8 shows the major measuring points on the front and rear stub frames for a unitized-construction vehicle. These measurements must be checked before starting a collision repair job. If they are not right, they must be corrected with the shop power equipment as a first step in body repair. On some cars, the stub frame has been reduced to a front-suspension cross member (Fig. 2-9).

≡ 2-5 BODY SHEET METAL

Figure 2-10 shows the major outer-body panels for a four-door sedan. However, there are many more parts that go into the body. Figures 2-11 and 2-12 show all interior and exterior parts that are formed separately and then welded together to make the body such as shown in Fig. 2-6. These two illustrations (Figs. 2-11 and 2-12) look complicated because they show many parts. However, you will rarely have to work with these separate parts. You will work with major assemblies such as shown in Figs. 2-5 and 2-6. Sometimes you will

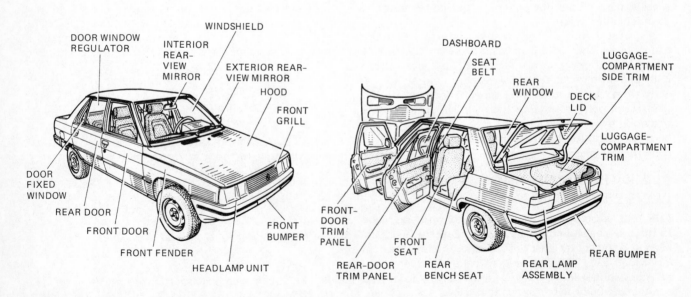

Fig. 2-10 Major body panels on a car. *(American Motors Corporation)*

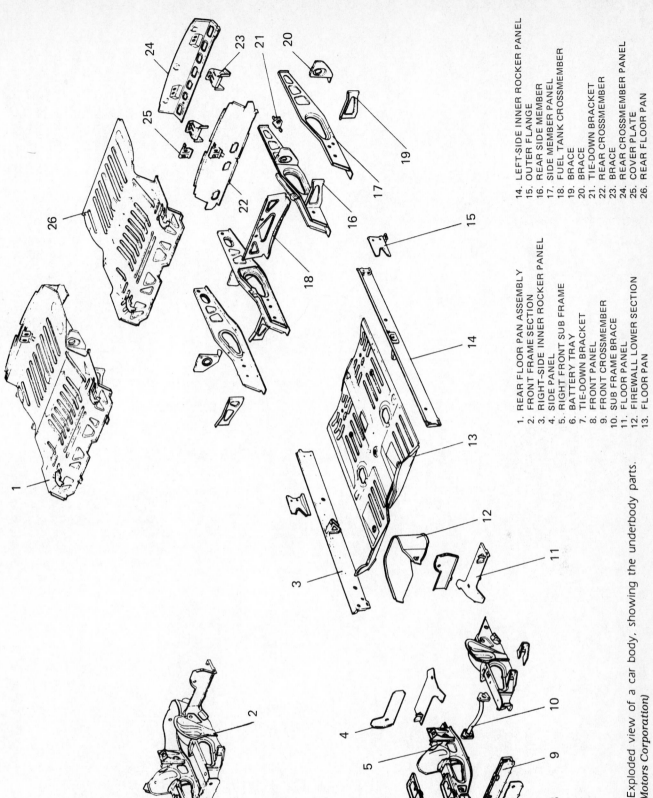

1. REAR FLOOR PAN ASSEMBLY
2. FRONT FRAME SECTION
3. RIGHT-SIDE INNER ROCKER PANEL
4. SIDE PANEL
5. RIGHT FRONT SUB FRAME
6. BATTERY TRAY
7. TIE-DOWN BRACKET
8. FRONT PANEL
9. FRONT CROSSMEMBER
10. SUB FRAME BRACE
11. FLOOR PANEL
12. FIREWALL LOWER SECTION
13. FLOOR PAN

14. LEFT-SIDE INNER ROCKER PANEL
15. OUTER FLANGE
16. REAR SIDE MEMBER
17. SIDE MEMBER PANEL
18. FUEL TANK CROSSMEMBER
19. BRACE
20. BRACE
21. TIE-DOWN BRACKET
22. REAR CROSSMEMBER
23. BRACE
24. REAR CROSSMEMBER PANEL
25. COVER PLATE
26. REAR FLOOR PAN

Fig. 2-11 Exploded view of a car body, showing the underbody parts. *(American Motors Corporation)*

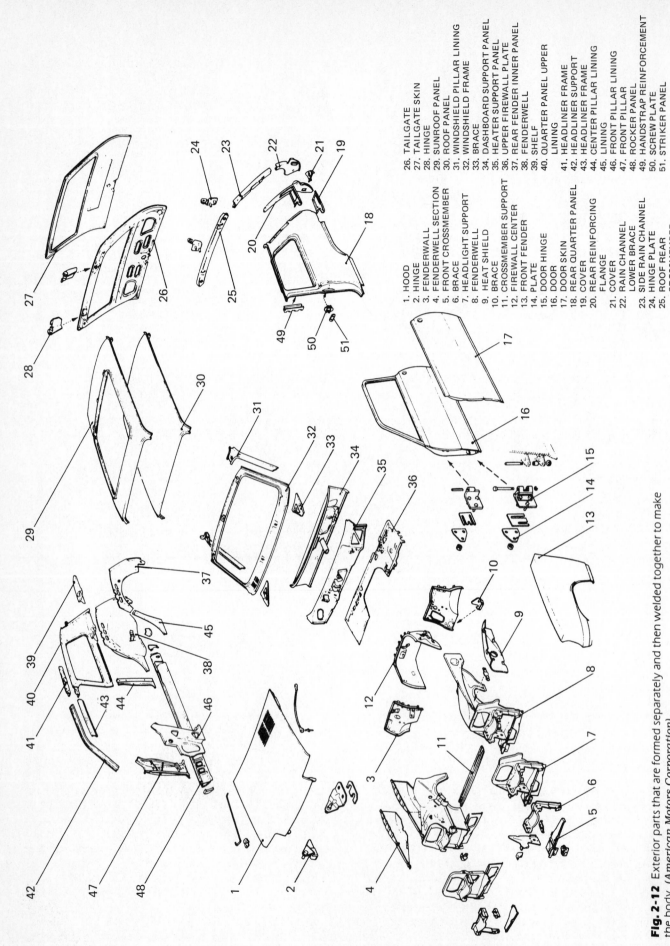

1. HOOD
2. HINGE
3. FENDERWALL
4. FENDERWELL SECTION
5. FRONT CROSSMEMBER
6. BRACE
7. HEADLIGHT SUPPORT
8. FENDERWELL
9. HEAT SHIELD
10. BRACE
11. CROSSMEMBER SUPPORT
12. FIREWALL CENTER
13. FRONT FENDER
14. PLATE
15. DOOR HINGE
16. DOOR
17. DOOR SKIN
18. REAR QUARTER PANEL
19. COVER
20. REAR REINFORCING
    FLANGE
21. COVER
22. RAIN CHANNEL
    LOWER BRACE
23. SIDE RAIN CHANNEL
24. HINGE PLATE
25. ROOF REAR
    CROSSMEMBER

26. TAILGATE
27. TAILGATE SKIN
28. HINGE
29. SUNROOF PANEL
30. ROOF PANEL
31. WINDSHIELD PILLAR LINING
32. WINDSHIELD FRAME
33. BRACE
34. DASHBOARD SUPPORT PANEL
35. HEATER SUPPORT PANEL
36. UPPER FIREWALL PLATE
37. REAR FENDER INNER PANEL
38. FENDERWELL
39. SHELF
40. QUARTER PANEL UPPER
    LINING
41. HEADLINER FRAME
42. HEADLINER SUPPORT
43. HEADLINER FRAME
44. CENTER PILLAR LINING
45. LINING
46. FRONT PILLAR LINING
47. FRONT PILLAR
48. ROCKER PANEL
49. HANDSTRAP REINFORCEMENT
50. SCREW PLATE
51. STRIKER PANEL

Fig. 2-12 Exterior parts that are formed separately and then welded together to make the body. (American Motors Corporation)

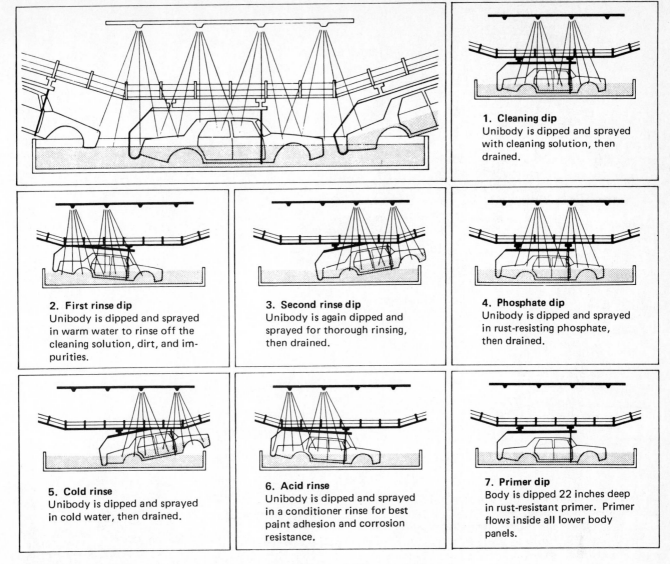

1. Cleaning dip
Unibody is dipped and sprayed with cleaning solution, then drained.

2. First rinse dip
Unibody is dipped and sprayed in warm water to rinse off the cleaning solution, dirt, and impurities.

3. Second rinse dip
Unibody is again dipped and sprayed for thorough rinsing, then drained.

4. Phosphate dip
Unibody is dipped and sprayed in rust-resisting phosphate, then drained.

5. Cold rinse
Unibody is dipped and sprayed in cold water, then drained.

6. Acid rinse
Unibody is dipped and sprayed in a conditioner rinse for best paint adhesion and corrosion resistance.

7. Primer dip
Body is dipped 22 inches deep in rust-resistant primer. Primer flows inside all lower body panels.

Fig. 2-13 Steps in the anticorrosion treatment given the body during manufacture of the car. *(Chrysler Corporation)*

cut away a badly damaged part and weld on a new or repaired part, such as a door panel.

Body parts are made of various materials. The body skin (or outer panels), if metal, is made of a special type of sheet steel or aluminum. Body panels are also made of various types of plastic and fiberglass. The internal parts shown in Figs. 2-11 and 2-12 are usually made of other types of sheet steel. They are usually of heavier-gauge (thicker) metal to support the attached components.

After the major parts are assembled to form the body, the body is dipped, sprayed, and redipped in an electroplating tank. This coats the metal surfaces to give the body additional antirust protection (Fig. 2-13).

Several subassemblies are attached to the body. These include doors, hood, trunk lid, and sun roof (if used). The body includes brackets and attachment plates to accept these parts. Figure 2-14 shows the parts and panels for a front end. Most of these are attached to the basic body structure after it has undergone the treatment described above.

≡ 2-6 METAL FOR BODY PARTS

The metal for body parts arrives at the body-stamping plant in large rolls. The metal is either steel or aluminum.

1. STEEL. Steel is a form of the element iron, combined or alloyed with carbon and other elements. The amount of carbon in steel is small, rarely as high as 2 percent. A high-carbon steel is a relatively hard, strong steel. A low-carbon steel is a relatively soft and less strong. Low-carbon steel, also called *mild* or *soft steel,* has less then 0.25 percent carbon. This is the type of steel used for body panels. The metal must be relatively soft so it can be bent and shaped easily.

For special purposes, other elements are added to steel to give it toughness, hardness, corrosion resistance, and wear resistance. Such steel may be used to fabricate other automobile parts such as axles, drive shafts, and engine valves.

2. STEEL FOR BODY-AND-FRAME CONSTRUCTION. When the body-and-frame construction is used,

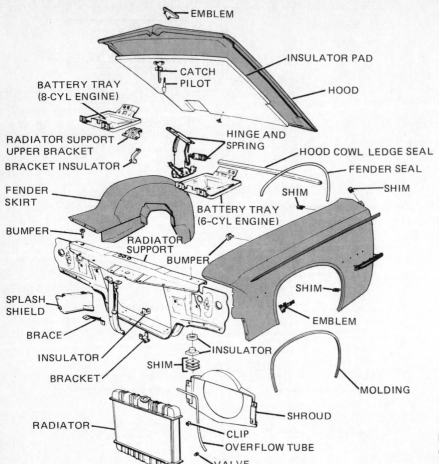

EMBLEM

INSULATOR PAD

CATCH PILOT

HOOD

BATTERY TRAY (8-CYL ENGINE)

RADIATOR SUPPORT UPPER BRACKET

BRACKET INSULATOR

HINGE AND SPRING

HOOD COWL LEDGE SEAL

FENDER SEAL

SHIM

SHIM

FENDER SKIRT

BATTERY TRAY (6-CYL ENGINE)

BUMPER

RADIATOR SUPPORT

BUMPER

SHIM

SPLASH SHIELD

EMBLEM

BRACE

INSULATOR

INSULATOR

BRACKET

SHIM

MOLDING

RADIATOR

SHROUD

CLIP

OVERFLOW TUBE

VALVE

Fig. 2-14 Sheet metal for the front end of a car. *(Pontiac Motor Division of General Motors Corporation)*

the body and its panels are not designed to be part of the basic support structure. The load is carried by the frame. It is the supporting member that supports both the body and the *running gear*—the engine, power train, suspension, steering, and brakes. The body is basically an enclosure for the passengers and load. Since the body panels carry little load, they are made of mild, relatively low-strength, low-carbon steel. This steel is easily shaped in presses. Then the panels can be welded together to form the body.

3. STEEL FOR UNITIZED BODY. The unitized-body construction uses the body itself as part of the load-bearing support structure. On the modern front-wheel-drive cars, the body and panels are made from a new family of high-strength, low-alloy (HSLA) steel. HSLA steel is lighter and thinner gauge, but provides the necessary structural strength. This saves weight so that the car is more fuel-efficient. However, HSLA body panels require different treatment during body-repair work, as explained later.

4. ALUMINUM. Aluminum alloys now are being used by some automotive manufacturers to make automotive sheet-metal parts. Figure 2-15 shows an all-aluminum hood. Note that it looks like the conventional steel hood, shown in Figs. 2-6, 2-10, and 2-12. These aluminum alloys have good strength and can be formed easily. When the same gauge (or thickness) of aluminum sheet is substituted for steel sheet, the aluminum parts weigh only one-third as much as the original steel parts.

Fig. 2-15 An all-aluminum hood, used on the car to save weight. *(Oldsmobile Division of General Motors Corporation)*

During the stamping process, some aluminum parts will develop marks, or "orange peel." This surface roughness can be removed, but usually these parts are nonvisible and so the surface roughness can be ignored.

14

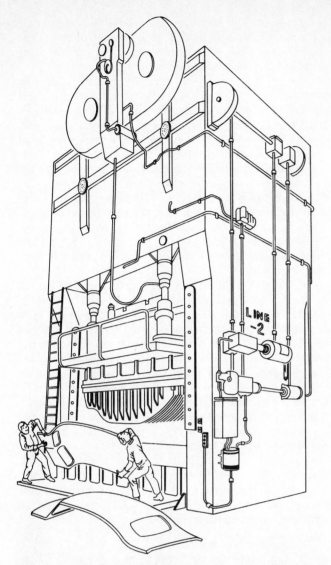

Fig. 2-16 Large stamping press which blanks out steel roofs for automobiles.

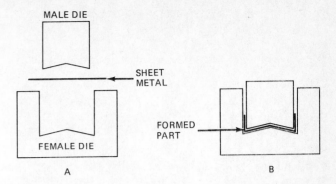

Fig. 2-17 A simple die set for stamping metal parts.

The metal aluminum does not occur in nature. As a result, all aluminum must be produced. Most aluminum comes from bauxite, a very plentiful aluminum ore which may contain as much as 45 percent aluminum oxide. The bauxite is processed to remove the aluminum oxide. Then the aluminum oxide is smelted to produce aluminum.

Aluminum and its alloys have good resistance to corrosion. Also, they are nonferrous metals. This means that they are not attracted by a magnet. Anytime you think a body panel or other part may be made of iron or steel, check it with a magnet. If the magnet is *not* attracted and if the part is made of a dull silvery-white metal, it probably is aluminum.

≡ 2-7 STAMPING BODY PARTS

Stamping is carried out in stamping presses. These presses vary from small units for stamping out small parts to the large presses used to form the car roof panel and other large parts (Fig. 2-16). For many large parts such as the roof panel, the sheet metal is cut into lengths of suitable size. These sheets are fed individually into the press.

The press uses a pair of dies, a male die and a female die, such as shown in Fig. 2-17. The sheet metal is placed between the dies, and they are then pressed together. This forces the metal to take the shape of the die faces. Figure 2-17 illustrates this. The male die is in the up position in Fig. 2-17A. The sheet-metal blank is positioned between the dies. When the press is operated, the movable die moves down (Fig. 2-17B). This forces the sheet-metal blank down so it takes the shape of the dies. Any excess metal on the formed part is cut off after the part is removed from the press. The new part may be given further treatment to remove sharp or uneven edges and to clean it.

≡ 2-8 EFFECT OF STAMPING ON SHEET METAL

Whenever sheet metal is worked—that is, whenever its shape is changed—it gets harder. The effect is called *work-hardening.* You can prove this for yourself by taking a piece of sheet metal and bending it a few times. You can feel that the metal in the bend becomes harder to bend. You get the same effect by laying a piece of sheet metal on a flat surface and hitting one section of it with a hammer several times. To do this, let the hammer blows fall on a line along one section of the sheet metal, as shown in Fig. 2-18. Then try to bend it at this spot. You will find it bends more easily on either side of the hammered area.

When a sheet-metal part is formed in a press, different areas will be bent different amounts. When a fender comes out of the press, varying curvatures have been stamped into it (Fig. 2-19). Where the sheet metal has been given a great amount of curvature, that area is said to have a high crown. Where the curvature is slight, the metal has a low crown. This ties in with what we said previously about work-hardening. The more that sheet metal is bent, the harder it gets. Therefore, the fender shown in Fig. 2-19, which has varying

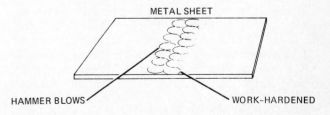

Fig. 2-18 Hammering on sheet metal work-hardens it.

Fig. 2-19 Low- and high-crown areas of a fender. *(Chrysler Corporation)*

amounts of curvatures or crown, varies considerably in its hardness. The high-crown area is considerably harder than the low-crown area. This is important to the body-repair technician. The amount of hardness an area of sheet metal has determines how the area will be distorted when damaged in a collision. Also, the hardness determines how the distortion must be treated to restore the original contour of the sheet metal. All this is covered in later chapters.

Hardness can be relieved by heating the metal to just a little under the melting point, as explained later. The heat changes the crystal structure of the metal. This relieves the internal strains that have caused the hardness. Working metal and then heating it was a routine procedure in the body shop for repairing damage to low-carbon body panels. Panels made of HSLA steel are now treated in a different way, as explained later.

≡ 2-9 PROPERTIES OF SHEET METAL FOR STAMPING

Steel is used for most body parts. The steel must have the proper chemical composition to permit it to be shaped in the stamping press without wrinkling, cracking, or otherwise failing.

The composition of the steel may be different for the outer panels that show than for the inner panels and parts that are hidden. An internal part may be required to be stronger, and the importance of its surface finish is not so great. Therefore, a higher-carbon steel might be used for an internal part. If you examine internal body parts, you may see wrinkling and roughness. These mean nothing as far as strength is concerned. But such roughness could not be tolerated on outside

body panels. The sheet metal for outside body panels must be such as to allow it to come out of the press smooth and clean. Also, the metal must take welding and painting with minimum problems.

The basic property of metal that permits it to be pressed into different shapes is called its *plasticity.* A mild steel is much more plastic than a high-carbon, or hard, steel. When flat sheet metal is shaped in a press, it is said to have undergone *plastic deformation.* That is, it has been deformed from a flat surface because it is *plastic.* It may be hard to think of steel as being plastic, because you may think of body filler or silicone when you hear the word "plastic." However, steel can be made to flow under pressure. If the steel is soft enough, it will do this without breaking, provided its yield point is not reached. *Yield point* is the point at which the metal actually breaks rather than continues to flow and become deformed.

Plastic deformation can result from a pull or a push on the metal. If you pull on metal, it is under tension and it will elongate, or stretch. This stretchability is called *ductility.* If the metal is subjected to a push that tends to compress it, and if it does change shape, the metal has *malleability.* An example here would be the metal used in the machines that form bolts. The metal enters the machine as a round rod. It is gripped, and a die with a recess shaped like a bolt head hits the end. Figure 2-20 shows the process. With the jaws open, the rod is positioned between the jaws. The jaws close, leaving the proper length of rod sticking out. The die then strikes the end of the rod. This forces the protruding rod to flow into the shape of a bolt head. This process is called *up-setting.* The material is forced to flow in compression. The ease with which it flows, or can be upset, is called its malleability.

≡ 2-10 PUTTING THE PARTS TOGETHER

Many parts go together to make up the body. The parts are attached by electric welding (Fig. 2-21). Electric welding uses electric current to heat the parts where they are touching each other. The metal gets so hot that it melts. Then, when the current stops, the metal cools and the parts have become attached by welds.

Today, many parts are attached by structural adhesives. Where properly used, they form joints that are stronger than some welded or riveted joints. Adhesives are described in Chap. 4.

Figure 2-22 shows the principle of electric welding. The parts to be joined are positioned between two electrodes. The electrodes are brought into contact with the two sides of the two metal sheets that are to be joined. A high current flows, and the metal between the two electrodes becomes so hot that it melts. When the electrodes are withdrawn and the spot cools, we have a spot weld. Now picture this on a large scale, with special machines called *robots* welding the body parts together. A modern version of this is shown in Fig. 2-23. The parts are positioned by clamps so they are held in place in readiness for the welds. Then the robots automatically extend electrodes that contact the parts and weld them together.

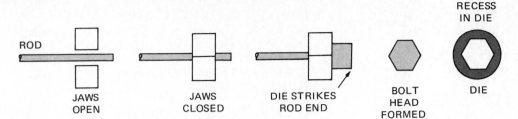

SIDE VIEW

ROD

JAWS OPEN

JAWS CLOSED

DIE STRIKES ROD END

END VIEW

RECESS IN DIE

BOLT HEAD FORMED

DIE

Fig. 2-20 Sequence of upsetting the end of a rod to form a bolt head.

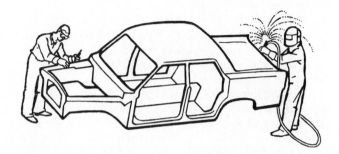

Fig. 2-21 Welding the parts together to form the body.

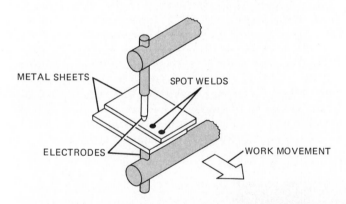

METAL SHEETS

SPOT WELDS

ELECTRODES

WORK MOVEMENT

Fig. 2-22 Principle of electric spot welding. Two metal sheets are overlapped, and two electrodes close on them to send current through the sheets. This melts the metal, forming the spot weld.

Fig. 2-23 Automated body welding is performed by a robot welder during the assembly of a unitized body. (*Buick Motor Division of General Motors Corporation*)

The surfaces on outside body panels are then given further treatment to eliminate weld marks. Next, the body is given a chemical treatment, as already explained (Fig. 2-13), and painted. It is then attached to the frame or stub frames for unibody construction.

≡ 2-11 PLASTIC BODY PANELS

A new way to assemble bodies has been developed at the Pontiac Motor Division of General Motors Corporation. A steel subframe is first fabricated by welding together a series of steel members (Fig. 2-24). This steel subframe, called a space frame, carries the entire load of the plastic body panels and the suspension, power train including the engine, and steering. The plastic body panels do not carry any part of the load.

To attach the body panels, a series of steel sheet-metal blocks, about an inch square, are welded to the subframe. These are placed at the points at which the plastic panels are to be attached. The sheet-metal blocks are filled with an epoxy compound. Then the subframe, with these epoxy-filled blocks, is positioned in a special drilling machine (Fig. 2-25). This machine has the same number of drills as there are epoxy-filled blocks on the subframe. The drills then all move into the epoxy-filled blocks. They first drill holes. Then a milling tool removes the proper amount of sheet metal

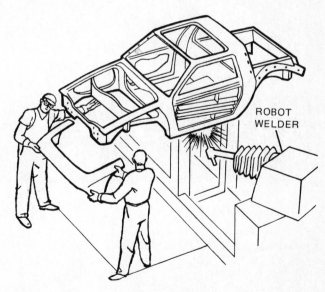

ROBOT WELDER

Fig. 2-24 Assembly of a space frame, to which plastic body panels are attached.

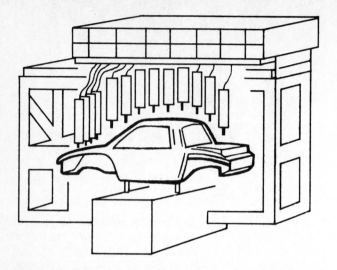

Fig. 2-25 Drilling the holes in the space frame for attaching the plastic body panels.

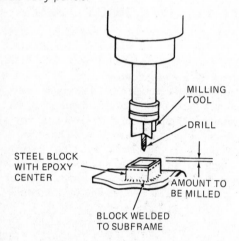

MILLING TOOL

DRILL

STEEL BLOCK WITH EPOXY CENTER

AMOUNT TO BE MILLED

BLOCK WELDED TO SUBFRAME

Fig. 2-26 As the drill is lowered, it makes the hole and then mills off the proper amount of sheet metal.

(Fig. 2-26). The result is that, in about 60 seconds, all the holes for attachment of the body panels are drilled. All are exactly positioned to accept the plastic panels and place them so that they fit with one another properly.

There is an advantage to this arrangement should the car be damaged and need repair. Then the damaged panel can be removed and a new panel installed, if the subframe is undamaged.

≡ 2-12 AIR RESISTANCE AND AERODYNAMICS

Air resistance is the resistance of the air to the passage of the car body through it. As car speed increases, so does the air resistance. At 90 miles per hour (mph) [145 kilometers per hour (km/h)], as much as 75 percent of the power that reaches the wheels is used to overcome air resistance. This power loss is due to the drag of the air on the car.

Even at lower speeds, the power required to overcome aerodynamic drag can reduce fuel economy by 2 miles per gallon or more. To improve fuel economy, modern automobiles are being made more "slippery" so that they slide through the air more easily. The process is called *streamlining*.

Figure 2-27 shows a new car design that has very low resistance to air. The light lines show how the air slides up and around the car. Note that the underbody is completely enclosed.

Air resistance is measured in terms of *drag coefficient* (C_d). The lower the drag coefficient, the less fuel required to move the car through the air. The car shown in Fig. 2-27 has a drag coefficient of 0.22. This is about 50 percent better than the ratings of cars produced before 1983. It can go about 2.5 miles farther on a gallon of fuel than a car of comparable size built before 1983.

In addition to the general shape of the car, the manner of placing the windows and external parts is care-

Fig. 2-27 Streamlining a car makes it more "slippery" so that it has less air resistance. The light lines show how the air moves up, over, and around the car. The bottom view shows how a cover is applied so that the bottom of the car presents minimum air resistance. *(Ford Motor Company)*

2-DOOR SEDAN

3-DOOR SEDAN

4-DOOR SEDAN

5-DOOR SEDAN

STATION WAGON

UTILITY VEHICLE

PICKUP TRUCK

CONVERTIBLE

VAN

LIMOUSINE

Fig. 2-28 *Various body styles.*

1. WINDOW ASSEMBLY
2. BELT TRIM SUPPORT RETAINERS
3. FRONT UP-TRAVEL STOP
4. REAR UP-TRAVEL STOP
5. LOWER-SASH UPPER GUIDE
6. LOWER-SASH LOWER GUIDE
7. LOWER-SASH GUIDE PLATE ASSEMBLY
8. GUIDE-TUBE ASSEMBLY
9. REMOTE CONTROL TO LOCK-CONNECTING ROD
10. INSIDE LOCKING ROD
11. DOOR OUTSIDE LIFT-BAR HANDLE
12. DOOR LOCK
13. WINDOW REGULATOR (ELECTRIC)
14. DOOR-LOCK REMOTE-CONTROL HANDLE
15. DOOR-LOCK SOLENOID
16. ROD INSIDE LOCKING TO SOLENOID

Fig. 2-29 Rear-door hardware. *(Copyright by Fisher Body Division of General Motors Corporation)*

fully designed to eliminate as much as possible any small eddy air currents. For example, windows are set as nearly flush with the surrounding body panels as possible (≡4-26).

≡ 2-13 TYPES OF AUTOMOTIVE VEHICLES

A variety of automotive vehicles are made. They are very similar under the skin—the body panels. All have an engine, a power train, steering and brake systems, wheels, and suspension. They vary in the type of body that covers these basic parts. Figure 2-28 shows different bodies. These include two-, three-, four-, and five-

door sedans, vans, convertibles, and small trucks. Convertibles are often called ''ragtops'' because the top, which can be folded back, is made of a cloth material.

≡ 2-14 DOORS

There are two general types of doors: closed style (with upper frames) and hardtop or convertible style (without upper frames). Doors contain a variety of devices (Fig. 2-29), including window regulators (opening and closing mechanisms), locks, cigarette lighters, windshield-wiper controls, seat-adjustment controls, rearview mirror and control, and door reinforcing strips. Window regulators can be mechanical, with a hand crank, or electric, with a reversible electric motor. Door locks can be mechanical, with a hand-operated button, or electric, with a two-way solenoid. Cigarette lighters and ashtrays are used in many doors. On some cars, the windshield-wiper control is located in the front left-hand door, as are the rearview mirror and its remote control. This location permits the driver to operate the controls as necessary.

1. DOOR ADJUSTMENT. Many doors have provisions for adjustment (Fig. 2-30). The holes in the hinges and the hinge-attachment points are enlarged or elongated. These allow the door to be shifted up or down, or forward or back, to fit the door opening properly. To make the adjustment, the screws are loosened slightly. Then the door is pried in the desired direction with a padded pry bar. When the adjustment is correct, the screws are tightened. If shifting the door throws the striker plate out of alignment, the striker plate then has to be adjusted.

2. GLASS ALIGNMENT. The doors have provisions for alignment of the glass if it does not close properly. When a glass is raised, it should fit watertight on the top and two sides. If it does not, the two supports at the bottom of the glass can be adjusted to correct the fit.

3. WINDOW REGULATOR. The window regulator may be operated either by a hand crank or by an electric motor. If something goes wrong, the door trim must be removed so the trouble can be corrected. There are many different arrangements. Figure 2-29 shows only one.

4. DOOR LOCK. The door lock is operated by a push button in the upper sash of the door. Many cars also have an electric solenoid to lock or unlock the door. If the car has electric door locks, there is a master control in the driver's door. The master control can be moved to prevent opening of any door or to permit any of the doors to be individually controlled by the passengers.

5. TRIM AND WEATHERSTRIPPING. Doors must have weatherstripping to seal them against the entrance of rain, dirt, and outside air (Fig. 2-31). The weatherstripping seals at all joints. Door trim includes handles and embellishment strips, attached by screws or locking catches.

≡ 2-15 TRUNK LID

The trunk lid, or rear-compartment lid, is attached at the forward end by two hinges. Most cars have some type of lid support assembly to assist in opening the lid

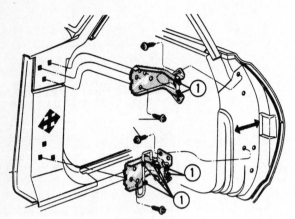

FRONT DOOR

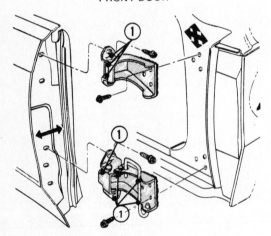

FRONT DOOR

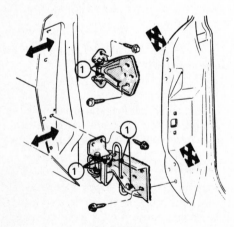

REAR DOOR

① LUBRICATION POINT - POLYETHYLENE GREASE

Fig. 2-30 Side-door hinge adjustments on various car models. *(Ford Motor Company)*

WEATHER STRIP

Fig. 2-31 Typical door weatherstrip. *(Chrysler Corporation)*

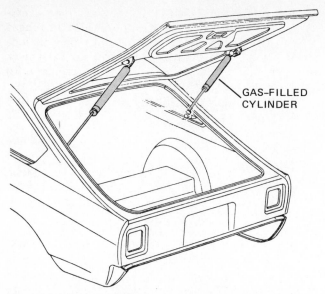

Fig. 2-32 Rear-compartment-lid attachment and support assembly. *(Copyright by Fisher Body Division of General Motors)*

(Fig. 2-32). Many trunk lids are supported in the open position by torsion bars. Others have a gas-filled cylinder, as shown in Fig. 2-32. The gas is under pressure, and when the lid is unlocked, the device extends to raise the lid. If this assembly requires replacement, it must be removed from the car in the fully extended

position. If it is detached with the trunk lid only partly open, it will instantly extend fully. This could injure you or damage the car.

Trunk lids have a lock that must be operated by a key. In some cars, the lid may be unlocked by an electric solenoid and a push button in the glove compartment.

≡ 2-16 FRONT HOOD

The front hood (Fig. 2-33) is attached to the body by two hinges, usually spring-loaded. The springs make it easier to open the hood and hold it open. Elongated or over-size holes permit the hood to be shifted as necessary to secure a good fit. In some cars the hood lock is at the front of the car. In others, the hood lock is connected by a cable to a control lever inside the passenger compartment.

≡ 2-17 TAILGATE, OR LIFTGATE

There are several styles of tailgate, or liftgate. In one, the tailgate is in one piece with a fixed window. With this arrangement, the tailgate is hinged at the top, just like the trunk lid. It is similar to the rear-compartment lid shown in Fig. 2-32. Another arrangement has the glass separate from the rest of the tailgate, which is hinged at the bottom. The glass can be retracted into the roof of the car by an electric motor. In some vehicles, the tailgate is hinged to swing down or to swing to one side. The tailgate can contain a variety of devices: lock-release solenoid, defogger, blower, and counterbalance

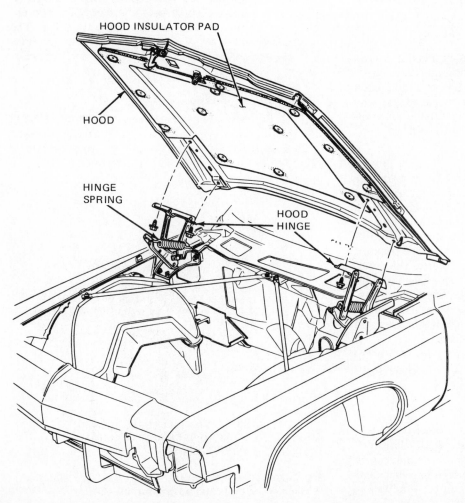

Fig. 2-33 Details of front-hood attachment. *(Buick Motor Division of General Motors Corporation)*

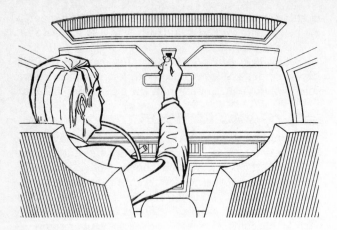

Fig. 2-34 Sun roof, partly open. *(ATW)*

support assemblies. In addition, it may have a warning system that turns on a warning light on the instrument panel if the gate is not closed when the ignition switch is turned on.

≡ 2-18 SUN ROOF

The sun roof is a metal panel in the roof of the car that slides back and forth on guide rails in the roof (Fig. 2-34). When it is slid back, the sun can shine down through the opening onto the passengers. On some cars the sun panel is operated by a two-way electric motor (Fig. 2-34). On other cars, the sun roof is operated by a hand crank.

≡ 2-19 SEATS

Seats are made in a variety of designs (Figs. 2-35 and 2-36). Some have a manual forward-and-back adjustment. Others have electric motors to move them back and forth or up and down. The latter are called four-way seats. Some seats are six-way. These have an additional control that changes the tilt of the seat.

≡ 2-20 SEAT BELTS

The purpose of seat belts (Fig. 2-37) is to restrain the drive and passengers if there is an accident. During a front-end crash, for example, the car is brought to a sudden stop. But everything inside the car continues to move forward until it hits some solid object. An unrestrained passenger would continue to move forward until he or she hit a part of the car such as the windshield or the instrument panel. It is these "second collisions" that hurt and kill people. However, if the passengers and driver are wearing seat belts, they will be restrained. They will not continue to move forward and will not hit some solid object in the car.

Older cars have two different kinds of seat belts; lap belts and shoulder belts. Most cars now have a continuous-loop seat-belt system (Fig. 2-37).

≡ 2-21 AIR BAGS

Air bags are a passive restraint to protect the driver (Fig. 2-38) and passengers in an accident. "Passive" means that the driver and passengers do not have to do anything to be protected by the air bags. This is in contrast with seat belts (≡2-20) that require an action—

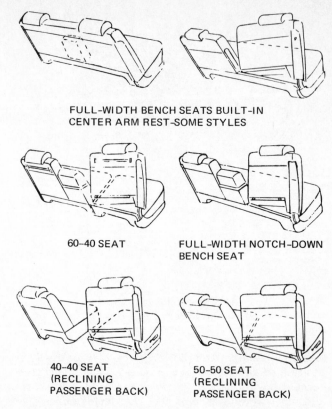

Fig. 2-35 Types of front seats (except bucket seats) for two-door cars. Front seats in four-door cars have nonfolding backs. *(Copyright by Fisher Body Division of General Motors Corporation)*

FULL-WIDTH BENCH SEATS BUILT-IN CENTER ARM REST-SOME STYLES

60-40 SEAT

FULL-WIDTH NOTCH-DOWN BENCH SEAT

40-40 SEAT (RECLINING PASSENGER BACK)

50-50 SEAT (RECLINING PASSENGER BACK)

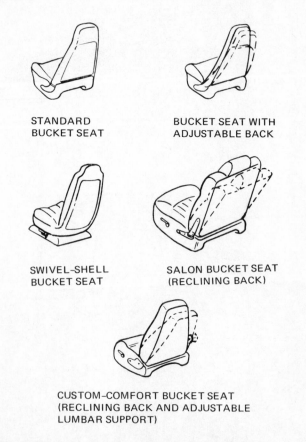

STANDARD BUCKET SEAT

BUCKET SEAT WITH ADJUSTABLE BACK

SWIVEL-SHELL BUCKET SEAT

SALON BUCKET SEAT (RECLINING BACK)

CUSTOM-COMFORT BUCKET SEAT (RECLINING BACK AND ADJUSTABLE LUMBAR SUPPORT)

Fig. 2-36 Types of bucket seats. *(Copyright by Fisher Body Division of General Motors Corporation)*

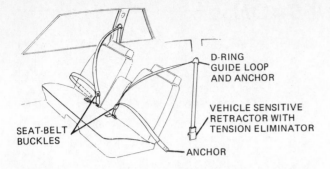

Fig. 2-37 Typical seat-belt installation for the front seat. *(Ford Motor Company)*

≡ 2-22 ENERGY-ABSORBING BUMPERS

The energy-absorbing bumper is required by law on late-model cars. It will withstand collisions at low speed without damage to the bumper or car. Most of these bumpers resume their original position after the collision. There are several types, used at both the front and the rear of late-model cars. One uses a leaf-spring assembly which supports the bumper, as shown in Fig. 2-39. On impact, the spring gives and absorbs the blow. The bumper then returns to its original position, if the impact was within the designed limits. If the impact was greater than the designed limits, damage may have occurred and repair may be required.

≡ 2-23 BODY ELECTRICAL EQUIPMENT

The body carries a considerable amount of wiring connecting the various electrically operated body devices. Some of these include power door locks, power windows, and power seats. In addition, the body carries several lights — headlights, taillights, turn-signal lights, and interior lights. Other electrical devices include the open-door warning buzzer and the theft alarm system. These are described in a later chapter.

buckling up. Many people do not buckle up because it is "too much trouble." As a result, there are far more highway injuries and deaths than there need be. Air-bag advocates believe that the air bag will save many lives and prevent many injuries.

The air bags inflate at the instant that a crash occurs. They then give the driver and passengers a cushion into which to move, as shown in Fig. 2-38. The air bags absorb the forward motion of the occupants. This prevents them from hitting anything hard that could injure them.

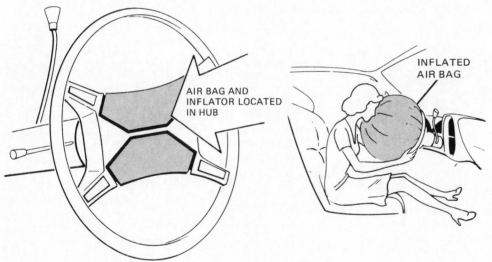

Fig. 2-38 Location of the air bag in the steering wheel. The illustration on the right shows the action when the air bag is inflated and the driver is thrown forward into it. *(General Motors Corporation)*

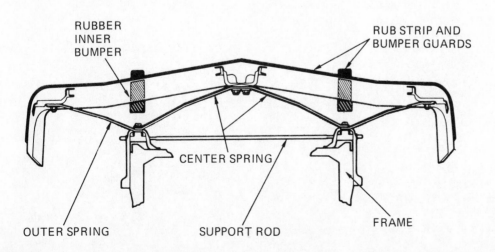

Fig. 2-39 Front-bumper system using a leaf-spring assembly to absorb the energy of a front-end impact. *(Pontiac Motor Division of General Motors Corporation)*

REVIEW QUESTIONS

Select the *one* correct, best, or most probable answer to each question. You can find the answers in the section indicated at the end of each question.

1. The two main types of automotive body construction are
   a. unibody and multibody
   b. body-and-frame and full body
   c. body-and-frame and unibody
   d. compact and truck
   (≡2-1)

2. The frame is supported by the (≡2-2)
   a. front- and rear-wheel springs
   b. body and engine parts
   c. driver and passengers
   d. body panels

3. In body-and-frame construction, the body is fastened to the frame by (≡2-3)
   a. welding
   b. plastic
   c. aluminum
   d. body bolts

4. A stub frame is used with some types of unibody construction to provide (≡2-4)
   a. front-wheel drive
   b. suspension-attachment points
   c. rear-wheel drive
   d. fuel-tank protection

5. To form the underbody, the metal stampings are (≡2-4)
   a. bolted together
   b. welded together
   c. soldered together
   d. dipped

6. Some body panels are made of (≡2-5)
   a. tin
   b. wood
   c. cast iron
   d. fiberglass

7. The steel usually used for body panels is (≡2-5)
   a. low-carbon steel
   b. high-carbon steel
   c. cast iron
   d. stainless steel

8. When the shape of sheet steel is changed, it gets
   a. hot
   b. cold
   c. harder
   d. softer
   (≡2-8)

9. Hardness in sheet metal can be relieved by (≡2-8)
   a. soaking the metal in acid
   b. cooling the metal
   c. heating the metal
   d. grinding the metal

10. The point at which metal breaks instead of flowing and deforming is its (≡2-9)
    a. yield point
    b. malleable point
    c. ductile point
    d. malleability

11. Mechanic A says that drag coefficient measures how "slippery" the car body is. Mechanic B says drag coefficient is a measure of the car's air resistance. Who is right? (≡2-12)
    a. mechanic A
    b. mechanic B
    c. both A and B
    d. neither A nor B

12. Adjusting the door is done by (≡2-14)
    a. bending the door
    b. shifting the hinges
    c. aligning the glass
    d. repositioning the window regulator

13. Doors are sealed against the entrance of water, dust, or outside air by (≡2-14)
    a. weatherstripping
    b. trim
    c. chrome
    d. glass thickness

14. An electric seat adjuster may be either (≡2-19)
    a. manual or hydraulic
    b. four-way or six-way
    c. one-speed or two-speed
    d. front-seat or rear-seat

15. Passive restraints include (≡2-21)
    a. seat covers
    b. seat belts
    c. air bags
    d. all of the above

CHAPTER 3
SAFETY IN THE SHOP

After studying this chapter, you should be able to:

1. Describe shop layouts.
2. Discuss shop safety.
3. List shop hazards due to various causes.
4. Discuss fire prevention in the shop, including various types of fire extinguishers and how to use them.
5. List the shop safety rules.

≡ 3-1 SHOPWORK

Shopwork is varied and interesting. The shop is where you will learn to do all sorts of automotive-body-repair jobs. These include cutting and welding, correcting sheet-metal and frame damage, repairing and replacing fiberglass and plastic panels, adjusting body panels, and servicing doors, sun roofs, seats, and stationary glass. You will also learn how to paint and refinish car bodies and interior parts.

However, before you work in the shop, you should know about safety. Safety in the shop means protecting yourself and others from possible danger and injury. This chapter describes the rules you should follow in the shop to protect yourself from harm. When everybody obeys the rules, the shop is a much safer place to work than your home! Many more people are hurt in the home than in the shop.

≡ 3-2 SAFETY IS YOUR JOB

Yes, safety is your job. In the shop, you are "safe" when you protect your eyes, your fingers, your hands—all of you—from danger. And just as important is looking out for the safety of those around you.

The rules of safety are listed and discussed in the next few pages. Follow the rules for your protection and for the protection of others.

≡ 3-3 SHOP LAYOUTS

The term "shop layout" means the locations of workbenches, car lifts, machine tools, and so on. Shop layouts vary. The first thing you should do in a shop is find out where everything is located. This includes the different machine tools and the workbenches, car lifts, and work areas. Many shops have painted lines on the floor to mark off work areas. These lines guide customers and workers away from danger zones where machines are being operated. The lines also remind workers to keep their tools and equipment inside work area lines.

Many shops have warning signs posted around machinery. Some of these signs may have the name OSHA, which stands for Occupational Safety and Health Administration. This is the federal agency with the responsibility of correcting conditions and equipment that present hazards to workers (≡3-4). The signs are posted to remind everyone about safety, and about how to use machines safely. Follow the posted instructions at all times. The most common cause of accidents in the shop is failure to follow instructions.

≡ 3-4 SHOP HAZARDS

Federal laws now require healthful and safe working conditions for employees. The federally established National Institute for Occupational Safety and Health (NIOSH) makes studies of shop working conditions and reports on potential hazards that should be corrected. Further, the law requires that the shops with such hazards must eliminate them. Hazards found are sometimes the fault of management, and sometimes the fault of the workers. The following three sections describe hazards that may be caused by working habits, faulty or improperly used shop equipment, and faulty or improperly used hand tools.

≡ 3-5 HAZARDS DUE TO FAULTY WORK HABITS OR CONDITIONS

Here are some of the major hazards that might be due to work habits of the employees or to the general working conditions:

1. Smoking while handling dangerous materials such as gasoline or solvents (Fig. 3-1). This can result in a major fire or explosion.

2. Careless or incorrect handling of paint, thinners, solvents, or other flammable substances. Figure 3-2 shows the correct arrangement for pumping a flammable liquid from a large container into a small one. Note the bond and ground wires. Without these, a spark might jump from the nozzle to the small container, causing an explosion and fire.

3. Blocking exits (Fig. 3-3). Areas around exit doors and passageways leading to exits must be kept free of all obstructions. If you wanted to get out in an

Fig. 3-1 Do not smoke or have open flames around combustibles such as gasoline or solvents.

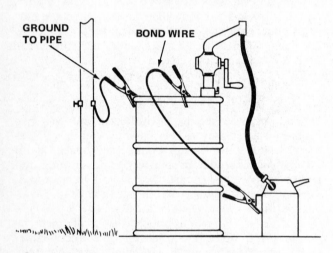

GROUND TO PIPE

BOND WIRE

Fig. 3-2 Setup for pumping a flammable liquid from a large container into a small one.

EXIT

Fig. 3-3 Exits must be kept free of obstructions. A blocked exit could mean injury or death if you needed to get out in a hurry.

emergency—for example, when a fire or an explosion occurred—a blocked exit could mean serious injury or even death.

4. Failure to wear a respirator (Fig. 1-6) when handling thinners, paints, and similar substances, when working with body-filler lead, or when sanding the car body or body filler. The vapor or dust from these substances, when breathed for a long time, can cause liver and lung damage. Proper ventilation of the work area and wearing of a respirator reduces this hazard to a minimum.

5. Other hazards caused by working habits and conditions in the body shop: Washing paint from the hands with thinner. Thinner can cause skin rashes and may be absorbed through the skin to cause liver damage. Plastic body filler, in the raw or uncured state, can also irritate the skin and should be washed off at once with soap and water. Wear rubber gloves while handling these materials.

≡ 3-6 HAZARDS DUE TO EQUIPMENT DEFECTS OR MISUSE

Here are the most common hazards in the shop due to equipment that is faulty or which is improperly used:

1. Incorrect safety guarding of moving machinery. For example, fans should have adequate guards (Fig. 3-4). Air compressors should have proper guards over the belt and pulley (Fig. 3-5).

2. Misuse of flexible electric cords, cords that are worn or frayed, or cords that have been improperly spliced. Flexible cord should not be run through holes in the wall or tacked onto the wall. Any of these could cause a fire or could electrocute someone.

3. Compressed-gas cylinders improperly stored or misused. These cylinders should never be stored near radiators or other sources of heat. They should never be kept in unventilated enclosures such as lockers or closets. There should be at least 20 feet [6.1 meters (m)] between stored oxygen and stored acetylene cylinders. Cylinders should not stand free but should be secured with a chain or lashing (Fig. 3-6). Cylinders should never be used as supports or as rollers to move an object. Such treatment could cause the cylinder to explode.

4. Hand-held electric tools not properly grounded. All such tools must have a separate ground lead (Fig. 3-7) or be double insulated to guard against shock.

5. Hydraulic car lifts improperly used. Passengers should not remain in the car when it is lifted. All doors, the hood, and the trunk lid should be closed. Otherwise, they could be damaged as the car is lifted. If the lift has a mechanical locking device, it should be engaged before you go under the lift. Do not use a lift that is not working properly and jumps or jerks when raised, settles slowly when it should not, rises or settles too slowly, blows oil out of the exhaust line, or leaks oil at the piston seal.

6. Using a wheel-and-tire balancer which does not have the safety hood in place. OSHA regulations now require wheel balancers of the spinner type to have hoods (Fig. 3-8). These hoods protect the workers if a stone or other object is thrown from the spinning tire tread.

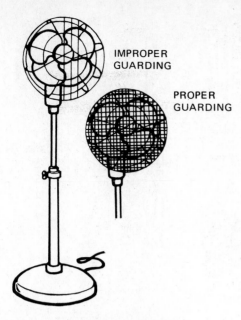

Fig. 3-4 A fan, improperly and properly guarded.

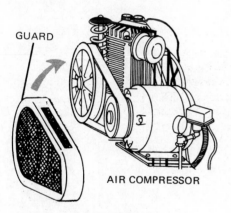

Fig. 3-5 Belts and pulleys on shop equipment should always be protected with guards.

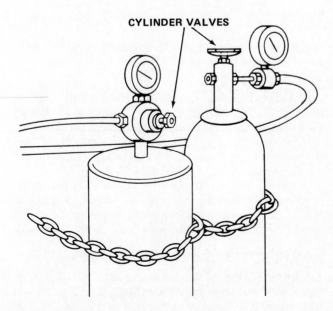

Fig. 3-6 Gas cylinders should not be allowed to stand freely but should always be secured with chains or lashing.

7. Letting tester leads fall into the engine fan. This can cut the leads. Also, the fan can throw out the leads, damage the tester, and possibly injure you.

8. Leaving the fan wire connected. Many engines that are mounted transversely (crosswise) at the front of the car have electric engine fans. These can run when the engine is turned off. As a safety precaution,

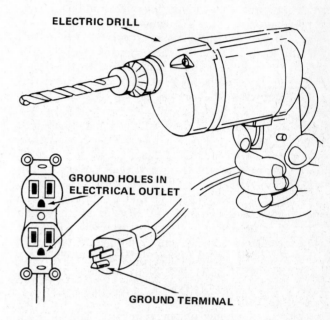

Fig. 3-7 Electric drill with three-wire cord. The third wire and terminal are to ground the electric-drill motor.

Fig. 3-8 An electronic wheel balancer used to check tire-and-wheel balance. The hood protects the technician from stones and other objects that might be thrown from the tire tread. The hood pivots down to a horizontal position before the wheel is spun. (Hunter Engineering Company)

when working around this type of engine and fan, disconnect the wire to the fan. Otherwise, if the engine is hot, the fan might start running unexpectedly and injure you.

9. Leaving a running machine unattended. Whenever you are using a power tool, and have to leave it for a moment, turn it off! If you leave it running, someone else might come along and, not realizing it is running, get a hand in the way of moving parts and be injured.

10. Playing with fire extinguishers. There have been cases where the workers thought it was fun to play with the fire extinguishers. But then some of them got hurt from slipping and falling down, or injured their eyes from the liquid or foam. Also, this leaves the extinguishers empty so they are useless if a fire should break out.

11. Using electric-arc- or gas-welding equipment which is faulty, or using it incorrectly. Gas-welding hose must be in good condition and not have leaks, burns, or worn places. Gas welding should be done in an area protected with screens, and there should be no combustibles nearby. Oil and grease must be kept away from gas-welding equipment. If high-pressure oxygen hits oil or grease, it will burst into flame with explosive violence. Electric-arc welding must also be done in a protected place, and the technician must wear a welding helmet or face shield (Fig. 3-9). In addition, the technician should wear fire-resistant clothes and gloves. A fire extinguisher should be nearby. The welding cable should never be coiled and must never be coiled around your body. Hot material should be marked to prevent someone from attempting to handle it.

≡ 3-7 HAND-TOOL HAZARDS

Hand tools should be kept clean and in good condition. Greasy and oily tools are hard to hold and use. Always wipe them before trying to use them. Do not use a hardened hammer or punch on a hardened surface. Hardened steel is brittle and can shatter from heavy blows. Slivers may fly out and enter the hand, or worse, the eye. Hammers with broken or cracked handles, chisels and punches with mushroomed heads, or broken or bent wrenches are other tool hazards that should be avoided.

Never use a tool that is in poor condition or that does not fit the job. Avoid hand-tool hazards so you won't get hurt. Proper use of hand tools is described further in Chap. 5.

≡ 3-8 FIRE PREVENTION

Gasoline is used so much in the shop that people forget it is very dangerous if not handled properly. A spark or lighted match in a closed place filled wth gasoline vapor can cause an explosion. Even the spark from a light switch can set off an explosion. So you must always be careful with gasoline. Here are some hints.

There will be gasoline vapors around, if gasoline is spilled or a fuel line is leaking. You should open the shop doors and run the ventilating system. Wipe up spilled gasoline at once. Put the rags outside to dry. Never smoke or light cigarettes around gasoline. When you work on a leaky fuel line, carburetor, or fuel pump, catch the leaking gasoline in a container or with rags.

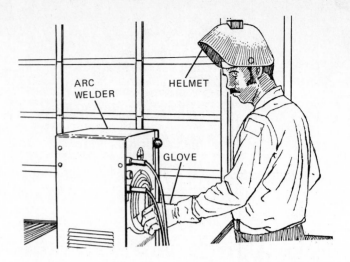

Fig. 3-9 When arc welding, you must wear a welding helmet and heavy gloves with cuffs.

Fig. 3-10 Always store gasoline and all flammable liquids in approved safety containers. (ATW)

Put the soaked rags outside to dry. Fix the leak as quickly as possible. Don't make sparks around the car, for example, by connecting a test light to the battery.

Store gasoline in an approved safety container (Fig. 3-10). Never store gasoline in a glass jug. The jug could break and cause an explosion and fire.

Oily rags can also be a source of fire. They can catch fire from spontaneous combustion, without a spark or flame. Oily rags and waste should be put into a closed safety container where they can do no harm (Fig. 3-11).

≡ 3-9 FIRE EXTINGUISHERS

Know the location of the fire extinguishers in the shop. Make sure you know how to use them. The quicker you begin to fight a fire, the easier it is to control. But you have to use the right kind of fire extinguisher, and use it correctly. Discuss any questions with your instructor.

Fig. 3-11 Safety container for the storage of oily rags.

≡ 3-10 SHOP SAFETY RULES

Some people say, "Accidents will happen!" But safety experts do not agree. They say, "Accidents are caused; they are caused by poor planning, carelessness, inattention to the job at hand, and using damaged or incorrect tools. And sometimes accidents are caused by just plain stupidity!"

To keep accidents from happening, follow these safety rules:

1. Work quietly and give the job your full attention.

2. Keep your tools and equipment under control.

3. Keep jack handles out of the way. Stand the creeper against the wall when it is not in use (Fig. 3-12).

4. Never indulge in horseplay or other foolish activities. You could cause someone to get seriously hurt.

5. Don't put sharp objects, such as screwdrivers, in your pocket. You could cut yourself or get stabbed. Or you could ruin the upholstery in a car.

6. Make sure your clothes are right for the job. Dangling sleeves or ties can get caught in machinery and cause serious injuries. Do not wear sandals or open-toe shoes. Wear full leather shoes with nonskid rubber heels and soles. Steel-toe safety shoes are best for shopwork. Keep long hair out of machinery by wearing a cap.

7. Do not wear rings, bracelets, or watches when working around moving machinery or electrical equipment. Jewelry can catch in moving machinery with very serious results. Also, if a ring or bracelet should accidentally create a short circuit of the car battery, the metal of the ring or bracelet could become white-hot in an instant. This would produce serious burns.

8. Wipe excess oil and grease off your hands and tools so that you can get a good grip on tools or parts.

9. If you spill oil, grease, or any liquid on the floor, clean it up so that no one will slip and fall.

10. Never use compressed air to blow dirt from your clothes. Never point a compressed-air hose at another person. Flying particles could put out an eye.

11. Always wear safety glasses, goggles, or a face shield when there are particles flying about. Always wear eye protection when using a grinder or machine that can throw chips or sparks (Fig. 3-13).

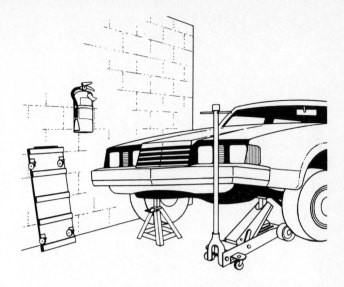

Fig. 3-12 When jacking up a car, always finish with the handle pointing up so no one can trip on it. When creepers are not in use, stand them up against the wall, wheels out. *(ATW)*

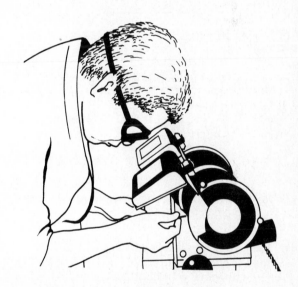

Fig. 3-13 Always wear safety glasses, safety goggles, or a face shield when using a grinder or machine that can throw chips or sparks.

12. Watch out for sparks flying from a grinding wheel or welding equipment. The sparks can set your clothes on fire.

13. To protect your eyes, wear eye protection when using chemicals, such as solvents. If you get a chemical in your eyes, wash them with water at once (Fig. 3-14). Then see the school nurse or a doctor as soon as possible.

14. When using a floor jack, make sure it is centered so that it won't slip. Never raise a car while someone is working under it! People have been killed when the jack slipped and the car fell on them! Always use safety stands or supports, properly placed, when going under a car (Fig. 3-15).

15. Always use the right tool for the job. The wrong tool could damage the part being worked on and could cause you to get hurt.

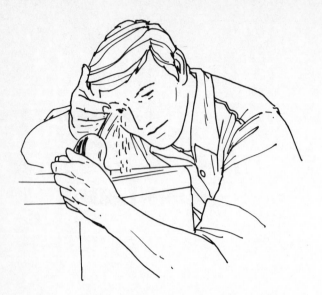

Fig. 3-14 If solvent or some other chemical splashes in your eyes, immediately wash them out with water.

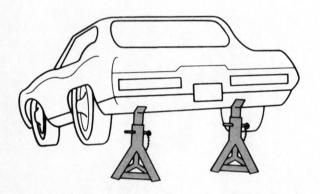

Fig. 3-15 Safety stands should be properly placed to support the car before you work under it.

16. Keep your hands away from the engine fan and belt when the engine is running. You could be badly cut or even lose fingers if your hand got caught in the fan or fan belt.

17. Do not stand directly in line with the engine fan when the engine is running. Some fans, especially the flex fans, have been known to throw off a blade when spinning. Anyone standing in line with the fan could get seriously hurt if hit by the blade.

18. Many transverse engines have electric fans which can run even if the engine is off, if the engine is hot. Disconnect the lead to the fan so there is no danger while you are working around an engine with an electric fan.

— **CAUTION** ———————

Never run an engine in a closed garage that does not have a ventilating system. The exhaust gases contain carbon monoxide. Carbon monoxide is a colorless, odorless, tasteless, poisonous gas that can kill you. In a closed one-car garage, enough carbon monoxide to kill you can collect in only 3 minutes.

≡ **3-11 USING POWER-DRIVEN EQUIPMENT**

A lot of power-driven equipment is used in the automobile shop. The instructions for using any equipment should be studied carefully before the equipment is operated. Hands and clothes should be kept away from moving machinery. Keep hands out of the way when using any cutting device, such as a brake-drum lathe. Do not attempt to feel the finish while the machine is in operation. There may be slivers of metal that will cut your hands. When using grinding equipment, keep hands away from rotating parts. Do not try to feel the finish with the machine in operation. Sometimes you will work on a device with compressed springs, such as a clutch or valves. Use great care to prevent the springs from slipping and jumping loose. If this happens, the spring may take off at high speed and hurt someone.

Never attempt to adjust or oil moving machinery unless the instructions tell you that this should be done.

≡ **3-12 WHAT TO DO IN EMERGENCIES**

If there is an accident and someone gets hurt, notify your instructor at once. The instructor will know what to do—give first aid or phone for the school nurse, a doctor, or an ambulance. Be very careful in giving first aid. You must know what you are doing. Trying first aid on an injured person can do more harm than good if it is done wrong. For example, a serious back injury could be made worse if the injured person is moved improperly. However, quick mouth-to-mouth resuscitation may save the life of a person who has suffered an electric shock. Talk to your instructor if you have any questions about this.

≡ **3-13 DRIVING CARS IN THE SHOP**

Cars have to be moved in the shop. They must be brought in for service, and may have to be moved from one work area to another. When the job is finished, they have to be moved out of the work area. Be careful when you drive a car in the shop. Make sure the way is clear. Make sure no one is under a nearby car. Someone might suddenly stick out an arm or a leg. Make sure there are no tools on the ground.

When you take a car out for a road test, *fasten your seat belt*, even though you're going only a short distance.

— **CAUTION** ———————

Always fasten your safety belt in a moving car, whether you are the driver or a passenger. Seat belts save lives; your seat belt could save yours. Buckle up for safety!

≡ **3-14 TOW-TRUCK OPERATION**

Driving a tow truck and doing emergency work at the scene of a collision takes experience. Each wreck is a special problem. Here are some recommendations for working with tow trucks.

1. Make sure the fire extinguisher is properly serviced, in good working condition, and mounted securely on the truck.

2. Do not exceed the unit's maximum hoisting capacity.

3. Make sure the truck floodlights are in good working condition.

4. The control mechanism for the hoist should be inspected periodically to make sure it is in good operating condition, and that the cable, hooks, drum, and other parts are okay.

≡ 3-15 WARNING SIGNS

Warning signs, such as shown in Fig. 3-16, are posted in shops to warn against hazards. They should be obeyed at all times to avoid injury and promote safety.

Fig. 3-16 Typical sign in many automotive shops, and other shops, reminding employees to obey the safety rules.

REVIEW QUESTIONS

Select the *one* correct, best, or most probable answer to each question. You can find the answers in the section indicated at the end of each question.

1. Safety in the shop means   (≡3-1)
   a. working safely
   b. protecting yourself from danger
   c. protecting others from danger
   d. all of the above

2. If there is an accident in the shop, you should (≡3-12)
   a. ignore it
   b. call the police
   c. notify your instructor
   d. call the hospital

3. The most common cause of accidents in the shop is
   a. failure to follow instructions   (≡3-3)
   b. following instructions
   c. taking shortcuts in your work
   d. following the wrong instructions

4. Failure to wear the proper respirator when handling thinners, paints, and similar materials   (≡3-5)
   a. will waste the materials
   b. can cause liver and lung damage
   c. can ruin the paint job
   d. can increase the time required for the job to dry

5. Never store gasoline in   (≡3-8)
   a. an approved container
   b. a glass jug
   c. steel tanks
   d. plastic fuel tanks

6. When working around transverse engines with electric fans,   (≡3-6)
   a. remove the fan
   b. disconnect the wire to the fan motor
   c. take off the blades
   d. remove the engine

7. Long loose sleeves around moving machinery   (≡3-10)
   a. protect your arms
   b. protect the machinery
   c. can get caught in the machinery and injure you
   d. keep you clean

8. A compressed-air hose must never be   (≡3-10)
   a. used in the body shop
   b. pointed at someone else
   c. left pressurized overnight
   d. used in the paint shop

9. Oil-soaked rags should be   (≡3-8)
   a. stored in a closed metal container
   b. piled out of the way under the workbench
   c. stored in the washroom
   d. burned in back of the shop

10. The reason it is dangerous to run an engine in a closed, unventilated garage is that   (≡3-10)
    a. carbon monoxide will accumulate in the garage
    b. carbon monoxide is a poisonous gas
    c. enough carbon monoxide can collect in 3 minutes to kill you
    d. all of the above

CHAPTER 4
FASTENERS, GASKETS, SEALANTS, AND ADHESIVES

After studying this chapter, you should be able to:

1. Discuss screw threads and explain pitch, series, and classes.
2. Explain how bolts, nuts, screws, and studs are marked to indicate their strength.
3. Explain how metric threads differ from USCS threads.
4. Define *prevailing-torque fastener*.
5. List four types of nonthreaded fasteners and describe their use.
6. Discuss the use of structural adhesives in automotive construction.
7. Describe clips and explain how they are used in automotive bodies.

≡ 4-1 FASTENERS

Fasteners are the parts that hold engines and automobiles together. *Fastener* is the name given to any device that holds or joins other parts together. Many are threaded. Examples are the screw, the nut and bolt, and the stud and nut (Fig. 4-1). Other types of fasteners include cotter pins, snap rings, keys, splines, and rivets. All these are covered in this chapter. Parts may also be attached by welding and by the use of structural adhesives. Welding is covered in a following chapter.

≡ 4-2 THREADED FASTENERS

A fastener that has some form of screw thread on it is a *threaded fastener.* Threaded fasteners let you remove and disassemble parts that may need repair during the life of the car. These parts usually are held together by screws, bolts, and studs (Fig. 4-1).

All threaded fasteners are not the same just because they look alike. For example, many metric fasteners and United States Customary System (USCS) fasteners are similar in appearance. But using the wrong one may "strip the threads," break the fastener, or cause a failure later while the car is on the road.

When you must install a new fastener, try to get a duplicate of the original fastener. If a duplicate is not available, the replacement fastener you install *must* be equivalent to the one removed. Be careful when selecting a replacement fastener.

≡ 4-3 SCREWS, BOLTS, AND STUDS

Screws and *bolts* are types of fasteners that have a head on one end and threads on the other. The screw is turned into a threaded hole in one of the parts being joined together. There are many different types and sizes of screws (Fig. 4-2). Most are turned, or "driven," with a screwdriver or wrench. Many engine and car parts are put together with *machine screws* and *cap screws.* These look like bolts. They are classed as screws because they do not use a nut. Most small

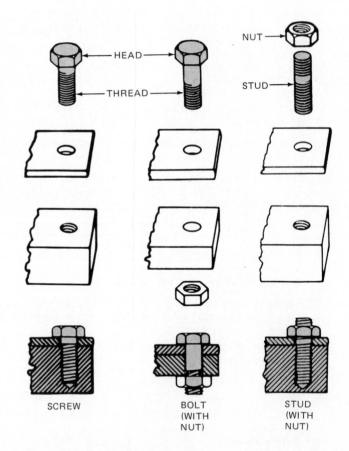

Fig. 4-1 Screw, bolt, and stud. Top shows the attaching parts separated, but aligned for assembly. Bottom shows the parts together.

screws have slotted heads. However, many Phillips-head and Reed-and-Prince-head screws are used in the car.

Bolts require nuts (Fig. 4-1). The parts that the bolt holds together have larger matching holes through which the bolt passes freely. Then a nut is turned onto the threaded end of the bolt and tightened. Sometimes

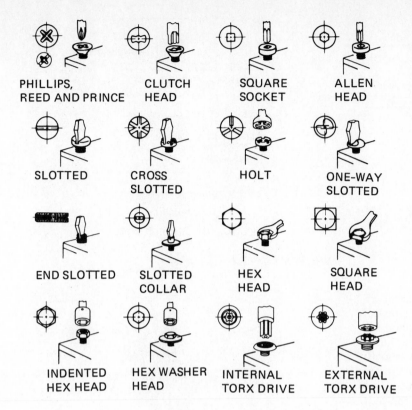

PHILLIPS, REED AND PRINCE   CLUTCH HEAD   SQUARE SOCKET   ALLEN HEAD

SLOTTED   CROSS SLOTTED   HOLT   ONE-WAY SLOTTED

END SLOTTED   SLOTTED COLLAR   HEX HEAD   SQUARE HEAD

INDENTED HEX HEAD   HEX WASHER HEAD   INTERNAL TORX DRIVE   EXTERNAL TORX DRIVE

Fig. 4-2 Screwdrivers and wrenches required to drive various types of screws. *(ATW)*

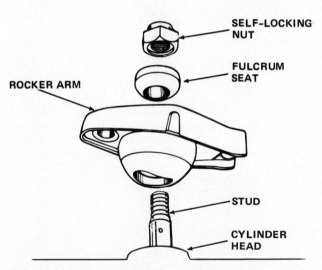

Fig. 4-3 An engine rocker-arm stud, threaded on only one end and using a self-locking nut. *(ATW)*

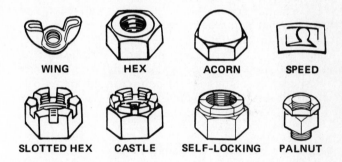

WING   HEX   ACORN   SPEED

SLOTTED HEX   CASTLE   SELF-LOCKING   PALNUT

Fig. 4-4 Nuts are made in various shapes and sizes. *(ATW)*

bolts and screws look the same. If they are used with nuts, they are bolts. If they are turned into a threaded hole, they are screws. However, on the engine, the cylinder head is fastened to the cylinder block without the use of nuts. It is general shop practice to call these particular fasteners "head bolts." Most common bolts have a hexagonal (six-sided), or "hex," head (Fig. 4-2).

A *stud* is a short piece of rod with threads on one or both ends so that it looks like a headless bolt (Fig. 4-1). If the stud is threaded at both ends, one end is screwed into a threaded hole. Then a part to be held in place is installed over the stud. A nut is then turned onto the

exposed end of the stud to hold the part in place. Many engines have rocker-arm studs that are threaded on only one end (Fig. 4-3). The other end is a *press-fit* into a hole in the cylinder head. The rocker arm and seat are placed over the stud. Then a nut is threaded onto it to hold the rocker arm in place.

≡ 4-4 NUTS

A *nut* is a removable fastener used with a bolt or stud to hold parts together (Fig. 4-1 and 4-3). The nut is made by threading a hole through the center of a piece of material (usually metal) which has been shaped to a standard size. Nuts are made in various shapes and sizes (Fig. 4-4). However, like bolt heads, most nuts used on cars have a hexagonal, or six-sided, shape. Slotted and castle (or "castellated") nuts are locked with a cotter pin. Other nuts are locked with lock washers. Cotter pins and lock washers prevent the nuts from working loose and dropping off. Some nuts are designed to be self-locking (Figs. 4-3 and 4-4).

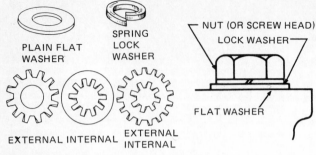

TOOTHED ("STAR") LOCK WASHERS

Fig. 4-5 Left, various types of washers. Right, a spring lock washer installed between a flat washer and a nut or bolt. (ATW)

≡ 4-5 WASHERS

A *washer* is a thin part with a hole in it for a screw, bolt, or stud to pass through. There are several types of washers (Fig. 4-5). The common types are the plain flat washer and the spring lock washer. The flat washer is used under nuts and bolt heads to provide a smooth bearing surface and to act as a shim. Flat washers are often used under lock washers (Fig. 4-5, right). This prevents them from damaging the surface of the part they are resting against.

Lock washers are used with screws and bolts. The lock washer is placed between the nut or screwhead and a flat washer (Fig. 4-5). The edges at the split (in the spring lock washer) cut into the nut or screwhead. This keeps it from turning and loosening. Toothed lock washers have many edges to improve the locking effect. Sometimes the flat washer is not used. The lock washer is placed directly against the part.

≡ 4-6 SCREW THREADS

Screws, bolts, and studs all have threads on the outside (Fig. 4-1). These are called *external* threads. Nuts and threaded holes have threads on the inside, or *internal* threads (Fig. 4-4). Most threads are made by "roll-forming" during manufacture. Threads can also be cut with taps and dies (Chap. 5). Threads, or *screw threads,* are described or "designated" in several ways, according to whether the threads are USCS threads or metric threads.

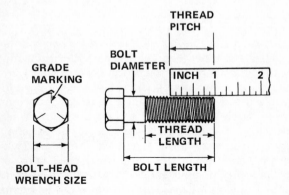

Fig. 4-6 Various measurements of a bolt. (ATW)

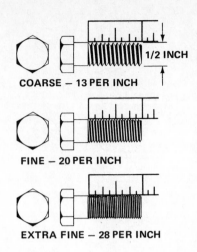

Fig. 4-7 Thread series on a ½-inch bolt.

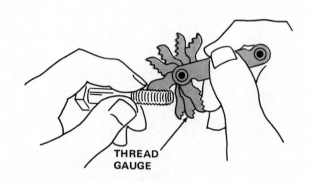

Fig. 4-8 Using a thread gauge.

There are other important measurements of a bolt (Fig. 4-6). These include the length of the bolt, diameter of the bolt, length of the thread, and size of the wrench required to turn the bolt head. Most bolts, screws, studs, and nuts have "right-hand threads." This means that you must turn the fastener clockwise (to the right) to tighten it.

≡ 4-7 THREAD PITCH

Nuts and bolts are made in many sizes, from very small to very large. Large nuts and bolts have *coarse* threads (Fig. 4-7). This means there are only a few threads per inch. Smaller nuts and bolts have *fine* threads, with more threads per inch. Very small nuts and bolts have *extra-fine* threads. These have even more threads per inch.

The number of threads per inch is called the *pitch.* On a bolt, you can find the pitch by counting the number of threads in 1 inch (Fig. 4-7). Or you can use a thread gauge to determine pitch. To use the thread gauge, find the blade that has the proper number of teeth to exactly fit the threads (Fig. 4-8). Then read the pitch from the blade. The number is marked on it.

≡ 4-8 THREAD SERIES

There are three thread series: coarse, fine, and extra-fine. These classifications refer to the pitch (number of threads per inch) on each size of threaded fastener. Fig-

Size	Diameter (Decimal)	Threads per Inch		
		Coarse (UNC or NC)	Fine (UNF or NF)	Extra-Fine (UNEF or NEF)
0	0.0600	. . .	80	
1	0.0730	64	72	
2	0.0860	56	64	
3	0.0990	48	56	
4	0.1120	40	48	
5	0.1250	40	44	
6	0.1380	32	40	
8	0.1640	32	36	
10	0.1900	24	32	
12	0.2160	24	28	32
¼	0.2500	20	28	32
⁵⁄₁₆	0.3125	18	24	32
⅜	0.3750	16	24	32
⁷⁄₁₆	0.4375	14	20	28
½	0.5000	13	20	28
⁹⁄₁₆	0.5625	12	18	24
⅝	0.6250	11	18	24
¾	0.7500	10	16	20
⅞	0.8750	9	14	20
1	1.0000	8	12	20
1⅛	1.1250	7	12	18
1¼	1.2500	7	12	18
1⅜	1.3750	6	12	18

Fig. 4-9 *Thread series for various sizes of USCS screw, bolt, stud, and nut.*

ure 4-9 shows the thread series for various sizes of screw, bolt, stud, and nut. For example, a ½-inch bolt could have coarse threads (13 threads per inch), fine threads (20 threads per inch), or extra-fine threads (28 threads per inch). A coarse thread shortens disassembly and reassembly time. Fewer turns are required to remove and install it. The fine and extra-fine threads are smaller than the coarse threads. Fine and extra-fine threads are used where greater bolt strength and additional accuracy of assembly are required.

≡ 4-9 THREAD CLASS

There are three thread classes. The difference is in the closeness of fit. Class 1 has the loosest fit. It is easiest to remove and install, even when the threads are dirty and battered. Class 2 has a tighter fit. Class 3 has a very close fit. An external thread, which is used on a bolt, screw, or stud, is called an A thread. An internal thread, which is used in a nut or threaded hole, is called a B thread.

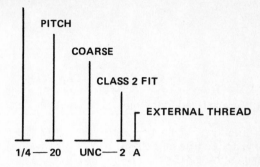

Fig. 4-10 *Thread designation in the USCS. (ATW)*

≡ 4-10 THREAD DESIGNATION

In the USCS, threads are designated by size, pitch, series, and class. Figure 4-10 shows the complete thread designation for a ¼-20 UNC-2A bolt. The bolt is ¼ inch in diameter. It has coarse threads (20 threads per inch). And the thread is an external, class 2 thread. After the thread designation, a number or fraction may appear (for example, ¼-20 x 1 ½). The "1 ½" is the bolt length in inches.

You cannot use a ¼-28 bolt with a ¼-20 nut because the threads do not match. The bolt size *and* the thread pitch must be the same for a bolt or screw to fit a matching nut or a threaded hole.

≡ 4-11 FASTENER STRENGTH MARKINGS

Bolts and hex-head screws are made of materials of different strengths. The table in Fig. 4-11 shows the head markings that tell the quality of the bolt or screw. The minimum tensile strength is the pull (in pounds) that a round rod with a cross section of 1 inch can stand before it breaks. High-quality screws are more expensive. They are used only where added strength is necessary.

Metric Fasteners

≡ 4-12 METRIC FASTENERS

Today many cars use metric fasteners. There are some similarities with USCS fasteners. For example, the wrench size for both types is determined by measuring across the flats of the bolt head (Fig. 4-12). Some metric fasteners are *almost* the same size as USCS fasteners. However, they are not interchangeable! The threads are not the same. Metric threads are measured in millimeters.

≡ 4-13 METRIC FASTENER SIZES

The sizes of metric fasteners are not as completely standardized as in the USCS. Many manufacturers follow the standard metric fastener sizes defined by the International Standards Organization (ISO). These are

Cap-Screw Head Markings	Cap-Screw Body Size Inches–Thread	SAE Grade 1 or 2 (Used Infrequently) Torque		SAE Grade 5 (Used Frequently) Torque		SAE Grade 6 or 7 (Used at Times) Torque		SAE Grade 8 (Used Frequently) Torque	
		ft-lb	N-m	ft-lb	N-m	ft-lb	N-m	ft-lb	N-m
Manufacturer's marks may vary. Three-line markings on heads shown below, for example, indicate SAE grade 5.	¼–20	5	6.7	8	10.8	10	13.5	12	16.2
	–28	6	8.1	10	13.5			14	18.9
	⁵⁄₁₆–18	11	14.9	17	23.0	19	25.7	24	32.5
	–24	13	17.6	19	25.7			27	36.6
	⅜–16	18	24.4	31	42.0	34	46.0	44	59.6
	–24	20	27.1	35	47.4			49	66.4
	⁷⁄₁₆–14	28	37.9	49	66.4	55	74.5	70	94.9
	–20	30	40.6	55	74.5			78	105.7
	½–13	39	52.8	75	101.6	85	115.2	105	142.3
	–20	41	55.5	85	115.2			120	162.6
	⁹⁄₁₆–12	51	69.1	110	149.1	120	162.6	155	210.1
	–18	55	74.5	120	162.6			170	230.4
	⅝–11	83	112.5	150	203.3	167	226.4	210	284.7
	–18	95	128.8	170	230.4			240	325.3
	¾–10	105	142.3	270	366.0	280	379.6	375	508.4
	–16	115	155.9	295	399.9			420	569.4
	⅞– 9	160	216.9	395	535.5	440	596.5	605	820.2
	–14	175	237.2	435	589.7			675	915.1
	1– 8	235	318.6	590	799.9	660	894.8	910	1233.7
	–14	250	338.9	660	894.8			990	1342.2

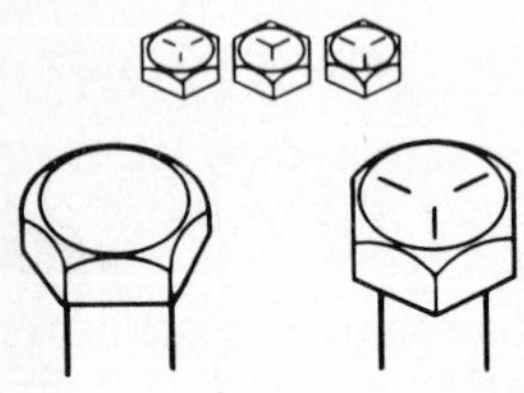

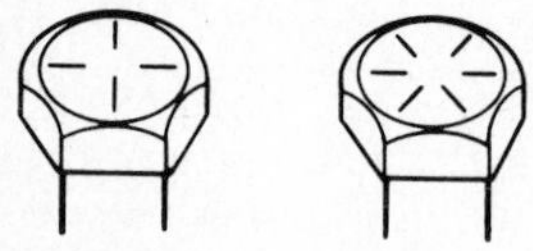

SAE 1 or 2   SAE 5

SAE 6 or 7   SAE 8

Fig. 4-11 Torque specifications and cap-screw head markings. *(American Motors Corporation)*

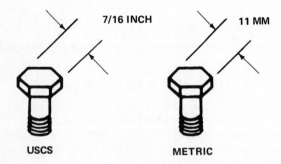

Fig. 4-12 Determining wrench size required for a bolt head.

shown in Fig. 4-13. This system reduces the number of different metric fasteners, while retaining the best strength qualities in each thread size. For example, the USCS ¼-20 and ¼-28 screws are replaced by the metric M6.0x1 screw. It has nearly the same diameter and 25.4 threads per inch. This places the thread pitch between the USCS coarse and fine.

≡ 4-14 METRIC THREAD DESIGNATION

Metric and USCS thread designations differ slightly. The difference is shown in Fig. 4-14. In the metric system, the "M8" indicates the bolt is 8 millimeters (mm) in diameter. The "1.25" is the distance between the threads. On the bolt designation shown in Fig. 4-14, the distance between each thread is 1.25 mm. This measurement is made from the crest of one thread to the crest of the next thread (Fig. 4-15).

≡ 4-15 METRIC FASTENER STRENGTH

Both USCS and metric bolts have head markings to show bolt strength. Slash marks on the head of a USCS bolt indicate its strength (Fig. 4-11). The more slash marks on the head, the stronger the bolt. Metric bolts have the "property class" number (Fig. 4-15, right) on

USCS Thread Size (inch)	Metric Thread Size Diameter (mm)	Pitch (mm)	USCS Thread Size (inch)	Metric Thread Size Diameter (mm)	Pitch (mm)	USCS Thread Size (inch)	Metric Thread Size Diameter (mm)	Pitch (mm)
	M1.5	x 0.35	¼-28				M22.0	x 2.50
0-80				M7.0	x 1.00		M22.0	x 2.00
	M1.6	x 0.35		M7.0	x 0.75		M22.0	x 1.50
	M1.8	x 0.35	5⁄16-18			7⁄8-9		
1-64			5⁄16-24			7⁄8-14		
1-72				M8.0	x 1.25		M24.0	x 3.00
	M2.0	x 0.45		M8.0	x 1.00		M24.0	x 2.00
	M2.0	x 0.40		M9.0	x 1.25		M24.0	x 1.50
2-56				M9.0	x 1.00		M25.0	x 2.00
2-64			3⁄8-16				M25.0	x 1.50
	M2.2	x 0.45	3⁄8-24			1-8		
	M2.3	x 0.40		M10.0	x 1.50	1-12		
	M2.5	x 0.45		M10.0	x 1.25		M26.0	x 3.00
3-48				M10.0	x 1.00		M27.0	x 3.00
3-56				M11.0	x 1.50		M27.0	x 2.00
	M2.6	x 0.45	7⁄16-14				M28.0	x 3.00
4-40			7⁄16-20				M28.0	x 2.00
4-48				M12.0	x 1.75	1⅛-7		
	M3.0	x 0.60		M12.0	x 1.50	1⅛-12		
	M3.0	x 0.50		M12.0	x 1.25		M30.0	x 3.50
5-40			½-13				M30.0	x 3.00
5-44			½-20				M30.0	x 2.00
	M3.5	x 0.60		M14.0	x 2.00	1¼-7		
6-32				M14.0	x 1.50	1¼-12		
6-40				M14.0	x 1.25		M32.0	x 3.50
	M4.0	x 0.75	9⁄16-12				M32.0	x 2.00
	M4.0	x 0.70	9⁄16-18				M33.0	x 3.50
8-32				M15.0	x 1.50		M33.0	x 3.00
8-36			5⁄8-11				M33.0	x 2.00
	M4.5	x 0.75	5⁄8-18				M34.0	x 3.50
10-24				M16.0	x 2.00	1⅜-6		
10-32				M16.0	x 1.50	1⅜-12		
	M5.0	x 1.00		M17.0	x 1.50		M36.0	x 4.00
	M5.0	x 0.90		M18.0	x 2.50		M36.0	x 3.00
	M5.0	x 0.80		M18.0	x 2.00		M36.0	x 2.00
12-24				M18.0	x 1.50		M38.0	x 4.00
12-28				M19.0	x 2.50			
	M5.5	x 0.90	¾-10					
	M6.0	x 1.00	¾-16					
	M6.0	x 0.75		M20.0	x 2.50			
	M6.3	x 1.00		M20.0	x 2.00			
¼-20				M20.0	x 1.50			

Fig. 4-13 Chart comparing USCS thread sizes with metric sizes.

Inch		Metric	
⁵⁄₁₆-18		M8x1.25	
Thread major diameter in inches	Number of threads per inch	Thread major diameter in millimeters	Distance between threads in millimeters

Fig. 4-14 Metric and USCS thread designations. *(Chrysler Corporation)*

the bolt head (Fig. 4-16). The higher the number, the greater the strength. Common metric bolt markings are 9.8 and 10.9. Nut strength markings are also shown in Fig. 4-16. Large studs may have the property class number stamped on them. Smaller studs are stamped on the end with a geometric code (Fig. 4-17).

≡ 4-16 PREVAILING-TORQUE FASTENERS

Many nuts and bolts are designed to have a continuous resistance to turning. This type of fastener is called a *prevailing-torque fastener.* No lock washer is required. The *interference fit* of the threads prevents the fastener from loosening.

For example, a prevailing-torque nut is designed to have an interference between the nut (Fig. 4-18) and the bolt threads. As a result, the nut resists loosening, even if it is not tightened down. The interference is often caused by distortion of the top of an all-metal nut. Another method is using a nylon patch on the threads in the middle of the held flat. A nylon insert may also be used between the nut and bolt threads.

A prevailing-torque bolt (Fig. 4-19) is designed to have an interference between the bolt and the nut threads or the threads of a tapped hole. The interference is caused by distorting some of the bolt threads or by using a patch of nylon or adhesive on the threads.

≡ 4-17 REUSE OF PREVAILING-TORQUE FASTENERS

Prevailing-torque fasteners which are rusty or damaged should be replaced with new ones of equal or greater strength. However, sometimes clean unrusted prevailing-torque nuts and bolts may be reused. Before installation, inspect each one as follows:

1. Clean any dirt and other foreign material off the nut or bolt.

2. Inspect the nut or bolt for cracks, elongation, or other signs of misuse or overtightening. If there is any doubt, discard the fastener.

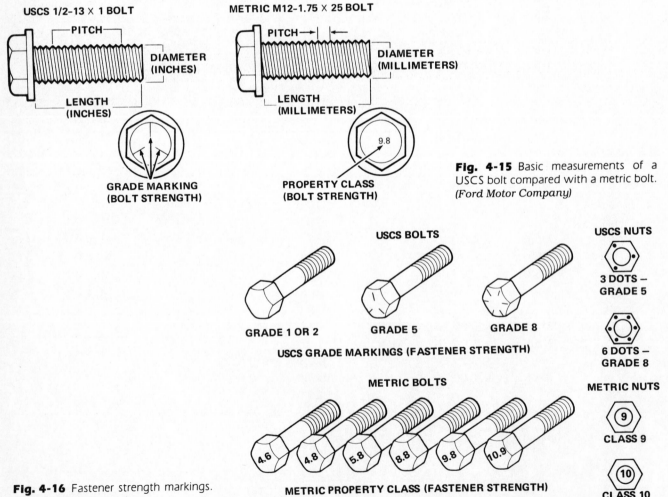

Fig. 4-15 Basic measurements of a USCS bolt compared with a metric bolt. *(Ford Motor Company)*

Fig. 4-16 Fastener strength markings. *(Ford Motor Company)*

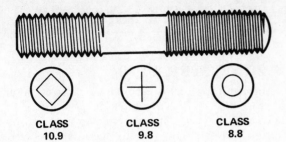

Fig. 4-17 Strength markings on a metric stud.

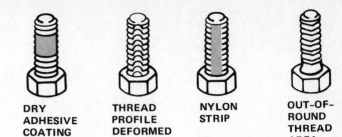

Fig. 4-19 Various types of prevailing-torque bolts. (*General Motors Corporation*)

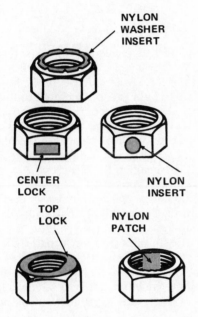

Fig. 4-18 Various types of prevailing-torque nuts. (*General Motors Corporation*)

3. Assemble the parts, and hand-start the nut or the bolt.

4. Before the fastener seats, check that the specified torque is required to overcome the resistance to turn. The torque specifications for most common sizes of prevailing-torque nuts and bolts are given in Fig. 4-20. If the fastener turns too easily, replace it. If installed, it will work loose.

5. Tighten the fastener to the installed torque specified in the manufacturer's service manual.

≡ 4-18 ANTISEIZE COMPOUND

The specifications for tightening a fastener are usually given for clean dry threads. However, most bolts are steel. Sometimes they fit into aluminum threads cut into an aluminum cylinder head or block. Cylinder-head bolts and main-bearing-cap bolts have high torque specifications. When such a bolt is removed from an aluminum part, the aluminum threads may be damaged or even pulled out by the bolt. This is because of corrosion, and because steel bolts tend to lock, or "seize," in aluminum threads.

To prevent this, an *antiseize compound* should be used on any bolt that goes into aluminum threads (Fig.

PREVAILING TORQUE FOR METRIC FASTENERS

	Millimeters	6 & 6.3	8	10	12	14	16	20
Nuts and all-metal bolts	N-m	0.4	0.8	1.4	2.2	3.0	4.2	7.0
	in-lb	4.0	7.0	12	18	25	35	57
Adhesive- or nylon-coated bolts	N-m	0.4	0.6	1.2	1.6	2.4	3.4	5.6
	in-lb	4.0	5.0	10	14	20	28	46

PREVAILING TORQUE FOR USCS FASTENERS

	Inch	¼	5⁄16	⅜	7⁄16	½	9⁄16	⅝	¾
Nuts and all-metal bolts	N-m	0.4	0.6	1.4	1.8	2.4	3.2	4.2	6.2
	in-lb	4.0	5.0	12	15	20	27	35	51
Adhesive- or nylon-coated bolts	N-m	0.4	0.6	1.0	1.4	1.8	2.6	3.4	5.2
	in-lb	4.0	5.0	9.0	12	15	22	28	43

Fig. 4-20 Torque specifications for common sizes of prevailing-torque nuts and bolts. (*General Motors Corporation*)

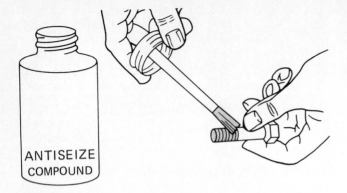

Fig. 4-21 Antiseize compound should be used on any bolt that goes into aluminum threads. *(ATW)*

4-21). A coating of antiseize compound on the threads prevents corrosion, seizing, galling, and pitting. Later, the bolt may be removed easily without damage to the threads.

≡ 4-19 THREAD INSERTS

Damaged or worn threads in a cylinder block, cylinder head, or other part can often be replaced with a thread insert (Fig. 4-22). To make the repair, you need a thread repair kit. First, drill out the hole using the same size drill that is equal in diameter to the bolt. For example, for a ¼-inch bolt, use a ¼-inch drill. Then tap the hole with the special tap from the thread repair kit. These taps cut the special threads for the insert.

Using the inserting tool from the thread repair kit, install the thread insert into the hole (Fig. 4-22). This brings the hole back to its original thread size. Now the original bolt can be used in it. After the thread insert is installed, apply antiseize compound to the inside thread of the insert. Then install the bolt and tighten to the specified torque.

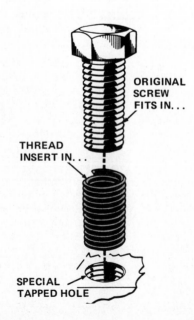

Fig. 4-22 Installing a thread insert into a tapped hole. *(Chrysler Corporation)*

Mechanical Fasteners

≡ 4-20 COTTER PINS

A *cotter pin* is a split soft-steel pin with a loop at one end for a head (Fig. 4-23). The cotter pin is inserted in a drilled hole (Fig. 4-24). The split ends are spread to lock the pin in position. This usually secures a castle nut (Fig. 4-24) or other type of pin. To use the cotter pin with a castle nut, tighten the nut until the nut slots are aligned with the hole. Then insert the cotter pin and bend the legs outward. One method is shown in Fig. 4-24.

≡ 4-21 RIVETS

A *rivet* (Fig. 4-25) is a headed metal fastener which joins parts together when a head is formed on the headless end. In the car, rivets hold the brake lining on the brake shoes. They also keep the clutch lining in place. Rivets are used to hold some transmission linkage together and to attach trim and upholstery to the car.

One end of the rivet has a head (Fig. 4-25). After the rivet is in place, a driver or a hammer-and-rivet set is used to form the head on the other end.

Blind rivets, or "Pop" rivets (Fig. 4-26), are special rivets for blind holes. These are holes where one end of the rivet cannot be reached to flatten it. To install a blind rivet, load the stem of the rivet into the rivet gun. Then insert the shank of the rivet into the hole. Squeeze the handle of the rivet gun. This pulls the stem of the rivet out until it breaks off. Now the rivet is set in place.

The head on the blind side of the hole is formed as the stem is pulled out. The small stem head pulls

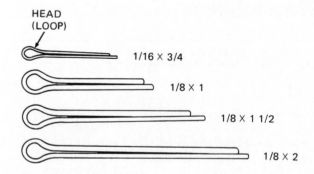

Fig. 4-23 Various sizes of cotter pins. *(ATW)*

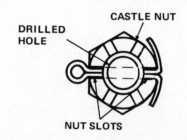

Fig. 4-24 A cotter pin is installed through a drilled hole to secure a castle nut in place. *(ATW)*

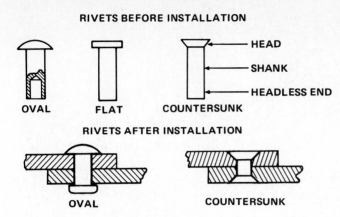

RIVETS BEFORE INSTALLATION

OVAL FLAT COUNTERSUNK
HEAD
SHANK
HEADLESS END

RIVETS AFTER INSTALLATION

OVAL COUNTERSUNK

Fig. 4-25 Rivets before installation (top) and after installation (bottom).

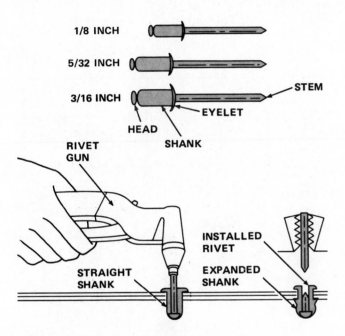

1/8 INCH
5/32 INCH
3/16 INCH
STEM
EYELET
HEAD
SHANK
RIVET GUN
STRAIGHT SHANK
INSTALLED RIVET
EXPANDED SHANK

Fig. 4-26 Installing a blind rivet. (ATW)

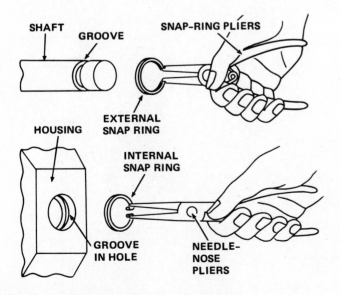

SHAFT GROOVE SNAP-RING PLIERS
EXTERNAL SNAP RING
HOUSING INTERNAL SNAP RING
GROOVE IN HOLE NEEDLE-NOSE PLIERS

Fig. 4-27 Internal and external snap rings. (ATW)

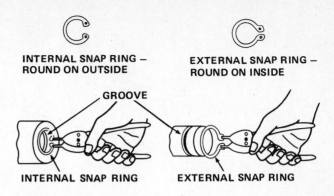

INTERNAL SNAP RING – ROUND ON OUTSIDE EXTERNAL SNAP RING – ROUND ON INSIDE
GROOVE
INTERNAL SNAP RING EXTERNAL SNAP RING

Fig. 4-28 Installing internal and external Truarc retaining rings. (ATW)

against the soft metal shank on the blind side of the hole. The shank collapses and expands before the stem breaks off. This secures the blind rivet in place.

Rivets are usually removed by cutting off one end with a chisel. They can also be driven out with a punch or drilled out.

≡ 4-22 SNAP RINGS

External retaining rings, or "snap rings," prevent end-to-end movement of a gear or bearing on a shaft (Fig. 4-27). Internal snap rings are used in housings to keep shafts or other parts in position. The external snap ring must be expanded, or stretched, with *snap-ring pliers*. Then it is slipped over the end of a grooved shaft and released to seat in the groove (Fig. 4-27, top). The internal snap ring must be squeezed so it can slip into the hole and then expand into a groove in the housing (Fig. 4-27, bottom). Many types of snap rings are used in automobiles. Some can be removed and installed with needle-nose pliers (Fig. 4-27). Others require the use of various types of snap-ring pliers (Figs. 4-27 and 4-28).

The Truarc retaining ring is a special type of snap ring. Its two lips have holes for the pin ends of special snap-ring pliers (Fig. 4-28). With the pins securely in the holes, there is less chance of the ring slipping off the pliers during removal and installation.

≡ 4-23 CLIPS

Clips of various types are used to hold interior trim and trim panels and exterior molding in place. For example, Fig. 4-29 shows the molding and clips used on one model of the Lincoln Continental. The clips are installed in holes in the body panels, and the molding is snapped onto the clips. Some molding is attached by adhesive.

Figure 4-30 shows an assortment of fasteners that are used in various cars to attach trim panels, as, for example, on the inside of doors and on quarter panels. Many of these are simply U-shaped brackets onto which the trim panels are slid. Trim panels also are held in place by screws. The screws may be covered by plates that snap into place.

≡ 4-24 KEYS AND SPLINES

Keys and splines are used to lock gears, pulleys, collars, and other similar parts to shafts so that they will rotate

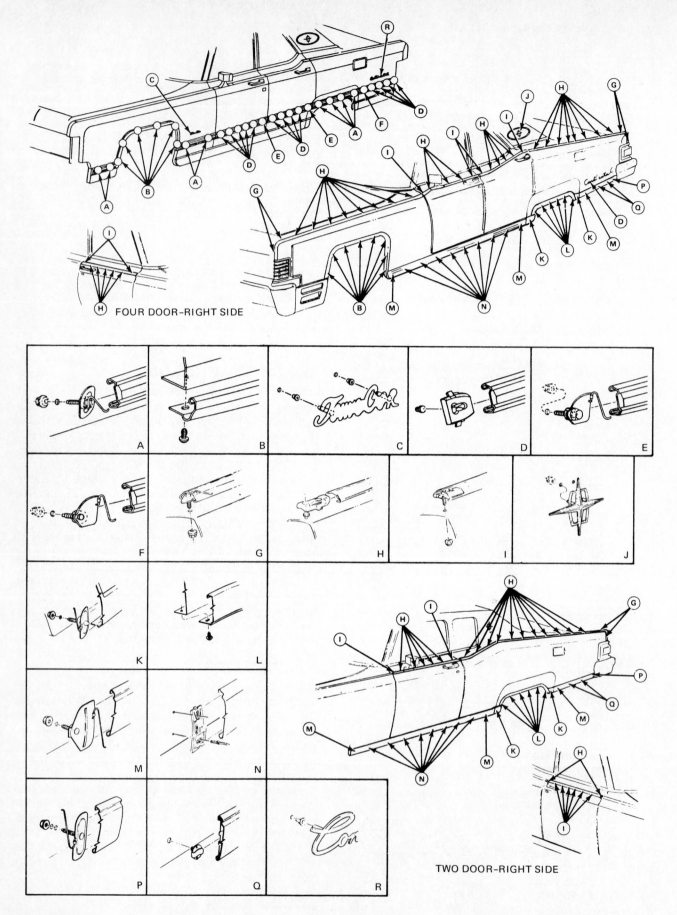

Fig. 4-29 Moldings and clips used on one model car. (*Ford Motor Company*)

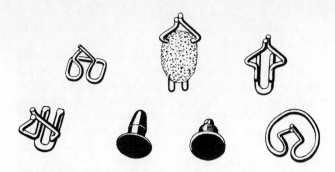

Fig. 4-30 Various types of trim-panel fasteners. *(Ford Motor Company)*

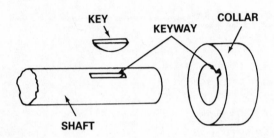

Fig. 4-31 A key locks parts together by fitting into slots called *keyways.*

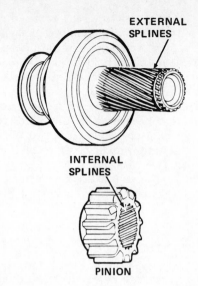

Fig. 4-32 Internal and external splines.

together. Figure 4-31 shows a typical key installation. The key is wedge-shaped and fits into slots called *keyways.* The keyways are cut in the shaft and collar (or other part being installed). The key locks the shaft and collar together.

To install the key, place the key into the keyway in the shaft (Fig. 4-31). Then slide the collar over the key until the collar is in place. If the collar or gear is to be installed on the end of the shaft, the keyway often extends to the end of the shaft. With this type of assembly, the collar is placed on the shaft so that the keyways match. Then a wedge-shaped key is driven into the two keyways for a tight fit. No other holding device is required to fasten the collar firmly to the shaft.

Splines are internal and external teeth cut in both the shaft and the installed part (Fig. 4-32). When the gear, pulley, or collar is installed on the shaft, it is the same as having many keys between the two parts. In many assemblies, the splines fit loosely so that the gear or other part is free to move back and forth on the splines. However, the splines force both parts to rotate together. Splines may be straight or curved (Fig. 4-32).

≡ 4-25 GASKETS

A *gasket* is a thin layer of soft material such as paper, cork, rubber, or copper. It is placed between two flat surfaces to make a tight seal (Fig. 4-33). When the gasket is squeezed by the tightening of fasteners, the soft material fills any small irregularities in the mating surfaces. This prevents any leakage of fluid, vacuum, or pressure from the joint. Sometimes the gasket is used as a shim to take up space.

Various types of gaskets are used throughout the automobile, especially in the engine. They seal joints between engine parts, such as between the oil pan, manifolds, or water pump and the cylinder head or block. In most joints, holes through the gasket allow it to seal in fuel, oil, or coolant. At the same time, it keeps out dirt, water, and air.

≡ 4-26 STRUCTURAL ADHESIVES

In some cars, welding certain body parts together has been replaced by structural adhesives. These adhesives are not ordinary "glue." They are the result of chemical research. Some joints can be made many times stronger with structural adhesives than with spot welds.

The new adhesives are of two types: single-part epoxies and two-part reactive acrylics. The two-part reactive acrylics use two chemical compounds which are mixed just before they are applied. Parts to be "glued" together have a bead of the mix applied to the joint. The two parts are then brought together and the mix cures in about 2 minutes to form a permanent joint.

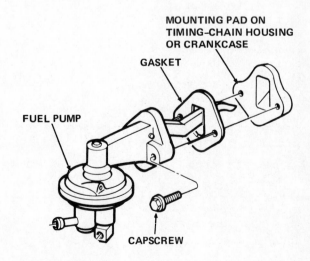

Fig. 4-33 Installation of a gasket.

The single-part epoxy requires heat to cure. It is inactive at room temperature and must be heated after the parts are joined. A common arrangement is to apply the epoxy and temporarily hold the parts in place with a jig. The joint is then cured in the paint oven at the end of the assembly line.

The future will bring increased use of structural adhesives in automobiles because the adhesives eliminate many welding operations and provide stronger joints. In addition, they make possible flush mounting of windows. This reduces air resistance and lowers the drag coefficient of the car (≡2-12). Also, when adhesives are used to install fixed glass in cars (windshield, back window, some side windows), the windows become part of the load-bearing structure. They actually add strength to the body.

You normally will not be concerned about the joints made with adhesives, because you will not be stripping the car down to these basic joints when you are repairing damage. However, there is one caution to observe. Repairing this type of joint by welding can release toxic gases. However, you would usually make repairs by working on the metal away from the joints—straightening metal, replacing damaged sections of panels by welding or riveting the replacement in place.

REVIEW QUESTIONS

Select the *one* correct, best, or most probable answer to each question. You can find the answers in the section indicated at the end of each question.

1. Fasteners that have threads on the outside are (≡4-3)
    a. nuts, bolts, and screws
    b. screws, bolts, and studs
    c. threaded holes and nuts
    d. splines, rivets, and screws

2. Pitch is the (≡4-7)
    a. number of threads per inch
    b. depth of the threads
    c. thread series
    d. thread classes

3. The three thread series are (≡4-8)
    a. class 1, 2, and 3
    b. series 1, 2, and 3
    c. coarse, fine, and extra-fine
    d. pitch, series, and class

4. An external thread is called (≡4-9)
    a. an A thread
    b. a B thread
    c. a C thread
    d. none of the above

5. The most common bolts (≡4-4)
    a. have hexagonal heads
    b. have six-sided heads
    c. have hex heads
    d. all of the above

6. The purpose of the cotter pin is to (≡4-20)
    a. fasten the cotter safely
    b. prevent the cotter from loosening
    c. prevent the nut from loosening
    d. prevent the splines from loosening

7. To keep the nut from loosening, use (≡4-4)
    a. a Palnut
    b. a cotter pin
    c. a lock washer
    d. any of the above

8. The two types of snap rings are (≡4-22)
    a. threaded and with teeth
    b. internal and external
    c. split and solid
    d. retainer and locking

9. Keys and splines (≡4-23)
    a. lock nuts to bolts
    b. lock plates and shafts together
    c. lock gears, pulleys, and collars to shafts
    d. fasten screws or studs in place

10. Thread inserts are used to (≡4-19)
    a. repair damaged internal threads
    b. repair damaged external threads
    c. replace faulty screws or studs
    d. repair damaged nuts

11. Clips are used to (≡4-23)
    a. attach body panels
    b. shorten the body length
    c. attach trim and molding
    d. clip on window glass

12. Two types of structural adhesives used in car bodies are
    a. glue and paste (≡4-26)
    b. epoxy and acrylic
    c. spot welds and solder
    d. arc welds and glue

13. Curing of single-part epoxy requires (≡4-26)
    a. pressure
    b. time
    c. heat
    d. addition of the curing agent

14. A prevailing-torque bolt will not loosen because
    a. it is used with a lock washer (≡4-16)
    b. the tightening torque is less
    c. it has an interference fit with the threads
    d. it requires the use of antiseize compound

15. A gasket is used to (≡4-25)
    a. seal in fuel, oil, or coolant
    b. seal out dirt, water, and air
    c. take up space
    d. all of the above

CHAPTER 5
HAND TOOLS

After studying this chapter, you should be able to:

1. Describe how and when to use screwdrivers, wrenches, sockets, and torque wrenches.
2. Discuss the various types of pliers.
3. Explain how to use sheet-metal cutters.
4. Describe hammers, body hammers, and slide hammers and explain how to use them.
5. Describe the purpose and use of pull rods.
6. Explain how to use suction cups, dollies, body spoons, and pry bars in body repair.
7. Discuss chisels, hacksaws, files, and punches and explain how to use them.

≡ 5-1 HAND TOOLS FOR THE BODY TECHNICIAN

The auto body technician needs a variety of hand tools. The professional body expert usually has a tool chest, as shown in Fig. 5-1, filled with the hand tools required to do the job. Although there are hundreds of tools in the chest shown, the technician knows where every one is because they are all neatly arranged in the drawers.

Fig. 5-1 The professional body technician owns a large tool chest filled with the special tools of the trade.

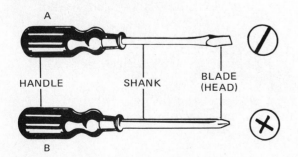

Fig. 5-2 (A) Typical slotted-head screwdriver. (B) Phillips-head screwdriver.

But the body technician does not acquire these tools all at once. He or she starts out with a basic set and then gets new tools as they are required. Note that the body shop is normally equipped with such power tools as pneumatic or electric lifts, hydraulic floor lifts, and pneumatic frame-and-body straighteners. Power tools are discussed in a following chapter.

≡ 5-2 SCREWDRIVERS

The common screwdriver is used to drive or turn screws with slotted heads. Figure 5-2A shows a typical slotted-head screwdriver. The screwdriver tip fits into the slot in the head of the screw. When the screw is turned one way, it goes into the workpiece. When it is turned the other way, it is removed from the workpiece.

Some screws have what seem to be two slots at right angles. The Phillips screw is one of these. The Reed and Prince screw is another. Each requires a special screwdriver with a tip that fits the crossed slots (Fig. 5-3). The Phillips screw is widely used on automobile trim and molding. It reduces the chances that the screwdriver will slip out of the slots and damage the finish.

Figure 4-2 shows a variety of screwheads and the special kinds of screwdrivers needed to turn them. Some of these screws do not have slotted heads. In-

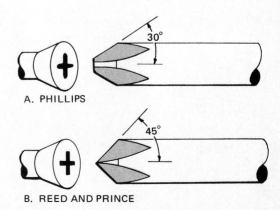

Fig. 5-3 Difference between the Phillips and the Reed and Prince screwdrivers.

stead, they have hexagonal (six-sided) heads. These "hex-head" screws require wrenches to turn them.

Always be sure to pick the right screwdriver for the job. For example, when choosing a screwdriver, make sure to pick one with a tip that properly fits the screw slot.

≡ 5-3 WRENCHES

Wrenches are used to turn screws or bolts that have hexagonal (six-sided heads). They are also used to turn nuts that are hexagonal. Bolts with six-sided heads are called *hex-head bolts*. Nuts with six sides (hexagonal) are called *hex nuts*. A stud goes into a threaded hole, and a nut is turned down on the other end. Figure 4-1 shows you the differences among screws, bolts, and studs.

The simplest wrench to use is the open-end wrench (Fig. 5-4). Select the proper size wrench to snugly fit the bolt head or nut, as shown in Fig. 5-5. Then pull or push the wrench to turn the nut or bolt.

≡ 5-4 BOX WRENCHES

The box wrench (Fig. 5-4) has an opening into which the bolt head or nut fits. The advantages of this wrench are that it will not slip off the bolt head or nut and that it can be used in restricted spaces because of the thinness of the wrench head. The typical box wrench has 12 notches in the head. Using this wrench, you can install a nut or bolt in an area where the wrench can be swung only about 15°. Figure 5-4 also shows a combination wrench that has the advantages of both the open-end and the box wrenches.

≡ 5-5 SOCKET WRENCHES

The socket wrench is the same as the box wrench except that the head, or socket, is detachable. Figure 5-6 shows different types of sockets. To use a socket wrench, first select a handle. There are several types of handles, as shown in Fig. 5-7. Select the socket that will fit the bolt head or nut. Next, snap the socket onto the handle. Finally, place the socket over the bolt head or nut and push or pull the handle.

The ratchet handle (Fig. 5-7) has a ratcheting device that releases in one direction but catches in the other. When you want to tighten a nut, just flip the lever on the ratchet-handle head to make the ratchet catch the socket only in the tightening direction.

The speed handle (Fig. 5-7) lets you spin a nut on or off very quickly.

If you are going to work on imported cars and trucks, you will need a set of metric sockets. USCS-sized tools will not fit some nuts and bolts on imported vehicles. Figure 5-8 shows the difference between metric and USCS sizes of sockets.

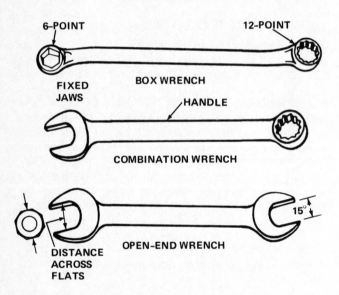

Fig. 5-4 Box, combination, and open-end wrenches. *(ATW)*

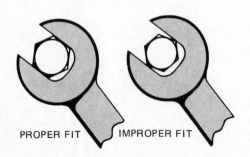

Fig. 5-5 An open-end wrench should fit the nut or bolt head securely.

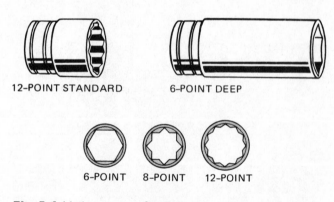

Fig. 5-6 Various types of sockets.

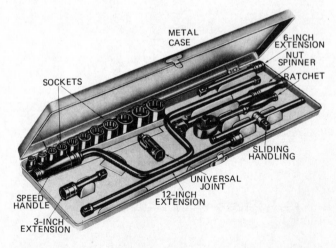

Fig. 5-7 Set of sockets with handles, extensions, and universal joint. *(Snap-on Tools Corporation)*

SOCKET	METRIC SIZE	DECIMAL EQUIVALENT IN INCHES		USCS SIZE	SOCKET	METRIC SIZE	DECIMAL EQUIVALENT IN INCHES		USCS SIZE
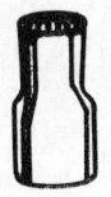	3 mm	0.118	0.125	$\frac{1}{8}$ INCH	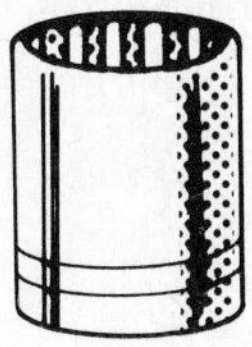	16 mm	0.630	0.625	$\frac{5}{8}$ INCH
	4 mm	0.157	0.187	$\frac{3}{16}$ INCH		18 mm	0.709	0.687	$\frac{11}{16}$ INCH
	6 mm	0.236	0.250	$\frac{1}{4}$ INCH	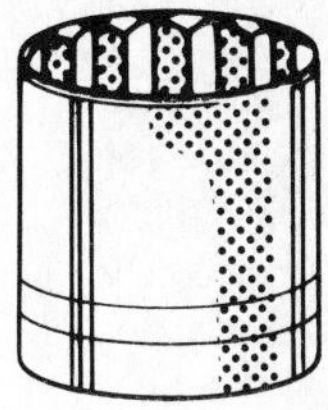	19 mm	0.748	0.750	$\frac{3}{4}$ INCH
	9 mm	0.354	0.312	$\frac{5}{16}$ INCH		20 mm	0.787	0.812	$\frac{13}{16}$ INCH
	10 mm	0.394	0.375	$\frac{3}{8}$ INCH	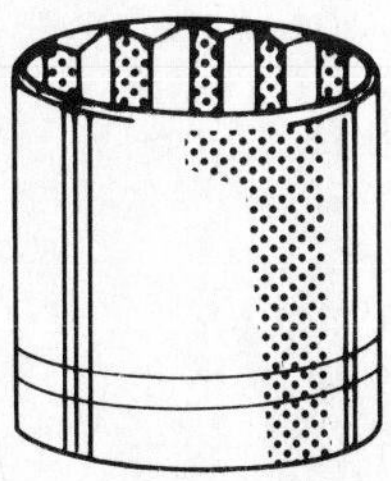	22 mm	0.866	0.875	$\frac{7}{8}$ INCH
	12 mm	0.472	0.437	$\frac{7}{16}$ INCH		24 mm	0.945	0.937	$\frac{15}{16}$ INCH
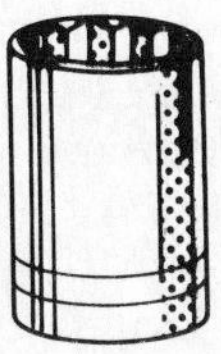	13 mm	0.512	0.500	$\frac{1}{2}$ INCH	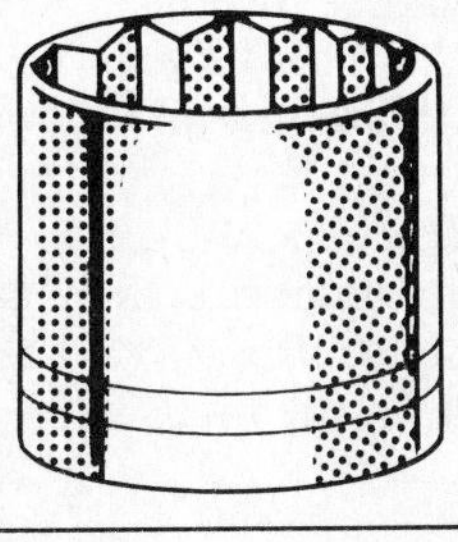	25 mm	0.984	1.00	1 INCH
	15 mm	0.590	0.562	$\frac{9}{16}$ INCH					

Fig. 5-8 Comparison of metric and USCS sockets. *(Dana Corporation)*

Metric nut and bolt sizes are expressed in millimeters. But the drive lugs on socket drivers are measured in inches throughout the world. The drive end of a socket is always made to accept ¼-inch, ⅜-inch, or ½-inch drive lugs (Fig. 5-9).

≡ 5-6 TORQUE WRENCHES

In automobiles, nuts and bolts must be tightened properly. Otherwise, they will loosen and something may fall apart. This could cause serious trouble, damage to the car, and possibly an accident. If nuts or bolts are tightened too much, they will be strained excessively and could break later, again with disastrous results.

To ensure proper tightening of nuts and bolts, you must use torque wrenches. For example, a specification might call for tightening a bolt to "20–24 lb-ft." This means that you have to put a 20- to 24-pound (lb) torque (or twist) 1 foot (ft) from the bolt. The torque

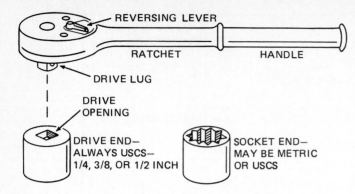

Fig. 5-9 Attaching the socket to the ratchet handle. *(ATW)*

wrench (Fig. 5-10) lets you do this accurately. You snap the correct socket on the torque wrench, fit the socket on the bolt head, and pull the wrench handle. Watch the indicator needle on the wrench as you gradually increase your pull. When it registers somewhere between 20 and 24, you know you have tightened the bolt correctly. This procedure is called *torquing* the bolt.

NOTE: Threads must be clean and in good shape. Dirty or damaged threads put a drag on the threads as the bolt is turned down. This prevents proper tightening of the bolt. Therefore, when assembling the various components, make sure that the threads are clean and in good condition.

On some torque wrenches, the amount of torque is registered on a dial or by a pointer as the handle is pulled (Fig. 5-10). On other types of torque wrenches, the specified torque is set by turning the handle (Fig. 5-10). A loud click is heard when that torque is reached. This type of torque wrench is called a *micrometer,* or *clicker, torque wrench.* Figure 5-10 shows how the specified torque is preset into the micrometer torque wrench by adjusting and locking the handle. This type of torque wrench permits very accurate tightening of nuts and bolts.

Most torque wrenches measure the torque in pound-feet (lb-ft). Some torque wrenches used on small nuts and bolts measure torque in pound-inches (lb-in). Twelve pound-inches equals 1 pound-foot. In the metric system, torque wrenches are scaled in kilogram-meters (kg-m), kilogram-centimeters (kg-cm), and newton-meters (N-m). Newton-meters is the preferred metric unit, although the others are still used in some manufacturers' specs. To convert pound-feet to kilogram-meters, multiply the pound-feet by 0.138. To convert to newton-meters, multiply pound-feet by 1.35.

≡ 5-7 PLIERS

Pliers (Fig. 5-11) are a special type of adjustable wrench. The jaws are adjustable because the two legs move on a pivot. Therefore, pliers can be used to grip or turn an object. But pliers must not be used on nuts or bolt heads. They will round off the edges of the hex and roughen the flats so that a wrench will no longer fit properly.

Some pliers have a side cutter, which can be used to cut wires. There are also regular nippers which have cutting edges instead of jaws. These are used to cut wire, thin sheet metal, and small bolts.

≡ 5-8 CHANNELLOCK PLIERS

These pliers are similar to the other pliers shown in Fig. 5-11. However, they have extra-long handles which make them a very strong gripping tool. These pliers have grooves on one jaw and lands on the other. To change the amount the jaws can open, the relative positions of the grooves and lands are changed. The groove-and-land design permits the jaws to be parallel to each other at any setting. This makes the pliers less likely to slip when gripping an object.

≡ 5-9 VISE-GRIP PLIERS

These pliers (Fig. 5-11) are locking-jaw pliers that can be locked onto an object. The screw at the end of the handle is used to adjust the size of the jaw opening. When the jaws are adjusted to grip an object, closing the handles will lock the jaws in place. They are released by pulling on the release lever.

A variety of locking-jaw pliers are used in the body shop. They are available in lengths from 6 to 12 inches. Some have flat jaws, as shown in Fig. 5-11. Another type has curved jaws and is used to grip pipe and other round objects. One special locking-jaw pliers has

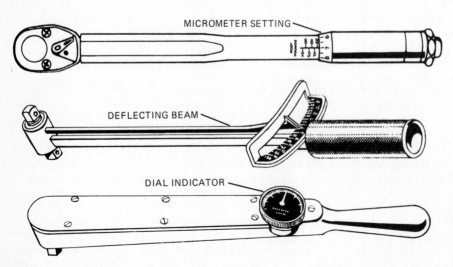

Fig. 5-10 Various types of torque wrenches. *(General Motors Corporation)*

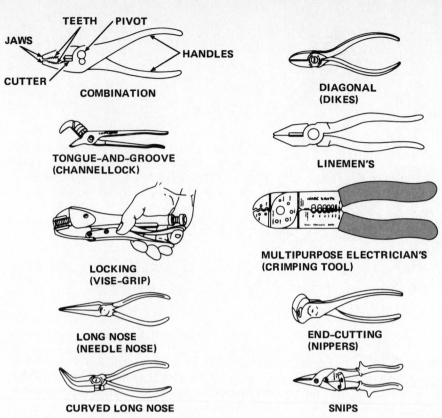

TEETH PIVOT

JAWS

CUTTER

HANDLES

COMBINATION

DIAGONAL
(DIKES)

TONGUE-AND-GROOVE
(CHANNELLOCK)

LINEMEN'S

LOCKING
(VISE-GRIP)

MULTIPURPOSE ELECTRICIAN'S
(CRIMPING TOOL)

LONG NOSE
(NEEDLE NOSE)

END-CUTTING
(NIPPERS)

CURVED LONG NOSE

SNIPS

GRIPPING PLIERS

CUTTING PLIERS

Fig. 5-11 Various types of gripping pliers and cutting pliers. *(ATW)*

smooth jaws and is used to hold sheet-metal panels together for welding or brazing. This leaves the hands free to do the job. These pliers are also useful on an upholstery job. They permit the cloth material to be pulled as necessary without damage.

NOTE: *All pliers and other tools should be kept clean and, when not in use, returned to your toolbox or the toolroom. If properly cared for, tools will last a long time. But if they are abused, their life will be short. Take care of your tools.*

≡ 5-10 SHEET-METAL CUTTERS

Sheet-metal cutters are used to cut thin sheet metal of the type used for body panels and trunk lids. To cut out a damaged area of a body panel — for example, part of a fender — special panel cutters are used. Figure 5-12 shows one of these. They are thin so they can be easily worked around on the body panels needing repair.

Regular metal cutters are shown in Figs. 5-11 and 5-13. These are called *snips,* or *shears.* Snips have sharp-edged jaws that produce the cutting action as the jaws move past each other. They must be treated with care, and cleaned and oiled periodically. Then they should be stored in a clean, dry place. Snips should never be used to cut anything except sheet metal. Cutting bolts or rods will ruin the cutting edges.

NOTE: *The body technician usually owns and uses an air-driven cutting tool that can cut out damaged sections of sheet metal very quickly. This tool is described in Chap. 7.*

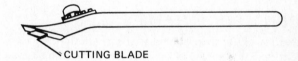

CUTTING BLADE

Fig. 5-12 Panel cutter.

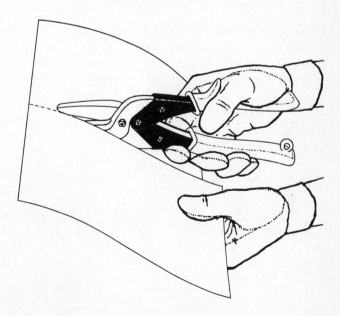

Fig. 5-13 Cutting sheet metal with snips.

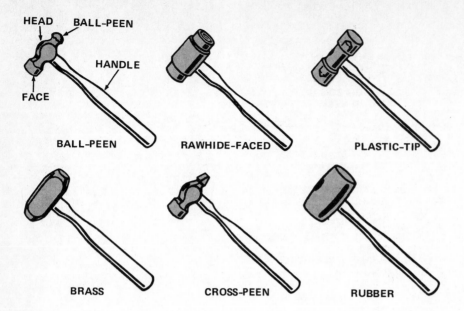

Fig. 5-14 Various types of hammers used in the auto shop.

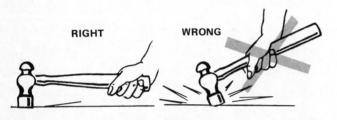

Fig. 5-15 Right and wrong way to hold a hammer.

≡ 5-11 SHOP HAMMERS

A variety of hammers are used in the automotive shop. Figure 5-14 shows some of the more common types. The soft-face hammers, tipped with plastic or rawhide or made of brass, are used on metal that has been dented or otherwise damaged. Figure 5-15 shows the wrong and right way to use a hammer. The handle should be gripped on the end. The blow should bring the face of the hammer down flat on the surface.

≡ 5-12 BODY HAMMERS

Figure 5-16 shows several body hammers. Each of these has its own special purpose. Some are used to align or rough out damaged sheet metal. Others are then used to smooth the damaged surface in preparation for final finishing. The pick hammers have a pointed end and a flat end. The pointed end is used to "pick up" small dents when the metal can be worked on from the underside (Fig. 5-17). Hitting the depressed area with the pick will push it up into place. Often, a dolly is used to help (Fig. 5-18). The *dolly* is a solid block of steel which backs up the panel. Dollies are described later in the chapter.

NOTE: Always use the right hammer for the job. For example, using a body hammer to drive a nail or a chisel will damage the working face of the hammer. A regular shop hammer should be used for such jobs. Check the head of the hammer occasionally to make sure it is firmly on the handle. A wedge or screw is used to spread the handle and tighten it in the eye of the hammerhead. Make sure it is tight. Someone could be injured if the head should fly off when the hammer is swung.

≡ 5-13 SLIDE HAMMER

Another way to raise the metal in a dent or depression is with a slide hammer (Fig. 5-19). The slide hammer has a weight that can be rammed against one or the other of

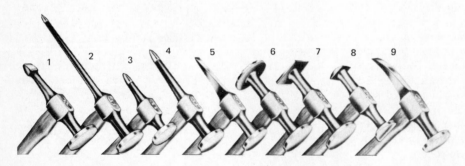

1. WIDE-NOSE PEEN HAMMER
2. LONG PICKING HAMMER
3. PICKING AND DINGING HAMMER
4. LONG, LOW SPOT PICK HAMMER
5. WIDE-NOSE, CROSS-PEEN HAMMER

6. SHRINKING HAMMER
7. WIDE-FACE SHRINKING HAMMER
8. REVERSE-CURVE LIGHT BUMPING HAMMER
9. SHORT-CURVED, CROSS-PEEN HAMMER

Fig. 5-16 Various types of body hammers.

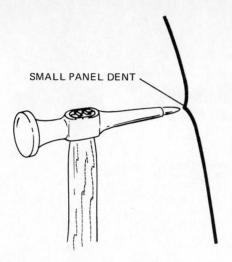

Fig. 5-17 The pick hammer is used to pick up, or flatten, dents in sheet metal, working from the reverse side.

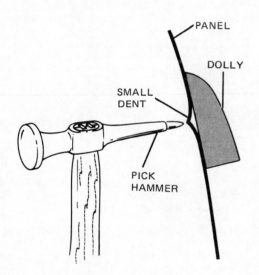

Fig. 5-18 The dolly block is used to back up the metal while the hammer is used to straighten the metal.

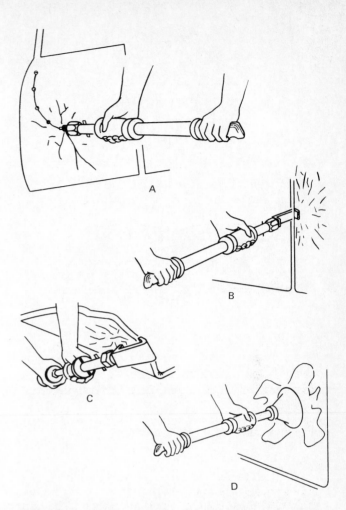

Fig. 5-19 Using a slide hammer. (A) Pulling out a crease or buckle in a body panel. (B) Pulling out the edge of the panel. (C) Pulling against the edge of the fender. (D) Used with a vacuum cup to pull out a dent in a panel. *(Guy-Chart Tools Limited)*

the two stops on the shaft. In use, the working end is attached to an object and the slide is rammed against the stop. This causes the working end to either pull or push on the object being worked on.

For example, a slide hammer can be used to raise a depressed area on a fender. First, holes are drilled in the depressed area (Fig. 5-19A). Then a sheet-metal screw is screwed into one of the holes. The slide hammer is then hooked onto the end of the screw, as shown. Careful operation of the slide hammer will then pull the sheet metal out into its approximate original contour. The technician moves the screw from one hole to another as necessary to do the job. Proper use of the slide hammer in this manner will get the sheet metal ready for the next steps—filing, filling, finishing, and painting.

Using the slide hammer as described above does not require any work from the inside of the panel. It is all done from the outside. Figures 5-19A, B, C, and D show various uses of the slide hammer.

≡ 5-14 PULL RODS

Pull rods (Fig. 5-20) are another type of tool that can be used to pull dents out. They will not work on larger dents or depressed areas as effectively as the slide hammer. To use a pull rod, a hole is drilled in the center of the dent. The hook end of the pull rod is then pushed through the hole and hooked on the back side of the sheet metal. This enables you to pull the dent out. Often, you can use a body hammer to tap lightly around the dent to help the metal spring back to its original contour.

Some body technicians prefer not to use pull rods or slide hammers unless there is no other way to pull out the dents. Use of a pull rod or slide hammer may leave a raised rim around each hole (Fig. 5-21). Then this has to be worked down or filed off.

≡ 5-15 SUCTION CUPS

The rubber suction cup (Fig. 5-22A) is another tool that can be used to pull out larger, but shallow, dents. For example, suppose a car door has been bumped so that a large area has been pushed in. If the metal has not been actually buckled (the metal upset), a suction cup can

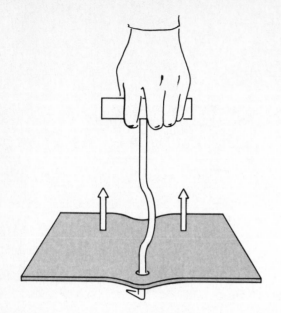

Fig. 5-20 Using a pull rod to straighten a dent.

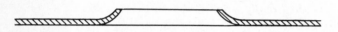

Fig. 5-21 A pull rod or slide hammer can leave a raised rim around the hole where the pull was made.

often be used to pull the metal out to its original contour. Figure 5-19D shows how this is done, using a slide hammer. The panel must be clean and wet. The cup should also be wet. It is pushed in at the center of the depression so that the air is expelled from the cup. The vacuum will then hold the cup against the panel. Now the cup can be pulled out, and if the operation is successful, the panel will snap back to its original contour.

Suction cups are sometimes used in groups of up to three to work on large panels such as a door panel (Fig. 5-22B) or a car roof (Fig. 5-22C).

≡ 5-16 DOLLIES

Up to now, the metal-straightening tools described can all be used on the outside. Therefore, these tools are very convenient where the damaged panel cannot be reached from the inside. This could occur where the panel is backed by trim and some mechanism, such as in the door, or by the internal structure, as on a quarter panel.

But there are many types of sheet-metal damage that require working from both sides of the panel. Besides, a better and smoother job can usually be done if it is possible to get a hand back of the panel. In such case, a dolly is used. Figure 5-23 shows several dollies.

The dolly is held in one hand either directly under the dent or off to one side. A body hammer is used to hammer against the other side of the sheet metal. There are two procedures called hammering *off the dolly* and hammering *on the dolly*. The general name for the procedure is *dinging*.

For example, Fig. 5-24 shows a dolly and body hammer being used to work out a small dent in sheet metal

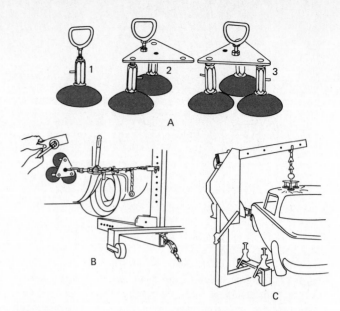

Fig. 5-22 Suction cups and their uses. (A) Suction cups are used singly or in groups of two or three. (B) Three suction cups being used to pull out a dent in a door panel. The technician is tapping the area above the dent to relieve the tension in the metal. (C) Using suction cups to pull up on a dent in a car roof. *(Guy-Chart Tools Limited)*

1. WING-DING SPOON DOLLY
2. LARGE COMMA WEDGE
3. GENERAL-PURPOSE DOLLY
4. HEEL DOLLY
5. TOE DOLLY

Fig. 5-23 Various types of metalworking dollies. *(Snap-on Tools Corporation)*

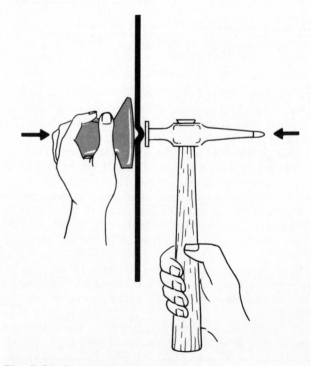

Fig. 5-24 On-the-dolly hammering.

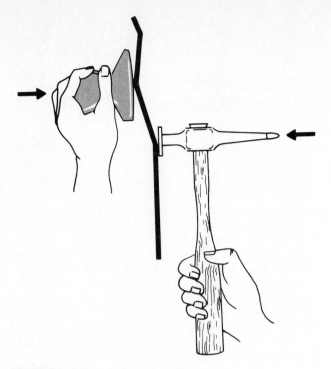

Fig. 5-25 Off-the-dolly hammering.

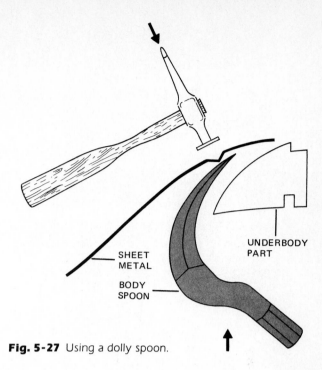

Fig. 5-27 Using a dolly spoon.

by the on-the-dolly process. The dolly provides the backing needed to counter the hammer blows.

The off-the-dolly procedure is used to work out a high spot and bordering low spot, or ridge, at the same time (Fig. 5-25). The hammer is working down a high spot while at the same time the dolly is working up the adjoining low spot.

The examples discussed here are only a small part of the many uses for dollies. They may be used by themselves, for example, to ding out low spots from inside a panel. A later chapter describes in detail how dollies are used.

≡ 5-17 BODY SPOONS

Body spoons (Fig. 5-26), or dolly spoons, have flattened ends which are curved or straight, depending on the purpose of the spoon. There are three general types, varying considerably in their size and shape. Here is how body spoons are used:

1. As dolly blocks with handles (Fig. 5-26). They can reach into places where a dolly or hammer cannot be used. For example, Fig. 5-27 shows a body spoon being used to back up a body panel which is partly

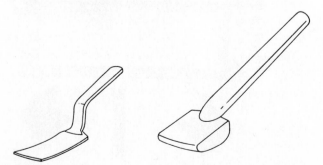

Fig. 5-26 Two of the many shapes of body spoons. *(Snap-on Tools Corporation)*

blocked off by the underbody construction. The spoon here acts as a dolly with the hammering being on the dolly.

2. To spread the blows of the hammer over a large area. For this purpose a flat body spoon can be laid down along a ridge. Hammering is done on top of the spoon to work the ridge down.

3. As a heavy-duty prying or driving tool. That is, the spoon itself is used to pry or drive against low spots to work them out. For example, this type of tool might be used to separate an outer panel from the inner construction when the two have been crushed together. We describe various uses of spoons in later chapters.

≡ 5-18 PRY BARS

Pry bars (Fig. 5-28) are available in various sizes and shapes. They are used to pry against low spots that are inaccessible unless other parts are removed. For example, Fig. 5-28 shows a pry bar being used to work out a low spot in a door panel. The pry bar has been inserted through a drain hole in the bottom of the door. If this operation is a success, the low spot can be pushed out without removing the door trim and internal mechanism.

≡ 5-19 WORKING HSLA STEEL

High-strength steel, used for the body panels of modern unitized-construction cars, is treated in a different manner from the steel used for body panels on the body-on-frame cars. For example, if these panels are heated above 700°F [372°C] for more than a few minutes, their strength will drop to that of mild steel. This loss of strength could seriously weaken the whole body structure.

In addition, HSLA panels are not easily worked with pulling hooks that can be used on thicker-gauge, body-and-frame cars. Also, HSLA panels cannot be successfully bead-welded, but must be MIG-welded. This is ex-

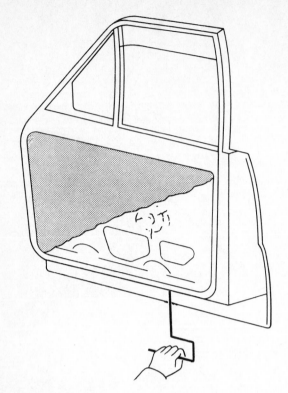

Fig. 5-28 Using a pry bar.

plained in later chapters. Some unitized-body parts cannot be straightened, even if only slightly bent. They must be replaced.

≡ 5-20 CHISELS

The chisel has a single cutting edge and is driven with a hammer to cut metal. Figure 5-29 shows different kinds of chisels. To cut a piece of sheet metal in two, the metal is clamped in a vise. Vises are described later.

While using a chisel, wear goggles. They protect the eyes from flying chips that could put out an unprotected eye.

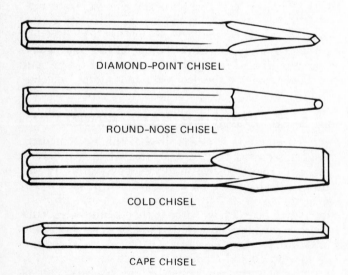

DIAMOND-POINT CHISEL

ROUND-NOSE CHISEL

COLD CHISEL

CAPE CHISEL

Fig. 5-29 Various types of chisels.

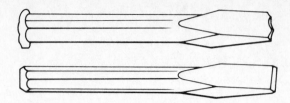

Fig. 5-30 Top, worn chisel with mushroomed head and dented cutting edge. Bottom, new or properly dressed chisel.

After a chisel has been used for a while, the cutting edge gets dull and the head tends to mushroom (Fig. 5-30). The mushroom must be ground off on a grinding wheel, as discussed in a later chapter. Grinding off the mushroom from the head of the chisel protects you from getting hurt. The turned-over metal could break off when the head is struck, and a piece of it could fly off and injure you. Figure 5-30 also shows how the chisel should look after it is ground.

NOTE: *The auto body technician uses an air-operated chisel or cutter to cut out damaged sheet metal. These tools are discussed in Chap. 7.*

— CAUTION —

Always wear eye protection when using, dressing, or sharpening a chisel.

≡ 5-21 HACKSAW

The hacksaw (Fig. 5-31) has a steel blade with a series of sharp teeth. The teeth act like tiny chisels. When the blade is pushed over a piece of metal, the teeth cut fine shavings, or filings, off the metal. Figure 5-31 shows how to hold and use a hacksaw. Each forward stroke should be full and steady and not jerky. On the back stroke, lift the saw blade slightly so that the teeth do not drag along the metal being cut.

When using a hacksaw, you should use a blade with the proper number of teeth for the metal piece you are going to saw. The teeth must be close enough so that at least two teeth will be working on the metal at the same time. If the teeth are too fine, they will get clogged and stop cutting.

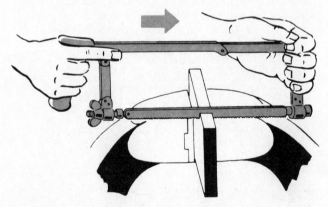

Fig. 5-31 How to hold and use a hacksaw.

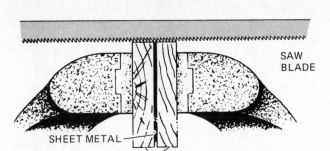

Fig. 5-32 To cut sheet metal with a hacksaw, clamp the sheet metal between two wood blocks in a vise. Saw through both wood and metal.

To cut sheet metal with a hacksaw, clamp the sheet metal between two wood blocks in a vise, as shown in Fig. 5-32. Then make the cut through both the wood and metal.

≡ 5-22 FILES

The regular shop file (Fig. 5-33) is a cutting tool with a large number of cutting edges, or teeth, each like a tiny chisel. There are many types and shapes of files (Fig. 5-34). The flat file is the most common. Files range in coarseness, or size of individual teeth, from "rough" or "coarse-cut," through "bastard" and "second-cut," to "smooth" or "dead-smooth."

Files also can be single-cut and double-cut. The single-cut file has a series of teeth, like knife blades, that are parallel to one another. The double-cut file has two sets of cuts on the face of the file that are at an angle to each other. The teeth on the double-cut file are pointed.

To use a file, strokes should be steady and the right amount of force should be used. Excessive force will clog the file teeth and could break the file. Insufficient force will not cut the metal and could cause the file to chatter or vibrate.

Regular shop files should be used with a handle, as shown in Fig. 5-33. The handle is tightened on the file tang by tapping the end of the handle on the bench.

Files should always be treated with care. When not in use, a file should be cleaned, wiped with a slightly oily cloth, and stored in a safe place where the file teeth will not be damaged. If the file is thrown into a drawer along with other tools, the teeth will be chipped and damaged and the file soon rendered useless. Never attempt to use a file as a pry bar or hammer on it. Files — particularly shop files — are brittle and could shatter dangerously. The tension on adjustable body files should be relieved so they will straighten out before they are put away. If left curved, a body file may break all by itself, owing to the internal stresses on the file.

≡ 5-23 BODY FILES

Body files are usually single-cut and made in a variety of sizes and shapes (straight, curved, round). The most common body file is used to semifinish a damaged area of sheet metal. The teeth are curved, as shown in Fig.

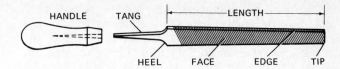

Fig. 5-33 Typical file and handle. (*General Motors Corporation*)

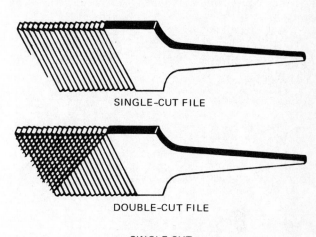

Fig. 5-34 Types of files and file cuts.

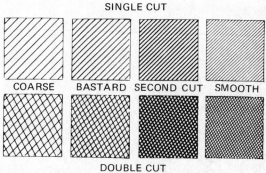

Fig. 5-35 Body file in a file holder.

5-35. This allows better cutting and easier cleaning of the teeth. Note that the file cuts in one direction only.

File holders are of two types: fixed and adjustable. The fixed holder (Fig. 5-35) has a pair of holes that match the holes in the file. The file is attached to the holder by a pair of screws. The adjustable file holder can be adjusted to bend the file so it will fit a curved surface.

There are several special-purpose body files, made to fit and work in tight places, as, for example, around windshields. Methods of using files are described in a later chapter.

The Surform (for surface forming), manufactured by the Stanley Tool Company, is a special form of file (Fig.

5-36) that is actually more like a cheese grater than a file. It has a series of open teeth, and is used to shape plastic body filler while the body filler is still soft. When it is used on the plastic, the cuttings come through the openings under the teeth. The Surform should not be used on hardened plastic, because this will dull the teeth. After the Surform has shaped the filler approximately to its correct contour, the filler is left to harden. Then the contouring is finished with an electric or air sander.

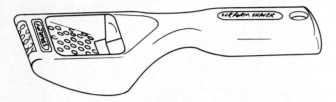

Fig. 5-36 A Surform, or "cheese-grater" type, file used to shape plastic body filler. *(Stanley Tool Company)*

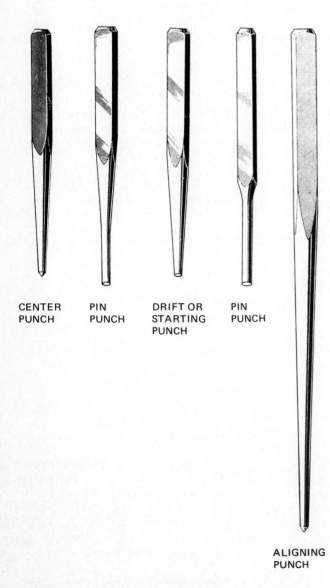

CENTER PUNCH   PIN PUNCH   DRIFT OR STARTING PUNCH   PIN PUNCH

ALIGNING PUNCH

Fig. 5-37 Various kinds of punches. *(General Motors Corporation)*

≡ 5-24 PUNCHES

Punches (Fig. 5-37) are used to knock out rivets and pins from parts that are being disassembled, to line up parts that are being assembled, and to mark locations of holes to be drilled. Let's discuss the different kinds of punches and how they are used for these jobs.

1. Knocking out rivets and pins. A starting punch and a pin punch are used to knock out rivets and pins. Some parts are held together by rivets and pins. When a pin is used, the ends of the pin are rounded off, or peened over, by a hammer. To remove the pin, first file off one of the rounded-off ends of the pin. Next, use a starting punch to break the pin loose. Then use a pin punch to drive the pin out.

2. Lining up machine parts. An aligning punch is used to line up, or align, parts. Some parts have holes that must align when the parts are assembled. To ensure proper alignment, place the aligning punch through each hole in each part. Then it will be easy to install a bolt or screw through the holes.

3. Marking locations of holes to be drilled. A center punch is used to mark locations of holes to be drilled. Marking the location of the hole gives the drill a place to start. This prevents it from wandering on the surface of the workpiece (Fig. 5-38).

4. Marking parts before disassembly. The center punch is also used for this purpose so that the parts can be put back together correctly. For example, suppose a cover plate could be put back on a housing in two positions, one right and one wrong. Before taking the cover plate off, put punch marks next to each other on the housing and the cover plate. Now there can be no question about which way the parts are to be reassembled.

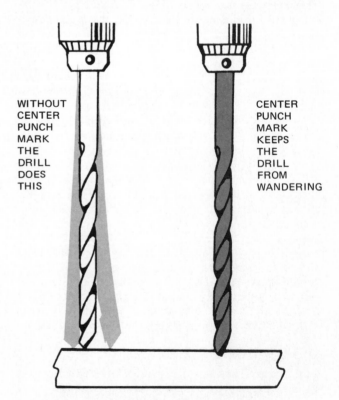

WITHOUT CENTER PUNCH MARK THE DRILL DOES THIS

CENTER PUNCH MARK KEEPS THE DRILL FROM WANDERING

Fig. 5-38 Center-punching a hole location prevents the drill bit from wandering. *(General Motors Corporation)*

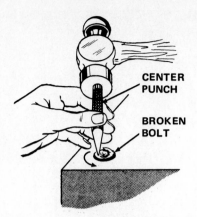

Fig. 5-39 Removing a broken bolt with a center punch and hammer.

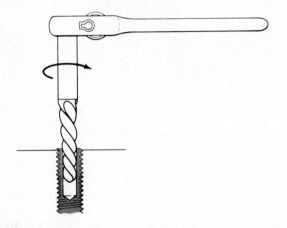

Fig. 5-40 Using a stud extractor to remove a broken stud.

Fig. 5-41 A tape measure is used for checking frame dimensions and making other measurements.

≡ 5-25 STUD EXTRACTOR

Sometimes a bolt or stud will break off and you have to get the bottom part out. If this part is rusted in, put some penetrating oil around the bolt and leave it in for a while. Then you may be able to remove the bolt with a center punch, as shown in Fig. 5-39. If this doesn't work, drill a hole down through the center of the broken bolt, as shown in Fig. 5-40. Then drive a stud extractor of the right size down into this hole. Next, use a wrench to turn the stud extractor, as shown in Fig. 5-40, to back the bolt out.

≡ 5-26 TAPE MEASURE

A tape measure, or steel tape (Fig. 5-41), is often required in the body shop. It is needed to make measurements when aligning body or frame parts and cutting sheet metal for patching damaged panels.

≡ 5-27 SCRAPERS

Scrapers (Fig. 5-42) are used in the body shop for such jobs as scraping off paint, undercoating, applying plastic filler, and caulking. A variety of scrapers are used by the body technician.

≡ 5-28 BRUSHES

Brushes are needed in the body shop to remove rust and old paint. The type of brush required depends on the job to be done. To remove dirt, for example, use a bristle brush. On rust, use a stiff wire brush.

Some wire brushes are made to be used with an air or electric drill. Figure 5-43 shows a cup-type wire brush for cleaning off rust spots and paint in depressions which are to be filled with body solder or plastic filler. Wear goggles when using wire brushes in drills. These brushes can throw off particles at high speed, and such particles could injure your eyes.

≡ 5-29 TRIM-PANEL TOOL

This tool (Fig. 5-44) is used to remove upholstery trim panels (also called *trim pads*) from the insides of doors and quarter panels. The tool is slipped under the trim at the points where it is attached, and the trim panel is then pried loose from the door. Properly done, the trim panel will come off with no damage.

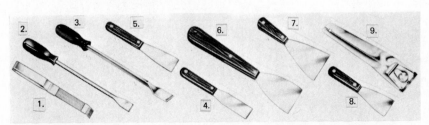

1. FLEXIBLE WIRE CARBON SCRAPER
2. RIGID CARBON SCRAPER
3. LONG, RIGID CARBON SCRAPER
4. STRAIGHT SCRAPER
5. CHISEL-EDGE SCRAPER
6. HEAVY-DUTY CHISEL-EDGE SCRAPER
7. 4-INCH [102-mm] BLADE PUTTY KNIFE
8. 2 1/8-INCH [54-mm] BLADE PUTTY KNIFE
9. WINDOW SCRAPER

Fig. 5-42 A variety of scrapers and "putty knives." (*Snap-on Tools Corporation*)

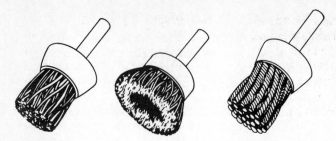

Fig. 5-43 Various cup-type wire brushes. *(Ford Motor Company)*

Fig. 5-44 A panel-trim tool.

≡ 5-30 DOOR WEATHERSTRIP TOOL

This tool (Fig. 5-45) is used to disengage the door weatherstrip from the fasteners which are hidden under the trim assembly.

≡ 5-31 MASKING STAND

Just before the car is rolled into the paint shop for painting, all parts that should not be painted are covered with masking tape and paper. This is called *masking.* A handy portable masking stand, such as shown in Fig. 5-46, makes this job easier and more quickly com-

Fig. 5-46 Masking-tape dispenser, or masking stand. *(3M Company)*

pleted. The masking stand is on wheels so it can be moved to the place where it is needed. The masking tape and paper are dispensed together, with the tape attached to the edge of the paper.

≡ 5-32 VISE

The bench vise (Fig. 5-47) is used to hold objects that are being worked on. When the handle is turned, a screw in the base of the vise moves the movable jaw toward or away from the stationary jaw. To protect objects that could be easily marred, "soft jaws" are put on the vise, as shown. These are caps made of a soft metal such as copper. They are less likely to scratch or dent the object being gripped.

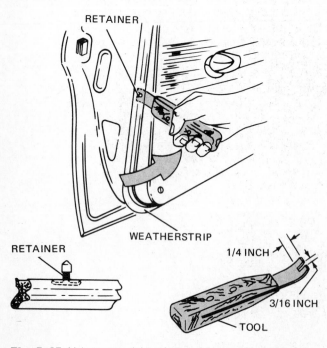

Fig. 5-45 Using a special tool to remove weatherstrip from the door edge. *(© Fisher Body Division of General Motors Corporation)*

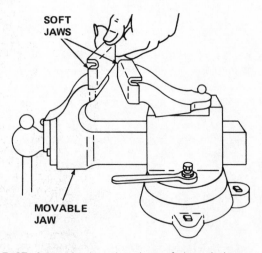

Fig. 5-47 A bench vise, showing soft jaws being put into place on the vise jaws.

REVIEW QUESTIONS

Select the *one* correct, best, or most probable answer to each question. You can find the answers in the section indicated at the end of each question.

1. The main difference between the box wrench and the socket wrench is that the socket wrench (≡5-5)
   a. is larger
   b. does not have an attached handle
   c. has more points in the head
   d. is a combination wrench

2. The purpose of the torque wrench is to (≡5-6)
   a. enable you to apply torque to a nut
   b. measure the torque applied while tightening a nut or bolt
   c. check the torque required to loosen a nut
   d. check the torque applied to the pry bar

3. Two types of pliers used in the shop are (≡5-8 and 5-9)
   a. adjustable and fixed
   b. Channellock and fixed
   c. Vise-Grip and Channellock
   d. two-leg and three-leg

4. The sheet-metal cutter (≡5-10)
   a. is used to cut sheet metal
   b. may be called snips, or shears
   c. should never be used to cut bolts or rods
   d. all of the above

5. A dent or depression in a sheet-metal panel can often be worked out with (≡5-13 to 5-15)
   a. a slide hammer
   b. pull rods
   c. suction cups
   d. all of the above

6. A dolly is used with a (≡5-16)
   a. file
   b. punch
   c. chisel
   d. body hammer

7. A body tool that has a flattened end that is either straight or curved is called a (≡5-17)
   a. body spoon
   b. body file
   c. body hammer
   d. dolly

8. When working with HSLA steel, you should (≡5-19)
   a. bead-weld it
   b. avoid overheating it
   c. avoid wire-welding it
   d. attach it with structural adhesive

9. Body files are usually (≡5-23)
   a. single-cut
   b. straight only
   c. used without a handle
   d. double-cut

10. The purpose of the masking stand is to (≡5-31)
    a. protect you from breathing sanding dust
    b. supply masking tape and paper in preparation for painting
    c. mask the car while it is being vacuumed
    d. take the place of the mask you should wear while painting

CHAPTER 6
BODY-SHOP ELECTRIC POWER TOOLS

After studying this chapter, you should be able to:

1. Explain how to use electric power tools safely.

2. Discuss electric drills and how to use them.

3. Describe the four basic sanders used in the body shop and discuss the cautions for working with them.

4. Explain how to use the grinder and the precautions to take.

☰ 6-1 BODY-SHOP POWER TOOLS

There are three types of body power tools: electric, pneumatic, and hydraulic. Electric tools, such as sanders, grinders, and drills, use electric motors. The word "pneumatic" means "of or pertaining to air." Therefore, pneumatic tools are air tools, operated by compressed air. They include air hammers, impact wrenches, air drills, air sanders, and air ratchets. The compressed, or high-pressure, air comes from the shop compressed-air system. Compressed-air systems and pneumatic tools are described in a following chapter.

The third category is hydraulic. The word "hydraulic" means "of or pertaining to a fluid or liquid." Hydraulic tools are tools that work because of the pressure of a fluid. The hydraulic tools used in the body shop include car lifts, power jacks, and body-and-frame aligners. They are powered either by a hand pump, by a pump driven by an electric motor, or by an air-driven pump. Hydraulic tools are described in Chap. 8.

☰ 6-2 USING POWER TOOLS SAFELY

When you use a power tool, you must use common sense, too, if you want to work safely. Common sense tells you that electricity can give you a severe and possibly fatal shock, that high-pressure air can cause serious injury if it is not used properly, and that you must respect moving parts and power tools when they are operating. Our descriptions of the various power tools include safety cautions for using these tools. Safety is as much a part of your job as dinging out fenders or painting a quarter panel. Review Chap. 3, which is devoted entirely to safety.

☰ 6-3 ELECTRIC DRILL

The electric drill (Fig. 6-1) has an electric motor that drives a chuck. The chuck has jaws that can be opened to accept a drill and then closed to grip it (Fig. 6-2). A special chuck key is used to turn the chuck collar and operate the chuck jaws. The electric drill uses twist drills, such as shown in Fig. 6-3. The twist drill has two cutting edges on the cutting end. Chips that these edges cut from metal pass up through the two helical grooves and away from the working area.

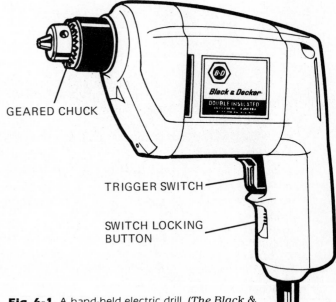

GEARED CHUCK

TRIGGER SWITCH

SWITCH LOCKING BUTTON

Fig. 6-1 A hand-held electric drill. (*The Black & Decker Manufacturing Company*)

To cut larger holes in sheet metal, a large-hole cutter such as shown in Fig. 6-4 is used. The drill goes into the metal first and then holds the hole cutter on center so the hole it cuts is smooth and round. A smaller version of this tool, shown in Fig. 6-5, is used to drill out spot welds. Drilling out spot welds is necessary to remove some body panels without major damage to them or to the underbody part to which the panel is spot-welded. Figure 6-6 shows how spot welds have been cut out with the tool.

NOTE: *The electric drill can be used for small sanding jobs using a small sanding disk or with a wire brush, such as shown in Fig. 5-43.*

Many body technicians prefer to use pneumatic or air-powered drills and other tools. They are usually lighter and more easily handled than electric tools. All body shops have a compressed-air system to supply air to operate air tools.

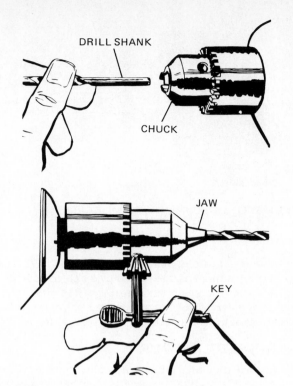

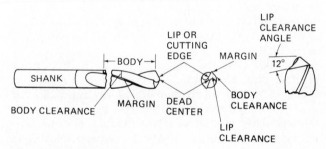

Fig. 6-2 Installing a twist drill in a drill chuck.

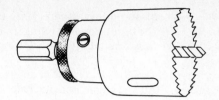

Fig. 6-4 A large-hole cutter.

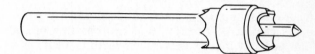

Fig. 6-5 A small *spot-weld cutter,* used to cut out spot welds.

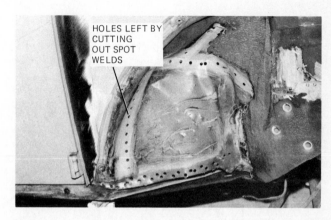

Fig. 6-3 Parts of a twist drill.

Fig. 6-6 Use of the spot-weld cutter. When used, it cuts out the metal in the spot weld, separating the sheet metal.

Here are some precautions to observe when using an electric drill:

1. Make sure that the drill is properly grounded (Fig. 6-7), with the third blade on the plug, or that the drill is double-insulated.

2. Make sure the cord is in good condition. Do not kink it or allow anyone to step on it or run a machine over it. Do not drag the drill around by its cord. Doing any of these things can damage the insulation so that someone could be shocked when using the drill.

3. Keep your hands and clothing away from the moving parts of the drill.

4. Do not drag electric tools around by their cords.

5. Keep a firm grip on the drill and be ready to shut it off if it jams. When a drill is about to break through metal, it sometimes tends to jam. Be prepared for this.

6. If a drill jams, do not try to break it free by turning the switch on and off. This can damage the drill. Instead, pull back on the drill to loosen it.

7. Do not leave the drill lying around on the floor or bench. When you are through with it, put it away where

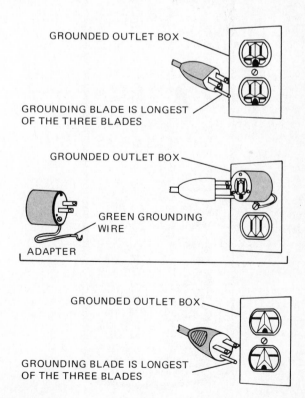

Fig. 6-7 Various methods of grounding electric tools.

it belongs. The drill should be wiped clean and oiled occasionally if it is the type requiring oiling. Some drills have preoiled bearings and require no additional oil.

If you want to check the size of a twist drill, use a drill gauge (Fig. 6-8). Find the gauge hole in which the drill fits snugly and then note the drill size as marked on the side of the hole.

≡ 6-4 POWER SANDERS

There are four types of power sanders used in the body shop. These are rotary (Fig. 6-9), reciprocating, orbital, and belt. Their purpose is to move abrasive disks or strips on body-panel surfaces. The abrasive action (called *sanding*) removes material from the surface. This smoothes the surface and brings it down to contour.

Sanders are powered by either electric motors or air motors (compressed air). Which type a body technician uses depends on personal preference. Some technicians prefer the air type, because it is lighter and easier to maneuver.

The various sanders are described later. To help you understand their job, the following section introduces

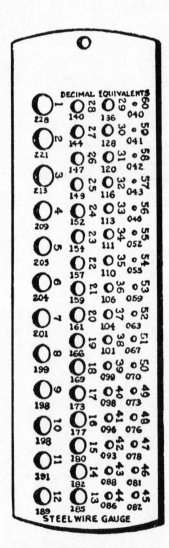

Fig. 6-8 A drill gauge. The number and size of the drill are shown beside the hole in which the drill fits snugly.

62

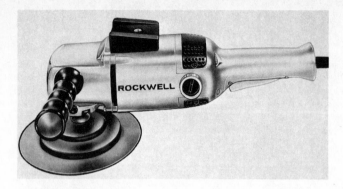

Fig. 6-9 An electric-powered disk sander. *(Rockwell International Corporation)*

abrasives—grinding disks and sandpaper. When attached to a sander and operated by a skilled body technician, the abrasive removes unwanted rust, paint, metal, or plastic. This is an important step in preparing sheet metal and other surfaces for refinishing.

≡ 6-5 ABRASIVES

Abrasive is the name given to any material that is used for cutting, grinding, lapping, or polishing metal or other materials or surfaces. For example, sandpaper is an abrasive. In the body and paint shop, abrasives are commonly used in three forms. These are sheets, disks, and belts. The choice depends on whether the sanding is to be done by hand or by use of some type of power sander (≡6-4).

The disk or rotary sander, shown in Fig. 6-9, uses a grinding disk. These are available in various sizes up to 9 inches [229 mm] in diameter. Grinding disks are made by applying very hard, sharp-edged pieces of aluminum-oxide or silicon-carbide grit to a fiber backing with glue or adhesive. The size of the particles, or grit, determines the coarseness of the disk and the speed with which it will cut. In the manufacturing process, the grit is graded by being sifted through a series of screens. The grit is passed down through the screens, each screen being finer than the one above it.

There are two types of grinding disks: open-grain and closed-grain. On the open-grain disk, the abrasive particles are separated, with some space between them. This type of disk is used to remove old paint and rust and to cut down solder or welds. Because the grits have space around them, the disks do not clog quickly. The paint or other material that is removed will not fill in the spaces, which would reduce the cutting ability of the disk. The closed-grain disk is used for finer work in which the material ground off is too fine to clog the spaces between the grits.

Grinding disks are also graded according to their coarseness. In refinishing, the grinding is started with a coarse grain. This removes material rapidly but leaves deep scratches. A finer-grain disk is then used to remove the scratches. This procedure is described later.

≡ 6-6 RECIPROCATING SANDER

The electric reciprocating, or straightline, sander is used mainly for finish-sanding of the metal or body filler. It uses a pad on which is mounted a strip of sand-paper. The sander moves this sandpaper back and forth. In general, the electric reciprocating sander is similar in appearance to the air reciprocating sander shown in Fig. 7-10. The air reciprocating sander is more widely used today.

≡ 6-7 ORBITAL SANDER

This sander is similar to the reciprocating sander except that the sandpaper moves in a circular or oval pattern. Some sanders have a switch that allows the technician to select the sanding action desired. Figure 7-12 shows an air-powered orbiting-reciprocating sander.

≡ 6-8 BELT SANDER

This sander (Fig. 6-10) uses an abrasive belt. It does the same job as the other sanders. It is usually equipped with a vacuum device that draws off most of the dust produced by the sanding operation. Which sander the body technician uses often depends on personal preference.

≡ 6-9 ABRASIVE CONES

In addition to disks, pads, and belts, some body jobs require abrasive cones for getting at sharp curves around moldings, and curved areas of doors and hoods. Figure 6-11 shows an abrasive-cone mandrel which is mounted on a disk grinder. The abrasive cone is then mounted on the mandrel.

≡ 6-10 CAUTIONS ON USING SANDERS

Safety and safe operating procedures are described in Chap. 3. However, there are certain hazards in using sanders that should be avoided. First, a sander raises dust. This dust can be irritating to the throat and lungs. Therefore, a respirator should be worn. This is especially important when plastic body filler is being sanded. The material is poisonous when ingested and can cause lung and liver damage.

Eye protection should be worn to protect the eyes from particles thrown off by the disk sander.

Before laying the sander down on the floor, make sure it is turned off and has stopped running. The electric disk grinder pulls air through it to keep it from overheating. If the grinder is laid on the floor while it is still running, it will pull dust in from the floor. This can cause dust buildup in the motor which causes damaging overheating.

In addition to the above, the precautions outlined in ≡6-1 and 6-2 also apply to electric sanders.

≡ 6-11 POWER POLISHERS

The power polisher (Fig. 6-12) is similar in construction to the power disk sander (≡6-5). However, the polisher is usually lighter and runs at higher speed. Instead of an abrasive disk, the polisher uses a wool buffing or polishing pad. When used on a surface after rubbing compound (≡31-12) or polish (≡31-13) is applied, the polisher gives a high luster (or shine) to the paint.

Some sanders can also be used as polishers after a suitable pad is installed. These sanders have two

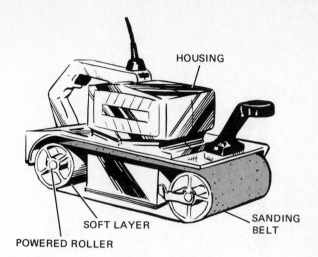

Fig. 6-10 An electric belt sander.

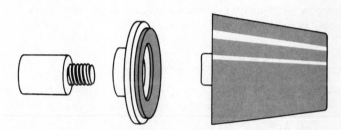

Fig. 6-11 A mandrel for an abrasive cone. *(3M Company)*

Fig. 6-12 An electric polisher with a polishing pad. *(Rockwell International Corporation)*

speeds controlled by a switch. When the sander is to be used as a polisher, the switch is moved to the high-speed position.

≡ 6-12 GRINDING WHEEL

The bench grinder (Fig. 6-13) has one or more grinding wheels made of abrasive material bonded together. When the wheel is rotated by the electric motor, objects

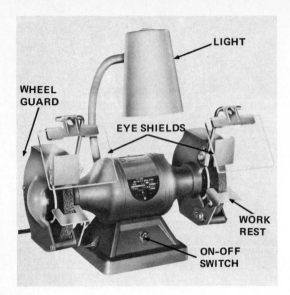

Fig. 6-13 A bench grinder. (*Rockwell International Corporation*)

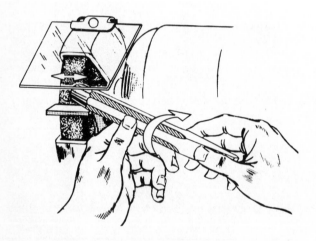

Fig. 6-14 Grinding the mushroom from the head of a chisel.

held against the wheel are ground down. Therefore, the grinder can be used to shape and sharpen tools.

There are many different sizes and grades of wheels. For coarse work, the abrasive particles are relatively large; they cut material rapidly. An example might be the grinding wheels used to take the rough edges off castings. For fine work, such as sharpening small tools, a relatively fine grinding wheel is used.

Figure 6-14 shows how to use the grinding wheel to grind the mushroomed head from a chisel. Figure 5-30 shows the chisel before and after it is ground.

Certain safety cautions should be followed when using a grinding wheel. These include:

1. Do not hammer on the wheel or apply excessive force to it.

2. When installing a grinding wheel, do not hammer on it or overtighten the spindle nut on the motor shaft.

3. Be alert against the danger from the heavy stream of sparks that fly off the wheel during the grinding of steel and other metals. These sparks are hot and can set fire to your hair or clothing and burn you.

≡ 6-13 VACUUM CLEANER

The vacuum cleaner (Fig. 6-15) is also used as a shop power tool. The body shop needs a vacuum cleaner to clean car interiors before they are painted and again before the car is returned to the customer. After the body panels have been prepared for painting, the car interior will be very dusty. It should be vacuumed to remove this dust.

A shop vacuum cleaner is also very useful for cleaning the shop floor. Even though the floor is dampened to hold down the dust, or floor-sweeping compound is sprinkled around, using a broom will raise dust. This is always troublesome, especially if painting is being done nearby. The vacuum cleaner will clean up the dust without raising it into the air.

The vacuum cleaner should have a long hose so it can reach into the car interior and trunk. It should have

Fig. 6-15 A shop vacuum cleaner. (*Rockwell International Corporation*)

Fig. 6-16 One type of paint shaker.

the proper accessories to get at corners and other places hard to reach. Some shops use a small, hand-held vacuum cleaner to clean car interiors.

≡ 6-14 PAINT SHAKER

When a can of paint sits on the shelf, the heavy materials in the can settle to the bottom. To mix the paint, the can must be shaken vigorously. Therefore, most body shops that do car painting have a paint shaker (Fig. 6-16). The can of paint is clamped in the shaker, and the shaker is turned on. An air or electric motor then drives an eccentric that shakes the clamp and can to assure thorough mixing of the paint. This is necessary, because if the paint is not properly mixed, the paint job will be defective.

Painters in shops that do not have a paint shaker take sufficient time, when they open a can, to stir the paint thoroughly.

≡ 6-15 PORTABLE INFRARED DRYERS

Many body shops have portable infrared dryers (Fig. 6-17) which are used following the application of primers and putties. The heat from the dryer will cure the materials in about 20 minutes. This then allows sanding to be completed sooner, while preventing many troubles that can later appear in the paint. However, to work properly, the dryer must be placed the proper distance from the surface.

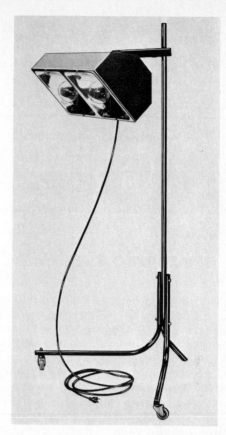

Fig. 6-17 A portable heat lamp, or dryer, for speeding up drying of putties and primers. *(The DeVilbiss Company)*

──── REVIEW QUESTIONS ────

Select the *one* correct, best, or most probable answer to each question. You can find the answers in the section indicated at the end of each question.

1. The jaws of an electric drill are adjusted with   (≡6-3)
   a. the ignition key
   b. a woodruff key
   c. a chuck key
   d. a square key

2. If the drill jams,   (≡6-3)
   a. turn the switch on and off to loosen it
   b. pull back on the drill to loosen it
   c. push harder on the drill to loosen it
   d. return the drill to the factory for repair

3. Power sanders can be rotary or   (≡6-4)
   a. reciprocating
   b. orbital
   c. belt
   d. all of the above

4. When sanding plastic body filler, always wear   (≡6-9)
   a. a coat
   b. rubber boots
   c. a respirator
   d. a hair net

5. The machine that mixes paint after it has been stored on the shelf is   (≡6-13)
   a. a vacuum cleaner
   b. an electric drill
   c. a paint shaker
   d. an abrasive cone

CHAPTER 7
PNEUMATIC TOOLS

After studying this chapter, you should be able to:

1. Explain how to use air tools safely.
2. Describe the basic types of air tools and how to use them.
3. Explain how to use the air chisel, nibbler, and air impact wrench.

≡ 7-1 OPERATING PNEUMATIC TOOLS

Pneumatic tools are operated by compressed air. The compressed air is supplied by the compressed-air system in the body shop. Compressed-air systems are described later in the chapter. The compressed air, as it enters the pneumatic tools, spins a rotor or causes a piston to move in a cylinder. Pneumatic, or air-powered, tools used in the body shop include impact wrenches, impact chisels, sanders, drills, floor jacks, and spray guns for painting cars. The air must be supplied at high pressure to the air tools and at a relatively lower pressure to the spray guns. For both, the air must be clean and dry. Dirt or moisture in the air will damage pneumatic tools and ruin paint jobs.

≡ 7-2 USING AIR TOOLS SAFELY

Air tools are safe and reliable if they are properly and sensibly used. However, compressed air can be dangerous, even deadly, when misused. Here are the safety rules for using any compressed-air tool in the shop:

1. Body shops have air nozzles—often called *blowguns*—used to blow parts dry and clean (Fig. 7-1). Never point this blowgun at yourself or anyone else. Do not use it to blow dust off your clothes. Dirt particles, driven at high speed by the compressed air, can penetrate the skin and eyes, causing serious injury. If high-pressure air is directed toward an open wound, it can send air into the bloodstream with fatal results.

2. Do not look into the air outlet or nozzle of any compressed-air tool.

3. Do not operate air impact chisels without a chisel installed. This can damage the tool.

≡ 7-3 BASIC TYPES OF AIR TOOLS

There are two basic types of air tools, aside from spray guns: (1) rotary and (2) reciprocating. The rotary type includes sanders, drills, and impact wrenches. The reciprocating type includes air hammers and chisels. The rotary type has a rotor that is driven by the compressed air. The reciprocating type has a piston that is moved back and forth in a cylinder by the air pressure.

Most air tools are very light for the power they develop. In addition, repeated overloading and stalling will not damage or overheat an air tool. These conditions will ruin many types of electric power tools.

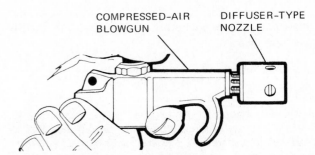

Fig. 7-1 A diffuser nozzle on a compressed-air blowgun. The maximum allowable discharge pressure is 30 psi [207 kPa]. (*Ford Motor Company*)

≡ 7-4 QUICK COUPLER

Air tools and blowguns are connected to the air hose through a *quick coupler* (Fig. 7-2). The connection is made by pulling back the collar on the coupler, inserting the nipple into the coupler, and then releasing the collar. The collar holds the coupler onto the nipple. Air pressure seals the connection.

On many air tools, the manufacturer recommends attaching a flexible *leader hose* to the air inlet on the

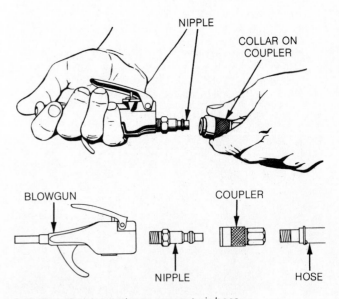

Fig. 7-2 Quick coupler to connect air hose.

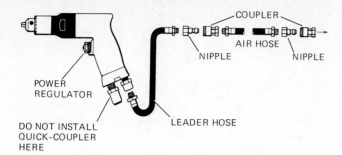

Fig. 7-3 Air drill with hose and couplings. *(Chicago Pneumatic Tool Company)*

tool (Fig. 7-3). Then the quick coupling is attached to the end of the hose that leads away from the tool.

≡ 7-5 AIR CHISEL

The air chisel, or *air hammer* (Fig. 7-4), uses reciprocating motion to drive a cutting or hammering tool. Figure 7-4 shows an air hammer being used to cut a nut that has rusted onto a stud. The air hammer repeatedly and rapidly drives a chisel against the nut. Air hammers can be used with a variety of tools—cutters, chisels, and punches—to do many jobs.

Figure 7-5 shows an air hammer equipped with a chisel being used to cut away the damaged part of a

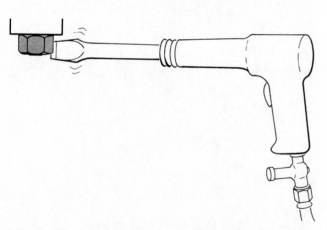

Fig. 7-4 Air hammer in operation, driving a chisel to cut a nut that has frozen onto a stud. *(Chicago Pneumatic Tool Company)*

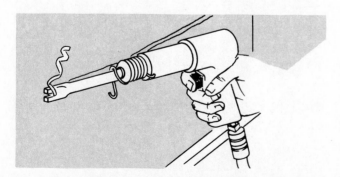

Fig. 7-5 Air hammer equipped with a panel-cutting chisel being used to cut out the damaged part of a panel. *(Snap-on Tools Corporation)*

body panel. This is done when the part is considered too damaged to be repaired with body hammers and dollies. After the damaged area is cut away, a patch will be riveted or welded on. Then the panel will be refinished.

≡ 7-6 AIR NIBBLER

The air nibbler (Fig. 7-6) works like a pair of scissors with one movable blade and two stationary blades. The two outer blades are stationary, and the center blade moves up and down between them. As the center blade moves up between the stationary blades, it cuts out a thin ribbon of metal, as shown in Fig. 7-7.

The name "nibbler" comes from the action of the tool. The nibbler takes small bites from, or it nibbles,

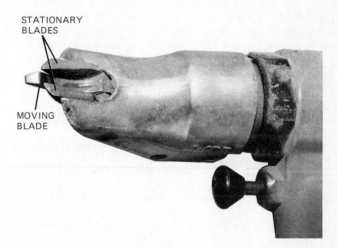

Fig. 7-6 An air-powered nibbler.

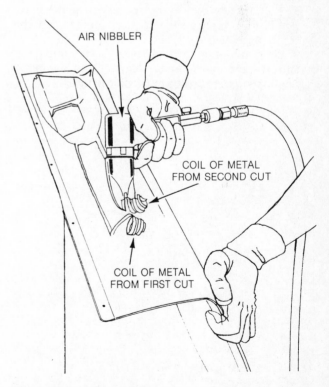

Fig. 7-7 Air nibbler cutting out a strip of metal from a discarded fender. The technician will use this strip to patch a body panel on a car.

the metal. To use the nibbler on a body panel, a hole large enough to get the nibbler started is first drilled in the metal. Then the movable blade is inserted in the hole, and the air valve is opened to start the nibbler. The tool is easily controlled so that a clean, accurate cut can be made. When a patch is being cut out for a panel from flat sheet metal, the cut is started from the edge of the sheet.

≡ 7-7 AIR IMPACT WRENCHES

Air impact wrenches (Fig. 7-8) use a pounding or impact force to loosen or tighten nuts or bolts. They do the job very rapidly and so are widely used in the shop. The direction of rotation can be changed by operating a reversing control on the wrench.

Most shop impact wrenches have a standard ½-inch [12.7-mm] socket drive. Only special impact sockets should be used with the impact wrench. Standard sockets will crack and round out when used on an impact wrench. Impact sockets are often black in color.

NOTE: Some impact wrenches are electric. These have an electric motor. They are usually larger and heavier than a comparable air impact wrench.

Here are some rules for using an air impact wrench:

1. Always use impact sockets with an impact wrench.

2. Use only the correct size socket for the bolt or nut.

3. Use the simplest possible assembly of sockets, extensions, and universal joint.

4. Use a deep socket, where possible, rather than a standard-length socket and extension.

5. Hold the wrench so the socket fits squarely on the bolt or nut. Apply a slight forward force to hold the socket in place before you operate the wrench.

6. Once a nut or bolt tightens, never impact it beyond an additional one-half turn. Continued impacting might strip the threads or break the bolt.

7. For accurate tightening of a bolt or nut to a specified tension, you must use a torque wrench (≡5-6).

8. Soak large rusty nuts or bolts with penetrating oil before impacting them.

≡ 7-8 AIR DRILL

Figure 7-3 shows an air drill with hose and couplings. This drill has a ¼-inch [6.35-mm] chuck capacity and a free speed of 2800 revolutions per minute (rpm). It develops ½ horsepower (hp).

≡ 7-9 AIR SANDERS

Figure 7-9 shows an air-powered disk sander. It is used in the same way that you use an electric disk sander. There are also air reciprocating sanders, such as shown in Fig. 7-10. In addition, there are orbital rotary sanders (Fig. 7-11). In these, the disk is off center, so it slowly moves around in a larger circle as it rotates. Another type of orbital sander is an orbiting-reciprocating type (Fig. 7-12). Some sanders have an attached vacuum device to pick up dust from the sanding operation.

Fig. 7-9 Using an air-powered disk sander.

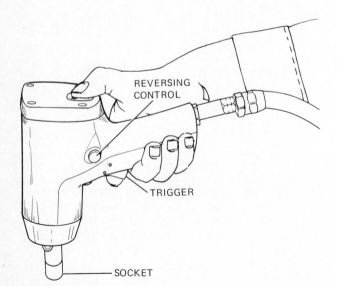

Fig. 7-8 Using an impact wrench.

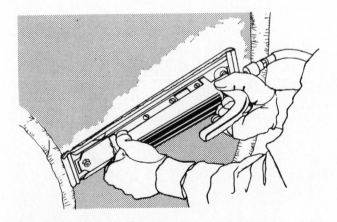

Fig. 7-10 Using an air reciprocating sander, or *air file.*

68

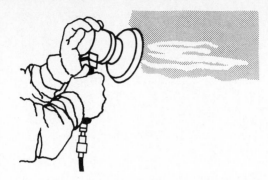

Fig. 7-11 Using a random orbital sander.

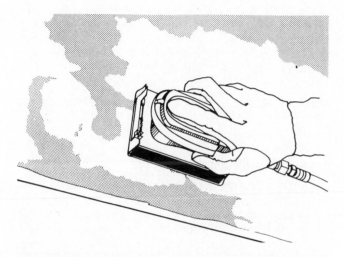

Fig. 7-12 An orbiting-reciprocating sander. (*Chicago Pneumatic Tool Company*)

Fig. 7-13 An air-powered bumper-type end lift, or air jack.

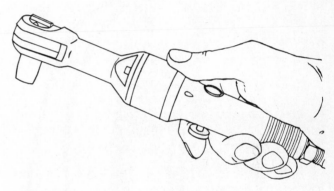

Fig. 7-14 An air ratchet.

≡ 7-10 PNEUMATIC FLOOR JACK

Many types of pneumatic jacks are used in the automotive body shop. The pneumatic floor jack, or bumper-type end lift (Fig. 7-13), uses compressed air to raise one end of the car. When the air valve is opened, compressed air flows into the jack cylinder, causing the ram to extend and raise the car. When the lever position is reversed, the air is released so the car settles back to the floor.

— CAUTION —

Never go under a car that is supported only by the jack. Always use safety stands placed under the car to support it safely before working under a car (Fig. 3-15). The pneumatic jack could slip or release, allowing the car to come down on you. This could seriously injure or kill you.

≡ 7-11 AIR RATCHET

The air ratchet (Fig. 7-14) usually has a ⅜-inch [9.53-mm] drive. It can use the sockets and attachments from a standard socket set. Since air ratchets deliver less force than an impact wrench, special impact sockets are not required.

≡ 7-12 PAINT SPRAY GUNS

There are two basic types of paint spray guns (Figs. 7-15 and 7-16): suction-cup and pressure-pot. The suction-cup spray gun is easier to move around. It is the most widely used, particularly for painting small sections and body panels that have been repaired. The suction-cup spray gun has a "cup" or container into which the paint is poured. Then, when the operating lever is pulled, compressed air passes through the gun, picking up paint from the container. The amount of paint picked up and the pattern that sprays from the gun can be changed by adjustments on the gun. These are described in a later chapter.

The pressure-pot spray gun (Fig. 7-16) is used for larger jobs such as repainting a complete car. The container holds considerably more paint than the cup on the suction-cup spray gun. The pressure-pot spray gun uses compressed air in the container to force paint through a hose to the spray gun.

Later chapters describe techniques for vehicle painting and explain how spray guns are used and the care they require.

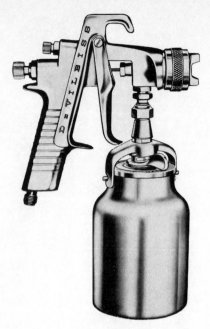

Fig. 7-15 A suction-cup paint spray gun. (*The DeVilbiss Company*)

Fig. 7-16 A pressure-pot paint spray gun. (*The DeVilbiss Company*)

≡ 7-13 CARE OF AIR TOOLS

Air tools should be given the same care as any other power tool. They should not be dropped on the floor or dragged around by the air hose. When not in use, they should be put on the workbench or on the designated shelf so they will not be carelessly handled. Every day, before using an air tool, apply three or four squirts of flushing oil to the air-tool inlet (Fig. 7-17). Then connect and operate the tool. This flushes out any dirt or moisture from the air motor and lubricates the moving parts. Any deposits are flushed out through the air exhaust.

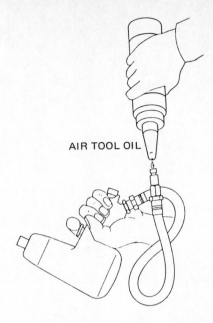

AIR TOOL OIL

Fig. 7-17 Squirting a few drops of air-tool oil into an impact-wrench air line. (*ATW*)

— **CAUTION** —————————————

Do not flush the wrench around an open flame. The mist coming out, which contains flushing oil, is flammable. Always point the tool air exhaust away from your body.

≡ 7-14 AIR SUPPLY

The auto body shop needs an adequate supply of compressed air to operate the various pneumatic tools used in the shop. Also, compressed air is needed to operate the spray guns used to paint cars. The air must be supplied at the correct pressure. In addition, the air must be clean and dry. Dirt or moisture in compressed air can damage pneumatic tools and ruin paint jobs.

≡ 7-15 SHOP COMPRESSED-AIR SYSTEMS

Figure 7-18 shows schematically a complete compressed-air system. It includes an electric motor that drives an air compressor. The air compressor draws air in from the surrounding space, compresses it, and forces it into the air tank. When the air pressure in the tank reaches a predetermined level, a switch automatically turns off the motor. The air tank is connected by pipes and flexible hoses to the various pneumatic tools and to the spray guns in the paint booths.

There are drains on the tank and in the lines. These are to drain out the water in the system. When air is compressed, the moisture in the air condenses into water. This water must be drained out so it will not get to the tools or spray guns.

In addition, the system has air filters or dryers to clean the air and regulators to regulate the air pressure

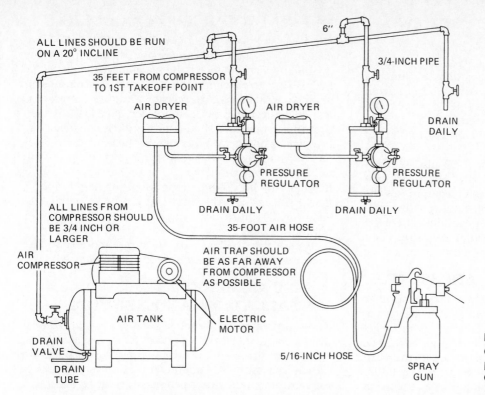

ALL LINES SHOULD BE RUN ON A 20° INCLINE

35 FEET FROM COMPRESSOR TO 1ST TAKEOFF POINT

6"

3/4-INCH PIPE

AIR DRYER

AIR DRYER

DRAIN DAILY

PRESSURE REGULATOR

PRESSURE REGULATOR

DRAIN DAILY

DRAIN DAILY

ALL LINES FROM COMPRESSOR SHOULD BE 3/4 INCH OR LARGER

35-FOOT AIR HOSE

AIR COMPRESSOR

AIR TRAP SHOULD BE AS FAR AWAY FROM COMPRESSOR AS POSSIBLE

AIR TANK

ELECTRIC MOTOR

DRAIN VALVE

DRAIN TUBE

5/16-INCH HOSE

SPRAY GUN

Fig. 7-18 Recommended layout of a compressed-air system for a body and paint shop. (*The Sherwin-Williams Company*)

going to the spray guns. Regulating the air pressure to the pneumatic tools is not important as long as the pressure is within the tool-operating range. But the air pressure at a spray gun is critical. If it is not correct within a very narrow range, the paint job will be bad.

≡ 7-16 AIR COMPRESSORS

The air compressor (Fig. 7-19) uses one or two pistons, moving up and down in cylinders, to compress the air and deliver it to the air tank. Each piston is attached by a connecting rod to a crank on a crankshaft, as shown in Fig. 7-19. The crankshaft is rotated by an electric motor. When the crankshaft is driven, it pushes and pulls on the connecting rod so the piston moves up and down.

On the down stroke, a partial vacuum is created above the piston. This allows atmospheric pressure to push the inlet valve down so that air can enter to fill the partial vacuum. At the same time, atmospheric pressure on the outlet valve holds it closed.

Then, on the up stroke of the piston, the air pressure increases above the piston as the air is compressed. This increasing pressure forces the inlet valve closed and the outlet valve open. The high-pressure air flows into the air tank. There is a check valve in the line from the compressor to the tank that prevents any backflow of air.

When the pressure in the tank reaches the preset value, a pressure switch is pushed open. This opens the electric circuit to the motor so the motor and compressor stop. Now the compressed air is available for any pneumatic tools or spray guns in the shop. When the pressure falls sufficiently as compressed air is used by the tools, the pressure switch closes. The motor starts again to bring the air pressure up to full again.

The actual pressure in the air tank varies according to the setting of the pressure switch. Most air tools require an air pressure of about 100 to 125 pounds per square inch (psi) [689 to 862 kilopascals (kPa)]. However, this is too high for spray guns, so a regulator is used to reduce the pressure at the spray guns.

Fig. 7-19 A two-stage, air-cooled air compressor. The large piston forces slightly compressed air into the cylinder with the small piston, which boosts air pressure higher. (*Lincoln St. Louis Division of McNeil Corporation*)

≡ 7-17 SINGLE-STAGE AND TWO-STAGE COMPRESSORS

Both single-stage and two-stage compressors are used to supply air for operating air tools and spray guns. In the single-stage compressor, the piston forces air from the cylinder directly into the air tank. Larger single-stage compressors have two pistons and cylinders. These may be satisfactory for small shops with limited compressed-air requirements.

The two-stage compressor (Figs. 7-19 and 7-20) has two cylinders, one larger than the other. Both work off a common crankshaft. The larger piston compresses the air to an intermediate pressure. This partly compressed air then enters the smaller cylinder. There the air is further compressed to the final pressure. Then the highly compressed air flows into the air tank.

≡ 7-18 COMPRESSOR AIR FILTER

The air entering the compressor must first pass through an air filter. Figure 7-20 shows the location of the air filter on a compressor. The purpose of the filter is to remove dust and dirt particles from the air so they do not enter the compressor. Dust particles in the compressor could scratch the piston, rings, and cylinder wall. Also, if dust gets into the air-supply system, it can cause trouble. Pneumatic tools can be damaged, and the spray gun will clog and stop working properly.

The compressor air filter should be cleaned or changed periodically. The service intervals depend on the type of filter and the amount of dirt in the air. Compressor manufacturers supply instructions which include recommendations on how often the filter should be cleaned or changed. These instructions should be followed to protect the compressor and the shop air system.

≡ 7-19 COMPRESSOR COOLING

Most compressors are air-cooled. A few are liquid-cooled. Air-cooled compressors have cooling fins on the cylinder block and head to help dissipate the heat. The heat results from compressing the air. The compressor should operate as cool as possible. A hot compressor is less efficient than a cool compressor. This is the reason that the compressor should be of sufficient capacity so that it does not have to run most of the time. A large-capacity compressor, with a large air tank, needs to run only a relatively small part of the time to supply the air needs of the shop. If the compressor is not large enough, it will run most of the time and not be very efficient. Also, it will require more frequent service and will wear out more quickly.

Where the air demands are large, more than one compressor will be required, working in parallel.

≡ 7-20 COMPRESSOR INSTALLATION AND SERVICE

The compressor, with motor, should be mounted on a level floor in a clean, well-ventilated place. All feet should rest firmly on the floor so there will be no strain on the assembly. Adequate ventilation is required to make sure that the heat produced by compressor action is carried away. Also, the compressor room must be clean so that the air going into the compressor is relatively free of dust particles.

All pipe connections from the main shop air line should be taken off at the top of the pipe, as shown in Fig. 7-18. This helps prevent any water in the system from flowing to air tools or spray guns. When air is compressed, it gets hot. Any moisture in the air condenses into water when the hot compressed air reaches the cooler pipes.

The air system and air tank are equipped with drain valves. They should be opened daily to drain out any water that has accumulated. Some compressors have an automatic device that opens a valve every cycle (starting and stopping of compressor). This releases any water that has accumulated.

Once a week, the compressor drive belts should be checked for wear, tightness, and alignment. At the same time, oil any bearings in the motor that require oiling.

The oil level in the compressor crankcase should also be checked weekly. If the oil level is low, add the type of oil recommended by the compressor manufacturer. At longer intervals (as recommended by the manufacturer), the oil should be drained and the crankcase refilled with fresh oil.

Blow the dust off the compressor cooling fins periodically. Dirty fins will not transmit heat as easily, causing the compressor to run hotter.

— CAUTION —

When checking the belt, oiling the motor, or performing any service around the compressor, shut off the electricity to the motor by opening the main switch. This will prevent the compressor from starting while you are working on it.

AIR FILTER

Fig. 7-20 A two-stage, horizontal-tank-mounted air compressor. (*Lincoln St. Louis Division of McNeil Corporation*)

≡ 7-21 AIR TRANSFORMER

The air transformer (Fig. 7-21) is actually a pressure regulator-separator assembly. It is connected in the line to the spray guns. Some transformers have a main-line pressure gauge and one or more regulated-pressure gauges. The main-line gauge indicates the pressure in the main-line air tank. The regulated-pressure gauge or gauges indicate the pressure in the lines to the spray guns. This pressure must be correct or the paint will not spray properly.

The pressure is regulated by a regulator valve. Turning the valve knob or handle one way or the other changes the air pressure going to the spray guns. Therefore, the paint technician can adjust the pressure to suit the requirements of the job.

The transformer also has a separator system to filter the air and remove any dust or water in it. There is a drain valve at the bottom of the regulator to drain off any water that has collected.

≡ 7-22 AIR-TRANSFORMER INSTALLATION

The air transformer should be mounted close to the paint technician so the pressure can be adjusted as needed. One recommendation is that it should be installed at least 25 feet [7.6 m] from the compressor. The takeoff should be from the top of the air line. The line should slope down and away from the takeoff (Fig. 7-18). This minimizes the possibility of water entering the transformer.

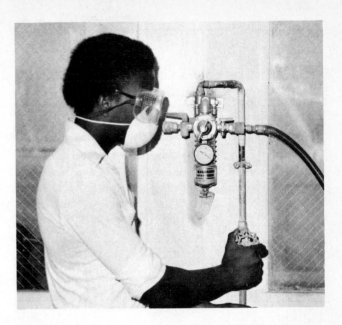

Fig. 7-21 An air transformer for cleaning and regulating compressed air.

≡ 7-23 AIR HOSE

The proper size air hose should be used. The tool and equipment manufacturer makes the recommendations for hose types and sizes (Fig. 7-18). These recommendations should be followed. Quick-disconnect couplings (Fig. 7-2) are used to connect and disconnect the tools to the air line.

REVIEW QUESTIONS

Select the *one* correct, best, or most probable answer to each question. You can find the answers in the section indicated at the end of each question.

1. When using the blowgun, (≡7-2)
   a. blow dust off your clothes
   b. first look into the nozzle to make sure it is clear
   c. never point it at anyone
   d. first load it with cartridges

2. Air tools provide either (≡7-3)
   a. rotary or reciprocating motion
   b. rotary or circular motion
   c. reciprocating or back-and-forth motion
   d. rotary or rotating motion

3. Mechanic A says the transformer is a pressure regulator. Mechanic B says it is a separator to remove dust and water from the air. Who is right? (≡7-21)
   a. mechanic A
   b. mechanic B
   c. both A and B
   d. neither A nor B

4. The air impact wrench (≡7-7)
   a. uses air pressure
   b. requires special impact sockets
   c. provides rotary motion
   d. all of the above

5. An advantage of an air drill is that it is undamaged by
   a. use underwater (≡7-8)
   b. lack of service
   c. water in the air line
   d. stalling

73

CHAPTER 8
HYDRAULIC BODY TOOLS

After studying this chapter, you should be able to:

1. Explain what *hydraulic* means and how hydraulic tools work.

2. Describe the operation of car lifts and jacks.

3. Discuss the purpose of the hydraulic press and how it is used.

4. Describe the types of body-and-frame aligners.

5. Explain the purpose of anchor pots and anchor rails.

≡ 8-1 OPERATING HYDRAULIC TOOLS

The word "hydraulic" means "of or pertaining to liquid or fluid." Therefore, hydraulic tools are tools that are operated by the pressure on a liquid. The brakes on automotive vehicles are operated by hydraulic pressure. When the brake pedal is pushed down, brake fluid at high pressure forces the brakes to apply. The hydraulic tools used in the body shop include car lifts, power jacks, and body-and-frame aligners. Lifts are powered by air or electric motors. Power jacks and aligners are powered by a hand pump, by a pump driven by an electric motor, or by an air-driven pump.

≡ 8-2 CAR LIFTS

Car lifts are either single- or double-post. Figures 8-1 and 8-2 show two types. Both have lift pads which can be positioned under lift points on the car frame or suspension. There is also the drive-on type, which has parallel tracks onto which the car is driven. The drive-on type is convenient for such jobs as draining the engine oil and working on the differential, clutch, and transmission. However, the type with lift pads is preferred for the body shop, because it can be adjusted to handle any size car without damage.

The lift is actuated by an air or electric motor that drives a hydraulic pump. The pump sends fluid to the cylinder or cylinders that form the post or posts. A piston or pistons are forced upward in the cylinder or cylinders by the fluid pressure. This raises the lift and the car on it.

── CAUTION ──

Do not allow anyone to remain in a car that is being lifted. Make sure all doors, the hood, and the trunk lid are closed; otherwise, they might get ripped off when the car is lifted. If the lift has a mechanical locking device, make sure it is engaged before you go under the lift. If a lift is not working properly, don't use it. Evidence of improper operation includes the following: the lift

Fig. 8-1 A single-post lift. The four lifting arms can be swiveled. They can also be extended or telescoped to fit a wide variety of cars and light trucks. *(Lincoln St. Louis Division of McNeil Corporation)*

Fig. 8-2 A two-post lift. The post under the front wheels can be moved forward or backward, as shown by the arrows, to accommodate vehicles of different lengths. *(Lincoln St. Louis Division of McNeil Corporation)*

may jerk or jump when raised, settle slowly when it should not, work too slowly, blow oil out of the exhaust line, or leak oil around the piston seal.

≡ 8-3 HYDRAULIC FLOOR JACK

The hydraulic floor jack (Fig. 8-3) is operated by pumping the handle. This raises the lifting saddle. Turning the top end of the handle or pulling a lever on the handle releases the hydraulic pressure so that the saddle and load on it will settle back down. When using the jack, be sure the saddle is firmly placed under the proper lift point on the car. If the saddle should slip, the car could drop and be damaged.

— CAUTION —

Never work under a car that is supported only by a jack. If it should slip, the car could fall on you. Place safety stands under the car at the proper lift points (Fig. 8-4). Then allow the car to rest on them before you go under the car. For some body and frame jobs, special support rods and stands are required (Fig. 8-5). The illustration shows only the frame supported on the stands. The body has been omitted to show how the frame of the car rests on the support rods.

≡ 8-4 PORTABLE CRANE

The portable crane (Fig. 8-6) is used to lift the engine out of the car. It is operated hydraulically by a hand

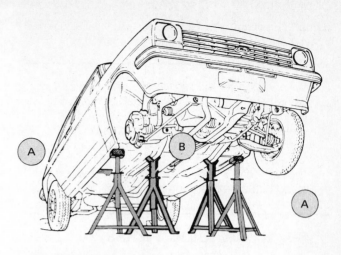

Fig. 8-4 Always place safety stands under a car at the proper lift points (A or B) before going under the car. *(Ford Motor Company)*

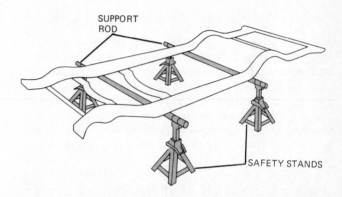

Fig. 8-5 Frame supported by support rods and safety stands. The body is omitted to show how the rods and stands are placed to support the car. *(Applied Power, Inc.)*

Fig. 8-3 A hydraulic floor jack.

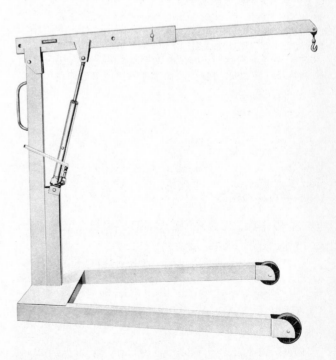

Fig. 8-6 A portable crane. *(Applied Power, Inc.)*

pump. The crane can be used for other jobs where a heavy object must be lifted and transported.

— CAUTION ——————————————

When using the portable crane or other lifting equipment, stand clear of the part that is being lifted. That way, you would not be injured if the part should slip or if the lift should topple. Never work on a part (such as an engine or transmission) that is suspended in the air. Instead, lower the part onto your workbench or into a support stand before working on it.

≡ 8-5 HYDRAULIC PRESS

The hydraulic press (Fig. 8-7) applies force to bent parts to straighten them. It is a general shop tool that has many uses. For example, it can be used to press bushings in or out, to press out rivets, and to straighten bent braces and brackets.

≡ 8-6 HYDRAULIC POWER JACK

This jack works on hydraulic pressure that is supplied by operating the handle on the pump (Fig. 8-8). Hydraulic fluid from the pump is forced into the jack, extending the piston. Most jacks of this type used with body-and-frame straightening equipment have an air-hydraulic pump that operates when the technician presses the treadle. See the Caution above (≡8-3) about the danger of working under a vehicle not properly supported.

≡ 8-7 TYPES OF BODY-AND-FRAME STRAIGHTENERS

The major hydraulic job in the body shop is to exert a force (a push or a pull) on bent sheet metal or the frame to straighten it. The operating components of the systems are hydraulic jacks and chains. These are attached to the vehicle so that the force can be exerted at the right place. Then hydraulic pressure is applied by a hand pump, or by an air or electric pump.

There are four types of body-frame straightening equipment. These are:

1. Portable (or rail) type (Fig. 8-9)
2. Floor-anchor (or anchor-pot) type
3. Stationary (or floor-rack) type
4. Bench (dedicated or universal) type

Each type has advantages and disadvantages, in addition to a difference in cost. These are described in the following sections.

≡ 8-8 PORTABLE BODY-FRAME STRAIGHTENERS

Figure 8-9 shows a typical portable body-frame straightener. It is basically a long steel beam (or rail) on wheels. The length of the beam can be adjusted. The hydraulic pump is hand-operated or driven by compressed air which is controlled by the technician's hand or foot.

Figure 8-9 shows a damaged front end being pulled into position with a portable body-frame straightener.

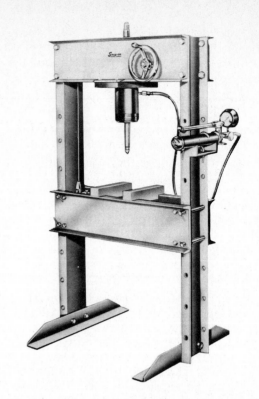

Fig. 8-7 A hydraulic press. *(Snap-on Tools Corporation)*

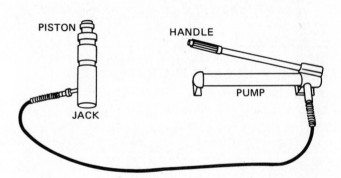

Fig. 8-8 A hydraulic power jack operated by a hand pump.

Fig. 8-9 A portable body-and-frame puller. *(Applied Power, Inc.)*

76

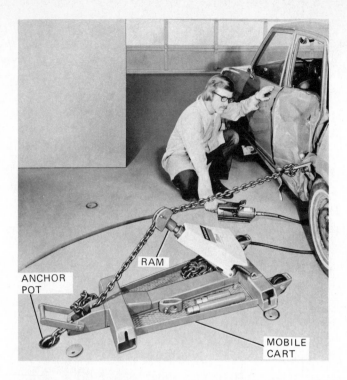

Fig. 8-10 A portable straightener that uses anchor pots set in the floor. *(Applied Power, Inc.)*

The post on the right end of the extension beam is anchoring the body in place. The pull is being exerted through the chain from the main post on the left.

The portable type of body-frame straightener costs less, can be easily moved to where it is needed, and then can be quickly moved out of the way for storage. However, heavy pulls cannot be made quickly and easily on all types of portable straighteners. Some equipment manufacturers recommend using anchor pots (≡8-9) with the beam for heavier pulling force.

≡ 8-9 FLOOR-ANCHOR BODY-FRAME STRAIGHTENERS

Another type of portable body-frame straightener is the floor-anchor straightener. One type uses anchor pots set in the floor to hold the mobile cart on which the hydraulic ram is mounted (Fig. 8-10). A pull chain is attached to the car. As the ram extends, the chain pulls the damaged metal back into position. The system shown in Fig. 8-10 can be set up to provide either a push or a pull.

Floor patterns for installing anchor pots in the shop floor are shown in Fig. 8-11. When placed at properly located spots, anchor pots can be used with chains and hydraulic equipment to exert pulls in almost any direction. Figure 8-12 shows how the pulling forces are ab-

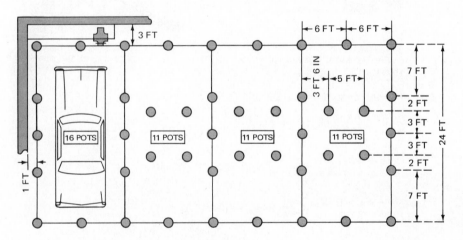

Fig. 8-11 Location of anchor pots in the floor. *(Guy-Chart Tools Limited)*

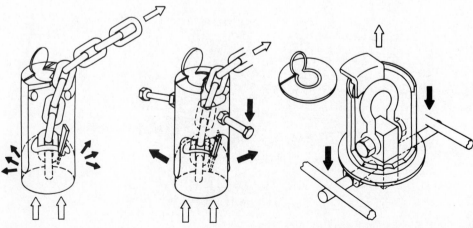

A. POT SET IN EXISTING FLOOR

B. POT SET IN NEW FLOOR

C. HEAVY-DUTY POT SET IN NEW FLOOR

Fig. 8-12 Methods of installing anchor pots. *(Guy-Chart Tools Limited)*

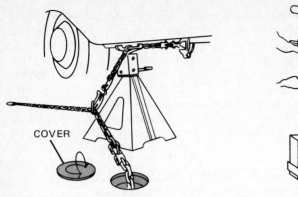

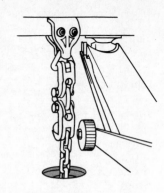

ANCHORING BETWEEN ANCHOR POTS.

COVER

ANCHORING UNIT DIRECTLY TO ANCHOR POT.

REVERSE PULL ON SILL. CHAIN IS REPLACEABLE IN SECONDS.

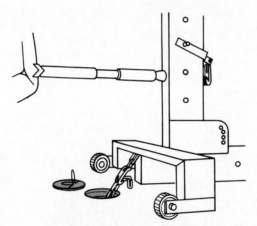

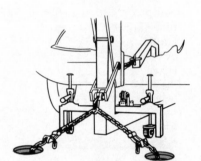

SECURING FRAME TO ANCHOR POT. THE HARDER YOU PULL THE TIGHTER IT GETS.

DEVELOPING A PUSH. RING IN POT PREVENTS CHAIN FROM CHIPPING CEMENT.

ANCHOR ANYWHERE IN YOUR SHOP. EACH LINK OF CHAIN IS AN ADJUSTMENT.

Fig. 8-13 Various ways in which anchor pots set in the shop floor can be used. *(Guy-Chart Tools Limited)*

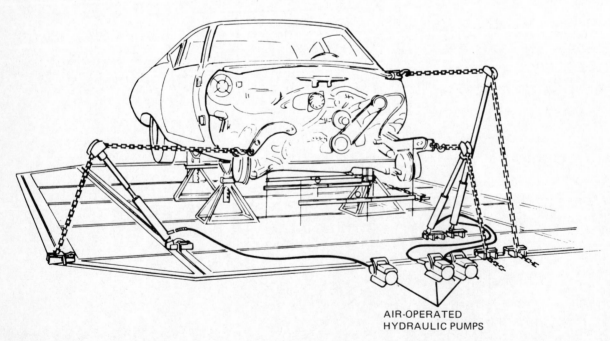

AIR-OPERATED HYDRAULIC PUMPS

Fig. 8-14 A floor-anchor type of body-frame straightener making pulls on the front end of a car. *(Applied Power, Inc.)*

sorbed by the pot. Figure 8-13 shows various setups for pushing, and for different kinds of pulls.

When anchor pots are not in use, they are protected with covers (Fig. 8-13). The covers prevent dirt from getting into the pots. They also prevent wheels or casters on jacks, carts, and creepers from getting caught in the pots.

Figure 8-14 shows another type of floor-anchor body-frame straightener. This uses a series of anchor rails embedded in the floor. The chain anchors are slid along in the slots in the anchor rails to the desired position. The setup shown in Fig. 8-14 includes three power rams. Each has its own air-hydraulic pump. Three separate and independently controlled pulls can be made at the same time. This is described in Chaps. 15 and 16.

When the tracks are not in use, the grooves can be filled with flexible plastic rail-slot covers (Fig. 8-15). The covers prevent dirt and other foreign material from getting into the slots.

The floor-anchor system allows the above-floor equipment (such as the mobile cart in Fig. 8-10) to be moved out of the way. Anchor pots or rails can be installed in every work area in the shop. Then every stall or bay can be used for body-and-frame straightening. However, positioning the chains for proper anchoring may take longer than using some other types of body-frame straighteners.

≡ 8-10 STATIONARY BODY-FRAME STRAIGHTENERS

Stationary body-frame straighteners may be mounted above the floor, in the floor, or in a pit. Once installed, they are not easily moved. Figure 8-16 shows an above-the-floor type of ramp-and-rack straightener. After the car is installed on the straightener, the upright beams are placed in the proper positions. Then hookups are made to the vehicle so that the pull can be exerted in the desired directions. For example, Fig. 8-17 shows a side pull being made on a body pillar to straighten it.

The floor-rack straightener has the ability to make three or four pulls at the same time. Some racks include turning-radius gauges for checking front-wheel alignment. However, because the rack is basically a permanent installation, its space in the shop cannot be used for other work. Even when the shop is busy, only one vehicle at a time can undergo body-and-frame straightening.

≡ 8-11 BENCH-TYPE BODY-FRAME STRAIGHTENERS

Most small cars are made with unibody construction and without a separate frame (Chap. 1). The metal body panels are stamped from high-strength steel (HSS). This type of sheet metal cannot be gas welded, arc welded, or heated without warping or weakening. Therefore, MIG welding must be used. MIG welding is described in Chap. 11.

A bench-type body-frame straightener can be used to repair many damaged unibody cars that would otherwise be "totaled." The bench (Fig. 8-18) consists of a steel frame with a machined top surface. A series of holes is drilled along both sides. Six transverse beams

Fig. 8-15 Floor-anchor grooves are protected with flexible plastic covers when not in use. *(Applied Power, Inc.)*

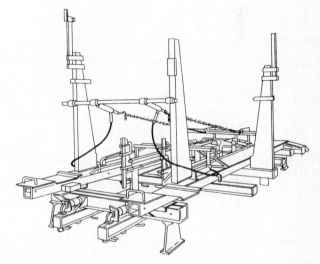

Fig. 8-16 An above-the-floor rack type of body-frame straightener. *(Applied Power, Inc.)*

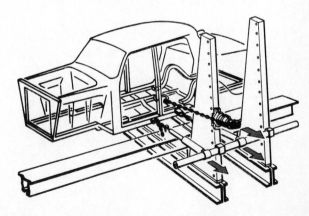

Fig. 8-17 Car in body-frame straightener with a side pull being exerted on a body pillar to straighten it. *(Applied Power, Inc.)*

Fig. 8-18 A bench-type body-frame straightener can be used to repair many cars with unitized bodies that would otherwise be totaled. *(Applied Power, Inc.)*

Fig. 8-19 Using a floor-anchor type of body-frame straightener to make pulls while the unibody car is on the bench. *(Applied Power, Inc.)*

are also machined and drilled with holes. Each hole is numbered. Fixtures bolt to the transverse beams and mate with the underbody of the car. If the fixtures fit the specified body control or reference-measurement points, the body of the car is in alignment. However, if the fixtures do not fit, the body must be straightened until the control points match the fixtures.

When welding is required, the fixtures can be used to hold the car while any structural members are being replaced. This prevents heat warpage that could return the body to an out-of-alignment condition. To make the pulls required, a floor-anchor body-frame straightener

is often used (Fig. 8-19). This allows the bench to be rolled into position. Then the pulls are made with the car on the bench.

REVIEW QUESTIONS

Select the *one* correct, best, or most probable answer to each question. You can find the answers in the section indicated at the end of each question.

1. The hydraulic tool that raises the entire car is the (≡8-2)
   a. floor jack
   b. portable crane
   c. car lift
   d. power jack

2. To remove an engine from a car, you would use a (≡8-4)
   a. portable crane
   b. car lift
   c. floor jack
   d. frame straightener

3. In the body shop, the major hydraulic job is to (≡8-7)
   a. remove engines
   b. lift cars
   c. align wheels
   d. straighten frames and sheet metal

4. Floor anchors are used with (≡8-11)
   a. portable body-frame straighteners
   b. bench-type body-frame straighteners
   c. both **a** and **b**
   d. neither **a** nor **b**

5. Most hydraulic rams used with body-frame straighteners are powered by (≡8-6)
   a. electric motors
   b. air-powered hydraulic motors
   c. hand pumps
   d. vacuum-powered hydraulic motors

PART 2

WELDING

Welding is a very important job in automotive collision repair. To weld two pieces of metal together, a very high heat is required. Sometimes molten filler metal must be added. Then, when the metals cool, they have *fused*, or melted together, to form one solid piece.

Five types of welding are used in automotive body shops. These are:

1. oxyacetylene (gas) welding
2. electric arc welding
3. metal inert-gas welding
4. compression (two-sided) resistance spot welding
5. noncompression (one-sided) resistance spot welding

Some shops may have equipment for all five types. Other shops may have only one or two. Each type has its advantages and disadvantages. But MIG welding is rapidly becoming the preferred procedure in automotive body shops.

All five types of welding, and other metal-cutting and joining processes, are described in this part of the book. Part 2 consists of three chapters:

Chapter 9   Oxyacetylene Welding and Cutting
Chapter 10 Brazing and Body Soldering
Chapter 11 Electric Welding

CHAPTER 9
OXYACETYLENE WELDING AND CUTTING

After studying this chapter, you should be able to:

1. Describe oxyacetylene-welding equipment and how to use it.

2. Discuss safety precautions required when using gas-welding equipment.

3. Explain the purpose and use of the regulators and the difference between the threads used on the two cylinders.

4. Explain how to light the torch.

5. Describe the various types of gas welds and how to make them.

6. Describe the procedure of cutting with a gas torch.

≡ 9-1 SHOP USE OF THE OXYACETYLENE TORCH

Gas welding and cutting are two ways in which oxyacetylene-welding equipment is used. The equipment is also called acetylene or gas-welding equipment. It uses two separate gases, oxygen and acetylene, to produce the flame.

The oxyacetylene torch has several uses in the body shop. It is used for welding metal parts together, as shown in Fig. 9-1. It also is used for cutting metal, heating metal to normalize or shrink it, brazing, and applying body solder.

≡ 9-2 WHAT IS WELDING?

Welding is a permanent type of metal-joining process that uses heat to form the bond. When metal is heated to a high enough temperature, it melts. In gas welding, the heat comes from a hot burning flame at the tip of the torch. (The torch is discussed in detail later in this chapter). As the temperature rises, the heat fuses, or melts together, the two adjoining pieces of metal. When the liquid metal cools, the two pieces have been joined together.

Two types of joining can be done with gas-welding equipment. These are welding, the procedure described above, and brazing. Brazing is covered in Chapter 10.

≡ 9-3 OXYACETYLENE-WELDING EQUIPMENT

The oxyacetylene-welding process uses highly flammable acetylene gas and burns it in pure oxygen to produce a flame with temperatures up to 6300°F [3482°C]. The temperature reached depends on the percentages of oxygen and acetylene delivered to the torch.

The oxyacetylene-welding equipment includes the following (Fig. 9-2):

1. Oxygen cylinder with regulator

2. Acetylene cylinder with regulator

3. Cart or hand truck with safety chains for the cylinders

4. Fire extinguisher, often mounted on hand truck

5. Hoses

6. Torch ("blowpipe") with handle, mixing chamber, check valves, and tip. Check valves, or *backfire arrestors*, are required by the Occupational Safety and Health Administration (OSHA) on manifolded equipment, which has two or more torches attached.

7. Eye shield or goggles for the technician

8. Torch lighter

Before we describe each of these and put them all together to explain the various ways the equipment can

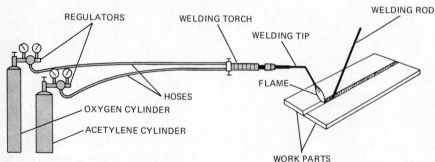

Fig. 9-1 Using gas-welding equipment. (*General Motors Corporation*)

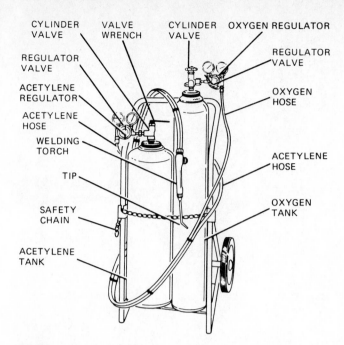

Fig. 9-2 Oxyacetylene-welding equipment mounted on cart. Chains secure the cylinders of acetylene and oxygen to the cart.

be used, we want to emphasize safety precautions that must be followed.

≡ 9-4 SAFETY

Special safety precautions must be observed when gas-welding equipment (Figs. 9-1 and 9-2) is used. The mixture of oxygen and acetylene is highly explosive. The flame is very hot. The materials worked on will reach high temperatures. All hose connections must be tight and leakproof. Hoses must be in good condition. Any leakage could result in an explosion and fire.

The cylinders must be treated with respect. The oxygen cylinder is holding between 2000 to 3000 psi [13,790 to 20,684 kPa] of pressure. Cylinders are supplied with valve-protection caps, or safety caps (Fig.

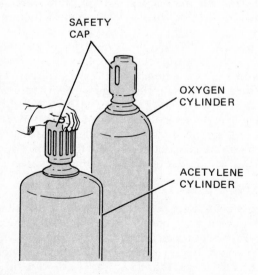

Fig. 9-3 Oxygen and acetylene cylinders with safety caps in place. *(Rego Company)*

9-3). The purpose of the cap is to protect the valve during transit. The cap should not be removed until after the cylinder is safely mounted on and chained to the cart or truck. If the cap is removed and the cylinder falls over, the valve might break off. If the cylinder contains oxygen, the compressed gas will be released at high pressure. This can turn the cylinder into a deadly missile which can actually ram through brick walls. Anyone in the way could be injured or killed. If the gas is acetylene, release of the gas by the breaking off of the valve could cause an explosion and fire.

— **CAUTION** —————————————

Some sheet steel is treated with rust-resistant zinc. When it is heated, as, for example, by gas welding, toxic zinc-oxide fumes are released. Adequate ventilation should be provided and respirators should be worn by technicians.

≡ 9-5 OXYGEN CYLINDER

The *oxygen cylinder* (Fig. 9-3) is a high-strength steel tank capable of holding pressures of 3000 psi [20,684 kPa]. Oxygen cylinders are painted either yellow or green so they can be easily identified. The cylinder has two valves: a safety valve and the operating valve. The safety valve is designed to open and release the gas if the pressure goes so high that the cylinder could explode. For example, in case of a fire, the safety valve opens. Release of the oxygen in this manner is much less hazardous than by a cylinder explosion.

The operating valve at the top of the cylinder is a *double-acting valve.* When it is turned all the way in, it seals the cylinder. When it is turned all the way out, it opens the cylinder to allow oxygen to flow to the regulator. Also, in the out position, the valve seals against the valve head to prevent any leakage of oxygen around the valve stem. When you use gas-welding equipment, turn the oxygen-cylinder valve all the way on in the open position to get this sealing effect.

Oxygen cylinders are filled to a pressure of 2200 psi [15,168 kPa] at 70°F [21.1°C]. However, cylinder pressure will go up as temperature increases. It will also go down as pressure decreases. For example, a fully filled cylinder at 0°F [−17.8°C] will have a pressure of only about 1780 psi [12,273 kPa]. If the cylinder is heated to 120°F [48.9°C], the pressure will go up to 2500 psi [17,237 kPa].

Oxygen cylinders are supplied in three sizes for most purposes. The large size used in auto body shops holds about 244 cubic feet [4.1 m³] of oxygen (if released at atmospheric pressure) at 70°F [21.1°C]. The two-stage oxygen regulator, described later and shown in Fig. 9-4, indicates the approximate amount of oxygen remaining in the cylinder.

≡ 9-6 ACETYLENE CYLINDER

Acetylene gas is produced by the action of a solid chemical, calcium carbide, when immersed in water. The gas is collected and stored in cylinders. The acetylene cylinder is somewhat different in construction from the oxygen cylinder (Fig. 9-2). Like the oxygen cylinder, the

Fig. 9-4 Two-stage oxygen-cylinder regulator. (*Harris Calorific*)

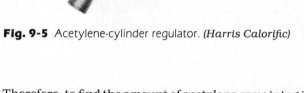

Fig. 9-5 Acetylene-cylinder regulator. (*Harris Calorific*)

acetylene cylinder is made of steel. However, it is lighter in construction because it does not have to contain such high pressures.

Free acetylene gas is very unstable at any pressure above 15 psi [103 kPa]. When the gas is put under pressure, it will explode. Therefore, a special process has been developed to store acetylene. The acetylene tank is filled with a porous substance such as charcoal, asbestos, or balsa wood. This material is saturated with the liquid acetone. Acetone has the peculiar property of being able to absorb large amounts of acetylene gas. Acetylene stored in this manner is safe provided normal precautions are taken, as explained below.

There are two general kinds of acetylene cylinders. One has a safety cap similar to the one for the oxygen cylinder to protect the cylinder valve. This type is shown in Fig. 9-3. The other type has the cylinder valve recessed so that a safety cap is not necessary.

— **CAUTION** ────────────

Never store an acetylene cylinder on its side. Always store it upright. The reason for this is that the cylinder is nearly filled with acetone liquid. If the cylinder is on its side, the acetone will cover the valve opening. Then, if the cylinder is used without being stood upright for a few minutes, liquid acetone will flow out. This can damage the welding equipment, and also it will leave a void in the cylinder and be a potentially serious explosion hazard.

However, because the pressure in the acetylene cylinder varies greatly with temperature, the regulator used with this cylinder indicates pressure, not the amount of acetylene left. The only accurate way to determine how much acetylene is left is to weigh the cylinder. One pound [0.45 kg] equals 14.74 cubic feet [0.42 m³] of acetylene gas (at atmospheric pressure)

Therefore, to find the amount of acetylene remaining in the cylinder (in cubic feet), weigh it (pounds), subtract the cylinder weight empty (pounds), and multiply the result by 14.74. Empty cylinder weight is stamped on the cylinder.

The acetylene cylinder has safety fuse plugs at top and bottom. These fuses will melt at a few degrees above the boiling point of water to release the internal pressure. This will prevent an explosion.

≡ **9-7 REGULATORS**

Each cylinder must be equipped with a regulator to reduce the internal pressures in the tanks to the low pressures required at the torch tip. Figures 9-4 and 9-5 show regulators for the oxygen cylinder and the acetylene cylinder. The oxygen-cylinder regulator, shown in Fig. 9-4, has two gauges. The gauge connected to the inlet side shows the tank pressure. The other gauge shows the outlet, or working, pressure to the torch. Turning the valve handle in increases the outlet pressure. This lets more of the tank pressure through the regulator. Turning the valve out reduces the pressure at the outlet.

The inlet-side oxygen pressure gauge may be marked to indicate both actual pressure and the amount of oxygen remaining in the cylinder. This is based on the volume the oxygen would occupy if released at atmospheric pressure.

The acetylene regulator, shown in Fig. 9-5, also has two gauges. One shows the cylinder pressure, and the other shows the outlet pressure to the torch. The outlet pressure can be changed by changing the valve setting.

≡ **9-8 REGULATOR THREADS**

It could be disastrous to accidentally install the wrong regulator on a cylinder—an oxygen regulator on an acetylene cylinder, or an acetylene regulator on an oxygen cylinder. To prevent this, the two regulator connections have different threads. The connecting nut of an oxygen regulator has right-hand threads to fit the right-hand threads on the oxygen-cylinder valve. The connecting nut on the acetylene regulator has left-hand threads that fit the left-hand threads of the acetylene-cylinder valve. In addition, some oxygen regulators are coded in green and acetylene regulators in red for easy identification.

≡ 9-9 HANDLING CYLINDERS

Compressed-gas cylinders provide safe and convenient sources of oxygen and acetylene. However, they must be treated with respect and handled with care. Cylinders must always be chained to the welding cart, to the wall, or to a post so they cannot fall. Always use the cylinders when they are in the vertical, or upright, position. Never use gas from cylinders that are lying on their side.

Many body shops have several sets of gas-welding equipment in use and do not store extra cylinders of oxygen or acetylene. When a cylinder is low, the shop foreman calls the local gas distributor, who sends over a truck with the required new cylinders. The truck driver then exchanges cylinders (Fig. 9-6).

Some shops keep extra oxygen and acetylene cylinders in reserve. Compressed-gas cylinders are sometimes found by safety inspectors to be improperly stored. They should not be stored near radiators or other sources of heat. They should be kept far away from combustible materials, stairs, or elevators. They should not be stored in unventilated enclosures such as lockers or closets. There should be at least 20 feet [6.1 m] between stored oxygen and acetylene cylinders. Or the cylinders should be separated by a fireproof barrier.

Cylinders should never be allowed to stand free but should be secured with a chain or lashing to keep them from toppling over (Fig. 3-6). Cylinders should always be plainly marked or painted to identify their contents.

≡ 9-10 EXCHANGING CYLINDERS

To safely remove an empty cylinder and put a full cylinder in its place, the following procedure must be followed. First, turn off the cylinder valve on the empty cylinder and disconnect the regulator. Then install a safety cap on the cylinder (Fig. 9-3). Next, unhook the chain holding the cylinder to the cart. Tip the cylinder on edge and roll it off the cart and to the place where cylinders of its type are stored. Chain it in place upright. Mark it "E" or "Empty" with a piece of chalk.

NOTE: Always handle "empty" cylinders the same as full cylinders. The empty ones may still have some gas in them.

Next, unchain the new cylinder, tip it on edge, and roll it to the cart. After you have put the cylinder on the cart, install the chain. Next, remove the safety cap. Before installing the regulator, "crack" the cylinder valve slightly to blow any dirt out of the valve opening (Fig. 9-7). To do this, stand to one side of the cylinder as shown in Fig. 9-7. Open the cylinder valve slightly, until you hear the hiss of escaping gas. Then immediately close the valve completely, but not too tightly.

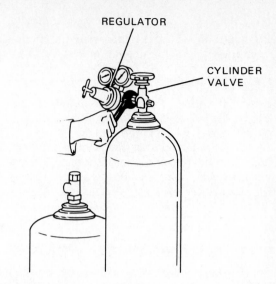

Fig. 9-6 Exchanging cylinders on the cart requires removal of the regulator from the empty tank and reconnecting it to the full tank. *(Rego Company)*

Fig. 9-7 Cracking the cylinder valve. *(Rego Company)*

― **CAUTION** ―――――――――――――――

Do not crack the acetylene-cylinder valve in a small or closed room or close to any open flame. For safety, roll the cart into an open area where no flame is present.

――――――――――――――――――――――――

Now attach the regulator (Fig. 9-6). Use an open-end wrench and turn the regulator attaching nut in the proper direction (clockwise for oxygen, counterclockwise for acetylene). Before you tighten the nut, position the regulator so the gauges are easy to read.

If the regulator connection leaks after you have applied the proper torque to the wrench, shut off the valve and remove the regulator. Carefully clean the threads and seat on the regulator and on the cylinder valve.

Should you find cross-threading, nicks, cracks, or other damage, do not use the damaged equipment. Call your welding-equipment supplier for service.

— **CAUTION** ——————————

Never lubricate the threads of the regulator nuts or cylinder valves. If high-pressure oxygen hits oil or grease, an explosion and fire can result. Technicians doing gas welding should not wear greasy or oily gloves or clothes while working with the gas torch. Oil and grease should be kept away from the gas cylinders and hoses.

___

≡ 9-11 SETTING UP TO WELD

Now let's discuss the procedure of setting up the gas-welding equipment and preparing to do a job. First, connect the regulators (≡9-10) if they are not already connected to the cylinders.

Next, select the torch body and tip that you need for the job. There are two basic types of torch bodies, one for welding (Fig. 9-8) and the other for cutting (Fig. 9-9). The basic difference is in the oxygen control. The welding torch has two rotary-type valves, one for oxygen and one for acetylene. They are adjusted to give the steady flame needed for welding or brazing. Some torches have the two torch connections identified with stampings such as OXY and ACET.

The cutting torch has four valves, three for oxygen and one for acetylene (Fig. 9-9). The torch oxygen valve (at the back of the torch) is opened to admit oxygen at the regulator pressure to the torch body, or handle. The second valve, the preheat oxygen valve, is used to adjust the amount of oxygen in the preheat flame. The

third valve, operated by a lever, releases additional oxygen at full regulator pressure into the flame. This produces an oxygen-rich flame which reacts with the white-hot metal to cut through it.

There are various types of welding tips (Fig. 9-10) and cutting tips (Fig. 9-11). The thicker the metal to be welded or cut, the larger the tip. Once the proper torch body and tip have been selected and assembled, the torch is ready to be connected to the cylinders. Hoses of the proper type and length are used. Both ends of the hoses have nuts, which are screwed onto the regulator and torch threads. Oxygen-hose nuts have right-hand threads. They are tightened clockwise on the oxygen regulator and the oxygen connection at the torch body. The acetylene-hose nuts have left-hand threads. They are tightened counterclockwise on the regulator and the acetylene connection at the torch body.

Complete welding outfits, such as shown in Fig. 9-12, are available. These provide all the basic parts needed for welding and cutting. The type of outfit to buy depends on the type of work you plan to do. For example, a light-duty outfit lets you cut steel up to 3 inches [76 mm] thick and to weld metal ¼ inch [6.35 mm] thick. The heavy-duty outfit shown in Fig. 9-12 lets you cut steel up to 6 inches [152 mm] thick and weld metal up to 1 inch [25 mm] thick. Both outfits will also heat and braze.

≡ 9-12 PURGING AND CHECKING HOSES AND TORCH

After all connections are made, the next step is to purge the lines and torch. Momentarily open the regulator valves to allow a quick spurt of gas to flow through. Then close the torch valves and check the hoses and connections for leaks. The steps in the procedure are listed below.

1. Loosen the regulator valve by turning it counterclockwise until the handle is loose. The valve is now closed. Open the cylinder valve. Oxygen will now enter the regulator. The cylinder pressure will be indicated on the regulator gauge.

NOTE: *Open the oxygen-cylinder valve all the way. This is a double-seating valve. Opening it all the way allows it to backseat in the open position. This prevents oxygen leakage around the valve stem.*

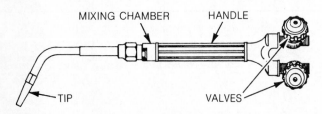

MIXING CHAMBER   HANDLE

TIP   VALVES

Fig. 9-8 A gas-welding torch.

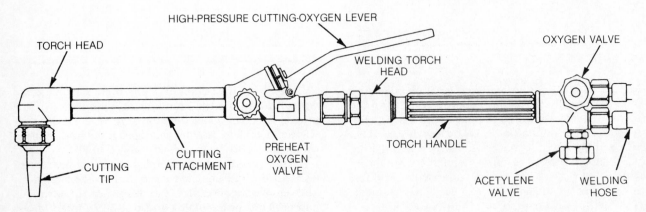

HIGH-PRESSURE CUTTING-OXYGEN LEVER

TORCH HEAD

WELDING TORCH HEAD

OXYGEN VALVE

CUTTING TIP

CUTTING ATTACHMENT

PREHEAT OXYGEN VALVE

TORCH HANDLE

ACETYLENE VALVE

WELDING HOSE

Fig. 9-9 A cutting torch. *(Rego Company)*

2. Check to make sure the oxygen valve on the torch is open. Then slowly turn the pressure-regulator valve in until oxygen begins to flow out of the torch tip. Now shut off the torch oxygen valve.

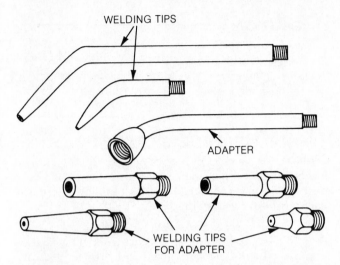

Fig. 9-10 Some of the various types of welding tips that can be attached to the welding torch. *(Harris Calorific)*

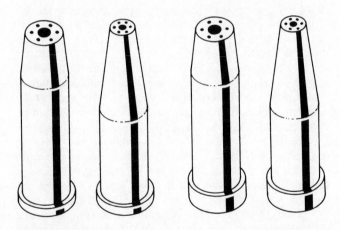

Fig. 9-11 A variety of cutting tips can be attached to the cutting torch. *(Harris Calorific)*

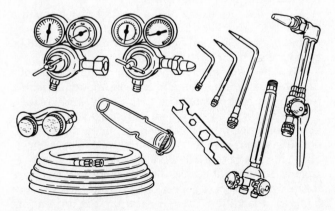

Fig. 9-12 A complete gas-welding outfit, which includes torches, regulators, tips, hose and other equipment.

3. There is now pressure in the hose and connections. To check for leaks, brush soapy water over the regulator, hose, and connections. Leaks will cause bubbles to form. Any leaks should be fixed before proceeding further.

4. If all connections are tight, turn the cylinder valve off. This shuts off the oxygen flow to the regulator and torch. Now back off the regulator valve to close it. This is a double assurance that gas will not be escaping from the cylinder.

NOTE: *Whenever finishing a welding job or stopping for a while,* always *close both valves — the cylinder valve* and *the pressure-regulator valve.*

5. The procedure for the acetylene regulator, hose, and torch is the same except for one step. Open the acetylene-cylinder valve only *one* turn (some recommendations are for one-half turn). This is not a backseating valve. The lower pressure in the acetylene cylinder can be retained by the packing around the valve stem.

CAUTION ―――――――――――――

Do not purge the acetylene hose and torch in an area where there are open flames or other conditions that could ignite the acetylene. Acetylene gas is highly explosive.

≡ **9-13 TORCH LIGHTER**

The torch lighter (Fig. 9-13) has a striker bar and a lighter flint to produce a spark which will ignite the torch. This is much like a cigarette lighter but larger and heavier, with a long handle so the hand can be kept safely away from the flame.

To use the lighter, hold the lighter cup under the torch tip. Then slightly open the acetylene valve on the torch. (The cylinder and regulator valves must be open.) The acetylene, being heavier than air, will fill the cup. Now squeeze the lighter handle. This strikes the flint on the bar and produces a spark that ignites the acetylene. You now have an acetylene flame which will be yellow and smoky. How to add oxygen and adjust the flame for welding is described in a following section.

CAUTION ―――――――――――――

Never try to light the torch with a match or cigarette lighter. You may get badly burned.

≡ **9-14 GAS PRESSURE FOR WELDING**

The pressures of the gas (oxygen and acetylene) as released by the regulators must be increased as the thickness of the metal being welded is increased. Thick metal requires more pressure. For example, Union Carbide recommends 5 psi [34 kPa] pressure for both the oxygen and acetylene when welding sheet metal up to

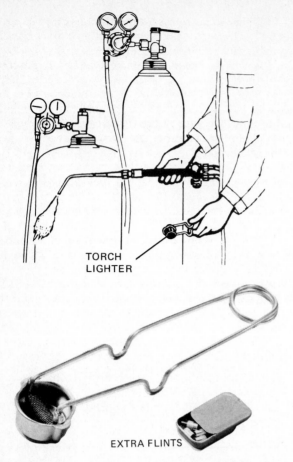

TORCH
LIGHTER

EXTRA FLINTS

Fig. 9-13 Top, using a torch lighter. *(Rego Company)* Bottom, torch lighter with extra flints. *(Harris Calorific)*

¼ inch [6.35 mm] thick. For metal from ¼ to ⅜ inch [6.35 to 9.5 mm] thick, the pressure should be 6 psi [41 kPa]. Then, ⅜-inch [9.5-mm] or thicker metal should have pressures of around 9 psi [62 kPa] for proper welding.

≡ 9-15 TIP CLEANERS

Tips must be kept clean. Two different kinds of cleaners are used (Fig. 9-14). One is a file that can be used to clean off the outside of the tip and reshape the tip if it has become damaged. The other type is a wire, or

Fig. 9-14 Tip cleaners. *(Harris Calorific)*

two wires twisted together, which is inserted into the tip hole or holes to clean them out. Wire of the correct size should be selected for the tip to be cleaned. If the wire is too small, it will not clean out all the soot that has formed. If the wire is too large, it might enlarge the tip hole or holes too much.

— **CAUTION** —

Tips must be kept clean. If a tip becomes clogged, the flame can back up inside the tip and cause a flashback. This is potentially dangerous because it can result in an explosion.

≡ 9-16 WELDING SAFELY

While there are certain hazards in gas welding, it is a safe job if the proper precautions are taken. Chapter 3 described the general safety rules to follow. Here are safety rules for gas welding:

1. Wear special dark welding safety goggles (Fig. 9-15). These goggles protect the eyes from flying sparks and from the intense light given off by the flame. This light can damage the eyes if they are not protected. The special welding safety goggles have dark lenses that filter out the harmful rays from the flame.

2. Wear leather gloves with wrist protectors (Fig. 9-16). They protect the hands and wrists from the white-hot sparks that the torch produces, particularly when cutting metal. Do not use cloth gloves. They can burn if a spark hits them.

3. Clothes should be worn that protect the arms, legs, and feet. A professional welder will wear heavy "leathers" or a jacket that is closed at the neck and a cap to protect the hair. A spark down the neck can be very painful. Hair can catch fire, especially if it is long.

4. Keep oil and grease away from the welding equipment. Never lubricate the threads on the nuts that attach the hoses. If oxygen hits a spot of grease or oil, it will burst violently into flame. For this reason, the welder's gloves and clothes must be free of grease or oil.

5. Welding should be done in a safe area, behind a shield that will protect others in the shop from sparks or from the intense light given out by the flame. There should be no flammable substances in the vicinity.

6. Keep the fire extinguisher handy. Make sure it is fully charged and working properly.

7. If a flashback occurs — if the flame backs up into the mixing chamber of the torch — *shut off the torch valves at once.* For safety, any torch you use should be equipped with backfire arrestors.

8. When welding a frame or other internal part of a car, stay away from fuel and air-conditioner lines. If a fuel line is broken, fuel could spurt out and create a serious fire before you could do anything about it. If an air-conditioner line or component, such as the condenser, is overheated, it could burst, releasing refrigerant. This is a potentially dangerous situation. The refrigerant comes out at a very low temperature. If you are in the way, you could get serious frostbite or severe eye damage. In addition, the refrigerant in the presence of an open flame will release a deadly poisonous gas. So locate and stay away from fuel and air-conditioner

Fig. 9-15 Gas-welding goggles. *(Harris Calorific)*

Fig. 9-16 Leather welding gloves. *(Marquette Division of Applied Power, Inc.)*

lines. If you have to work close to such lines, detach and move them to one side.

≡ 9-17 BASIC TYPES OF WELDS

Welding is much more than heating two pieces of metal until they melt together. To make good, strong welds, you must first know the types of welds that can be made. Figure 9-17 shows the six basic types of welds. Each weld is described below. Later sections describe the procedures for making each type of weld.

1. BUTT WELD. This weld (Fig. 9-17A) is made between two pieces of metal placed side by side, with or without a gap between them. In actual practice on car sheet steel, the butt weld is used to repair cracks or tears in a body panel or fender.

2. TACK WELD. This is not a final weld but a preliminary weld made before the complete weld is started. Figure 9-17B shows a tack weld. Its purpose is to hold the two pieces in place while the final weld is being made. Figure 9-17B shows how welds are made in

several spots to tack the two pieces together. This ensures that they will not move out of position during the final weld.

3. LAP WELD. This weld (Fig. 9-17C) is made by placing the edge of one piece on top of the other. Then the edge of the upper piece is welded to the flat surface of the lower piece. This is used when a patch is being applied to a body panel or when a replacement panel is being installed. Note that the weld is made on the outside and not on the underside. After the weld is completed, it must be hammered down to a level with the surrounding sheet metal. The irregularities are than smoothed down and filled, as described later.

4. CORNER WELD. The corner, or fillet, weld (Fig. 9-17D) is made to join two metal pieces at an angle. This type of weld is not often used in auto body sheet-metal work. However, sometimes it is necessary to use angle welding to repair frame and pillar members.

5. T WELD. This weld (Fig. 9-17E) joins one part to another to form an upside-down capital letter T. It is not often used in sheet-metal body work. The joint is stronger if the weld is made on both sides. To make this weld, the parts must be held in position with a vise or clamps.

6. EDGE WELD. This weld (Fig. 9-17F) joins two pieces along one edge. While this method can be used to join two body panels, MIG welding and electric spot welding are now preferred. The spot welds are made through the two sides rather than along the edges. Spot welding and MIG welding are described in Chap. 11.

≡ 9-18 ADJUSTING THE WELDING FLAME

After the torch is lit, it must be adjusted to give a welding flame. This type of flame is called a *neutral flame.* It results from a mixture of about equal parts of oxygen and acetylene coming out of the torch tip. The flame picks up some oxygen from the air, so the flame is composed of about one part of acetylene to about two parts of oxygen.

The proper proportions of the two gases are required to achieve a good welding flame. Too much acetylene will produce a carbonizing flame that has unburned carbon in it. This carbon will deposit on the pieces to be welded, and they will not weld properly. Too much oxygen will produce an oxidizing flame that will burn or

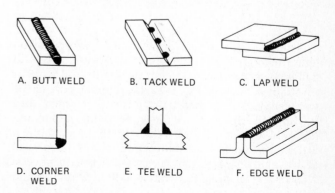

A. BUTT WELD   B. TACK WELD   C. LAP WELD

D. CORNER WELD   E. TEE WELD   F. EDGE WELD

Fig. 9-17 Six basic types of welds. *(General Motors Corporation)*

oxidize the metal. The resulting weld, even if successful, may be too hard, so that it would crack later.

The flame is adjusted by turning the two valves at the back end of the welding torch. To start with, when the torch is first lighted (Fig. 9-13), only the acetylene valve is opened (about one-quarter turn). The torch is then burning acetylene only. This gives a yellowish flame which is not hot enough for welding (Fig. 9-18). Note that this flame is wavy and sooty. To adjust the acetylene gas flow, gradually turn the acetylene valve on the torch, increasing the gas flow, until the flame just leaves the end of the tip. Then close the valve just enough to allow the flame to settle back onto the tip.

NOTE: *The actual adjustment of the acetylene valve depends mainly on the size of the welding tip. A large tip will pass more gas. Therefore, the valve must be opened wider to make the correct adjustment.*

Next, slowly open the oxygen valve on the torch. This causes the flame to sharpen and change color (Fig. 9-19). The flame takes on a bluish tinge. Also, the flame stops wavering and sharpens into a steady flame. As the oxygen valve opens further, when the flame is neutral, the yellow flame will have vanished into the blue inner cone of the flame, as shown in Fig. 9-20. This is the flame needed for welding.

NOTE: *When a sheet-steel body panel needs to be heat-shrunk, a flame slightly heavy with acetylene is used. This is not as hot or as pointed a flame. So it can heat a fairly large area without danger of burning the metal.*

If there is too much oxygen in the flame, the inner cone will shrink and almost vanish. This flame makes a hissing noise. It is not a good welding flame because it can cause the molten metal to bubble and spark, resulting in a poor weld. The extra oxygen also changes the chemical composition of the metal and causes it to become harder.

≡ 9-19 MAKING A BUTT WELD

To make any weld, including a butt weld (Fig. 9-17), you need the gas-welding equipment and welding rods, as shown in Fig. 9-1. Welding rods are made of metal and are melted by the heat so the molten metal flows into the joint and becomes part of it. For practice in making butt welds, two pieces of metal are laid out on the special firebricks set on the welding bench, as shown in Fig. 9-21.

Then you put on your goggles, cap, and gloves and light the torch. Adjust the torch valves to get a neutral flame. Next, you hold the torch and welding rod at about the angles shown in Fig. 9-22. Start at one edge of the two pieces of sheet metal. Bring the torch down until the tip of the inner core of the flame is almost touching the welding rod and metal. Back up the torch flame a little on the rod. You want to melt the end of the rod and at the same time melt the edges of the two metal sheets. As soon as the metal begins to puddle—which should take only a few seconds—you start the weld.

Keep the torch flame moving up and down the welding rod, so the rod melts, and at the same time moving

Fig. 9-18 Acetylene flame immediately after lighting.

Fig. 9-19 Acetylene flame with some oxygen in it. The flame has sharpened and shortened, and an inner cone has formed in it.

Fig. 9-20 Welding flame. The yellow flame has vanished and the inner blue cone has sharpened.

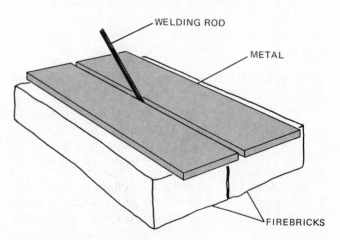

Fig. 9-21 Setup to make a butt weld.

WELDING ROD

METAL

FIREBRICKS

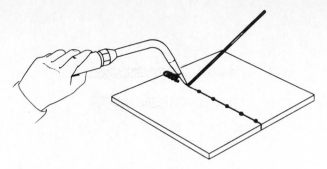

Fig. 9-22 Positions of torch and welding rod to start a weld.

across the gap between the two pieces of metal. Make sure you are melting the edges of the metal sheets and at the same time melting enough rod to fill the gap. It takes practice to make a uniformly smooth weld across the metal sheets. Make several butt welds until you learn to control the torch and rod. Move the torch flame up from the end of the rod just a small amount—just enough to melt the end of the rod. At the same time, you swing the flame a little from side to side so the edges of the metal sheets also melt.

The welding process described above is called *running a bead*, because you run a bead across the weld. The weld metal, which rises above the level of the surrounding metal, is ground, hammered, or sanded down (as necessary) during the final finishing procedure.

Figure 9-23 shows some good and bad welds. The bad welds are caused by not enough or too much heat or by failure to move the torch flame uniformly across the metal pieces as the weld is being made. When a person is just starting to learn welding, the torch is often moved in a jerky fashion. It is held in one spot a little too long and then moved too quickly, held more or less stationary for a few seconds and then again moved too fast.

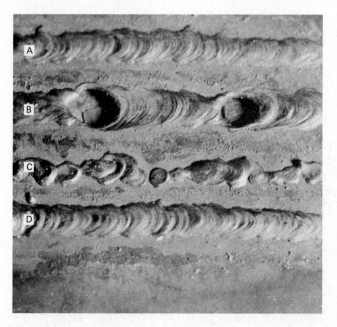

Fig. 9-23 A and D show good welds. B and C show bad welds. *(Union Carbide Corporation)*

Keep the torch moving smoothly up and down the end of the welding rod, and at the same time from side to side to heat the metal pieces. Continue to work smoothly across and along the joint being welded.

After the metal has cooled, turn it over and examine the back side. See if the weld has penetrated properly and if you have uniform welding all along the seam between the two metal pieces. Sometimes a weld looks good from the top. But when you turn the metal over you find there are places where the undersides of the pieces are not properly joined. The weld is not filled in.

NOTE: On your first butt welds, you may prefer to tack-weld the two pieces, as shown in Fig. 9-17B. This will hold them in position.

≡ 9-20 TACK WELDING

In tack welding (Fig. 9-17B), you want to weld the two metal pieces together in several spots. This means you select a spot and heat it and the welding rod so you get a puddle of molten metal. You repeat this in two or more spots along the joint. Later, when you make the weld, these spots will blend in with the rest of the joint.

≡ 9-21 LAP WELDING

This weld (Fig. 9-17C) is made the same way as the butt weld. However, when you are working with relatively thin sheet metal, you must be careful not to blow holes through the bottom sheet. Stay close to the joint as you move the flame from side to side. This joint can be made without using a welding rod if the metal pieces are not too thin. To do this, you apply most of the heat to the lower piece so the puddle starts to form there. It takes more heat to puddle the flat surface than to puddle the edge of the upper piece.

≡ 9-22 OTHER WELDS

The other welds—corner, T, edge—are all made in about the same way as the butt and lap welds. With these other welds, jigs or clamps are required to hold the parts in place while the welds are being made. In the shop, you should practice making these various welds until you can complete them properly.

≡ 9-23 WELDING POSITIONS

The previous sections describe the welding of metal pieces that are lying flat on a workbench. The pieces are horizontal and the torch flame and welding rod are pointed down. However, most welding jobs on the car must be done on metal that is upright or overhead. These require that the torch flame and welding rod be pointed up.

Figure 9-24 shows how to hold the torch and rod to weld a horizontal joint in sheet metal that is in a vertical position. This is the sort of job you might be doing to fix a horizontal tear in the side of a fender, for example. In this type of job, you would first straighten the metal and bring the two torn edges together. Then run a bead along the edges to make the weld. Hold the torch and rod pointed upward, as shown in Fig. 9-24, to control the puddle so it will not dribble down.

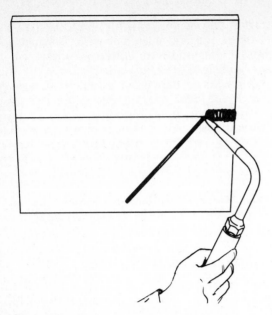

Fig. 9-24 Making a horizontal weld on vertical pieces.

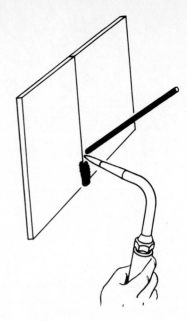

Fig. 9-25 Making a vertical weld on vertical pieces.

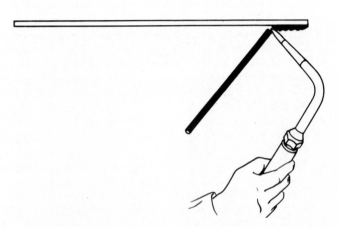

Fig. 9-26 Making an overhead weld.

If you are welding a vertical joint between two vertical metal pieces, hold the torch and rod as shown in Fig. 9-25. The flame is pointed upward to control the puddle so it does not run down. Move from bottom to top in making the weld. The welding rod is pointed downward toward the puddle. With this type of weld, the rod requires less heating from the flame because the heat from the puddle rises toward the rod.

Overhead welding (Fig. 9-26) is the most difficult and most hazardous. An example of this type of job might be going under a car on the rack to weld a broken joint in the car frame. In doing this type of weld, keep to one side so that molten metal or sparks will not drop on you. Gloves with protective cuffs, and a cap and a welding jacket that is fastened tightly around the neck, should be worn.

Point the torch flame up at about a 45° angle, with the rod pointed up at about the same angle (Fig. 9-26).

≡ 9-24 LEARNING TO WELD

To become an expert welder, you must practice making the various joints. Also, you should practice making horizontal and vertical welds on work that is held upright, or in a vertical position (Figs. 9-24 and 9-25). Practice making welds on overhead work, as shown in Fig. 9-26. Once you have mastered the technique, you will be able to make smooth, even, perfect welds every time. Later, you will make welds on actual cars. This will enable you to see how the proper welds contribute to restoring cars to their original condition.

≡ 9-25 SHUTTING DOWN

When you finish a weld, turn off the torch. Close the acetylene valve on the torch first. Then close the torch oxygen valve. If you are stopping for a short time, also turn off the oxygen and acetylene regulator valves. Then open and close the oxygen and acetylene valves on the torch to release any pressure in the torch and hoses.

If you stop work for a longer time or at the end of a welding session, you should also close the cylinder valves on the oxygen and acetylene cylinders. You should then close the regulator valves. Finally, open and close the torch valves to release all gas in the hoses and torch. When you leave the job, all valves should be closed—cylinder, regulator, torch.

≡ 9-26 EFFECT OF WELDING ON METAL

Whenever metal is heated, by a torch or otherwise, it undergoes certain changes. For one thing, it expands. If you heat one edge of a piece of sheet metal, for example, it will expand and warp, as shown in Fig. 9-27. The reason for this is that the metal along the edge, as it expands, has to go someplace. So the warp, or ripple, develops to take care of this expansion.

This can be a problem in welding body sheet metal, as, for example, when you are welding a patch onto a damaged fender. To guard against the ripple, you would first tack the patch to the fender in several places. This

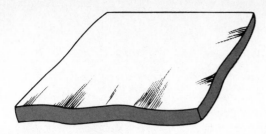

Fig. 9-27 Effect of heating one edge of a metal sheet. It expands when hot and then, when it cools, it warps and wrinkles.

would then tend to hold the two pieces being joined in place so warping would not occur.

NOTE: This expansion of the metal with heat is one reason that body technicians prefer other methods of patching body sheet metal and repairing rips in the metal. Expansion caused by heating the metal must be taken care of to bring the surface back to contour. For this reason, many body technicians use MIG welding (≡11-22), electric spot welding (≡11-19), screws, or Pop rivets (≡4-21) to attach patches.

Heating sheet metal to near its melting point changes its crystal structure so it becomes softer (≡11-21). When sheet metal is bent, it becomes hard, or work-hardens. The more it is bent, the harder it becomes. The same thing happens when sheet metal is hammered. The hammered area gets harder. It also tends to expand as the metal is pushed out and away from the hammer blows.

The two effects, work-hardening and expansion, result whenever body sheet metal is straightened and aligned. The two conditions—hardening and expansion—can be eliminated by heating the metal with a torch. Heating the area softens the metal. If the area is then worked with a hammer and dolly, the heating shrinks it. Cooling the area with water is part of this procedure. Heat shrinking is one of two procedures used to take care of the expansion or stretching of sheet metal. The procedure for heat shrinking sheet steel is described in a later chapter.

≡ 9-27 CUTTING METAL

To cut metal, a special cutting torch and tip are required (Figs. 9-9 and 9-11). The cutting torch has four valves, one for acetylene and three for oxygen. The acetylene valve, when open, admits acetylene to the torch. The torch oxygen valve admits oxygen to the torch when it is open. It should be opened all the way when the torch is in use. The preheat oxygen valve admits oxygen to the preheat flame. The cutting oxygen valve is operated by a lever and sends oxygen through the center hole of the torch tip (Fig. 9-28).

The outside holes in the tip release a mixture of oxygen and acetylene which forms the neutral flame for preheating the metal to be cut. When the metal turns dark red and is close to the melting point, the cutting oxygen lever is pressed to release oxygen from the center hole of the tip. This produces the cutting action. The procedure is described in following sections.

NOTE: The cutting torch is not often used in the body shop. Body technicians do not like to use it to cut sheet-metal panels because the resulting heat causes the panels to warp. This then requires additional work to relieve the expansion and warpage. Instead, body technicians use air chisels or nibblers to cut body panels (Figs. 7-5 to 7-7). If a frame member needed to be cut out so a new member could be welded into the frame, the cutting torch would be used for this job. But this is a rare and seldom recommended procedure.

≡ 9-28 SETTING UP TO CUT

Follow the procedure outlined for setting up to weld (≡9-18). However, attach a cutting torch with the appropriate tip to the oxygen and acetylene hoses. The size of tip you select is determined by the thickness of the metal to be cut. A thick piece requires a larger tip, which can deliver more preheat and more cutting oxygen than a thin piece. Likewise, a thick piece requires more gas pressure than a thin piece. For example, Union Carbide recommends the pressures shown in Fig. 9-29 for cutting metal of various thickness.

The metal to be cut should be marked with a cutting line to indicate where the cut is to be made. The cutting line can be made with chalk or soapstone. It should be easily visible because the dark goggles make faint lines harder to see.

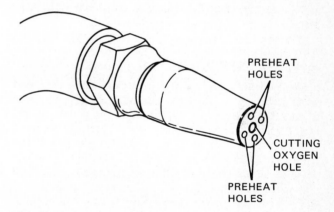

Fig. 9-28 Construction of a cutting tip.

Metal Thickness inch (mm)	Oxygen Pressure psi (kPa)	Acetylene Pressure psi (kPa)
⅛ [3]	15–20 [103–138]	3–5 [21–34]
¼ [6]	20–35 [138–241]	3–5 [21–34]
⅜ [10]	20–35 [138–241]	3–5 [21–34]
½ [13]	30–40 [207–276]	3–5 [21–34]
1 [25]	40–50 [276–345]	3–5 [21–34]
2 [50]	60 [413]	3–5 [21–34]

Fig. 9-29 Recommended oxygen and acetylene pressures to cut metal of various thicknesses. *(Union Carbide Corporation)*

After you have the torch set up and have the piece to be cut marked and on the workbench, put on your goggles, cap, and gloves. Adjust the regulators to the required pressures. Open the torch oxygen valve all the way. This admits oxygen to the torch. Depress the cutting oxygen valve momentarily to purge the torch. Release the lever.

Open the torch acetylene valve about a quarter turn and use the torch lighter to light the acetylene. Gradually open the acetylene valve until the flame moves off the tip. Then close the acetylene valve just enough so the flame backs up to the tip again. The torch is now feeding the proper amount of acetylene.

Next, turn the preheat oxygen valve to admit oxygen to the preheat flames. These are the flames produced by the gas coming out of the outside, or preheating, holes in the tip (Fig. 9-28). These separate flames more or less blend into a single, fairly broad flame suitable for preheating the metal to be cut. If any of the smaller flames coming from one of the preheating holes is small or missing, that hole is clogged. The torch should be shut off. After it has cooled, the tip should be cleaned or replaced.

When the right amount of oxygen is feeding to the preheating holes, the combined flame will be neutral. The yellowish acetylene flame will have practically disappeared into the central blue cone.

Now squeeze the operating lever momentarily to make sure cutting oxygen will flow out of the cutting oxygen hole in the tip. The flame will now change to an intense blue and will become longer and narrower. Release the cutting-oxygen-valve lever.

You are now ready to cut.

≡ 9-29 CUTTING

Many technicians rest their goggles on their forehead so they can see what they are doing while getting ready to cut. Then, when ready, they pull the goggles down over their eyes and start cutting. Here is the procedure:

Find the cutting line on the workpiece. Direct the preheating flame at the cutting line on the edge of the workpiece. Hold the preheating flame at this point until the metal becomes dark red and is ready to melt (Fig. 9-30). The torch is tilted so the flame hits the metal at an angle. The flame points toward the edge of the workpiece.

Squeeze the cutting-valve lever to release cutting oxygen. This additional oxygen starts the cutting action. As the metal cuts through, move the torch slowly along the cutting line to continue the cut. As the cut starts, straighten the torch so the cutting flame hits the metal more nearly straight on, as shown in Fig. 9-31. This reduces the thickness of metal that the flame must cut through. However, when cutting sheet metal, tilt the torch so the flame strikes the metal at an angle of up to 30°, as shown in Fig. 9-32. This blows away slag and makes a cleaner cut.

To cut a rivet or bolt head, preheat the head until hot. Then remove the head with the cutting flame.

≡ 9-30 GAS-WELDING ALUMINUM

Welding aluminum is more difficult than welding steel. Aluminum does not give any warning that it is hot

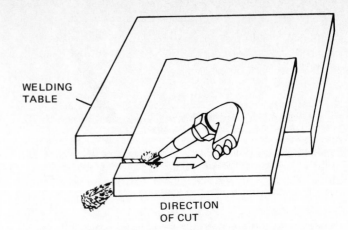

Fig. 9-30 Starting the cut. *(Rego Company)*

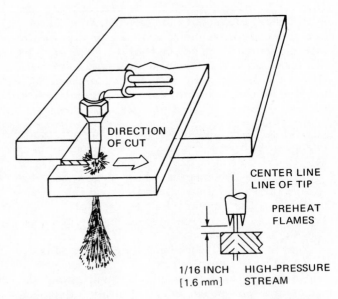

Fig. 9-31 Cutting-torch action in making the cut. *(Rego Company)*

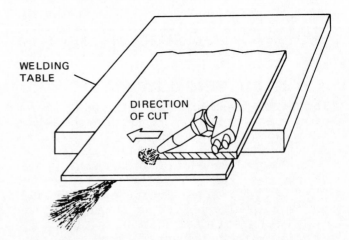

Fig. 9-32 Cutting sheet metal. *(Rego Company)*

enough to weld, by changing color. Instead, it will suddenly collapse, because it becomes very weak when it nears its melting temperature. Also, aluminum has a very high degree of heat conductance. This means much more heat must be directed to the joint. The heat is conducted away from the hot area very rapidly by the aluminum itself.

As the aluminum gets hot, it oxidizes. This oxide can form a coating that prevents a good weld. However, all these problems can be overcome if the right technique is followed.

Some body technicians who work with aluminum recommend goggles with blue-tinted lenses. These enable you to see the actions at the weld. The flame is slightly acetylene-rich. The inner cone should be a little fuzzy. This flame will appear rather yellow with ordinary welding goggles, and so you can't see the metal under the flame. Wearing goggles with blue lenses enables you to see the metal.

The aluminum surfaces to be welded must be absolutely clean. Oxide forms readily on aluminum, and it must come off, along with any dirt. Chemical cleansers are available, but new wire brushes will do the job. Flux is necessary to prevent the accumulation of aluminum oxide at the weld. The flux floats the oxide away. You can use aluminum welding rods which are coated with flux, or have the flux available so you can dip the rod into it before the weld starts. The rod should be heated and dipped into the flux. Flux will cool the rod and adhere to it.

Thin sheets of aluminum can be butt-welded. For thicker aluminum sheets, notching is recommended, as shown in Fig. 9-33. Aluminum sheets thicker than ½ inch [12.7 mm] should be both notched and beveled on the edges to be joined.

Preheat the surfaces to be welded and apply flux on both sides. The flux prevents formation of oxide on the surfaces. Now hold the welding rod at the work. Start at one edge of the aluminum sheets. Heat the rod and sheets at the same time, keeping the torch flame moving in a small circle to distribute the heat. Aluminum does not change color as it reaches melting temperature. Instead, it just gets mushy all at once. Be prepared for this so you can run the bead at just the right moment and temperature. Hold the rod and torch at a flatter angle than when welding steel. Also, the flame should be directed more toward the unwelded part of the joint to preheat the metal.

≡ 9-31 HEATING HSS/HSLA STEEL

For many years, cars were built using a type of steel called *mild steel*. It has a *yield strength* (or "stretch resistance") of up to 35,000 pounds per square inch (psi). This was the most common type of steel in cars. Everything from fenders to frames has been made from it. On some unibody cars, outer body ("skin") panels are still made from it. The procedure described so far in this chapter covers the oxyacetylene cutting and welding of mild steel. However, most car bodies built today are made of other types of steel.

Steel that has a yield strength from 40,000 psi to more than 150,000 psi is called *high-strength steel* (HSS). *High-strength low-alloy* (HSLA) *steel* is one of several types of HSS used in unibody cars.

HSS is used by car manufacturers to reduce car weight without reducing strength, and also for other

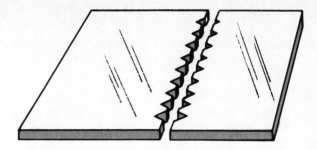

Fig. 9-33 *Notching thick aluminum sheets for welding.*

reasons. HSS can be heated up to its *critical temperature* and then allowed to cool without affecting its strength. However, when HSS is heated above its critical temperature, the metal becomes weaker and when cooled will be weaker than it was originally. The further above the critical temperature that HSS is heated, the weaker it gets. After heating to 1700°F (927°C), HSS may lose as much as 40 percent of its original strength.

Different types of HSS (such as HSLA) are used in cars today, and each type has its own critical temperature. You cannot tell by looking at a piece of steel what type it is, or its critical temperature. Therefore, automotive manufacturers recommend that you treat *all* steel as if it were HSS.

Most steel of any type can safely be heated to the 900-to-1200°F (482-to-649°C) range. If a piece of steel is dented or bent smoothly in a collision, you can probably straighten the damage cold, or by heating to the safe range. But if the metal cannot be straightened within the safe range, or if the metal is kinked or has sharp bends, replace it. Side-guard door beams and bumper reinforcements must *never* be heated. Chrysler cautions against heating certain pieces above 700°F (371°C).

In collision-repair work, you have two choices. One is to try to keep up with and follow the latest recommendations of the automotive manufacturers. The other is to be safe and not use heat at all.

If you must use heat, it must be carefully controlled. Blackhawk recommends the following:

1. Use a small torch tip with a neutral flame. Always remember that thin metal heats very fast.

2. Keep the torch moving evenly. Never hold it in one spot. A weak spot could be created by destroying the grain structure of the metal even in a small area.

3. Draw several lines across the area you are going to heat with a temperature-indicating crayon. (These are available from welding suppliers.) When the lines start to melt, stop heating or move to another area.

4. Don't cool the heated area with water or an air hose. Let the area cool naturally in the air.

5. Don't heat in one area for a total of more than three minutes.

Only by following the above recommendations can a torch be used in collision-repair work without weakening the part being heated. If sheet-steel panels must be welded together, or if the car body must be sectioned, then MIG welding must be used if there is any possibility that the metal is HSS/HSLA steel. MIG welding is described in Chap. 11.

REVIEW QUESTIONS

Select the *one* correct, best, or most probable answer to each question. You can find the answers in the section indicated at the end of each question.

1. The cylinder with the highest pressure contains   (≡9-5)
   a. hydrogen
   b. oxygen
   c. acetylene
   d. air

2. The oxygen cylinder has   (≡9-5)
   a. no valves
   b. one valve
   c. two valves
   d. three valves

3. When using gas-welding equipment, turn the oxygen-cylinder operating valve   (≡9-5)
   a. all the way closed
   b. all the way open
   c. halfway open
   d. open just enough to get a flow of oxygen

4. Acetylene gas is stored in a cylinder   (≡9-6)
   a. under high pressure
   b. filled with charcoal or similar material
   c. that should always lay flat
   d. that has no valves

5. Mechanic A says the acetylene cylinder should always be stored lying on its side. Mechanic B says it should always be stored upright. Who is right?   (≡9-6)
   a. mechanic A
   b. mechanic B
   c. both A and B
   d. neither A nor B

6. The two gauges on the oxygen-cylinder regulator show
   a. internal and external pressures   (≡9-7)
   b. oxygen and acetylene pressures
   c. tank and torch pressures
   d. atmospheric and vacuum pressures

7. Oxygen-hose nuts have   (≡9-8)
   a. left-hand threads
   b. right-hand threads
   c. lock washers
   d. cotter pins

8. Oil and grease must be kept away from the gas cylinders and hoses because   (≡9-10)
   a. oxygen hitting oil or grease can cause them to explode
   b. they will prevent welding
   c. they can prevent the oxygen and acetylene from mixing
   d. they can cause the cylinders to rust

9. Always light the torch with   (≡9-13)
   a. a cigarette lighter
   b. a match
   c. a lighted cigarette
   d. the special torch lighter

10. When welding aluminum,   (≡9-30)
   a. do not overheat it
   b. keep the surfaces to be welded very clean
   c. use flux
   d. all of the above

CHAPTER 10
BRAZING AND BODY SOLDERING

After studying this chapter, you should be able to:

1. Discuss brazing and explain how it is done with various materials.

2. Explain the purpose of body soldering and how it is done.

3. With the proper equipment, protective clothing, and instruction, demonstrate brazing and body soldering.

≡ 10-1 INTRODUCTION TO BRAZING AND BODY SOLDERING

Brazing and body soldering are much like oxyacetylene welding. The same gas-welding equipment is used and the procedure is similar. However, when brazing or soldering, the metal to be joined is not heated to the melting point. Also, the rods used usually are made of brass or lead. They have a lower melting point than the steel welding rods used for welding. If the filler rod melts above 840°F [450°C], the process is defined as *brazing*. If the filler rod melts below 840°F [450°C], the process is called *soldering*. Both processes are sometimes referred to as low-temperature welding.

≡ 10-2 WHAT IS BRAZING?

Brazing is a process that requires the use of a filler material (a brazing rod). The metals to be joined are heated along with the filler rod. At a temperature above 840°F [450°C] but below the melting temperature of the metals being joined, the rod melts. The joint is formed as shown in Fig. 10-1. In brazing, the metals being joined do not melt. Instead, the rod melts and then solidifies to hold the two pieces in position. As you can see in Fig. 10-1, the brazed joint made this way is similar to the joining together of two pieces of wood with glue. The strength of the joint is determined by the strength of the filler material. Some brazed joints can be very strong, depending on the material in the filler rod used.

≡ 10-3 BRAZING RODS

A brazing rod is a convenient form in which to handle the brass filler material. Actually, brazing rods are classified and sold as types of gas-welding rods. Like welding rods, brazing rods are usually 36 inches [914 mm] long. They are available in various diameters. Popular sizes of brazing rods are 1/16 inch [1.5 mm], 3/32 inch [2 mm], and 1/8 inch [3 mm]. Gas-welding rods (including brazing rods) are sold by the pound. Brazing rods are very expensive compared to steel gas-welding rods. Also, some flux-coated brazing rods are available.

≡ 10-4 BRAZING FLUX

When brazing, a flux must be used to produce a clean, strong joint. A *flux* is a special powder or paste that is

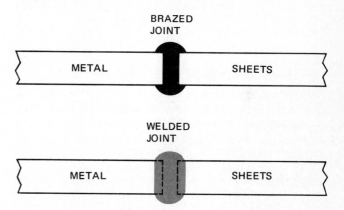

Fig. 10-1 Top, a brazed joint. The two metal sheets being joined did not melt. Bottom, a welded joint. The two metal sheets have melted together.

melted with the rod to dissolve any oxides and to help remove any dirt that may be on the surfaces. However, the surfaces should be cleaned before brazing begins. In addition, the flux promotes the free flow of the melted rod.

Most fluxes are mainly borax or boric acid. Probably the most frequently used flux in the body shop comes in 1-pound [0.45-kg] cans. However, many shops order and use flux-coated brazing rods. These rods have a flux coating the length of the rod. No additional flux normally is necessary when they are used.

≡ 10-5 ADVANTAGE OF BRAZING

Many people prefer brazing to welding when repairing brackets and other parts. One reason is that less heat is required. Therefore, there is less distortion of the metal. The more distortion, the more additional body work that will be required. Also, brazing is a faster procedure because the metal does not have to be heated to as high a temperature. However, brazing is seldom used on body sheet metal.

NOTE: *By definition, brazing usually means the use of a brass (copper and zinc) filler rod. You can identify a brazed joint because of its color, which is brassy or yellowish. Figure 10-2 shows a braze on a front-fender underbracket.*

Fig. 10-2 Brazing job on a bracket on a fender underbody.

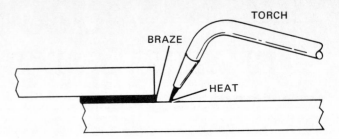

Fig. 10-3 Brazing an overlapped joint.

≡ 10-6 BRAZING SHEET METAL

Thin sheet metal can be brazed in an overlapped position joint. Thick metal may be brazed in a butt joint. The edges of the thick metal must be beveled first to form a V in which the brazing will be made. This process is covered in a following section.

The size of the torch tip and the gas pressures are determined by the thickness of the metal to be brazed. The major difference from welding is in the type of flame used. In welding, a neutral flame is required. In brazing, a slightly oxygen-starved flame is used. This is a carbonizing flame. The acetylene flame does not quite disappear into the central cone as in the welding flame.

NOTE: In many body shops, brazing of body sheet metal is seldom done. Instead, other methods of attaching patches or sheet-metal parts are used, such as riveting or electric MIG welding or spot welding. Electric welding is covered in the following chapter.

≡ 10-7 BRAZING OTHER MATERIALS

Brazing can be used to fasten together two different metals. (In welding, you fasten together two pieces of the same metal.) Softer metals such as brass or copper can be brazed. These metals cannot be welded easily. They melt at relatively low temperatures and are not as easy to handle as steel.

≡ 10-8 BRAZING THIN SHEET METAL

Thin sheet metal can be brazed in an overlapping joint. To braze an overlapping joint (Fig. 10-3), first make sure the surfaces to be joined are clean. In brazing, the brass melts and penetrates into the heated surfaces of the metal being joined. These surfaces must be free of any oxide or other material that would prevent this penetration.

The surfaces should be scrubbed with a very clean or new wire brush (to avoid putting grease or dirt on the surface from a used brush). Position the two pieces of sheet metal. Use flux-coated brazing rods. If these are not available, you can coat the rods with flux when the job begins. This is done by heating the rod and dipping it into a container of flux. The flux helps clean the metal being brazed and prevents the brass and other metal from oxidizing. The flux floats to the surface of the braze. There it protects the brass from the oxygen in the air, which could otherwise form a film of oxide. This could prevent good adhesion of the brass to the metal surfaces.

Now put on your goggles, cap, and gloves and make sure your clothing is right for the job. Light the torch and adjust the flame so it is slightly oxygen-starved. This is a carbonizing flame which is not quite as hot as a neutral welding flame. Fairly low regulator gauge pressures are used. Around 6 psi [41 kPa] for both oxygen and acetylene is about right for most brazing jobs.

NOTE: The size of torch tip depends on the job, particularly on the thickness of the metal and the brazing rod.

When brazing, do not hold the torch as close to the work as in welding. If you hold it too close, the flame could blow the melted brass away. Then it would be hard to get a good braze.

Heat the edges of the sheet metal, at the same time holding the brazing rod just above the joint. Move the flame up and down and in a circular pattern to distribute the heat over the sheet metal and rod. Only the brass rod melts, not the metal. When the metal and rod are heated enough, the rod starts to melt and it flows into the joint. As it cools, it solidifies and forms the brazed joint.

For larger patches and panels, tack-braze the sheet metal in several places. This will hold its position during the complete job.

≡ 10-9 BRAZING THICK METAL

Thick metal should be butt-brazed, not lap-brazed. The edges to be joined should be beveled at about a 45° angle (Fig. 10-4). When heating the V be careful not to overheat the top edges. Keep the flame pointed directly down and do not move it from side to side too much. When the metal is hot enough, the brass rod will melt and flow onto it. You may need to run several beads, one on top of the other, if the metal is very thick (Fig. 10-4). The first bead just fills the bottom of the V. The final pass over the joint should just fill the V with a little extra so there will be no voids. The extra may then be ground off if a smooth surface is desired.

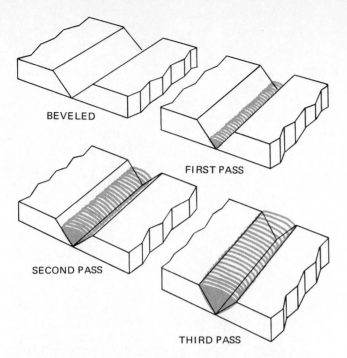

Fig. 10-4 Steps in brazing thick metal.

≡ 10-10 CLEANING THE BRAZE

After a braze is completed, it will be covered with soot and flux. The soot comes from the oxygen-starved brazing flame. The soot and flux will have to be cleaned off and the braze leveled and smoothed before the area is finished.

≡ 10-11 BODY SOLDERING

Solder is an alloy, or mixture, of tin and lead. It is widely used for making electrical connections. At one time, it was the preferred way to fill in damaged body-panel spots. Today, it has been largely replaced by plastic fillers which go on faster and are more easily worked. However, body soldering (or body leading) is still the best repair for some jobs, even though it takes longer and costs more than plastic.

Solder can be painted in the same way as other metal surfaces. It will adhere to the metal if properly applied and will not crack, peel, or flake off. It will last as long as the panel to which it has been applied. The disadvantage is that it takes longer, is messy, and is harder to work with. However, unlike other metals, solder does not change from a solid to a liquid at a certain temperature. Instead, as heat is applied, it becomes soft and plastic. This characteristic makes solder useful as an automotive body filler.

≡ 10-12 HAZARDS OF WORKING WITH LEAD

If lead gets into the human body, the lead can cause trouble. When working with solder, which is largely lead, certain precautions should be taken. Lead can enter your body if you are using solder as a filler on sheet metal. First, the fumes rising from the solder as it is melted have lead in them. Second, when a sander is being used to smooth the filled area, lead dust will be thrown off the sanding disk.

To guard against inhaling these fumes and dust, wear a respirator. The filter should be changed frequently. After using lead, wash your hands before you eat or smoke. In addition, the area should be vacuumed to pick up any lead dust that might have settled on the floor.

≡ 10-13 MATERIALS FOR BODY SOLDERING

In addition to the torch with a soldering tip, you need several sticks (or bars) of body solder, a roll of acid-core solder, some clean rags, a wooden soldering paddle (Fig. 10-5), and lacquer thinner (to remove acid from the soldered area).

≡ 10-14 BODY-SOLDERING A PANEL

There are several steps in the procedure of preparing a damaged body panel for body solder and then applying the solder. As a first step, the area on the body panel must be cleaned of all paint and dirt. Solder will not stick to a dirty surface. The cleaning can be done with a power grinder or sander or with a new and clean wire brush.

Next, the area to be soldered must be tinned. For small areas, the tinning can be done with acid-core solder. For larger areas, the tinning may be done with acid while a preliminary coat of solder is applied. The purpose of the tinning is to put a clean coat of solder over the surface so it is protected until the final soldering job can be done. The solder will adhere to the tinned surface much more easily.

To tin the area with acid-core solder, first heat the area with the torch. The torch should be equipped with a soldering tip, and the flame adjusted to be heavily carbonizing. That is, it should have an excess of acetylene. This gives a fairly cool flame, which is good because high temperatures are not needed for soldering.

As the area is heated, the end of the acid-core solder is applied to the metal under the flame. The solder will melt if the temperatures are right and will tend to

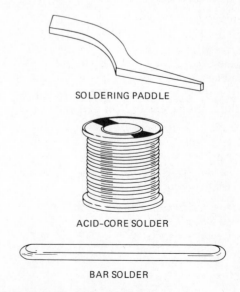

Fig. 10-5 Materials for body soldering.

spread over the prepared surface. Once the whole area is properly tinned, application of solder can begin.

Hold the end of the stick of body solder onto the metal surface and at the same time apply heat with the torch. When the temperature is high enough, the solder will begin to melt. Keep the torch and stick of solder moving. Try to spread the solder as evenly as possible over the area being repaired. You will not be able to spread it very evenly, so don't try at this point. Instead, after you have covered several inches with solder, lay aside the stick of solder and pick up the wooden soldering paddle (Fig. 10-6). While the solder is still molten, spread it evenly. Repeat the procedure until the entire area has been filled in and is reasonably smooth.

≡ 10-15 FINISHING THE SOLDERED AREA

After the soldered area has cooled, it must be finished with a metal body file and a sander. Edges should be featheredged with a fine grade of sandpaper. Next, the area must be treated to neutralize the acid used in the flux. Unless the acid is removed, it will cause the paint job to fail. Even a trace of acid will soon cause the new paint to peel. The area can be cleaned of acid with lac-

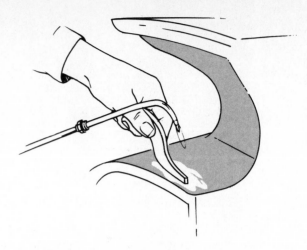

Fig. 10-6 Using the soldering paddle.

quer thinner. Be careful when wiping the area with thinner. Do not get any of it on surrounding painted areas. It will spot and damage the old paint. After the lacquer thinner has evaporated, the area is ready for priming and painting.

REVIEW QUESTIONS

Select the *one* correct, best, or most probable answer to each question. You can find the answers in the section indicated at the end of each question.

1. In brazing, the metals being joined together   (≡10-2)
   a. melt together
   b. are riveted together
   c. do not melt
   d. are soldered together

2. When brazing, the flux used   (≡10-4)
   a. promotes free flow of the melted rod
   b. helps maintain clean surfaces being joined
   c. helps dissolve any oxides that form
   d. all of the above

3. A brazing rod is made of   (≡10-3)
   a. steel
   b. brass
   c. lead
   d. solder

4. Mechanic A says brazing is better than welding because less heat is required. Mechanic B says brazing is faster than welding. Who is right?   (≡10-5)
   a. mechanic A
   b. mechanic B
   c. both A and B
   d. neither A nor B

5. Brazing can be used to fasten together   (≡10-7)
   a. two pieces of the same metal
   b. two different metals
   c. a crack in cast iron
   d. all of the above

6. Mechanic A says brazing of body sheet metal is seldom done. Mechanic B says it is better to rivet or spot-weld body sheet metal. Who is right?   (≡10-6)
   a. mechanic A
   b. mechanic B
   c. both A and B
   d. neither A nor B

7. Brazing flux is   (≡10-4)
   a. sulfuric acid
   b. boron
   c. mainly borax or boric acid
   d. activated lime

8. Solder is a mixture of   (≡10-11)
   a. lead and zinc
   b. lead and tin
   c. copper and bronze
   d. steel and lead

9. One important action required after a body-solder job is to   (≡10-15)
   a. neutralize the flux
   b. remove the solder from the panel
   c. fill in the rivet holes
   d. none of the above

10. To smooth the molten solder, use   (≡10-14)
    a. a torch
    b. sandpaper
    c. a grinder
    d. a solder paddle

CHAPTER 11
ELECTRIC WELDING

After studying this chapter, you should be able to:

1. Describe the hazards of arc welding and the protective clothing and helmet that must be worn.
2. Describe spot welding and explain how it is done.
3. Describe the operation and use of an arc welder using a rod electrode.
4. Compare ac and dc welders.
5. Describe the operation and use of a MIG welder.
6. Describe the basic types of welds and what good and bad welds look like.
7. Explain the operation of the Panelspotter.

≡ 11-1 BASIC TYPES OF ELECTRIC-ARC WELDING

There are three basic types of arc welding used in the automotive body shop. These methods are spot, arc, and metal-inert-gas (MIG). In spot welding, two sheet-metal panels are overlapped. Then a flow of current is sent through them at one spot. The current heats the metal at that spot, causing it to melt. The metal from the two panels, now being liquid, mixes together, or fuses. When the metal cools, the two panels are spot-welded together. In the actual job, the spot welder repeats the weld at many places along the joint where the two panels overlap.

In arc welding, the heat from a low-voltage, high-current electric arc causes the metal to melt. Two metal pieces can be joined at the joint between them by this melting process. Usually, some metal is added from a rod or a wire (the *electrode*). The resulting melt joins the two metal pieces after the metal cools.

Two variations of electric-arc welding are shown in Fig. 11-1. In one, the arc is struck between the workpiece and a metal rod, or electrode. This is often called "stick welding" because a "stick," or rod, electrode is used. In a second variation, the electrode is a metal wire that continually feeds from a wire feeder to the arc. This system is usually equipped with a gas cylinder that feeds an inert gas (argon, for example) around the arc. This forms an inert-gas shield, or envelope, that prevents contamination of the weld by gases in the atmosphere (such as oxygen and nitrogen). The system is called *metal-inert-gas (MIG) welding*.

MIG welding is required for welding the thinner, high-strength steel (HSS) used for body panels on late-model, lighter-weight vehicles. However, the type of steel used in a body panel or other part is very difficult to identify. For this reason, most manufacturers now recommend MIG welding for automotive body repairs on all cars. This includes the lower-strength, mild-steel

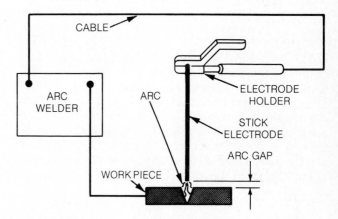

STICK ARC WELDING

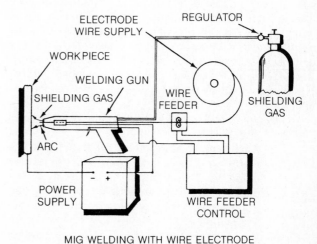

MIG WELDING WITH WIRE ELECTRODE

Fig. 11-1 Types of electric-arc welding.

sheet metal used in older cars. MIG welding is described in detail in ≡11-21 and ≡11-22.

≡ 11-2 ARC WELDING AND SAFETY

There are several special safety cautions that must be observed when electric-arc welding. These include such hazards as:

1. Electric shock
2. Fumes and gases from the welding process
3. Ultraviolet rays that can damage the eyes and cause sunburn
4. Sparks from the welding process that could burn you or cause fires
5. Droplets of molten metal (splatter) that fall from the welding arc

Each of these is discussed below.

— **CAUTION** —————————

MIG welders include a compressed-gas cylinder. Observe the proper procedure for handling and storing cylinders (≡3-6 and ≡9-4).

_____

1. ELECTRIC SHOCK. Electric shock can kill. Always be aware that you are handling an electrically "hot" electrode when the welder is on. Also, the metal workpiece itself is electrically "hot."

Although spot and arc welding require a heavy flow of current, sometimes amounting to several hundred amperes, the voltage is very low. Voltage is the "push" that forces the amperes through the circuit. In the spot welder, the circuit is through the two metal sheets being welded. In the arc welder, the circuit is through the electric arc.

This low voltage is not ordinarily dangerous, because it is not high enough to give you a shock. The voltage needed for arc welding is only a few volts, not enough to present any hazard. However, there is always some risk in operating and handling any electrical equipment. Therefore, you should always make sure that the cable is in good condition and that the insulation is intact. If you are using a portable machine which has a long power cable, make sure the cable is not damaged by being stepped on or driven over. If the power-cable insulation is bad and if the cable is on a wet floor or in contact with metal being welded, a short circuit could develop that could give you a serious shock.

   a. Wear dry, hole-free leather gloves with cuffs (Fig. 9-16).

   b. Always make sure you are insulated from the metal workpiece and from the ground by using dry insulation. If you are welding in a damp location, or on a metal floor or grating, make sure you are completely insulated from the metal.

   c. Never dip the electrode holder in water to cool it.

   d. When working above floor level, protect yourself from a fall if you should get a shock.

   e. Maintain the equipment—electrode holder, work clamp, welding cable, and welding machine—in good condition. Make sure that the cables to the welder are not stepped on or run over. This could damage the insulation and create an electric shock or fire hazard.

   f. The welding cable should not be coiled up, nor should it be coiled around your body. Sometimes a technician may think it is easier to handle the cable if it is coiled around the body. However, this can be hazardous because it could establish a circuit through the body.

2. FUMES AND GASES. Welding can produce fumes and gases that are a health hazard. Avoid breathing these fumes and gases. Keep your head out of the fumes. Use enough ventilation to carry away the fumes. The hazard is more serious when welding galvanized, or lead- or cadmium-plated, steel. The fumes from these materials are highly toxic.

Do not weld in locations near chlorinated-hydrocarbon vapors from degreasing, cleaning, or spraying equipment. The heat and rays from the arc can react with solvent vapors to form phosgene, a highly toxic gas.

3. ULTRAVIOLET RAYS. The welding arc produces strong ultraviolet rays which can cause severe sunburn on skin exposed to them for only a few minutes. Ultraviolet rays can seriously damage the eyes in only a few seconds if you look directly at the arc.

— **CAUTION** —————————

You can get "sunburned" from the arc through light, thin clothing. A thin cotton shirt is not adequate protection for heavy arc welding.

_____

4 and **5.** SPARKS AND SPLATTER. These hazards are the reason that full-time arc welders do a complete "cover-up" when on the job. Anytime you are arc welding, wear a welding helmet that completely covers the face, as shown in Fig. 11-2. The helmet has a window of special tinted glass. The tint filters out the harmful ultraviolet and therefore protects the eyes. In front of this special glass is a window of ordinary glass which serves to protect the special glass. Metal splatters when arc welding is in progress. The ordinary glass, which can be cheaply replaced, guards the more expensive special tinted glass against damage.

Helmets have hinges which permit the technician to swing the helmet up when welding is not in progress, as when getting ready to weld (Fig. 11-3A). It is difficult to see things in ordinary light through the special tinted glass. Then, just before striking an arc, the technician swings the helmet down (Fig. 11-3B).

NOTE: Helmets are made in different styles and with various features. A deluxe helmet model has a hinged window which can be swung up to give the welder a clear view of the work before starting to weld. When welding is about to begin, the window is swung down to protect the eyes.

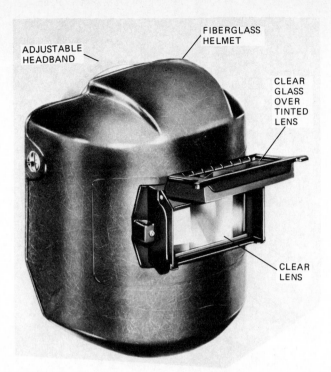

Fig. 11-2 A helmet with a special tinted-glass lens must be worn anytime you are arc welding. *(Marquette Division of Applied Power, Inc.)*

In addition to the helmet, the arc welder wears leather gloves with cuffs (Fig. 9-16). Also, a complete set of leathers may be worn to protect the arms, neck, and chest. Some technicians, when arc welding, wear leather aprons which provide adequate cover for the front of the body. Leather is preferred because it will not burn or catch fire as some clothing materials might. The degree of cover-up a technician uses when arc welding depends on how heavy a job is being done. For relatively light jobs, such as welding sheet-metal

panels, fairly light protection might be appropriate. But for heavy-duty welding, such as welding a truck frame, full body protection is best.

— CAUTION ——————————

If another person is helping you weld, the assistant must have adequate protection also. It is sometimes believed that the assistant, being several feet further away from the arc than you, does not need as much protection. However, the assistant should have a face shield or helmet, gloves, and clothing that provides complete coverage of the skin.

In addition, welding in the shop should be done in an area away from other technicians. When an arc-welding job is in progress, shields should be erected around the area and signs posted warning of the danger. Otherwise, a customer, child, or anyone passing by might suffer eye damage from casually looking at the arc.

≡ 11-3 SPOT-WELDING HAZARDS

During spot welding (Fig. 11-4), sparks will fly, just as with arc welding. The amount of sparking depends on the size of the job being done. With the spot welders found in the usual body shop, the sparking is not as severe as when an arc-welding job is in progress. Therefore, you may find spot welders being used in body shops by technicians not wearing any protection. This is wrong, because a single stray spark can put out an eye. As a minimum, goggles and gloves should be worn. Clothing should be buttoned or zipped up around the neck.

Since no arc is formed with spot welding, there is no hazard from the light. However, there are hazards from the sparks.

A   B

Fig. 11-3 How the helmet is used. (A) The technician has swung the helmet up to adjust the welder. (B) The technician is welding, so the helmet has been swung down to protect the face and eyes.

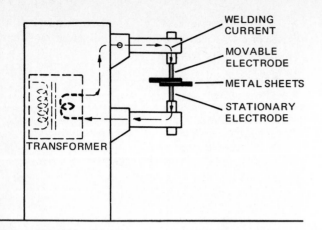

Fig. 11-4 Basic principle of spot welding. Current flows through two overlapped metal sheets, from one electrode to the other, causing the metal to fuse in the spot. *(General Motors Corporation)*

≡ 11-4 FIRE HAZARD

The welding area should be free of any flammable materials. One spark hitting a pile of oily rags can cause it to burst into flames. All flammable materials should be cleared away before welding begins. As an added safety precaution, position a fire extinguisher nearby.

When welding a frame or other internal part of a car, stay away from fuel and air-conditioner lines. If a gasoline line is broken, gasoline could spurt out. Then you would have a serious fire before you could do anything about it. If an air-conditioner line or component part such as a condenser is overheated, it could burst, releasing refrigerant. This can be very dangerous. The refrigerant comes out at a very low temperature. If you are in the way, you could get serious frostbite or severe eye damage. In addition, the refrigerant, in the presence of an open flame or arc, will produce a deadly poison gas.

Before welding, locate the fuel and air-conditioner lines and stay away from them. If you have to work close to such lines, detach them from their supports and move them to one side. Do not disconnect them unless it is absolutely necessary. Chapter 38 describes how to check air-conditioning systems for damage.

≡ 11-5 DISCONNECTING THE CAR BATTERY

The car battery gives off hydrogen gas while charging. Therefore, welding near an engine that has been run recently, or a battery that has been charging, could cause a violent explosion. Always disconnect the grounded battery cable from the battery. Then remove the battery from the car before starting to perform any type of electric welding (≡12-8). Unless this is done, the welding voltage could send a high current through the battery and the car electrical equipment, possibly ruining them. This is especially important on late-model cars which have several types of sensitive electronic devices.

≡ 11-6 SPOT WELDING

Spot welding is the simplest electric-welding procedure. Two pieces of sheet metal, cleaned on both sides,

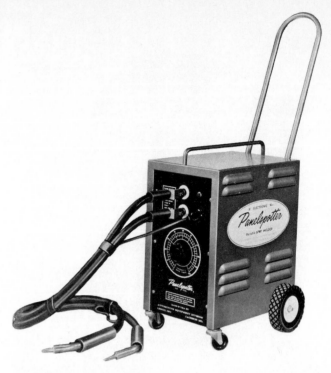

Fig. 11-5 A spot welder used in automotive body shops. *(Lenco, Inc.)*

are overlapped, as shown in Fig. 11-4. Then two electrodes are brought up against the two sheets. A heavy electric current at low voltage flows from one electrode to the other, through the sheet metal. This melts the metal at the spot. When the electrodes are withdrawn and the spot cools, the metal has fused to form a spot weld. The metal must be clean, because any dirt, paint, rust, or grease can prevent a good weld.

A great variety of spot welders are available (Fig. 11-5). They all operate in a similar manner. The typical spot welder has a transformer which steps down the shop 220 voltage to only a few volts. The spot welder includes a pair of heavy conductors on the ends of which are attached electrodes. The electrodes are copper, which offers low resistance and can pass a high current. The current is 100 amperes or more. This can produce almost instantaneous heating and fusing of the metal clamped between the two electrodes.

≡ 11-7 FAULTY SPOT WELDS

Technique does not enter into spot welding. You simply press the two electrodes to the two sides of the metal panels. Then close the switch that is located on one of the electrodes. The current flow does the rest. Faulty spot welds will result if the pressure is not correct or if the areas to be welded are not clean. Figure 11-6 shows good and faulty spot welds.

≡ 11-8 ARC WELDING WITH ROD (STICK) ELECTRODES

Arc welding is one of three electric welding processes used in the body shop (≡11-1). These machines may have a continuous electrode fed from a spool of wire. Others use a single welding rod, or stick electrode, at a time. This is sometimes called "stick" welding.

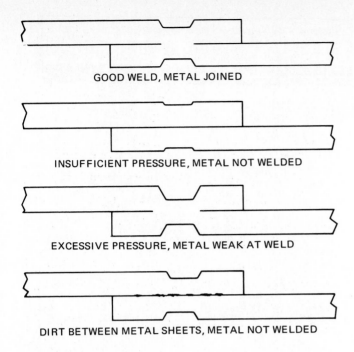

GOOD WELD, METAL JOINED

INSUFFICIENT PRESSURE, METAL NOT WELDED

EXCESSIVE PRESSURE, METAL WEAK AT WELD

DIRT BETWEEN METAL SHEETS, METAL NOT WELDED

Fig. 11-6 Good and bad spot welds.

The arc-welding machine supplies a high amperage at low voltage. The current may be as high as 250 amperes or more. This produces enough heat to melt the rod (stick) electrode and weld body sheet metal and frames.

Amperage, or heat, varies with the thickness and type of metal. The thicker the metal to be welded, the higher the amperage, or heat, required. Instruction manuals supplied with the welders give you specific instructions on the correct adjustments for different thicknesses of metal.

In the arc welder which uses rod electrodes (Fig. 11-7), the heavy current flows between the electrode and the metal workpiece. The end of the electrode is held a short distance from the workpiece so that an arc is formed. The heat from this arc melts both the end of the electrode and the immediate area of the metal

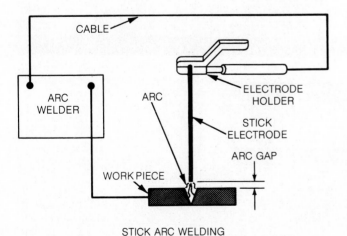

STICK ARC WELDING

Fig. 11-7 Basic principle of arc welding. *(General Motors Corporation)*

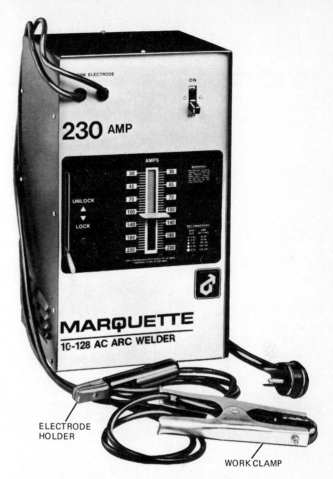

ELECTRODE HOLDER

WORK CLAMP

Fig. 11-8 An arc welder. *(Marquette Division of Applied Power, Inc.)*

workpiece. As the electrode is moved along, the melted metal cools and solidifies. This forms the weld. The action is called *running a bead.*

There are two basic types of arc welders: alternating-current (ac) and direct-current (dc) (Fig. 11-8). The ac welder uses a transformer to reduce, or step down, the 220 shop voltage to just a few volts. Only a few volts are needed to maintain the arc after it is started. However, two hundred or more amperes may flow in the arc. The heat from the arc produces the high welding temperature.

The dc arc welder has a means of stepping down the 220 ac voltage and also converting it into dc. The voltage reduction is produced by either a transformer or a motor-generator set. If a transformer is used, there is also a converter. Like a rectifier, the converter uses electrical check valves that change the ac to dc. If a motor generator is used, the shop ac runs the motor, which then drives the dc generator. The generator produces the dc directly. Dc welders usually have a polarity switch. It can change the direction of the current flow. When current flows from the electrode to the work, it is called *straight polarity*, or dc−. But when the polarity switch is thrown, the current flows from the work to the electrode. This is called *reverse polarity*, or dc+. Each polarity requires a separate type of electrode.

Welders have either a current-adjustment rheostat or several plug-in jacks so that the correct amperage for the job can be selected.

ELECTRODE DIAMETER AND CURRENT RANGE (AMPERES)

COATING COLOR	AWS CLASS	ELECTRODE POLARITY (+) = REVERSE (−) = STRAIGHT	5/64 INCH	3/32 INCH	1/8 INCH	5/32 INCH	3/16 INCH	7/32 INCH	1/4 INCH	5/16 INCH
ELECTRODES FOR MILD STEEL										
LIGHT TAN	E6010	DC (+)						200–275	250–325	280–400
BRICK RED	E6010	DC (+)		40–75	75–130	90–175	140–225			
TAN	E6012	DC (−) AC			80–135 90–150	110–180 120–200	155–250 170–275	225–290 250–320	245–325 275–360	
LIGHT TAN	E6011	AC DC (+)			75–120 70–110	90–160 80–145	120–200 110–180	150–260 135–235	180–300 170–270	
RED BROWN	E6011	AC DC (±)			80–130 70–120	120–160 110–150				
DARK TAN	E6013	AC DC (±)		75–105 70–95	100–150 90–135	150–200 135–180	200–260 180–235			
GRAY–BROWN	E7014	AC DC (−)			110–160 100–145	150–225 135–200	200–280 180–250	260–340 235–305	280–425 260–380	
BROWN	E6013	AC DC (±)	45–80 40–75	75–105 70–95	100–150 90–135	150–200 135–180	200–260 180–235	250–310 225–280	300–360 270–330	360–460 330–430
BROWN	E6011	AC DC (+)		40–90 40–80	60–120 55–110	115–150 105–135				
GRAY	E7024	AC DC (±)		65–120 60–110	115–175 100–160	180–240 160–215	240–300 220–280	300–380 270–340	350–440 320–400	
BROWN	E6027	AC DC (±)				190–240 175–215	250–300 230–270	300–380 270–340	350–450 315–405	
GRAY	E7024	AC DC (±)			115–175 100–160	180–240 160–215	240–315 215–285	300–380 270–340	350–450 315–405	450–600
GRAY	E7018	DC (+) AC		70–100 80–120	90–150 110–170	120–190 135–225	170–280 200–300	210–330 260–380	290–430 325–440	375–500 400–530
GRAY	E7018	DC (+) AC		70–100 80–120	85–150 100–170	120–190 135–225	190–260 180–280			
GRAY–BROWN	E7028	AC DC (+)				180–270 170–240	240–330 210–300	275–410 260–380	360–520	
ELECTRODES FOR LOW ALLOY, HIGH-TENSILE STEEL										
PINK	E7010-A1	DC (+)		50–90	75–130	90–175	140–225			
PINK	E7010-A1	DC (+)					140–225			
TAN	E7010-G	DC (+)			75–130	90–185	140–225	160–250		
TAN	E7010-G	DC (+)			75–130	90–185	140–225			
WHITE	E8010-G	DC (+)			75–130	90–185	140–225			
GRAY–BROWN	E8018-C1	DC (+) AC			90–150 110–160	120–180 140–200	180–270 200–300		250–350 300–400	
GRAY–BROWN	E8018-C3	DC (+) AC			90–150 110–160	120–180 140–200	180–270 200–300	210–330 250–360	250–350 300–400	
GRAY	E8018-B2	DC (+) AC			90–150 110–160	110–200 140–230	160–280 200–310			
GRAY	E11018-M	DC (+) AC			95–155 115–165	120–200 145–230	160–280 200–310	190–310 240–350	230–360 290–410	
ELECTRODES FOR STAINLESS STEEL										
PALE GREEN	E308-15	DC (+)			30–70	50–100	75–130	95–165	150–225	
GRAY	E308-16	DC (+); AC	20–45	30–60	55–95	80–135	115–185		200–275	
GRAY	E308L-16	DC (+); AC		30–65	55–100	80–140	115–190			
GRAY	E309-16	DC (+); AC		30–60	55–95	80–135	115–185		200–275	
PALE GREEN	E310-15	DC (+)		30–70	45–95	80–135	100–165			
GRAY	E310-16	DC (+); AC		30–65	55–100	80–140	120–185		200–275	
GRAY	E316L-16	DC (+); AC		30–65	55–100	80–140	115–190			
PALE GREEN	E347-15	DC (+)		30–70	50–100	75–130	95–165			
GRAY	E347-16	DC (+); AC		30–60	55–95	80–135	115–185			
ELECTRODES FOR BRONZE AND ALUMINUM										
PEACH	E-CuSn-C	DC (+)			50–125	70–170	90–220			
WHITE	Al-43	DC (+)		20–55	45–125	60–170	85–235			

ELECTRODES FOR CAST IRON

COATING COLOR	AWS CLASS	ELECTRODE POLARITY	1/8″ SIZE	5/32″ SIZE	3/16″ SIZE	1/4″ SIZE
LIGHT TAN	ESt	DC (+); AC	80–100			
BLACK	ENi-CI	DC (±) AC	60–110 65–120	100–135 110–150		
ELECTRODES FOR HARDSURFACING						
BLACK		DC (±) AC	40–150 50–165	75–200 80–220	110–250 120–275	150–375 165–410
BLACK		DC (+); AC			60–150	
BLACK		DC (+); AC			60–150	
DARK GRAY		DC (±) AC		145–210 155–225	180–280 200–290	230–360 255–375
DARK GRAY		DC (±) AC		120–180 135–230	160–260 165–285	200–350 220–385
DARK GRAY		DC (+) AC			110–275 125–275	150–400 200–400

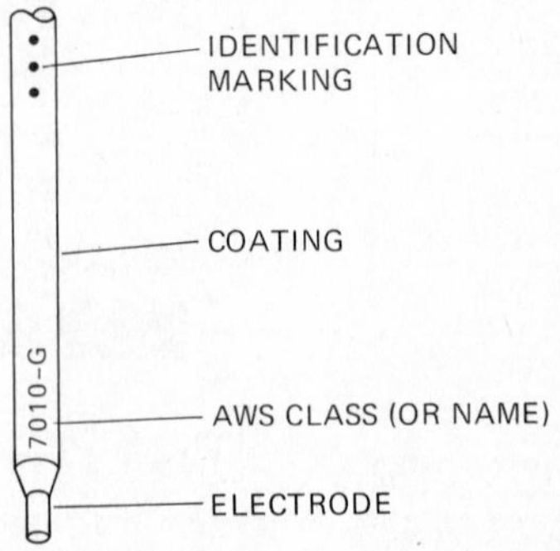

IDENTIFICATION MARKING

COATING

7010-G

AWS CLASS (OR NAME)

ELECTRODE

Fig. 11-9 Types of arc-welding rods, or electrodes.

≡ 11-9 COMPARING AC AND DC ARC WELDERS

Direct-current welding permits a uniform, continuous flow of current to help maintain a smooth welding arc. For straight-polarity (dc−) welding, the current flows from the electrode to the metal workpiece. A negative electrode is required. For very thin material or when only minimum penetration of the weld is desired, dc− welding is preferred.

In dc+ welding, the current flows from the metal workpiece to the electrode. A positive electrode is required. The positive electrode, with the current flowing to the electrode, allows maximum penetration of the weld. It is most suitable for such applications as welding on heavy frame members.

The steady flow of dc makes it easier to weld with small-diameter electrodes. These might be used on sheet metal, and also when welding in tight spots.

When welding with ac, the current changes directions 60 times a second (60-cycle ac). This means that the welding current passes through zero 120 times each second. Special ac electrodes are required which will maintain the arc through the rapid changing in the direction of current flow. A hissing sound, due to the alternating current, characterizes ac welding. For larger electrodes and for applications where arc blow is encountered, ac welding is usually preferred. *Arc blow* is the tendency for the arc to bounce back (for example, when trying to weld in a corner). Ac welding reduces this tendency.

≡ 11-10 TYPES OF ELECTRODES

The arc between the electrode and the work melts both the electrode and the work. There are many types of electrodes, each designed to be used on a specific metal of a specific thickness (Fig. 11-9). The electrodes are usually heavily coated with a flux. The purpose of this flux is to provide a gas shield around the molten pool of metal so the gases in the atmosphere cannot react with it and spoil the weld. Figure 11-10 shows welding being done with a bare electrode. The nitrogen and oxygen are free to get to the molten metal and react with it. These gases form chemicals, such as iron oxide, that

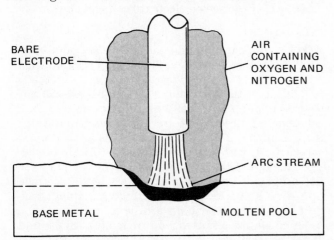

Fig. 11-10 When arc welding with a bare electrode, the molten metal reacts with the oxygen and nitrogen in the air to cause a poor weld.

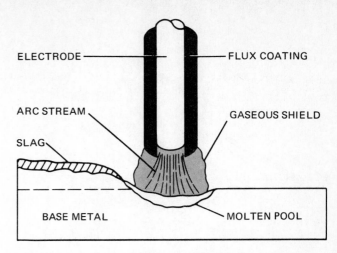

Fig. 11-11 When arc welding with a flux-coated electrode, the coating melts and forms a gaseous shield over the molten metal. This protects it from the oxygen and nitrogen in the air.

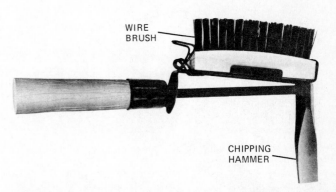

Fig. 11-12 Combination chipping hammer and wire brush for cleaning arc welds. *(Marquette Division of Applied Power, Inc.)*

combine with the molten metal so that the weld will be very weak.

Figure 11-11 shows welding being done with a coated electrode. The coating is melting and forming a gaseous shield over the molten pool. In addition, the coating floats up to the top of the weld, carrying with it impurities in the metal so that a purer and stronger weld is formed. After the weld is completed and cooled, this slag must be chipped off with a chipping hammer (Fig. 11-12).

NOTE: *When a weld is interrupted (for example, when you stop to put a new electrode in the holder), chip off the slag at the point where you stopped. This ensures a good union at that point when you start to weld again.*

≡ 11-11 TYPES OF ARC WELDS

Figure 11-13 shows a variety of welds that can be made by electric arc. Note that the electric-arc welder can make the same welds as gas-welding equipment — butt, lap, edge, tack, and T.

Butt welds are difficult on thin metal, particularly if the two edges are not perfectly aligned. The arc is so hot that it can quickly burn holes in thin metal. In butt-

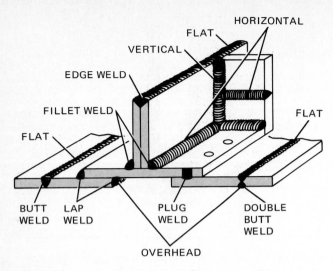

Fig. 11-13 Types of weld made with an arc welder.

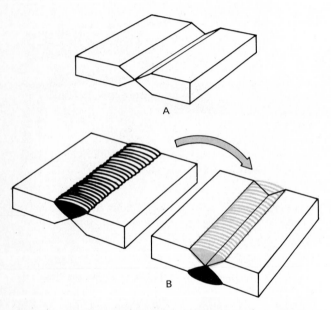

Fig. 11-14 Double V-butt weld. (A) The pieces are ground to form a V on both sides. (B) After the weld is made on one side, the piece is turned over to weld the other side.

welding thicker metals, the edges should be beveled so a V is formed. A double butt weld is often used on thick metals (Fig. 11-14). The two pieces are ground on both edges to form a V on both sides (A in Fig. 11-14). One side is welded. Then the piece is turned over so the other side can also be welded (Fig. 11-14B).

≡ 11-12 COMPARING GAS AND ARC WELDING

The type of welding done in a shop depends on the preferences of the shop owner and the technicians. There are advantages and disadvantages to both types of welding. For example, heavy-duty arc welders can cut metal, but high voltage and amperage are required. The arc welders found in body shops are not normally used to cut metal.

The gas welder is more versatile in many ways, because it can be used for cutting as well as welding. In addition, the gas flame can be used to braze and to apply body solder. Also, the gas flame is used in heat shrinking. Sometimes it is used in body-panel work.

The electric-arc welder, properly used, welds faster and causes less heat distortion. The heat is more concentrated in a small area. With gas welding, the superheated gas surrounding the flame heats a much larger area. This can cause considerable expansion and distortion of the metal. The greater the metal distortion due to heat, the more "extra work" the body technician has to do to correct it.

A second advantage of the arc welder is that there is less of a fire hazard than with gas. However, the arc welder throws out sparks which can burn anything they hit.

≡ 11-13 ARC WELDING

A typical arc-welding job is the butt-welding of two metal plates. First, the plates are beveled along the edges to be welded. They are then placed on the workbench and clamped so they will be held in position during the welding operation.

Next, the equipment is set up for the job. Plug the machine into the 220-volt shop outlet. Connect the welding cables to the machine and the ground clamp to the workpiece or worktable. Select the correct electrode for the job and put it into the electrode holder.

Now turn on the welder, adjust it to the correct amperage, put on your gloves and face shield, and lower the shield to protect your face. Be sure that you are completely covered and that your shirt is buttoned up to protect your neck. Arc welding and safety is discussed in ≡11-2.

You are now ready to strike an arc. This is done by either of two methods, tapping or scratching. Scratching is preferred by most welders, especially when welding with ac. This is just like striking a match (Fig. 11-15). The tip end of the electrode is scraped across the work and then raised slightly. If done correctly, the arc will form between the electrode and the work. Do not scratch just any place on the work. Scratch where the weld is to begin. The work and end of the electrode must be clean so a good electrical connection is made.

NOTE: *If you stop moving the electrode when scratching, the electrode will stick.*

The tap method of striking the arc (Fig. 11-16) consists of tapping the end of the electrode on the work. If this is done correctly, the arc will start when the electrode is lifted slightly off the work. This method works satisfactorily with dc but not as well with ac. If the electrode is raised from the work just as the current alternates and starts to flow from the work to the electrode, no arc will form. However, repeating the tapping procedure several times should start the arc.

Once the arc is started, you are ready to run a bead. Take the welding position (Fig. 11-17) as follows (assuming you are right-handed):

1. Hold the electrode holder in your right hand.

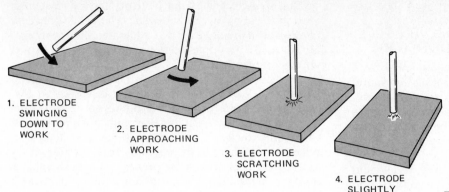

1. ELECTRODE SWINGING DOWN TO WORK

2. ELECTRODE APPROACHING WORK

3. ELECTRODE SCRATCHING WORK

4. ELECTRODE SLIGHTLY ABOVE WORK. ARC FORMED

Fig. 11-15 *Sequence of striking an arc by the scratch method.*

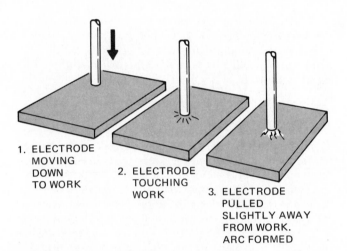

1. ELECTRODE MOVING DOWN TO WORK

2. ELECTRODE TOUCHING WORK

3. ELECTRODE PULLED SLIGHTLY AWAY FROM WORK. ARC FORMED

Fig. 11-16 *Sequence of striking an arc by the tapping method.*

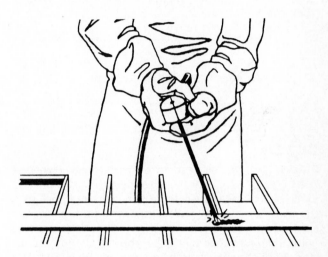

Fig. 11-17 *Running a bead, using two hands to steady the electrode holder.*

2. Put your left hand under the right as a means of supporting it.

3. Tuck your left elbow into your left side.

This position helps steady the electrode so that it can be moved smoothly across the work. It gives you better control of the electrode. (If you are left-handed, reverse the hand positions.)

Hold the electrode at a slight angle with its end at a distance from the work about equal to the diameter of the electrode (Fig. 11-18). The electrode should be tilted in the direction that it is moving.

When running a bead, keep the electrode moving steadily. Also, maintain the same air gap between the end of the electrode and the work. If you move jerkily, the weld will be jerky—too much metal in one place, not enough in another. Likewise, if you vary the length of the arc, you will have poor welding action in some places. The "sound" way of determining whether or not the length of the arc is correct is described in ≡11-14.

Watch the puddle of molten metal behind the arc. Do not watch the arc itself. It is the appearance of the puddle and the ridge in back of the arc where the molten puddle solidifies that indicates correct welding speed. The ridge should be about ⅜ inch [9.5 mm] behind the electrode (Fig. 11-19). Most beginners tend to weld too

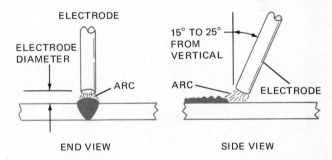

ELECTRODE

ELECTRODE DIAMETER

ARC

END VIEW

15° TO 25° FROM VERTICAL

ARC

ELECTRODE

SIDE VIEW

Fig. 11-18 *Correct positioning of the end of the electrode above the work.*

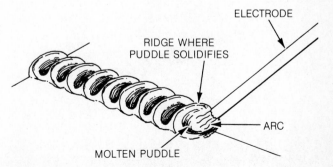

ELECTRODE

RIDGE WHERE PUDDLE SOLIDIFIES

ARC

MOLTEN PUDDLE

Fig. 11-19 *Correct welding speed is indicated when the ridge forms about ⅜ inch [9.5 mm] behind the electrode.*

fast. This produces a wormy-looking bead, because they are not watching the molten metal.

≡ 11-14 SOUND OF A GOOD ARC

When the electrode is held at the proper distance from the work, the arc will give off a sharp crackling sound which some technicians call the "frying-egg" sound. Actually, it is a sort of sputtering or frying sound that is a little sharper than you would get frying eggs. If the arc is too long, which means poor welding, you will hear a more subdued humming noise. Have an experienced welder strike an arc. If you listen carefully, you should be able to distinguish the difference between the sound from an arc of the right length and the sound from an arc that is too long. If the electrode is moved too far away from the work, the arc will not be able to jump the gap. Then the arc will die out.

— CAUTION —

Do not look at the arc without your helmet on and your eyes protected by the lens!

≡ 11-15 STRINGER AND WEAVE BEADS

Stringer and weave beads are the two basic types of bead (Fig. 11-20). The stringer bead (Fig. 11-20A) is made by moving the electrode in a straight line across the work at a steady pace. After striking the arc, the electrode should be held momentarily at the starting point to ensure good melting of the metal and good fusion. Then the electrode should be moved smoothly and at a steady pace along the joint being welded. The correct length of arc should be maintained.

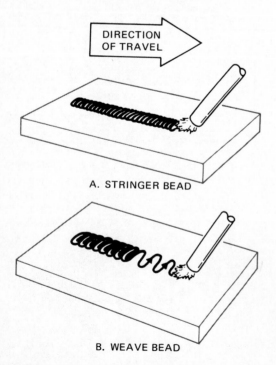

Fig. 11-20 Stringer and weave beads.

The stringer bead is satisfactory for most welding around the shop, except where a wider bead is needed. A wider bead might be needed to join two slightly irregular edges, for example, or to finish off a closed V-butt weld, as shown in Fig. 11-14B. To make the weave bead, weave the end of the electrode from one edge of the space to be filled to the other, as shown in Fig. 11-20B. Continue this weaving motion at the same time that you move forward along the bead. You should hesitate momentarily at each edge of the weave. This supplies as much heat to the edges as at the center.

Figure 11-21 shows the procedure of butt-welding on thick metal. Four beads are shown being laid. Bead 1 runs along the bottom of the V. Then you add beads 2 and 3 along the two sides of the V. Finally, make a weave bead to finish off the weld.

NOTE: After each bead is completed, chip off the slag from the top of the bead before starting the next bead. If you do not do this, a poor weld will result. The upper weld will not fuse satisfactorily through the layer of slag.

≡ 11-16 ANALYZING GOOD AND BAD BEADS

Some bad beads are caused by incorrect movement of the electrode on the work. Others are caused by incorrect selection of the current, or heat (Fig. 11-22).

A in Fig. 11-22 shows an uneven bead, caused by uneven speed of movement across the work. In some places, the technician moved slowly and a good bead was formed. Then the technician moved too fast, and so very little bead was formed. There was very little penetration in these places, so the weld is weak. This weld is unsatisfactory.

B in Fig. 11-22 shows just the opposite situation. The bead is too thick in places, as a result of uneven and excessively slow movement in spots. Where the bead has piled up, that part of the bead probably is porous and burned because of the excessive heat resulting from holding the electrode there too long. This weld is unsatisfactory.

C in Fig. 11-22 shows too much spatter, which occurs when the metal "splashes" away from the bead.

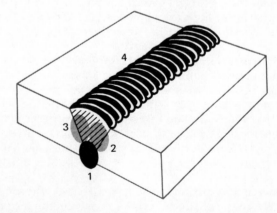

Fig. 11-21 Procedure for making a V-butt weld on thick metal. Four beads are shown, and they should be made in the numbered sequence.

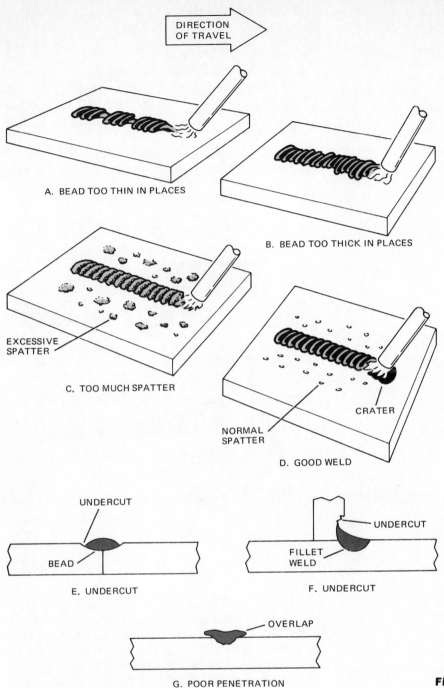

DIRECTION OF TRAVEL

A. BEAD TOO THIN IN PLACES

B. BEAD TOO THICK IN PLACES

EXCESSIVE SPATTER

C. TOO MUCH SPATTER

CRATER

NORMAL SPATTER

D. GOOD WELD

UNDERCUT

BEAD

E. UNDERCUT

UNDERCUT

FILLET WELD

F. UNDERCUT

OVERLAP

G. POOR PENETRATION

Fig. 11-22 *Good and defective arc welds.*

The usual cause is an arc that is too long. The length of the arc should be about the thickness of the electrode being used. An excessively long arc gives off more of a humming sound than a crackling sound (≡11-14).

D in Fig. 11-22 shows a good weld being made. The bead is uniform and there is only a little spatter.

E and F in Fig. 11-22 show the same defect. This is called *undercutting* and is due to failure to fill the depression created by the arc. This is caused by moving the arc too rapidly along the work. There is not enough time for the electrode to melt and fill the crater.

G in Fig. 11-22 shows another kind of defective weld, called *overlap*. The edges of the bead overlap the base metal beyond the sides of the crater. This overlap

does not fuse to the work. There are several possible causes of this condition, including too low a welding current (heat), too long an arc, or excessive travel. To avoid overlap, try a higher heat, a shorter arc, and slower electrode movement.

Another condition sometimes causes a beginner trouble. This is when the electrode sticks to the work. The cause of this condition is allowing the electrode to remain in contact with one area for too long. When this happens, the electrode welds to the base metal. To release the electrode, bend it from side to side to break it free. The instant an arc is struck, you should move the electrode away from the spot—along the joint to be welded.

≡ 11-17 PRACTICING ARC WELDING

To develop proper arc-welding technique, try welding with the welder turned off. Practice holding the electrode the proper distance from the work and moving it smoothly along the joint you want to weld. Some technicians find that using both hands helps to steady the electrode. Also, keeping the elbows close to the body reduces the tendency to weave the electrode as you move it. Do this practice with your face shield up so you can see what you are doing. There will be no arc with the welder turned off, so there is no danger. When practicing, try to keep the end of the electrode only about ¹⁄₁₆ to ⅛ inch [1.6 to 3 mm] from the work as you move it along the weld.

In actual welding, the electrode melts away. Therefore, you must keep moving the electrode holder down toward the work in order to maintain the proper length of arc (Fig. 11-23).

— CAUTION —————————————

Always have the helmet down to protect your eyes and face before striking the arc and beginning to weld.

≡ 11-18 MAKING DIFFERENT KINDS OF WELDED JOINTS

After you have mastered the basic welding technique and have made a good butt weld on two metal plates on the bench, try other types of welds (Fig. 11-13). As you develop skill, you should begin performing the basic welds on actual cars.

≡ 11-19 ARC SPOT WELDING

Figure 11-24 shows an arc spot welder. This is a semi-automatic machine that makes arc welds in spots. A typical job would be to spot-weld two overlapping panels together. The arc spot weld is similar in many ways to the resistance spot weld described in ≡11-6. However, the arc spot weld adds filler metal to the weld so that a small bump is left.

— CAUTION —————————————

Goggles should be worn even though this type of welding does not throw as many sparks as the other types already described. There will still be sparks, and it takes only one spark to put out an eye.

≡ 11-20 USING THE PANELSPOTTER

The Panelspotter (Fig. 11-25) does spot welding with two electrodes applied to only one side of a panel or metal sheet. Figure 11-26 shows the principle. The electric current flows into the metal from one electrode, through the metal, and out through the other electrode. The two spots where the electrodes are applied become hot enough for welding to take place.

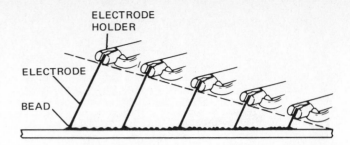

Fig. 11-23 As the electrode melts away while running a bead, you must move the handle steadily downward to maintain the same length of the arc.

Fig. 11-24 An arc spot welder with three receptacles for low, medium, and high heat. (*Marquette Division of Applied Power, Inc.*)

Figure 11-27 shows a patch being applied to a rear deck which has rusted out along the edge of the back window. To make a weld, the surfaces to be welded must be clean. The rusted-out area on the car, shown in Fig. 11-27, was first sandblasted to remove all old rust and expose clean metal. Then the sheet-metal patch was cut to fit, cleaned, and spot-welded to the old metal.

To make a weld, the machine must be plugged in and turned on. Then the two electrodes are pressed against the patch, as shown in Fig. 11-27. Next, the electrode handle is pressed. This turns on the current. It flows from one electrode, through the work, to the other electrode. The heat produced at the two electrodes produces two welds. The amount of time that the current flows is automatically controlled by a setting on the machine. After this time has lapsed (only a few seconds), the machine shuts off the current and the welds are completed.

The Panelspotter is a very handy welder for installing replacement panels. To start with, the parts have to be cleaned so that there is clean metal-to-metal contact between the edge of the sheet metal on the car and the

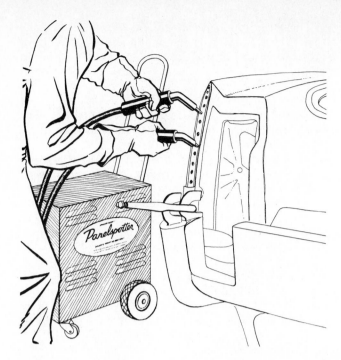

Fig. 11-25 Spot-welding the rear end of a left quarter panel to the underbody. *(Lenco, Inc.)*

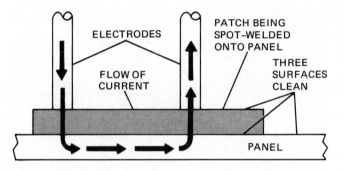

Fig. 11-26 Basic principle of noncompression-resistance spot-welding with a Panelspotter.

edge on the replacement panel. Then the replacement panel should be held in position, either by tacking in several places or by clamps. Next, the machine is used to make as many welds as necessary to secure the replacement panel in place.

Many other uses will be found for the Panelspotter. Figure 11-25 shows it being used to weld the crimped-over rear end of a left quarter panel to the underbody. Figure 11-28 shows how the front end of a right quarter panel was welded to the underbody.

Fig. 11-28 Front end of a right quarter panel after it is spot welded to the underbody. *(Lenco, Inc.)*

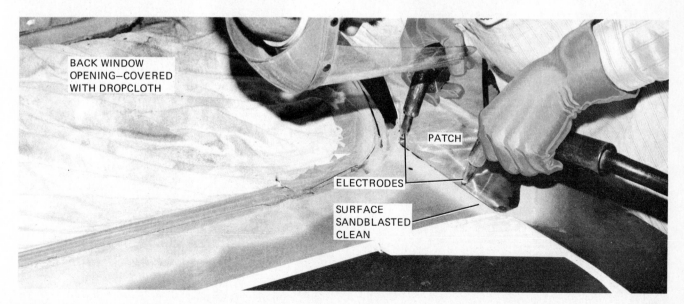

Fig. 11-27 Using the Panelspotter to spot-weld a patch on the rear deck.

≡ 11-21 REASONS FOR MIG WELDING

MIG welding is the recommended method of welding HSS. This is because MIG welding produces an acceptable *heat-effect zone* (Fig. 11-29). This is the width of the metal on each side of the weld that is weakened by the heat from the welding process.

Spot welding produces a smaller heat-effect zone (Fig. 11-30). However, with oxyacetylene spot welding, the heat-effect zones may overlap. This creates a continuous line of weakened steel. Compression resistance spot welding produces a very small heat-effect zone (Fig. 11-30). However, you cannot get to both sides of most repair jobs to use compression spot welding. In addition, good welds can be made only on clean panels without paint or rust.

Noncompression (single-sided) resistance spot welding should not be used on structural panels. The welds may be weak because the two pieces to be joined are not compressed together.

With MIG welding, there is no overlap of the heat-effect zones if the spot welds are placed far enough apart.

There are several reasons for using MIG welding, especially on the thinner gauges of HSS. Welds are made quickly on all types of steel. A low welding current is used, which reduces the heat distortion of thin metals. No extensive training is necessary. MIG-welding equipment takes up little more room than a set of cylinders used in oxyacetylene welding. MIG spot welding is more tolerant of gaps and misfits of the metals being welded. Severe gaps can be spot-welded by making several spots on top of each other. Vertical and overhead welds can be made easily. Metals with different thicknesses can be welded with the same diameter of wire. Almost all steels can be welded with one common type of weld wire.

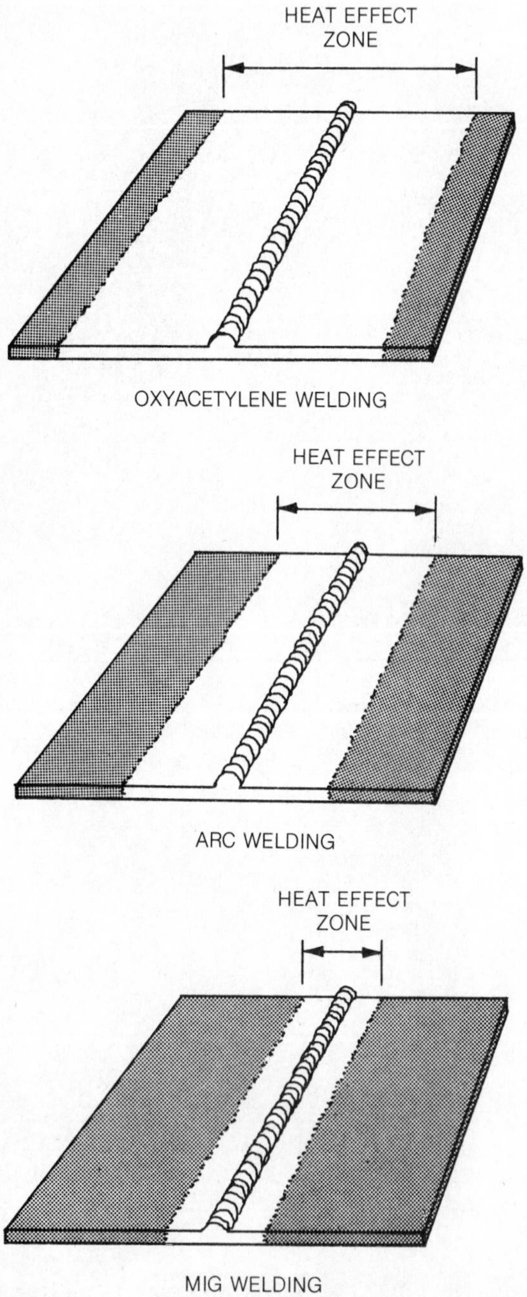

HEAT EFFECT
ZONE

OXYACETYLENE WELDING

HEAT EFFECT
ZONE

ARC WELDING

HEAT EFFECT
ZONE

MIG WELDING

Fig. 11-29 Heat-effect zones with different types of continuous welding. *(Applied Power Inc.)*

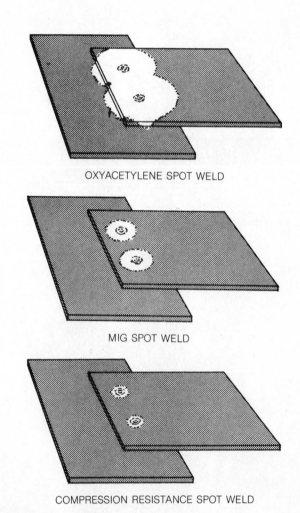

OXYACETYLENE SPOT WELD

MIG SPOT WELD

COMPRESSION RESISTANCE SPOT WELD

Fig. 11-30 Heat-effect zones around various types of spot welds. *(Applied Power Inc.)*

≡ 11-22 THE MIG-WELDING PROCESS

MIG welding is a form of electric-arc welding. Metals are joined together by heat from an electric arc that forms between the electrode and the metal workpiece (Fig. 11-31). However, instead of a coated rod electrode as used in arc welding, a continuous fine-wire electrode is used as the filler metal. The wire is not coated, so a shielding gas such as carbon dioxide (CO_2) or argon (an inert gas) protects the molten metal from contamination by the surrounding air. In addition, the shielding gas helps to stabilize the arc. After the arc is struck, the wire electrode is automatically fed at a predetermined rate into the puddle of molten metal.

A MIG-welding setup includes the following (Fig. 11-32):

1. A MIG-welding machine connected to an electric power supply.

2. A wire-feed control to feed the wire at the required speed.

3. A welding gun that you hold to direct the weld to the weld area.

4. A supply of shielding gas to protect the molten weld pool from contamination.

5. A spool of electrode wire of the proper type and diameter. For automotive work, typical wire diameter is from 0.030 to 0.035 inch [0.8 to 1.0 mm].

When the electrode advances to contact the work, a short circuit occurs. Resistance heating of the end of the wire causes the end to melt down onto the work surface. Then the end of the wire "burns back" toward the torch at a faster rate than the wire is being fed forward.

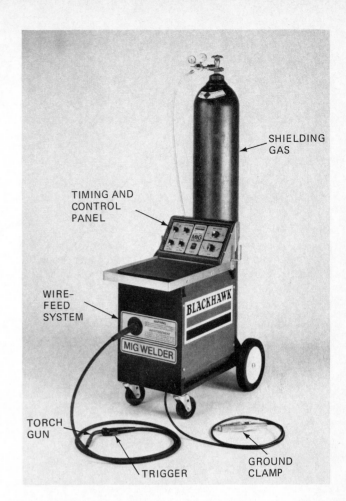

Fig. 11-32 A MIG welder widely used in automotive body shops. *(Applied Power Inc.)*

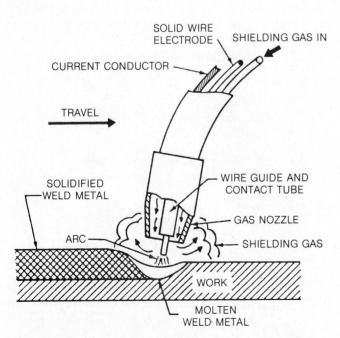

Fig. 11-31 Basic principle of MIG welding. A continuous solid-wire electrode is fed to the gas-shielded arc. *(The Lincoln Electric Company)*

After the end of the wire has melted off, the force of the arc flattens the molten metal against the surface being welded. Then the wire feed overcomes the burnback, and again advances the end of the wire into contact with the work.

This cycle all takes place in a fraction of a second. Generally, this type of MIG welding is limited to metals less than ¼-inch [6-mm] thick, with arc voltage that seldom exceeds 20 volts.

The MIG-welding machine can be used to run a bead, stitch- or step-weld, and to spot- and plug-weld (Fig. 11-33).

The basic principle of MIG welding is the same as when using a rod electrode with an arc welder. There are two differences. A wire is used instead of a rod, and the shielding gas flows from a cylinder instead of being released as the flux on the rod melts. An advantage to the MIG-welding procedure is that the wire is automatically fed to the arc at the correct speed. Usually, the gun rests on the joint. Then the wire-feed control feeds the wire into the arc so that the proper arc is maintained. Basically, all the technician must do is to move the gun along the joint at the proper speed.

Figure 11-33 shows the setup for welding a body panel in place. For welding steel, the shielding-gas cylinder is filled with an inert-gas mixture of argon and

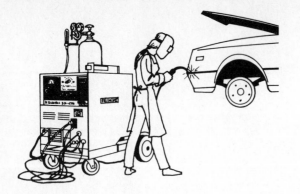

Fig. 11-33 Using a MIG welder to weld a body panel in place. The cylinder is filled with inert gas, such as a mixture of argon and carbon dioxide, which shields the molten metal from atmospheric gases. *(The Lincoln Electric Company)*

carbon dioxide, under pressure. For welding aluminum, 100 percent argon gas is used for best results.

As with other arc-welding processes, a welding helmet, gloves, and protective clothing must be worn. Welding starts when you place the end of the wire on the place where you want to begin. Then you press or pull the trigger on the welding-torch gun. The arc begins, and the wire feeds into the arc with inert gas.

The same basic MIG-welding equipment can be used in the "no-gas-cylinder" mode. The shielding of the arc and molten metal is provided by welding with a self-shielding *flux-cored-wire* electrode. As the wire melts, the flux releases a gaseous shield. This action is similar to welding with a *coated-rod electrode* (≡11-10). However, the large diameter wire that is flux-cored is not normally used for automotive body and collision repair.

REVIEW QUESTIONS

Select the *one* correct, best, or most probable answer to each question. You can find the correct answers in the section indicated at the end of each question.

1. Two types of electric welding are   (≡11-1)
   a. oxygen and acetylene
   b. brazing and soldering
   c. heating and cutting
   d. arc and spot

2. When arc welding, you must always wear   (≡11-2)
   a. a helmet
   b. special gloves
   c. leather to protect the arms, neck, and chest
   d. all of the above

3. Arc-welding electrodes are coated with a flux to   (≡11-10)
   a. prevent air from reaching the molten metal
   b. provide more oxygen for better melting
   c. add nitrogen for stronger welds
   d. allow the use of lower "heats"

4. Striking an arc is done by   (≡11-13)
   a. matches or torch lighter
   b. tapping or scratching
   c. adding flux
   d. breaking away the slag

5. The machine that adds filler material to the spot weld is
   a. an arc spot welder   (≡11-20)
   b. a resistance spot welder
   c. an ac welder
   d. a dc welder

6. Types of arc welding include   (≡11-8)
   a. MIG
   b. rod-electrode
   c. spot
   d. all of the above

7. MIG means   (≡11-1)
   a. metal-inert-gas
   b. major-iron-gauge
   c. metal-internal-gauging
   d. minor-interference-gas

8. Major hazards from arc welding include electric shock, fumes and gases from the welding process, sparks, and
   a. electric-holder breakdown   (≡11-2)
   b. bad cables
   c. ultraviolet rays
   d. high-voltage surges

9. Mechanic A says always disconnect the car battery before welding on the car because the welding voltage could send a high current through the electrical equipment. Mechanic B says the purpose of disconnecting the battery is to protect the electronic equipment on the car. Who is right?   (≡11-5)
   a. mechanic A
   b. mechanic B
   c. both A and B
   d. neither A nor B

10. In rod-electrode arc welding, watch   (≡11-13)
    a. the puddle of molten metal
    b. the ridges that form back of the puddle
    c. the ridges for uniform size and spacing
    d. all of the above

PART 3

CORRECTING SHEET-METAL AND FRAME DAMAGE

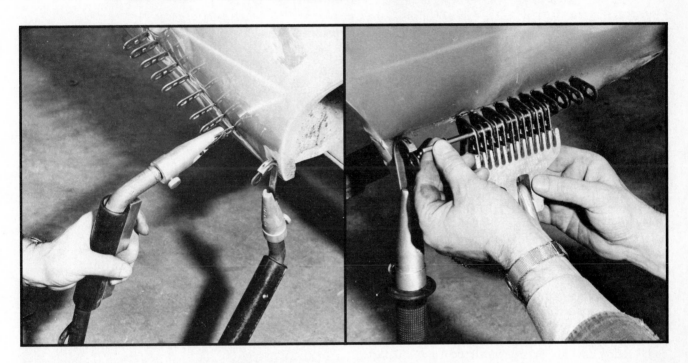

This part discusses sheet-metal and frame damage and describes the tools and their use to correct such damage. The purpose of such work is to restore the frame and body to their original alignment and body contours. Discussions include methods of removing and replacing damaged parts such as trim, bumpers, air-conditioning components, engine radiator, and battery. Often these parts must be removed before work can begin on the damaged sheet metal and frame. Later chapters in this part describe sheet-metal repair and frame straightening. Part 3 consists of five chapters, as follows:

Chapter 12 Basic Operations in Collision Repair
Chapter 13 Methods of Sheet-Metal Repair
Chapter 14 Repairing Sheet Metal
Chapter 15 Fundamentals of Body-and-Frame Straightening
Chapter 16 Using Body-and-Frame Straighteners

CHAPTER 12
BASIC OPERATIONS IN COLLISION REPAIR

After studying this chapter, you should be able to:

1. Describe the sequence of operations in the repair of a damaged vehicle.
2. Explain how to remove molding.
3. Describe the removal of bumpers and the special cautions to observe.
4. Explain how to remove and install the battery and the special cautions to observe.
5. Discuss the automotive air conditioner and the special cautions to observe when working with air-conditioning components.
6. Discuss the cooling-system radiator and the transmission oil cooler and how to handle these when repairing a damaged vehicle.
7. Describe checking of the suspension and headlight aiming after repair work has been completed.

≡ 12-1 PRELIMINARY WORK REQUIRED FOR COLLISION REPAIR

This chapter describes the preliminary work required before actual work begins on sheet metal and the frame. This preliminary work can include removing such parts as moldings, grills, headlight assemblies, bumpers, air-conditioning components, cooling-system radiator, and battery. For example, the car shown in Fig. 12-1 suffered a right-front collision. The right fender was so badly damaged it had to be replaced. There was also damage to the frame. The first thing the body technician did was remove all the front-end parts that were damaged and pile them to one side for later examination. The only part that could be saved was the radiator. It was repaired and reinstalled. The grills, headlight assemblies, front panel, fender marker lights, and trim were so badly damaged they were junked. However, the bumper was sent to a bumper recycler, where it was straightened and rechromed so it could be reused.

≡ 12-2 SEQUENCE OF OPERATIONS

A vehicle that has been in a collision is given a preliminary estimate to determine whether or not it is worth repairing. Generally, if the cost of repair exceeds 75 percent of the value of the vehicle, it is declared a "total." This means that the vehicle is not repaired, but is sold for salvage, usually to a salvage yard. If the preliminary estimate of the cost of repair falls below this percentage and the insurance adjuster agrees, then a detailed estimate is made. This written estimate lists every new part needed and every labor operation required to repair the vehicle.

When the vehicle owner or the insurance company agrees to pay the repair costs on the estimate, the car is ready to become a job in process. Then the parts needed to repair the car are ordered. The car is assigned to a

Fig. 12-1 Car damaged by a right-front collision. It has been set on safety stands, and damaged front-end parts have been removed.

body technician and moved into a stall in the body shop. The body technician then takes the following steps:

1. Analyzes the damage and determines the course of action
2. Removes damaged parts that are in the way of assessing the job and making necessary alignment checks
3. Makes alignment check
4. Straightens sheet metal and frame, as required
5. Checks and corrects the fit of doors, hoods, trunk lids, and other parts
6. Fills damaged areas of sheet metal with plastic body filler

7. Sands off the plastic body filler in preparation for priming and painting

8. Sends the vehicle to the paint shop

If the damage is extensive, there may be additional steps in the procedure. For example, if the windshield or rear glass requires replacement and if door pillars have been repaired, the car may make two trips between the body shop and the paint shop. It will go to the paint shop for painting of door pillars, interior of the trunk, and other interior parts that will show. At the same time, the painter may put on primer coats. Next, the car is returned to the body shop for installation of the glass and other exterior parts. Then it goes back to the painter for final painting.

☰ 12-3 REMOVING MOLDING

Molding is installed by various methods. Some is put on with adhesive. Other molding is attached to the body panels with screws, nuts, or plastic studs. Figure 12-2 shows typical attachment methods. The molding is removed by special tools that can be inserted under the molding to snap it free. Care must be used in doing this to avoid damaging the paint if the body panel is in good condition and does not need any work.

☰ 12-4 REMOVING BUMPERS

Bumpers have energy-absorbing components. These were described in Chap. 2. The energy absorbers (or *isolators*) are often hydraulic shock absorbers very similar to those used in suspension systems. Figure 12-3 shows how the hydraulic units are fitted to the

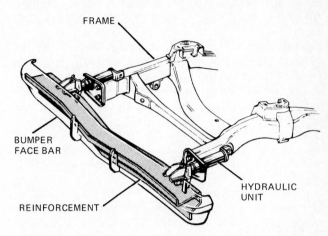

Fig. 12-3 Energy-absorber installation in back of the front bumper. *(Chrysler Corporation)*

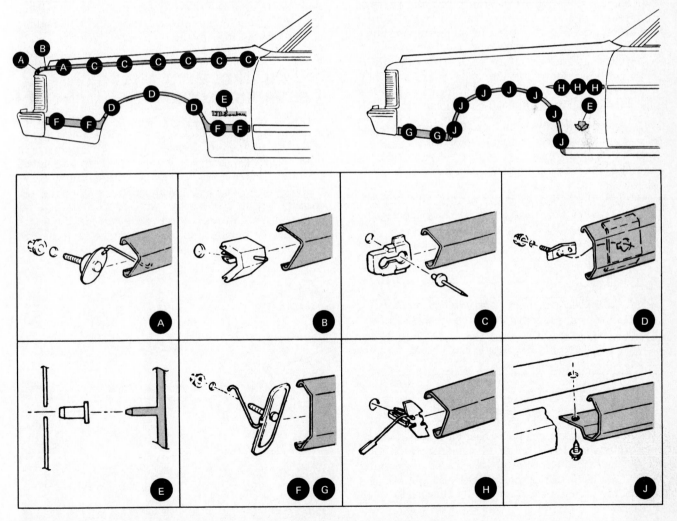

Fig. 12-2 Methods of attaching front exterior side molding. *(Ford Motor Company)*

front bumpers. Their purpose is to permit the bumpers to withstand collisions at low speeds without damage to the bumper or car.

The energy absorbers shorten in length during the impact. Then they will resume their original length after the collision. At high speeds, the energy absorbers will probably be damaged and require replacement. In any event, you must use care in removing and handling these absorbers, regardless of whether they appear to be in good condition or not. If they are to be junked, the gas-filled type must have a hole drilled in it (as explained later) so the gas pressure will be released. This renders the absorber harmless. Unless this is done, someone could be severely injured if a compressed absorber suddenly extended or if it were heated and exploded.

The gas-filled energy absorber is shown in one car in Fig. 12-3. An energy-absorbing bumper, using a spring instead of gas to provide the return force, is shown in Fig. 2-39.

When starting work on a car that has had a front or rear collision, use care when removing the bumper and energy absorbers. You should not disconnect the bumper from one absorber and then let the bumper swing down to the floor. This twists the piston in the other absorber and damages the seal. Instead, support the bumper until you detach it from the other absorber.

Often you will remove the bumper and absorbers as an assembly, detaching the absorbers at their inner ends from the frame. Do not let the bumper swing down so the piston in the other absorber will be twisted.

Here is the caution that the vehicle manufacturers give regarding removal of a damaged energy absorber:

"When an energy absorber is bound up as a result of a collision, observe the following cautions:

1. Stand clear of the bumper. The absorber might release and snap the absorber out suddenly.

2. Use a chain or cable to apply positive restraint to the energy absorber so it will not suddenly pop out to its original length.

3. Drill a small hole in the piston tube near the bumper bracket (Fig. 12-4) to relieve the gas pressure, as explained in ≡ 12-7. Wear goggles!

4. After the gas has escaped, remove the absorber from the vehicle."

--- CAUTION ----------------------------------

Many energy absorbers contain gas at high pressure. Never attempt to repair, weld, or apply any heat to the unit. Applying heat to the unit could cause it to explode like a bomb.

≡ 12-5 CHECKING ENERGY ABSORBERS ON THE CAR

First, examine the energy absorber for leakage around the seal between the cylinder tube and the piston tube. A stain or trace of oil on the piston tube near the seal is normal. But if oil is dripping from the seal or stud end of the unit, the energy absorber should be replaced.

Examine the bumper bracket, piston tube, frame bracket, and cylinder tube for evidence of visible distor-

Fig. 12-4 Drilling a hole in the piston tube to relieve the gas pressure before discarding a defective energy absorber. *(Chevrolet Motor Division of General Motors Corporation)*

tion. Scuffing of the piston tube, if the unit has been stroked, is considered normal. If there is obvious damage, the unit and associated damaged parts should be replaced.

≡ 12-6 CHECKING ENERGY-ABSORBER ACTION

The energy-absorber action can be checked with the unit on the car, as shown in Fig. 12-5. Each energy absorber should be checked separately. The test is made with the engine not running, the transmission in PARK, the parking brake set, and a brake-applying tool holding the service (foot) brakes. Any suitable barrier can be used, such as a pillar, wall, or post. Then install a device that can apply force. For example, put a jack between the barrier and one side of the bumper (Fig. 12-5). Protect the bumper with rags. Apply force to see

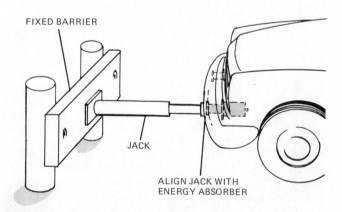

FIXED BARRIER

JACK

ALIGN JACK WITH ENERGY ABSORBER

Fig. 12-5 Testing an energy absorber. *(General Motors Corporation)*

if the energy absorber will move inward ⅜ inch [9.5 mm] or more. Then release the force. The bumper should return to its original position. Be sure to apply the force squarely to the bumper so the jack does not slip off.

A bench check can also be made of the energy absorber in a shop press. The unit should compress at least ⅜ inch [9.5 mm] and then return to its normal length when the force is released. If the unit does not, discard it.

≡ 12-7 SCRAPPING AN ENERGY ABSORBER

If an energy absorber is to be scrapped, the internal gas pressure must be released. Put the energy absorber in a vise. Drill a small hole in the piston tube, as shown in Fig. 12-4. Use the caution label as a locator for drilling. Drill either in front of or through the label.

≡ 12-8 REMOVING BATTERY

If the accident to the vehicle has pushed metal in enough to press against the battery, you will need to remove the battery. Even if the metal has not been pushed in that much, you may still want to remove the battery so you can work on the metal. The first thing you must do is examine the battery to see whether its case has been damaged. If the case has been damaged, the battery liquid (called the *electrolyte*) may have leaked out. This liquid, which contains sulfuric acid, is highly corrosive. It will eat holes in your clothes, give you severe burns if it gets on your skin, and can injure your eyes if it gets into them.

If the battery case has been damaged and the electrolyte has leaked out, the battery must be junked. Battery cases cannot be repaired. Proceed as follows to remove the battery, regardless of whether or not the case has been damaged:

1. First disconnect the grounded battery-terminal cable from the battery-terminal post. This guards against accidental shorting across the battery when the insulated battery-terminal cable is being disconnected. If the grounded terminal is not disconnected first and the battery is still charged, there can be sparks if the wrench accidentally touches metal. The wrench would be shorting directly across the battery.

2. There are various types of battery connectors. Some have a cable clamp that is attached to a terminal

on top of the battery (Fig. 12-6). If the clamp is of the nut-and-bolt type, loosen it with battery pliers. If you use an open-end wrench or ordinary pliers, you may break the battery top. As you turn the wrench or pliers, the jaw could swing around and hit the top, breaking it. Use a battery-terminal puller, as shown in Fig. 12-7, to pull the clamp off if it sticks. Do not try to pry the clamp off, as this can damage the battery.

3. The spring-ring type of battery connector (Fig. 12-8) is loosened with pliers, as shown.

4. The side-terminal battery connector (Fig. 12-9) requires a wrench to disconnect the screws.

5. Some batteries have stainless-steel screw-type terminals. These take nuts which require wrenches to loosen them.

Fig. 12-6 Using battery pliers to loosen the nut-and-bolt type of battery-cable clamp.

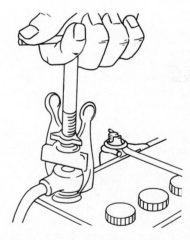

Fig. 12-7 Using a battery-clamp puller to pull the cable from the battery terminal.

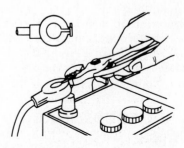

Fig. 12-8 Using pliers to loosen the spring-ring type of cable clamp from a battery post.

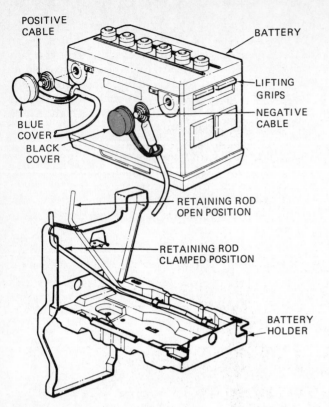

Fig. 12-9 Cable connection and battery mounting arrangement. *(Cadillac Motor Car Division of General Motors Corporation)*

Fig. 12-10 If solvent or other chemical splashes in your eye, immediately wash your eye with water.

— **CAUTION** —————————————

If the battery case has been cracked or broken, electrolyte probably has leaked out. When removing the battery, try to avoid getting electrolyte on you. Attach a battery carrier or carrier straps to the battery and lift it from the vehicle. Set the battery outside in a safe place where leakage of electrolyte will not harm anything. If you get electrolyte on you, wash it off at once with plenty of water. If you get electrolyte in your eyes, wash them out with plenty of water (Fig. 12-10). Then see a doctor immediately.

Electrolyte will eat the paint on the car and also eat away vinyl and upholstery. You can neutralize the electrolyte with a baking soda solution. Mix baking soda and warm water and put it on the spilled electrolyte. After the foaming stops, flush the area with water.

When reinstalling the battery, connect the insulated battery-terminal cable first. Then connect the grounded battery-terminal cable. The condition of the battery should be checked, and the battery should be charged, if necessary. Also, the charging system on the car should be tested before the car is returned to the owner.

☰ 12-9 AIR-CONDITIONER CONDENSER

The condenser for the air conditioner is up front, in front of the engine radiator (Fig. 12-11). Therefore, it is

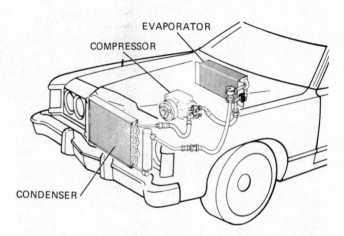

Fig. 12-11 Basic components of the automotive air conditioner. *(Ford Motor Company)*

frequently damaged during a front-end collision. The purpose of the condenser is to dispose of the heat that the air conditioner takes out of the passenger compartment. The air conditioner does its job by circulating a refrigerant called Freon between an evaporator in the passenger compartment and the condenser.

The evaporator absorbs heat from the passenger compartment as Freon evaporates inside it. The vapor then passes through the compressor, where the vapor is compressed to a high pressure. This increases the temperature of the compressed vapor. When the vapor passes through the condenser, the vapor gives up this heat and condenses back into a liquid again. The liquid flows back into the evaporator where it evaporates. This is a brief description of the refrigeration cycle. It continues as long as the compressor is operating.

The thing you have to watch out for when working around an air-conditioning system is that the refrigerant is under high pressure in the system. This means that, if the system has not been punctured, there is gas inside at high pressure. You must be careful. Escaping refrigerant can be very dangerous.

To start work on a car with air conditioning which has been in a front-end crash, take a good look at the condenser. Has it been pushed back? Are there signs that it has been punctured? If it has been punctured, the refrigerant has already leaked out. However, even if the condenser appears to be in good condition, a connecting tube may have been damaged or twisted so leakage has occurred.

If the front end has been pushed in, you may have to take the condenser off so you can work on the metal, regardless of whether or not the air-conditioning system is okay. If the condenser appears to be in good condition, you will have to release the refrigerant from the system. Attach a gauge set and discharge the system as shown in Fig. 12-12. Some technicians discharge the refrigerant by barely cracking the attaching nut on one of the lines connected to the condenser. However, observe the following safety cautions for air conditioners.

— CAUTION

1. Put on your safety glasses or goggles when discharging refrigerant. The refrigerant is under pressure, and when it comes out, it will instantly freeze anything it touches. If it hits your hand, it can freeze the flesh. If it hits your eyes, it can freeze them so you could lose your sight!

2. Do not release the refrigerant in an enclosed space. As the refrigerant evaporates, it displaces the air around it. If you release the refrigerant in a completely closed and unventilated space, for example, it could push the air out and you could suffocate. Follow the procedure of discharging the refrigerant into the shop exhaust outlet, as shown in Fig. 12-12.

SYSTEM CAN BE OPENED WHEN PRESSURE DROPS TO 5 PSI [34.5 kPa]. (LEAVE GAUGES INSTALLED.)

SHUT OFF AT REFRIGERANT TANK OR VACUUM PUMP

OPEN BOTH VALVES SLIGHTLY FOR SLOW DISCHARGE

WATCH FOR COMPRESSOR OIL. REDUCE DISCHARGE RATE IF OIL APPEARS

CENTER HOSE TO EXHAUST OUTLET

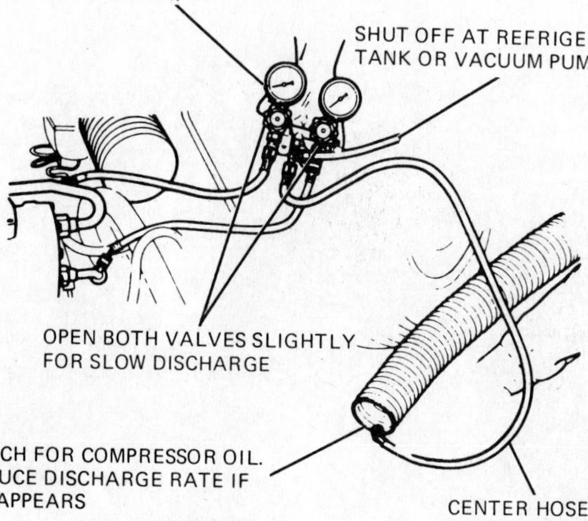

Fig. 12-12 *Using a gauge set to discharge the refrigerant.* *(Ford Motor Company)*

3. Never release the refrigerant around an open flame. When the refrigerant hits a flame, it turns into a deadly gas.

4. Heat in any form must never be applied to any refrigerant line or any component of the air-conditioning system. The refrigerant is under pressure. Heating the refrigerant could increase the pressure enough to cause an explosion. Therefore, never steam-clean any air-conditioner component or line. When welding, remove these components and move refrigerant lines out of the way.

A special refrigerant oil that lubricates the compressor circulates with the refrigerant. If the refrigerant escapes slowly, little oil will be lost (Fig. 12-12). However, if the refrigerant escapes rapidly, it will carry most of the oil out with it. This oil must be restored to the system when it is repaired or the compressor will fail from lack of lubrication.

≡ **12-10 INSTALLING CONDENSER AND RECHARGING SYSTEM**

Installing a condenser, or any other component of the air-conditioning system, is a job for the trained technician. You must connect the condenser and attach it to the car. When a new condenser is installed, a specified amount of fresh, clean refrigerant oil must be added to it. After the condenser is installed, a gauge set, a vacuum pump, and a container of refrigerant must be connected to the system. Then the system must be purged and recharged. *Automotive Air Conditioning,* another book in the McGraw-Hill *Automotive Technology Series,* covers the servicing of air conditioners in detail.

≡ **12-11 COOLING-SYSTEM RADIATOR**

Check the coolant level in the radiator. If it is still full, then the radiator has not been damaged, even though it may have been pushed back. What often happens is that the radiator is shoved back into the engine fan and the fan cuts into the radiator before the engine stalls. Then the radiator may be so badly damaged that it must be replaced. However, if the damage is slight, the radiator can be repaired and used again.

You may have to remove the radiator to straighten the front-end metal, even though the radiator is not damaged. In such case, you must decide whether or not to save the coolant. Generally, if the coolant has been in the system for a year or longer, it probably should be replaced anyway. Drain out the coolant and discard it. You can then disconnect the hose clamps and remove the attaching nuts or screws holding the radiator to the car.

≡ **12-12 TRANSMISSION OIL COOLER**

On some cars, the radiator has a built-in oil cooler that cools the automatic-transmission oil (Fig. 12-13). The automatic transmission is connected by oil-cooler lines to the oil cooler in the outlet tank of the radiator. When

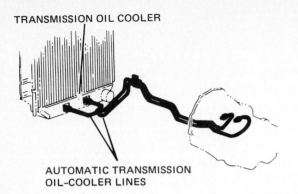

Fig. 12-13 Automatic-transmission oil cooler and lines. *(Ford Motor Company)*

the engine is running, transmission oil flows through the tubes to the radiator, where the oil is cooled. It then flows back to the transmission. If the radiator is damaged so that oil has been lost, or if the radiator has to be removed, oil must be added to the transmission. This is done after the radiator has been reinstalled and reconnected. *Automotive Automatic Transmissions* another book in the McGraw-Hill *Automotive Technology Series*, covers the procedure in detail.

≡ 12-13 INSTALLING RADIATOR AND FILLING COOLING SYSTEM

If the vehicle has high mileage, it may be desirable to flush out the engine water jackets while the radiator is off. (However, this is not a job routinely performed by the auto body technician.) This is done with the thermostat removed, as shown in Fig. 12-14. Sending water through the water jackets in the reverse direction helps to remove scale.

After the radiator is reinstalled and the hoses are reconnected (including the transmission oil lines if used), the cooling system should be filled. Add the proper amount of antifreeze to get adequate protection against freezing at the lowest temperature expected in your area. Then add water. This mixture is called the *coolant*. The cooling-system thermostat will be closed when water and antifreeze are added. This may prevent complete filling of the cooling system. The thermostat has a small hole in it that permits the air to leak out. But this takes some time. You may have to wait and refill

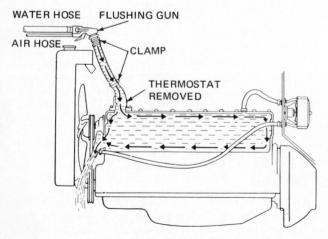

Fig. 12-14 Reverse-flushing the engine water jackets.

the radiator a couple of times. The engine can be started and run for a few minutes until the thermostat heats up and opens. Then the system can be completely filled.

Install the radiator cap. Run the engine for a few minutes to check for leaks. The complete servicing procedure for engine cooling systems is covered in detail in *Automotive Fuel, Lubricating, and Cooling Systems,* another book in the McGraw-Hill *Automotive Technology Series*.

≡ 12-14 SUSPENSION SYSTEM

If a front end has suffered a relatively severe impact, the damage might extend back into the front suspension. For example, the vehicle shown in Fig. 12-15 received a severe impact on its left front. The body technician has removed all parts that might get in the way of checking alignment. Note that extensive straightening has already been done. The underfender, for example, has been straightened. The left door panel has been straightened and plastic body filler has been added to it.

While checking the suspension on the left front, the technician found that the lower arm had been bent back. Therefore, a new lower arm was installed. You can see the label on the new arm in Fig. 12-15. It may be that the upper arm was also bent, but it showed no evidence of this. However, after the car has gone through the body and paint shop, it will be taken to the alignment rack. There, front alignment will be checked. These checks may show that the upper arm is also bent and it will also be changed.

Front-suspension service is covered in detail in *Automotive Brakes, Suspension, and Steering,* another book in the McGraw-Hill *Automotive Technology Series*.

≡ 12-15 HEADLIGHT AIMING

After any front-end collision, regardless of whether the headlight assemblies are replaced, the aiming of the headlights must be checked. Aiming is checked with a special aiming device and adjusted by turning screws (Fig. 12-16). Each headlight has two screws, one for vertical adjustment and one for horizontal adjustment.

Fig. 12-15 Car damaged by a severe left-front collision. The car is on safety stands, and the fender and other parts have been removed.

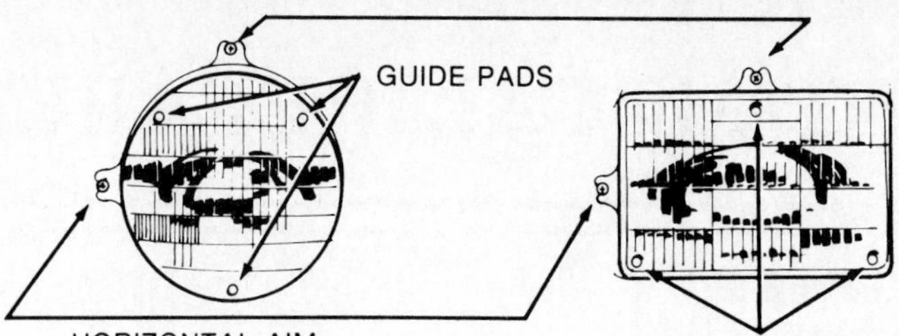

VERTICAL AIM ADJUSTING SCREWS

GUIDE PADS

HORIZONTAL AIM
ADJUSTING SCREWS

ROUND HEADLIGHT

GUIDE PADS

RECTANGULAR HEADLIGHT

Fig. 12-16 Adjusting screw locations for round and rectangular headlights.

REVIEW QUESTIONS

Select the *one* correct, best, or most probable answer to each question. You can find the answers in the section indicated at the end of each question.

1. A car is usually considered totaled if the cost of repair exceeds (≡12-2)
   a. $500
   b. 75 percent of the value of the vehicle
   c. 50 percent of the value of the vehicle
   d. 30 percent of the value of the vehicle

2. You should never attempt to repair, weld, or apply heat to (≡12-4)
   a. a fender
   b. a door
   c. an energy absorber
   d. a molding

3. To check an energy-absorber action, (≡12-6)
   a. drive slowly into a wall
   b. use a jack to apply force
   c. heat it to see if it acts normally
   d. remove it from the vehicle and put it in a vise

4. After a front-end collision, always check the battery for (≡12-8)
   a. overcharging
   b. a cracked case
   c. shorts
   d. overheating

5. A safety precaution to take if the battery case is cracked is to (≡12-8)
   a. avoid getting electrolyte on you
   b. recharge it safely
   c. send it out for case repair
   d. keep it connected so it will not discharge

6. The part of the air-conditioning system that is most likely to be damaged in a front-end collision is the
   a. compressor (≡12-9)
   b. evaporator
   c. condenser
   d. drive belt

7. A safety precaution when you are discharging refrigerant from the air-conditioning system is (≡12-9)
   a. wear safety glasses or goggles to protect your eyes
   b. do not allow the discharging refrigerant to touch your flesh
   c. never discharge refrigerant around an open flame
   d. all of the above

8. If the cooling-system radiator is still full after a front-end collision, then probably (≡12-11)
   a. it needs a change of coolant
   b. the radiator is all right
   c. the engine is still running
   d. none of the above

9. If the cooling system has lost liquid, after repair is completed, (≡12-13)
   a. add water
   b. add antifreeze
   c. add both water and antifreeze
   d. send the radiator out for repair

10. After the front-collision damage has been repaired,
    a. front alignment should be checked (≡12-14)
    b. control arms should be replaced
    c. wheels should be replaced
    d. the frame should be checked for tracking

CHAPTER 13

METHODS OF SHEET-METAL REPAIR

After studying this chapter, you should be able to:

1. Describe the procedures for straightening sheet metal and explain the meaning of *work-hardening.*

2. Discuss the effect of plain and sculptured panels on repair methods.

3. Explain how to classify damage and how to determine how the damage occurred.

4. Discuss direct and indirect damage and explain how they are related.

≡ 13-1 REPAIRING SHEET METAL

There are various methods of sheet-metal repair. Which repair method or methods are used on a particular job depends on several things:

1. Quality of job required

2. Repair equipment in the shop

3. Type of damage

4. Type of vehicle construction — body-and-frame or unitized body

5. Type of sheet metal — low-carbon, soft steel or high-strength, low-alloy (HSLA) steel

For small dents or ridges, you would select one repair method. If the damage is extensive, you would select another repair method, or perhaps three or four procedures. Also, the value of the car must be considered. If the car is relatively new and expensive, the owner might insist on the most expensive methods of repair. If it is an older car being reconditioned for resale, you would probably use less expensive repair methods.

≡ 13-2 WORKING SHEET METAL

When sheet metal arrives at the stamping plant, the sheet metal is uniform in thickness and softness (or *ductility*). But when it goes through a press and is shaped into a body part — a fender, for example — its hardness is changed in some places. Whenever sheet metal is bent, it becomes harder. This is called *work-hardening,* which was described in Chap. 2 (Fig. 2-19). The area where the metal has been bent considerably (the high-crown area) has become harder than the area which has been bent very little (the low-crown area).

Pounding on sheet metal with a hammer will also work-harden the metal. Heating the metal, as with a gas torch, will relieve the hardness, regardless of whether the hardness resulted from bending or hammering. This is one method used in straightening sheet metal. First, the damage is dinged out with a body hammer and dolly. Then the area is heated to soften and also shrink the metal so it is restored to approximately its original contour.

When a body panel is bent in a collision, the part that is bent is work-hardened. It has bent beyond its elastic limit. The *elastic limit* is the limit to which the

metal can be bent and not be deformed. The bottom of an oil can, for example, can be bent (pushed in). Then it will return to its original contour when the force is relieved. The metal has not been bent to its elastic limit. If it had been, it would not return to its original shape.

Often, when a body panel has been damaged by an impact, part of the sheet metal will be bent beyond its elastic limit. But other areas, even though pushed out of shape, may not. They have simply "oil-canned." When you straighten the area that has been bent beyond its elastic limit, this other part often will spring back to its original contour. If you should start your work on the "oil-can" area, you could *add damage to* instead of *remove damage from* the panel.

NOTE: Heating body panels made of high-strength, low-alloy (HSS/HSLA) steel is described in ≡9-31.

≡ 13-3 METHODS OF SHEET-METAL REPAIR

There are at least 12 methods of repairing damaged sheet metal. On some jobs you will use only one method. Other types of damage might require you to use two or more of the basic methods. Which method and how many you use depend upon the damage that is to be corrected. New tools and straightening methods are being developed all the time. However, if you learn the basics, you will be able to use any new tool and procedure that is developed.

Although it is desirable to restore the sheet metal as nearly as possible to its original contour, this is a practical impossibility for many jobs. Your aim should be to restore the sheet metal to *near* its original shape and then fill it with plastic body filler or body solder. The filler is then finished to the final contour, and the panel is painted.

Here are the 12 repair methods. Each one is described in detail later in the chapter.

1. Pulling out an oil-can dent with vacuum cups. This procedure can often be used on a panel which has been pushed in but has suffered little or no bending beyond its elastic limit.

2. Pulling out a crease or dent with pull rods or a slide hammer. This method might be used on a panel

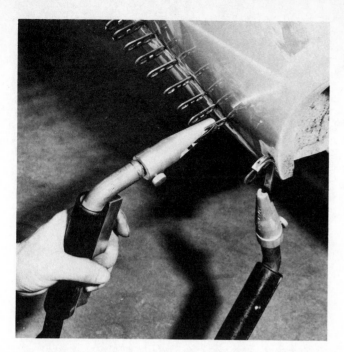

Fig. 13-1 Pull tabs being welded to a crease in a panel. *(Guy-Chart Tools Limited)*

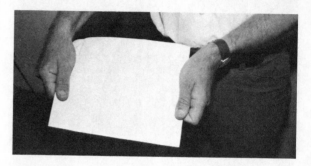

Fig. 13-3 A sheet of paper which has been wrinkled (A) can be partly straightened out by pulling on the two ends (B).

which cannot be easily worked on from the inside. Such metal has been bent beyond its elastic limit and must be pulled out working from the outside only.

3. Using pull tabs. When pull rods or a slide hammer are used to pull out a crease or dent, there are two ways of doing the job. One is to drill holes into the panel so the pull rods or slide hammer can have someplace to hook onto. The other is to weld a series of pull tabs to the panel. The *pull tab* is a small steel tab (Fig. 13-1) one end of which is welded to the body panel at the point where it needs to be pulled out. As many of the tabs as necessary can be welded to the panel (Fig. 13-2). With

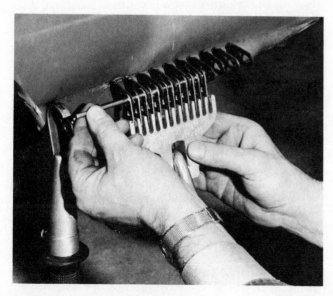

Fig. 13-2 After the pull tabs are welded to the crease, a rod is threaded through the holes in the tabs so a puller can be attached to them. *(Guy-Chart Tools Limited)*

pull tabs, no holes need be drilled or inner panels cut to get to the back side of the body panel. The procedure of using pull tabs is described later.

4. Pulling out a panel from two sides to straighten the sheet metal. This is like straightening a sheet of paper which has wrinkles in it by pulling on two edges, as shown in Fig. 13-3. The pull can be done by attaching appropriate clamps or solder pads to the sheet metal and then exerting the pull with a power ram. Figure 13-4 shows a body clamp and methods of attachment of the clamp to sheet metal. The holes drilled in the sheet metal to attach the clamps are filled later. Some body clamps do not require drilled holes but can be clamped onto the edge of the metal (Fig. 13-5).

5. Using a pry bar to get behind a dent and push it out.

6. Using a spread ram.

7. Using a hammer and dolly where both sides of a damaged panel are accessible.

8. Using a hammer, dolly, and body file where both sides of a damaged panel are acccessible. This method, called the *pick-and-file* procedure, prepares the metal for painting. No filling is necessary.

9. Using a bumping spoon.

10. Heat-shrinking a panel which has been stretched by the impact and by the work of straightening the panel.

NOTE: Care must be exercised when heating HSLA panels in order to avoid overheating. Excessive heating destroys the strength of the metal and the integrity of the car body. Do not heat-shrink HSLA body panels.

11. Filling low areas with plastic body filler. All the above procedures, with the exception of the pick-and-file procedure, require bringing the sheet metal out to

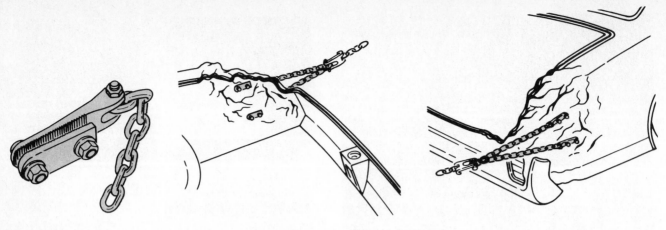

Fig. 13-4 The clamp shown requires that holes be drilled in the panel so the clamp can be firmly attached. Then the pull can be made. *(Guy-Chart Tools Limited)*

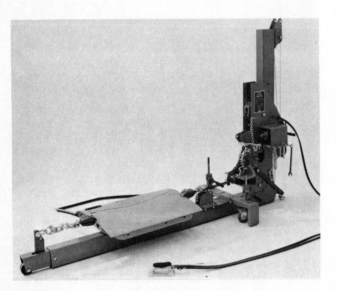

Fig. 13-5 Pulling out a door with body clamps and hydraulic equipment. *(Guy-Chart Tools Limited)*

approximately its correct contour. Then the irregularities are filled with plastic body filler, as described in a following chapter.

12. When a panel is severely damaged, the repair probably would be to install a new or salvaged panel in its place. Whether to repair or replace is a matter of materials and labor cost. With severe damage, the labor cost required to make a correction would approach or exceed the cost of buying a new or salvaged panel and

Fig. 13-6 A fender with smooth curves is relatively easy to repair.

installing it in place of the old panel. Then replacement probably would be the preferred repair procedure.

≡ 13-4 EFFECT OF PLAIN AND SCULPTURED PANELS ON REPAIR METHOD

Many earlier cars had fenders and other body panels that were fairly simple in design. They had relatively smooth curves, going from flat surfaces to curved surfaces gradually (Fig. 13-6). When a fender of this type was damaged, it was comparatively easy to work out the damage to approximately the original contour. However, late-model cars have *sculptured* body panels. These are body panels with reverse curves leading to ridges or to raised accents or ridges around the wheel openings (Fig. 13-7). Not only does this sculpturing effect add style to the car, but also the curved panels are stronger than flat panels. Because of this and because automotive manufacturers must make cars lighter, thinner sheet metal can be used for many body panels. Another factor permitting the use of thinner sheet metal for body joints is that the sheet metal used today, although lighter, also is stronger and tougher (HSLA).

The combination of curves with thinner and tougher metal makes it more difficult for the body technician to straighten damaged panels. As a result, it has become more common in recent years to replace damaged parts rather than attempt to repair them.

≡ 13-5 CLASSIFYING DAMAGE

Damage to a panel can be analyzed in terms of collision-caused bends, tears, or holes which have occurred to the panel. Tears or holes have to be patched or filled. Bends can be of several types, requiring several types of repair. Let us analyze just what a simple bend is, and then look at the more complex bends that actually occur.

Take a strip of sheet metal and bend it over the edge of the workbench, as shown in Fig. 13-8. Figure 13-9 shows what happens. The top area has been stretched. The bottom area has been pushed together or shrunk. Both areas have been work-hardened.

Fig. 13-7 Sculptured fenders with reverse curves and sharp ridges or bends are relatively difficult to repair after damage.

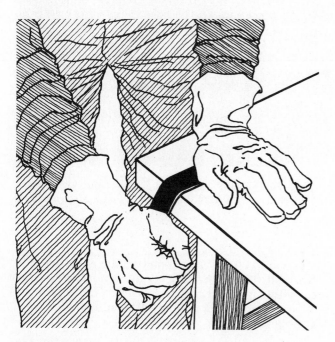

Fig. 13-8 Bending a strip of sheet metal work-hardens it at the bend.

In common shop talk, the metal has buckled, and the area which has bent is called a *buckle*. Figure 13-9 is a simple buckle which you will not find in car body damage. The reason is that there are no perfectly flat sheet-metal panels on the car. When curved panels buckle, the buckles are more complicated.

For example, look at the curved panel on a car door (Fig. 13-10). If you tried to bend this panel along its vertical centerline, as shown in Fig. 13-11, you would get a much more complex bend. The upper and lower

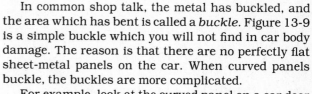

Fig. 13-10 Door panel typically has a curve from top to bottom. *(Ford Motor Company)*

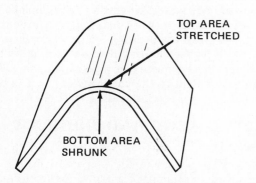

Fig. 13-9 The changes to a strip of sheet metal that is bent.

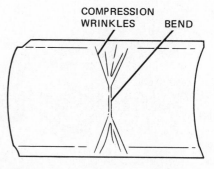

Fig. 13-11 What happens when a curved panel, such as a door panel, is bent at the middle in a vertical direction.

edges would wrinkle, because the metal, under compression, has to go someplace.

Another example is shown in Fig. 13-12. It shows a box section similar to those used in car frames. If this box section is bent, the top part will be stretched and the bottom will be compressed and wrinkled (Fig. 13-13). This type of damage is called a *collapsed box* and is more typical of what occurs in collision accidents. The reason is that many of the body sheet-metal parts are in the form of partial boxes. Look at a fender, for example (Fig. 13-14). If you simplified it, as shown in Fig. 13-15A, you would have half a box section. Now if you bent it, as shown in Fig. 13-15B, you would have compression wrinkles radiating from the top to the lower edge. This is a partially collapsed box.

With an actual fender, you may have a still more complex situation (Fig. 13-16) because of the curves, or crowns, in the metal. The metal along the side collapses, as before, but it sends creases up into the crown. These creases are known as *rolled buckles*.

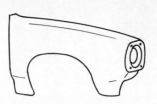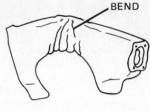

A. FENDER SIMPLIFIED   B. FENDER BENT FROM FRONT HIT

Fig. 13-15 (A) The fender is basically a semibox section. (B) When the fender is hit from the front, the top bends. Then the side wrinkles as the metal collapses.

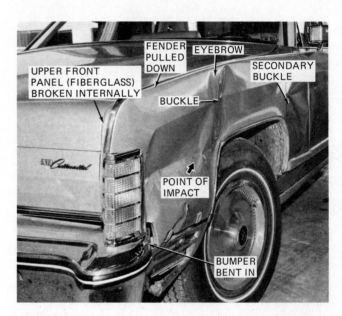

Fig. 13-16 Effects of a near frontal impact on a left fender. The "eyebrow" is the curved ridge that marks the upper end of the buckle.

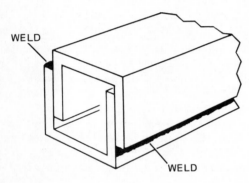

WELD

WELD

Fig. 13-12 Box section made by welding together two U-shaped members.

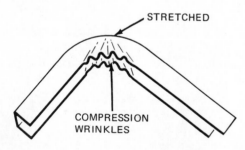

STRETCHED

COMPRESSION WRINKLES

Fig. 13-13 What happens when a box section is bent.

Fig. 13-14 The fender of a car is a modified form of a half-box section. (*Ford Motor Company*)

They tend to end at some point in the crown with a sharp dent. The ridge above is called an *eyebrow*. The metal all along the creases has been shrunk. When correction is made, the metal must be straightened and also expanded.

☰ 13-6 VISUALIZING HOW DAMAGE OCCURRED

If you were able to watch, in slow motion, just what happens to body panels when they are damaged, you would know exactly how the metal came to be bent and the order in which the bending occurred. For example, suppose you hit the side of a door panel a heavy blow (Fig. 13-17). The sequence of illustrations shows the resulting deep dent in the panel and, as this is being made, a series of creases radiating out from it.

☰ 13-7 DIRECT AND INDIRECT DAMAGE

Direct damage occurs at the place where an object strikes or pushes against the panel. Indirect damage

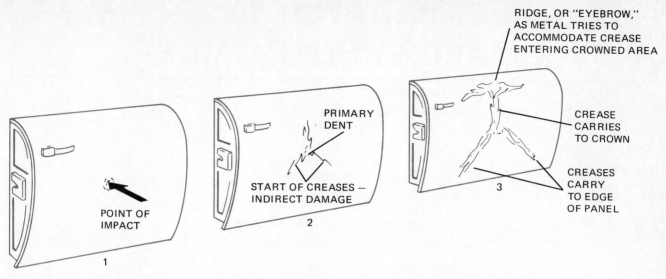

Fig. 13-17 *Sequence of events following an impact on a door panel.*

RIDGE, OR "EYEBROW," AS METAL TRIES TO ACCOMMODATE CREASE ENTERING CROWNED AREA

CREASE CARRIES TO CROWN

CREASES CARRY TO EDGE OF PANEL

PRIMARY DENT

START OF CREASES — INDIRECT DAMAGE

POINT OF IMPACT

occurs at other places on the panel, owing to the direct damage. Figure 13-17 shows direct and indirect damage. The direct damage occurs at the spot where the panel is struck. Then radiating out from this spot is the indirect damage.

It is important to recognize direct and indirect damage. Normally, you start work on the indirect damage first, working back to the direct damage. Going the other way, from the direct to the indirect damage, would probably make the situation worse. Many times, the technician will work out the indirect damage and then fill the direct-damage spot with plastic body filler. Using filler eliminates a lot of expensive, time-consuming labor, because direct damage is sometimes difficult to completely work out.

━━━ REVIEW QUESTIONS ━━━

Select the *one* correct, best, or most probable answer to each question. You can find the answers in the section indicated at the end of each question.

1. On sheet metal, the area that is bent gets (≡13-2)
   a. softer
   b. harder
   c. rusty
   d. shorter

2. An oil-can dent can be pulled out with (≡13-3)
   a. a hammer and dolly
   b. vacuum cups
   c. a ram
   d. a bumping spoon

3. Compared with flat panels, sculptured panels are (≡13-4)
   a. weaker
   b. thicker
   c. stronger
   d. cheaper

4. A fender is similar to a (≡13-5)
   a. box
   b. round bar
   c. half box
   d. square frame

5. Indirect damage is the result of (≡13-7)
   a. the direct damage
   b. the tow truck
   c. hitting a stationary object
   d. hitting a moving object

CHAPTER 14

REPAIRING SHEET METAL

After studying this chapter, you should be able to:

1. Explain how to use vacuum cups.
2. Describe the use of pull rods and slide hammers.
3. Discuss the use of the hydraulic ram to pull out dents.
4. Explain how to use pull to straighten a panel.
5. Discuss the use of a pry bar in space-limited areas.
6. Describe a spread ram and how to use it.
7. Discuss the two basic techniques of using a hammer and dolly.
8. Explain how to use the body file on metal and on plastic.
9. Discuss the use of the bumping spoon.
10. Explain the use of heat shrinking and its limitations.
11. Discuss patching or installing a panel.

≡ 14-1 INTRODUCTION TO SHEET-METAL REPAIR

The previous chapter listed 12 methods of repairing sheet-metal panels. This chapter describes in detail how each of these methods is used. Don't think that each repair method is a separate entity all by itself. Usually, two or three or more of the methods are used to repair a single panel. For example, you might use a spread ram to push out a fender. Then you would use one of the pull methods to pull out a buckle. During this procedure you might use the hammer to relieve the stresses in the metal. Finally, you would sand and fill the damaged area with plastic body filler.

≡ 14-2 PULLING ON SHEET METAL

There are several different methods of pulling on sheet-metal panels. The purpose is to pull out buckles and creases to restore, as nearly as possible, the original contour of the panel. In the past, with the low-carbon, soft sheet steel, it was relatively easy to pull out panels that were not too badly damaged. However, with the newer HSLA panels, it is more difficult to pull out damages. The pull must be distributed over a larger area. And the pulling force must be applied more gradually so the metal does not tear.

Also, the problem is more complex with the unibody because the panels form a structural part of the vehicle. In any impact that damages a panel, the entire body may be pushed out of line. Pulls and pushes may be required to straighten body panels and to reestablish proper alignment of the body itself. This is covered in the next chapter.

— CAUTION —

Heat should not be used to straighten a panel made of HSS/HSLA steel, except as described in ≡9-31. If the panel is bent, straighten it. If the panel is torn or kinked, replace it.

In following sections describing various straightening methods, it is stated that the panel being straightened should be tapped with a hammer. This relieves stress and prevents pullback. *Pullback* is what happens when a panel is pulled out and released without hammering. The panel can move back toward its damaged position. Often, the technician will lay a block of wood (such as a 2 by 4) on the panel and hammer on it. This prevents local work-hardening of the metal. The theory is that the shock of hammering jars the molecules of the metal so they are "shaken" out of their stressed positions. The problem here is knowing just where to hammer. Usually it is in or around the area of maximum damage.

≡ 14-3 USING VACUUM CUPS

Vacuum cups can be used to correct oil-can damage to sheet metal. If the paint has not been damaged and if the metal has not been bent beyond its elastic limit, the depression often may be pulled out without damaging the paint. Under ideal conditions, this would be a repair job that would take only a few minutes. However, if there is paint damage and direct damage to the metal (metal bent beyond elastic limit), then the pull-out is only the first step in the repair job.

To use a vacuum cup, first make sure that the body panel is clean. All dirt should be washed off so the paint will not be scratched when the vacuum cup is used. Wet the cup and press it in against the panel, at the center of the depression (Fig. 14-1). When the air has been squeezed out of the cup, it will grip the metal. Pull out steadily to bring the metal out to its original contour. Sometimes the use of a slide hammer, as shown in Fig. 14-1 is necessary to apply adequate force. This procedure will work if the metal has not been buckled or bent beyond its elastic limit. It will not work on crowned surfaces, because the cup will not be able to grip the curved surface. Also, if there is a depression on a crown, the metal probably has been stressed beyond its elastic limit. When this has occurred, another repair method will be required.

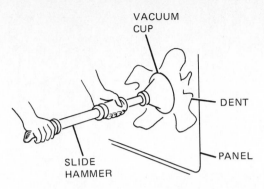

Fig. 14-1 Using a vacuum cup to pull out a dent in a panel. *(Guy-Chart Tools Limited)*

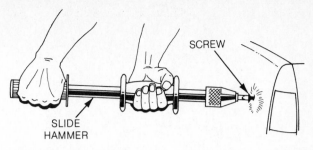

Fig. 14-3 Using a slide hammer to pull out a crease, or buckle, in a body panel. *(ATW)*

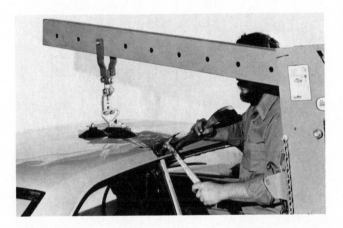

Fig. 14-2 Using vacuum cups to pull up on a dent in a car roof. At the same time, the technician is using a body spoon and hammer to tap down the ridge at the edge of the roof. *(Guy-Chart Tools Limited)*

For working on large areas, such as a damaged roof, vacuum-cup assemblies with three cups are available (see Fig. 5-22). They are attached to a plate which has a handle that can be pulled out by hand or by a crane. Figure 14-2 shows a roof panel being repaired by this method. The technician is using a body spoon and hammer to work out a ridge while the pull is being made.

≡ 14-4 USING PULL RODS AND SLIDE HAMMERS

If the dent has sharp edges or is too deep or irregular, the vacuum cup will not work. If it is also difficult to get behind the panel, then the pull has to be made from the outside. This requires pull rods or a slide hammer.

There are two ways of attaching the pull rods or slide hammer to a panel. These are to drill into the panel or to weld pull tabs onto the panel. If holes are drilled, they must be filled later. If pull tabs are used, they must be twisted off later.

A slide hammer is used with holes drilled or punched in the panel. Screw a sheet-metal screw into a hole near one end of the crease. When it takes hold, hook on and operate the slide hammer (Fig. 14-3). This will create enough force to pull the crease out. To operate the slide hammer, hold the hammer handle in one hand and slam the slide against the stop. Be careful not

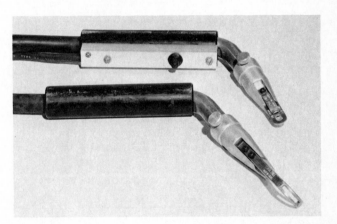

Fig. 14-4 Special attachments for electrodes when pull tabs are to be welded onto a panel. *(Guy-Chart Tools Limited)*

to use excessive force because the screw might pull out. Go from one hole to the next until you have pulled the dent out. Use a body hammer to tap around the outside of the damage while the pull is being exerted. This helps to release the tension that was introduced by the impact. As this tension is released, the dent can be raised more easily.

Pull tabs (Figs. 13-1 and 13-2) are used with a spot welder (Chap. 11). The welding electrodes are fitted with special attachments to take the pull tabs (Fig. 14-4). One of these is for the ground tip. It has a slot so it can be hooked over the first pull tab to be welded onto the panel. The other holds the pull tabs, which are then welded onto the panel. Here is the procedure:

Install the spot-tip pull-tab holders over the spot-welder electrodes. Adjust welder to a low setting (1 in Fig. 14-5). Grind a small area of about a square inch (or a few square centimeters) to a clean metal (2 in Fig. 14-5). This ensures good contact for the first pull tab to be welded on. Put a pull tab in the clip on the welding electrode. Hold the ground tip and pull tab close together on the bare area, and pull the trigger to weld the first pull tab to the panel (3 and 4 in Fig. 14-5). Now hook the ground tip onto the first pull tab, as shown at 5 in Fig. 14-5. Be sure the back side of the ground tip makes good contact with the panel. Now weld additional pull tabs to the panel (Fig. 13-1). The edges of the pull tabs are sharpened and will cut through paint with little force. Therefore, the whole area does not need to be sanded to use pull tabs.

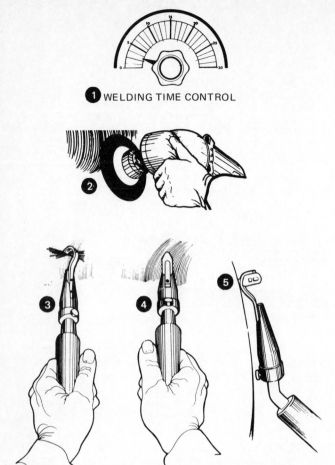

① WELDING TIME CONTROL

Fig. 14-5 Sequence of actions to weld pull tabs onto a panel. Each step is explained in the text. *(Guy-Chart Tools Limited)*

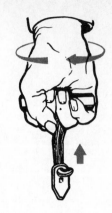

Fig. 14-7 Twisting off a tab. *(Guy-Chart Tools Limited)*

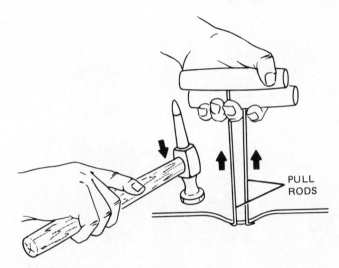

PULL RODS

Fig. 14-8 When pulling on a panel, a body hammer is often used to tap on the high spots near the dent being pulled out.

After the necessary number of pull tabs have been welded on, a pull-plate assembly is attached by interlocking the pull tabs with the tabs on the pull plate, as shown in Fig. 13-2. Then the slide hammer is attached so the pull can be made, as shown in Fig. 14-6. The number of pull tabs to be used varies with the size and type of damage to the panel. During the pull, tap with a body hammer on the high spots around the crease to

relieve the set of the metal and help it settle down to contour. After the pull is completed, the pull tabs can be twisted off, as shown in Fig. 14-7. Only a small mark will be left, which can then be touched up and refinished (if the panel has been brought back to contour).

NOTE: *Any pull equipment in the shop including the hydraulic body-frame straighteners (Chap. 16), can be hooked onto the pull tabs. When the pull tabs are welded in a series, as described above, you can pull up to 4000 pounds [17,792 newtons (N)].*

Slide hammers have a variety of pulling attachments, as shown in Fig. 5-19. They take care of pulling on edges of fenders, door posts, and other parts.

Pull rods can be used instead of a slide hammer, although not as much force can be exerted with pull rods. Figure 14-8 shows pull rods being used to pull out a small dent. The procedure is similar to that for the slide hammer. You weld pull tabs or make holes into which the hooked end of the pull rod can be inserted. Then you pull out to raise the dented metal. A hammer can be used to tap around the damaged area and release the tension that has locked the dent into the metal (Fig. 14-8). Sometimes, with larger dents or creases, more than one pull rod can be used in adjacent holes. With three or more pull rods hooked to the metal, the pull can be exerted over a larger area.

Fig. 14-6 Using a slide hammer to pull on the pull tabs. *(Guy-Chart Tools Limited)*

The holes left after using a slide hammer or pull rods are later filled with plastic body filler. Some body technicians do not like to drill holes and use pull rods or slide hammers. Sometimes these tools can raise ridges around the holes (Fig. 5-21), which then require additional work to correct.

≡ 14-5 USING HYDRAULIC RAM TO PULL OUT DENT

If the dent is too big to be pulled out with a slide hammer or pull rods, a hydraulic ram can be used. To pull out the large dented area shown in Fig. 14-9, the body technician drilled holes and used special adapters. Three of the adapters are shown in Fig. 14-10. The two thin ones

Fig. 14-9 Left quarter panel damaged by an impact from the side.

Fig. 14-10 Pull tools made by the technician.

Fig. 14-11 Using hydraulic equipment to pull out the damage.

are for placement behind sharp creases. The flat adapter is for pulling out a large dent, such as shown in Fig. 14-9.

The adapter is used by unscrewing the plate from the hook, inserting the threaded rod through a hole in the sheet metal, and then screwing the hook onto the rod from the back of the panel. The technician was able to get behind the panel by removing the rear seat and trim. This permitted the technician to attach the plate to the threaded rod.

NOTE: *The body technician could have used a series of pull tabs welded to the panel, as described in ≡14-3, instead of drilled holes and special adapters to pull out the dent. Then the technician would not have needed to remove the rear seat and interior trim to get behind the panel.*

Figure 14-11 shows the hookup for making the pull. The chain was attached to the hook at one end and to the hydraulic pull mechanism at the other. (This mechanism is described in Chap. 16.) The technician actuated the hydraulic pump, and the dent was pulled out. Actually, the procedure was a little more complicated than this. The technician used a hammer at certain points on the panel to relieve stress. Also, an additional hole was drilled to pull out from a different point. In addition, the technician worked from behind the panel with a hammer and pry bar. Figure 14-12 shows the panel restored approximately to its correct contour. Note the two pull holes have been welded closed. The panel can now be filled, sanded, and filed in readiness for painting.

≡ 14-6 USING PULL TO STRAIGHTEN A PANEL

If a panel has been crushed or shortened by an impact, it can often be straightened by a combination of pulling and working with a hammer and dolly or other tools. This is similar to straighteening a crumpled sheet of

Fig. 14-12 Panel restored to its approximate contour in readiness for sanding, filling, and painting.

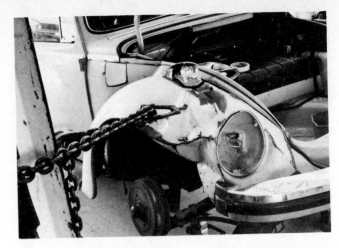

Fig. 14-14 Pulling out a right fender of a Volkswagen.

Fig. 14-15 Using a body hammer to tap on high spots while a pry bar inserted in the hole for the quarter-panel side-marker light works on low spots from the inside.

paper by pulling on two edges (Fig. 13-3). For example, the right quarter panel shown in Fig. 14-13 has been shortened by a rear-end impact. If the pull is exerted in a line vertical to the wrinkles and in line with the shortening, most of the damage can be pulled out. A force is exerted in a direction exactly opposite to the impact force that caused the damage.

Pull may be applied to the panel by using a power jack (or ram) with clamps, or with solder plates. Solder plates are seldom used today because they are messy, slow, and cause heat distortion of body panels. Where clamps can be used, it is the preferred method because it is much quicker and less messy. The clamps are at-

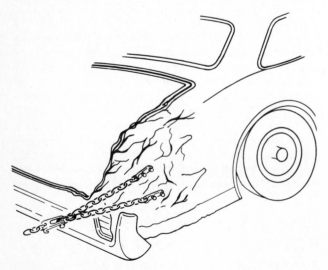

Fig. 14-13 Right quarter panel shortened by a rear-end impact. A pull in the reverse direction will pull out much of the damage. (Guy-Chart Tools Limited)

tached by welding on pull tabs (Fig. 14-5) or by boring holes in the sheet metal so the clamps can be attached. Tightening the nuts tightens the hold of the clamps on the metal. The clamps are large enough to spread the pull so there is less chance of tearing the metal. Figure 13-4 shows a typical clamp. Some clamps do not require bored holes to take hold (Fig. 13-5).

Sometimes the pull has to be made in a direction about vertical to the sheet metal so clamps cannot be used. Then a hole can be drilled in the panel so that a special adapter can be fitted to transfer the pull to the panel. Figure 14-14 shows the setup for pulling out a right fender of a Volkswagen which has been crumpled by a front-end impact. The adapter being used is homemade and is one of the thin adapters shown in Fig. 14-10. It is in back of the fender, resting squarely against the crease in the metal.

While the pull is being exerted on a panel by the power ram, a body hammer is used to tap against high spots (Fig. 14-15). If a dolly, pry bar, or pick bar can be worked behind the panel, it can work on high spots on the underside (which would be low spots on the outside). Sometimes the torch is also used to relieve work-hardening in the damaged area. The heat also makes the metal more plastic so the area can be worked down to contour easily.

NOTE: *The power ram does not do all the work. It merely puts the panel in tension. It cannot pull out all the damage. The damage must be worked out with hammer, dolly, pick or pry bar, and torch. As the damage is worked out, the panel will elongate. Therefore, the hydraulic ram must be adjusted to maintain adequate tension on the panel as the damage is worked out.*

Care must be used when pulling against sheet metal with the hydraulic ram. Excessive pull can tear the sheet metal and present you with a very difficult repair job.

≡ 14-7 PULLING WITH SOLDER PLATES

Solder plates are seldom used today. However, on certain jobs, some technicians may prefer to use them. The solder plates are soldered onto the body panel at the proper spots so the pull can be exerted in the right direction.

To use solder plates, first sand off the paint from the two spots. Then the plates are soldered to those spots. The procedure of preparing a body panel for the application of body solder is described in Chap. 10. The area is cleaned and tinned, and then solder is applied, using the oxyacetylene torch to supply the heat. At the same time, the face of the solder plate is tinned. With hot solder on both and the temperature right, the plate is pressed to the panel and quenched with water. After a few seconds, the solder cools to form a solid joint. With two solder plates soldered to the panel in this manner, the power ram has something to work on. The ram, when installed between the plates and activated, subjects the panel to a pull which is the reverse of the force that damaged the panel.

While the pull is being exerted, the area to be straightened should be worked on with a body hammer and dolly or with other tools. At the same time it should be heated with the torch, as previously explained.

After a panel is straightened, the solder plates are removed by heating them with the torch. Then the panel is heated enough to melt the solder, and the solder is wiped off. That part of the panel is then ready for final finishing after you have wiped it with lacquer thinner to remove any trace of acid. Don't get lacquer thinner on the paint!

NOTE: *The heat injected into the sheet metal by the soldering and unsoldering operation can distort the metal and change the contour. When this happens, additional work will be required to correct the problem. This is another reason most body technicians don't use solder plates.*

≡ 14-8 USING A PRY BAR

Damage in some places is hard to reach from the inside, for example, a dent in a door panel. Various means of working out this type of damage by using a vacuum cup, pull rods, or a slide hammer have been described. Pull

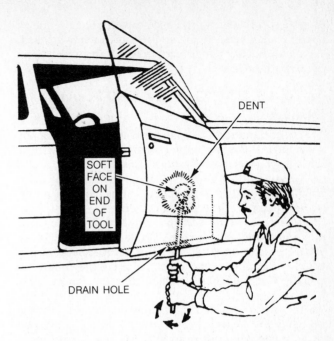

Fig. 14-16 *A pry bar inserted through the drain hole in the bottom of the door is used to push out low spots.*

rods or a slide hammer leave holes that must be filled. An alternative is to use a pry bar inserted into drain holes (or holes drilled) in the bottom edge of the door, as shown in Fig. 14-16. It is often possible to put the end of the bar on the spots that have to be pushed out. Then the pry bar is used to pry the spots out to approximately restore the original contour.

≡ 14-9 USING A SPREAD RAM

The spread ram (Fig. 14-17) is like a pair of pliers in reverse. The two jaws are placed between a damaged panel and the underbody. The ram is then activated and the two jaws are spread. This exerts a straightening force on the damaged panel. Note that the jaws of the ram are covered with ridged rubber so they will not slip.

For example, the spread ram can be used to apply force to a fender that has been crushed inward. The spread ram forces the damaged area outward approximately to its original contour. After this operation, a

Fig. 14-17 *A spread ram. When the ram is operated, the jaws open.*

hammer and dolly can be used to work out the major irregularities still left. Before the spread ram is used, there may not be enough room to get a hand with a dolly up behind the fender.

≡ 14-10 USING A HAMMER AND DOLLY

The right hammer and dolly must be used to ding out sheet metal. On low-crown surfaces, a dolly with a fairly flat face is used. On high-crown surfaces, a dolly with a curved face is used. The curvature of the dolly should be slightly greater than the final contour of the surface being worked on (Fig. 14-18).

Figure 14-19 shows the proper way to hold the hammer and dolly. Note that the dolly is held rather loosely with the palm exerting the force on it. The hammer should be gripped fairly loosely, close to the end of the handle. The dolly is held on one side of the metal, and the hammer strikes the other side (Fig. 14-20). There are two basic techniques: hammer-on-dolly and hammer-off-dolly. Learn both techniques. Practice both on scrap sheet metal until you have mastered them.

≡ 14-11 HAMMER-ON-DOLLY

This is the simpler of the two techniques. The hammer blows fall on the metal under which the dolly is held, as shown in Fig. 14-21. The metal, in effect, is squeezed between the hammer and dolly. This lowers the raised metal. The action also spreads the metal. This action is resisted by the metal surrounding the point where the hammer blows fall. The result is a slight bubble raised in the metal, as shown in Fig. 14-22A. There is no way that further hammering will flatten this bubble. In fact, additional hammering will spread the metal still more and increase the size of the bubble. There are two ways of dealing with this problem. One is to tap the bubble and drive it below the surface of the original contour (Fig. 14-22B) and then to fill the depression with plastic body filler.

The second way of reducing the bubble, used on the earlier low-carbon, soft-steel panels, was to heat the bubble with a gas torch and then cool it. The process is called *heat shrinking* and it is not recommended for HSLA panels. Heat shrinking can weaken high-strength steel and reduce the integrity of the unibody structure.

Both methods of taking care of a problem such as shown in Fig. 14-22 are described later. Also, ≡14-17 discusses repair methods.

Here are some hints on how to hammer-on-dolly that will help you learn the technique. First, hold the dolly out in front of you so you can see it. Then tap the dolly face lightly with the hammer (Fig. 14-19). This helps you learn how to guide the hammer so it will strike the center of the dolly face. Once you move the dolly behind a panel, you cannot see it. Therefore, you must sense exactly where it is so you can strike the metal that is directly above the dolly. You must have a good feel for exactly where your hidden hand and the dolly are. Hold the dolly out in front of you again and, with your eyes closed, tap the center of the dolly face with the hammer. Practice this until you can tap the center of the dolly face every time.

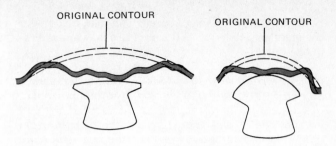

Fig. 14-18 Curvatures of dollies for working on areas with low crowns and high crowns. Curves should fit the final contours.

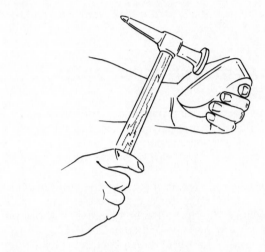

Fig. 14-19 Proper way to hold dolly and hammer.

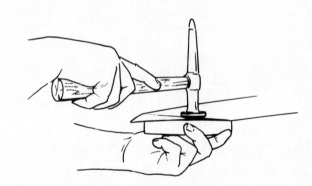

Fig. 14-20 The dolly is held on one side of the sheet metal, and the hammer strikes the other side.

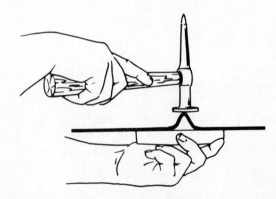

Fig. 14-21 How to work down a raised dent in sheet metal. Hold the dolly under the center of the dent and tap it with the hammer.

Fig. 14-22 (A) Driving down the dent expands the metal and leaves a bubble of raised metal. (B) The metal has been driven down below the surface so it can be sanded and filled in preparation for painting.

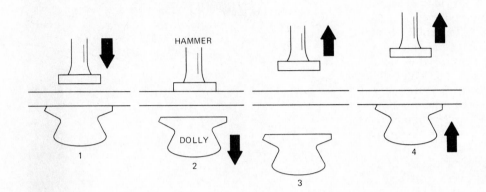

Fig. 14-23 Sequence of actions when hammering-on-dolly.

Hold the hammer lightly. Swing the hammer from the elbow, with only enough force to strike the metal lightly. Hard blows will spread the metal and work-harden it too much.

Now let's work on a dent, such as is shown in Fig. 14-21. Make a dent in a discarded body panel by hitting it with a pick hammer. Hold the dolly firmly against the lower side of the panel. Swing the hammer, allowing the flat face of the hammer to fall squarely on the metal (Fig. 14-21). If you cock the hammer, the edge of the face will make small dents in the metal and these will be hard to work out. When the hammer strikes the metal, the force of the blow goes through the metal and into the dolly. This momentarily drives the dolly away from the metal (Fig. 14-23). At almost the same instant, the springiness of the metal causes the hammer to bounce up from the metal surface. Then the hand force on the dolly pushes it upward so it strikes a blow on the underside of the metal.

Note the sequence in Fig. 14-23 carefully. The metal is struck twice, once from above with the hammer, and once from below with the dolly. The effect of these two blows is determined by the amount of force back of them. For example, when working a large depressed area, the dolly is held with heavy force against the metal. Now, after the dolly is driven down by the hammer blow, it snaps back up against the metal with that heavy force. This action is effective in raising the metal as the blows are repeated over the surface of the metal.

≡ 14-12 HAMMER-OFF-DOLLY

Another way to pound out dents is to use the hammer-off-dolly technique. Figure 14-24 shows the procedure on a large dent that has been made in a low-crown area. The metal has been pushed down at the point of impact. The metal above and below has been raised as a result of the impact. The metal on the two sides of the impact has not been moved to any extent. Figure 14-25 is a top

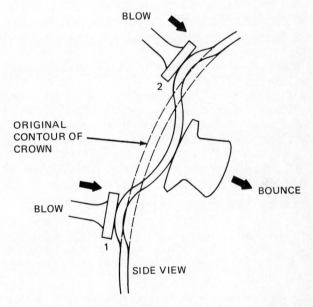

Fig. 14-24 Side view of a panel which has been pushed in, showing the hammering-off-dolly technique to bring the metal back to contour.

Fig. 14-25 Top view of the panel shown in Fig. 14-24. The metal has not been distorted on two sides of the dent. The distortion of metal has taken place above and below the dent owing to the crown in the metal.

view of a section through the dent. The contour of the metal allows the metal to expand horizontally from the effect of the blow. But the crown resists the expansion and causes the ridges ("eyebrows") that appear above

139

and below the point of impact. Bending the metal produces work-hardening. The crown shown in Fig. 14-25 was made by bending the metal in a vertical direction. Therefore, it is harder above and below the dent. This is why the metal resists expansion from the impact.

Now, to work the dent up and the ridges down, hold the dolly in the center of the dent. Then hammer on the two ridges above and below the dent, as shown at 1 and 2 in Fig. 14-24.

The action is different from the hammer-on-dolly procedure. When the hammer strikes a ridge, it drives the ridge down. The spot is not supported by the dolly. The movement of the metal carries the force of the blow to the dolly, causing it to bounce off the metal. Even before this happens, the springiness of the metal bounces the hammer back off the metal. The hand force on the dolly carries the dolly back up to the metal, striking a blow in the center of the dent. The sequence is as follows: (1) hammer strikes ridge, (2) hammer rebounds, (3) dolly rebounds, (4) dolly strikes center of dent.

Once the metal has been worked back close to its original contour, hammer-on-dolly work can begin. When the hammer-and-dolly work is finished, the metal will have expanded as a result of this work and also will have been work-hardened. With the older low-carbon, soft-steel panels, the expansion can be taken care of by heat shrinking and filling with plastic body filler. However, HSLA panels should not be heat-shrunk (≡14-20). This weakens the panel and reduces the strength of the body.

The metal on the two sides of the dent is not touched with the hammer and dolly. This metal has been pushed below its original level. Working on this metal would expand it further and act against bringing the dented metal out toward its original contour.

Here are two general rules for using the hammer-off-dolly process:

1. Start the hammer blows on the raised metal that is farthest from the dent. Work inward from this point, alternating from one side to the other.

2. Never strike metal that is below the original level, only that which has been raised above the original level.

≡ 14-13 USING THE BODY FILE

The body file (Fig. 5-35) has a series of curved teeth. When the file is pushed across a body panel, the teeth remove thin shavings of metal. The body file is normally not used if the body technician is planning to fill a panel after straightening the metal. However, if the technician is going to bring the metal itself out to its original contour and then, with no further work, prime and paint it, the body file is an essential tool. The procedure of using the file in this manner is called the *pick-and-file* method.

Sometimes the body file is also used on plastic filler after it has hardened or set up. For example, some body panels, such as a hood or trunk lid, are fairly flexible. Suppose damage to such a panel has been repaired and filled with plastic body filler. Next, the filler has set and requires sanding, as explained in a following chapter. If

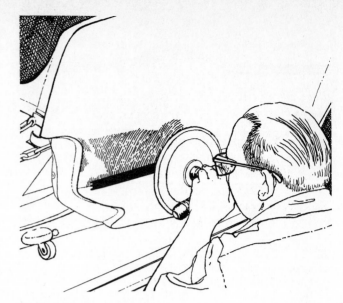

Fig. 14-26 Sanding the panel with a disk sander to remove the paint.

an oscillating air or electric sander is used, the weight might cause the panel to flex while the sanding is going on. This would prevent a smooth and level panel finish. In such case, the body technician may use the body file to bring the body filler to contour. Then the job is finished by hand-sanding the body filler (Chap. 17).

≡ 14-14 USING BODY FILE ON METAL

At one time, fenders and other body panels were of heavier metal and were simpler in contour. In addition, they were often more accessible from the inside than they are today. Therefore, it was easier to work from both sides of the panel, using hammers, dollies, and picks, to restore the metal to approximately its original contour. At the same time, the body file was used to check the panel being worked on for low spots. The combination of tools brought the metal back to its original shape, ready for finishing and painting.

The body file is still used to some extent today for this same purpose. Let's assume that the right quarter panel on a car is damaged by a rear-end impact that put a crease or buckle in the panel. Working from the inside, the technician has succeeded in pushing and bumping the crease out.

Once the metal is about where it should be, sanding and filing begin. Figure 14-26 shows the start of the sanding operation with an air-powered disk sander. The sanding operation is described in detail in Chap. 17. After the sander has removed most of the paint and has exposed bare metal, the file is used. Figure 14-27 shows the technician stroking the file across the bare metal. Notice that the technician is looking at a sharp angle at the surface. Any place the file does not remove metal is low and should be worked up. Figure 14-28 shows a spot at the top of the panel where no paint has been removed. This is the top of the crease. Figure 14-29 shows the technician, working from inside the panel, using a pick hammer to work the low spot out.

Fig. 14-27 Stroking the body file across the freshly sanded area.

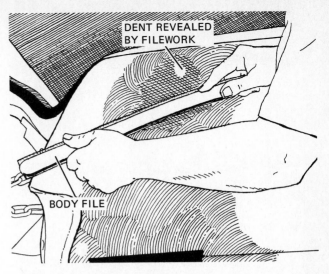

Fig. 14-28 The body file has revealed a low spot in the metal.

The file is used in an "X," or crossing, pattern, as shown in Fig. 14-30. Therefore the file crosses the metal surface in two or more directions. This reveals the low spots. If the file were used in only one direction, low spots might not be revealed.

NOTE: The body file is generally used today on un-filled body panels only when the body technician is bringing the metal out to its original contour and no filling with plastic body filler is planned.

≡ 14-15 USING BODY FILE ON PLASTIC

The weight of the air or electric sander on some body panels can cause the panel to flex. This prevents a smooth and level finish. Therefore, on such surfaces, the plastic filler is smoothed off with a body file. The force on the file can be controlled accurately so that the body panel is not flexed as the file is moved across its surface.

≡ 14-16 FILING OR FILLING

Sometimes new body panels arrive slightly damaged in transit. The replacement part has a dent or crease in it, put there by careless handling during shipping. The body technician can fill this with plastic body filler or straighten it with hammers, dollies, picks, and body file. Since the new body panel is off the car, it is relatively easy to work on it from both sides. Therefore, the preferred repair method is to use the body file.

≡ 14-17 REPAIRING LARGER DAMAGED AREAS

A dolly and hammer can remove simple dents in body panels. However, at the end of the procedure, you will still be left with an area that must be filled with plastic body filler.

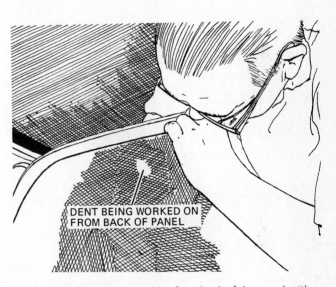

Fig. 14-29 Technician working from back of the panel with a pick hammer to raise the low spot.

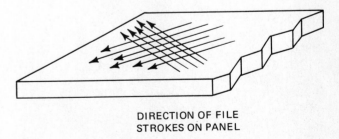

DIRECTION OF FILE STROKES ON PANEL

Fig. 14-30 Directions of file strokes on a panel.

If the area is larger and includes several dents, ripples, or creases, there may be considerable stretching of the metal as a result of the damage. You add to this stretch as you work the area down (or up) to near its original contour. As a result, you could end up with a

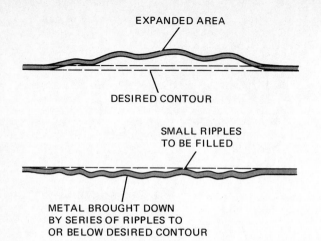

EXPANDED AREA

DESIRED CONTOUR

SMALL RIPPLES
TO BE FILLED

METAL BROUGHT DOWN
BY SERIES OF RIPPLES TO
OR BELOW DESIRED CONTOUR

Fig. 14-31 How to bring the expanded area down to and below contour by producing a series of small ripples to be filled.

Fig. 14-32 Body technician filling a left quarter panel.

Fig. 14-33 Technician sanding the filled area down to contour.

large bulge or depression. This can be removed, at least partly, by heat shrinking, as described later.

Another and more practical way, used by some body technicians, is to put a series of small ripples into the expanded area. These, in effect, absorb the expansion. Figure 14-31 shows the procedure. The small depressions that form the ripples are not too deep and can be filled satisfactorily. Figure 14-32 shows a body technician using plastic body filler to fill a left quarter panel which has been treated this way. Figure 14-33 shows the technician sanding the hardened plastic in preparation for painting. Using plastic body filler is covered in a following chapter.

NOTE: Another method of shrinking sheet metal, used by some body technicians, is to work the expanded area with a shrinking hammer (Fig. 14-34). This is described in ≡14-20.

≡ 14-18 BUMPING SPOON

The bumping spoon (Fig. 14-35) is held between the damaged metal and the hammer. The hammer blows fall on the bumping spoon. This distributes the force of the blows over a larger area than does the use of the hammer alone. The bumping spoon is effective in working down long ridges or buckles that are not too large. These ridges could be reduced with a hammer, but it would take longer. Also there is always the chance that you would leave hammer marks, which would then require additional work.

Bumping spoons are made with flat faces or with faces of various contours.

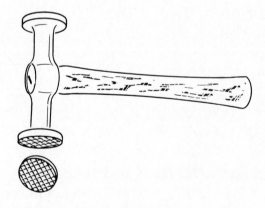

Fig. 14-34 A shrinking hammer.

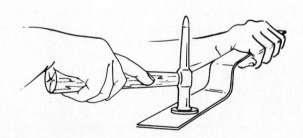

Fig. 14-35 Using a bumping spoon.

≡ 14-19 PICKING SMALL DENTS

Small dents can be picked up with a pick hammer, as shown in Fig. 5-17. You must be careful when using the pick end of the pick hammer. The pointed end can easily punch holes in the metal or push dents in it. Make sure the point hits the center of the dent and strike only light blows.

Figures 14-28 and 14-29 show a practical application of the procedure discussed above. In Fig. 14-28, the body technician has showed up a dent by using a body file which files the metal that is level. The paint on the dent is untouched, showing clearly that there is a significant dent or low spot. In Fig. 14-29 the technician is using a pick hammer behind the panel to work out the dent. The hammer and the technician's hand are hidden behind the panel.

Small dents can often be raised with a pry bar if they cannot be reached from the inside with a pick hammer. For example, a small dent in a door panel can often be leveled with a pry bar stuck through a drain hole in the bottom of the door.

≡ 14-20 HEAT SHRINKING

Heat shrinking is for use on the older low-carbon steel panels. It is not recommended for the HSLA panels. This treatment could seriously weaken them.

Most impact forces will cause metal to stretch. The two examples used in discussing hammer-on-dolly and hammer-off-dolly procedures (Figs. 14-21 and 14-24) both result in stretched metal. Hammering on the metal stretches it. There is too much surface area for the metal to settle back into the original contour. There are two ways to correct this. One is to work the metal into a series of small ripples as shown in Fig. 14-31. The other way is to heat-shrink the area. By either method, the metal will still have irregularities that must be filled with plastic body filler.

NOTE: The use of a shrinking hammer can also restore the metal to nearly its original contour. The shrinking hammer (Fig. 14-34) has a "waffle" face with a series of grooves running vertically to each other. When this face strikes sheet metal, it imprints this waffle pattern on the metal. The metal is therefore drawn in, or shrunk. The shrinking hammer is seldom used today. HSLA steel is weakened by this treatment.

To understand the heat-shrinking process, let us first look at what happens when metal is heated and cooled. When metal is heated, it expands. When it cools, it contracts. As a simple example, look at what happens when you heat a spot in a flat panel (Fig. 14-36). To heat the spot, use the oxyacetylene-welding torch adjusted to a neutral flame. Direct the flame at the spot, keeping the inner, or blue, flame about ½ inch [12.7 mm] away from the metal. Do not overheat the metal. It is easy to burn a hole in thin sheet metal.

As the metal gets hot, it expands, causing the bulge shown at 2 in Fig. 14-36. Then, when the metal cools, it contracts, as shown at 3. If this were the whole story, heating and cooling a spot in a metal panel would not be

Fig. 14-36 Sequence of actions when a sheet-metal panel is heated. At 1, a gas torch is applying heat. This causes the metal to expand and form a bulge as shown at 2. When the metal cools, it shrinks slightly and forms the depression shown at 3.

helpful because you would be left with a slight sag, as shown at 3 in Fig. 14-36. However, the hot metal can be worked with a hammer and dolly, and then quenched (cooled) with water, to make the shrinking effective.

NOTE: Some body technicians believe that the only reason for water-quenching the heated metal is to cool the surface quickly so they can feel the surface to determine how much bulge remains. They believe that the quick quenching can crystallize the metal and make it harder to work on. The metal will crystallize if it is quenched when it is too hot.

The procedure that can be used to shrink a bulge and bring it down to the level of the surrounding metal starts with a bulge in a panel (Fig. 14-37). This is the result of working out a dent. The metal has been smoothed, but it has been stretched by having been worked with a hammer and dolly.

You must work fast when heat-shrinking. This means you must have everything ready before you start—oxyacetylene-welding equipment, body hammer, dollies, a bucket of water, and a sponge or rags.

As a first step, the torch is lit and adjusted to a neutral flame. The flame is pointed at the center of the bulge and held so the inner cone of the flame is about ½ inch [12.7 mm] away from the metal (Fig. 14-37). Heat a small area about the size of a dime until it is cherry red. Do not overheat it! You can burn a hole in the metal very quickly.

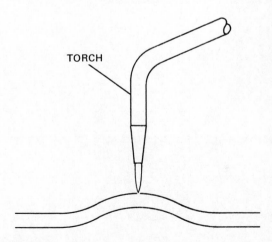

Fig. 14-37 Heat the center of the bulge with a torch.

As soon as the area turns cherry red, put aside the torch and pick up the hammer and dolly. The dolly should have a face of the correct curvature for the panel. In our example, the panel is flat.

Hit the center of the heated area with the body hammer, as shown in Fig. 14-38. Hit it several times to drive the center down. This produces a ridge around the center. Quickly bring the dolly (a body spoon can also be used) up under the work area, as shown in Fig. 14-39. Strike blows, as shown at 1, 2, 3, and 4 in Fig. 14-39. This brings the ridge down. Striking the ridges pushes the ridge metal toward the heated spot. The heated spot, being soft, can accept this metal without any great tendency to bulge. The heated metal becomes thicker. However, there will be a tendency for a bulge to occur. This is where the quenching with water comes in. Figures 14-40 and 14-41 show a body technician working down a dent in a panel by heating and hammering.

After the area has been worked so it is smooth except for a slight bulge, it should be quenched to flatten it. This is done by running a wet sponge or rag over the heated area, as shown in Fig. 14-42. If the area does not level completely, it will require reheating, further working, and quenching.

NOTE: Quench only after the color has left the metal and it has turned black. If you quench the metal when it is too hot (has some color), the steel will become very hard. It will be difficult to file and sand in preparation for painting. If the metal is very hot when it is quenched, it could crack.

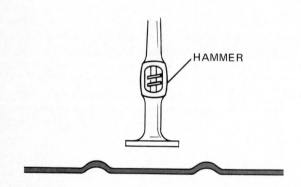

Fig. 14-38 Hit the center of the heated area to drive it down.

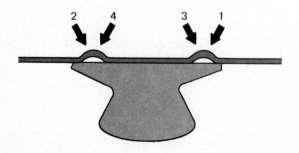

Fig. 14-39 With dolly under, strike hammer blows in the numbered sequence.

The description above covers the basic steps in heat shrinking. However, the procedure can be more complicated. For example, when heat-shrinking a large panel, such as a quarter panel, do not heat the whole panel. Instead, heat a number of small spots, quenching each before going on to the next. The spots should be fairly widely spaced so that there will be strong metal between them. If this is done properly, the panel will be brought down to contour. If the hot spots are too closely spaced, they can cause wrinkles, because a large area will be shrunk. Heating one spot after another is sometimes called *sequence shrinking*.

≡ 14-21 FILLING

Filling can be done with body solder or with plastic body filler. The application of body solder is described in Chap. 10. However, body solder is seldom used today. Body solder is put on hot. Plastic filler is put on cold. The surface preparation for the application of plastic filler is similar to that for body solder. The surface must be clean and sanded down to bare metal. Then the plastic filler is mixed and applied with a putty knife or squeegee. After the plastic has set up (hardened), it can be filed and sanded in preparation for painting, just as for metal. The use of plastic body filler is covered in detail in a following chapter.

≡ 14-22 PATCHING OR INSTALLING A PANEL

If an area of damage is not too large but is severe (tears, holes, rusted-out metal), you can cut out the damaged area and apply a patch. The patch can be made from scrap discarded from another job, or from flat sheet metal especially purchased for patch work. The patch may be riveted, spot- or arc-welded, or brazed into place. Spot welding is the method preferred by many body technicians, because it is fast and does not distort the metal. Arc welding and brazing can heat and distort the sheet metal and produce expansion, which must then be worked out.

The rivets, welds, or brazed spots are driven below the level of the surrounding metal, and the low areas are filled with plastic. The area is then filed and sanded in preparation for painting.

If a major damage has been done to a body panel, the decision will probably be to replace it entirely. The decision is usually based on two factors:

1. The cost of making repairs as compared to the cost of replacing the panel

2. The general condition and value of the car

Let us look at item 1 first. Suppose there is a fender that is badly crushed. It could be straightened, patched, and restored so it looks like new. But it would take several hours. If labor is billed at $25 an hour and it took 8 hours to do the job, the labor cost would be $200. And the result would still be an old, repaired fender. To buy and install a new fender might cost only a little more and would be the preferred way to do the job.

Now let us look at item 2. Here we have an unknown factor—the owner's desires. The owner may be proud

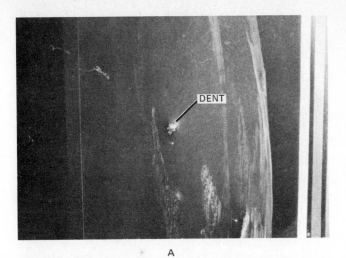
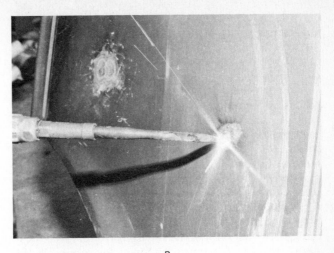

A   B

Fig. 14-40 (A) Dent in a panel. (B) Heating the panel as the first step in heat shrinking.

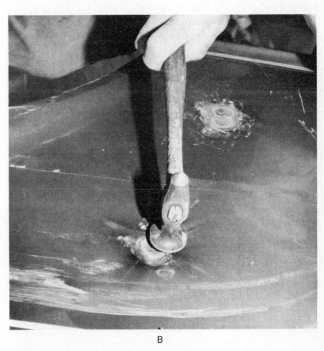

A   B

Fig. 14-41 (A) Hitting the center of the heated area with a body hammer. (B) Working around the heated area which has been driven in.

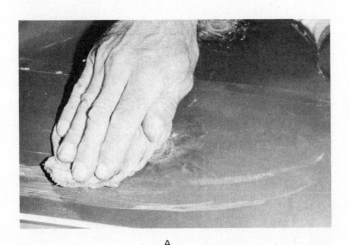
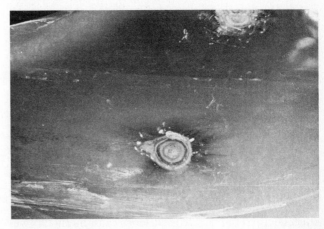

A   B

Fig. 14-42 (A) Quenching the heated area. (B) The area flattened.

of the car and want only the best. So you install a new fender. If the car is fairly old or is for sale, the owner will not want to put too much money in it. So if the damage can be repaired at less cost than by replacement, the old panel is repaired.

If a replacement panel is called for, the shop might get a new replacement part or a part that comes from a salvage yard. These car "graveyards" are places where cars damaged in collisions are brought. Generally, these cars have been totaled. This means that it would have cost more to fix them than they were worth.

However, totaled cars are not necesssarily completely junked. They usually have many usable parts. Alternators, air conditioners, engines, undamaged body panels, and many other parts can be salvaged and reused. The operator of the salvage yard removes these parts and stores them in readiness for resale. Or the operator merely leaves the junked cars in rows in the yard. When you need a part, you search out the model car for which the part is needed. Then, if that car has the part you need undamaged, you remove it yourself.

Some of the larger parts the salvage yard may remove and store in readiness for resale include front clips and rear clips. These are substantial parts of the car body. Figure 14-43 shows a rear clip. When a rear clip is used, the car being repaired has the rear part of its body removed so the replacement rear clip can be installed in its place.

The front clip is sometimes called the *doghouse*. It includes all the front and body parts. Sometimes a side clip (Fig. 14-44) is also used.

Often, when a salvage part is used, it is not from a car exactly identical to the car being repaired. This means that the part must be adapted by cutting and fitting.

≡ 14-23 REPLACING BODY PANELS

Some body panels can be replaced by removing bolts. For example, the fender shown in Fig. 14-45 is removed by removing the front bumper, rocker-panel molding, and fender liner and clips. Then the fender can be unbolted and removed from the car.

Other body panel replacement requires more work. For example, Figure 14-46 shows body panels that can be purchased from the car dealer. The new panel can be installed after the damaged panel is cut out or removed. Before the new panel is welded in place, the body must be restored to its original shape so the new panel will fit properly. The welding should be done with a MIG welder.

≡ 14-24 SELECTING THE REPAIR PROCEDURE

There are a variety of sheet-metal repair procedures. Which method you select for a specific job depends on several factors: first, what kind of damage has been done; second, what equipment you have available; third, the quality of job required.

It takes knowledge and experience to determine which methods to use when you are confronted with a sheet-metal repair job. The various repair methods give you choices from which you can select the best way under the circumstances.

Fig. 14-43 A rear clip.

Fig. 14-44 A side clip.

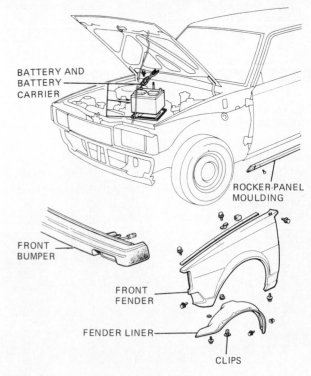

BATTERY AND BATTERY CARRIER

ROCKER-PANEL MOULDING

FRONT BUMPER

FRONT FENDER

FENDER LINER

CLIPS

Fig. 14-45 Some body panels, such as this front fender, can be replaced by removing bolts.

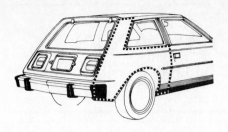
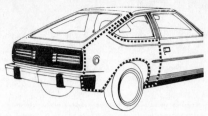
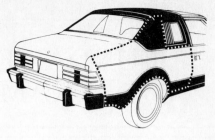

SPIRIT SEDAN/EAGLE KAMMBACK

SPIRIT/EAGLE SX/4 LIFTBACK

CONCORD-EAGLE
TWO-DOOR SEDAN

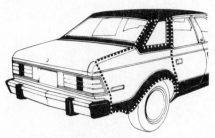

CONCORD-EAGLE
FOUR-DOOR SEDAN

CONCORD-EAGLE
WAGON

Fig. 14-46 New body panels that can be purchased from the manufacturer through the dealer's parts department. *(American Motors Corporation)*

REVIEW QUESTIONS

Select the *one* correct, best, or most probable answer to each question. You can find the answers in the section indicated at the end of each question.

1. To ding out sheet metal, you use (≡14-10)
   a. vacuum cups
   b. a slide hammer
   c. a hammer and dolly
   d. a pry bar

2. Pull tabs are attached with (≡14-4)
   a. screws
   b. a spot welder
   c. a torch
   d. epoxy

3. The purpose of tapping a panel when it is being straightened is to (≡14-2)
   a. help relieve stress
   b. prevent pullback
   c. both **a** and **b**
   d. neither **a** nor **b**

4. Straightening metal by hammering on a dolly will cause the metal to (≡14-11)
   a. shrink
   b. bubble
   c. tear
   d. rust

5. A dent in a door panel can often be worked out by
   a. a vacuum cup (≡14-8)
   b. pull rods
   c. a slide hammer
   d. all of the above

6. A body file can be used to (≡14-14)
   a. locate low spots
   b. pry out bubbles
   c. hammer down bubbles
   d. ding out dents

7. The pick hammer is used to (≡14-19)
   a. pick holes in panels
   b. pick up small dents
   c. shrink the metal
   d. pick up screws from panels

8. A doghouse is (≡14-22)
   a. a rear clip
   b. a side clip
   c. the car body
   d. a front clip

9. The process of restoring stretched metal to its original contour is (≡14-20)
   a. heat shrinking
   b. hammering-on-dolly
   c. hammering-off-dolly
   d. pulling

10. The purpose of plastic body filler is to (≡14-21)
    a. prevent rusting of damaged spots
    b. fill in low spots
    c. help ding out dents
    d. cushion hammer blows when using a dolly

CHAPTER 15
FUNDAMENTALS OF BODY-AND-FRAME STRAIGHTENING

After studying this chapter, you should be able to:

1. Explain how to check frame-and-body alignment.
2. Discuss the construction of body-and-frame and unitized-body cars.
3. Describe the four controlling points in body-frame straightening.
4. Discuss the basic types of body-frame misalignment.
5. Explain how to diagnose body-frame damage.
6. Discuss the diagnosis of unitized-body damage.
7. Describe how to prepare a body-and-frame car and a unitized-body car for straightening.
8. Explain the purpose of reference measurement points and how they are used.

≡ 15-1 CHECKING FRAME-AND-BODY ALIGNMENT

Whenever a car has been damaged by a collision, rollover, or other accident, the alignment of the frame and body should be checked. This should be done even though damage appears slight. For example, a car that struck a large animal, such as a horse or cow, may appear to receive only light damage. Because the animal was large and the impact took place over a large area of the car, little visible damage may be seen. However, since the impact was heavy, the shock could have carried back into the body structure and frame, causing misalignment that should be corrected. Always check body-and-frame alignment whenever any possibility of misalignment exists.

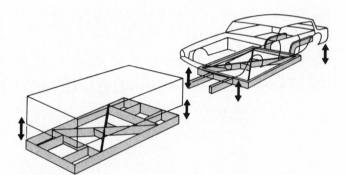

Fig. 15-1 Major resistance to twist is offered by the frame. *(Applied Power, Inc.)*

≡ 15-2 BEGIN WITH BODY-AND-FRAME ALIGNMENT

Before you attempt to do any work on body sheet-metal panels, you should check alignment and make whatever corrections are required. Straightening the body structure or frame also straightens, to some extent, the body sheet metal.

Never work on sheet metal before the frame and body have been properly realigned. Suppose you did straighten some sheet metal first. When you put the power equipment to work on the car to align the frame, you would probably pull the sheet metal out of line again. Chapter 8 describes various types of body-and-frame straightening equipment. This equipment and its use are described in the following chapter.

≡ 15-3 TYPES OF FULL FRAMES

Various types of frames are used in cars having a full frame. Two types are the *ladder* (often used in trucks) and the *perimeter* (Fig. 2-2). With this construction,

the major resistance to twist or other body-frame distortion is offered by the frame itself (Fig. 15-1). The frame is somewhat flexible, but it is made of steel beams of various shapes that provide great strength. In recent years, the tendency has been to reduce weight. However, at the same time, steels of greater strength, and scientific design of the structural parts of the frame, have improved the impact resistance and basic strength of the frame. Figure 15-2 shows the intricate shapes into which the frame parts are formed. This frame illustrates the scientific principles of getting strength from relatively light weight.

≡ 15-4 UNITIZED BODIES

In the unitized body, the body itself forms the support for the engine, suspension, and drive train. Figure 15-3 shows a unitized body. The body includes heavy structural sills, box-section rails, and lower-body reinforcing members to add strength to the assembly and provide support for the engine and suspension system. Figure 2-6A shows another unitized body.

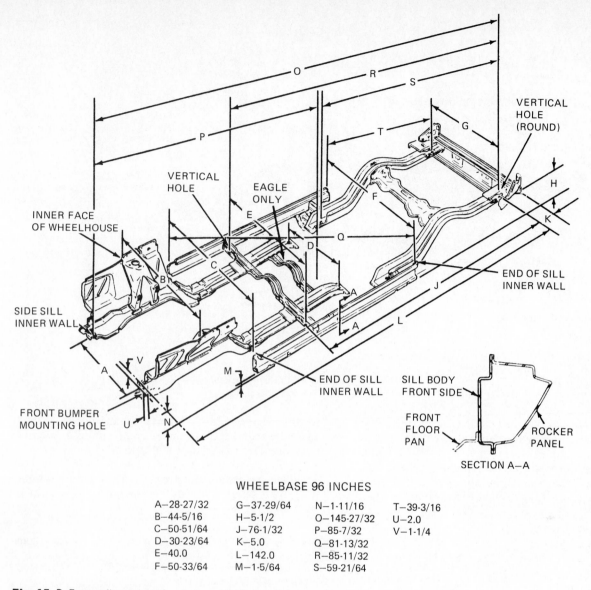

VERTICAL
HOLE (ROUND)

VERTICAL
HOLE

EAGLE
ONLY

INNER FACE
OF WHEELHOUSE

END OF SILL
INNER WALL

SIDE SILL
INNER WALL

FRONT BUMPER
MOUNTING HOLE

END OF SILL
INNER WALL

SILL BODY
FRONT SIDE

FRONT
FLOOR
PAN

ROCKER
PANEL

SECTION A–A

WHEELBASE 96 INCHES

A—28-27/32	G—37-29/64	N—1-11/16	T—39-3/16
B—44-5/16	H—5-1/2	O—145-27/32	U—2.0
C—50-51/64	J—76-1/32	P—85-7/32	V—1-1/4
D—30-23/64	K—5.0	Q—81-13/32	
E—40.0	L—142.0	R—85-11/32	
F—50-33/64	M—1-5/64	S—59-21/64	

Fig. 15-2 Frame dimensions for one model of car. *(American Motors Corporation)*

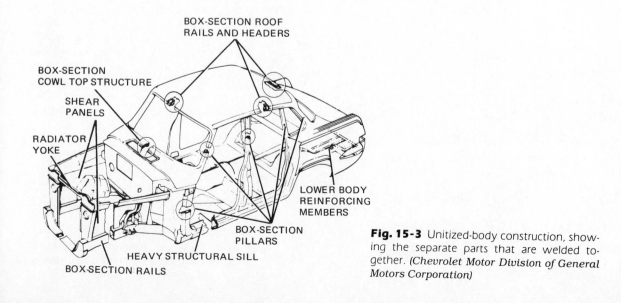

BOX-SECTION ROOF
RAILS AND HEADERS

BOX-SECTION
COWL TOP STRUCTURE

SHEAR
PANELS

RADIATOR
YOKE

LOWER BODY
REINFORCING
MEMBERS

BOX-SECTION
PILLARS

HEAVY STRUCTURAL SILL

BOX-SECTION RAILS

Fig. 15-3 Unitized-body construction, showing the separate parts that are welded together. *(Chevrolet Motor Division of General Motors Corporation)*

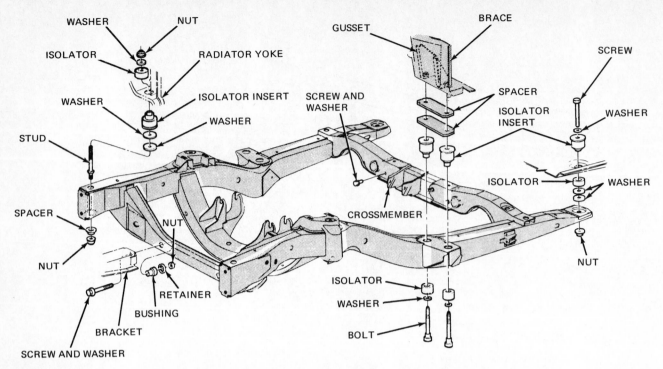

Fig. 15-4 Stub frame used at the front of a unitized-body vehicle. *(Chrysler Corporation)*

Many unitized bodies use a stub frame at the front (Fig. 15-4). It is attached to the body by bolts through isolators. The isolators absorb road and suspension vibration and prevent it from carrying up to the body.

Figure 15-5 shows a similar stub frame. The structural parts are formed to provide strength and support for the engine and other parts. In some unitized-body cars, the stub frame is basically a front cross member that supports the transaxle (Fig. 2-9).

In unitized and semiunitized bodies, the body itself provides the structural strength. This is illustrated in Fig. 15-6, where the body is shown as part of a struc-

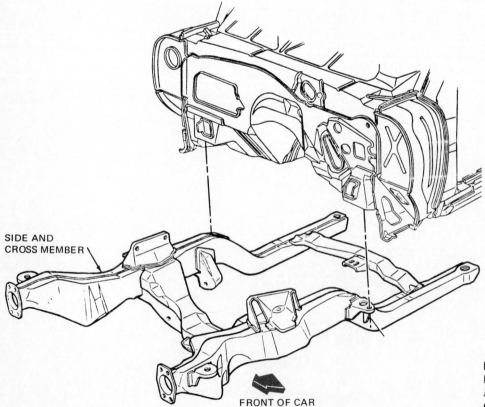

Fig. 15-5 Stub frame, showing how it fits under the body. *(Buick Motor Division of General Motors Corporation)*

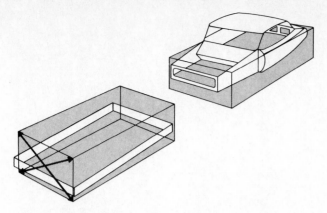

Fig. 15-6 With unitized-body construction, the body becomes part of the structural assembly and supplies structural strength. *(Applied Power, Inc.)*

tural box section. This contrasts with the full-frame assembly, shown in Fig. 15-2, where the body itself does not greatly add to the basic strength of the assembly. In the full-frame car, the body is dropped onto the frame and the frame is the supporting and strenghtening member.

≡ 15-5 UNITIZED-BODY REFERENCE POINTS

The body technician must have drawings to show reference points and measurements between them. These drawings, called *underbody dimensions,* are found in the manufacturers' shop manuals. For example, Fig. 15-7 shows the underbody of a Volkswagen Rabbit, with the dimensions between reference points given in

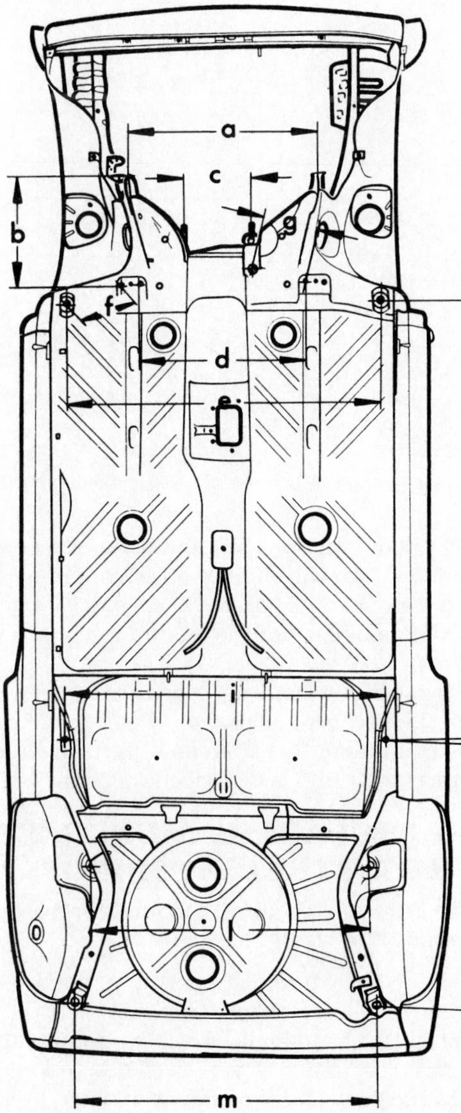

Dimension	Location	Millimeters (Inches)
a	Between front subframe (hole centers)	683 mm (26⅞ in)
b	Between front and rear subframe mounting points	365^{+1}_{-3} mm ($14\frac{3}{8}^{+1/32}_{-1/8}$ in)
c	Between subframe mountings (bolt centers)	272 mm (10²³⁄₃₂ in)
d	Between rear mounting holes (hole centers)	586 mm (23¹⁄₁₆ in)
e	Between front locating holes (hole centers)	1110 mm (43¹¹⁄₁₆ in)
f	Between rear subframe mounting holes and locating holes (hole centers)	204 mm (8¹⁄₃₂ in)
g	Between locating hole and subframe mounting hole (hole centers)	192 mm (7⁹⁄₁₆ in)
h	Between locating holes and holes in rear side member (hole centers)	1478 mm (58³⁄₁₆ in)
i	Between holes in rear side members (hole centers)	1142 mm (44³¹⁄₃₂ in)
k	Between rear locating holes and holes in rear side members (hole centers)	888 mm (34³¹⁄₃₂ in)
l	Between rear-axle coil-spring mountings (buffer mount centers)	1020 ± 4 mm (40⁵⁄₃₂ ± ⁵⁄₃₂ in)
m	Between rear locating holes (hole centers)	1057 mm (41⅝ in)

Fig. 15-7 Underbody dimensions for a Volkswagen Rabbit. *(Volkswagen of America, Inc.)*

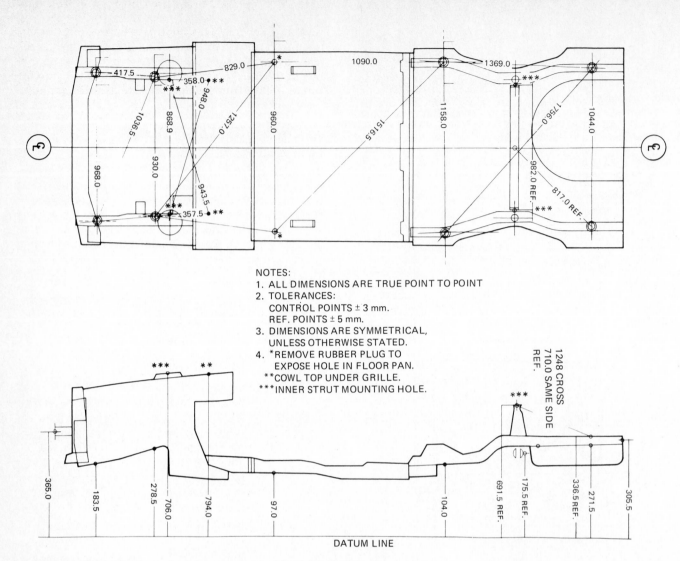

NOTES:
1. ALL DIMENSIONS ARE TRUE POINT TO POINT
2. TOLERANCES:
   CONTROL POINTS ± 3 mm.
   REF. POINTS ± 5 mm.
3. DIMENSIONS ARE SYMMETRICAL,
   UNLESS OTHERWISE STATED.
4. *REMOVE RUBBER PLUG TO
   EXPOSE HOLE IN FLOOR PAN.
   **COWL TOP UNDER GRILLE.
   ***INNER STRUT MOUNTING HOLE.

DATUM LINE

Fig. 15-8 Underbody dimensions for one model of Ford. *(Ford Motor Company)*

millimeters and inches. Figure 15-8 shows the underbody dimensions of one model of Ford. These dimensions must be correct before work is started on the upper part of the body.

In the lower illustration in Fig. 15-8, notice the use of the *datum line* (or *datum plane*). This is an imaginary line from which the height dimensions are given for points on the car body or frame. Gauges can be used to quickly establish the datum line. When frame gauges are hung from the vehicle, the top of the gauge becomes the datum plane. This provides a method of checking any section of the frame against the specifications given by the manufacturer in the underbody dimensions.

Use of the datum line, or datum plane, enables the technician to measure how much damage is in the body. Then an estimate can be prepared of how much time it will take to correct it. For accuracy, during measuring the vehicle should be supported on its wheels or suspension system. Lifts or stands that support the car weight at other points will cause inaccurate measurements.

When the basic underbody measurements have been corrected, then work can start on the upper struc-

ture of the body. Figure 15-9 shows reference points and dimensions for the engine compartment of the car shown in Fig. 15-7. Figure 15-10 shows reference points and dimensions for the rear ends of various unitized bodies.

All of these dimensions must be correct before work begins on the sheet-metal and body panels. The use of hydraulic equipment to realign body parts to obtain the correct measurements is described in Chap. 16.

≡ 15-6 PREPARING A UNITIZED BODY FOR STRAIGHTENING

Here is the general procedure to follow when preparing a unitized body for straightening:

1. Jack up the car and support it on stands.

2. Remove bumpers and trim only if necessary. Straightening unitized bodies usually requires that all components remain on the vehicle. These parts are integral with the body and should stay in place during the straightening operation. They add support while the straightening pull or push is applied.

3. Remove suspension parts and wheels that will interfere with checking alignment.

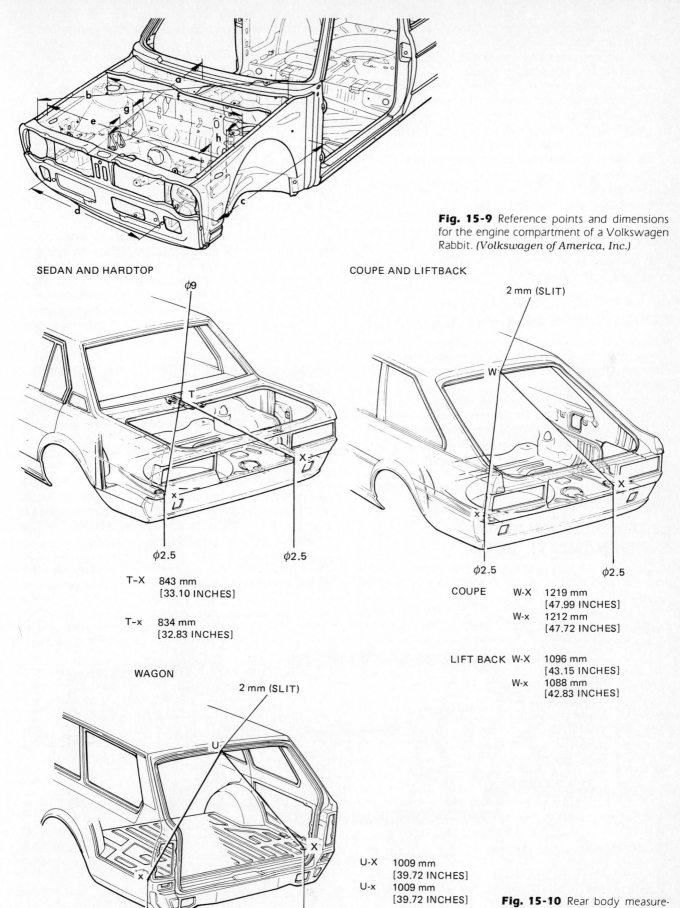

Fig. 15-9 Reference points and dimensions for the engine compartment of a Volkswagen Rabbit. *(Volkswagen of America, Inc.)*

SEDAN AND HARDTOP

$\phi 9$

$\phi 2.5$ $\phi 2.5$

T–X   843 mm
       [33.10 INCHES]

T–x   834 mm
       [32.83 INCHES]

COUPE AND LIFTBACK

2 mm (SLIT)

$\phi 2.5$ $\phi 2.5$

COUPE   W-X   1219 mm
                [47.99 INCHES]
         W-x   1212 mm
                [47.72 INCHES]

LIFT BACK W-X 1096 mm
                [43.15 INCHES]
           W-x 1088 mm
                [42.83 INCHES]

WAGON

2 mm (SLIT)

$\phi 15$ $\phi 15$

U-X   1009 mm
       [39.72 INCHES]
U-x   1009 mm
       [39.72 INCHES]

Fig. 15-10 Rear body measurements for various models of cars with unitized-body construction. *(Toyota Motor Sales, Inc.)*

4. Rough out badly damaged areas before taking measurements for squaring up a body. If necessary, remove unbroken glass from the damaged area to prevent glass breakage during straightening.

5. If there has been severe damage, it may be necessary to remove or cut reinforcement brackets or other inner construction to permit restoration of the outer shell and pillars. Straighten, install, and secure all such parts in place before attempting to align the body.

6. The underbody must be restored to its correct dimensions first.

7. Use the factory reference measuring points to determine how much parts are out of line (≡15-5).

NOTE: Use of push and pull must be carefully controlled. There is a difference between the gauge (thickness) of the metal in the sub-body and the stress points of the body panels.

≡ 15-7 REPAIRING MAJOR COMPONENTS IN A UNITIZED BODY

If inner construction parts in a unitized body are broken or cracked, it is often possible to weld the break. Only electric (MIG) welding should be used to avoid weakening the parts.

When a reinforcing plate is welded to a body member, run the welds lengthwise along the sides of the reinforcement. This avoids welding across the damaged part, which could weaken it at that point. If a damaged component is replaced, use the same method of attachment as was used for the original member. If new bolts are used, always use bolts of the same specifications as the original bolts.

≡ 15-8 ALIGNMENT OF FULL-FRAME VEHICLES

In checking alignment of frames in full-frame vehicles, refer to the manufacturer's service manual for the drawing giving the underbody reference points and dimensions between them (≡ 15-5). Following sections describe procedures for checking frame alignment.

≡ 15-9 BODY-FRAME VEHICLE CONTROLLING POINTS

There are four controlling points in body-frame straightening (Fig. 15-11). These are:

1. The front cross member
2. The cowl cross member
3. The cross member at the rear-door area
4. The rear cross member

These are the four reference points for any checks and straightening operations. The frame, in effect, is divided into three sections: the front or engine section, the center or passenger section, and the rear or trunk section. Each section is bordered by a cross member, or controlling point. Hookups of straightening equipment are usually applied at or near any of the controlling points.

≡ 15-10 BASIC TYPES OF FRAME MISALIGNMENT

There are five basic types of frame misalignment (Figs. 15-12 and 15-13). These are sidesway, sag, mash, diamond, and twist.

Three basic kinds of sidesway are shown in Figs. 15-12A to 15-12C. The cause of each type is indicated in the illustration. Figures 15-12D and 15-12E show frame sag from front or rear impact. Figures 15-12F and 15-12G show mashed and buckled frames. Sometimes a frame will have a diamond misalignment or twisted frame (Figs. 15-13A and 15-13B).

All frame damage is not as simple as shown in Figs. 15-12 and 15-13. A severe impact can produce a combination of the basic conditions shown. But regardless of

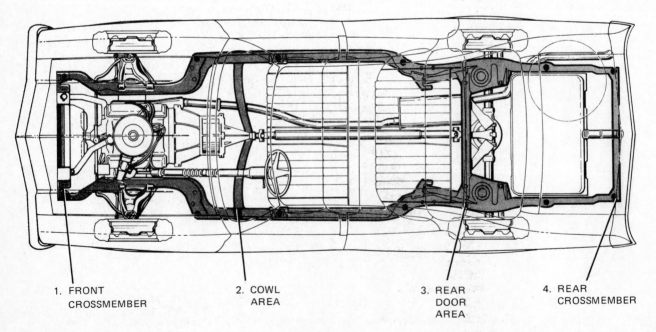

1. FRONT CROSSMEMBER   2. COWL AREA   3. REAR DOOR AREA   4. REAR CROSSMEMBER

Fig. 15-11 *The four controlling points in body-frame straightening.*

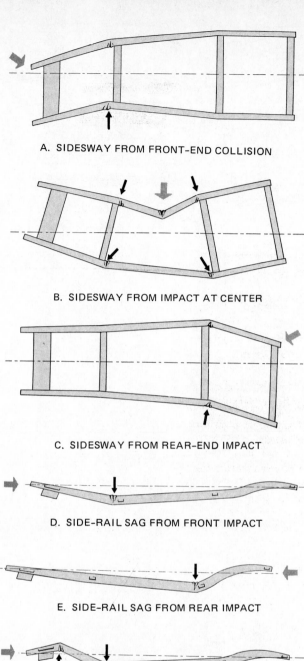

A. SIDESWAY FROM FRONT-END COLLISION

B. SIDESWAY FROM IMPACT AT CENTER

C. SIDESWAY FROM REAR-END IMPACT

D. SIDE-RAIL SAG FROM FRONT IMPACT

E. SIDE-RAIL SAG FROM REAR IMPACT

F. FRAME MASHED AND BUCKLED
FROM FRONT-END IMPACT

G. FRAME MASHED AND BUCKLED
FROM REAR-END IMPACT

Fig. 15-12 Basic types of frame misalignment. (*Applied Power, Inc.*)

A. DIAMOND MISALIGNMENT

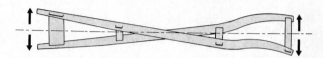

B. TWISTED FRAME

Fig. 15-13 Frames with diamond and twist misalignment. (*Applied Power, Inc.*)

force. This, in effect, "undoes" the impact. Procedures are described in following sections.

≡ 15-11 PREPARING TO CORRECT BODY-FRAME DAMAGE

Whenever a frame is damaged, the body sheet metal, trim, bumper, and related parts also are damaged. In your analysis of an impact-damaged vehicle, look at the frame first to determine whether the impact has been severe enough to penetrate through the body and underbody and reach the frame. This is done by checking the frame alignment.

You do not loosen body bolts attaching the body to the frame or stub frame when checking and correcting alignment. Alignment of the frame and body are corrected together. Then body sheet-metal work is completed.

≡ 15-12 DIAGNOSING BODY-FRAME DAMAGE

As a first step, the body technician removes from the damaged car all parts that would get in the way of making a careful analysis of the damage to the body and frame. Figure 12-1, for example, shows a car damaged in a right-front-end collision. The front grill, right front wheel, radiator, and other parts have been removed and stored out of the way. However, they are available for further examination, or repair and reuse. In the car shown in Fig. 12-1, the radiator was damaged but it was repaired and reused.

With the damaged parts off, the alignment is checked. There are several types of alignment-checking (frame-gauging) tools. One type has a set of rigid centering gauges, as shown in Fig. 15-14. These are placed at the three front controlling points shown in Fig. 15-11. One is placed at the front cross member, one at the cowl area, and one at the rear-door area. In Fig. 15-14A, the vertical alignment points do not line up. This indicates frame sidesway. Figures 15-14B and 15-14C show sag and twist.

Figure 15-15 shows the locations of the centering gauges. This illustration shows four centering gauges being used. Figure 15-16 shows methods of attaching centering gauges to the frame.

the type of damage, the body technician must analyze the condition of the body and frame. The first step is to determine the direction of the impact that caused the damage. Then, using a pull or push with hydraulic equipment, the technician reverses the impacting

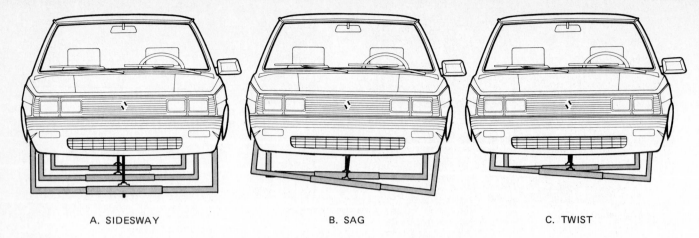

A. SIDESWAY   B. SAG   C. TWIST

Fig. 15-14 Using frame centering gauges to check frame alignment. *(Applied Power, Inc.)*

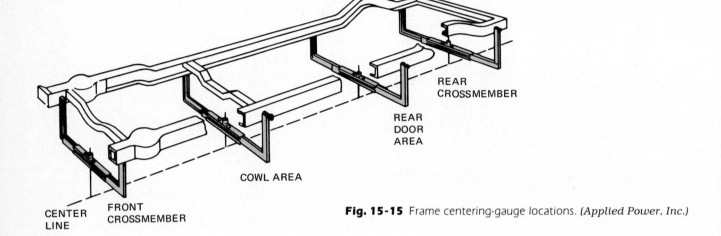

REAR CROSSMEMBER

REAR DOOR AREA

COWL AREA

CENTER LINE

FRONT CROSSMEMBER

Fig. 15-15 Frame centering-gauge locations. *(Applied Power, Inc.)*

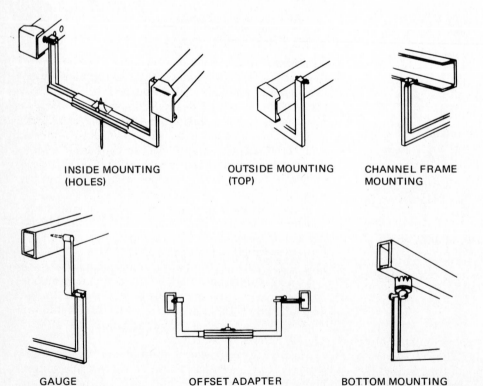

INSIDE MOUNTING (HOLES)

OUTSIDE MOUNTING (TOP)

CHANNEL FRAME MOUNTING

GAUGE EXTENSION

OFFSET ADAPTER

BOTTOM MOUNTING (MAGNETIC HOLDERS)

Fig. 15-16 Methods of attaching centering gauges to frame. *(Applied Power, Inc.)*

Fig. 15-17 Frame alignment-checking tool that uses pendants and vertical rods. The rods are out of line, showing that the frame has sidesway.

A second type of alignment-checking tool uses chains and pendants with vertical rods (Fig. 15-17). Three of these are hung at the controlling points noted above. Figure 15-17 shows that the frame has sidesway. This is the same car shown in Fig. 12-1.

A third type of alignment-checking tool uses a laser beam. It has a laser-beam projector, a movable mirror, and several special gauges (Fig. 15-18). The laser beam hits the mirror and is turned 90° so it passes through the two gauges. The two gauges are attached to the lower body or frame at the specified gauging points. As the laser beam passes through the gauges, it produces a bright spot on each gauge. If the spots line up, the frame or body at that point is in line. If they do not, the body or frame must be pulled or pushed to produce alignment. The mirror is moved along the track to the various controlling points. These are the points at which alignment checks are made.

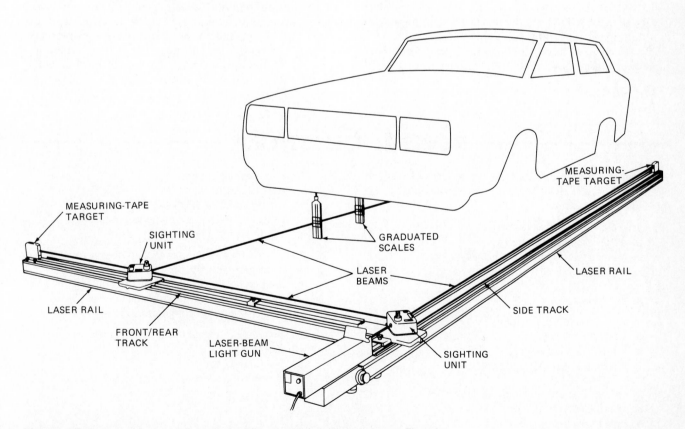

Fig. 15-18 Body-and-frame alignment-checking system using a laser beam. The mirror can be moved on the track to various locations where the gauges are hung. *(Nicator, Inc.)*

≡ 15-13 PREPARING THE CAR FOR STRAIGHTENING

Where collision damage has been light, the body technician may not use the alignment gauges to check the frame alignment. However, if there is the slightest doubt, check the frame alignment. Failure to check and correct frame alignment is the reason you occasionally see a car going down the highway with wheels that do not track.

Tracking is the following of the rear wheels in proper alignment behind the front wheels (Fig. 15-19). If the rear wheels do not track properly, the frame is probably out of line. A car that fails to track properly after a body-frame repair job has not been properly repaired. The technician who did the job did not take the time to check and correct frame alignment. This is the reason for the necessity of checking alignment (≡15-1) whenever there is the possibility of damage. While not all collision jobs are the same, the following steps are usually required. They apply to full-frame vehicles. Unitized-body alignment was described in ≡15-5.

1. Jack up the car and support it on safety stands.
2. Remove wheels, bumpers, and other parts that might interfere with checking alignment.
3. *Do not remove or loosen body bolts!*
4. Remove suspension parts that might interfere.
5. Check alignment as described earlier. Use the factory measurement reference points to determine how much parts are out of line (≡15-5).
6. Examine frame for buckles or breaks.
7. If the frame is cracked or broken, weld it (≡15-14). Observe the safety cautions outlined in Chaps. 9 and 11. This step is necessary to prevent further damage and tearing of the sheet metal.
8. If parts still on the car will interfere with straightening, remove them. If necessary, remove un-

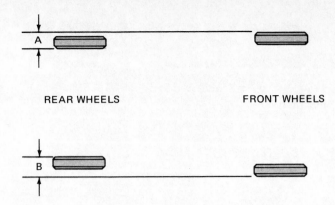

Fig. 15-19 Checking rear-wheel tracking. A should equal B on most cars. *(Ford Motor Company)*

broken glass from the damaged area to prevent the glass being broken during the straightening.

9. Having determined the extent and direction of the misalignment, make necessary hookups and apply the straightening force. These steps are described in Chap. 16.

≡ 15-14 FRAME REPAIR

If a frame is cracked or broken, it may be possible to weld the break. Electric-welding equipment should be used for all frame welding. Heat must be kept to a minimum so that the hardness of the metal will not be affected.

When a reinforcing plate is to be welded to a frame side member, run the welds lengthwise along the sides of the reinforcement. If a damaged frame member is to be replaced, use the same method of attachment as was used for the original frame member. Also, new bolts, required for reattachments of parts to the new member, must have the same specifications as the original bolts.

REVIEW QUESTIONS

Select the *one* correct, best, or most probable answer to each question. You can find the answers in the section indicated at the end of each question.

1. Before sheet-metal work starts,   (≡15-2)
   a. alignment must be checked
   b. frame and body must be properly aligned
   c. hydraulic equipment must be used, if necessary to correct alignment
   d. all of the above

2. In the full-frame car, the frame   (≡15-3)
   a. is somewhat flexible
   b. is made of steel beams
   c. has beams welded together
   d. all of the above

3. The purpose of unitized-body isolators is to   (≡15-4)
   a. allow full-frame construction
   b. isolate the stub frame from the body
   c. isolate the floor pan from the body
   d. insulate the electrical system from the body

4. Reference points are points   (≡15-5)
   a. from which bending starts
   b. where damage is most likely to occur
   c. between which measurements are taken
   d. to refer to for specifications

5. The reason for removing unbroken glass is to   (≡15-6)
   a. install it on another car
   b. avoid breaking it during straightening
   c. concentrate on the sheet metal
   d. protect the frame from rupture

6. When welding on a unitized-body vehicle, use   (≡15-7)
   a. MIG welding
   b. gas-torch welding
   c. carbon-arc welding
   d. none of the above

7. The controlling points in body-frame straightening are the points (≡15-9)
   a. where the frame parts are welded together
   b. where reference checks are measured
   c. at which the body is connected
   d. used to measure service work

8. A vehicle that fails to track has a (≡15-13)
   a. flat tire
   b. broken spring
   c. bent frame
   d. defective shock absorber

9. Sidesway, sag, and mash are types of (≡15-10)
   a. frame misalignment
   b. frame construction
   c. front-end collision
   d. body-frame assembly

10. Three types of alignment-checking tools are centering gauges, chains and pendants, and (≡15-12)
    a. laser beam
    b. hydraulic puller
    c. light ray
    d. X-ray

CHAPTER 16
USING BODY-AND-FRAME STRAIGHTENERS

After studying this chapter, you should be able to:

1. Explain how hydraulics operates the straighteners.
2. Discuss the safety cautions that must be observed when using pulling equipment.
3. Describe the types of body-and-frame straighteners and the types of attachments they use.
4. Explain the difference between portable and stationary straightening equipment.
5. Describe the special procedures required to correct diamond misalignment, mash, sag, sidesway, and twist of frames.
6. Explain what **overcorrection** means and why it is used.

≡ 16-1 USING BODY-AND-FRAME STRAIGHTENERS

No two collisions are identical. Therefore, the damages to the cars are never the same. This means that you must look at each straightening job as unique. You must figure out just how the damage occurred — where the impact or impacts took place, the direction of the impact, and how the push forced the body and frame parts out of line. Then you must apply a force that is opposite to the force that caused the damage. Most straighteners use pull to correct damage. The procedure is described later in detail.

The body panels and frame are not straightened by pull alone. As the pull is exerted, the body technician uses body tools to help the metal move back to its original contour. The combination of pull and hammering on or off the dolly, for example, will usually simplify the straightening of a buckled body panel. The procedure usually requires pulling a little beyond the original shape and then releasing the pull. There will be some springback when the pull is released. Pulling slightly beyond will allow the metal to spring back to its approximate original shape. Sometimes the body technician applies heat from a gas torch to the damaged area to help relieve the "set" of the metal.

≡ 16-2 HYDRAULIC PRINCIPLES

Body and frame straighteners operate on hydraulic principles. The word "hydraulic" means "of or pertaining to liquids" such as water and oil. Our special interest, so far as body-frame straighteners are concerned, is in the pressure that can be developed in liquids. This is called *hydraulic pressure.*

Force and motion can be transmitted from a piston in one cylinder to a piston in another cylinder (Fig. 16-1). As the piston in cylinder A is moved, the liquid flows through a tube to cylinder B, forcing the piston in cylinder B to move.

Pressure can be transmitted by a liquid (Fig. 16-2). If the piston shown in Fig. 16-2 has an area of 1 square

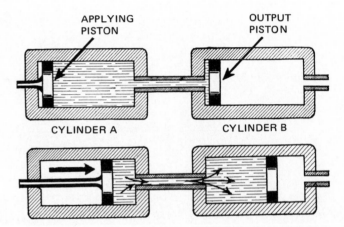

Fig. 16-1 Force and motion can be transmitted through a tube from one cylinder to another by hydraulic pressure. *(Pontiac Motor Division of General Motors Corporation)*

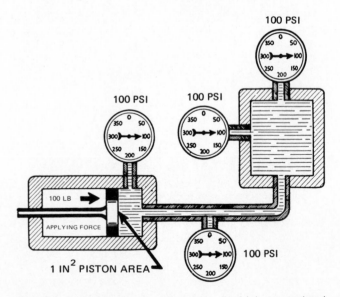

Fig. 16-2 The pressure applied to a liquid is transmitted equally in all directions. *(Pontiac Motor Division of General Motors Corporation)*

inch, and if it is pushed with a force of 100 pounds, the pressure on the liquid is 100 pounds per square inch (100 psi). Regardless of where the reading is taken, the pressure is the same throughout the hydraulic system.

Figure 16-3 shows how the same pressure can be used to produce different output forces. The bigger the output piston, the greater the output force. For example, the output piston to the right has an area of 2 square inches. Since the pressure is 100 psi, the total force on this piston is 200 pounds.

Now let us apply this to a hydraulic system used in body-frame straighteners. This equipment uses hydraulic rams. A *hydraulic ram* is simply a tube with a piston inside it. The piston is attached to a rod. When hydraulic fluid is sent into the tube, the fluid pushes on the piston so the piston and rod move.

The basic hydraulic system for a hydraulic ram is shown in Fig. 16-4. The pump has a small piston (1-square-inch area). The ram has a larger piston (4-square-inch area). If the pump handle is operated to develop a pressure of 500 psi, then a force of 2000 pounds is acting on the piston in the ram.

The length of the pump handle, or lever, determines the amount of force acting on the pump piston. If you push on the pump handle with a force of 50 pounds, the force acting on the pump piston is 500 pounds. This is because of the mechanical advantage produced by the length of the pump-handle lever. Therefore, a push of 100 pounds on the lever will produce an output force of 4000 pounds.

Many body-frame systems use a hydraulic pump operated by air pressure from the compressed-air system in the body shop. Figure 8-10 shows one of these.

≡ 16-3 SAFETY WITH PULLING EQUIPMENT

When pull is exerted by hydraulic equipment on body panels or frame, the pull can increase to more than 4000 pounds [17,792 N]. If a clamp is not secured properly, if a chain is defective, or if the body or frame member is rusted or cracked, something could "let go." Then the broken chain or clamp with chain that has slipped off could whip around the shop with deadly force. Anyone standing in the way could be seriously or fatally injured. For that reason, special safety cautions must be observed when working with pulling equipment.

1. When using a clamp on a body part, make sure that the undercoating is removed so the clamp gets a firm hold on the metal and will not slip.

2. Make sure that the clamp teeth are clean and sharp so they will grip well. They should be cleaned periodically with a wire brush.

3. Check the clamps and chain for wear before each use. Worn clamps and chains with nicked or otherwise damaged links should be replaced.

4. Be careful about attaching a clamp to a rusted panel. The panel may be so weak it will pull apart with very little tension. Tack-weld a supporting brace across the weakened part.

5. If the vehicle is on a stand when the pull is made, make sure the vehicle is tied down securely so it will not roll off.

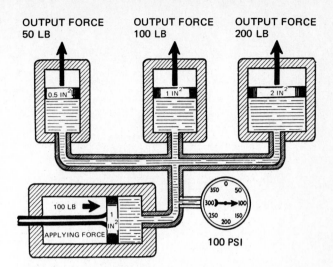

Fig. 16-3 The force applied to the output piston is the pressure in the system in pounds per square inch times the area of the output piston. *(Pontiac Motor Division of General Motors Corporation)*

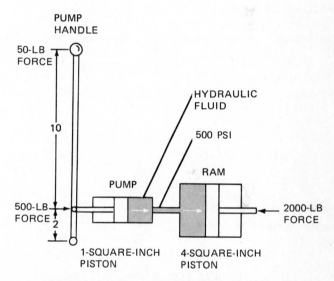

Fig. 16-4 How the lever (pump handle) provides a mechanical advantage which acts with the hydraulic system to increase the force applied to the ram-piston rod.

6. Double the chain, using two in parallel, for extra-heavy pulls.

7. Cover the chain and clamp with a heavy blanket. If anything lets go, the blanket will help muffle the chain and clamp and prevent it from whipping.

8. Never stand in a direct line with chains.

9. Use care in pulling on unitized bodies with HSLA panels. These panels are of thinner-gauge steel and can tear more easily. A tear usually requires replacement of the panel.

≡ 16-4 TYPES OF BODY-FRAME STRAIGHTENERS

Body-frame straighteners are classed as either portable or stationary. The various types are described and illustrated in Chap. 8. Find out which type is available in

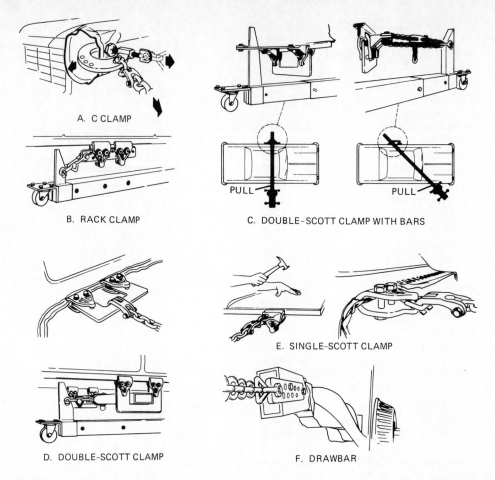

Fig. 16-5 Various types of clamps and how they can be used. (*Guy Chart Tools Limited*)

A. C CLAMP

B. RACK CLAMP

C. DOUBLE-SCOTT CLAMP WITH BARS

PULL

PULL

D. DOUBLE-SCOTT CLAMP

E. SINGLE-SCOTT CLAMP

F. DRAWBAR

your shop. Then study the manufacturer's operating instructions to learn the specific procedures for the straightener you will be using. Typical procedures are covered in following sections.

≡ 16-5 TYPES OF ATTACHMENTS

Most attachments for pulling body and frame metal are clamps. Strong chain usually indirectly connects the chain to the hydraulic ram of the body-frame straightener.

A variety of clamps for attaching to body and frame parts are shown in Fig. 16-5. Some clamps are attached by drilling holes in the sheet metal to accommodate the clamp bolts. Other clamps attach to the sheet metal without drilling holes. The clamp jaws have teeth that grip the metal.

Hooks are often used to pull on the frame. They can be inserted in reference or structural holes in the frame members. Figure 16-6 shows finger hooks, spiral screws, wedge tips, and hook extensions. The spiral screw (Fig. 16-6B) can be screwed into a hole from 1 to 1½ inches [25 to 38 mm] in diameter. Then a finger hook is inserted in the hole in the center of the spiral screw. The screw distributes the pull over half the circumference of the hole. This minimizes the possibility of distorting or tearing the metal.

Full-Frame Vehicles

≡ 16-6 USING PORTABLE BODY-FRAME STRAIGHTENERS

Figure 16-7 shows various pulls that can be made using portable body-frame straighteners. Each of the five types of body-frame misalignment—sidesway, sag, mash, diamond, and twist—can also be corrected using the portable body-frame straightener. Figures 15-12 and 15-13 show each type of body-frame misalignment.

When using any type of body-frame straightener, you usually want to pull in a direction opposite to the direction of the force that caused the damage. Visualize the damage and the impact that caused it. Then visualize applying your hands at the proper places to pull out the damage (Fig. 16-8). Using this principle, you can quickly decide where the pull must be applied.

≡ 16-7 CORRECTING DIAMOND MISALIGNMENT

Figure 16-9 shows the setup to correct diamond misalignment of the frame. The back end of the portable

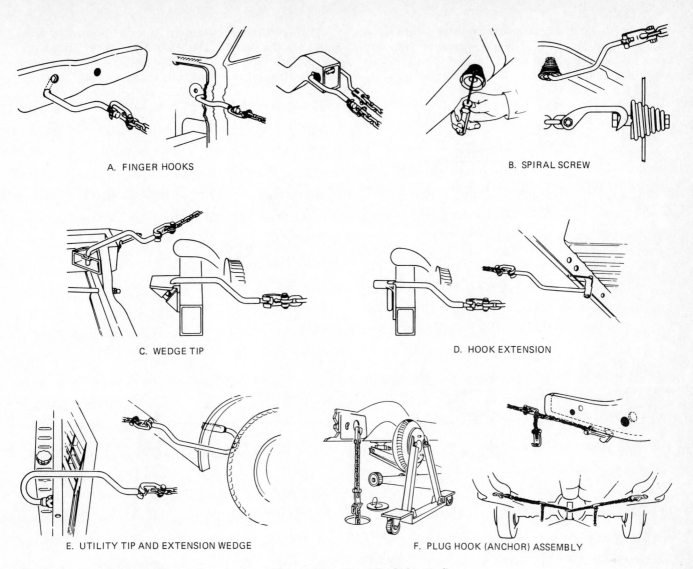

A. FINGER HOOKS

B. SPIRAL SCREW

C. WEDGE TIP

D. HOOK EXTENSION

E. UTILITY TIP AND EXTENSION WEDGE

F. PLUG HOOK (ANCHOR) ASSEMBLY

Fig. 16-6 Hookups for making pulls on body and frame. *(Guy Chart Tools Limited)*

straightener is attached by a chain to the frame near the rear. A plate is bolted to the left front horn of the left rail. The pump is then operated to exert a pull on the left side rail. This will usually pull the rail back into line. During the straightening procedure, you will be taking measurements from various reference points to determine when correction is completed. For example, Fig. 16-10 shows that the impact which moved the left rail back caused measurement 2 to become greater than measurement 1. When the pull has moved the left rail forward enough so that the two measurements are equal, the diamond misalignment has been removed.

NOTE: The distortions shown in the various illustrations of diamond, mash, sag, and other misalignments are exaggerated so the specific misaligned conditions can be easily seen. Also, there will probably be more than one type of distortion in a car that has had a severe impact. For example, a car might have diamond, mash, and sag distortion.

≡ 16-8 CORRECTING MASH

Figure 16-11 shows the setup to correct mash. If there is diamond misalignment, it must be removed first. Then mash is corrected. The pull in Fig. 16-11 is being exerted on the horn of the rail that has been mashed. When it is pulled out to the same dimension as the other rail, the mash has been corrected. Mash at the rear is corrected in the same manner, except that the connections are reversed.

≡ 16-9 CORRECTING SAG

Figure 16-12 shows the setup to correct sag. Generally, sag and mash occur together. As a rail is mashed in, it tends to sag at some point. Sag and mash are removed at the same time. The basic difference between the procedures for removing them is the direction in which the pull is exerted (Figs. 16-11 and 16-12). An upward pull is used to correct mash. A downward pull is used to correct sag. In Fig. 16-12, a jack has been placed under the rail at the cowl area. In addition, there is a tie-down at the front and another at the rear-door area. These are required to ensure that, when the pull is exerted, the rail will be bent downward to the straightened position.

If heavy force is required, always use steel plates between the jack and chains and the frame. The plates spread the force away from the center point. This prevents the rail from being crushed at that point.

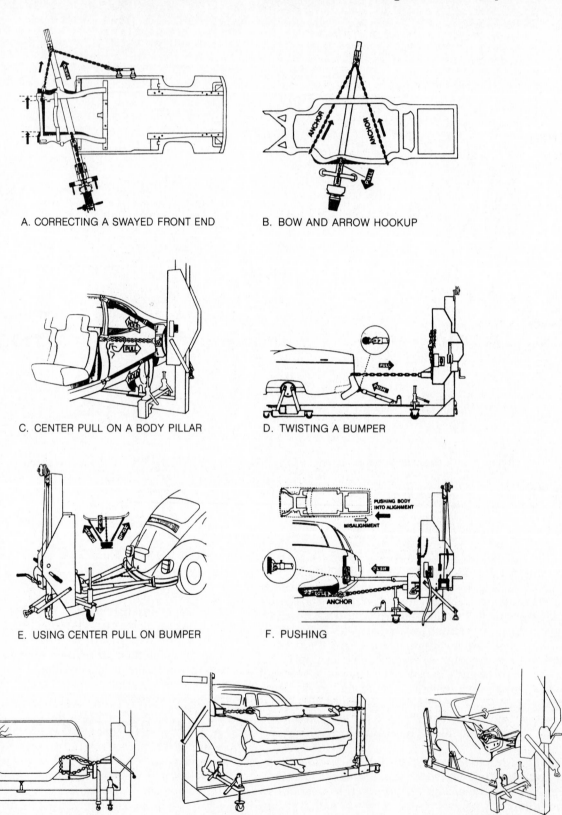

A. CORRECTING A SWAYED FRONT END

B. BOW AND ARROW HOOKUP

C. CENTER PULL ON A BODY PILLAR

D. TWISTING A BUMPER

E. USING CENTER PULL ON BUMPER

F. PUSHING

G. STRAIGHTENING A CROSSMEMBER

H. TRUNK LID REPAIR

I. STRETCHING A PANEL

Fig. 16-7 Variety of hookups for pulling, pushing, and twisting. *(Guy Chart Tools Limited)*

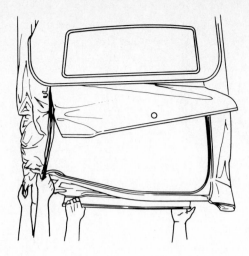

Fig. 16-8 The hydraulic equipment gives you, in effect, strong hands to pull on the metal wherever you wish. *(Applied Power, Inc.)*

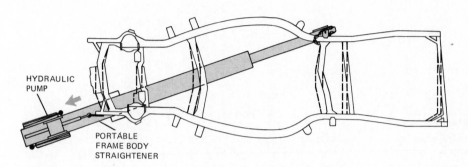

HYDRAULIC PUMP

PORTABLE FRAME BODY STRAIGHTENER

Fig. 16-9 Setup to correct diamond misalignment of frame. *(Applied Power, Inc.)*

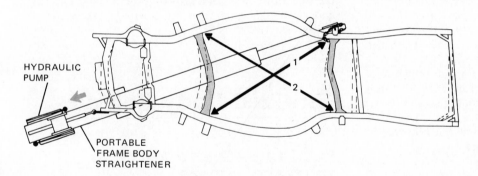

HYDRAULIC PUMP

PORTABLE FRAME BODY STRAIGHTENER

Fig. 16-10 The impact that produced the diamond misalignment caused measurement 2 to become greater than measurement 1. When the two measurements are the same, the misalignment has been corrected. *(Applied Power, Inc.)*

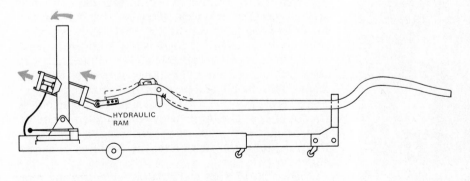

HYDRAULIC RAM

Fig. 16-11 Pull to correct mash. *(Applied Power, Inc.)*

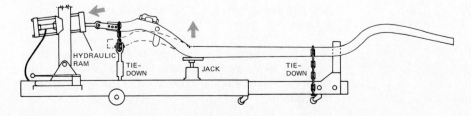

HYDRAULIC RAM

TIE-DOWN

JACK

TIE-DOWN

Fig. 16-12 Pull to correct sidesway. *(Applied Power, Inc.)*

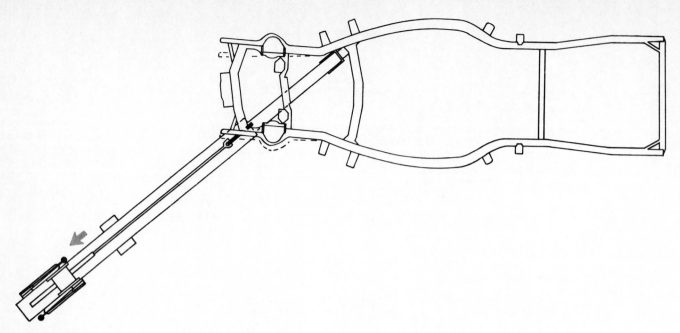

Fig. 16-13 Hookup on car with frame to correct sidesway. *(Applied Power, Inc.)*

≡ 16-10 CORRECTING SIDESWAY

Once diamond, sag, and mash misalignments have been corrected, sidesway should be eliminated. Figure 16-13 shows the setup to correct sidesway on a vehicle with a full frame. Note that the sidesway has affected the front part of the frame clear back to the cowl area.

The three centering gauges should be in place, as shown in Fig. 15-17. Sidesway is corrected when the three gauges line up.

During a relatively minor front impact, only one of the front horns may be bent. In this case, the pull should be made against this horn alone to straighten it. Figure 16-14 shows pull being exerted on the right front horn. The rod stuck through holes in the horn is to prevent the chain from slipping back.

Fig. 16-14 Pulling on the right frame horn to straighten it.

≡ 16-11 CORRECTING TWIST

If a frame has been twisted (shown exaggerated in Fig. 16-15), an untwisting force must be applied. In the setup shown in Fig. 16-15, two jacks are used to force the two frame rails back into alignment. The centering gauges should be installed (Fig. 15-17). The condition is corrected when they line up.

Unitized-Body Vehicles

≡ 16-12 SAG AND MASH IN UNITIZED BODIES

For vehicles with unitized bodies, sag and mash are treated together. A typical setup to correct front-end mash and sag is shown in Fig. 16-16. Two separate pulls are being used and there is a jack under the cowl area. The rear end is tied down. One pull is high—at the wheelhousing panel. The other is low—on the stub frame. This double pull permits the frame and body to be pulled out together. Of the two pulls, the upper pull is the lead force. The upper body will usually have to be pulled out more than the lower structural members. At the same time, the jack under the cowl area removes sag.

Figure 16-17 shows the setup for correcting rear mash on a unitized body. Do not tie down the front when making this pull. To do so could cause the roof to crease.

NOTE: Padding for unitized-body pulls should be wood blocks. Wood provides greater protection for body rails and sills when placed between tie-downs and jacks.

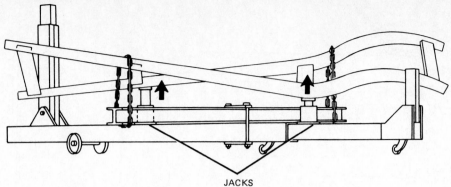

Fig. 16-15 Hookup to correct frame twist. *(Applied Power, Inc.)*

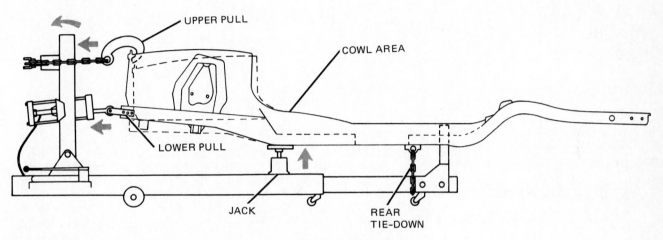

Fig. 16-16 Hookup to correct front-end mash and sag. *(Applied Power, Inc.)*

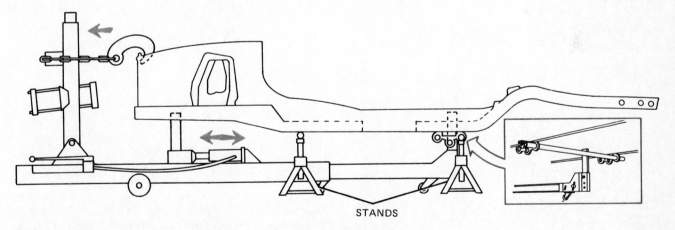

Fig. 16-17 Hookup on unitized body to correct rear mash. *(Applied Power, Inc.)*

≡ 16-13 UNITIZED-BODY SIDESWAY

To correct sidesway in a vehicle with unitized-body construction, an additional pulling force must be added to the wheelhousing panel (Figs. 16-18 and 16-19). Sidesway is corrected when the three centering gauges line up and also when the measurements at the wheelhousing panels are correct (Fig. 15-9).

Sidesway at the rear is corrected in the same manner as for sidesway at the front. Figure 16-20 shows a setup to correct sidesway at the rear of a unitized vehicle. Note that one pull is being exerted at the right rear quarter panel and a second pull is being exerted under the car.

≡ 16-14 UNITIZED-BODY TWIST

Figure 16-21 illustrates the setup for correcting unitized-body twist. The forces are applied to move the underbody and the body in the untwisting direction.

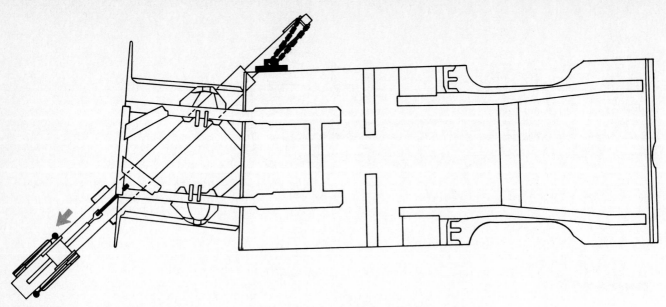

Fig. 16-18 Hookup on unitized body to correct sidesway. (*Applied Power, Inc.*)

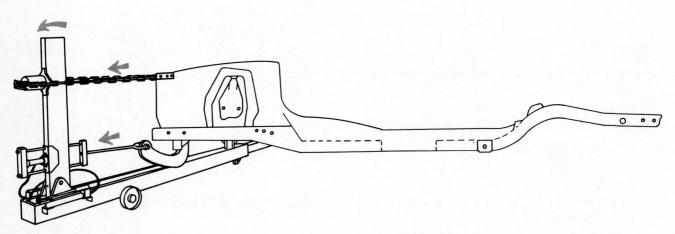

Fig. 16-19 Side view of hookup on unitized body to correct sidesway. (*Applied Power, Inc.*)

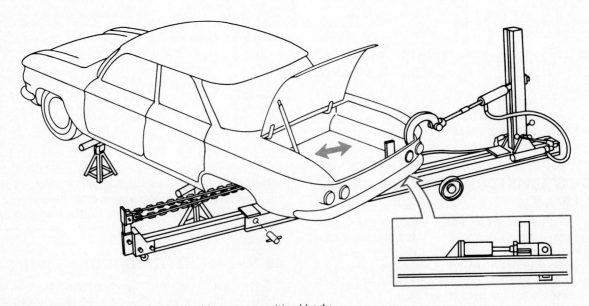

Fig. 16-20 Hookup to correct underbody sidesway on unitized body. (*Applied Power, Inc.*)

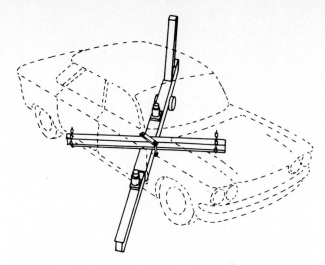

Fig. 16-21 Hookup to correct unitized-body twist. *(Applied Power, Inc.)*

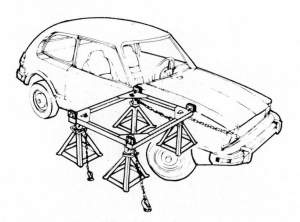

Fig. 16-22 Blackhawk Quadri-Clamp with a car mounted on it. The basic system uses a set of four clamps arranged in a rectangle. *(Applied Power, Inc.)*

≡ 16-15 QUADRI-CLAMP FOR UNITIZED BODIES

This system uses a set of four clamps arranged in a rectangle (Fig. 16-22). The supporting beams are adjustable to accommodate cars of various sizes. The clamps are connected to the pinch welds of the rocker panels as shown in Fig. 16-23. First, clean off any undercoat so the clamps can get a good hold. Make sure the clamps clear the small lips which are on some cars. Tighten the clamps to make sure they are firmly fastened and will not slip. Make sure the clamp teeth are pointed in the proper direction for any pull you make.

When making a pull, watch what is happening carefully to be sure that nothing tears or breaks. Observe the cautions listed in ≡16-3.

≡ 16-16 OVERCORRECTION

When pull is exerted on a frame or body member, the member is forced to move in the direction of the pull. When the pull is relaxed, the member will spring back slightly. Therefore, whenever you are pulling, you

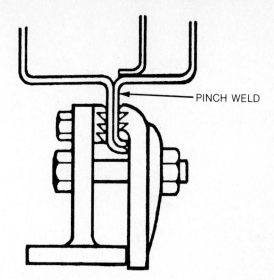

PINCH WELD

Fig. 16-23 Clamp shown in place on the pinch weld of a rocker panel.

should overcorrect slightly. Then when the springback occurs, the member will settle into its correct position.

The amount of overcorrection needed is learned from experience. If you don't pull enough, the springback will carry the member back too far. But if you pull too much, the member may be damaged or tear.

≡ 16-17 UPPER-BODY PULLS

Figures 16-24 and 16-25 show upper-body pulls. In Fig. 16-24, the pull is being made at the door post. In Fig. 16-25, the pull is being made at the front of the roof panel. Figure 16-26 shows a portable straightener set up to hold in two places and pull in a third to straighten a door post.

≡ 16-18 USING HEAT AND THE HAMMER

Frame buckles, if not too severe, can be pulled out. To assist the straightening operation, some heat may be applied to the buckled part with a gas torch. Be sure to remove—or move to one side—all fuel and air-conditioning lines so they will not be heated. A fuel line heated by the torch could break. Then the spilled fuel could start a fire. An air-conditioner line or component, if overheated, could burst, releasing refrigerant. The refrigerant, expanding as it is released, could freeze anything it touches—your hands, face, eyes. Also, the refrigerant, in the presence of an open flame, turns into deadly, poisonous phosgene gas. So be cautious when working near fuel and air-conditioner lines.

Ford recommends that if heat is needed to straighten a frame member, the temperature of the metal should be kept below 1200°F [649°C]. Excessive heat can weaken the metal so that the member could fail later on the highway.

As the buckle is heated, further pull can be applied. The general rule is to pull the member slightly beyond proper alignment. It will tend to spring back when the pull is released.

169

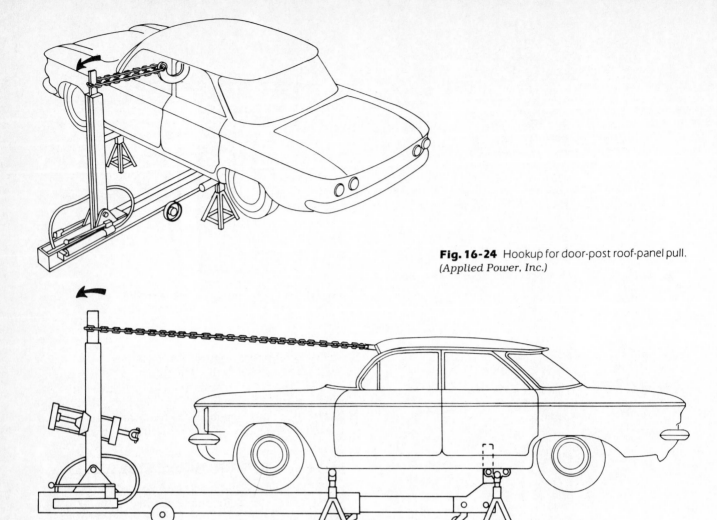

Fig. 16-24 Hookup for door-post roof-panel pull. *(Applied Power, Inc.)*

Fig. 16-25 Hookup for roof pull at front. *(Applied Power, Inc.)*

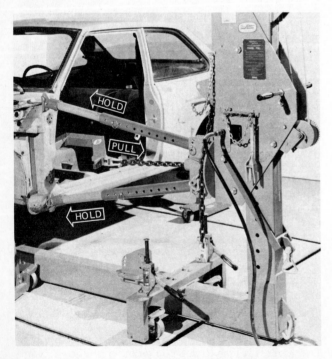

Fig. 16-26 Hookup for a portable straightener which holds in two places and pulls at a third. *(Guy Chart Tools Limited)*

Frame members that are badly buckled can sometimes be repaired by cutting out the buckle and welding in a good section. Otherwise, the frame member should be replaced.

Sheet metal is often tapped with a body hammer while it is being pulled (see ≡14-2). This helps release the set of the metal. One recommendation (by Bear) for low-carbon, soft steel is that while the pull is being exerted on the panel, tap around the buckle and continue to pull until a silver streak begins to appear in the heart of the buckle. Then apply heat from a neutral flame to heat the buckled area to a cherry red, at the same time continuing the pull. The neutral flame from a large welding tip is used so the heat is not concentrated in a small area. A larger area that includes the worst part of the buckle should be heated, and not a small spot.

NOTE: Many sheet-metal damages can be worked out with hammer, dolly, pry bar, pull rods, and other tools without heat. It is only the large buckles and sheet-metal damage that might require heat to work out.

Careful Heating of the panel applies to the heavier-gauge, low-carbon steel used on older cars. HSLA panels should be heated very carefully, if at all. Usually HSLA panels that cannot be straightened cold should be replaced.

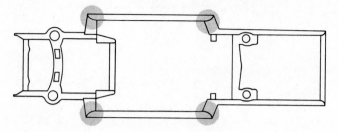

Fig. 16-27 Four anchor points on a car with a perimeter frame. *(Applied Power, Inc.)*

≡ 16-19 USING A TRACK-ANCHOR STRAIGHTENER

This type of straightener (Fig. 8-15) furnishes the anchor points for pulling and the anchor points to hold down the car frame or body. The anchors can be slid along the track into any position that will provide the desired pull or push. There are four anchor points for full-frame cars (Fig. 16-27). They are at the cowl and rear-door area. These are the four points at which holddown chains can be attached (Fig. 16-28).

In unitized-body cars, the four anchor points are at the ends of the rocker sills. These are the two sills that run along the two sides of the body. To secure or tie-down these two points, attach underbody clamps as shown in Figs. 16-20, 16-24, and 16-29. Figure 16-30 shows how to set up the equipment for pushing instead of pulling.

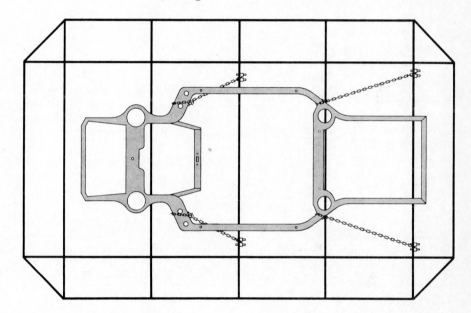

Fig. 16-28 Attachment points for holddown chains on a perimeter frame. *(Applied Power, Inc.)*

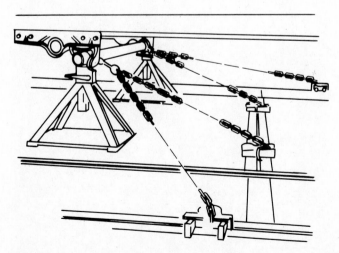

Fig. 16-29 Attachment of underbody clamps and cross tube to get the necessary holddowns on a unitized body. *(Applied Power, Inc.)*

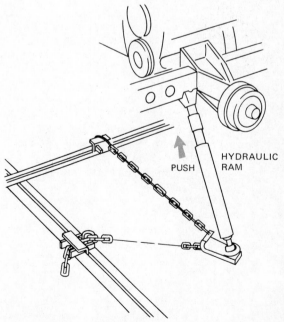

PUSH HYDRAULIC RAM

Fig. 16-30 Setup for making a push from underneath the car. *(Applied Power, Inc.)*

Figure 8-14 shows a car being straightened on a track-anchor straightener. The centerline gauges are in position so the technician can see the amount of straightening being done. When the pointers line up, *after the pull is relaxed*, the technician knows alignment has been achieved.

REVIEW QUESTIONS

Select the *one* correct, best, or most probable answer to each question. You can find the answers in the section indicated at the end of each question.

1. Body-and-frame straighteners are operated by   (≡16-2)
   a. hydraulic pressure
   b. vacuum
   c. air pressure
   d. hand power

2. The purpose of covering a pulling chain and clamp with a blanket is to   (≡16-3)
   a. prevent pulling heat from escaping
   b. keep the chain tight
   c. prevent the chain from whipping if it should let go
   d. keep your hands clean

3. Most attachments for pulling body and frame metal are
   a. plastic   (≡16-5)
   b. clamps and hooks
   c. solder plates
   d. brazed plates

4. For unitized bodies, sag and mash are   (≡16-12)
   a. not treated
   b. treated separately
   c. treated together
   d. none of the above

5. The Quadri-Clamp   (≡16-15)
   a. uses a set of four clamps
   b. is an adjustable rectangle
   c. can be used on cars of various sizes
   d. all of the above

6. Mechanic A says that the purpose of overcorrection is to compensate for springback. Mechanic B says it is to strengthen the metal. Who is right?   (≡16-16)
   a. mechanic A
   b. mechanic B
   c. both A and B
   d. neither A nor B

7. When using a clamp on a body part,   (≡16-3)
   a. remove undercoating where the clamp is to be attached
   b. make sure clamp teeth are sharp and clean
   c. be sure clamps and chain are in good condition
   d. all of the above

PART 4

BODY FILLER, FIBERGLASS, AND PLASTIC REPAIR

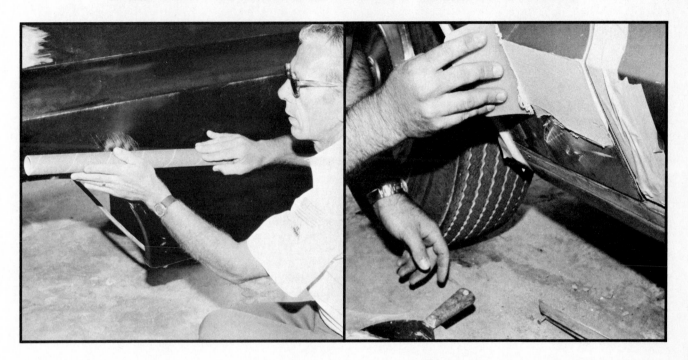

This part covers the preparation of body panels for filling with the application of body filler. The procedure of mixing and applying plastic body filler is described, and how the filler is then sanded in preparation for painting is explained. A chapter is included in this part on the use of fiberglass and the procedure for making fiberglass repairs. There is also a separate chapter on plastic repairs. There are three chapters in Part 4. They are:

Chapter 17   Using Plastic Body Fillers
Chapter 18   Fiberglass Repair
Chapter 19   Plastic Repair

CHAPTER 17
USING PLASTIC BODY FILLER

After studying this chapter, you should be able to:

1. Explain how to sand body filler.
2. Describe the zoom stick and its use.
3. Explain how to prepare body filler for priming.
4. Discuss the safety cautions to observe while using plastic body filler.
5. Describe how to prepare the panel surface for filling and how to mix and apply plastic body filler.
6. Explain how to finish plastic body filler.
7. Describe plastic-body-filler failures and their causes.

≡ 17-1 PREPARING TO USE PLASTIC BODY FILLER

Chapters 13 and 14 described the various methods of restoring damaged sheet-metal panels to an approximation of their original contours. The aim of the body technician is to bring the metal back, as nearly as possible, to its original shape. At the same time, the technician must keep the correction at the level of the original contour or slightly below. Various methods are used to accomplish this, including working on the original metal, patching the metal, and replacing complete body panels. This chapter describes how to prepare a sheet-metal panel for filling and then how to use plastic body filler to fill it.

≡ 17-2 PREPARING TO SAND PLASTIC BODY FILLER

After the body technician has straightened the damaged panel approximately to its original contour, the next steps are to check the fit of doors, hood, trunk lid, and sun roof. If everything fits properly, then clean the surface in preparation for sanding.

Checking and correcting the fit of doors, trunk lids, hoods, and sun roofs is covered in Parts 5 and 6. All of

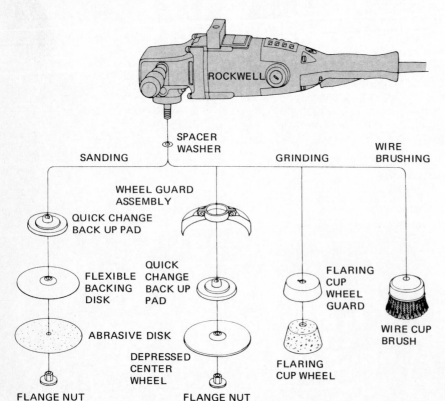

Fig. 17-1 Electric disk sander with attachments. *(Rockwell International Corporation)*

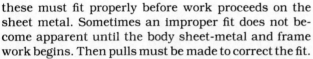

Fig. 17-2 Using a 9-inch [229-mm] disk sander. *(ATW)*

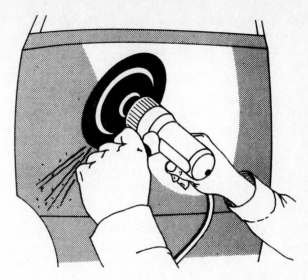

Fig. 17-3 Using a 7-inch [178-mm] disk sander. *(ATW)*

these must fit properly before work proceeds on the sheet metal. Sometimes an improper fit does not become apparent until the body sheet-metal and frame work begins. Then pulls must be made to correct the fit.

All such corrections must be made, as described elsewhere in the book, before sanding and filling. The area to be sanded should then be cleaned with a shop cloth and wax-and-silicone remover to remove all grease and wax. These can clog the sanding disk and prevent its cutting properly.

≡ 17-3 USING THE DISK SANDER

Disk sanders are electric (≡6-4) or air (≡7-9). Both types are made for 7-inch [178-mm] disks and for 9-inch [229-mm] disks. Figure 17-1 shows how to set up a 9-inch [229-mm] electric disk sander for sanding, grinding, and wire brushing. For sanding, the backup pad, backing disk, and abrasive disk are required.

To start sanding, the body technician selects a sander and disk of the correct size and grit for the job. To sand large areas, use a 9-inch [229-mm] disk (Fig. 17-2) of the correct size and grit for the job. For smaller areas, use a 7-inch [178-mm] disk (Fig. 17-3).

The grit selected depends on the preference of the technician. Some might use a 24-grit open-coat disk. Others might select a 16-grit open-coat disk. The coarser the grit, the deeper the scratches in the metal. The scratches are not harmful if they are in the area where filling is to be done. However, if the scratches are at the edge of the area, where there is good painted metal, they will have to be removed as the repair is blended into the surrounding good paint.

Figure 17-4 shows the right and wrong ways of applying the rotating disk to the metal surface. The disk should be tipped, or applied at a slight angle, so that most of the face will be on the metal surface. If only the tip is applied, it may cut through the metal. The sander should be moved back and forth in long, sweeping strokes that overlap. Do not hold the sander in one place or you will burn the metal. Do not move the sander in circles. When you do this, some spots (where the circles overlap) will be sanded more than others.

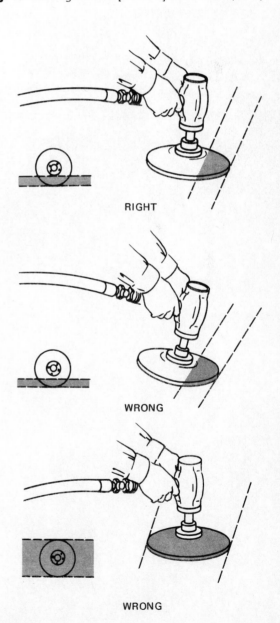

RIGHT

WRONG

WRONG

Fig. 17-4 Right and wrong ways to apply the rotating disk to the metal.

NOTE: Many body shops have a disk cutter. This device trims a worn 9-inch [229-mm] disk into a usable disk of smaller diameter.

≡ 17-4 SANDING SMALLER SPOTS

You will often have relatively small spots to sand. For example, the technician had to apply a patch to the lower front edge of the right quarter panel shown in Fig. 17-5. The technician used a 7-inch [178-mm] disk (shown in Fig. 17-5) to sand the patch and the surrounding metal. The results are shown in Fig. 17-6. How to apply plastic body filler to this patch is described later.

≡ 17-5 OCTAGONAL DISKS

The round disks cannot get into contoured surfaces with reverse curves. There are two ways of getting into

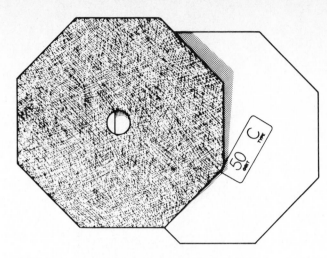

Fig. 17-7 An octagonal (eight-sided) disk.

Fig. 17-5 Sanding the patch and surrounding area with a disk sander.

Fig. 17-6 Sanding completed, in readiness for filling.

these curved surfaces: with an octagonal (eight-sided) disk and with an abrasive tube (≡17-6). The octagonal disk (Fig. 17-7) can work into reverse curves. The points are flexible and will bend to conform to the curves. Many body shops cut old, discarded round 9-inch [229-mm] disks to an octagonal shape.

≡ 17-6 ABRASIVE TUBE

Another way to sand reverse curves is to use an abrasive tube, or "zoom stick" (Fig. 17-8). This is a cardboard tube with a sheet of abrasive paper glued to it. The tube will fit into most curved areas. Working the tube back and forth will remove paint and metal to prepare the surface for filling. The abrasive tube is also used to shape body filler after it has hardened.

To handle a greater variety of sanding jobs, the tube is available in several different grits. A typical abrasive tube has a 1½-inch [38-mm] diameter and an 18-inch [457-mm] width. It can be cut to length and crimped to fit into any radius. Like any other abrasive paper, the tube is discarded when worn out.

Sandpaper applied by hand is also used in hard-to-get-at areas. Instead of an abrasive tube, some body technicians wrap sandpaper around a piece of old radiator hose to work into curved areas. Another way of getting into difficult areas is to use a wire-cup brush attached to the disk sander (lower right in Fig. 17-1).

≡ 17-7 USING THE RECIPROCATING SANDER

The reciprocating sander or air file (Fig. 7-10), moves a strip of abrasive paper back and forth. To finish the preparation of the panel for filling, a strip of 40-grit open-coat abrasive paper is put into the sander. The sander is then used to rough up the edges of the paint, featheredging into the paint. This provides a rough surface for plastic body filler. It will adhere to a rough surface much better than to a smooth surface.

≡ 17-8 TYPES OF BODY FILLER

There are several different types and grades of body plastic filler. They vary in the materials used to make them. Some have fiberglass in them. Others have alu-

176

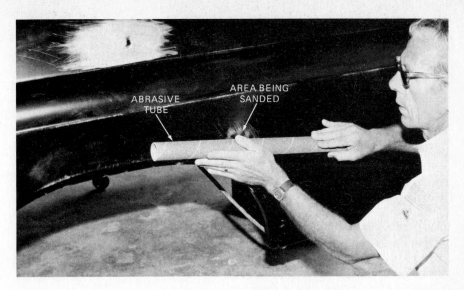

Fig. 17-8 Sanding a reverse curve with an abrasive tube.

minum or steel. These are claimed to provide added strength to the plastic when it is applied and hardens.

Plastic body filler is supplied in two parts (Fig. 17-9). These are the base material and the catalyst, or hardener. In the standard commercial grade of plastic body filler used in auto body shops, the base material usually is a mixture of about 50 percent powdered talc and 50 percent polyester resin, which is a thick, syrupy liquid. After mixing, this base material is packaged in cans of quart, half-gallon, and gallon sizes. The gallon can is used in most body shops. The catalyst, or hardener, may be either a liquid or a cream.

Figure 17-9 shows a tube of cream hardener on top of a gallon can of base material (plastic body filler). When the correct amount of catalyst is mixed with the base material, the plastic sets up, or hardens, in a few minutes. Then it can be filed and sanded in preparation for painting.

NOTE: Plastic and fiberglass repair procedures are not the same. Plastic body filler is a paste that is mixed with a cream or liquid hardener. The fiberglass comes in mats or cloth. It requires the use of a

liquid resin material and a hardener. Fiberglass is used primarily to repair fiberglass panels.

≡ 17-9 SAFETY CAUTION FOR PLASTIC BODY FILLER

When handling plastic body filler, try not to get it on your hands. It can dry the hands. But it can also be absorbed through the skin. This could cause liver and other damage to your body. For this reason, a particle mask or respirator should be worn when filing and sanding plastic body filler. If you breathe the dust, it can cause lung trouble and liver damage. This applies especially to those body technicians who use plastic filler every day. Occasional exposure will normally cause little harm. However, day-after-day use could cause the material to accumulate in the body and result in serious illness. To be safe, always wear a dust mask or respirator when sanding plastic body filler.

≡ 17-10 WHERE PLASTIC BODY FILLER CAN AND CANNOT BE USED

Because plastic body filler is so easy to use, some technicians try to use it in places where it will not survive. The plastic material should be applied to relatively rough, but clean, metal surfaces. It should not be applied in thick coats to fill deep creases or dents. Nor should it be applied out to the edge of a panel. (Lead should be used here.) When plastic body filler is used to build up an edge, it can soon break off or be knocked off. Here are the "dos and don'ts" about using plastic body filler:

1. It can be used to bring panels back to their original contour after they have been roughed out. Be careful not to leave any high spots in the metal, because these cannot be worked down after the plastic is applied.

2. It can be used to fill seams left when sheet metal has been repaired by welding or brazing, or where new sheet metal has been riveted, welded, or brazed on the panel.

3. It cannot be used satisfactorily to fill out to the edge of a panel. If it extends to the edge, moisture can

Fig. 17-9 Can of plastic body filler and a tube of cream hardener.

work up under the edge between the metal and plastic, and the plastic will fall off. Also, bumping the edge can break off the plastic.

4. It should not be used to fill depressions deeper than about ¼ inch [6 mm]. Thicker fills can crack and break off.

5. The metal surface must be worked up to its final shape before the plastic filler is applied. After the filler is on and has hardened, no further work on the metal should be done. This would knock off the plastic. Plastic body filler is not like body solder. After soldering, you can do some additional work to drive down high spots, for example, and then do further soldering on the panel.

6. Any flexing of the panel can cause the plastic filler to crack and fail. Plastic is not flexible like body solder. The plastic filler is rigid when it sets up.

≡ 17-11 PREPARING THE SURFACE FOR FILLING

When all panels are close to contour and everything fits, the surface to be filled must be cleaned. Wash the vehicle with detergent and water to remove dirt and water-soluble contaminants. Then rinse with water.

Now clean the surface to be filled with a wax-and-silicone remover (*not* solvent from the shop parts cleaner). This will remove dust, dirt, oil, grease, and fingerprints. If the surface is not cleaned before sanding begins, the contaminants could stick to the sanding disk and smear onto bare metal. A loss of adhesion could result that, after painting, would allow the new paint to flake off. Then sand or grind the surface to be filled down to bare metal.

Clean the surface again, using a prefinishing cleaner, or solvent. Then sand with a 24-grit open-coat disk. Follow this by featheredging the edges of the bare metal into the paint. (Featheredging is described later.) Use a reciprocating sander (air file) with 40-grit paper for this job. When you are finished, the surface preparation is complete. The surface is now ready for the application of plastic body filler.

≡ 17-12 MIXING PLASTIC BODY FILLER

Before mixing up a batch of plastic body filler, carefully read the safety cautions on the hardener and the instructions on the can (Fig. 17-10). Only a small amount of hardener is needed. If too much hardener is used, the filler will set up (harden) before you can apply it. If too little hardener is used, the filler sets up too slowly. Then you will have to wait a long time before the filler surface can be smoothed and sanded in preparation for painting.

The amount of hardener to use is proportionate to the amount of body filler used. For example, Fig. 17-9 shows a tube of cream hardener and a can of plastic body filler. If you were preparing to use the entire can of filler, you would add the entire tube of hardener. If you planned to use only half the can of body filler, then you would add half the tube of hardener. However, many jobs require only a small amount of body filler. To an amount the size of a golf ball, squeeze a 2-inch [51-mm] ribbon of cream hardener from the tube.

Easy-To-Use Directions

Sand area to be repaired, using approximately 16 or 24 grit paper. Area must be clean, free of paint, oil, moisture. Do NOT wipe with oil or solvent-soaked rag. Place required amount of Plastic Body Filler on clean, hard surface. Using spatula or putty knife, mix in Creme Hardener: ¼ teaspoon for golf ball–size lump or 1 oz to every 3 lbs. Mix thoroughly and quickly. If Filler hardens too quickly, use less Hardener.

"Wipe" thin coat of mixed Plastic Body Filler on area to be repaired, assuring good bond, and then fill entire dent or hole with filler.

Mixed as directed, Plastic Body Filler will harden in approximately 10 minutes. For quicker hardening, add a little extra Hardener while mixing.

Never return mixed Filler to can: keep can closed and in a cool place. Under 85°F (29°C).

Caution:

Vapors harmful. Do not take internally. If taken internally, induce vomiting. Consult a physician. Wash hands after use and before smoking or eating. Keep away from heat and open flame. Use only with adequate ventilation. Avoid prolonged breathing of vapor. Avoid prolonged or repeated contact with skin. In case of contact, flush skin or eyes with plenty of water. **KEEP OUT OF REACH OF CHILDREN.**

Fig. 17-10 *Directions on a can of plastic body filler.*

You will learn from experience how much hardener to use. On a cold day, the plastic body filler is slower to set up. More hardener should be used. On a hot day, the plastic body filler hardens faster. So use less hardener. Always follow the instructions on the can (Fig. 17-10).

Here are the things to look out for:

1. On your first jobs, use less hardener rather than more. This will give you more time to work the body filler onto the prepared surface.

2. Never mix more body filler than you can apply in a few minutes. Properly mixed body filler sets up in about 30 minutes or less. However, after about 10 minutes it becomes harder to apply and work.

3. Never return *any* mixed body filler to the container. The catalyst will contaminate the base material and cause it to harden.

4. Mix the ingredients on a clean sheet of safety glass or sheet metal (Fig. 17-11). A piece of cardboard can be used in an emergency, but safety glass or sheet metal is easier to use.

5. The base material is white. The hardener is colored. The purpose of this color difference is to ensure thorough mixing. Mixing should continue until the mix has a uniform color throughout.

6. Use a wide-bladed putty knife to mix the two ingredients. Make sure the putty knife and mixing board or glass are clean.

7. Mix the two ingredients by scooping the mixture up from the bottom and turning the putty knife over to press down on the mixture. Continue to mix until the

Fig. 17-11 Mixing plastic body filler and hardener. (ATW)

mixture is smooth and creamy and has a uniform color throughout.

8. Do not whip the material. This will create air bubbles which would cause trouble later.

9. Always thoroughly clean the putty knife and mixing sheet after each use. Any old body filler remaining on these will put crumbs in your next mix.

≡ 17-13 APPLYING PLASTIC BODY FILLER

Apply the body filler immediately after it is mixed. Use a wide-bladed putty knife, a rubber squeegee, or a plastic spreader or applicator (Fig. 17-12). The squeegee, being soft, is sometimes preferred because it can follow the contours of the surface more easily. Apply a thin coat of filler on the area to be filled. Then apply more filler with even strokes all in one direction. When applied with moderate force, this helps remove air bubbles from the filler. After hardening, trapped air bubbles show up as pinholes that have to be filled.

NOTE: Notice the masking tape on the rear edge of the door. The purpose of the tape is to protect the edge of the door from the plastic body filler and final sanding of the filler. These could harm the paint on the door.

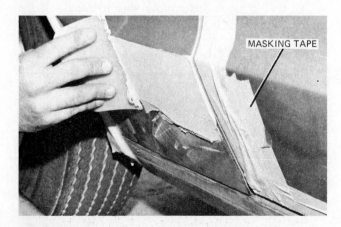

Fig. 17-12 Applying plastic body filler over the patched area.

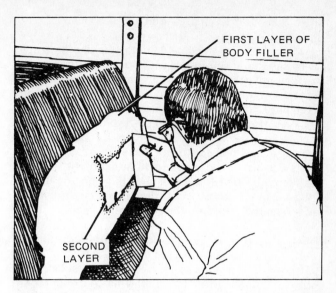

Fig. 17-13 Applying a second coat of plastic body filler over the first coat.

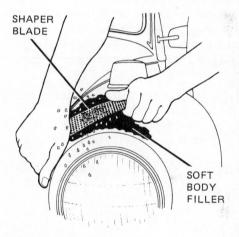

Fig. 17-14 Using a body-filler shaper blade ("cheese grater") before the filler has hardened.

Repeat the application until the filler is slightly higher than the surrounding surface. This buildup of filler provides the material to be removed during sanding. However, try to make the final surface of the filler as smooth as possible. If there is a crease or gouge to fill, the filler must be applied in layers (Fig. 17-13).

When the filler is hard enough to resist scratching with your fingernail, the filler has set up. Now you can sand and featheredge the patch into the desired contour and finish (≡17-14).

≡ 17-14 SHAPING AND FINISHING PLASTIC BODY FILLER

Some technicians use a body-filler shaper blade ("cheese grater") for rough shaping before the filler is fully cured and hard (Fig. 17-14). This removes excess material and brings the filled surface down to near the final contour. The blade is often used without a file holder by flexing the blade slightly, as shown in Fig. 17-14. Move the blade very lightly over the soft body filler. You do not want to take off too much material or to gouge the surface.

Many body technicians do not use a cheese grater. They say that if they apply the body filler properly, the surface will not need this preliminary smoothing. They let the sanding operation that follows take care of any irregularities in the filler surface.

After the plastic body filler has hardened, some technicians use a rotary grinder with a 50-grit open-coat disk on the filled surface. This smooths the rough spots and brings the surface nearly to contour. Then an air file with 40-grit paper is used (Fig. 17-15). This is followed by 80-grit paper to bring the surface to contour and to featheredge into the surrounding paint.

NOTE: These grits are the recommendations of some technicians. Other technicians may use paper with different grades of coarseness. The selection of abrasive-paper grades is often a matter of personal preference.

In the paint shop, the final smoothing is done with a fine grade of sandpaper (360 or 400 grit). The final surface preparation and application of primer and paint are covered in later chapters.

Fig. 17-15 Finish-sanding the filled area with a reciprocating sander, or air file.

── CAUTION ──

The catalyst, or hardener, used when mixing plastic body filler is poisonous (toxic). It is also irritating to the skin and eyes. Technicians working daily with plastic body filler should wear rubber gloves to protect their hands. Dust from sanding plastic body filler is dangerous to breathe. Wear a particle mask or respirator while sanding. The area in which plastic body filler is sanded should be cleaned daily with a vacuum cleaner. Other safety cautions for working with plastic body filler are covered in ≡17-9.

≡ 17-15 CAUSES OF PLASTIC-BODY-FILLER FAILURE

Plastic body filler can fail for many different reasons. These include:

1. Failing to properly prepare the metal surface. Oil, wax, or traces of paint on the metal surface will prevent proper adhesion. Therefore, the plastic body filler will fail by breaking, or by flaking off.

2. Applying the plastic body filler too thickly. Generally, ¼ inch [6 mm] is about the thickest layer that should be applied to a panel.

3. Trying to fill over large holes or tears in the metal. Small holes, such as those left in by pulling out a crease with pull rods, can be filled. But plastic body filler will not bridge over larger holes or tears satisfactorily. It will soon crack or chip away. These holes should be closed by welding.

4. Trying to cover up rusted spots. Good adhesion will not occur unless the metal is clean. Rusted spots should be patched.

5. Trying to build up the edge of a panel with plastic body filler, such as the bottom edge of a door. Water from under the edge of the door will work up between the body filler and metal. This causes the plastic body filler to fail. In addition, the door edge is vulnerable to bumps. Any bump can crack or break off body filler. When applying plastic body filler, featheredge out to the edge of the panel. But the layer of body filler must stop before it reaches the edge.

6. If filling to the edge of a panel, use lead.

── REVIEW QUESTIONS ──

Select the *one* correct, best, or most probable answer to each question. You can find the answers in the section indicated at the end of each question.

1. Plastic body filler can fail if   (≡17-16)
   a. the metal surface has not been properly prepared
   b. the body filler has been applied too thickly
   c. you try to cover rusted spots
   d. all of the above

2. After the damaged panel has been straightened to about its original contour, the next step is to   (≡17-11)
   a. paint the panel
   b. prime the panel
   c. clean the panel
   d. apply plastic body filler

3. The sanding disk should be applied (≡17-3)
   a. at right angles to the metal
   b. flat against the metal
   c. at a slight angle to the metal
   d. with fast reciprocating motion

4. The octagonal disk is used on (≡17-6)
   a. surfaces with reverse curves
   b. surfaces with positive curves
   c. flat surfaces
   d. the back sides of panels

5. To sand large areas with the disk sander, you would use
   a. a 7-inch [178-mm] disk (≡17-3)
   b. an octagonal disk
   c. a 9-inch [229-mm] disk
   d. a square disk

6. The area to be sanded should be cleaned of grease and wax because they (≡17-3)
   a. would make the disk cut too rapidly
   b. could clog the sanding disk
   c. would overheat the metal
   d. would crack the plastic body filler

7. To get into reverse curves for sanding, use
   a. a body file (≡17-5 and 17-6)
   b. a body spoon
   c. an abrasive tube or an octagonal disk
   d. a belt sander

8. When using plastic body filler, (≡17-9)
   a. keep it off your hands
   b. do not breathe the sanding dust
   c. wear a dust mask or respirator while sanding
   d. all of the above

9. Mechanic A says that if you are careful, you can fill a panel out to its edge with plastic body filler. Mechanic B says body filler at the edge will fall off or get knocked off. Who is right? (≡17-10)
   a. mechanic A
   b. mechanic B
   c. both A and B
   d. neither A nor B

10. If you must fill to the edge of a panel, you should
   a. use lead (≡17-15)
   b. use plastic body filler
   c. use fiberglass
   d. use the arc welder

CHAPTER 18
FIBERGLASS REPAIR

After studying this chapter, you should be able to:

1. Describe the construction of fiberglass parts.

2. Name the fiberglass repair materials and explain how to use them.

3. Discuss safety cautions for mixing and using resin.

4. Explain how to repair a damaged fiberglass panel.

≡ 18-1 MAKING FIBERGLASS REPAIRS

This chapter describes the repair of fiberglass body panels with fiberglass. *Fiberglass* is a synthetic (manufactured) fiber, or thread, made from glass. Usually, we think of glass as a rigid pane that forms the transparent part of a window, or as a drinking glass. When someone mentions glass, we think of how easily it can break. However, if molten glass is squeezed into threads, the threads become very flexible and strong (for their size).

≡ 18-2 CONSTRUCTION OF FIBERGLASS PARTS

When fiberglass thread is woven into cloth or made into a mat, the glass fibers form a strong, flexible material that can be used to make fiberglass panels or fiberglass car bodies (Fig. 18-1). The Chevrolet Corvette (Fig.

18-1) entered production in 1953. It was the first mass-produced car to have a fiberglass body. Today, fiberglass bodies are used on many limited-production vehicles, such as racing cars, sports cars, dune buggies, and recreational vehicles.

The way these bodies and other parts are made is very similar to the way you will use fiberglass to patch plastic and fiberglass panels. The fiberglass material is laid in a mold which has the desired shape. Then resin with hardener is applied to the fiberglass. When this has set up (the setting process is also called *curing*, *drying*, or *hardening*), the panel is taken out of the mold.

Now the new part is ready for finishing. Actually, the procedure is a little more complicated. The general idea is that fiberglass can be shaped as desired and then set permanently in that shape by the addition of the resin hardener. However, the fiberglass cannot be removed from the mold until the new part has set up. This means that manufacturing fiberglass parts is a

Fig. 18-1 Fiberglass body panels have been used on the Chevrolet Corvette since production began in 1953. *(Chevrolet Motor Division of General Motors Corporation)*

HOOD

FIBERGLASS INSULATION

Fig. 18-2 Fiberglass insulation used under the hood to reduce engine noise.

very slow, expensive, labor-intensive process. When it is advantageous not to make a part of metal, plastic (not fiberglass) parts often can be made reasonably at a fairly high rate of production. Plastic parts and their repair are described in Chapter 19.

≡ 18-3 CHARACTERISTICS OF FIBERGLASS BODIES

Body panels made of fiberglass have several advantages. They are very strong, highly resistant to fire and corrosion, and waterproof. When damaged by an impact, the damage does not spread over a large area as with sheet metal. Instead, the damage is usually confined to the immediate area of the impact. In severe impacts, sheet-metal parts crumple. However, similar fiberglass parts crack and tear badly. To repair severely torn fiberglass, the technician cuts off the damaged area and installs a new section. Fiberglass panels usually are easy to repair.

For the automobile manufacturer, the major disadvantage of fiberglass as a body material is that making a body panel of this material is a slow process. With sheet metal, the parts are stamped out, sometimes hundreds an hour. They are then welded together quickly to form the body shell. With fiberglass, however, the fiberglass matting or cloth is laid in the mold, the resin with hardener is applied, and the material is left until cured. This is the reason why only a few specialty low-production cars, such as the Chevrolet Corvette, have all-fiberglass bodies. However, many body parts such as hoods, deck lids, and quarter-panel extensions on high-production cars now are made of fiberglass. Also, fiberglass insulation is used under the hood of many cars to reduce engine noise (Fig. 18-2).

≡ 18-4 FIBERGLASS REPAIR MATERIALS

The basic materials to make fiberglass repairs can be obtained in kits. These kits include a can of fiberglass resin (also called *polyester resin*), a small tube or can of hardener, and fiberglass mat or fiberglass cloth (Figs. 18-3 and 18-4). In a shop where extensive fiberglass repair is performed, the materials are purchased in larger quantities.

Fiberglass mat (Fig. 18-4) is a blanket of randomly arranged glass fibers. It is comparatively thick, and used when a rapid buildup of material is needed to speed the job. The fiberglass mat is very pliable when

RESIN   HARDENER

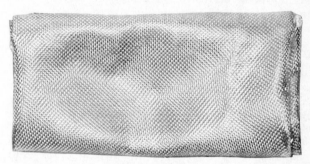

FIBERGLASS CLOTH

Fig. 18-3 Materials required to make a fiberglass repair.

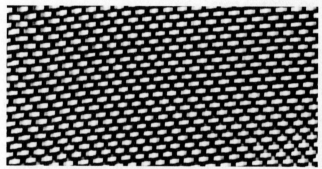

A. FIBERGLASS CLOTH

B. FIBERGLASS MAT

Fig. 18-4 Difference in texture between fiberglass mat and fiberglass cloth.

saturated with resin. This makes it ideal for repairing compound curves.

Fiberglass cloth (Fig. 18-4) is made from continuous glass fibers woven on regular textile machinery. It is much stronger than fiberglass mat and is used where the most strength and least thickness are required.

The resin and hardener are mixed just before the job is to be completed. The fiberglass mat or cloth is saturated with the mixture. Then the mat or cloth is applied to repair the previously prepared surface. These procedures are described in following sections.

≡ 18-5 WORKING SAFELY WITH FIBERGLASS

Always wear a respirator and goggles when grinding or sanding fiberglass to avoid breathing the dust or getting it in your eyes. The resin and fiberglass dust can irritate your skin, and breathing it is a health hazard. To avoid skin rashes or other skin problems, wear rubber gloves or use a commercial protective skin cream before starting a fiberglass repair job. Your sleeves should be rolled down. Your neck should be covered by buttoning your shirt to protect your skin from the dust. After working with resin materials and fiberglass, wash your hands.

NOTE: The proper way to apply the protective skin cream is to work it into your cuticles, under and around your fingernails, between your fingers, and around your wrists. Then add a second coat. Hold your hands under cold running water for a few seconds to set the cream.

≡ 18-6 THE FIBERGLASS REPAIR PROCEDURE

In the repair process, the purpose of the fiberglass cloth or mat is to provide a strong reinforcement across the damaged area. The resin is a liquid that has little strength. However, when applied to the fiberglass cloth, the resin acts to bind the strands of glass together. Then, when the resin dries, the repaired area is ready for sanding.

But getting the resin to dry can be a problem. Applied by itself, the resin might not dry for days. This is too long a time for practical purposes. The solution to the problem is the liquid hardener. When a few drops of hardener are added to the resin, curing time may be reduced to as little as 30 minutes.

Curing is a heat process brought about by mixing the hardener and resin. This causes a chemical action. As a result of the chemical action, the resin gets hot and largely dries itself. You can actually feel this heat with your hand. To aid in the drying and to reduce drying time even more, heat lamps can be turned on to warm the patched area. On very cold days, drying takes longer. Because the chemical action creates heat all through the fiberglass, it all is dry at the same time. When the outside surface of the fiberglass is hard, it is hard all the way through.

≡ 18-7 REPAIRING A FIBERGLASS PANEL

The extent of damage determines the repair procedure. If the damage is only a scratch, it may be repaired by

hand-sanding and then painting. Deeper scratches or dents require a fiberglass buildup using fiberglass cloth. If a panel is cracked or fractured (has lost some pieces), the repair procedure varies. A different procedure is used if the panel is accessible from underneath. These procedures are described in following sections.

≡ 18-8 REPAIRING MINOR SCRATCHES

A *minor scratch* is a scratch that extends through the paint, but makes little entry into the fiberglass. Some types of plastic body filler (Chap. 17) can be used to repair minor damage to a fiberglass panel. A fiberglass-reinforced body filler is widely used. It is mixed with a hardener, applied, shaped, and finished in the same way as other plastic body filler (Chap. 17). However, the fiberglass-reinforced body filler is claimed to be twice as strong as regular body filler.

To repair a minor scratch, first clean the surface with a wax-and-silicone remover. Then hand-sand the scratch with 400-grit sandpaper. Do not sand too deeply or you will have to build up the surface with body filler before painting it.

Featheredge out to the undamaged paint. Clean the surface with a tack rag. (A *tack rag* is a cheesecloth pad that has been soaked with a sticky, nondrying varnish.) It will pick up any lint or dust remaining on the surface. Then mask off the area and paint it, using the recommended refinishing system. Chapters 31 to 37 cover painting and refinishing.

≡ 18-9 REPAIRING DEEPER SCRATCHES AND PITS

Deep scratches and pits that have penetrated the fiberglass can also be repaired with body filler. However, be sure that the label on the body-filler container states that it is recommended for use on fiberglass. To start the repair procedure, clean the surface with a wax-and-silicone remover.

1. Put on your respirator and goggles, and protect your neck, arms, and hands (≡18-5). Use sandpaper or a grinder to remove the paint from around the damaged area.

2. If the sandpaper or grinder does not remove the paint from pits, use a cup-type wire brush (Fig. 5-43) to remove the paint. If the wire brush cannot remove all the paint, use a reamer to cut out the painted surface.

3. Rough-sand the area. Wipe the area with a tack cloth.

4. Mix the body filler and hardener, following the directions on the containers (≡18-12). Apply the body filler with a putty knife or squeegee. Build up the surface slightly higher than the final contour. After the filler sets up, sand it down to contour (≡17-14). Then finish-sand, clean, mask, and paint the area (Chaps. 31 to 37).

≡ 18-10 REPAIRING CRACKED PANELS

A cracked panel is broken, split completely through. In fiberglass, even small cracks should be repaired. Without repair, they will grow (lengthen) into large cracks.

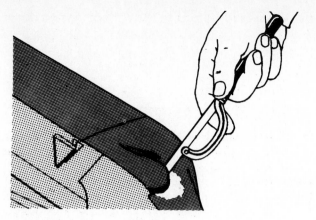

Fig. 18-5 *Using a hacksaw blade to enlarge the crack. (ATW)*

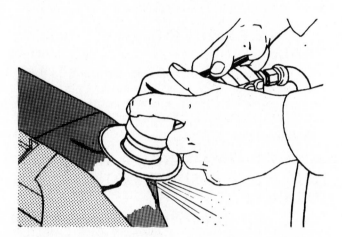

Fig. 18-6 *Sanding off paint around the crack. (ATW)*

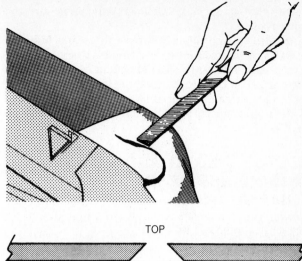

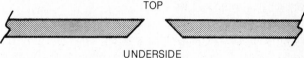

TOP

UNDERSIDE

Fig. 18-7 *Filing a taper in the crack. (ATW)*

There are two procedures for repairing cracks in fiberglass. One is used if the panel is accessible from underneath. The other is used if the panel cannot be worked from underneath.

≡ 18-11 REPAIRING CRACK ACCESSIBLE FROM UNDERNEATH

This and the following section explain how to repair a crack that is accessible from underneath. How to repair a cracked panel that is not accessible from underneath is described in ≡18-13.

When the area is accessible from underneath, first clean the area outside and underside with a wax-and-silicone remover. Protect your hands, arms, and neck. Put on your respirator and goggles (≡18-5).

1. Use a hacksaw blade or a power hacksaw to saw away the rough edges (Fig. 18-5). This should leave a gap of about ⅛ inch [3 mm]. Use a grinder to remove the paint around the crack (Fig. 18-6).

2. Use a file to file down the edges to form an inverted V, tapering out from the top to the underside (Fig. 18-7). Mask the area around the crack with nonstaining masking tape to protect the good paint from the resin. If necessary, use C-clamps to align the two sides of the break. They must be in exact alignment.

3. Cut two strips of fiberglass cloth large enough to overlap the crack by about 2 inches [51 mm]. If clamps

have been used, cut smaller strips to cover these areas after the clamps have been removed.

4. Clean the repair area with a dry tack cloth. Protect your hands with hand cream or rubber gloves (≡18-5). Mix the fiberglass resin and hardener, carefully following the instructions on the containers (≡18-12).

5. Spread a piece of cellophane or polyethylene film (clear plastic warp) on a flat surface. Lay a strip of fiberglass cloth on the film. Thoroughly saturate the fiberglass cloth with the mixture of hardener and resin (Fig. 18-8). Apply the cloth on the underside of the crack. Repeat with the second strip.

6. Use a heat lamp to speed up drying time. However, do not let the temperature exceed 200°F [93.6°C]. Higher temperature can cause vapor bubbles to form under the patch. The surface layers will set up too fast. Then, when the bottom layers begin to harden and release vapor, bubbles will form. This will require that the area be worked over again.

7. After the patch has set up, remove any clamps that were used. Fix and apply the small strips on any

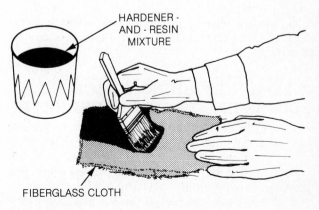

HARDENER - AND - RESIN MIXTURE

FIBERGLASS CLOTH

Fig. 18-8 *Preparing fiberglass cloth for installation by applying the hardener-and-resin mixture to it. (ATW)*

marks left by the clamps, following the procedure outlined above.

8. Fill in and slightly build up the top of the V groove, and surrounding area, using fiberglass-reinforced body filler. After the filler has hardened, sand the surface to the proper contour. Inspect the surface for imperfections. Repair any that are found.

9. Clean, mask, and refinish the area (Chaps. 31 to 37).

≡ 18-12 MIXING AND USING FIBERGLASS RESIN

Always follow the instructions on the containers when mixing fiberglass resin and hardener. In addition, the following should be observed:

1. Make sure the cup in which you mix the resin and hardener is clean. Use a clean spatula or putty knife to mix the resin and hardener. Make sure they are mixed thoroughly.

2. Never mix any more resin and hardener than you can use in a few minutes.

3. Never return unused resin-hardener mix to the resin can. You will ruin the resin in the can.

4. When using fiberglass and resin, wear rubber gloves. The hardener-resin mixture is toxic (poisonous). It can be absorbed through the skin and can cause liver damage.

5. Work out all air bubbles as you apply the layers of resin-saturated fiberglass. Any bubble will show up later and can ruin an otherwise good job.

6. Make sure that the fiberglass layers are completely saturated with the resin-hardener mixture. One way to do this is to lay the fiberglass patch on cellophane or polyethylene film (clear plastic wrap). Then pour on or brush on the resin. Be sure the fiberglass is thoroughly soaked with the resin. Then pick up the patch and lay it face down across the prepared surface. Brush on additional resin to make sure the exposed side of the fiberglass is covered. Work out all air bubbles with a putty knife.

7. Put the brush and other tools in lacquer thinner to remove the resin remaining on them. If the resin hardens, it is difficult to get off and the brush will be ruined.

8. Make sure the area you are working in is well ventilated. In addition, wear a respirator. The vapor is toxic.

9. Always wear a respirator and safety goggles while sanding the finished patch. Fiberglass dust is also toxic.

≡ 18-13 REPAIRING CRACK NOT ACCESSIBLE FROM UNDERNEATH

If a cracked panel is accessible only from the outside surface, a different fiberglass repair procedure is required. First, clean the damaged area with wax-and-silicone remover. Then cut away all ragged edges and sand off the paint for about 3 inches [76 mm] from the edge of the crack. Scuff-sand the surface around the damage so the resin will bond well.

─ **CAUTION** ─────────

Put on a respirator and safety goggles before beginning any fiberglass repair. Also, protect your hands, arms, and neck from fiberglass dust (≡18-5).

────────────────

Clean the area with a tack cloth. Mask the area around the crack with masking tape to protect the paint from the resin. Cut several pieces of fiberglass cloth large enough to overlap the crack about 2 inches [51 mm] on all sides. Saturate the strips with the mixture of resin and hardener (≡18-11). Then apply the strips to the prepared area. After the patch has set up, sand the repaired area down to the proper contour. Then clean, mask, and refinish the area (Chaps. 31 to 37).

≡ 18-14 REPAIRING FRACTURED PANEL

A *fractured panel* is a panel that has a hole in it because a piece has been knocked out. If the panel is accessible from underneath, one procedure is used. If the panel is not accessible from underneath, a different procedure is required.

≡ 18-15 REPAIRING FRACTURED PANEL ACCESSIBLE FROM UNDERNEATH

Protect your hands, arms, and neck. Put on your respirator and safety goggles. Cut away all edges. Clean the outside and underside with wax-and-silicone remover. Sand or grind off the paint for about 3 inches [76 mm] from the edges of the fracture. File the edges to a tapered V. The taper should be from the inside to the outside if the underside is accessible (Fig. 18-7).

Wipe the area with a clean tack cloth. Protect the adjacent areas with masking tape and masking paper. Cut several pieces of fiberglass cloth, each large enough to overlap the fractured area about 2 inches [51 mm] on all sides.

Cut a piece of cardboard the same size. Lay it on top of the fracture. Drill enough holes through the cardboard and the panel so that the patch can be secured with sheet-metal screws when it is applied (Fig. 18-9).

Lay the cardboard on a flat surface and place a sheet of clear plastic wrap on top of the cardboard. Put the pieces of fiberglass cloth, a layer at a time, on the plastic wrap. Then saturate each layer of fiberglass cloth with resin-hardener mixture (≡18-11).

Brush a coat of resin-hardener mixture over the damaged area (underneath). Then position the patch, with the plastic wrap and cardboard, on the underside of the panel with the fiberglass cloth next to the panel. The cloth should overlap about 2 inches [51 mm] on all sides. Align the holes bored in the cardboard and panel. Secure the patch to the panel with No. 6 or 8 sheet-metal screws. Brush wax on the screws before inserting them. This permits easy removal.

Brush more resin-hardener mixture over the patched area. After the patch has cured, remove the

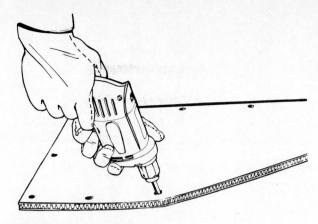

Fig. 18-9 Drilling holes through the cardboard and the damaged panel. These holes will be used to attach the patch with rivets or screws. *(Ford Motor Company)*

screws, the cardboard, and the plastic wrap. Grind away any loose strands of fiberglass from the edge of the cloth.

Counterbore the screw holes to a 45° angle (Fig. 18-10). Fill the screw holes and low spots in the cloth patch with body filler (Chap. 17). After it dries, grind to contour, clean with a tack cloth, and refinish (Chaps. 31 to 37).

≡ 18-16 REPAIRING FRACTURED PANEL NOT ACCESSIBLE FROM UNDERNEATH

The same basic repair procedure should be followed as outlined for repairing a panel from underneath (≡18-15). However, you have to work from the top or outside surface. First, cut away enough material in the

Fig. 18-10 Counterboring the screw holes to a 45° angle. *(ATW)*

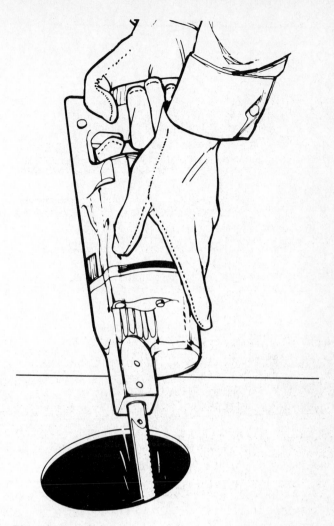

Fig. 18-11 Using a power hacksaw to cut out the damaged area of a panel. *(ATW)*

damaged area to allow working space for the buildup of fiberglass patching strips. Cut a hole large enough (Fig. 18-11). If it is too small, the patch will not lay below the original body surface.

Then file a wide taper around the edge of the hole (Fig. 18-12). This taper provides the bonding surface for the patch. Now follow the instructions given in ≡18-11 for preparing resin-soaked fiberglass-cloth strips. Lay the strips one at a time over the hole (Figs. 18-13 and 18-14). Continue the buildup until the center of the patch is above the original contour of the panel (Fig. 18-14). As each strip is applied, its center is pressed down to get a secure bond with the underlayers.

After the patch is cured, it should be ground down to the original contour (Fig. 18-15). Then the area should be refinished as required.

≡ 18-17 REPLACING PANEL SECTION

If a panel is so badly damaged that it cannot be repaired by any method outlined above, the damaged area or complete panel must be replaced. In either case, a replacement panel must be obtained.

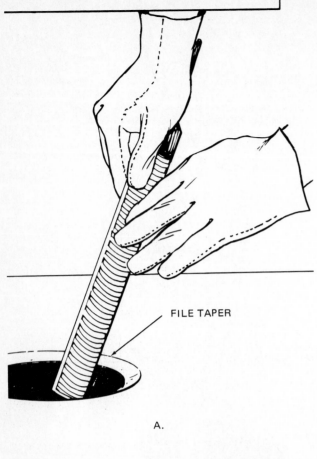

FILE TAPER

A.

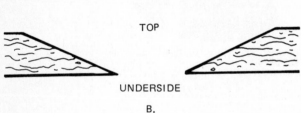

TOP

UNDERSIDE

B.

Fig. 18-12 Filing a taper around the edge of the hole. *(ATW)*

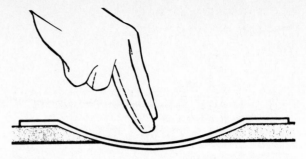

Fig. 18-13 Applying the first layer of resin-soaked fiberglass cloth. *(ATW)*

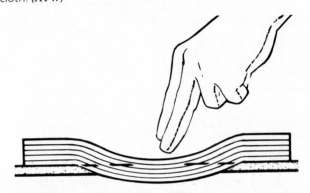

Fig. 18-14 Continue applying the layers until the center of the patch is above the original contour of the panel. *(ATW)*

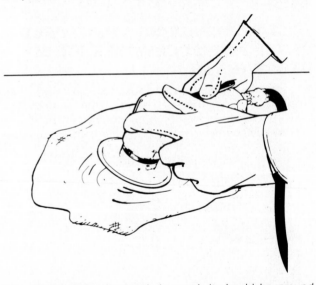

Fig. 18-15 After the patch is cured, it should be ground down to the original contour. *(ATW)*

FENDER FLARES

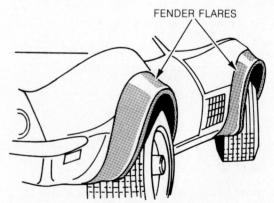

Fig. 18-16 Fender flares for front and rear fenders. *(ATW)*

Sometimes the fragments that have been broken out can be used to make a repair. The fragments can be patched together and then restored to the panel, using the procedures outlined previously in the chapter.

If repair is not possible, the damaged area of the original panel must be cut away and the rough edges smoothed at an angle. The replacement panel must be cut to obtain a piece that will restore the damaged panel to its original contour. The edges of the replacement part should be smoothed at an angle to match the angle on the original panel. Then, using C-clamps and the procedures outlined earlier in the chapter, the replacement panel can be secured to the original.

≡ 18-18 INSTALLING FENDER FLARES

To give a car or truck a more sporty look, and allow the use of wider tires, some owners install plastic or fiberglass fender flares (Fig. 18-16). On some vehicles, the flares can be bolted on.

☰ 18-19 REPAIRING PLASTIC PANEL WITH FIBERGLASS

Figure 18-17 shows the steps in a general procedure that can be used to patch a hard plastic (or fiberglass) panel. The crack is shown before any work is done on it in Fig. 18-17A. At B, the crack has been widened and smoothed. Then the top edges are beveled, as shown in C. Next, if the underside of the crack is accessible, the inner edges of the crack are beveled, as shown at D.

Cut the strips of fiberglass cloth, three for the underside and three for the top surface. One recommendation is to cut the strips for each side slightly larger than the one below it, as shown at Fig. 18-17E.

Mix the resin-hardener mixture, and apply it to each strip as described earlier. Work out all air bubbles as each layer is applied. After the patch is dry, sand down the top patch until there is a slight depression, as shown in F. Then apply body filler, until the patch area is slightly higher than the desired contour, as shown in G. After the filler has hardened, sand it to contour, as at H. Now the surface is ready for refinishing as required.

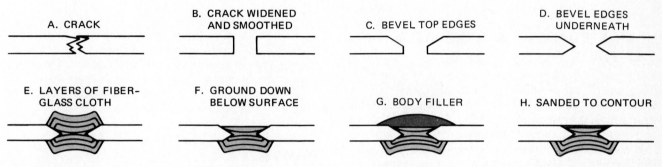

Fig. 18-17 Steps in repairing a plastic panel with fiberglass.

—— REVIEW QUESTIONS ——

Select the *one* correct, best, or most probable answer to each question. You can find the answers in the section indicated at the end of each question.

1. Fiberglass cloth can be used to repair fiberglass panels and   (☰18-19)
   a. hard plastic panels
   b. cracked windshields
   c. trim
   d. frames and sills

2. To speed up the drying time of a fiberglass patch,
   a. add more resin   (☰18-11)
   b. keep the patch moist
   c. apply heat
   d. use less resin

3. Fiberglass cloth is made of   (☰18-2)
   a. ground glass
   b. sheet glass
   c. resin
   d. glass threads

4. A fiberglass repair kit includes   (☰18-4)
   a. fiberglass cloth or mat
   b. fiberglass resin
   c. hardener
   d. all of the above

5. The purpose of the hardener is to   (☰18-6)
   a. produce a glossy finish
   b. shorten the curing time
   c. keep the patch cool
   d. require heat lamps

6. Precautions to observe when working with fiberglass and resin to make repairs include   (☰18-5)
   a. wear rubber gloves or use protective skin cream to protect your hands
   b. cover your arms and neck
   c. wear safety goggles and respirator
   d. all of the above

7. No air bubbles should remain in the patch because they
   a. can slow the curing process   (☰18-12)
   b. ruin the job
   c. overspeed the curing process
   d. prevent normal curing

8. The purpose of the resin is to   (☰18-6)
   a. provide strength
   b. prevent overheating
   c. bind the fiberglass threads together
   d. speed up the drying process

9. The type of repair procedure required depends on the
   a. material in the damaged panel   (☰18-7)
   b. amount of damage
   c. type of vehicle
   d. temperature in the shop

10. To saturate the fiberglass cloth before applying it to the damaged area, place the strip on   (☰18-11)
    a. clear plastic wrap
    b. a piece of laminated safety glass
    c. a flat piece of sheet metal
    d. none of the above

CHAPTER 19
PLASTIC REPAIR

After studying this chapter, you should be able to:

1. Explain the differences between thermoplastic and thermosetting materials.

2. Explain how to identify plastic parts and their type.

3. Describe the procedures for repairing soft plastic parts.

4. Discuss hot-air plastic welding and explain how it is done.

≡ 19-1 PLASTIC AUTOMOTIVE PARTS

Many parts of the automobile are made of plastic. In fact, nearly 100 percent of the car interior is made of some type of plastic. Industry predictions are that in future cars, even more body and underhood parts will be plastic. One important advantage of plastic parts is that they are lighter than the steel parts they replace. This results in a lighter car with better fuel economy.

Like fiberglass (Chap. 18), plastics are synthetic (manufactured) materials. Many of the plastics used in automobiles today are made from petroleum.

≡ 19-2 TYPES OF RESIN

Resins are natural or synthetic compounds. Their normal state varies from thick fluids and gums to solids. Various resins are mixed with fillers, plasticizers (softening agents), and other materials to make the group of materials known as "plastics."

There are many types of resins, but two are widely used for automotive plastics. These are (1) thermoplastic resin and (2) thermosetting resin. The word "thermo" means of or pertaining to heat. "Plastic" means soft and pliable. "To set" means to harden. Now, let's take another look at the names of the two types of resins.

"Thermoplastic" means heat softens. A thermoplastic resin is a material that softens when heat is applied to it. This occurs every time you heat it. Resins that are thermosetting have different characteristics. "Thermosetting" means heat hardens. Therefore, thermosetting resins are materials that harden the first time that heat is applied. Then, if heat is applied a second time, the thermosetting material is destroyed.

This is why the body technician must correctly identify the type of plastic being worked on. For example, if a piece of vinyl from a vinyl top is heated, the vinyl becomes soft and pliable. It is a thermoplastic resin, or a material that softens when heated. In fact, heat can be applied to vinyl many times to soften it without damaging it. This is a characteristic of thermoplastic resin.

Fiberglass (Chap. 18) is a thermosetting material. To cure fiberglass, it is heated one time, usually from the chemical release of internal heat aided by heat lamps. This heat cures and hardens the resin. Should you apply high heat to fiberglass a second time, it does not soften or melt. Instead, the material is ruined. These two examples point out the importance of knowing the type of plastic you are working on. Using the wrong servicing procedure can ruin the part instead of repairing it. Also, the type of plastic determines the proper refinishing procedure to use.

≡ 19-3 IDENTIFYING PLASTIC PARTS

Figure 19-1 shows the exterior parts on one model of car which are made of plastic. It is difficult for even the most experienced body technician to be certain which plastic is used for each part.

The first step in repairing a plastic part is to find out of which plastic the part is made. There are three general types of plastics used for interior car parts. These are ABS plastic (the initials of the compound *acrylonitrile-butadiene-styrene*), polypropylene plastic, and vinyl plastic. Polypropylene parts are hard, and vinyl parts are soft. However, the problem of identification arises because of the wide use of ABS. This plastic has several forms, and both hard parts and soft parts are made of it.

Here are two simple tests that will help you identify the type of plastic you are about to repair.

≡ 19-4 IDENTIFYING POLYPROPYLENE AND ABS

From a hidden back-side portion of the plastic part, remove a sliver of the material with a sharp knife. Hold the sliver with tweezers and ignite it with a match (Fig. 19-2). Watch the burning plastic closely. Polypropylene burns with no readily visible smoke. ABS burns with a readily visible black smoke residue that hangs temporarily in the air.

≡ 19-5 IDENTIFYING VINYL

Heat a copper wire in the flame of a propane torch until the wire glows and turns red. Then touch the heated wire to the back side or hidden surface of the material being tested. Some of the material must stick on the wire.

Return the wire with the material on it to the flame (Fig. 19-2C). Look for a green-turquoise-blue flame. If the flame is in this color range, the material is vinyl.

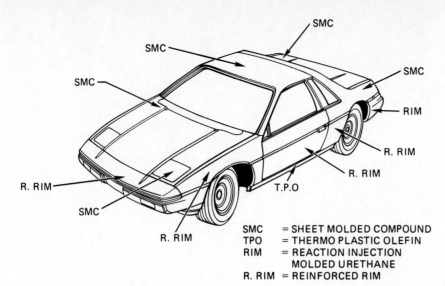

SMC = SHEET MOLDED COMPOUND
TPO = THERMO PLASTIC OLEFIN
RIM = REACTION INJECTION
        MOLDED URETHANE
R. RIM = REINFORCED RIM

Fig. 19-1 Exterior body panels made of various types of plastic. *(Pontiac Motor Division of General Motors Corporation)*

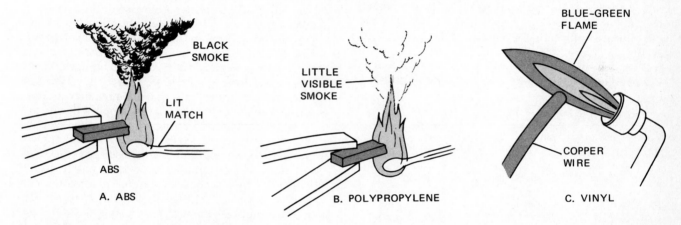

Fig. 19-2 Flame test to identify the various types of plastic. *(Ditzler Automotive Finishes Division of PPG Industries, Inc.)*

≡ 19-6 PLASTIC REPAIR PROCEDURES

Hard parts made of ABS, nylon, Lexan, Noryl, and fiberglass can be repaired with fiberglass. Follow the fiberglass repair procedures outlined in Chap. 18.

Soft parts made of ABS/vinyl, and vinyl tops and interior trim, can be repaired with vinyl patching kits. This procedure is covered in Chap. 29. Other soft plastic materials can be repaired after backing with aluminum auto-body-repair tape. Then the damaged area is filled with 3M Flexible Parts Repair Material, 3M Structural Adhesive, or another similar product. Follow the instructions on the containers for surface preparation, mixing, and curing time.

Repairs to thermoplastic materials can be made with hot-air plastic welding. This is covered in a later section.

≡ 19-7 REPAIRING FLEXIBLE PLASTIC PARTS

Flexible plastic parts are being used more and more on the exterior of automobile bodies (Fig. 19-1). Typical examples include front- and rear-bumper filler panels or sight shields, valance and end panels, quarter-panel extensions, front- and rear-bumper upper and lower covers, and bumper center moldings.

Many of these plastic parts are replaced when they are damaged. However, a punctured, gouged, or torn plastic panel can be restored to its original appearance by following the procedure below. Figure 19-3 shows a punctured flexible plastic panel that we will repair.

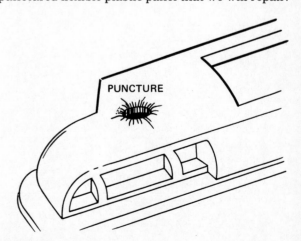

Fig. 19-3 A punctured flexible plastic panel that can be repaired. *(General Motors Corporation)*

Fig. 19-4 Grinding away the damaged material. *(General Motors Corporation)*

1. Clean the damaged area with a general-purpose adhesive cleaner and wax remover. If the damage is through the thickness of the part, clean both sides. Then grind away the damaged material with a 36-grit disk (Fig. 19-4). Featheredge the paint around the damage using a 180A-grit disk.

2. Lightly singe the repair area with a propane torch for approximately 15 seconds (Fig. 19-5). This will improve adhesion. Be careful not to burn the plastic!

3. Apply auto-body-repair tape (Fig. 19-6) or a new or used adhesive-back disk to the back side of the dam-

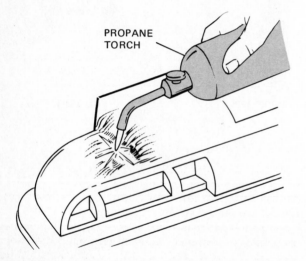

Fig. 19-5 To improve adhesion, lightly singe the repair area with a torch. *(General Motors Corporation)*

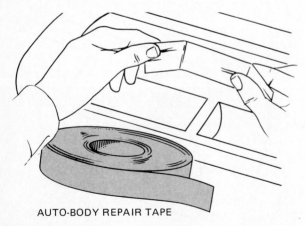

Fig. 19-6 Applying auto-body-repair tape to the back side of the damage. *(General Motors Corporation)*

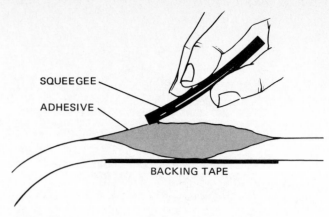

Fig. 19-7 Filling the damaged area with adhesive. *(General Motors Corporation)*

age. This will prevent the patch material from falling through. Clean the damaged surface.

4. Using 3M Structural Adhesive or an equivalent available from your supplier, mix the adhesive according to the instructions on the package. Use a putty knife or the stick enclosed in the package to thoroughly mix the two-part adhesive. To prevent air bubbles during mixing, the adhesive should be scraped together and spread thinly on the mixing board. Do not lift the adhesive from the mixing board. Always apply a downward force while mixing the two materials together.

5. Scrape the mixture from the board and apply a thin coat to the damaged area with a soft squeegee (Fig. 19-7). Heat for 15 minutes at approximately 180°F [82°C] with a heat lamp or heat gun. Temperature can be checked with an inexpensive cooking thermometer. Mix and apply a second coat of adhesive.

6. Sand the patch level with the surrounding area using a 240A-grit disk. Check for pinholes and low areas. If necessary, mix more adhesive and apply it to low areas.

7. Bake 15 minutes at 180°F [82°C]. Then sand, using a 320A-grit disk. Next, scuff-sand the entire panel with a 320-grit disk. Do this by hand or with a random orbital sander. Then refinish the repaired area.

≡ 19-8 HOT-AIR PLASTIC WELDING

Hot-air welding is a process that repairs damaged thermoplastics by fusing (melting) them together. (Thermoplastics soften when heat is applied.) The process uses a *hot-air welding torch* that electrically heats low-pressure compressed air. Figure 19-8 shows some of the shapes of available welding torches. Figure 19-9 shows the construction of one type of torch. In general, they use compressed air at 2 to 3½ psi [14 to 24 kPa] and a 115-volt heating element in the 300- to 500-watt range. The air is heated to between 400 and 750°F [204 and 399°C]. This is hot enough to partially melt thermoplastic materials.

There is some variation in the construction of hot-air torches, as shown in Fig. 19-8. Follow the manufacturer's operating instructions. In operation, the barrel of the torch gets hot enough to burn you. Be careful not to touch it. Also, the low volume of hot air from the torch can burn you if the hot air is directed against the skin

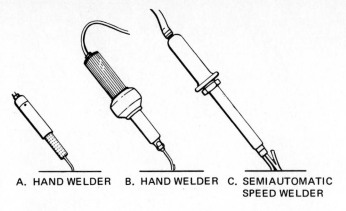

A. HAND WELDER B. HAND WELDER C. SEMIAUTOMATIC
SPEED WELDER

Fig. 19-8 *Various types of hot-air welding torches. (General Motors Corporation)*

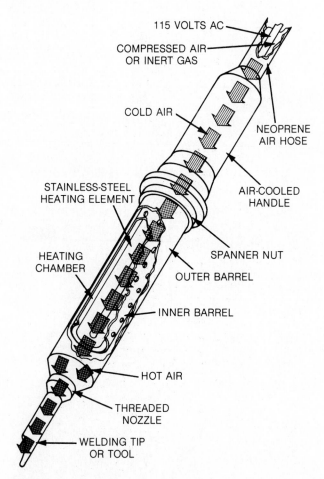

Fig. 19-9 *Heating element and hot-air flow through one type of hot-air welding torch. (Kamweld Products Company, Inc.)*

long enough. However, accidental fanning of the torch-heated air over your hands produces a warm sensation with adequate warning to move the torch or your hand.

The torch is used with a plastic "welding rod" made from the same material as the plastic being repaired. By using a welding rod of the same material, the strength, hardness, and flexibility of the repair is the same as those of the original part. You can make your own welding rod from scrap material of the same type being repaired or from the underside of the piece you are repairing. However, the material may be stressed and may

not produce a good weld. Various types of plastic welding rods may be obtained from your local plastics suppliers.

≡ 19-9 THE PLASTIC WELDING PROCEDURE

Good plastic welding requires the following:

    1. Correct welding-rod material and shape
    2. Correct temperature
    3. Correct force
    4. Correct angle between the welding rod and the part being welded
    5. Correct speed

In the welding of thermoplastics, the material is fused together by the application of heat and force. In hand welding, this is achieved by heating the rod and base material at the same time and pushing on the rod to get proper force. Too much force stretches and distorts the weld. Too much heat will char, melt, or distort the material. Too little heat or force results in poor welds.

Here is the repair sequence for hot-air plastic welding:

    1. Prepare the damaged area.
    2. Align the damaged area.
    3. Weld.
    4. Cool.
    5. Sand. If pinholes or low spots are present, bevel the edges of the problem area and add another bead of weld. Then resand.
    6. Paint.

≡ 19-10 PREPARING THE DAMAGED AREA

The tear or break should be trimmed to a V shape with a knife or by sanding. As in metal welding, this provides a surface to heat and a space to fill with softened rod. Types of welds for plastics using round welding rods are shown in Fig. 19-10. Figure 19-11 compares welds made with round and triangular rods. Use of the triangular rod reduces the number of passes necessary to complete the weld.

Some tears can be heat-welded by melting the material along the crack. However, this usually does not provide complete bonding or excess material to sand off for a smooth finish. Wipe any dust or shavings from the joint with a clean, dry rag. Solvents should not be used for cleaning damaged plastics. On plastics, solvents tend to soften the edges and cause poor welds.

≡ 19-11 OPERATING THE HOT-AIR WELDING TORCH

This torch requires a source of clean compressed air. The compressed air always must be flowing before the torch is plugged into an electric outlet.

To start the torch, turn on the compressed air. Adjust the air pressure to approximately 2 ½ psi [17 kPa]. The pressure needed depends on the type of plastic to be welded. The higher the air pressure, the lower the welding temperature. Conversely, the lower the air pressure, the higher the welding temperature.

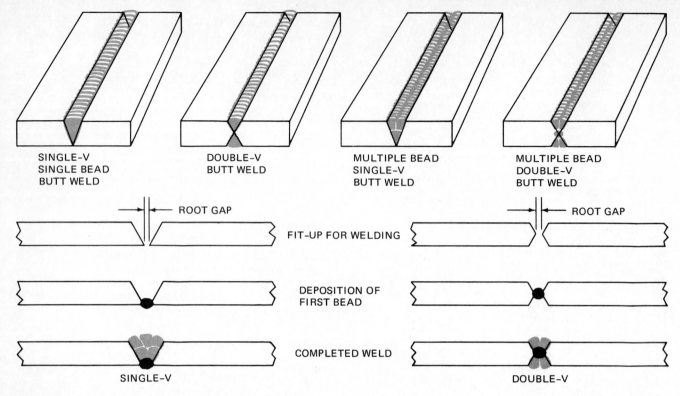

Fig. 19-10 Various types of welds for plastic. *(General Motors Corporation)*

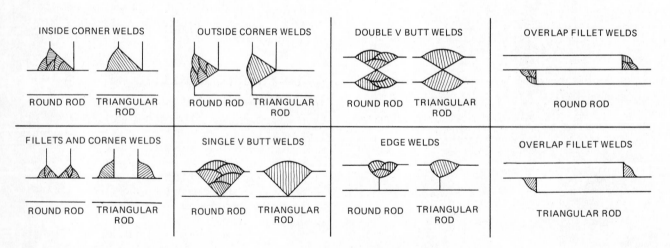

Fig. 19-11 Various types of welds made with round rod and with triangular rod. To complete the weld, several passes must be made with the round rod. *(Kamweld Products Company, Inc.)*

After the pressure is set and air is flowing, plug the torch into a 115-volt electric outlet. Allow the torch to preheat for 5 to 10 minutes. Then check the hot-air temperature by holding a thermometer ¼ inch [6 mm] from the hot-air end of the torch. The temperature should be in the 400–750°F [204–399°C] range for most thermoplastics. Information supplied with the torch usually includes a chart of welding temperatures.

To shut off the torch, disconnect the electric plug. Be sure to continue the compressed-air flow for approximately 10 minutes after unplugging the electric cord. This cools the heating element in the torch before disconnecting the compressed air line.

≡ 19-12 WELDING PLASTIC PARTS

The edges to be joined should be aligned as necessary (Figs. 19-10 and 19-11). If a tear is long and you have difficulty getting a backing strip on it, tack-weld it (Fig. 19-12). Small tack welds can be made along the tear to hold the two sides in place while you are performing the finish weld.

To tack-weld plastic, hold the damaged area in its correct position. Use clamps and other fixtures, as necessary, to hold the pieces in position. With the torch, apply hot air to each side of the damage until some material from each side melts together.

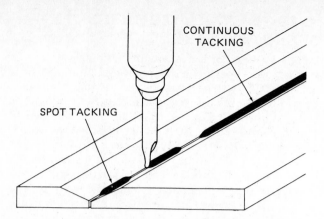

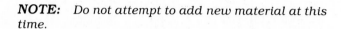

Fig. 19-12 Tack-welding with plastic rod. The tacks can be made in spots, or continuously. The purpose is to hold the two pieces together when the final welding starts. *(Kamweld Products Company, Inc.)*

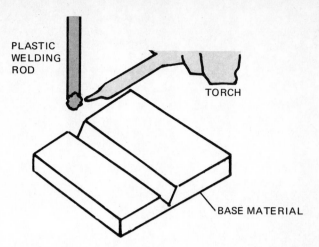

Fig. 19-13 Position of the torch and rod for plastic welding. *(General Motors Corporation)*

NOTE: *Do not attempt to add new material at this time.*

To start the weld, hold the torch ½ inch [13 mm] from the damaged area (Fig. 19-13). Hold the end of the welding rod at a 90° angle to the base material. The welding rod should be pointed straight up. The welding rod also should be ½ inch [13 mm] from the torch. Move the torch back and forth between the rod and the material, as shown in Fig. 19-14, to evenly preheat both until they are shiny and tacky. Now move the rod down to barely touch the base material. If the rod and the material have been preheated sufficiently, the rod will stick.

Continue moving the torch between the material and the rod. At the same time, press the rod directly into the weld area with a force of about 3 pounds [13 N]. When you can see molten plastic where the rod meets the base material, the rod will bend and begin to move forward.

NOTE: *Do not overheat the base material. It will char or melt.*

In welding, a good start is essential, because this is where most plastic weld failures begin. For this reason, starting points on multiple-bead welds should be staggered whenever possible.

Once the weld has been started, continue to fan the torch from rod to base material, as shown in Fig. 19-15. Because the base material has greater bulk, a greater amount of heat must be directed at it than at the rod. Experience will help you to develop the proper technique.

In the welding process, the rod will gradually be used up. This makes it necessary for you to renew your grip on the shortened rod. Unless this is done carefully, the release of force may cause the rod to lift away from the weld bead. This allows air to become trapped under the weld and results in a weak weld. To eliminate this problem, continuously apply force on the rod while repositioning your fingers on it. This can be done by applying force with the third and fourth fingers while moving the

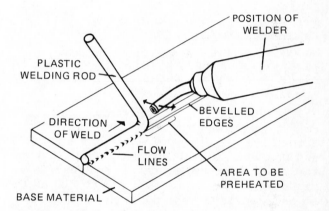

Fig. 19-14 The process of hot-air plastic welding. The hot air softens both the plastic welding rod and the beveled edges of the workpieces. *(Kamweld Products Company, Inc.)*

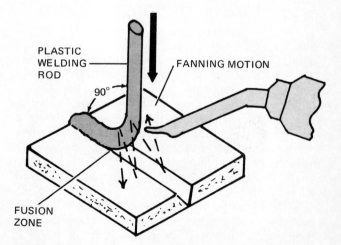

Fig. 19-15 The torch should be kept moving as shown, between the two workpieces that are to be joined and the plastic welding rod. *(General Motors Corporation)*

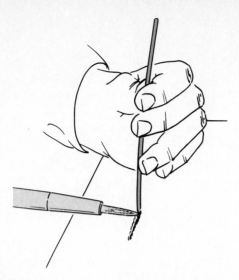

Fig. 19-16 While plastic welding, you must apply a steady force on the rod. *(General Motors Corporation)*

thumb and first finger up the rod. Another way is to hold the rod down into the weld with the third or fourth finger, while repositioning the thumb and first finger. This technique is shown in Fig. 19-16. The welding rod should be cool enough to do this, because only the bottom of the rod should be heated. However, always be careful in touching new welds or aiming the torch near your fingers.

≡ 19-13 COMPLETING THE WELD

When the weld is to be ended, stop the forward motion and direct the heat at the intersection of the rod and base material. Remove the torch and maintain downward force on the rod for several seconds. This allows the rod to cool and prevents the bead from being pulled out. After a few seconds, cut the extra rod from the weld with a knife.

A plastic weld does not develop full strength until completely cool. This takes 15 to 30 minutes unless compressed air or cold water is applied to speed the cooling process. Any attempt to test a weld by bending it before it has cooled may result in weld separation.

≡ 19-14 SMOOTHING THE WELD

First, remove any excess plastic with a sharp knife. The welded area then can be smoothed by grinding it with a coarse 36-grit disk of emery or sandpaper. A 9-inch [229-mm] disk on a 5000-rpm air-powered polisher will remove large weld beads.

The weld area will soften from the heat generated by grinding it. Be careful not to allow the welded plastic to overheat. During grinding, you should frequently apply water to the weld area to cool it. This will speed up your work and prevent damage to the weld.

After rough grinding, the weld should be checked visually for defects. Bending the part across the welded area should not produce any cracks. The weld should be as strong as the original material. Any pinholes, low spots, or cracks make the weld unacceptable.

Finish sanding the welded area using 220-grit sandpaper, followed by 320 grit. Use a belt or an orbital sander, plus hand sanding as required.

≡ 19-15 SEMIAUTOMATIC SPEED WELDING

Figure 19-17 shows a semiautomatic speed-welding torch. It has a special tip that allows you to control heat and pressure with one hand while the rod is fed automatically. The rod is preheated as it passes through the tube in the welding tip. The base material is heated by hot air coming out of the tip ahead of the rod tube. A shoe on the end of the tip applies pressure to the rod at the point of weld, and at the same time smooths the weld. The forward motion pulls the rod through the tip.

Figure 19-18 shows how to start the weld, lay the bead, and end the weld. Figure 19-19 shows how to use

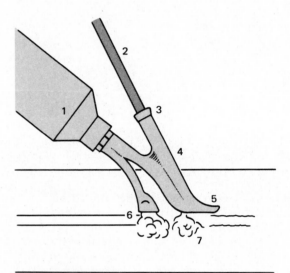

1. ELECTRIC TORCH
2. WELDING ROD
3. SPEED TIP
4. ROD IS PREHEATED IN TUBE
5. SHOE PROVIDES PRESSURE
6. ORIFICE PREHEATS AREA TO BE WELDED
7. HEAT

Fig. 19-17 Semiautomatic speed-welding torch for plastic welding. *(General Motors Corporation)*

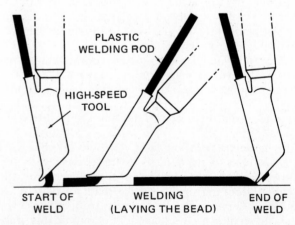

Fig. 19-18 How the semiautomatic speed welder works to start the weld, weld, and end the weld. *(Kamweld Products Company, Inc.)*

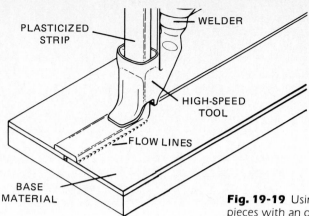

PLASTICIZED STRIP

WELDER

HIGH-SPEED TOOL

FLOW LINES

BASE MATERIAL

a high-speed welder that applies a strip to weld two flat plastic pieces together.

A good speed weld in a V joint will have a slightly higher crown and more uniformity than a hand weld. The speed weld will appear smooth and shiny with a slight bead on each side. For best results, the tip should be cleaned occasionally with a wire brush.

Fig. 19-19 Using a special semiautomatic speed welder to weld two flat pieces with an overlapping flat strip. *(Kamweld Products Company, Inc.)*

REVIEW QUESTIONS

Select the *one* correct, best, or most probable answer to each question. You can find the answers in the section indicated at the end of each question.

1. Two types of plastic are   (≡19-2)
   a. plastic and resin
   b. thermoplastic and thermosetting
   c. resin and glass
   d. hot and cold

2. A plastic that softens when heated is   (≡19-2)
   a. a thermoplastic resin
   b. fiberglass
   c. a thermosetting resin
   d. a body filler

3. Plastic parts can be identified by the   (≡19-3 to 19-5)
   a. acid test
   b. way they tear
   c. flame test
   d. weight and color

4. Punctured flexible plastic panels   (≡19-7)
   a. can be patched with adhesive
   b. must be replaced
   c. cannot be painted
   d. are repaired by cold soldering

5. The welding rod used in hot-air plastic welding is made of   (≡19-8)
   a. steel
   b. bronze
   c. the plastic being patched
   d. fiberglass

PART 5

ADJUSTING BODY PANELS

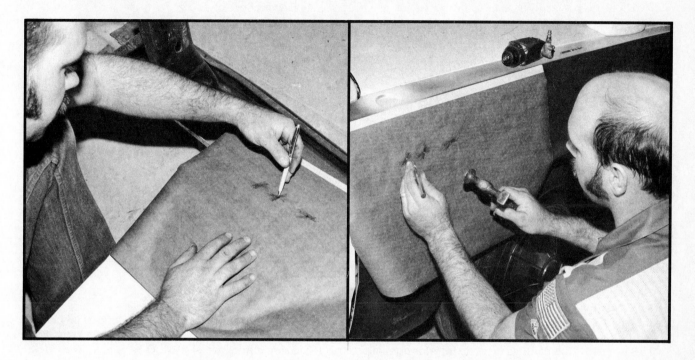

In this part, you will learn how certain body panels are adjusted. These include the fenders, doors, hoods, and trunk or luggage-compartment lids. All these panels are attached to the body with hinges.

Doors, hoods, and trunk lids may be made of sheet metal, sheet aluminum, fiberglass, or plastic. Regardless of the material, the adjusting methods for each of these panels are the same. In general, part of the procedure is to reposition the panel hinges.

Fenders are securely fastened in place. However, the other panels are each a type of door that provides access to a compartment. The hood provides access to the engine compartment. The doors provide access to the passenger compartment. The trunk lid provides access to the luggage compartment.

Part 6 covers the servicing of doors, tailgates, lift gates, sun roofs, and the special mechanisms — such as door locks and window regulators — that they contain.

There are three chapters in Part 5. These are as follows:

Chapter 20   Adjusting Body Panels
Chapter 21   Fitting Fenders and Doors
Chapter 22   Fitting Hoods and Trunk Lids

ADJUSTING BODY PANELS

After studying this chapter, you should be able to:

1. Discuss the reasons for adjusting body panels.
2. Explain the purpose of shims and how to use them.
3. Discuss the purpose of slotted holes and caged or floating anchor plates.
4. Explain the purpose of adjustable stops.

≡ 20-1 REASONS FOR ADJUSTING BODY PANELS

There are three reasons why body panels must fit and open and close properly:

1. SAFETY. Doors latch in two positions: the safety position and the closed, or locked, position. The door, when closed, should move past the safety-latch position and into the fully closed position. If the door and latch are improperly positioned, only the safety latch will catch. This endangers the passenger sitting by the door. Hoods also have a safety-latch position.

2. APPEARANCE. A fender that does not properly line up with the adjacent metal will look bad. The fender must fit on the sides, back, and front (Fig. 20-1). Likewise, misalignment of a door or trunk lid will show up and indicate poor workmanship.

3. SEALING. All openings into the interior of most cars are closed by swinging panels—doors, hoods, trunk lids, tailgates, and lift gates. Exceptions are the sliding sun roof and the removable hatch roof (T roof). Regardless of whether the panels swing, slide, or "pop out," they all must fit properly. This means they must fit without binding, yet fit tightly enough to prevent the entrance of water, wind, and dust. Although sealing is not critical with the hood, all other panels use weatherstripping to complete the fit and seal.

Fig. 20-1 For good appearance, the body panels must have proper alignment and fit. *(Chrysler Corporation)*

≡ 20-2 ADJUSTING METHODS

Various methods are used to shift body panels with respect to the car body so that they will fit properly. Four mechanical devices are used. These are:

1. Shims
2. Slotted holes
3. Caged or floating anchor plates
4. Adjustable stops

In addition, bending of metal is also used to secure a proper fit. Each of these adjustment methods is described in a following section.

≡ 20-3 SHIMS

Body *shims* are thin pieces of metal that can be placed between a part being attached and the car body (Fig. 20-2). Some shims are slotted. Others look like thick, flat washers.

Shims are available in various sizes and thicknesses. Frequently used thicknesses of body shims are $\frac{1}{16}$ inch [1.6 mm], $\frac{1}{8}$ inch [3 mm], and $\frac{3}{16}$ inch [5 mm].

Installing a shim moves the part out from the body. If shims are present, removing a shim moves the part in. For example, Fig. 20-3A shows a part attached to the body with two shims between the part and body. Figure 20-3B shows the part attached with the shims removed. The part is moved closer to the body member.

Note that the lower shims shown in Fig. 20-2 are slotted. Slotting permits them to be added or removed without taking the bolt out. If the bolt or nut is loosened enough so there is space between the part and the body member, the shim can be slipped into place. It will be held there when the bolt or nut is tightened.

Where and how many shims to install are matters of judgment. For example, if a fender fits too closely at the front edge, one or more shims can be installed between it and the body bracket to move the fender out. The experienced body technician can look and decide whether to install one, two, or more shims to make the adjustment.

≡ 20-4 SLOTTED HOLES

Slotted, or elongated, holes, either in the body bracket or post or in the part to be attached, can be used to

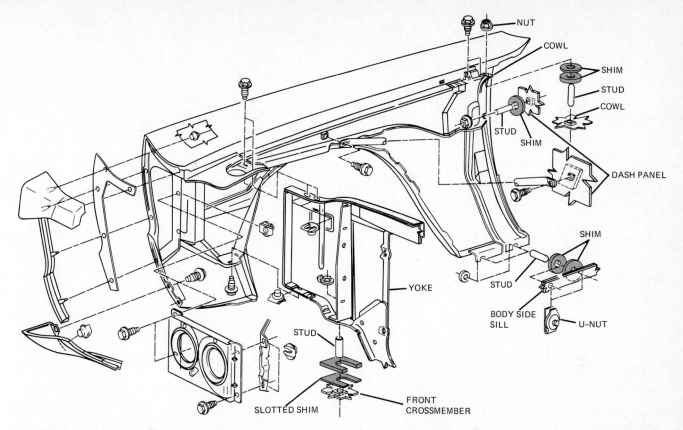

Fig. 20-2 Shims are placed between the fender and the car body to achieve proper alignment. *(Chrysler Corporation)*

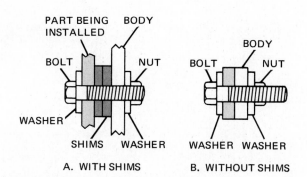

Fig. 20-3 How shims position a part away from or closer to the car body.

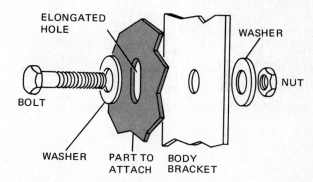

Fig. 20-4 Elongated holes in some parts are used to secure alignment of attaching parts.

secure alignment. Figure 20-4 shows the principle. The bolt is run through the washer, the part to be attached, the body bracket, the other washer, and the nut. The nut is not tightened until the part is moved up or down as necessary to get alignment. Then it is tightened.

In some cars, the holes are enlarged to permit movement in any direction so that proper alignment can be obtained. On these, there is no need to elongate the oversize holes.

≡ 20-5 CAGED OR FLOATING ANCHOR PLATES

Caged or floating anchor plates are like oversized nuts which are mounted inside the part to be attached or the body bracket. Some door hinges, for example, are fas-

tened to caged anchor plates. Figure 20-5 shows the principle with a striker plate mounting. The anchor plate is in a pillar and is caged on the inside so it will not fall down when the bolt is removed. The hole in the pillar is enlarged so the plate can be shifted around as necessary. The adjustment procedure is described later.

≡ 20-6 ADJUSTABLE STOPS

The body of many cars has several adjustable stops which position the hood when it is closed (Fig. 20-6). These stops have rubber heads. When the hood is closed, dimples in the underhood rest on these rubber heads. The stops properly position the hood when it is closed. They also isolate the hood from the other panels

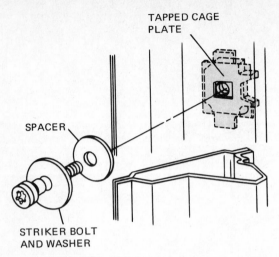

Fig. 20-5 Tapped caged plate in the pillar does not fall when striker bolt is removed. (© *Fisher Body Division of General Motors Corporation*)

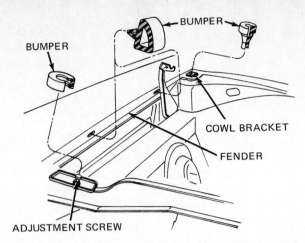

Fig. 20-7 Triangular-shaped rubber bumpers fit in slots along the inside edge of the fender to isolate hood vibration from other parts of the car. *(Chrysler Corporation)*

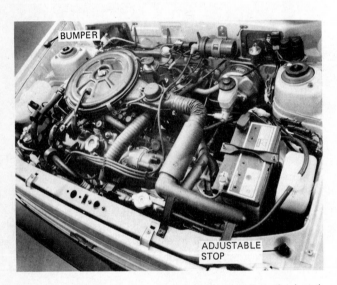

Fig. 20-6 Adjustable stops are used for aligning the hood. *(Chrysler Corporation)*

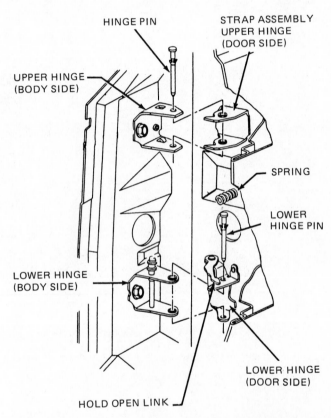

Fig. 20-8 Front-door hinge system for a compact car. The hinge half of each hinge is welded to the side of the door. The other hinge half is bolted to the pillar. *(Chevrolet Motor Division of General Motors Corporation)*

of the car. This prevents any vibration of the hood from passing into other parts of the car. Assisting in this isolation, on many cars, is a series of rubber bumpers placed along the fender in slots (Figs. 20-6 and 20-7). The hood, when closed, rests on these rubber blocks, which provide the hood with solid support. At the same time, they serve as isolators and keep hood vibrations from passing into the fenders and body.

Turning the adjustable stop out or in raises or lowers that part of the hood which is over the stop.

≡ 20-7 ADJUSTING DOOR FIT

In many cars, especially the smaller, down-sized vehicles, the hinges are welded to the door. The matching hinges are bolted to the body hinge pillars (Fig. 20-8). On these vehicles, there is no provision for adjusting the door fit. The hinges on the door and pillar are connected by hinge pins. If a door hinge is damaged, it can

be removed and a new hinge installed with a bolt. This requires the use of a tapped anchor plate behind the door edge.

On these cars, if a collision has thrown off the door alignment, then a door pillar has been pushed out of line. This requires a push or a pull with the body-straightening hydraulic ram to move the pillar back into position (Fig. 20-9).

Fig. 20-9 Bending the door pillar so the door will fit. (*Guy Chart Sales Inc.*)

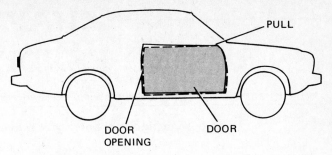

Fig. 20-10 Door sag caused by impact to the right front fender.

Some cars have door hinges that are attached through slotted, or elongated, holes. Adjustment is made by loosening the attaching bolts slightly and shifting the door to correct the fit. Sometimes a collision has pushed the pillar back so far that adjustment with the slotted holes will not correct the fit. Then hydraulic staightening of the pillar is required (Fig. 20-9). Figure 20-10 shows the effect of an impact and the results of

that push. Chapter 21 describes in detail adjusting the fit of a door.

≡ 20-8 AVOIDING PAINT CHIPPING

When shifting a body panel around, it is possible to accidentally chip paint off the edge. For example, when shifting the hood to improve the fit, you could shift it too far. Then, when you close the hood to check its fit, its edge could strike the edge of the fender. This could chip off paint. Then you would have the job of touching up the spots that have lost paint. Always be careful when shifting a body panel. Its edge must not strike an adjacent stationary edge when the panel fit is checked.

───── REVIEW QUESTIONS ─────

Select the *one* correct, best, or most probable answer to each question. You can find the answers in the section indicated at the end of each question.

1. Four methods of panel adjustment are shims, slotted holes, caged anchor stops, and (≡20-2)
   a. welding
   b. adjustable stops
   c. brazing
   d. cotter pins

2. Safety, appearance, and sealing are reasons why (≡20-1)
   a. new cars are popular
   b. lower speeds are required today
   c. the car passes safety inspection
   d. the body panels must fit properly

3. Doors and hoods have (≡20-1)
   a. three hinges
   b. only torsion-bar springs
   c. a safety-latch position
   d. no method of adjustment

4. Body shims may be (≡20-3)
   a. slotted or adjustable
   b. slotted or washer type
   c. adjustable or rubber
   d. caged or anchored

5. A caged anchor plate (≡20-5)
   a. is held in position by the cage
   b. falls to the floor when the screws are removed
   c. is welded in place
   d. is not used today

CHAPTER 21
FITTING FENDERS AND DOORS

After studying this chapter, you should be able to:

1. Explain how to remove, install, and adjust the alignment of a fender.

2. Describe how to locate the emblem on a newly installed fender.

3. Discuss the procedures for fitting doors and adjusting door alignment.

≡ 21-1 FENDER ALIGNMENT

A fender must fit properly (Fig. 20-1) to avoid unsightly gaps that could cause air, dust, and water leaks. An even gap on each side, between the fender and hood and between the fender and door, usually is considered a good fit. Damage to the fender may result from a gap that is too small. If the fender is too far back (toward the door), it will be struck by the forward edge of the door as it opens. A fender too far in (toward the hood) may be hit by the hood as it closes. This can happen when sufficient space is not left for the hood to close into. Striking a misaligned fender with a hood or door probably will chip the paint on the fender, and it may cause dents.

Figure 21-1 shows how the fore-and-aft and the in-and-out adjustments are made. By using slotted holes,

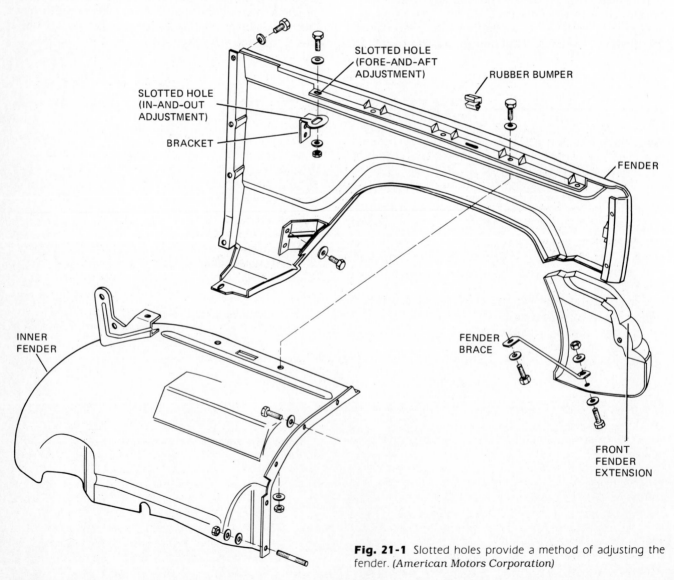

Fig. 21-1 Slotted holes provide a method of adjusting the fender. (*American Motors Corporation*)

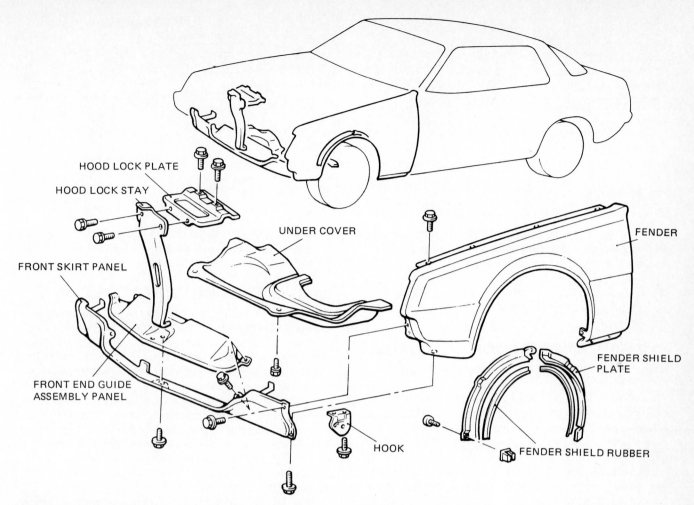

Fig. 21-2 Fender and other parts for attachment to a unitized body. (*Chrysler Corporation*)

HOOD LOCK PLATE

HOOD LOCK STAY

FRONT SKIRT PANEL

FRONT END GUIDE ASSEMBLY PANEL

UNDER COVER

HOOK

FENDER

FENDER SHIELD PLATE

FENDER SHIELD RUBBER

the attaching bolts are permitted some movement in the desired direction. The slotted holes at the bottom of the fender allow a separate in-and-out adjustment for each end of the fender. Figure 20-2 shows how shims are used to make the up-and-down adjustment.

≡ 21-2 PREPARING FOR FENDER REMOVAL

Figure 21-1 shows the attachment of an inner and outer fender. Figure 21-2 shows a fender and other parts to be attached to a unitized body.

When a fender is removed, be careful not to chip the paint on it. Also, care must be taken not to chip paint from the door. Wraparound bumpers leave little space between the fender and other panels. It requires skill and proper masking to remove a fender without damaging the paint.

One way to avoid chipping paint on the fender is to apply several layers of masking tape over the edge of the bumper on its end, as shown in Fig. 21-3. This will prevent the rough edges of the bumper from damaging the paint should the fender drag against the bumper while being removed.

Disconnect the battery ground cable. If the radio antenna is mounted on the fender, the antenna must be

MASKING TAPE

Fig. 21-3 Mask the edge of the bumper to prevent damaging the paint on the fender.

removed. This is done by disconnecting the antenna wire from the radio in the dash. Tie a long string to the antenna wire. Then remove the antenna assembly from the fender. The string is used to guide the antenna wire back into position when you reinstall the fender.

Place several layers of masking tape over the front edge of the door, as shown in Fig. 21-4. This will prevent paint damage should the fender strike the door during removal. If the fender has a wheel lip molding, you may have to remove it. Then turn the steering wheel in the same direction as the fender being re-

MASKING TAPE

Fig. 21-4 Removing the fender.

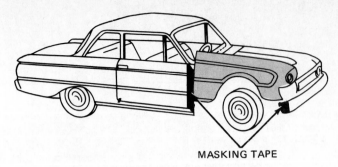

MASKING TAPE

Fig. 21-6 Lifting the fender.

moved. If you are removing a right fender, turn the steering wheel to the right. This will allow you to get to the attaching screws more easily.

NOTE: The parts of a car are named by their position when you are sitting in the driver's seat and facing forward.

≡ 21-3 REMOVING FRONT FENDER

Remove the splash guard or inner-fender mounting bolts from inside the fender (Figs. 21-1 and 21-5). You may have to hunt for these screws, as they often are covered with undercoating and dirt. Next, take out all other screws that attach the fender to another part. The screw holes shown in Fig. 21-1 are typical locations. In general, the fender fastens on all edges except around the wheel opening. This area of the fender is supported and protected by an attached splash guard or inner fender, as shown in Fig. 21-1.

Today the fenders on many cars contain headlamps, parking lamps, and side-marker lamps. On these, you must disconnect the wiring for each and then remove the lamp. Some fenders may have moldings that must be removed to prevent damage to them. When the fender is free of all attachments, you are ready to remove it.

To remove the fender, first tilt the top of the fender out at the front. Then lift the fender at the rear and

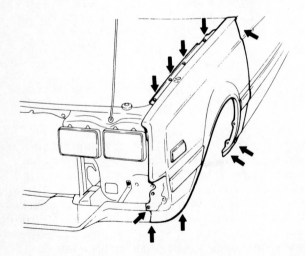

Fig. 21-5 Arrows point to locations of fender-attachment bolts. *(Chrysler Corporation)*

remove it from the car, as shown in Fig. 21-6. Be careful not to scrape the paint or make dents while you are lifting and removing the fender.

≡ 21-4 FENDER INSTALLATION

To install the fender, tilt the rear of the fender up and carefully position it in place. Align the fender (≡21-1) and install the attaching screws. Brush or spray undercoating onto the underside of the fender and the entire splash-guard-to-fender contact area. This area must be sealed to prevent rust.

Install in the new fender any lamps, moldings, or other parts that were removed. Connect the wiring for the lights. Use the string attached to the radio antenna to pull the antenna wire back through the fender. Reconnect the antenna to the radio. Then install the antenna assembly on the fender. Connect the battery ground cable to the battery.

The fender should be adjusted to provide for equal spacing at the cowl, door front edge, and door top panel edge. On the fender shown in Fig. 20-2, these adjustments are made with shims in three areas: at the bottom of the body side sill, at the cowl top panel, and at the yoke.

≡ 21-5 LOCATING THE EMBLEM

Many cars have small moldings and names in fancy script or lettering attached to the fenders. Several examples of these emblems are shown in Fig. 21-7. When a damaged fender is removed, it is often possible to remove the emblem and install it on the new fender after the fender has been put in place. Figures 21-8 and 21-9 show how to locate the emblem correctly. In Fig. 21-8, the technician carefully positions paper on the old fender after the emblem has been taken off. The exact locations of the holes are marked on the paper. Then the technician transfers the paper to the new fender. Now a punch and hammer are used to mark the locations of the holes to be drilled for the emblem in the new fender (Fig. 21-9).

≡ 21-6 FITTING DOORS

In many cars, the holes through which the hinge attaching bolts pass (in the door or door pillar) are slotted or enlarged. This enables the technician to shift the hinges up or down, or sideways, to get proper door fit. Figure 21-10 shows how moving the hinge-to-body and

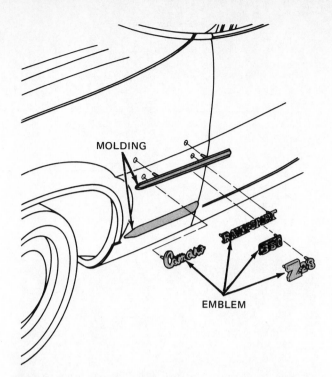

Fig. 21-7 Small moldings and emblems can sometimes be removed from the old fender and installed on the new fender. *(Chevrolet Motor Division of General Motors Corporation)*

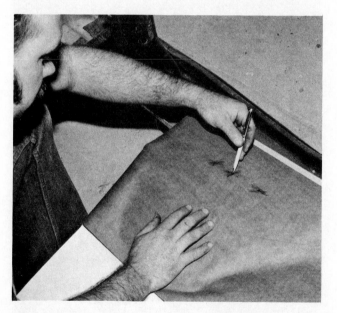

Fig. 21-8 Position the paper on the discarded fender. Then mark the exact locations of the holes where the emblem was attached.

Fig. 21-9 After the new fender is installed, position the paper on it. Then use a punch to mark the locations of the holes for drilling.

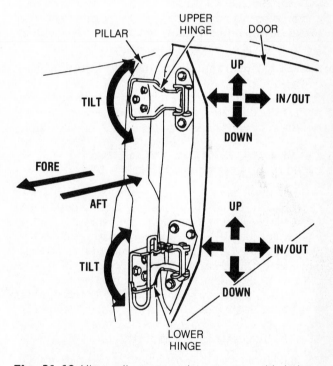

Fig. 21-10 Hinge-adjustment points on cars with bolt-on hinges. *(Chrysler Corporation)*

hinge-to-door bolts provides the door alignment adjustments.

By moving each end of the upper and lower hinges, the door can be shifted fore and aft (forward and backward), up and down, and in and out. In addition, the tilt of the door can be changed. However, after all these adjustments are made, the latch pin (or striker bolt) may require adjustment to ensure proper latching of the door when it is shut. In some cars, adjustment must

be made by applying a push or pull on the door pillar (Fig. 20-9).

NOTE: *Chapter 24 covers door services other than adjusting fit. These include servicing window regulators and latching and locking devices. Chapter 23 covers weatherstripping, water-testing door seals for leaks, and also locating and eliminating wind noise, air leaks, and water leaks.*

≡ 21-7 DOOR ALIGNMENT

Proper alignment is achieved when the gaps between the edges of the door and the surrounding panels are uniform all the way around (Fig. 21-11). In addition, the door should open and close without binding. It should not move up or down as it latches. If it does, the latch and striker bolt are not properly aligned.

As the door closes, the latch should move through the safety-latch position and into the fully latched, or locked, position. There are two latching positions on a car door. The first is the safety-latch position. The second is the fully closed, or fully latched, position. Open and close a car door slowly to check this out for yourself. Sometimes, when adjustments have been made to the door and striker bolt, the door will latch in only the first, or safety-latch, position. This creates a dangerous riding condition for the person sitting next to the improperly latched door. Correct adjustment allows the door to close into the full-latched, or locked, position.

If the door is shifted rearward during an adjustment, the switch on the door jamb which controls the dome light or interior courtesy lights may require adjustment. The switch may have to be shifted rearward. If it is not adjusted, the switch might not open and turn off the courtesy lights in the car when the door is closed.

Sometimes a hinge or striker plate is moved enough to expose unpainted metal. When this occurs, touch up the unpainted area with paint of the proper color.

NOTE: When rebuilding a wrecked car, it is especially important to achieve proper door fit, not only from the standpoint of safety. The customer often judges the quality of the body-repair job by the way the doors open, close, fit, and sound (when closing).

≡ 21-8 GENERAL MOTORS DOOR ADJUSTMENTS

Some General Motors cars have the hinges welded onto the doors and door pillars. No adjustment is possible on these doors except by using the hydraulic pulling equipment to pull on the pillars supporting the doors. To service the hinges, the welds must be drilled out. Then new hinges can be installed with the bolts supplied with the hinges so the door can be reattached.

The General Motors door-adjustment procedure for doors attached by bolts is described below. This procedure applies to General Motors cars using bolts to attach the hinges to doors and pillars.

1. Before checking door alignment and fit, and before making any adjustments, remove the striker bolt (Fig. 20-5) from the door pillar. This allows the door to hang freely on its hinges. When a front door is being adjusted, you may want to loosen the front fender so that it will not interfere.

2. The fit is checked by observing the variations in the gap between the edges of the door—at the top, sides, and bottom of the door—and the adjacent panels (Fig. 21-11). If the fit is not about the same all around, adjustment is required.

3. Adjust the door up or down, or fore or aft, at the body-hinge-pillar attachments (Fig. 21-12). The bolts attaching the hinges to the pillar are loosened so the

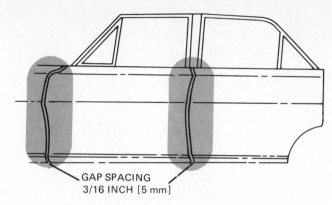

Fig. 21-11 Typical gap spacing around a door.

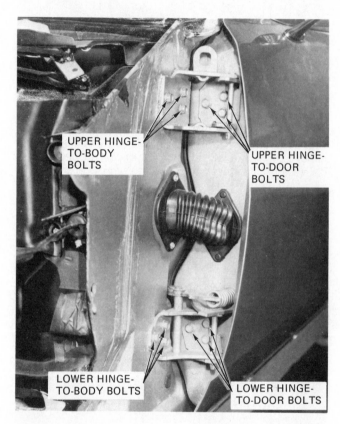

Fig. 21-12 Hinge-adjustment points on General Motors cars with bolt-on hinges. (© *Fisher Body Division of General Motors Corporation*)

door can be shifted up, down, fore, or aft. Use a pry bar padded heavily with shop cloths to avoid damaging the edge of the door. Loosen the bolts only enough to permit the door to be shifted with light force. Tighten the bolts when the adjustment is correct.

4. To move the door in or out, loosen the bolts attaching the hinges to the door. Then shift the door as required and tighten the bolts to the specified torque.

5. The striker bolt (Fig. 20-5) must be adjusted so that it is centered in the door latch when the door is closed. General Motors recommends checking this adjustment with a small amount of modeling clay or caulking compound (Fig. 21-13), as follows:

a. Make sure door is properly aligned.

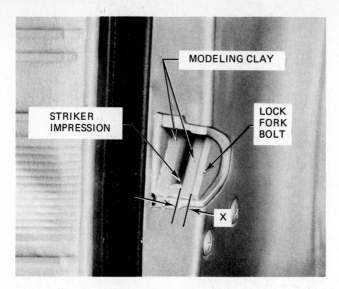

Fig. 21-13 Checking striker-bolt adjustment with modeling clay. (© Fisher Body Division of General Motors Corporation)

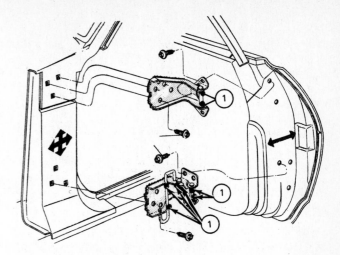

Fig. 21-14 Front-door adjustments on some Ford models. Lubricate the numbered points with polyethylene grease. (Ford Motor Company)

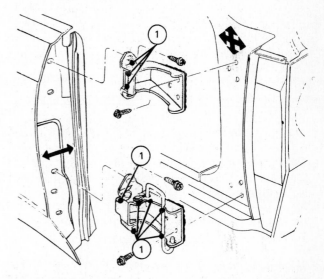

Fig. 21-15 Front-door adjustments on other Ford models. (Ford Motor Company)

b. Apply modeling clay or caulking compound to the lock-bolt opening as shown in Fig. 21-13.

c. Close door only as far as necessary for the striker bolt to form an impression in the clay or caulking.

NOTE: Do not close the door completely or you will jam the clay or caulking compound into the door lock. This may cause the problem of how to remove it.

d. The striker-bolt impression should be centered fore and aft, as shown in Fig. 21-13.

e. The striker bolt can be shifted up or down, or sideways, by loosening it and moving it to make the adjustment. It screws into a caged anchor plate.

f. Spacers can be inserted under the striker bolt, as shown in Fig. 20-5, if necessary.

g. When adjustment is correct, tighten the bolt to the specified torque.

6. Make sure the door fully latches and that the door-jamb switch is correctly adjusted (≡21-7).

≡ 21-9 FORD DOOR ADJUSTMENTS

The holes in the hinges or the holes at the hinge attaching points are either slotted (elongated) or enlarged to permit door alignment. Figure 21-14 shows the adjustments of the front door of some Fords. The vertical and horizontal arrows (to the left) on the pillar to which the door hinges are attached indicate that the holes are enlarged so the hinges can be shifted in any direction. The horizontal arrow on the door jamb (to the right) indicates that the hinges can be shifted only horizontally on the jamb.

Proper alignment is achieved when the gap between the edge of the door and the surrounding panels is uniform all around (Fig. 21-11). In addition, the door should open and close without binding. Also, the door should latch and hold closed.

Figures 21-15, 21-16, and 21-17 show the front- and rear-door adjustments on other Ford-built cars.

Figure 21-18 shows the adjustments of the door-latch striker pin. The adjustments are made as follows:

1. Check the fit of the door to determine how it must be moved to obtain proper fit all around. Open and close the door and note whether the latch is working properly. The striker pin should center in the latch assembly. The latch should close around the pin at the proper distance from the end of the pin as shown in Fig. 21-18.

2. If the door does not fit properly or if the striker pin is not properly located, adjustments must be made.

NOTE: Do not try to cover up a poor door adjustment by readjusting the striker pin.

3. Pad a pry bar by wrapping several layers of shop cloths around it.

4. Loosen the door hinge bolts just enough to permit movement of the door. Use the pry bar to move the door in the direction required to make the adjustment.

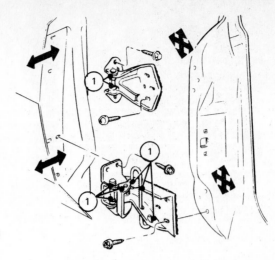

Fig. 21-16 Rear-door adjustments on some Ford cars. *(Ford Motor Company)*

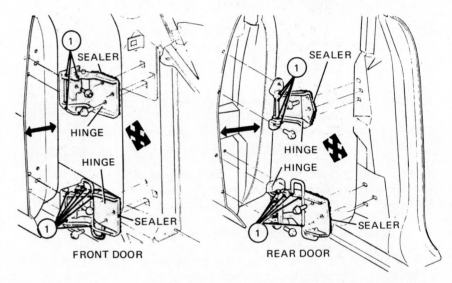

FRONT DOOR   REAR DOOR

Fig. 21-17 Door hinge adjustments on some Ford hardtop models. Apply lubricant to the numbered points. *(Ford Motor Company)*

Tighten the hinge bolts and recheck the fit. Make sure there is no interference with adjacent panels. Making this adjustment will probably throw off the striker-pin adjustment. Check it after the door fit is corrected.

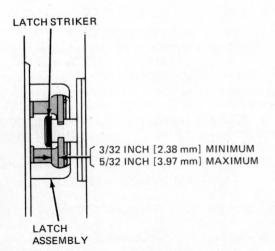

LATCH STRIKER

3/32 INCH [2.38 mm] MINIMUM
5/32 INCH [3.97 mm] MAXIMUM

LATCH
ASSEMBLY

Fig. 21-18 Proper adjustment of the door-latch striker pin. *(Ford Motor Company)*

5. You may need to repeat the adjustment procedure more than once to get the correct door fit. Once the fit is correct, tighten the hinge bolts to the specified torque. Recheck the fit of the striker pin.

6. The striker pin can be adjusted sideways and up and down. Its threaded end goes through an enlarged hole in the door pillar and into a threaded anchor plate behind the pillar. When the pin is loosened (with a Phillips screwdriver), it can be shifted in the direction required. The pin should be located so that it centers in the latch when the door is closed.

If the latch is not closing on the pin within the dimension range given in Fig. 21-18, you may have to add or remove shims (spacers) under the pin plate. To check the clearance, or the point at which the latch is contacting the pin, apply a thin coat of dark grease on the pin. Then close and open the door. Examine the marks in the grease to see where the latch has hit the pin. Shim as necessary. Wipe off the dark grease so it won't get on a customer's clothes.

When the adjustment is completed, the latch should close over the pin smoothly with no upward or downward movement of the door. The door should open smoothly without dragging on the pin.

7. Make sure that the door fully latches and that the door-jamb switch is correctly adjusted (≡21-7).

≡ 21-10 CHRYSLER DOOR ADJUSTMENTS

Figure 21-19 shows the tool Chrysler recommends for loosening and tightening door hinge bolts. Figure 21-20 shows the arrangement of the front-door hinges and striker pin. Figure 21-21 shows the rear-door hinges.

The doors can be shifted up and down on the door pillar, forward or backward, or in and out, as follows:

1. Up-and-down adjustment. This is made at either the pillar or door hinges. The hinge bolts holding the hinge to the door can be loosened to make the adjustment. Or the hinge bolts holding the hinge to the pillar can be loosened to make the adjustment.

2. In-and-out adjustment. If the door panel is not flush with the surrounding metal, the door must be moved in or out. This adjustment is made at the door hinge half. Adjust only one hinge at a time. Raising the outer end of the door (door open) moves the upper part of the door into the door opening (when door is closed). Lowering the outer end of the door (door open) moves the lower part of the door into the door opening (when door is closed).

3. Fore-and-aft adjustment. The fore-and-aft adjustment is made at the pillar hinge half. Adjust only one hinge at a time. Raising the outer end of the door (with door open) moves the upper part of the door forward (with door closed). Lowering the outer end of the door (with door open) moves the lower part forward (when door is closed).

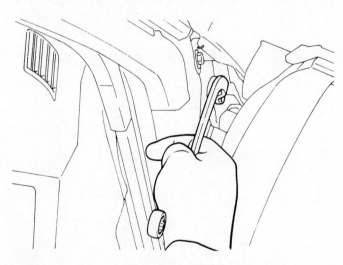

A. ADJUSTING DOOR

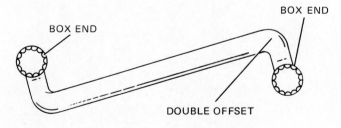

B. HINGE-ADJUSTING TOOL

Fig. 21-19 Adjusting a front-door hinge. (Chrysler Corporation)

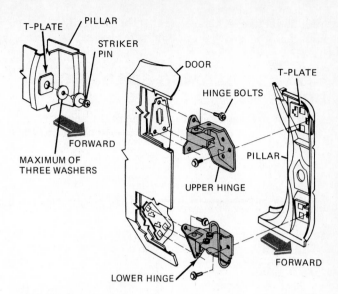

Fig. 21-20 Front-door hinge-and-striker-pin arrangement on some Chrysler-built cars. (Chrysler Corporation)

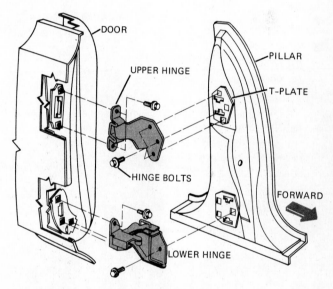

Fig. 21-21 Rear-door hinge arrangement on some Chrysler-built cars. (Chrysler Corporation)

4. Check the position of the striker pin as the door latches, and make the necessary adjustments to center the pin in the latch. Make sure the pin is entering the latch deeply enough. The latch must close over a central part of the pin.

5. Make sure that the door fully latches and that the door-jamb switch is correctly adjusted (≡21-7).

≡ 21-11 AMC DOOR ADJUSTMENTS

The adjustments on the doors of cars made by American Motors are similar to those described previously. The striker bolt should be removed and the fit of the door noted as the door hangs freely in the door opening. In-and-out adjustments are made by loosening the hinge bolts at the door. Up-and-down or fore-and-aft adjustments are made by loosening the hinge bolts at the door pillar. The striker bolt should be tightened after it is adjusted. Make sure that the door fully latches and that the door-jamb switch is properly adjusted (≡21-7).

≡ 21-12 CHECKING SEAL AROUND DOOR

After any car-door adjustment, check the seal around the door to make sure it is still watertight and wind-noise-tight. Sometimes shifting the door reduces the sealing effect of the weatherstrip. This could result in water leaks. Also, improper sealing can cause an annoying air leak into or out of the car. Air leaks often produce a bothersome noise. Chapter 23 covers the testing of weatherstripping for water leaks. The chapter also explains how to check for air noise and correct the condition causing it.

—— REVIEW QUESTIONS ——

Select the *one* correct, best, or most probable answer to each question. You can find the answers in the section indicated at the end of each question.

1. Fenders must be adjusted for proper fit in (≡21-1)
   a. one direction
   b. two directions
   c. three directions
   d. four directions

2. For safety, the battery ground cable should be disconnected before removing a (≡21-2)
   a. door
   b. fender
   c. door hinge
   d. striker bolt

3. Usually, the door fits properly when the gap (≡21-7)
   a. is narrower at the front
   b. is narrower at the rear
   c. does not exceed ¼ inch [13 mm]
   d. is the same all around

4. After adjusting a door, you may have to readjust the
   a. headlights (≡21-7)
   b. brake lights
   c. dome lights
   d. glove-box light

5. The door-latch mechanism on a car door has (≡21-7)
   a. only one position
   b. two positions
   c. three positions
   d. four positions

CHAPTER 22
FITTING HOODS AND TRUNK LIDS

After studying this chapter, you should be able to:

1. Explain how to adjust hoods and hood latches.
2. Describe the procedures for adjusting trunk lids and trunk-lid latches.
3. Discuss hold-open springs and torsion bars and the adjustments they require.
4. Describe weatherstripping and how to adjust or install new trunk-lid weatherstripping.
5. Explain how to check the trunk-lid seal with water.

≡ 22-1 HOOD HINGE LOCATIONS

Most hoods are hinged at the back with the latch at the front of the car, above the radiator. Some are hinged at the front with the latch at the cowl. The latch control ("hood release") is located inside the driver's compartment on many cars. This makes it harder for thieves to get into the engine compartment. If the car is locked, a door key is needed to gain easy access to the car and unlatch the hood.

≡ 22-2 ADJUSTING HOODS

Hoods have two hinges, one on each side of the car. The opposite end of the hood has the latching arrangement (Fig. 22-1). The hood has bumpers which cushion the hood when it is closed and produce a tight and rattle-

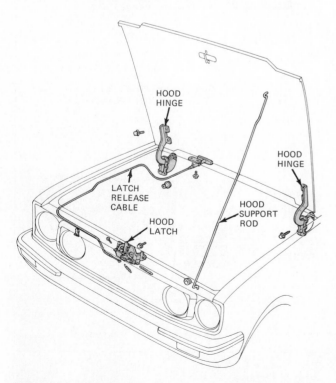

Fig. 22-1 Hinges and latching arrangement on a hood. *(Toyota Motor Sales, Inc.)*

free fit. Some of these bumpers are adjustable (Fig. 20-7).

Many times, you will be required to adjust the fenders along with the hood. For example, if one of the fenders is out of line, it will change the gap between the fender and hood and require adjustment. Figure 22-2 shows various types of misalignment and possible corrections. Chapter 21 covers fender adjustments. Hood hinges and hood latches have slotted holes which allow sufficient movement to correct the alignment. Shims may also be required to correct the fit. The adjustable bumpers are used not to secure alignment but to secure snug latching. This holds the hood tight at all four corners and along the sides so it will not rattle or flutter.

NOTE: The adjustable bumpers on the cowl (back of hood) must not be used to adjust the hood fit. The fit of the hood is adjusted by the slotted holes as explained above. Only after this adjustment is completed do you adjust the bumpers to take up any play and eliminate the possibility of rattles. To explain why this is the proper procedure, here is an example:

Suppose the right rear corner of the hood is too low. You could raise this by backing out the adjustable bumper. Then when the hood was closed, it would hit this bumper and be lifted up to align with the fender. However, every time the hood was closed the sheet metal would be bent up. You could end up with a bent hood that would require work to straighten it out. This would not happen if you adjusted the hood hinge first and then adjusted the bumper.

In many cars, the hinges have a special coil-spring arrangement that holds the hood up when it is raised (Fig. 22-3). The springs, in effect, go over center to produce the "hold-open" tension. Then as the hood is moved down to the closed position, the springs go back over center to produce a "hold-closed" tension. Without some such arrangement, a support rod is required to hold the hood open (Fig. 22-1).

Instead of coil springs in the hinges, many cars made by Chrysler use torsion bars to produce the counterbalancing action. Figure 22-4 shows the torsion-bar arrangement.

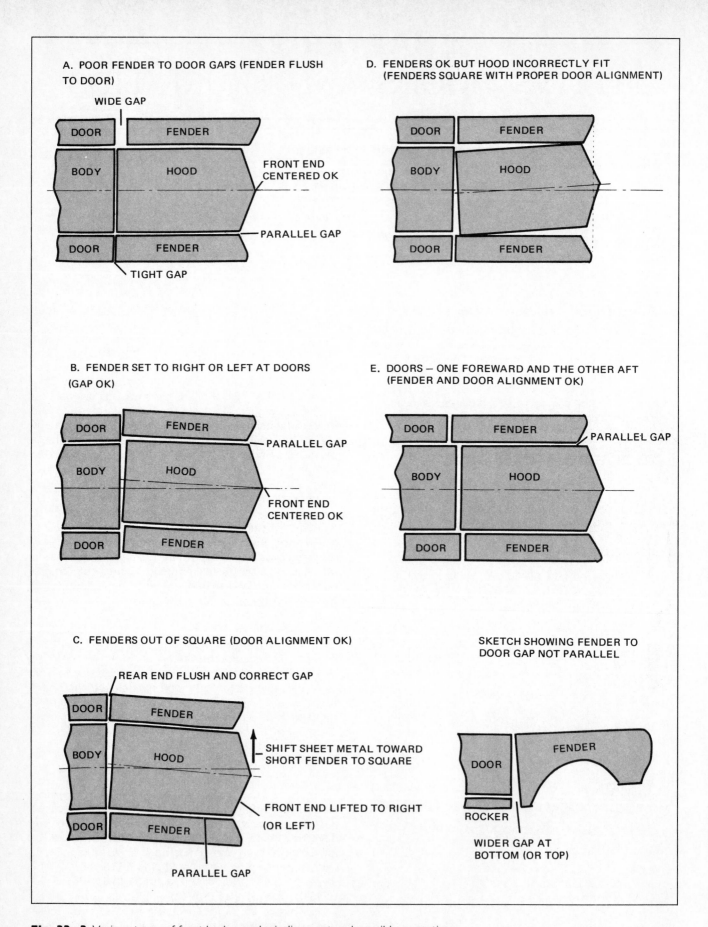

Fig. 22-2 Various types of front body-panel misalignment and possible corrections. *(Chrysler Corporation)*

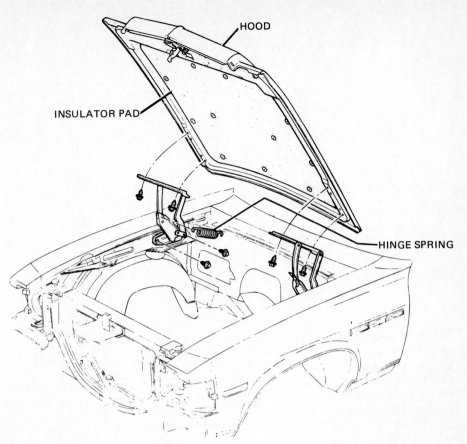

Fig. 22–3 Hood mounting on hinges using coil springs for counterbalancing. *(Buick Motor Division of General Motors Corporation)*

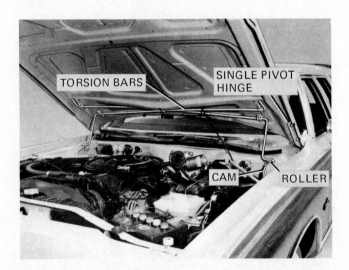

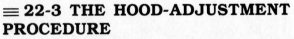

Fig. 22–4 Torsion bars used to counterbalance the hood. *(Chrysler Corporation)*

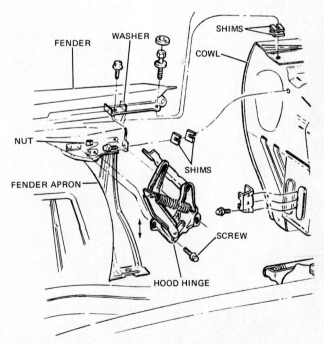

Fig. 22–5 Hood hinge installation on some Ford and Mercury cars. *(Ford Motor Company)*

≡ 22-3 THE HOOD-ADJUSTMENT PROCEDURE

First, check the hood fit at the back, front, and sides. If fenders are misaligned, adjust their fit as explained in Chap. 21. Then note hood alignment. Loosen the hinge screws as necessary to shift the hood fore and aft, or sideways, to secure proper alignment. Figures 22-3 to 22-5 show various attachment methods. The hinge screw holes are elongated or oversize to permit the hood to be shifted to secure the proper fit. Shims are used under the hinges in many cars to align the hood, as shown in Fig. 22-5.

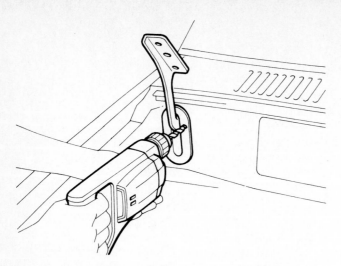

Fig. 22–6 A damaged hood hinge can be removed from many vehicles by drilling out the spot welds. *(Chrysler Corporation)*

NOTE: *When checking fit, make sure that the edge of the hood does not strike any adjacent panel when the hood is closed. This could knock paint off and require retouching the paint.*

As a final step in checking hood fit, test the latch to make sure it operates correctly and holds the hood tight. Make sure that the hood meets the adjustable bumpers when it is closed. Also, see that all the bumpers along the sides of the hood (if used) are in place.

If the hood hinges must be removed from the front deck (Fig. 22-6), drill out the spot welds. Then install the new hinge with the new bolts that are packaged with it.

≡ 22-4 HOOD LATCH

Hoods have two latches: the locking latch and the safety, or auxiliary, latch. When the hood release is operated, the locking latch releases, allowing the hood to pop up to the safety-latch position. The safety latch is then released by reaching in under the hood and operating a lever by a finger. The hood release is located inside the passenger compartment in some cars (Fig. 22-7). In other cars, the hood release is located at the front of the car, as shown in Fig. 22-8. With either location, when the release is pulled, a cable carries the movement to the latch, causing it to release. A pop-up spring (Fig. 22-9) then pushes the hood up to the safety-latch position. The safety latch is released by reaching in under the partly open hood.

≡ 22-5 ADJUSTING HOOD LATCH

The hood latch can be moved from side to side, and up or down, to secure the proper fit. You must first make sure that the hood hinges are properly adjusted before attempting to adjust the latch. Then loosen the nuts or screws attaching the latch and make the adjustment. If an up or down adjustment must be made, first loosen the adjustable stop screws at the front and turn them in so they will not interfere with the adjusting procedure. Then adjust the latch so that the hood aligns along the sides and at the front. Tighten the hood attaching screws. Then turn the adjustable stops up so they snug up against the hood when it is closed. Tighten the lock nuts.

Check the action of the safety latch (Fig. 22-9). Open and close the hood several times to make sure that the safety latch works.

≡ 22-6 TRUNK-LID ADJUSTMENT

The trunk, or rear-compartment, lid is attached at the forward end with hinges. A locking latch is centered at the rear (Fig. 22-10). The hinge screw holes are elongated or enlarged so that the lid can be shifted one way or the other to get proper alignment. To make the adjustment, loosen the screws slightly and shift the lid as necessary. Then tighten the screws.

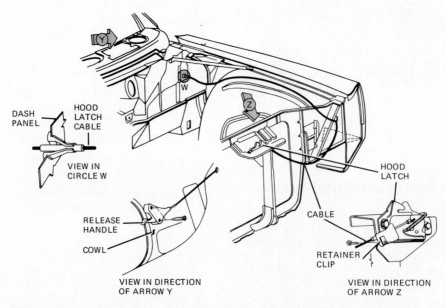

Fig. 22–7 An inside, or remote-control, hood release. *(Chrysler Corporation)*

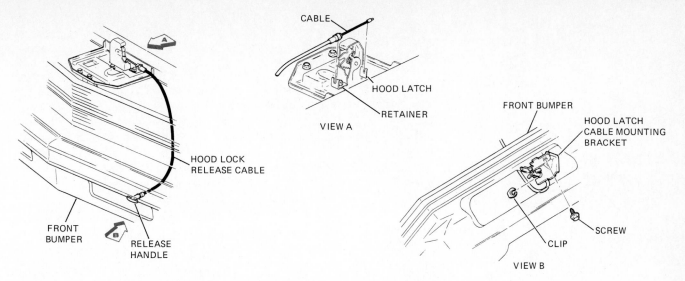

Fig. 22–8 A front-mounted hood release. (*Buick Motor Division of General Motors Corporation*)

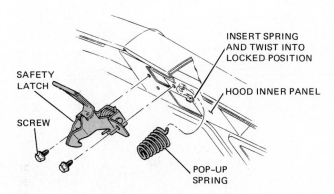

Fig. 22–9 Location of the pop-up spring and safety latch. (*Buick Motor Division of General Motors Corporation*)

≡ 22-7 TRUNK-LID LATCH

The trunk lid latches in the locked position when it is closed. It is released by a key. When the key is turned, the lock is unlatched and the trunk lid opens. In some cars, the lid can also be unlocked by an electric solenoid and a push button in the glove compartment. (Ignition switch must be in the ON or accessory position.) The lid latch is adjusted by loosening the attaching screws and moving the latch up or down as required, or by moving the striker.

NOTE: When adjusting the electric lid latch, avoid placing excessive tension on the latch. This could prevent the solenoid from releasing the latch.

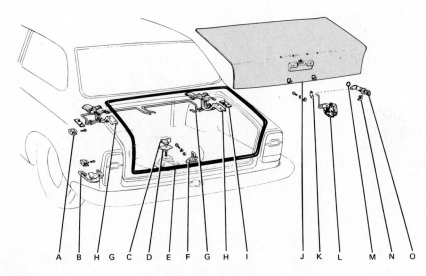

A. JACK HANDLE CLAMP
B. JACK CARRIER
C. SPARE WHEEL CLAMP SCREW
D. SPARE WHEEL CLAMP PLATE
E. WEATHERSTRIP
F. STRIKER
G. TORSION BAR
H. HINGE
I. SHIM
J. TRUNK
K. ROD SNAP
L. LOCK
M. LOCK CYLINDER GASKET
N. LOCK CYLINDER RETAINER
O. LOCK CYLINDER

Fig. 22–10 Trunk and trunk-lid components. (*Toyota Motor Sales, Inc.*)

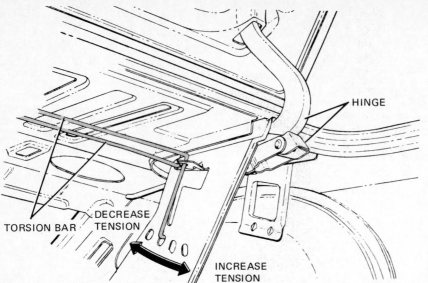

Fig. 22-11 Adjustment of the torsion-bar springs. *(Ford Motor Company)*

≡ 22-8 HOLD-OPEN SPRINGS

Two types of hold-open springs are used: torsion-bar (Figs. 22-10 and 22-11) and spiral (Fig. 22-12). Both work in the same way. When the lid is unlocked, the springs counterbalance the weight of the trunk lid. They supply most of the effort of moving the lid up to the fully opened position. The torsion bars can be adjusted if they do not supply sufficient tension to hold the lid open (Fig. 22-11).

≡ 22-9 ADJUSTING TORSION BARS

If the lid does not open properly, the torsion bars are not supplying enough tension. This requires a readjustment that will increase the tension. Figure 22-11 shows the principle. The end of the torsion bar is lifted from one of the adjustment holes and moved to the next adjustment hole. Figure 22-13 shows the use of Vise-Grip pliers to make the adjustment. Note that in Fig. 22-11 the arrangement uses adjustment holes. In Figure 22-13, there is a series of adjustable slots. With either arrangement, moving the end of the torsion bar from one position to another changes the tension.

≡ 22-10 WEATHERSTRIP

The joint between the trunk and the surrounding metal is closed by a rubberlike weatherstrip (Figs. 22-10 and 22-14). The shape of the weatherstrip varies with the car, but its purpose is the same. When the lid closes, the

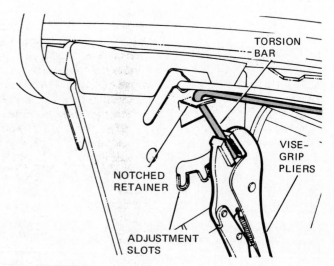

Fig. 22-13 Using Vise-Grip pliers to adjust the torsion bar. *(American Motors Corporation)*

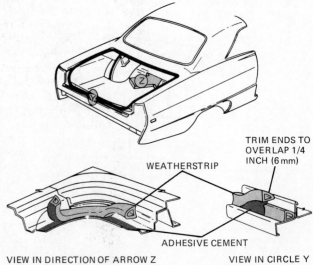

VIEW IN DIRECTION OF ARROW Z   VIEW IN CIRCLE Y

Fig. 22-14 Weatherstripping around trunk lid. *(Chrysler Corporation)*

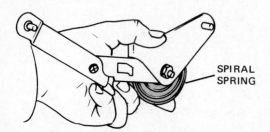

Fig. 22-12 Spiral type of counterbalancing spring. *(American Motors Corporation)*

218

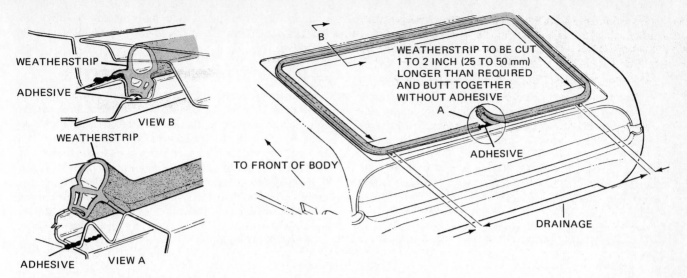

Fig. 22–15 Installing new weatherstrip around trunk lid. No adhesive should be applied around the drainage depressions. *(Ford Motor Company)*

weatherstrip mashes down to form a tight seal between the deck lid and the surrounding panels. Figure 22-15 shows another shape of weatherstrip.

To install weatherstrip, first make sure that all the old weatherstrip and cement have been removed from the trough into which the new weatherstrip is to be installed. Different manufacturers have different methods of installing the weatherstrip. For example, Chrysler recommends the following method: Apply an even, continuous coat of rubber cement to the weatherstrip-contact surface in the deck-lid opening and also to the contact surface of the weatherstrip (Fig. 22-14).

Then install the weatherstrip. Locate the joint at the bottom as shown at Y in Fig. 22-14. Make sure that the weatherstrip molded corners are correctly positioned. Avoid puckering or stretching the weatherstrip around corners. Trim ends to overlap ¼ inch [6 mm]. Apply cement to the ends, and when it becomes tacky, compress the ends into position. Wipe off any excess cement with a cloth moistened with a suitable solvent.

Ford supplies these instructions (Fig. 22-15): Apply a ¼-inch [6 mm] bead of rubber cement in the bottom of the weatherstrip trough except at the drainage depressions (to right in Fig. 22-15). Position the new weatherstrip as shown in Fig. 22-15. Cut the weatherstrip about 1 to 2 inches [25 to 50 mm] longer than required. Butt the two ends together without adhesive. Apply a 3⁄32-inch [2 mm] bead of rubber cement under the outboard lip of the weatherstrip between the points shown in Fig. 22-15.

≡ 22-11 LEAK-CHECKING TRUNK-LID SEAL

With the lid down, direct a mild stream of water at the joint between the lid and adjacent quarter panel (Fig. 22-16). Carry the water stream all the way around the lid and also on the rear window and taillights. Then open the lid and look for wet spots on the inside of the weatherstrip and for water on the floor of the trunk. If the water-leak test shows low spots at body-solder or weld joints, you'll need to build up these low points with plastic filler and then paint the repaired area. Or you can shim out the weatherstrip with vinyl foam strip to improve the seal.

If seams or pinholes are the cause of the leakage, repair them with air-dry vinyl or equivalent sealer. Then touch up with paint.

If end extension or taillights are the cause of leakage, first check for loose or missing nuts or screws. Install and tighten the screws and nuts as necessary. Apply caulking material around screws and nuts to seal them.

If water leakage is found around the lower edge of the rear window, it will be necessary to replace the weather seal around the window. Servicing rear windows is covered in Chap. 26.

Fig. 22–16 To check for water leaks, direct a mild stream of water at the joint between the trunk lid and the adjacent quarter panel. *(ATW)*

On vinyl-roof vehicles, check molding-retainer studs for looseness or leaks at the upper deck panel.

≡ 22-12 LID LOCK

The lid lock is held in position by a retainer which is attached with a rivet or screw (Fig. 22-17). To remove the lock, work from the inside of the lid (lid open). Remove the screw or rivet and then the lock cylinder retainer. The lock cylinder is now free and can be pulled out of the lid.

Remove the latch attaching screws. Disconnect the electric latch wire (if the car is equipped with an electric lid release). Remove the latch.

Before reinstalling the lock cylinder, clean and lubricate it. Alcohol can be used to clean it. Blow out the cylinder with compressed air to make sure all solvent is evaporated. Then use a silicone lubricant to lubricate the cylinder. Chapter 24 describes servicing the lock cylinder.

≡ 22-13 TRUNK-LAMP SWITCH

Some cars are equipped with a trunk lamp. It turns itself on and off automatically as the trunk lid is raised and lowered. The trunk-lamp switch is a mercury switch. When the trunk lid is raised, the switch is tilted into the ON position. The mercury runs to the low end of the switch and covers the two terminals in the switch. This completes the circuit to the battery and the light comes on. When the lid is closed, the opposite end of the switch becomes the low end. The mercury runs to that end, away from the terminals. This opens the circuit, and the light goes off.

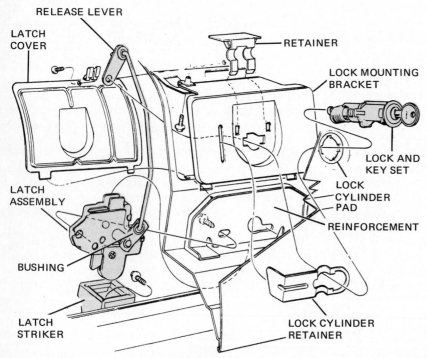

Fig. 22-17 Trunk-lid latch and lock arrangement. *(Ford Motor Company)*

REVIEW QUESTIONS

Select the *one* correct, best, or most probable answer to each question. You can find the answers in the section indicated at the end of each question.

1. Hoods may be hinged   (≡22-1)
   a. only one way
   b. at the front or back
   c. at the front only
   d. at the back only

2. Adjustable bumpers under the hood are used to (≡22-2)
   a. prevent rattle or flutter
   b. secure alignment
   c. prevent water leaks
   d. secure the proper gap

3. To get proper alignment, hoods and trunk lids can
   a. be shimmed   (≡22-3 and 22-6)
   b. have thicker weatherstripping added
   c. have stronger springs installed
   d. be shifted one way or the other

4. The main purpose of weatherstripping around the trunk opening is to prevent   (≡22-10)
   a. trunk-lid flutter
   b. water leaks
   c. wind noise
   d. rattles

5. The trunk-lid seal can be checked with   (≡22-11)
   a. shims
   b. an air hose
   c. a water hose
   d. a flashlight

PART 6

SERVICING DOORS, TAILGATES, LIFT GATES, AND SPECIAL ROOFS

In this part, you will learn about the mechanisms inside doors, tailgates, and lift gates and how to service them. In addition, you will learn about special roofs and possible services they may require.

Doors contain two basic types of mechanisms. One raises and lowers the windows, either mechanically with a crank or electrically with a motor. The second mechanism latches and unlatches the door using a locking device that may be operated mechanically with a knob or electrically with a solenoid.

Front doors contain additional devices. The left front door on the driver's side has, on some cars, a rearview mirror control, trim, door pull, armrest, electric door-lock switch, window regulators, ashtray, cigarette lighter, and control switches for the electrically operated seat adjuster.

Tailgates can be more complex than doors. They may contain a mechanical or electrical device for raising or lowering the back window. They also contain a handle and latching device that permits the tailgate to be lowered. The latching device includes a lock. In addition, dual-action tailgates have a second hinging arrangement that permits them to swing to one side like a door. Some tailgates also include a window wiper (like the windshield wiper) and a window heater to remove any frost or mist that could impede vision to the rear.

In contrast, lift gates are comparatively simple. The sun roof is also comparatively simple. It is a sliding cover that can be mechanically or electrically moved back to provide an opening in the roof. All of these body panels are described in this part. There are three chapters in Part 6, as follows:

Chapter 23 Door Trim, Moldings, and Weatherstrip
Chapter 24 Door Latches, Locks, and Window Regulators
Chapter 25 Rear-Opening Doors and Special Roofs

DOOR TRIM, MOLDINGS, AND WEATHERSTRIP

After studying this chapter, you should be able to:

1. Describe the various components of a car door.

2. Explain how to remove and install door trim.

3. Discuss the purpose and location of the water deflector.

4. Explain how to remove and replace door exterior moldings.

5. Discuss weatherstripping for doors and explain the two basic types.

6. Explain how to leak-test door seals.

7. Describe how to check glass-to-weatherstrip fit.

8. Explain how to diagnose wind noise and how to correct it.

≡ 23-1 DOOR COMPONENTS

The typical car door (Fig. 23-1) includes:

- Door latch
- Door lock
- Window regulator
- Weatherstrip
- Interior trim
- Exterior moldings

In addition, doors have armrests, door pulls, ashtrays (some with cigarette lighters), and litter bags. The door on the driver's side may contain additional devices such as rearview-mirror control, seat-adjuster switches (for electrically adjusted seats), a door-lock switch for all doors, and separate master switches for each electric window in the car. This chapter describes the door trim, molding, and weatherstrip. Door-latch and lock mechanisms, and window regulators, are covered in Chap. 24.

≡ 23-2 DOOR PULLS

Each door on a car must have some way for a person seated next to it to safely and conveniently pull it closed. *Door pull* is the name given to any of a variety of

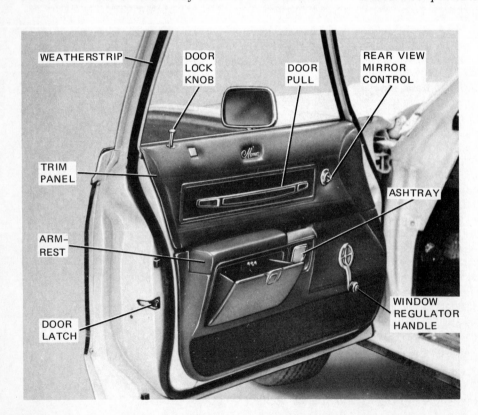

Fig. 23-1 A typical car door. *(Chrysler Corporation)*

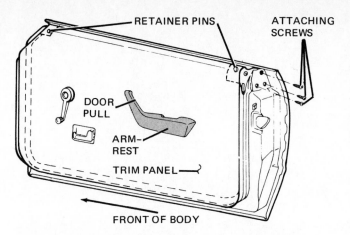

Fig. 23-2 A solid-type door pull combined with the armrest. *(Ford Motor Company)*

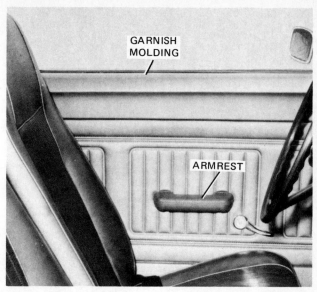

Fig. 23-3 Armrest that is basically a padded bracket. *(Ford Motor Company)*

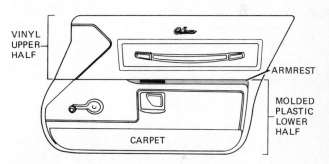

Fig. 23-4 Armrest molded into the lower half of the trim panel. *(Chrysler Corporation)*

simple "hand-holds" that a person can grasp and pull to close the door while seated inside the car.

Door pulls are either straps (Fig. 23-1) or handles such as shown in Fig. 23-2. On most cars with pull straps, the strap is attached with screws. Then a cover is snapped into place to hide the screw. Some cars have covers that are attached with screws. Figure 23-2 shows a solid-type door pull that is combined with the armrest. It is fastened to the door with screws.

≡ 23-3 ARMRESTS

Armrests vary greatly in style. A simple bracket can be made into an armrest by padding it, as shown in Fig. 23-3. Some armrests contain a variety of switches to control windows, door locks, seat position, and rear-view mirrors. Figure 23-4 shows another type of armrest. It is molded into the lower half of the door trim panel and then covered with a pad.

≡ 23-4 DOOR TRIM

Any cloth or plastic material used to line the interior of a door is called *door trim*. Usually the various pieces of trim for a door are assembled into one-piece or two-piece "trim pads" or "trim panels." Figures 23-1 to 23-4 show different styles of door trim panels.

A variety of fastening methods are used to attach door trim to doors. Figure 23-5 shows a typical attachment method for a one-piece door trim panel. Others are similar, although various types of fasteners are used. The removal and installation of door trim panels on various Ford-built cars is described below. This procedure will show you how to get into and out of a door. While these instructions apply in general to many similar vehicles, refer to the manufacturer's shop manual for the car you are working on.

NOTE: Some of the steps given below do not apply to all vehicles. If they do not, skip them and go to the next step. Figures 23-5 to 23-7 show the details of attachment.

REMOVAL

1. Remove the door-lock knob and the garnish molding (Fig. 23-3).

2. Remove the window-regulator handle and the door-latch handle (Fig. 23-6). These are attached in various ways. Sometimes there is a screw cover which is removed first. This exposes the screw (or screws) that attaches the handle.

3. Remove the armrest assembly. If the armrest contains electric switches, disconnect the switch wiring before removing the armrest.

4. Remove the mirror remote-control bezel nut.

5. Remove the door-trim retaining screws (Fig. 23-5).

6. Use a putty knife or trim-panel clip remover and lift the trim-panel retaining clips from the door inner panel to disengage the panel (Fig. 23-7).

7. Disconnect all wiring as necessary to remove the trim panel.

8. If the trim panel or armrest requires replacement, transfer the pull-handle rivets and retaining screws, retaining clips, trim moldings, and other parts to the new assembly. If the watershield (also called *water dam* and *water deflector*) has been removed or damaged, replace it (Fig. 23-8). Check that the watershield is positioned and sealed correctly (≡23-5) before installing the trim panel.

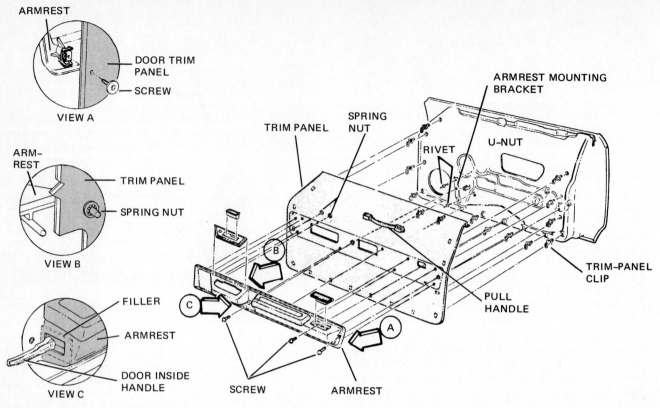

Fig. 23-5 Method of attaching one-piece trim panel to the door. *(Ford Motor Company)*

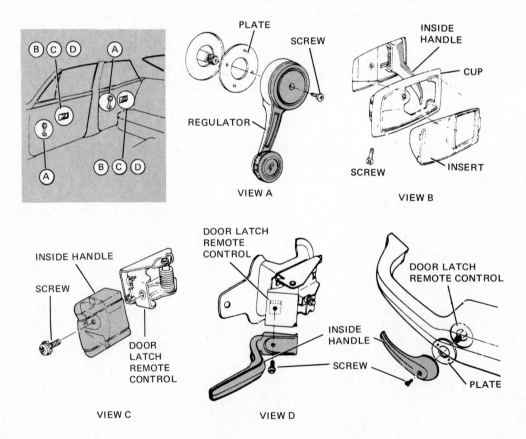

Fig. 23-6 Typical installations of door and window-regulator handles. *(Ford Motor Company)*

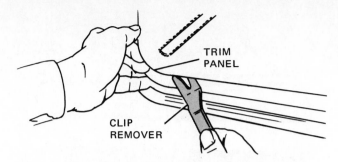

Fig. 23-7 Removing trim-panel clips. *(Ford Motor Company)*

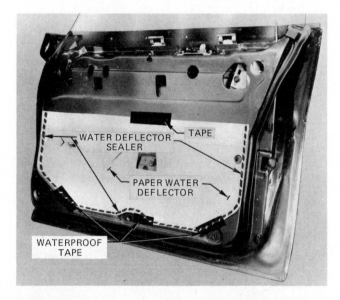

Fig. 23-8 Watershield, or water deflector, sealed in place in door. *(© Fisher Body Division of General Motors Corporation)*

9. Make sure the armrest screw U-nuts are properly positioned on the door inner panel. If they have been dislodged, they must be repositioned before the watershield is installed.

INSTALLATION

1. Position the trim panel on the door inner panel and connect wiring (if so equipped). Route the mirror control cable through the hole in the trim panel.

2. Replace any damaged trim-panel clips. Then push the trim panel and retaining clips into the holes in the inner door panel (Fig. 23-5). Install the retaining screws.

3. Install the remote-control-mirror bezel nut.

4. Connect the wiring (if any) to the armrest, position the armrest on the trim panel, and install the retaining screws.

5. If the armrest has a finish panel or trim, install it.

6. Position the door-latch and window-regulator handles and secure them with the attaching screws (Fig. 23-6). Reinstall the screw-access covers. If they were originally cemented into place, clean off the old cement with alcohol. Special tape (adhesive on both sides) is required to tape the covers back into place.

7. Install the garnish molding and door-lock knob (Figs. 23-1 and 23-3).

≡ 23-5 WATER DEFLECTOR

The purpose of the water deflector (Fig. 23-8) is to seal the door inner panel and prevent the entry of water into the body. The deflector is attached by a sealing material that is loaded with string and by waterproof sealing tape. The deflector is made of tough waterproof paper or plastic film. Whenever work is done on the doors that disturbs the deflector, it must be reattached and resealed (as explained below) to prevent water leaks.

1. Put a bead of sealer on the deflector as shown in Fig. 23-8, making sure there are no gaps so water will be guided into the drain slots.

2. Make sure the sealing area on the door inner panel is clean and dry. Position the deflector on the door inner panel. Insert the lower edge of the deflector in the retaining slot. Then firmly press or roll the edges of the deflector to get a good seal between the door panel and deflector.

NOTE: If you are merely resealing the old deflector which you have only partly detached, you may need additional sealer. Use body caulking compound or strip caulking on the inner panel at the unsealed areas.

3. Seal the lower edge of the deflector with a waterproof body tape.

4. On the doors that have inner-panel hardware attachments below or outside of the water deflector, seal the screwheads and panel holes with body caulking compound.

If the deflector is damaged, it should be replaced. The material comes in rolls. To fabricate a new deflector, cut off a length of the paper, lay the old deflector on it, and cut out a new deflector of the same size and shape.

NOTE: The complete procedure of removal and installation that follows may not be required if the deflector is only partly detached to get to the internal door mechanism.

REMOVAL

1. Remove the door-trim assembly and the waterproof body tape attaching the top of the water deflector to the door inner panel.

2. Use a putty knife to break the seal between the deflector and panel. Work down both sides of the deflector. Make sure the tool blade is between the inner panel and the string that is embedded in the sealer.

3. Remove the tape from the inner panel at the lower edge of the water deflector (Fig. 23-8). Disengage the deflector from the inner-panel drain slot and remove it.

INSTALLATION

Inspect the deflector. If it is torn or has holes, repair it with waterproof body tape applied to both sides of the deflector. If the deflector is in bad shape, use it as a template to cut out a new deflector from the roll of special paper.

≡ 23-6 DOOR EXTERIOR MOLDINGS

Door exterior moldings are attached in various ways. The following procedures cover the removal and replacement of the moldings used on the doors of General Motors cars. The procedures are similar for cars made by other manufacturers. If you find a different sort of attachment, refer to the shop manual covering the specific model of car you are working on.

NOTE: *The procedure for removing and replacing moldings that are secured by adhesive tape is described in ≡23-7.*

Refer to Figs. 23-9, 23-10, and 23-11. Figure 23-9 numbers the different moldings for reference when you look at the chart in Fig. 23-11. Figure 23-10 illustrates the various door molding attachments, as follows:

1. Weld stud retained plastic clip

2. Weld stud retained plastic clip with attaching screws and/or T bolt clip and nut retaining molding end or ends in the hem flange

3. Adhesive bonded with either tape or urethane sealant

4. Spring or clinch type (self-retained)

5. Attaching screw with integral or separate belt molding

To determine the removal procedure for any piece of molding, first refer to Fig. 23-9 to determine its reference number. Then refer to Fig. 23-11 to find this number in the vertical column to the left. To the right of this reference number you will find the molding described and also, in the right-hand column, the attachment reference. Use this reference to go back to Fig. 23-10 to find the illustration showing the attachment method.

POINTS TO WATCH

1. Protect the adjacent painted surface with masking tape to prevent damaging it.

2. Use the proper tools, and exercise care to avoid damaging the molding.

3. Holes in body panels for screws, bolts, or clips may allow water to leak into the body interior if they are not sealed off. Use body caulking compound or presealed screws, nuts, or clips.

4. If a weld stud on an outer panel becomes damaged or is broken off, drill a small hole in the panel next to the original weld-stud location. Insert a self-sealing screw through the original clip and into the outer panel. Or you can replace the damaged weld stud with a self-sealing screw-type weld stud.

≡ 23-7 ADHESIVE BODY MOLDINGS

The procedure that follows applies to door moldings and to all moldings that are applied to body panels with adhesive tape. Separate procedures are included for reattaching loose ends of moldings and for completely removing and replacing moldings.

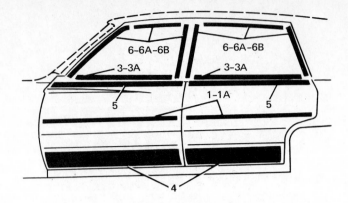

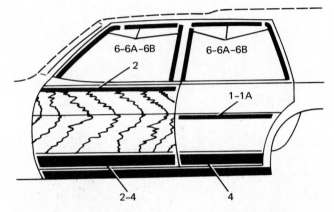

Fig. 23-9 Typical door exterior moldings. Numbers in the illustration refer to the usage (Fig. 23-11) and to the method of attachment (Fig. 23-10). (© Fisher Body Division of General Motors Corporation)

NOTE: *The panel surface should be warm (70 to 90°F) [21 to 32°C] and free of any wax or oil film.*

REATTACHING LOOSE ENDS

If only one end of the molding has come loose, proceed as follows:

1. Wash the panel area from which the molding has come loose with detergent and water. Wipe dry. Wipe the panel and adhesive side of the molding with oil-free naphtha or alcohol.

2. If you need a guideline, apply a length of masking tape to the panel. You can also use a straightedge.

3. If the molding has separated from the adhesive back, with the tape remaining on the body panel, do not remove this tape. Instead, wipe the back of the molding and the tape on the body panel with naphtha or alcohol.

4. Apply adhesive compound to the back of the molding and press it in place. Follow the instructions on the adhesive container. For example, one type requires that you hold the molding in place with constant force for 30 seconds. Another type requires that you tape the molding in place with masking tape for 15 minutes or longer, or until the adhesive sets.

REMOVING AND ATTACHING MOLDING

If the molding has to be completely removed or if it has come off, proceed as follows:

1. After removing the molding, wash the affected panel area with detergent and water and wipe it dry.

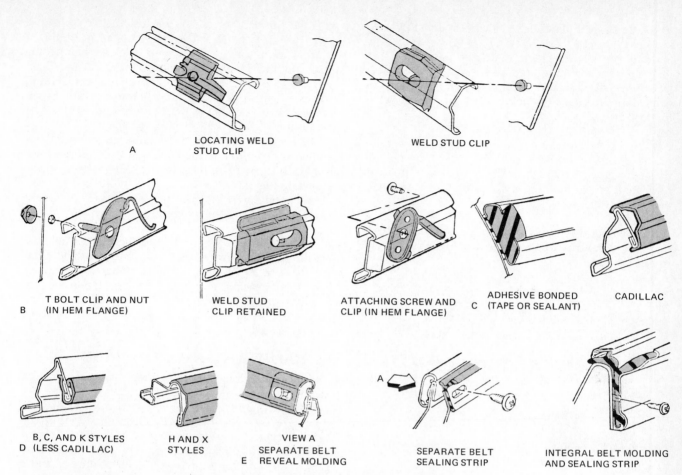

A LOCATING WELD STUD CLIP WELD STUD CLIP

B T BOLT CLIP AND NUT (IN HEM FLANGE) WELD STUD CLIP RETAINED ATTACHING SCREW AND CLIP (IN HEM FLANGE) C ADHESIVE BONDED (TAPE OR SEALANT) CADILLAC

D B, C, AND K STYLES (LESS CADILLAC) H AND X STYLES E VIEW A SEPARATE BELT REVEAL MOLDING SEPARATE BELT SEALING STRIP INTEGRAL BELT MOLDING AND SEALING STRIP

Fig. 23-10 Methods of attaching exterior door moldings. (© *Fisher Body Division of General Motors Corporation*)

MOLDING DESCRIPTION (USAGE)	MOLDING REFERENCE NUMBER (FIG. 23-9)	ATTACHMENT REFERENCE (FIG. 23-10)
Body Side (Front and Rear Door)	1	A or C
Body Side (Front and Rear Door) If attaching screws or nuts are visible in front and/or rear hem of door	1A	B
Body Side – Upper and/or Lower – Woodgrain Transfer Finishing (Front and Rear Door)	2	A or B
Door Belt Reveal (Front and Rear Door) When integral part of outer belt sealing strip	3	E
Door Belt Reveal (Front and Rear Door) When separate from outer belt sealing strip	3A	E
Front Door Belt Reveal –Front "A" Body Styles	3B	E
Door Outer Panel – Lower (Front and Rear Door)	4	B
Door Outer Panel – Upper Peak (Front and Rear Door)	5	A or B
Door Window Upper Frame Scalp "B, C, K" Body Styles less Cadillac (Front and Rear Door)	6	D
Door Window Upper Frame Scalp Cadillac Style (Front and Rear Door)	6A	D
Door Window Upper Frame Scalp "H and X" Body Styles (Front and Rear Door)	6B	D

Fig. 23-11 Name and installation chart for exterior door moldings on many General Motors cars. (© *Fisher Body Division of General Motors Corporation*)

Wipe the panel and adhesive side of the molding with alcohol.

2. If you need a guide, mark the position of the molding with masking tape as shown in Fig. 23-12. (Figures 23-12, 23-13, and 23-14 show the application of molding to a quarter panel. The principle is the same for doors.)

NOTE: *If the adhesive tape has separated from the molding and remains on the body panel, do not remove the tape from the panel. Instead, wipe the tape and back of the molding with alcohol and proceed with step 3.*

3. Temporarily attach the molding, following with masking-tape strips applied every few inches as shown in Fig. 23-13.

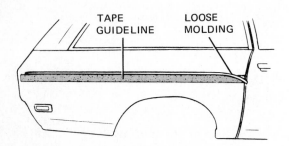

Fig. 23-12 Before removing a molding, mark its position with masking tape. *(General Motors Corporation)*

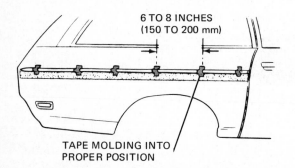

Fig. 23-13 Hold the molding in place with strips of masking tape. *(General Motors Corporation)*

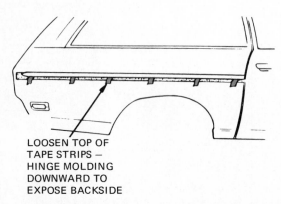

Fig. 23-14 Use the strips as hinges to swing down the molding so weatherstrip adhesive can be applied to the back side. *(General Motors Corporation)*

4. If the body is cold—well below 70°F [21°C]—warm the body panel with a heat lamp or heat gun.

5. Loosen the top of the tape strips so the molding can be hinged downward as shown in Fig. 23-14. Then, using a circular motion, quickly apply a thin film of weatherstrip adhesive (GM recommends 3M Super Weatherstrip Adhesive) to the adhesive part of the molding.

6. Immediately align the molding to previously installed tape guideline and firmly press it into place. Hold it there by reapplying the masking-tape strips as shown in Fig. 23-13. Allow it to set for at least 15 minutes. Then remove the masking-tape strips, using care to avoid detaching the molding.

Although the adhesive cures sufficiently to hold the molding in place after about 15 minutes, it will not completely cure for at least 24 hours. Therefore, the car should not be washed by any high-pressure method for at least a day after the molding has been applied. If any adhesive has squeezed out, clean it off with a cloth dampened with alcohol.

≡ 23-8 WEATHERSTRIPPING

There are two basic types of doors, each requiring a somewhat different method of weatherstripping. The weatherstripping must be water-, wind-, and dust-proof. The two types of doors are the sedan type and the hardtop type. The sedan-type door (Fig. 23-15) has an upper frame which surrounds the glass when it is raised. The hardtop-type door (Fig. 23-16) has no upper frame. The sedan door has weatherstripping all the

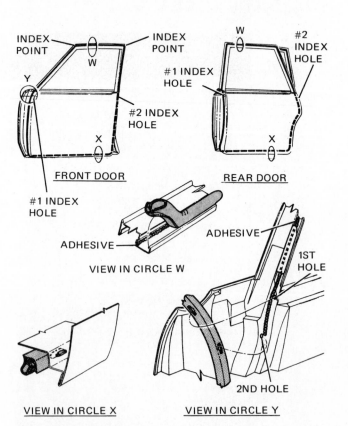

Fig. 23-15 Weatherstrip installation on a sedan door. *(Chrysler Corporation)*

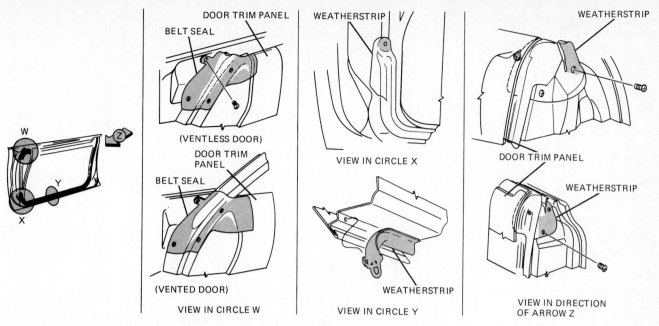

Fig. 23-16 Weatherstrip installation on a hardtop door. *(Chrysler Corporation)*

way around the edge, including the upper frame. On the hardtop door, the weatherstrip for the glass is in the roof rail. Following sections describe the removal and installation of this weatherstripping.

≡ 23-9 SEDAN-TYPE-DOOR WEATHERSTRIPPING

This type of door and its weatherstripping are shown in Fig. 23-15. When new weatherstripping is required, remove all the old weatherstrip particles and cement before applying the new weatherstrip. Do not stretch the weatherstrip or pucker it when applying it around a curve. The typical procedure that follows applies to Chrysler-built cars. Other cars may require a slightly different procedure. However, the following generally applies to all cars:

1. Refer to Fig. 23-15. Apply the lower half of the weatherstrip, starting at the No. 1 index hole and ending at the No. 2 index hole. Use the fasteners on the weatherstrip to locate and attach the weatherstrip.
2. For the upper half of the weatherstrip, start by applying a ⅛-inch [3-mm] bead of cement to the weatherstrip seating area on the door upper half.
3. Install the upper half of the weatherstrip to the door, indexing it as shown in Fig. 23-15. Work the weatherstrip from the index holes to points midway between, making sure that it is not stretched or puckered.
4. On Ford-built cars the weatherstrip is partly retained by pins inserted into holes in the door panel. Adhesive is also used where needed.

≡ 23-10 HARDTOP-DOOR WEATHERSTRIPPING

This type of door does not have the upper frame. Therefore, the weatherstrip for the glass is installed in the roof rail. Figure 23-16 shows how the weatherstrip is

installed in this type of door used on Chrysler-built cars. The procedure is as follows:

1. Position and attach the molded end of the weatherstrip with fasteners at the door hinge pillar (view X in Fig. 23-16).
2. Index and install the weatherstrip on the door, using fasteners at locating points. Work from the hinge-pillar side of the door completely around to the lock pillar.
3. Install lock-pillar seal on lock pillar with fasteners as shown in view Z in Fig. 23-16.
4. Install front-belt seal with screws as shown in view W in Fig. 23-16.
5. The hardtop roof-rail weatherstrips are attached to the weatherstrip retainers as shown in Fig. 23-17. The retainers are installed first. Then the weatherstrips are pressed into place. The quarter-window-belt outer water seal is held in place by screws. The weatherstrip retainers are adjustable. They have elongated attaching holes. This allows the weatherstrip to be moved in or out as necessary to get the required sealing action.

NOTE: When the glass is up against its stop and the roof-rail weatherstrip and the glass are properly adjusted, the outer lip of the weatherstrip will seal along the top outer edge of the glass. The inner lip of the weatherstrip will seal along the top inside edge of the glass (Fig. 23-18).

≡ 23-11 DOOR BELT-LINE WEATHERSTRIP

A weatherstrip is required at the door belt-line so that the door outer panel will seal against the glass regardless of its position (up or down). Figure 23-19 shows one way the glass belt-line weatherstrip is installed. By sealing between the glass and the outer door panel, the

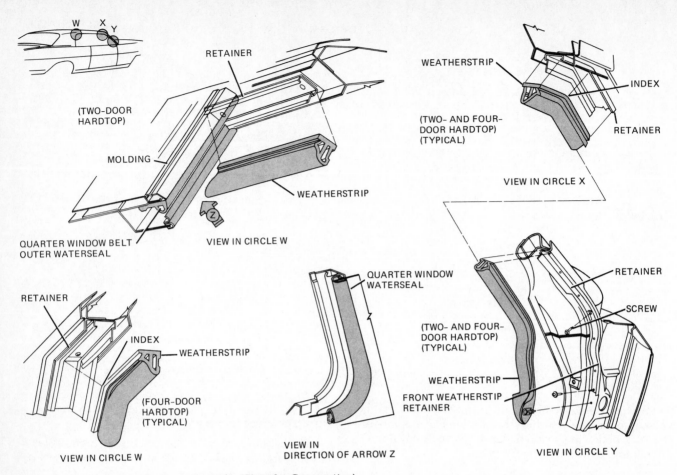

Fig. 23-17 Hardtop roof-rail weatherstrip. *(Chrysler Corporation)*

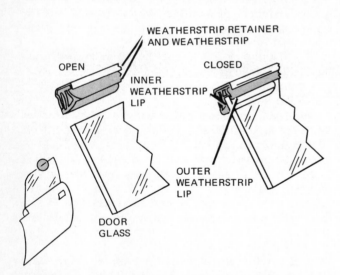

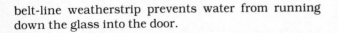

Fig. 23-18 Action of the roof-rail weatherstrip with the door open and with the door closed. *(Chrysler Corporation)*

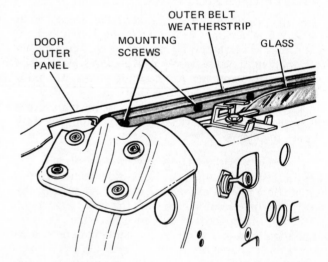

Fig. 23-19 Typical installation of a door belt-line weatherstrip. *(Chrysler Corporation)*

belt-line weatherstrip prevents water from running down the glass into the door.

≡ 23-12 LEAK-TESTING DOOR SEALS

Only a small stream of water is needed to find a leak. If you use too much water pressure, the water may be forced past even a good weatherstrip. Water with too much pressure also can splash over the suspected area and make it difficult for you to locate the source of the leak.

Hold the pressure down to get about a 3-inch [76-mm] stream (Fig. 23-20). Have an assistant sit inside and watch for water coming in as you work the hose around the gap at the door edge on the outside. Start at the lower edge of the door and work upward. If you start at the top, the runoff will wet the untested

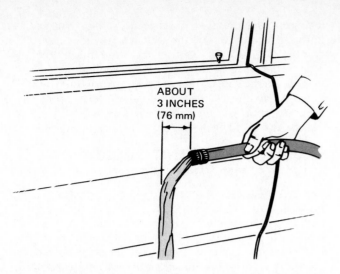

Fig. 23-20 Proper water stream to use for locating body water leaks. *(Chrysler Corporation)*

area and make any leak harder to locate. If your assistant locates leaks, mark the leaky area with chalk or tape.

If you find a leak, take necessary steps to fix it. If the cause is low spots at body-solder or weld joints or other places around the door opening, build up these low points. Use body filler and repaint the repaired area. Or you can shim out the weatherstrip with vinyl foam strip.

There might be more than one leaky point. Correct leaks you find at the lower places before proceeding with the test above them. Make sure the areas to be fixed are dry before you try to apply plastic or cement.

Run water along the belt line and check the inside trim panels for dampness, especially at the bottom. If you find water there, it means the plastic watershield is damaged or has come loose. It should be fixed (Fig. 23-5).

For a general overall check for water leakage, position the car under water-test stands (Fig. 23-21).

≡ 23-13 CHECKING GLASS-TO-WEATHERSTRIP FIT

On hardtops, the door glass must make good contact with the weatherstrip, especially along the top. The upper edge of the glass should not be visible when the

Fig. 23-21 Water-test stands positioned for an overall test of weatherstrip on the car. *(© Fisher Body Division of General Motors Corporation)*

door is closed. A quick test is to cut several strips of masking paper about 2 inches [50 mm] wide. Lay them across the top of the glass and close the glass. The paper strips should be clamped firmly between the top edge of the glass and the weatherstrip. Try pulling on them. If they pull out easily, the weatherstrip is not fitting tightly enough. Check further by the water test (≡23-12).

If there is leakage between the glass and the weatherstrip, the glass may need adjustment. If leakage is occurring over the weatherstrip, the weatherstrip probably is loose or deteriorated. Examine it and repair or replace it as necessary. Adjust the glass in the door if required.

≡ 23-14 DIAGNOSING WIND NOISE

The source of wind noise is sometimes difficult to locate. The spot where the noise is heard may not be the place where the wind leakage is occurring. Wind leaking into or out of the vehicle can set up a whistling noise that is very annoying. Most wind-noise complaints are caused by air leaks in the upper area (Fig. 23-22).

There are various causes of wind noise. The shape of the vehicle causes air to flow around the windshield and alongside the vehicle as it moves forward (Fig. 23-23). This causes a low-pressure area to develop outside the car, especially in the window areas (Fig. 23-24). Now, inside the car, the ventilating and air-conditioning or heating system build up pressure. So there is a combination of low pressure outside and high pressure inside the car.

If the weatherstrip is loose fitting at any point, air will escape from the car around the loose weatherstrip.

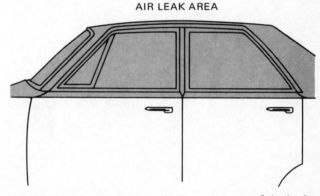

Fig. 23-22 Most air leaks are in the upper area of the body. *(Chrysler Corporation)*

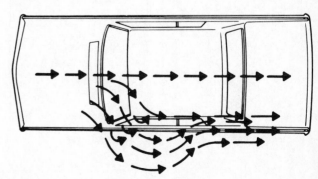

Fig. 23-23 Airflow over and around vehicle as it moves forward. *(Ford Motor Company)*

231

Fig. 23-24 Low-pressure area develops around windows of a moving car. *(Ford Motor Company)*

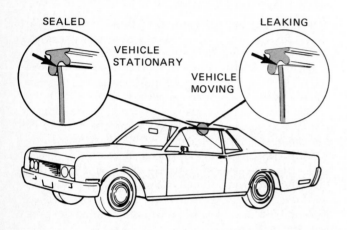

Fig. 23-25 Actions of a defective seal when the car is stopped and when the car is moving. *(Ford Motor Company)*

The seal may appear satisfactory when the car is standing still but may allow air leaks when the car is moving (Fig. 23-25). To the left, the circled drawing shows that the glass apparently fits against the weatherstrip. To the right, however, you can see that the fit is poor. When the car is moving, the internal pressure tends to push the glass out. This allows air leakage along the top of the glass.

≡ 23-15 CHECKING POSSIBLE CAUSES OF WIND NOISE

First take a good look at the weatherstrip and adjoining metal around the doors and glass (Fig. 23-26). Often it is easy to spot the cause of wind noise because you can see where the poor fit is. If the cause is loose, torn, or distorted weatherstrip, you can usually fix it by repositioning, patching, or replacing the weatherstrip. Figure 23-27 shows one method of building up the weatherstrip at a weak point where it does not fit properly. Slit the weatherstrip and insert the vinyl. Vinyl should be coated with adhesive. Also look for holes in the sheet-metal joints on the front and rear faces of the door. Seal any openings you find. Even a small hole can produce a whistling, or "pop-bottle," sound. Blow across the top of a soft-drink bottle to hear this sound.

If you don't see any obvious cause of wind leak, set the heater or air-conditioner controls to bring in outside air. Start the engine to move any vacuum-operated air doors into position. Then switch the ignition to the accessory position to keep the blower running with the engine off. Close the car doors. Now the passenger compartment will be pressurized.

Run your hand slowly around the edges of the doors

A. IMPROPERLY INSTALLED OR MISROUTED WEATHERSTRIP

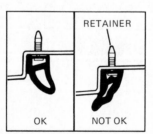

B. COLLAPSED WEATHERSTRIP

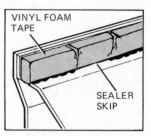

C. SEALER SKIPS AND VINYL FOAM TAPE TORN OR OMITTED

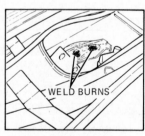

D. OMITTED WELDS OR WELD BURNS

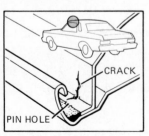

E. CRACKS AND/OR PIN HOLES IN BODY AREAS

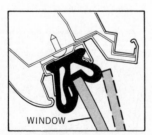

F. ALIGNMENT OF DOORS AND WINDOWS

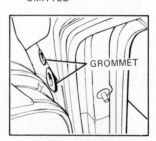

G. LOOSE, IMPROPERLY SEATED AND/OR MISSING GROMMETS AND BODY PLUGS

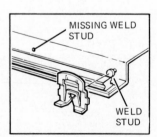

H. MISSING WELD STUD

Fig. 23-26 Sources of wind and water leaks. *(Ford Motor Company)*

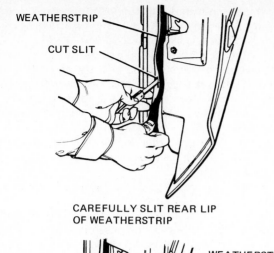

WEATHERSTRIP

CUT SLIT

CAREFULLY SLIT REAR LIP
OF WEATHERSTRIP

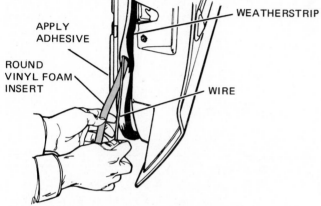

APPLY
ADHESIVE

ROUND
VINYL FOAM
INSERT

WEATHERSTRIP

WIRE

POSITION FOAM INSERT INTO CAVITY OF
COLLAPSED WEATHERSTRIP USING A WIRE

Fig. 23-27 Building up weatherstrip with vinyl. *(Ford Motor Company)*

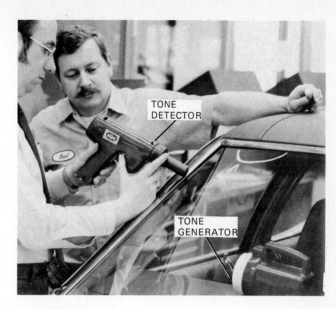

TONE
DETECTOR

TONE
GENERATOR

Fig. 23-28 Electronic leak detector can locate the source of wind noise. *(Ford Motor Company)*

≡ 23-16 USING CARPENTER'S CHALK

To make a chalk test, open the door and run chalk all around the weatherstrip (Fig. 23-29). Use white chalk for a dark car, and blue for a light-color car. Then gently close the door, holding the button so the door does not latch. Now open the door and look around the door opening for chalk transfer. Where the weatherstrip has made good contact, you will find chalk on the door. Where there is poor contact, little or no chalk will transfer.

≡ 23-17 USING TRACING POWDER

To use tracing powder, you need a powder syringe (Fig. 23-30). Close the doors and windows. Squeeze the sy-

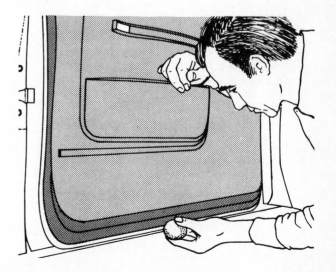

Fig. 23-29 Using carpenter's chalk to check around weatherstrip for leaks. *(ATW)*

and vent, and all around the window glass. Mark any place you feel air coming through so you can check these points later. If you moisten your hand with water, you can feel the air leakage more easily.

Listen for any hissing noise. You can improve your chances of hearing any hiss by using a short length of small-diameter hose. Hold one end of the hose to your ear and pass the other end slowly around the door and glass edges. Even a small leak will usually make enough noise for you to hear it through the hose.

If feeling and listening do not help you locate the source of the wind noise, you can use an electronic leak detector. This detector includes a tone generator and a tone detector (Fig. 23-28). The tone generator is placed inside the vehicle. It produces a high-pitched (ultrasonic) tone that is inaudible to the human ear but travels out through a leak. While the tone generator is operating, the technician moves the detector around the edges of the door and glass. A meter in the detector measures the strength of the signal being received. The signal will be strong at the point of leakage.

If you do not have an electronic leak detector, there are two other ways to check for air leaks. These use carpenter's chalk (≡23-16) and tracing powder (≡23-17).

Fig. 23-30 Using tracing powder in a powder syringe to check for leaks. *(ATW)*

ringe to blow powder around the edges of the doors and windows. Then open the doors and look for powder on the inside. There is loose weatherstrip at any point where powder has blown in.

≡ 23-18 CORRECTING WIND NOISE

Correction of wind noise, once the source of trouble is located, requires sealing holes, building up low spots in the metal, shimming up the weatherstrip, or repositioning or replacing the weatherstrip. These procedures were described earlier.

The technician should take the car out on the road to try to locate the cause. If you hear the noise while driving and can get a general idea of where it is coming from, pull over to the side of the road. Then seal the suspected area with masking tape. Apply tape over the joint between the door and adjoining body metal, or between the glass and adjoining metal. Then drive some more. If the tape stops or reduces the noise, you've pinpointed the source.

Sometimes accessories that have been installed on the car exterior will cause noise. Check outside mirrors, wind deflectors, roof racks, antennas, hood ornaments, and any other accessory as possible sources of noise. Also, check air ducts for debris such as leaves, twigs, and paper. If the noise persists on a new car, the manufacturer may have issued a service bulletin on how to correct it.

NOTE: Always *recheck after having made any repair for wind noise. In addition, be sure to clean the car before returning it to the customer.*

———— REVIEW QUESTIONS ————

Select the *one* correct, best, or most probable answer to each question. You can find the answers in the section indicated at the end of each question.

1. Door pulls are used to   (≡23-2)
   a. pull the door open
   b. pull the door closed
   c. raise the window
   d. latch the door

2. The material lining the interior of a door is called (≡23-4)
   a. door rest
   b. door material
   c. door trim
   d. opener

3. The water deflector is located   (≡23-5)
   a. between the inner and outer body shells
   b. under the windshield
   c. under the hood
   d. in the doors

4. Mechanic A says door exterior moldings are attached with adhesive. Mechanic B says they are attached with weld studs. Who is right?   (≡23-6)
   a. mechanic A
   b. mechanic B
   c. both A and B
   d. neither A nor B

5. Two types of doors are the   (≡23-9 and 23-10)
   a. two-door and four-door
   b. hardtop door and sedan door
   c. front door and back door
   d. hood and trunk

CHAPTER 24
DOOR LATCHES, LOCKS, AND WINDOW REGULATORS

After studying this chapter, you should be able to:

1. Describe door internal mechanisms.
2. Discuss window regulators and explain how to service dual U-run, tube-run, and flex-drive regulators.
3. Describe how to service a tumbler lock.

≡ 24-1 DOOR AND WINDOW MECHANISMS

The various mechanisms in doors may require service. These include the window regulators that raise and lower the glass, the latching mechanism that holds the door closed but allows it to be opened when operated, and the locking device.

The mechanisms and service procedures that follow are typical examples only. Specific door models may vary from those described. When servicing a car door, refer to the manufacturer's body-service manual for the car you are working on. If this manual is not available, make notes and sketches of the mechanism as you take it apart. In your drawings, show where each rod connects, how each lever is attached, and so on. If you run into trouble when trying to reassemble a mechanism, remove the trim from another similar door, or the door on the opposite side of the car. Then see how it is assembled.

≡ 24-2 DOOR INTERNAL MECHANISMS

Inside the door are two mechanisms. One, called the *window regulator*, raises and lowers the window. The other is a latching and locking mechanism. Figure 24-1 shows these mechanisms in a rear door. In this door, the door lock is operated by an electric solenoid (item 15 in Fig. 24-1).

Figure 24-2 shows a hardtop door with the parts named in considerably greater detail. This illustration also shows, outside the door, a manual door lock and window regulator. Examine various car doors to see if they have manual or electric controls. The servicing of the internal mechanisms in doors is described in following sections.

≡ 24-3 DOOR-LATCH MECHANISMS

The latch mechanism for a front door is shown in Fig. 24-3. When the door handle is operated, either from the inside or outside, a rod is moved. This causes the latch to release so the door can be opened. Then, when the door is closed, the latch operates to hold it closed. How

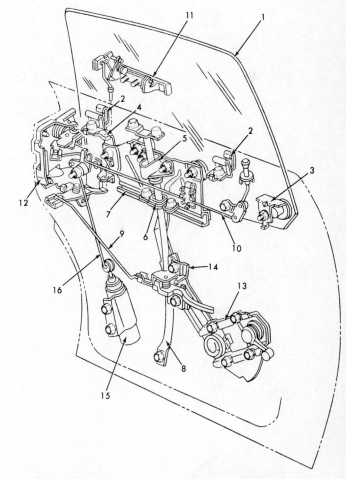

1. WINDOW ASSEMBLY
2. BELT TRIM SUPPORT RETAINERS
3. FRONT UP-TRAVEL STOP
4. REAR UP-TRAVEL STOP
5. LOWER-SASH UPPER GUIDE
6. LOWER-SASH LOWER GUIDE
7. LOWER-SASH GUIDE PLATE ASSEMBLY
8. GUIDE-TUBE ASSEMBLY
9. REMOTE CONTROL TO LOCK-CONNECTING ROD
10. INSIDE LOCKING ROD
11. DOOR OUTSIDE LIFT-BAR HANDLE
12. DOOR LOCK
13. WINDOW REGULATOR
14. DOOR-LOCK REMOTE-CONTROL HANDLE
15. DOOR-LOCK SOLENOID
16. ROD INSIDE LOCKING TO SOLENOID
17. WINDOW-REGULATOR HANDLE

Fig. 24-1 Rear-door hardware. (© Fisher Body Division of General Motors Corporation)

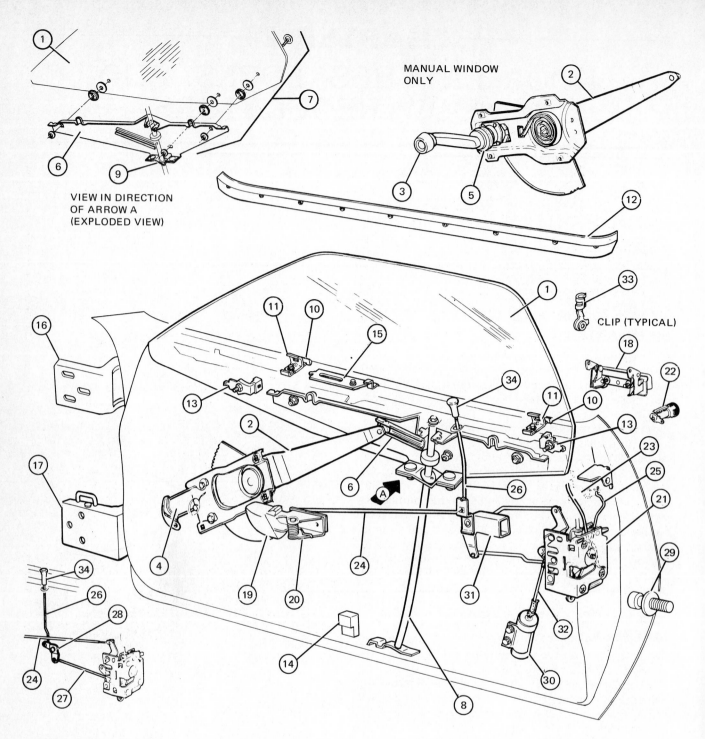

MANUAL WINDOW ONLY

VIEW IN DIRECTION
OF ARROW A
(EXPLODED VIEW)

CLIP (TYPICAL)

MANUAL DOOR LOCK ONLY

1. DOOR GLASS
2. REAR DOOR REGULATOR
3. REGULATOR HANDLE
4. MOTOR
5. REGULATOR HANDLE SPACER
6. GLASS LIFT CHANNEL
7. GLASS LIFT CHANNEL FASTENER
8. TRACK, TUBE TYPE
9. TRACK GUIDE

10. GLASS STABILIZER
11. GLASS STABILIZER TRIM SUPPORT BRACKET
12. OUTER BELT WEATHERSTRIP
13. UPSTOP
14. DOWNSTOP BUMPER
15. LIFT CHANNEL STABILIZER
16. UPPER HINGE
17. LOWER HINGE
18. OUTSIDE DOOR HANDLE
19. INSIDE REMOTE HANDLE

20. REMOTE CONTROL
21. DOOR LATCH
22. DOOR LOCK CYLINDER
23. LINK, OUTSIDE HANDLE TO LATCH
24. LINK, REMOTE CONTROL TO LATCH
25. LINK, LOCK CYLINDER TO LATCH
26. LINK, PUSHROD TO LATCH LOCK CONTROL

27. LINK, LATCH LOCK CONTROL TO LATCH
28. LATCH LOCK CONTROL
29. DOOR LATCH STRIKER
30. LOCK SOLENOID
31. LOCKING SWITCH ASSEMBLY
32. LINK, SOLENOID TO LATCH
33. LINKAGE CLIPS
34. LOCKING KNOB

Fig. 24-2 Details of the internal mechanisms in a door. (*Chrysler Corporation*)

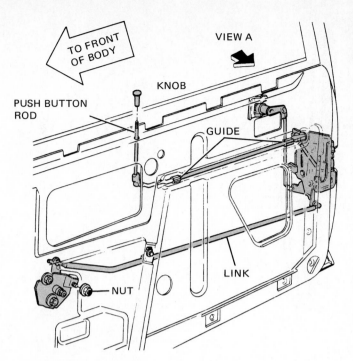
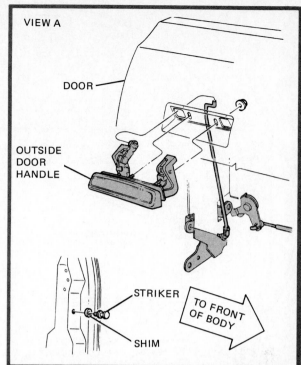

Fig. 24–3 Latch mechanism for a front door. (*Ford Motor Company*)

to adjust the latch and striker bolt was described in Chap. 21.

The door lock is part of the latching mechanism. When the locking knob is pushed down (mechanical type) or when the solenoid is actuated (electrical type), the latch is disconnected from the operating handles. Figure 24-3 shows the location and connections of the solenoid to the linkages.

≡ 24-4 DOOR-LATCH SERVICE

All door latches are similar in construction and linkage to the handles and lock. The first step in door-latch service is to remove the trim panel and watershield (deflector) as explained in Chap. 23. You can then get to the mechanism through the access holes in the inner door panel. Detach connecting rods and remove screws and nuts as necessary to replace defective parts. Before reinstalling the watershield and trim panel, operate the door latch several times to make sure it is working properly.

Servicing the lock cylinder is covered in detail in ≡24-13.

≡ 24-5 WINDOW REGULATOR

Windows are raised or lowered either mechanically by turning a crank or electrically with a motor. Both types are shown in Figs. 24-1 and 24-2.

Window regulators also differ in the glass guidance system. There are three basic types. These are the *dual U-run*, the *tube run* or *glass run*, and the *flex-drive*. Each type is described below.

1. DUAL U-RUN WINDOW REGULATOR. This type of regulator is shown installed in a door in Fig. 24-4. It is

shown removed from the door in Fig. 24-5. The crank or electric motor (on electric units) has a gear which meshes with the gear segment. The gear segment is part of the primary lever. When the gear segment is activated by rotation of the crank or motor gear, the primary lever pivots up or down.

When the window is being lowered, the gear segment turns, so the primary lever pivots and moves downward (Fig. 24-4). The roller on the end of the lever rolls in the glass channel. At the same time, the secondary lever is forced to pivot downward because it is fastened at the middle to the primary lever. The roller on the end of the secondary lever also rolls in the glass channel.

With both lever rollers rolling in the glass channel, and moving downward, the glass must follow, so it is lowered. The two runs, which are vertical channels, guide the glass as it moves down or up.

2. TUBE-RUN (GLASS-RUN) REGULATOR. This regulator is shown in Figs. 24-1, 24-2, and 24-6. The tube guides the glass as it moves up and down. As the gear on the crank or electric motor turns, it causes the gear segment to turn. This moves the lever and puts an up or down force on the channel in the glass bracket. The bracket and glass attached to it are forced to move. The tube guides the glass so it moves in the proper direction. Figure 24-7 shows the tube and guide removed from the door.

3. FLEX-DRIVE REGULATOR. This regulator (Figs. 24-8 and 24-9) uses a flexible toothed belt that moves in a T-shaped track to push the window up or pull it down. The end of the track is fastened to the window by a stud through the lower edge of the glass. As the gear on the crank or electric motor rotates, it

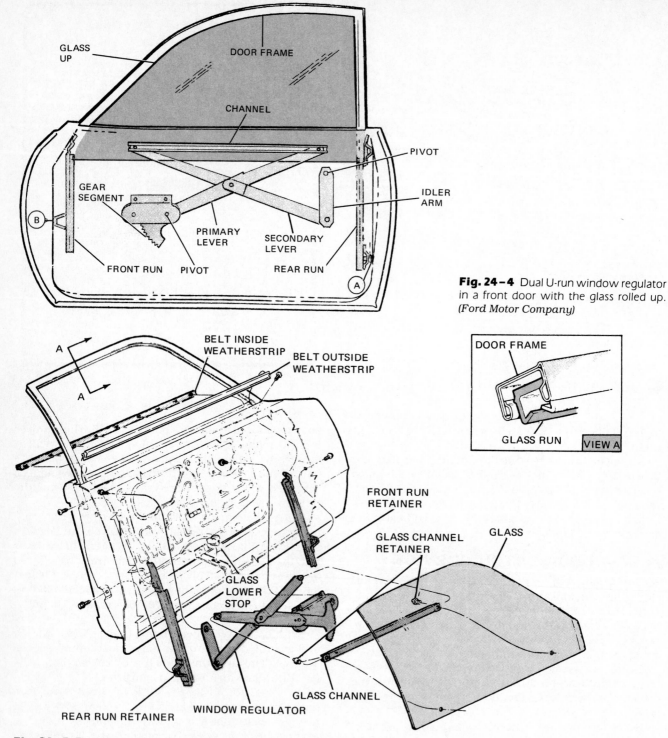

GLASS UP

DOOR FRAME

CHANNEL

PIVOT

IDLER ARM

GEAR SEGMENT

B

PRIMARY LEVER

SECONDARY LEVER

FRONT RUN

PIVOT

REAR RUN

A

Fig. 24-4 Dual U-run window regulator in a front door with the glass rolled up. *(Ford Motor Company)*

DOOR FRAME

GLASS RUN

VIEW A

A

A

BELT INSIDE WEATHERSTRIP

BELT OUTSIDE WEATHERSTRIP

FRONT RUN RETAINER

GLASS CHANNEL RETAINER

GLASS

GLASS LOWER STOP

REAR RUN RETAINER

WINDOW REGULATOR

GLASS CHANNEL

Fig. 24-5 Dual U-run window regulator removed from the door. *(Ford Motor Company)*

causes the flexible belt to slide along the T-shaped track. This moves the glass up or down.

≡ 24-6 SERVICING FORD DUAL U-RUN WINDOW REGULATORS

This regulator (Fig. 24-4) is used in many Ford-built cars. It is shown disassembled in Fig. 24-5. To remove the glass, proceed as follows:

REMOVING AND INSTALLING THE GLASS

1. Remove the trim panel and watershield.

2. Lower the glass until the glass retainers are visible at the access holes in the door inner panel. Remove the front and rear glass retainers by pushing the center pins from the retainers with a small drift punch.

3. Support the glass and pry the retainer from the drive-arm bracket and glass. Insert a screwdriver behind the glass retainer flange and pry carefully.

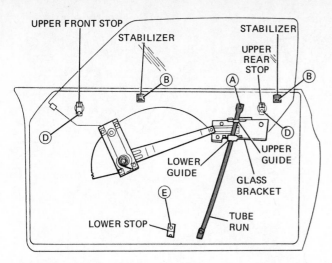

Fig. 24-6 Window regulator using a tube run to guide the glass. *(Ford Motor Company)*

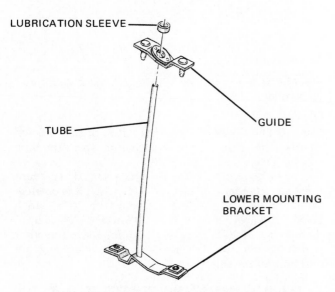

Fig. 24-7 Tube-run type of glass track. *(Chrysler Corporation)*

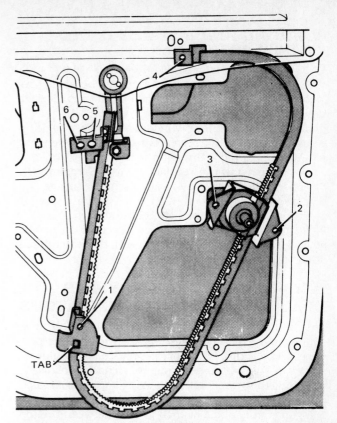

Fig. 24-8 Manually operated flex-drive. The numbers indicate the positions of the attaching rivets and also the proper sequence in which to tighten the replacement bolts. *(Chrysler Corporation)*

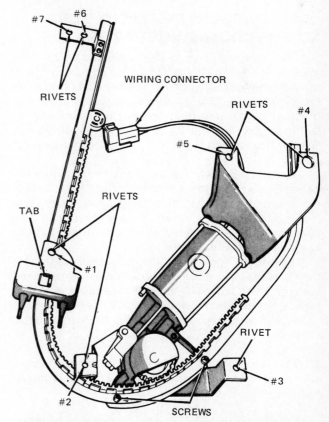

Fig. 24-9 Electrically operated flex-drive. The numbers indicate the positions of the attaching rivets and also the proper sequence in which to tighten the replacement bolts. *(Chrysler Corporation)*

4. Remove the front-run lower attaching screw.

5. Tip the front end of the glass in a downward position, and lift the glass out of the door, working from the outside.

6. To reinstall the glass, insert it into the door and tip it into normal position. Hold the drive-arm bracket to the glass, and push the glass rear retainer into the hole. Then install the glass retainer pin by pushing it into the retainer hole until the end of the pin is flush with the retainer flange. Install the glass front retainer by the same procedure. Then, with the glass positioned in the two runs, install the run attaching screws. Adjust as indicated in step 7.

7. To adjust the glass, check the weatherstrip to make sure it is in good condition. Then raise the glass to the top. Loosen the two run-retaining screws (A and B in Fig. 24-4). Lower the glass until the top edge is about 4 inches [100 mm] above the belt line. Tighten the run retainer screws. Cycle the window up and down several times to make sure it works properly.

REMOVING AND INSTALLING THE WINDOW REGULATOR

1. Remove the trim panel and watershield.

2. Support the glass, and remove the screw attaching the window-regulator equalizer arm to the door inner panel.

3. Remove the four window-regulator attaching screws. Disengage the regulator from the channel, and remove the regulator through the lower access hole.

4. To reinstall the regulator, put the regulator in the door through the lower access hole. Engage the regulator arm rollers in the channel. Position the regulator and secure it with the attaching screws. Then attach the equalizer (idler) arm with a screw. Check the adjustment. If it is satisfactory, install the watershield and trim panel.

☰ 24-7 SERVICING CHRYSLER DUAL U-RUN WINDOW REGULATORS

This regulator, shown in Fig. 24-10, is serviced in a similar manner to the Ford unit, covered in the previous section. However, Chrysler uses a pivot guide as shown in Fig. 24-10. Adjustment is made as follows.

Check the weatherstrip to make sure it is in good condition. Raise the glass almost all the way up so there is a gap of only about ⅛ inch [3 mm] between the top edge of the glass and the glass run at the top of the door frame. Loosen the pivot-guide attaching screws so the glass can be adjusted to make the top edge parallel to the door frame. Then tighten the fasteners.

☰ 24-8 ADJUSTING FORD TUBE-RUN WINDOW REGULATORS

This regulator is shown in Figs. 24-6 and 24-11. The glass must be repositioned if it has been replaced or if considerable fore-and-aft adjustment of the door hinges has been done. To adjust the glass, remove the trim panel and watershield. Loosen the upper-guide attaching screw (A in Fig. 24-6) and reposition the glass. Position the upper guide and tighten the attaching screw.

The stabilizers (B in Fig. 24-6) hold the glass in position and prevent it from wobbling. If the glass wobbles, remove the trim panel. With the glass up, loosen the front-stabilizer screw. Push the stabilizer in firmly against the glass. Tighten the screw. Repeat these steps for the rear stabilizer.

The "in-out" position of the glass determines how the top of the glass meets the weatherstrip as the glass goes up. It is adjusted by loosening the lower-guide attaching screws and moving the top of the glass in or out as required to get a good seal at the top. Then tighten the screws.

NOTE: *On right doors, the lower-guide rear screw should be tightened first, followed by the lower-guide front screw.*

The upper stops are adjusted to properly limit the amount that the glass can be raised. Remove the trim panel to adjust them. Raise the window all the way. Make sure there is no interference when the door is

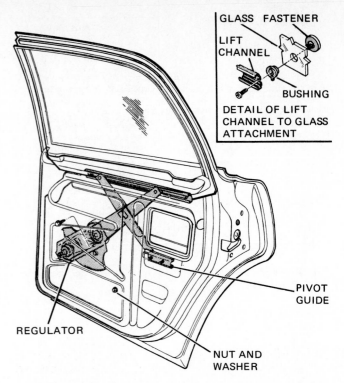

Fig. 24–10 Chrysler dual U-run window regulator. *(Chrysler Corporation)*

opened. Then position the upper stop brackets down against the glass stops and tighten the attaching screws (D in Fig. 24-6).

The lower stop (E in Fig. 24-6) is adjusted to prevent the glass from moving down too far when it is opened. To make the adjustment, remove the trim panel. Loosen the lower-stop screw and lower the glass until its top edge is flush to ¼ inch [6 mm] above the outer panel. Then raise the stop against the glass bracket and tighten the screw.

☰ 24-9 SERVICING FORD TUBE-RUN WINDOW REGULATORS

The services described below include removing and installing the glass, the window regulator, the window motor, and the guides or run.

REMOVING AND INSTALLING THE GLASS

Remove the trim panel, watershield, glass stabilizers, and upper stops. Remove the center pins from the rivets attaching the glass bracket to the glass (Fig. 24-11) with a drift punch. Then drill out the rivet heads with a ¼-inch [6-mm] drill.

NOTE: *Do not attempt to pry the rivets out. You can break the glass or bracket this way.*

Push the rivets out. Move the glass forward until the rear upper stop aligns with the access notch in the inner panel of the belt line. Lift the rear of the glass up and out. Then move the glass rearward until the front upper stop is aligned with the access hole and remove the glass. To remove the stops from the glass, remove the rivets as explained above.

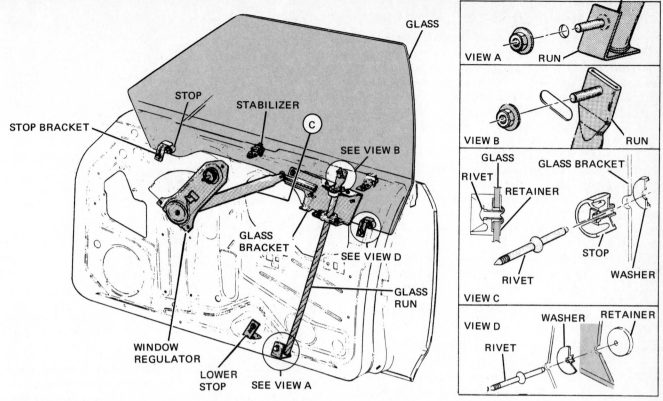

Fig. 24-11 Attachments of the Ford tube-run window regulator. *(Ford Motor Company)*

NOTE: *The bolts and nuts recommended to install the glass are ¼-20 × 1 inch hex bolts and ¼-20 nuts, tightened to 6 to 11 lb-ft [8 to 15 N·m] torque.*

To install the glass, first attach the upper stops with bolts, washers, and nuts. Then insert the glass into the door, using the access notch to move the stops below the belt line. Position the glass on the glass bracket and secure with bolts, washers, and nuts.

Then install the upper-front- and rear-stop brackets and the glass stabilizers. Adjust the stops and stabilizers (≡24-7). Install the watershield and trim panel.

REMOVING AND INSTALLING THE WINDOW REGULATOR

Remove the door trim panel and watershield. Support the glass in the up position. If the door has electric windows, remove the center pin from the motor bracket-to-inner-panel attaching rivets with a drift punch. Then drill the heads from the rivets with a ¼-inch [6-mm] drill.

Remove the center pin from the rivets attaching the window regulator. Drill the heads from the rivets. Disengage the regulator arm from the glass bracket and remove the regulator from the door.

If the motor is in good condition (electric windows) but the regulator is defective, remove the motor and install it on the new regulator. First drill a ⁵⁄₁₆-inch [8-mm] hole through the regulator sector gear and the regulator plate. Install a ¼-inch [6-mm] bolt through the hole. This prevents the sector gear from moving (it is under spring tension) when the motor is removed.

To install the window regulator, first lubricate it (Fig. 24-12). Position the regulator in the door and insert the roller into the glass bracket channel. Secure the regulator to the panel with ¼-20 × ½ inch screws and washers. Attach the motor bracket to the inner panel (electric windows). Check the regulator operation. Install the watershield and trim panel.

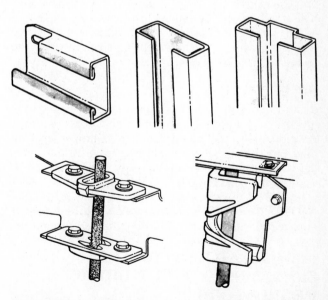

Fig. 24-12 Lubrication points for the tube-run window regulator. Apply an even coating of polyethylene grease to all window-regulator rollers, shafts, and the entire length of roller guides as shown by the shaded areas. *(Ford Motor Company)*

MOTOR AND DRIVE REMOVAL AND REPLACEMENT (ELECTRIC WINDOWS)

Remove the trim panel, watershield, and radio speaker. Many cars have holes punched in the door inner panel for motor and drive removal. On other cars, drill three ¾-inch [19-mm] holes with a hole saw in the door inner panel at the dimples. The pilot drill for the hole saw should not extend more than ¼ inch [6 mm] beyond the saw. This is to keep the drill from damaging the internal door parts.

Disconnect the motor wires at the connector. Working through the access holes, remove the three attaching screws and remove the motor and drive.

To install the motor and drive, attach it snug (but not tight) with the three screws. Connect the motor wires at the connector. Run the glass up and down to ensure gear engagement. Then tighten the motor attaching screws. Install body tape over the drilled holes. Install the radio speaker. Recheck the window operation. Then install the watershield and trim panel.

REMOVING AND INSTALLING GUIDES AND RUNS

Remove the door trim panel and watershield. Support the glass in the up position and remove the two attaching screws from the upper and lower guides. Remove the glass-run upper and lower attaching screws and remove the guides and run from the door. To install, lubricate the areas shown in Fig. 24-12. Then reinstall the run and guides. Remove the glass support and adjust the glass (≡24-7).

≡ 24-10 SERVICING CHRYSLER FLEX-DRIVE REGULATORS

REMOVAL

This regulator is shown in Figs. 24-8 and 24-9. To remove the drive, first remove the trim panel. Then position the glass to the access hole. Remove the shoulder bolt attaching the glass drive arm to the flex belt.

Block the glass in the up position in the door. Drive the center pins from the mounting rivets. Rotate the regulator drive belt out of the access hole.

INSTALLATION

Clean the flex-drive belt and make sure it is properly lubricated. Rotate the regulator into the access hole. Position it with the mounting tab in its proper locating hole. Bolt the regulator into place using ¼-20 bolts. Follow the sequence shown in Figs. 24-8 and 24-9. Tighten the bolts to 90 lb-in [10 N·m].

NOTE: The tightening sequence must be followed to prevent any twist or binding of the flex-drive unit.

≡ 24-11 ADJUSTING AND SERVICING OTHER WINDOW REGULATORS

The procedures given above for various window regulators are typical of adjusting and servicing procedures for most cars.

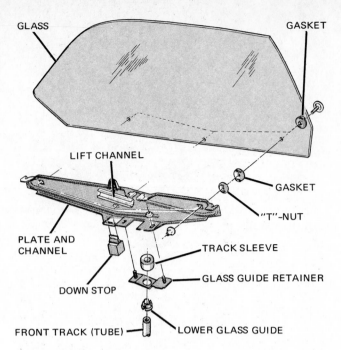

Fig. 24-13 *Attaching glass to a channel. (Ford Motor Company)*

However, one difference is the way the glass is attached to the window regulator. On many cars, the glass is attached to a channel or plate with nuts and gaskets or bushings. This method is shown in Figs. 24-10, 24-11, and 24-13. On other cars, the channel is held in place by epoxy (Fig. 24-14). A two-part adhesive is used. The two parts are mixed thoroughly and placed in the channel at three locations as shown in Fig. 24-14. Spacer clips are installed. The channel is applied to the glass at the previously determined location and taped in place so it will not move until the adhesive has cured. (Curing takes about 1 hour.)

NOTE: Two types of adhesives have been used during original assembly to secure the channel to the glass: plastisol (which is tan) and urethane (which is black). If the adhesive is tan, it is permanent and the glass and channel are replaced as an assembly. If the adhesive is black, the channel can be removed from the glass by applying heat from a gas-welding torch with a No. 2 or 3 tip. Slowly pass the flame along the full bottom length of the channel for about 1 to 1½ minutes. This should soften the adhesive so the channel can be pulled off the glass with pliers.

— CAUTION —

Do not breathe the fumes which result from heating the urethane. They are toxic! Wear a respirator.

≡ 24-12 LOCKS AND KEYS

The key has a series of notches. When the key (Fig. 24-15) is inserted into the lock cylinder, a series of tumblers (Fig. 24-16) are raised to the correct height. This lines up the notches on all the tumblers. At the same time, a side bar is pushed into the notches by two small

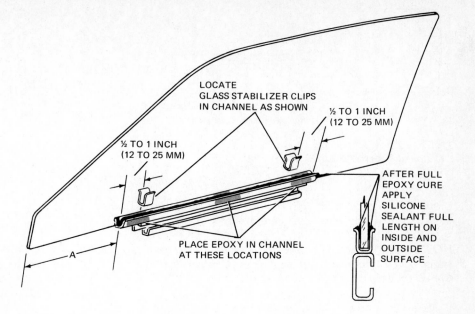

Fig. 24-14 Glass held in the channel by epoxy. *(© Fisher Body Division of General Motors Corporation)*

LOCATE GLASS STABILIZER CLIPS IN CHANNEL AS SHOWN

½ TO 1 INCH (12 TO 25 MM)

½ TO 1 INCH (12 TO 25 MM)

AFTER FULL EPOXY CURE APPLY SILICONE SEALANT FULL LENGTH ON INSIDE AND OUTSIDE SURFACE

PLACE EPOXY IN CHANNEL AT THESE LOCATIONS

A

springs. When this side bar moves into the notches, it clears the space between the lock cylinder and the lock housing. This allows the key to turn the cylinder so that unlocking occurs.

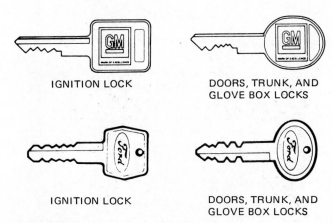

IGNITION LOCK

DOORS, TRUNK, AND GLOVE BOX LOCKS

IGNITION LOCK

DOORS, TRUNK, AND GLOVE BOX LOCKS

Fig. 24-15 Typical car keys. Many keys have notches on both sides so they can be inserted in the lock either way.

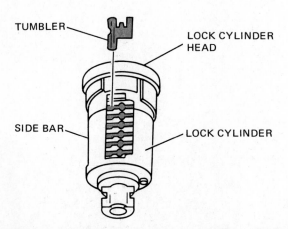

TUMBLER

LOCK CYLINDER HEAD

SIDE BAR

LOCK CYLINDER

Fig. 24-16 Location of tumblers in a lock cylinder. *(© Fisher Body Division of General Motors Corporation)*

When the cylinder is turned to the locked position and the key withdrawn, the tumblers return to their original positions. The side bar moves back into the cylinder so it is positioned between the cylinder and the cylinder housing. This is the locked position. The cylinder cannot turn.

NOTE: *This is one of several arrangements in locks. The description above is for General Motors locks except glove and console compartment locks. Many keys have notches on both sides (Fig. 24-15) so they can be inserted in the lock in either position.*

≡ 24-13 SERVICING LOCKS AND KEYS

Locks do not normally require service. However, if a lock becomes defective, it will require replacement. The cylinders and tumblers are supplied separately, and you must assemble them properly so the key will work the lock. A special code, available to owners of key-cutting equipment, lists the parts numbers of the tumblers and their positions in the cylinder for every lock arrangement. This tells you what tumbler to put where in the cylinder. There are six tumblers in the cylinder shown in Fig. 24-16. They must be so arranged that when the key is inserted, the notches on the sides of the tumblers will line up. This allows the side bar to move out of the way so the cylinder can be rotated.

If the code is not available, you can still determine which tumblers to insert in which positions in the cylinder. Lay the key on the key-code diagram in Fig. 24-17 so the key is outlined by the diagram. Start at the head of the key blade (position 1 in Fig. 24-17). Note and write down the lowest level (which is the tumbler number) that is visible in No. 1 position. Repeat this for positions 2 through 6. You now have the tumbler numbers and positions that are to be inserted into the cylinder.

Pull out the side bar with your fingers so the tumblers will drop into place. Insert the properly numbered tumbler into its correct space in the cylinder. Insert a

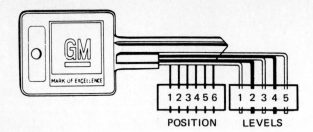

Fig. 24–17 *Using the key-code diagram.* (© *Fisher Body Division of General Motors Corporation*)

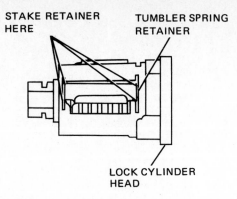

STAKE RETAINER HERE

TUMBLER SPRING RETAINER

LOCK CYLINDER HEAD

Fig. 24–18 *Installing the spring retainers.* (© *Fisher Body Division of General Motors Corporation*)

tumbler spring in the space provided above each tumbler. Install all tumblers in this manner.

NOTE: If the springs become entangled, do not pull them apart. Instead, unscrew them. Pulling them apart can stretch and ruin them.

Insert the end springs of the spring retainer into the slots at the ends of the cylinder (Fig. 24-18). Push the spring retainer down into place temporarily while you check the lock action. Insert the key into the cylinder. If the tumblers are properly installed, the side bar will drop down. If the bar does not drop, springs and tumblers are incorrectly installed.

NOTE: If improperly assembled, tumblers can be removed by holding the cylinder, tumbler slots down. Pull the side bar out with your fingers and jar the cylinder to shake the tumblers out.

When the key works as explained above, the tumblers are correctly installed and the spring retainer should be staked into place. Put the cylinder into a vise, using leather or wood at each vise jaw to prevent damage to the cylinder. Use a staking tool to lightly stake the spring retainer as shown in Fig. 24-18.

REVIEW QUESTIONS

Select the *one* correct, best, or most probable answer to each question. You can find the answers in the section indicated at the end of each question.

1. The job of the window regulator is to   (≡24-5)
   a. raise or lower the window
   b. prevent water leaks
   c. clean the window
   d. regulate the speed of movement

2. Window regulators may be operated by turning a crank or by   (≡24-5)
   a. air motors
   b. hydraulic motors
   c. electric motors
   d. vacuum motors

3. The purpose of the tube run is to   (≡24-5)
   a. drain water
   b. align the glass
   c. guide the glass
   d. lock the door

4. When you see the channel secured to the glass with black adhesive, you know that the   (≡24-11)
   a. glass and channel are replaced as an assembly
   b. channel can be removed by applying heat
   c. wrong adhesive has been used
   d. window cannot be adjusted

5. Automotive keys usually are cut by   (≡24-13)
   a. a hacksaw
   b. a key cutter
   c. hand filing
   d. a lathe

CHAPTER 25
REAR-OPENING DOORS AND SPECIAL ROOFS

After studying this chapter, you should be able to:

1. Describe the various types of rear-opening doors.

2. Discuss servicing of lift gates and tailgates.

3. Describe sun roofs and explain how they are serviced.

≡ 25-1 TYPES OF REAR-OPENING DOORS

There are several different types of gates and doors which close the rear opening of automotive vehicles that do not have a separate luggage compartment. One type, often used on small station wagons, is called a *lift*

gate (Fig. 25-1). It is hinged at the top and opens by swinging up. Many small cars use this type of lift gate as a rear-compartment lid, as shown in Fig. 25-2. The body style frequently is called a *hatchback*.

A second type of rear-opening door is shown in Fig. 25-3. It is called a *single-action tailgate*. This tailgate swings down (as a drop gate) and is hinged at the bottom. A third type, called a *dual-action tailgate*, can swing down like the single-action tailgate, as shown in Fig. 25-3. In addition, the dual-action tailgate can swing to one side and open like a door, as shown in Fig. 25-4. The dual-action tailgate has two sets of hinges,

Fig. 25-1 Small station wagons often use a lift gate, which is hinged at the top and opens by swinging up. *(Ford Motor Company)*

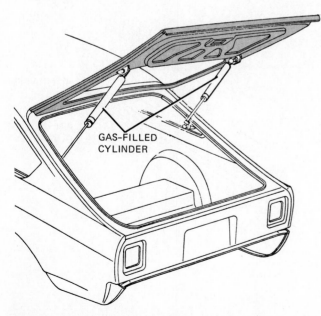

Fig. 25-2 A rear lid on a hatchback. *(© Fisher Body Division of General Motors Corporation)*

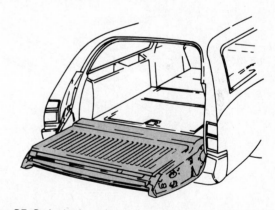

Fig. 25-3 A single-action tailgate is hinged at the bottom. *(Chrysler Corporation)*

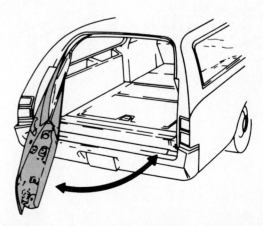

Fig. 25-4 A double-action tailgate can open down as shown in Fig. 25-3 or swing open as a door. *(Chrysler Corporation)*

one set along the bottom and one set at the side. The hinges can be selectively uncoupled, one set at a time. The side hinges can be uncoupled so the tailgate can swing down (Fig. 25-3), or the bottom hinges can be uncoupled so the tailgate can be swung to the side like a door (Fig. 25-4).

Some tailgates, such as the type that opens by swinging up (Fig. 25-1), have fixed glass. Others, which are hinged at the bottom (or bottom and side), have movable glass that can be raised or lowered by a window regulator. The regulator may be mechanically operated or, on some cars, operated by an electric motor.

≡ 25-2 LIFT-GATE SERVICE

The lift gate, or rear-compartment lid, is hinged at the top and is swung up to gain access to the interior of the car (Fig. 25-1). It has a fixed glass and two supports. The supports act as springs to hold the lid up when it is raised. The support, in the car shown in Fig. 25-2, consists of a gas-filled cylinder with a piston in it. (Another type of support contains a coil spring.) The pressure of the gas pushes the piston outward when the lid is raised, and this holds the lid up.

Some lift gates have a solenoid, actuated by a switch controlled by the driver, to unlock them. This is similar to the electric door locks, described earlier. Also, some lift gates are equipped with an electric windshield wiper.

Figure 25-5 shows a disassembled lift gate, or lid, for a hatchback. Removing and replacing the parts does not require any special procedures. A defective support is removed and a new support is installed. However, be careful when working with either the gas-

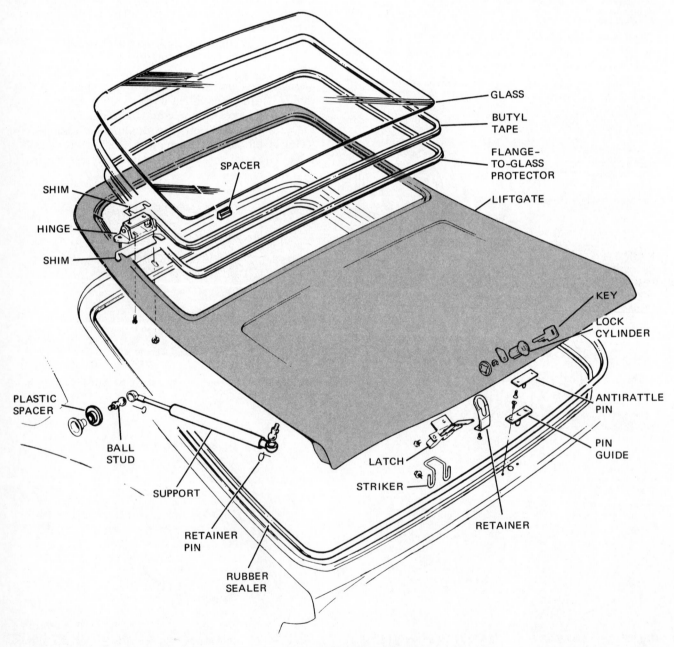

Fig. 25-5 Components of a hatchback lid. *(American Motors Corporation)*

filled or spring-type support. Never try to detach the support with the lift gate closed.

CAUTION

The supports contain high-pressure gas (or a strong spring) and may injure you or damage the car if you try to detach them with the lift gate closed. Never try to repair or dismantle the supports.

☰ 25-3 DEACTIVATING DEFECTIVE SUPPORT CYLINDERS

To dispose of a defective gas-filled support, you must first release the pressurized gas that is in it. Clamp the support horizontally in a vise (Fig. 25-6). Put at least four layers of shop towels over the end of the cylinder. Measure about 1 ¼ inches [32 mm] from the end of the cylinder. Strike a sharp-pointed center punch with a hammer to drive a small hole into the cylinder so the gas can escape. Hold the towels and punch in place until all the gas has escaped. This takes several seconds. Then, still holding the towels over the support, push the shaft into the cylinder. This forces out the remaining oil. Remove the towels and discard them. Now you can safely throw away the support.

CAUTION

Always wear eye protection while depressurizing a support. The support is filled with high-pressure gas, and when it is released, it can spurt out, carrying oil with it. If the gas or oil hits your eye, the eye can be injured.

The spring-type support is made safe for disposal as follows: Tape two pieces of ¼-inch [6-mm] steel rod about 4 inches [100 mm] long to the jaws of a bench vise

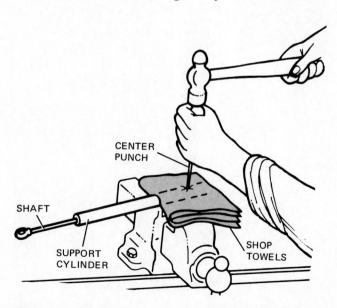

Fig. 25-6 Releasing the gas pressure in a support. *(American Motors Corporation)*

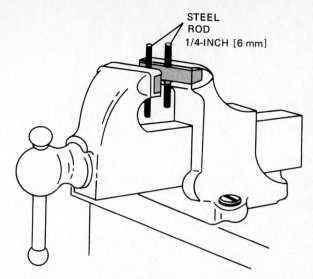

Fig. 25-7 To disable a spring-type support, first tape two pieces of steel rod to the jaws of a vise. *(© Fisher Body Division of General Motors Corporation)*

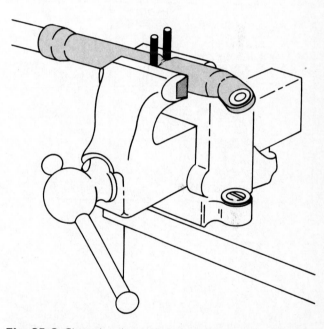

Fig. 25-8 Close the vise until each rod has made a crimp in the cylinder. *(© Fisher Body Division of General Motors Corporation)*

as shown in Fig. 25-7. Start at the back end of the support. Put the support in the vise, and tighten the jaws to put a crimp in the cylinder about 4 inches [100 mm] from the end (Fig. 25-8). Depth of the crimp should be about ¼ inch [6 mm]. Repeat the crimping operation at 6-inch [150-mm] intervals along the tube. Do not crimp closer than 2 inches [50 mm] from the end. The support can now be safely thrown away without danger of injury to someone trying to work on it.

☰ 25-4 SINGLE-ACTION-TAILGATE SERVICE

This type of tailgate (Fig. 25-9) has hinges at the bottom only and swings down when opened so it is flush with the floor of the station wagon. When the handle is oper-

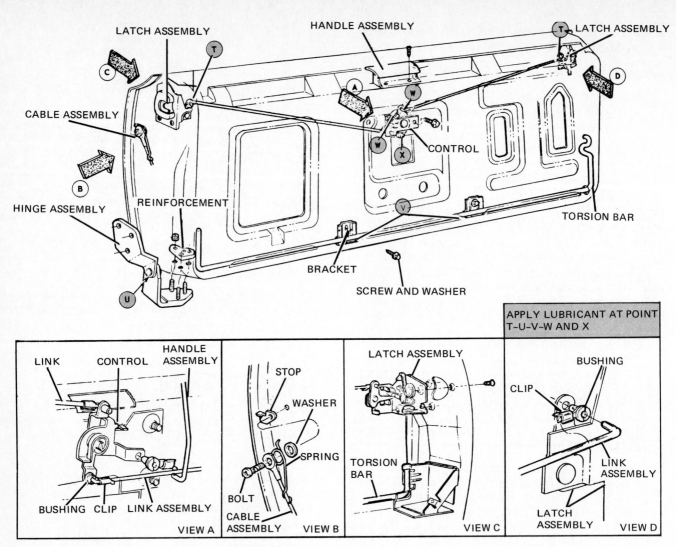

LATCH ASSEMBLY

HANDLE ASSEMBLY

LATCH ASSEMBLY

CABLE ASSEMBLY

CONTROL

HINGE ASSEMBLY

REINFORCEMENT

TORSION BAR

BRACKET

SCREW AND WASHER

APPLY LUBRICANT AT POINT T-U-V-W AND X

VIEW A

LINK   CONTROL   HANDLE ASSEMBLY

BUSHING   CLIP   LINK ASSEMBLY

VIEW B

STOP

WASHER

SPRING

BOLT

CABLE ASSEMBLY

VIEW C

LATCH ASSEMBLY

TORSION BAR

VIEW D

BUSHING

CLIP

LINK ASSEMBLY

LATCH ASSEMBLY

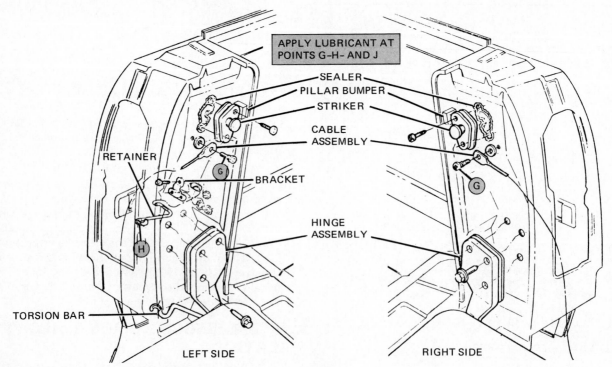

APPLY LUBRICANT AT POINTS G-H- AND J

SEALER

PILLAR BUMPER

STRIKER

CABLE ASSEMBLY

RETAINER

BRACKET

HINGE ASSEMBLY

TORSION BAR

LEFT SIDE

RIGHT SIDE

Fig. 25-9 Single-action-tailgate mechanism. *(Ford Motor Company)*

ated, the cables pull on the latches on the two sides of the tailgate, releasing the latches so the tailgate can be lowered. The assembly includes a torsion bar which is twisted when the tailgate is lowered. This makes it easier to close the tailgate, because the torsion in the twisted bar supplies much of the closing force as the bar untwists.

Some single-action tailgates have a solenoid, actuated by the driver, to unlock them. This is similar to the electric door locks, discussed earlier.

The tailgate fit can be adjusted, on some station wagons, by loosening the hinge attaching screws and shifting the tailgate as required. Then, when the fit is corrected, the screws are tightened.

Figure 25-10 shows the weatherstrip and inside cover assembly for a dual-action tailgate. The weatherstrip and inside cover assembly for the single-action tailgate is similar. Several types of weatherstrip are used on tailgates, but all weatherstrips work the same way. They provide a seal around the sides and bottom of the tailgate and along the sides and top of the glass when it is raised.

Other services for the tailgate include replacing hinges and the latch and also replacing internal parts of the latching mechanism. Steps in these procedures are given in following sections.

≡ 25-5 REPLACING RIGHT-SIDE HINGE

The steps in replacing the right-side hinge on a single-action tailgate are as follows:

1. Open the tailgate and remove the trim panel, watershield, and access cover. Mark the hinge location on the tailgate and body.

2. Support the tailgate with a suitable prop and remove the three hinge-to-body bolts. Then remove the hinge-to-tailgate nuts and remove the hinge.

3. To replace the hinge, install the hinge, bolts, and nuts. Align the tailgate and hinge with the marks previously made. Then tighten the bolts and nuts. Install the access cover, watershield, and trim panel.

≡ 25-6 REPLACING LEFT-SIDE HINGE

Replacing this hinge is more difficult than replacing the right-side hinge. This is because you must release the tension of the torsion bar.

1. Open the tailgate and mark the location of the hinge on the body and tailgate. Remove the trim panel, watershield, and access cover.

2. Hold the torsion bar in place with a deep socket and extension.

3. Remove the torsion-bar retainer-bracket screws. Then release the torsion bar and remove the bracket and retainer.

4. Support the tailgate with a suitable prop and remove the three hinge-to-body bolts. Disconnect one end of the cable assembly.

5. Remove the hinge-to-tailgate nuts and remove the hinge.

6. To install the hinge, position it on the tailgate and attach it with the nuts. Install the three hinge-to-

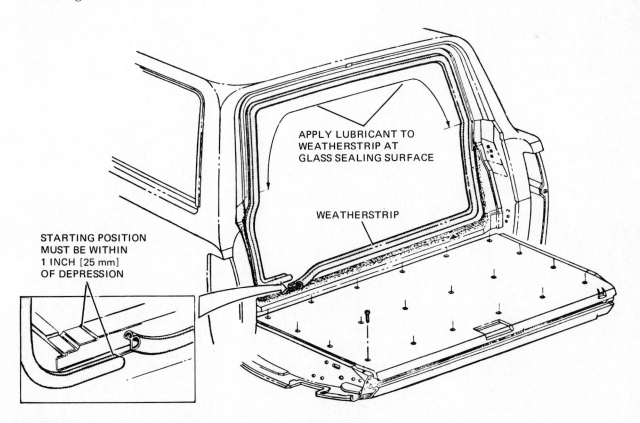

Fig. 25-10 Weatherstrip around a dual-action tailgate. (*Ford Motor Company*)

body bolts. Align the tailgate and tighten the nuts and bolts.

7. Apply tension to the torsion bar and install the torsion-bar bracket and retainer.

8. Install the access cover, watershield, and trim panel.

≡ 25-7 LATCH SERVICE

1. To remove the latch, open the tailgate and remove the trim panel. Disconnect the latch release cable from the latch. Remove the three latch attaching screws and take off the latch.

2. To install the latch, reverse the removal procedure.

≡ 25-8 DUAL-ACTION-TAILGATE-SERVICE

Figure 25-11 shows one arrangement of the mechanisms for the dual-action tailgate. All work in a similar manner. The tailgate is hinged along the bottom and also along one side. When the tailgate is lowered (as a drop gate), the bottom hinges are effective. The side hinges are disconnected. When the tailgate is opened as a door, the hinges along the bottom are disconnected. The glass can be raised or lowered, just as with side doors. In some tailgates, the glass is regulated by a mechanical crank. In others, a motor does the job. The motor can be actuated by a switch at the driver's seat or by the tailgate key, inserted into the tailgate lock. Figure 25-12 shows the circuit with the instrument-panel switch closed to cause the window to move up.

The adjustments of the dual-action tailgate are more complicated than for a side door. This is because the dual-action tailgate has two sets of hinges. Some adjustments are made by adding or removing shims. Other adjustments are made by shifting the hinges as shown in Fig. 25-13. The holes are enlarged to permit this. Figure 25-14 shows a typical method of adjusting the strikers, using shims and also taking advantage of the enlarged holes so the strikers can be shifted up or down, or fore or aft.

≡ 25-9 SPECIAL ROOFS

Several types of decorative roofs are available on many models of cars (Fig. 25-15). These include vinyl roof covers, fixed-glass roofs, manual and electric sliding sun roofs, pop-up and removable sun roofs, and hatch roofs (T roofs) which have two removable panels.

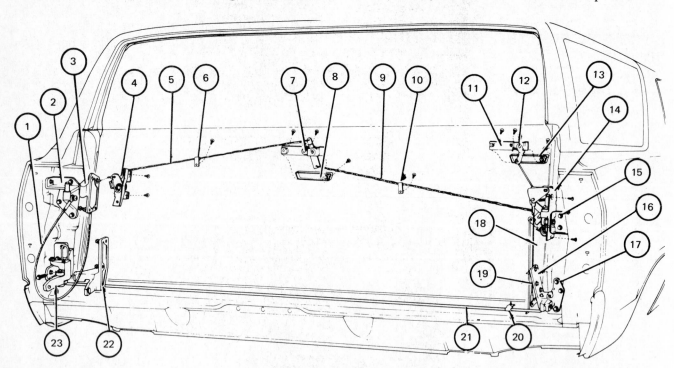

1. TAILGATE SUPPORT CABLE
2. LEFT UPPER-HALF HINGE AND ECCENTRIC ROLLER PIN ASSEMBLY
3. LEFT UPPER BODY HALF HINGE AND LATCH ASSEMBLY
4. LEFT UPPER HINGE HORIZONTAL LATCH RELEASE BELL-CRANK
5. LEFT LATCH RELEASE ROD
6. RELEASE ROD CLIP
7. HORIZONTAL REMOTE CONTROL
8. HORIZONTAL RELEASE HANDLE
9. RIGHT LATCH RELEASE ROD
10. RELEASE ROD CLIP
11. VERTICAL RELEASE REMOTE CONTROL
12. VERTICAL RELEASE BELL-CRANK
13. VERTICAL RELEASE HANDLE
14. TAILGATE LATCH ASSEMBLY
15. LATCH STRIKER AND BRACKET ASSEMBLY
16. RIGHT LOWER-HALF HINGE AND LATCH ASSEMBLY
17. RIGHT LOWER BODY HALF HINGE AND LATCH ASSEMBLE
18. UPPER LATCH TO LOWER–HINGE RELEASE CABLE
19. GLASS OPERATED SAFETY RELEASE ROD
20. TORSION ROD RETAINER CLIP
21. TORSION ROD
22. LEFT LOWER-HINGE ASSEMBLY DOOR HALF
23. LEFT LOWER-HINGE ASSEMBLY BODY HALF

Fig. 25-11 Dual-action-tailgate mechanism. *(American Motors Corporation)*

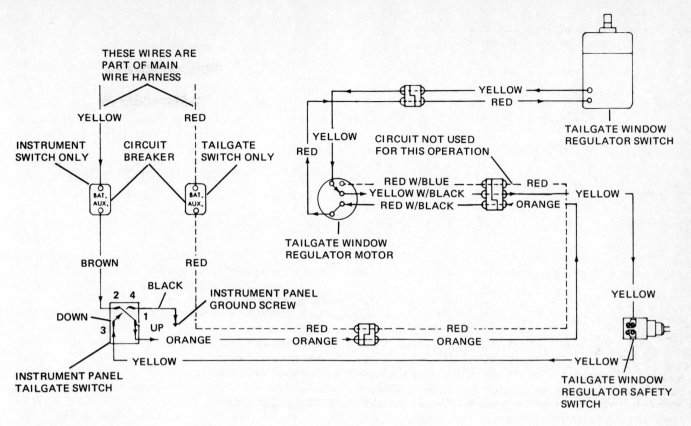

Fig. 25-12 Wiring circuit for an electrically operated glass in a tailgate. *(American Motors Corporation)*

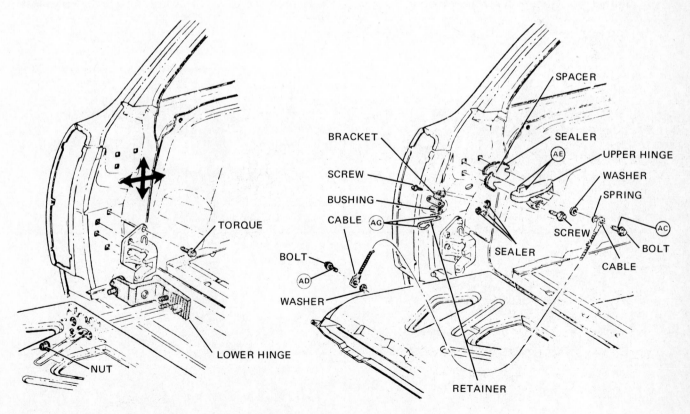

Fig. 25-13 Dual-action tailgate is adjusted by shifting the hinges. Apply lubricant at the points indicated by lettered circles. *(Ford Motor Company)*

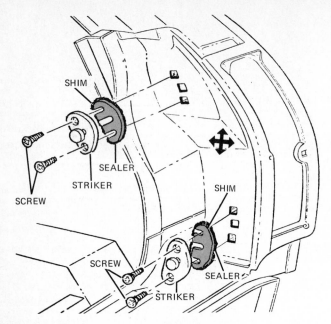

Fig. 25-14 *Adjusting the tailgate striker using shims and the oversize holes. (Ford Motor Company)*

Many buyers of special roofs would have purchased a convertible. However, with fewer convertibles now being manufactured than in past years, many people buy cars with some type of special roof, or have one installed. The owner then has a car that provides the open-air effect, while being more theft-resistant than a convertible. In addition, the hard roof panels are much more durable than the soft convertible top.

Vinyl roofs are usually a pad and vinyl cover glued to the top of the car (Fig. 25-15). This provides a distinctive appearance desired by many owners. The vinyl cover may be placed over the entire roof, or only over the rear section of the roof. This is called a *Landau vinyl top.* It can be installed on the same car that has a sun roof, or a removable hatch roof. Repair and replacement of vinyl roofs is described in Chap. 29. Following sections describe the construction and servicing of various types of special roofs.

≡ 25-10 TYPES OF SUN ROOF

In addition to the roof with a fixed-glass panel in it, there are three basic types of sun roofs. These are the pop-up or removable type (Fig. 25-16), the manual slide type, and the electric slide type (Fig. 2-34). The manual and electric slide types are basically the same. The difference is the method of opening and closing them.

The sun-roof panel may be metal, plastic, or tinted glass. Sun-roof glass may be either monolithic (single-layer) or laminated (safety) glass. Usually, the glass is tinted during manufacture. This reduces the amount of heat and light that enters the passenger compartment through the sun roof.

NOTE: *Ford calls its clear sun roof a moon roof.*

≡ 25-11 REMOVABLE SUN ROOF

This sun roof can be raised a small amount to serve as a vent. Forward movement of the car creates a draft which pulls air from the car. Figure 25-17 shows how to open the sun roof to the vent position. Move the release lever as far forward and upward as it will go. This raises

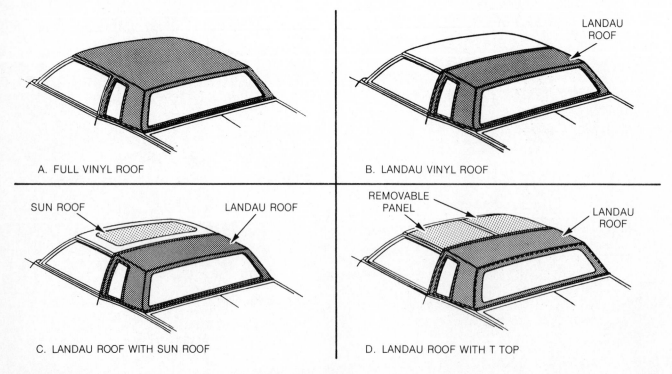

A. FULL VINYL ROOF

B. LANDAU VINYL ROOF

C. LANDAU ROOF WITH SUN ROOF

D. LANDAU ROOF WITH T TOP

Fig. 25-15 *Various types of decorative roofs. (ATW)*

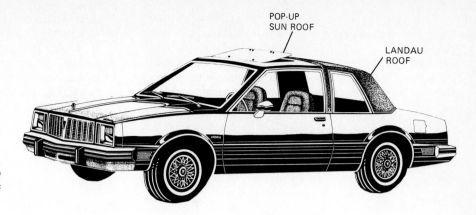

Fig. 25-16 Car with a Landau top and a pop-up sun roof. *(General Motors Corporation)*

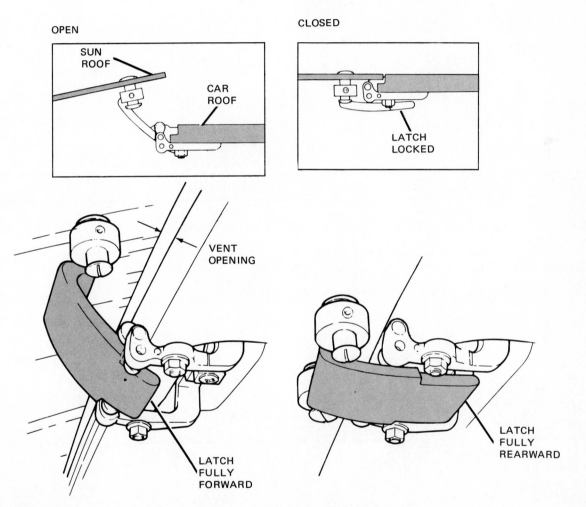

Fig. 25-17 Left, sun roof open. Right, sun roof closed. *(Ford Motor Company)*

the sun roof. The sun roof is closed by moving the lever back.

To remove the sun roof, move the release lever to its midposition. Then squeeze the attaching links together to disengage the latching mechanism from the roof panel. From outside the car, raise the glass at the rear edge and remove it by lifting upward and pulling rearward.

There is a place to stow the sun roof in the car. On two-door models, the stowage bag rests against the rear-seat back at the bottom edge. It clips to the drain trough beneath the weatherstrip at the top edge. On three-door models, the stowage bag is strapped to the rear floor on the passenger side of the car.

— **CAUTION** ————————————

The sun roof should never be stored any other place in the car. If you store it elsewhere, it may break and hurt someone.

253

To install the sun roof, align the two hinges at the front of the glass with the hinge sockets in the roof panel (Fig. 25-18). The hinges should be fully seated in their sockets before the rear edge of the panel is lowered. From inside the car, squeeze the connecting links together and insert them into their respective sockets. The glass can then be locked into position by operating the release lever.

If the sun roof is broken, the new glass panel is installed as follows: Transfer all attaching screws on the hinges and latching mechanism from the old glass to the new (Fig. 25-18). The part of the latch that is at-

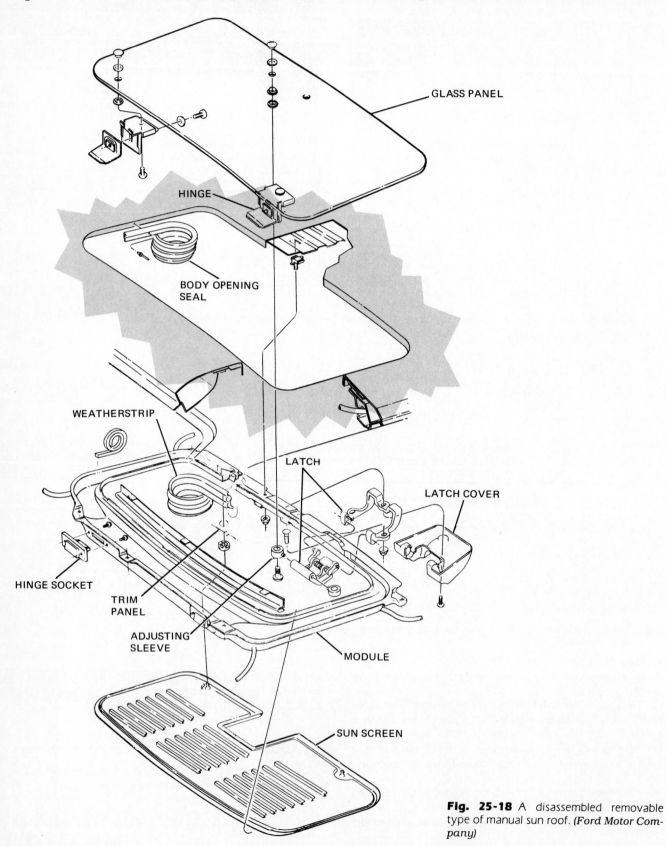

GLASS PANEL

HINGE

BODY OPENING SEAL

WEATHERSTRIP

LATCH

LATCH COVER

HINGE SOCKET

TRIM PANEL

ADJUSTING SLEEVE

MODULE

SUN SCREEN

Fig. 25-18 A disassembled removable type of manual sun roof. *(Ford Motor Company)*

tached to the roof panel can be adjusted fore and aft by loosening the attaching bolts and shifting the latch.

The weatherstrip is very important because it must seal tightly overhead. The body-opening seal is secured by Pop rivets. The new seal should be secured in a similar way. The roof-opening weatherstrip is secured by the shape of the weatherstrip and the channel into which it fits. Figure 25-18 shows both the body seal and the roof-opening weatherstrip.

≡ 25-12 MANUAL SLIDING SUN ROOF

The manual sliding sun roof (Fig. 25-19) is a sliding panel that slides fore and aft on guide rails. It is operated by a crank or handle. The crank, located overhead on the header assembly, is splined to a shaft and pinion that drive two flexible cables. Each cable is attached to

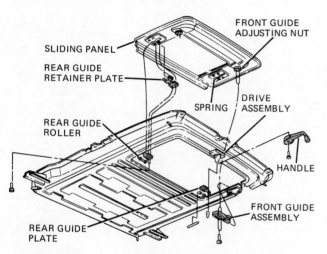

Fig. 25-19 Handle, sliding panel, and guide mechanism for a manual sun roof. (Chrysler Corporation)

a slide that moves on guide rails. The cable-drive arrangement is shown in Fig. 25-20.

When the crank is turned to open the sun roof, the sun roof is moved downward and rearward. It moves on the guide rails into the storage position between the headlining and the roof.

When the crank is turned to close the sun roof, the sun roof moves forward on the guide rails. As it nears the end of its forward travel, the rear part moves up on two ramps. Then the lifter raises the sun roof flush with the roof. The sun roof seals tightly against the weatherstrips.

Many sun-roof installations include a roof drainage system to drain water away from the seam between the roof panel and the sun roof. Tubes carry the water from the drain channel down the sides of the car so the water can discharge onto the ground.

The two adjusting nuts (Fig. 25-19) raise or lower the front of the sun roof so a good seal between the sun roof and the car roof panel can be achieved. The rear end of the sun roof can be raised or lowered to get a good seal. On Chrysler-built cars, loosen the screw located under the rear guide linkage (Fig. 25-19). Raise or lower the sun-roof rear end as necessary to get a good seal. Then tighten the screw.

To make other adjustments, remove the trim panel (headliner) of the sun roof. The procedures are covered in the manufacturer's service manual.

≡ 25-13 ELECTRIC SLIDING SUN ROOF

The electric sliding sun roof is basically the same as the manual sliding sun roof (≡25-12). However, the electric sun roof has a reversible electric motor to open and close the sun roof (Fig. 2-34). Also, there is a manually operated backup system which can be used to close the roof in case of electrical failure. A crank is stored in the glove compartment to use for this purpose.

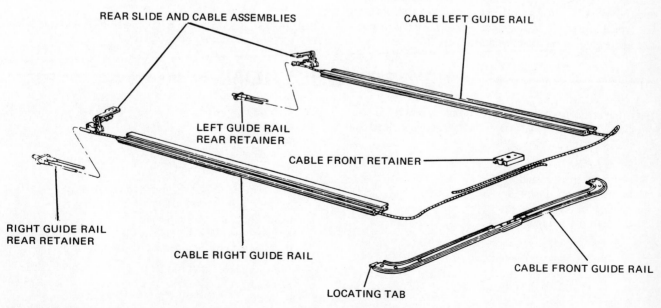

Fig. 25-20 Guide rail and cable system for a manual sun roof. (Ford Motor Company)

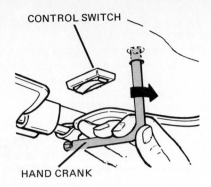

Fig. 25-21 Using the hand crank to manually close an electric sun roof. *(Ford Motor Company)*

To manually close the electric sun roof, insert the drive end of the crank handle into the auxiliary socket (Fig. 25-21). Turn the crank to close the roof.

≡ 25-14 REMOVABLE HATCH ROOF (T ROOF)

Figure 25-22 shows a car that has a T roof, with the hatch panels removed. Most T roofs are very similar in design. A major difference among them is how the hatch fastens to the car. One type of T roof has two locking pins which secure the hatch to striker plates on the car (Fig. 25-23A). Another type has two end fittings that actually grip the edges of the striker plate (Fig. 25-23B).

Another difference among T roofs is the location of the weatherstripping. On some cars, the weatherstrip is part of the removable panel, or hatch (Fig. 25-23A). Other cars have the weatherstrip installed on the body of the car (Fig. 25-23B).

≡ 25-15 SERVICING SPECIAL ROOFS

No periodic service is required on fixed-glass roofs, sun roofs, or T-roofs. The most frequent complaint is water leaks, and sometimes noise or air leaks. On some cars, the roof panel can be adjusted to provide a tighter fit. If the weatherstrip is damaged or out of position, reposition or replace it as described in Chap. 23.

Fig. 25-22 A T roof, with the hatch panels removed. *(Chrysler Corporation)*

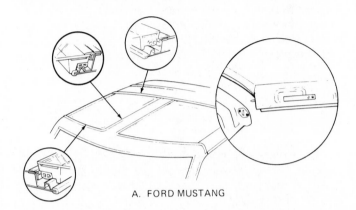

A. FORD MUSTANG

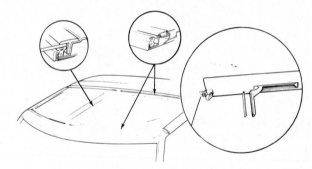

B. FORD THUNDERBIRD

Fig. 25-23 Locking pins and weatherstrip around two types of T roofs. *(Ford Motor Company)*

——— REVIEW QUESTIONS ———

Select the *one* correct, best, or most probable answer to each question. You can find the answers in the section indicated at the end of each question.

1. Rear-opening doors are called (≡25-1)
   a. hoods and trunk lids
   b. lift gates and tailgates
   c. hatchbacks and sun roofs
   d. sun roofs and moon roofs

2. A dual-action tailgate is hinged (≡25-8)
   a. at the top and at the bottom
   b. at the left side and at the right side
   c. in the middle and at the bottom
   d. at the bottom and at one side

3. A lift gate is used on a (≡25-1)
   a. pickup truck
   b. large sedan
   c. van
   d. small station wagon

4. In a tailgate, an electric motor can be used to (≡25-1)
   a. open and shut the tailgate
   b. lock and unlock the tailgate
   c. open and close the tailgate glass
   d. change from top opening to side opening

5. The special roof that has two removable panels is the
   a. hatch roof (≡25-14)
   b. T roof
   c. both **a** and **b**
   d. neither **a** nor **b**

PART 7

STATIONARY GLASS SERVICE

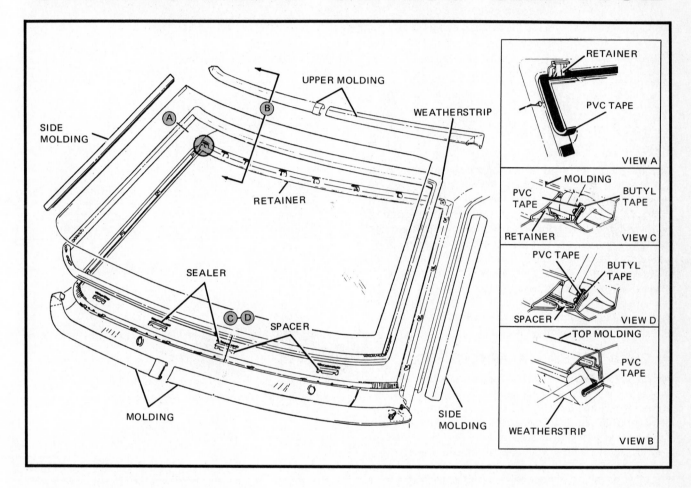

SIDE MOLDING

UPPER MOLDING

WEATHERSTRIP

RETAINER

SEALER

SPACER

MOLDING

SIDE MOLDING

RETAINER

PVC TAPE

VIEW A

MOLDING

PVC TAPE

BUTYL TAPE

RETAINER

VIEW C

PVC TAPE

BUTYL TAPE

SPACER

VIEW D

TOP MOLDING

PVC TAPE

WEATHERSTRIP

VIEW B

In this part, you will learn how to remove and install stationary glass in a car. This includes the windshield, rear window, and stationary side windows.

There are two basic types of automotive glass: laminated safety glass, used for the windshield, and solid tempered plate glass, used for side and back glass. The laminated safety glass consists of a layer of plastic material sandwiched between two layers of glass. The plastic material greatly reduces the possibility that the glass will shatter. If the glass does break, the plastic prevents the broken pieces from flying off. Tempered glass is less brittle than ordinary plate glass. When tempered glass is broken, it tends to crumble into very small pieces. There are no large pieces with sharp edges from the break that could cause injury to passengers.

There is one chapter in Part 7:

Chapter 26 Stationary Glass Replacement

CHAPTER 26
STATIONARY GLASS REPLACEMENT

After studying this chapter, you should be able to:

1. Discuss the types of adhesives used to install windshields.

2. Explain how to replace a windshield by using the short method and by using the extended method.

3. Discuss the additional steps required if the windshield has a built-in antenna.

4. Explain how to remove and install a noncemented windshield.

5. Describe how to service rear windows, side windows, and quarter windows.

≡ 26-1 STATIONARY GLASS INSTALLATION

The stationary glass in the car includes the windshield and the rear and quarter, or opera, windows. Often the glass is bonded to the body opening with a synthetic rubberlike adhesive. Other stationary glass, such as the windshield, is bonded to the body with a special polyvinyl chloride (PVC) tape, as shown in Fig. 26-1. Some station-wagon back windows and quarter windows are retained in rubber channels. The first step in removing a stationary glass is to take off all the trim and hardware surrounding the glass. This may include reveal moldings, garnish moldings or finishing lace, and windshield-wiper arms.

≡ 26-2 TYPES OF ADHESIVE

An *adhesive* is a glue that is applied as a liquid or as a paste. After it cures, or hardens, the adhesive forms a rubberlike material. Dry adhesive sheet and tape also are available. Adhesives are used in many places on the automobile. They are used to join two materials together when mechanical fastening, such as rivets or nuts and bolts, is not possible or would impair the appearance. For many jobs, the use of liquid or paste adhesive lowers the assembling costs and at the same time seals the joint against water leaks.

In windshield installations, there are two basic types of adhesive caulking materials used to bond the glass to the glass opening. These are both synthetic, self-curing, rubberlike adhesives:

1. Polysulfide adhesive
2. Urethane tape

A special tape made of butyl PVC is used on some cars to bond the windshield or other glass to the opening (Fig. 26-1). Also, some glass, such as quarter windows, is set in rubber channels or gaskets and is not otherwise bonded to the opening.

In some cars, body strength is increased by using the stationary glass as an integral part of the body structure. Body rigidity is reduced when softer or noncuring adhesives are used to bond replacement windshields. Squeaks and rattles can develop when a windshield or

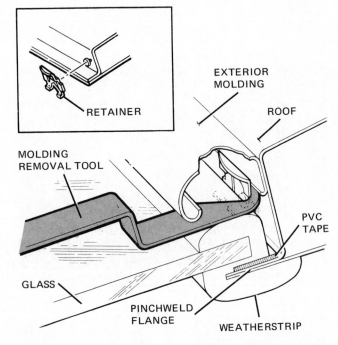

Fig. 26-1 Using a special tool to remove the exterior molding from around the windshield. *(Ford Motor Company)*

back glass is not securely bonded to the body opening with adhesive of the proper strength.

General Motors recommends using its urethane adhesive caulking kit whenever a windshield is replaced in an older-model vehicle. When you are replacing glass on other cars, use the same adhesive as was originally used.

NOTE: Before using a liquid or paste adhesive on a windshield installation, check that the windshield or the rubber gasket will not be damaged by the adhesive you are planning to use. For example, polysulfide adhesive may attack butyl rubber and cause or enlarge water leaks. Similarly, there is a problem with some sealants which are used to fill in areas and prevent water leaks. If the wrong sealant is used, it may attack the plastic center of the windshield around the

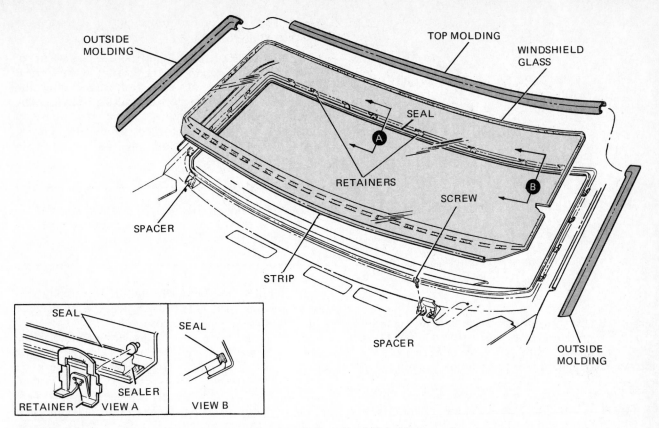

Fig. 26-2 Typical windshield and exterior molding installation. *(Ford Motor Company)*

edges. This will cloud the plastic, and bubbles may appear in it.

≡ 26-3 WINDSHIELD REPLACEMENT—SHORT AND EXTENDED METHODS

There are two methods of replacing the windshield. These are called the short method and the extended method.

The *short method* is recommended when the windshield is removed intact and the body opening does not require any repairs or straightening. After the glass is removed, a carefully controlled bead of adhesive is applied to the pinchweld flange. The pinchweld flange (Fig. 26-1) is the flange formed by the bent-down edge of the roof and the sheet metal welded to it. The bead of adhesive or adhesive tape laid down on this flange serves as a base for the glass when it is installed.

The *extended method* is recommended where there is a considerable loss of adhesion between the original adhesive material and the body opening. It is also recommended in cars where the body opening requires repair. In these cars, all old adhesive materials must be removed from the pinchweld flanges.

≡ 26-4 REMOVING TRIM AND HARDWARE

The first step in windshield replacement is to remove all trim and hardware that could be in the way. Trim is any part that is attached to the body after it is painted.

Some manufacturers refer to the molding that surrounds the glass and hides the joint as *reveal* molding. Others call it simply top, exterior, or outside molding (Figs. 26-1 to 26-3). The molding is clipped in a variety of ways. A screwdriver or special tool (Figs. 26-1 and 26-3) is used to unclip it. If the molding is to be used again, be careful not to bend it as you take it off.

≡ 26-5 WINDSHIELD REMOVAL— ADHESIVE-BONDED TYPE

First remove the trim and hardware as indicated in the previous section. Then put protective covering around the area where the glass is being removed so that the paint will not be damaged. Windshield removal is the same for the short and the extended installation

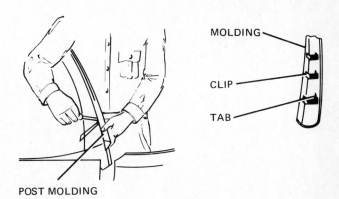

Fig. 26-3 Removing a post molding. *(Chrysler Corporation)*

259

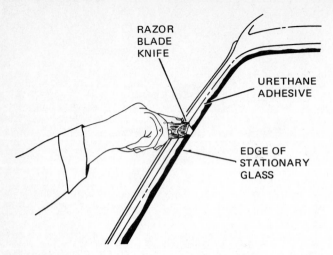

RAZOR
BLADE
KNIFE

URETHANE
ADHESIVE

EDGE OF
STATIONARY
GLASS

Fig. 26-4 Cutting the adhesive from the edge of the glass with a razor blade. *(American Motors Corporation)*

methods. However, when the short installation method is used, extra care is required during windshield removal to make sure that an even, uniform bead of adhesive material remains on the window opening. This bead will serve as the base for the replacement glass.

If the windshield has a radio antenna built into it, disconnect the antenna lead at the lower center of the windshield. If the windshield is to be reused, fold and tape the lead wire onto the outer surface of the windshield. This prevents the wire from being damaged during removal and installation of the glass.

Now, using the edge of the glass as a guide, cut adhesive material from the edge of the glass with a razor knife (Fig. 26-4). This is in preparation for the use of a cutting knife or steel music wire to complete the cutting of the adhesive from the glass.

Either a cutting knife or music wire can be used to cut the adhesive. There are two types of cutting knives:

cold and hot. The procedure for cutting the adhesive and removing the glass is as follows:

1. USING THE KNIFE. Figure 26-5 shows the use of the hot knife. It has an electric heating element in it that heats the blade hot enough to easily soften the adhesive. Note that two types of blades are shown. The standard blade is used where there is no adhesive on the back, or inside, of the glass. The special curved blade is used to cut through adhesive that is adhering to the back of the glass.

— **CAUTION** —————————————

When using the hot knife, do not inhale the fumes of the burning material. Always have adequate ventilation in the work area.

————————————————————————

Do not allow the hot-knife blade to remain stationary at any one spot. This will overheat the adhesive so that it will become permanently soft.

The cold-knife method is similar to the hot-knife method. However, it requires a considerably greater force—greater physical strength—to pull the knife through the adhesive. However, if the knife is kept sharp, it can be done satisfactorily.

In addition to keeping the hot-knife blade sharp, it should be cleaned immediately after use, while still hot, with steel wool. If the blade is cool, wash the adhesive off with a suitable solvent.

2. USING MUSIC WIRE. Music wire can be used to cut through the adhesive as shown in Fig. 26-6. Note that the music wire has been wrapped around pieces of wood which serve as handles. With a helper working on the other side of the glass, carefully pull the wire through the adhesive material around the entire outside edge of the windshield. If the short method of installation is to be used, hold the wire as close to the

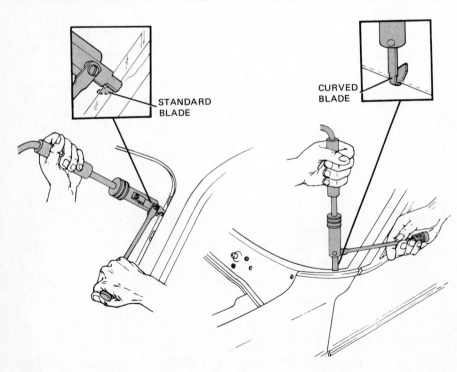

STANDARD
BLADE

CURVED
BLADE

Fig. 26-5 Cutting adhesive with a hot knife. *(American Motors Corporation)*

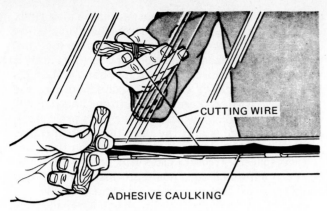

Fig. 26-6 Using steel music wire to cut the adhesive in which the glass is set. *(Chrysler Corporation)*

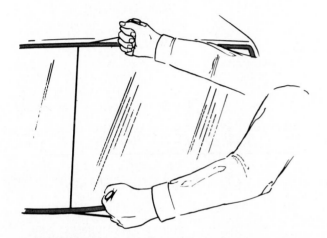

Fig. 26-7 One body technician can cut the adhesive from the windshield with music wire. *(© Fisher Body Division of General Motors Corporation)*

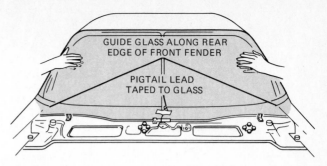

Fig. 26-8 Two body technicians are needed to remove and install a windshield. *(© Fisher Body Division of General Motors Corporation)*

inside of the glass as possible. This leaves a good bed of adhesive for the replacement glass. Keep tension on the wire throughout the cutting job to avoid kinking or breaking it. One person can do the job as shown in Fig. 26-7.

3. REMOVING THE WINDSHIELD. After the adhesive is cut, have an assistant help you remove the glass from the car (Fig. 26-8). First push from the inside of the glass to make sure it is free. Then you and the assistant should be on each side of the car, as shown in Fig. 26-8. Place one hand on the inside of the windshield and the other hand on the outside. Tilt the windshield out so you can move your hands around the posts. Then lift the windshield off the car.

If the original windshield is to be reinstalled, put it on a protected bench. Use a razor blade or sharp scraper to remove old adhesive from the glass edges. Any remaining trace of adhesive can be wiped off with denatured alcohol or lacquer thinner applied with a clean cloth.

NOTE: When cleaning laminated glass, such as the windshield, do not allow any solvent to get onto the edges of the glass and touch the plastic center layer. The plastic will absorb the solvent and cause discoloration of the glass.

≡ 26-6 WINDSHIELD INSTALLATION — SHORT METHOD (ADHESIVE-BONDED TYPE WITHOUT ANTENNA)

Use a clean, lint-free cloth dampened with a suitable solvent and rub it briskly over the original adhesive material remaining on the pinchweld flange. This smooths the original adhesive in preparation for installing the windshield.

If a new windshield is being installed, check to see if it has a mirror bracket. If it does not, you must install one. This requires a special adhesive. The bracket is cemented to the windshield in the proper spot.

The procedure for windshield installation by the short method is as follows:

1. A special windshield installation kit is required which contains all the materials needed for the job:
a. Instruction sheet
b. Cartridge of urethane adhesive
c. Standard dispensing nozzle
d. Glass blackout primer
e. Pointed dispensing nozzle
f. Dauber to apply primer
g. Support spacers

You will need, in addition, an adhesive dispensing gun, solvent, masking tape, and standoff spacers (for properly spacing the glass in the opening). In addition, when the pinchweld flange must be cleaned (and for the extended method), you will need paint primer to prime the flange.

2. Check the molding retaining clips and replace any that are broken or loose. Install the lower support spacers where used (Fig. 26-9).

3. Check the relationship of the glass to the adhesive material on the pinchweld flange. Gaps in excess of ⅛ inch [3 mm] must be corrected by applying more adhesive.

4. Put the glass in the proper position in the opening. Apply pieces of masking tape from the edge of the glass to the adjacent pillar or body part. Then slit the tape at the joint and remove the glass. The tape will serve as guides when you make the final installation of the windshield.

5. To make the cleanup job easier after the windshield is installed, apply a strip of masking tape 1 inch [25 mm] wide to the inside of the glass, ½ inch [13 mm]

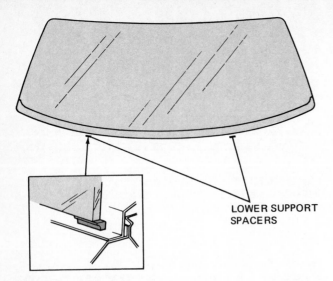

Fig. 26-9 Installation of the lower support spacers. *(American Motors Corporation)*

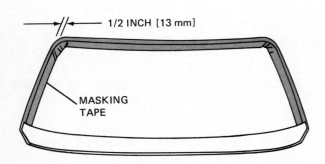

Fig. 26-10 Applying tape to make the cleanup job easier. *(American Motors Corporation)*

glass to the opening, two technicians are required (Fig. 26-8). Each carries the glass with one hand inside and one hand outside the glass. At the window opening, put the glass in a horizontal position. One technician then reaches inside the car with the upper hand and brings it back on the glass. The other technician does the same. Now, with one hand inside and one hand outside the car (Fig. 26-8), they can raise the glass to a vertical position and set it into the opening. With the tape guides aligned, and with the windshield on the lower support spacers, press the glass in against the adhesive on the pinchweld flange. Avoid excessive force, which could cause excessive squeeze-out of the adhesive.

11. Use a small disposable brush or a flat-bladed tool to paddle additional adhesive around the edge of the

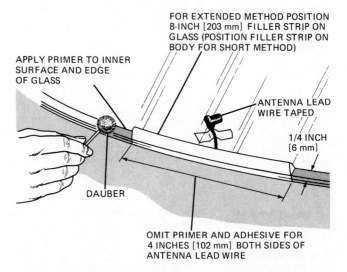

Fig. 26-11 Preparing for application of the adhesive. *(© Fisher Body Division of General Motors Corporation)*

inboard from the edge (Fig. 26-10). Apply it to the sides and top only, not to the bottom. After the job is completed, you remove this tape, leaving a smooth, even edge to the adhesive.

6. Use a clean cloth, dampened with isopropyl alcohol, to wipe the surface of the glass between the masking tape and the outer edge. This is where a bead of adhesive will be applied.

7. Use the dauber to apply blackout primer around the entire inner surface and edge of the glass (Fig. 26-11).

NOTE: *Figure 26-11 shows a windshield with an antenna, but the general procedure of applying the primer is the same for any windshield. The purpose of the primer is to secure good sticking of the adhesive to the glass.*

8. Use care in applying the primer. It will damage trim and painted surfaces.

9. After waiting 10 minutes for the primer to dry, apply a smooth, continuous bead of adhesive around the entire inner edge of the glass (Fig. 26-12). The bead should be ⅛ to 3/16 inch [3 to 5 mm] in diameter.

10. Now, using the tape guides, carefully position the glass on the fenders next to the opening. To bring the

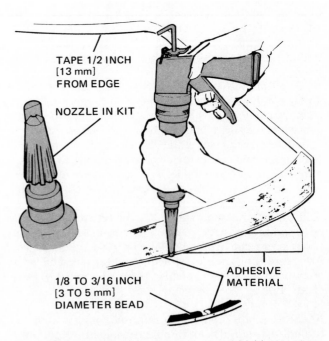

Fig. 26-12 Applying adhesive to the windshield. *(American Motors Corporation)*

glass as necessary to fill voids and ensure a good seal all around.

12. Water-test the windshield at once. Use a cold-water spray and allow the water to spill over the edge of the glass. Do not direct a hard stream of water at the adhesive because it has not set up yet. If you see any leaks, apply extra adhesive at the leaking points.

13. Install moldings and remove masking tape from the inner surface of the glass. Clean up the glass as necessary with a cloth dampened with solvent.

14. Install the inside rearview mirror on the bracket and tighten the screw.

NOTE: When the windshield is originally installed, a rubber sealing strip or dam is used around the inside edges of the glass to prevent excessive squeeze-out of the adhesive materials. Installations made in the field do not require the dam. Masking tape applied around the perimeter of the glass enables you to pick up and remove excessive squeeze-out as you take off the tape.

15. Allow the vehicle to set in a room temperature of 72°F [22.2°C] for 6 hours to complete the cure of the adhesive. Some manufacturers recommend cementing rubber spacers to both sides of the glass. This prevents the glass from slipping to one side or the other while the adhesive is curing.

≡ 26-7 WINDSHIELD INSTALLATION—SHORT METHOD (ADHESIVE-BONDED TYPE WITH ANTENNA)

If the windshield has an antenna built into the glass, some additional steps and precautions are required during installation. Figure 26-8 shows how the antenna wire is taped up out of the way before the windshield is installed. When installing the windshield, note the following:

1. On the type with a butyl strip at the bottom center of the windshield (at antenna lead pigtail), mark the location of each end of the strip at the edge of the glass with tape or grease pencil. After glass removal, replace the original butyl strip with the new strip provided in the installation kit. Stretch or cut a new strip to fill the existing gap on the body.

2. On the type without the butyl strip at the bottom center of the windshield opening, measure 4 inches [102 mm] on both sides of the body centerline. Use tape or a grease pencil to mark the location on both the body and the glass. After the windshield removal, cut the original adhesive material from between the marks and insert the filler strip provided with the kit.

3. Apply primer around the outer edge of the glass as shown in Fig. 26-11, omitting the area between the two marks, or tape, established in steps 1 and 2 above. Also, when applying adhesive (Fig. 26-12), do not apply it in the area between the two marks.

4. To ensure a good seal between the filler strips and the adjacent adhesive material, paddle additional material at the edges of the butyl strip.

≡ 26-8 WINDSHIELD INSTALLATION—EXTENDED METHOD (ADHESIVE-BONDED TYPE)

The windshield installation by the extended method is similar to the installation by the short method, with the following additional requirements:

1. Use a sharp scraper or chisel to remove old adhesive from the flanges on which the glass rests. Work all the way around the opening. If butyl or some other adhesive has been used, all traces of it must be removed.

2. Make whatever repairs are necessary to the opening and flanges. The flanges must be even all the way around. If any part of the flange is bent downward, poor adhesion and a water leak could develop at that point. If any part of it is bent upward, it could cause the windshield to crack at that point either during installation or later.

3. If refinishing or painting of the area is required, or if original paint has been exposed by removal of the adhesive, apply the special primer (provided in the repair kit) to the flange. Primer should also be applied to the glass edge as explained in the previous section covering the short method. Make sure the primer is thoroughly stirred and agitated before applying it. Allow the primer to dry for 5 minutes.

4. Install flat rubber spacers in the positions shown at B in Fig. 26-13. These support and hold the glass off the flange to provide uniform space for the adhesive.

5. Use black weatherstrip adhesive or adhesive material to cement the rubber spacers into place.

6. Note the two spacers (A in Fig. 26-13) which support the bottom of the glass.

7. With the aid of a helper, temporarily place the windshield into the opening. Check the spacing be-

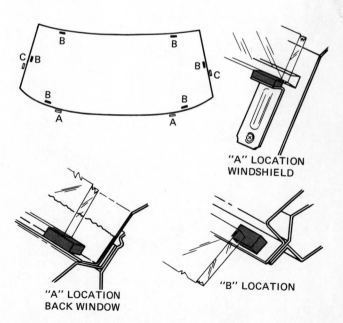

"A" LOCATION WINDSHIELD

"A" LOCATION BACK WINDOW

"B" LOCATION

Fig. 26-13 *When installing the windshield, place the glass spacers in the positions shown at B. (© Fisher Body Division of General Motors Corporation)*

tween the glass and the pinchweld flange all the way around. This space should be no less than ⅛ inch [3 mm] and no more than ¼ inch [6 mm]. If it is not correct at any spot, try the following:

a. Reposition the flat spacers.

b. Try another windshield if available. Its contour may be different.

c. Rework the pinchweld flange.

d. Plan to add more adhesive at the areas where the spacing is excessive.

8. Check the location of the glass in the opening. The glass should overlap the pinchweld flange at least 3/16 inch [5 mm]. Overlap across the top of the windshield can be corrected by repositioning the lower supports.

9. After final adjustments have been made, apply strips of tape across the body and glass. Cut the tape at the joint between the two. The tape is lined up when the windshield is installed in the correct position.

10. The remainder of the installation job is the same as for the short method. Tape is applied around the inner surface of the windshield, ¼ inch [6 mm] inboard from the edge of the glass. Then the glass edge is cleaned and primed (Fig. 26-11). Adhesive is then applied to the edge of the glass (Fig. 26-14). The nozzle has been enlarged to lay down an extra-heavy bead of adhesive. This is required for the extended method to replace the adhesive removed from the pinchweld.

11. After the adhesive is applied to the glass, the glass is then installed as for the short method and pressed down into place. Additional adhesive should be paddled into place as necessary in order to fill any gaps. Note the special precautions that must be taken if the windshield has an antenna embedded in it (≡26-7).

12. Water-test the seal and apply additional adhesive if required to eliminate water leaks. Allow the seal to cure 6 hours before moving the car.

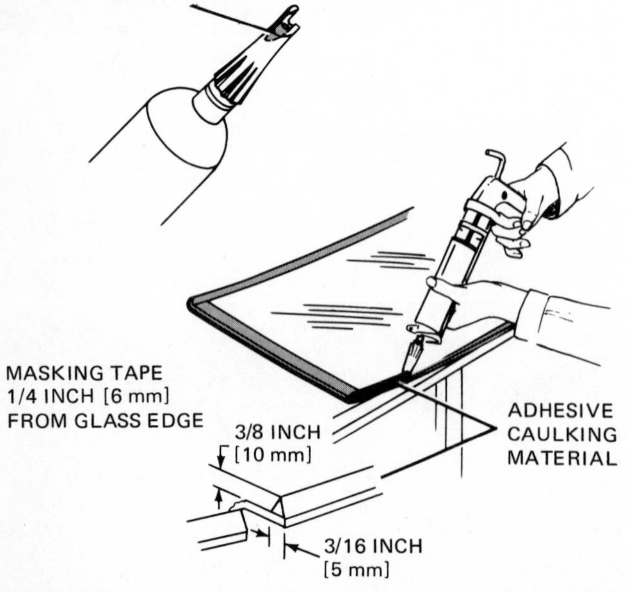

Fig. 26-14 Applying adhesive in the extended method. (© *Fisher Body Division of General Motors Corporation*)

≡ 26-9 WINDSHIELD SERVICE—TAPE-SEALED WEATHERSTRIP TYPE

This type of installation (Fig. 26-1) uses adhesive tape to seal between the pinchweld flange and the glass weatherstrip. Removal and installation of the windshield are described below (Fig. 26-15).

WINDSHIELD REMOVAL

1. Remove molding and windshield-wiper blades as previously explained.

2. From inside the vehicle, push the windshield out of the opening.

3. Remove the weatherstrip from the glass.

WINDSHIELD INSTALLATION

1. Clean all adhesive from the pinchweld flange. Check molding retainers and replace any that are defective or loose.

2. If PVC tape is to be used, apply sheet-metal primer to the flange. Then apply the tape (butyl or PVC) to the flange.

3. Install the weatherstrip on the glass (Fig. 26-1).

4. Insert a draw cord into the pinchweld opening of the weatherstrip all the way around, overlapping the cord about 18 inches [457 mm] at the lower center of the glass (Fig. 26-16). Tape the ends of the cord to the glass (Fig. 26-17).

5. Position the windshield in the opening. With an assistant applying hand pressure from the outside, pull the draw cord out of the pinchweld flange in the weatherstrip. This will pull the lip of the weatherstrip up and over the flange.

6. Water-test as described previously.

7. Install moldings and windshield-wiper blades.

≡ 26-10 WINDSHIELD SERVICE—TAPE-SEALED GLASS TYPE

When the windshield is sealed directly to the pinchweld flange with tape, make sure there is a seal all the way around during installation. Look closely at the glass edge before installing the molding. Dull spots indicate areas where the tape is not adhering to the glass. Press down at these areas to get a good seal.

The flange and glass must be prepared as for other installation procedures. The glass and flange must be clean. The flange must be even so there will be uniform spacing between the glass and the flange all the way around. Spacers must be used. Also, after the windshield is installed, a bead of sealer must be applied to the edge of the glass, all the way around the windshield. This ensures a good seal between the glass and the adjacent metal of the body opening.

≡ 26-11 WINDSHIELD SERVICE—NONCEMENTED TYPE

This type of installation (Figs. 26-18 and 26-19) uses an interlocking weatherstrip. Before removing the windshield, you must unlock this weatherstrip from the glass. You do this by prying the lip away from the glass.

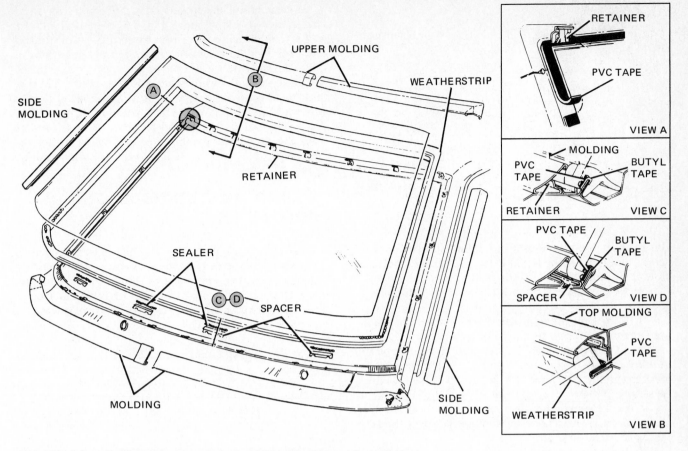

Fig. 26-15 Installation of a tape-sealed windshield. *(Ford Motor Company)*

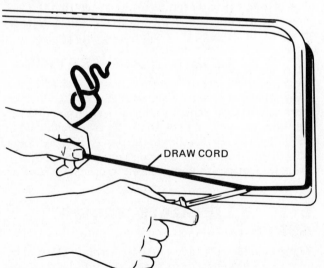

Fig. 26-16 Working the draw cord into the pinchweld opening of the weatherstrip. *(Ford Motor Company)*

Fig. 26-17 Tape the ends of the cord to the glass. *(Ford Motor Company)*

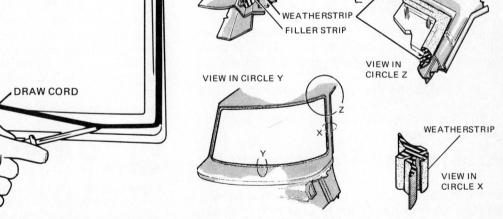

Fig. 26-18 Interlocking weatherstrip used to hold a windshield. *(Chrysler Corporation)*

Then insert a fiber wedge and work it all the way around the glass. With the weatherstrip unlocked, have an assistant help you remove the glass.

The installation procedure is as follows:

1. If the glass has cracked, perhaps owing to some irregularity, check the pinchweld flange for any irregu-

265

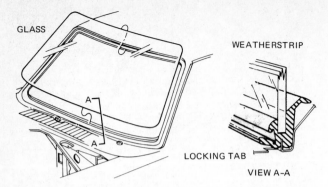

Fig. 26-19 Windshield installation using an interlocking weatherstrip. *(Chrysler Corporation)*

larity that could have put undue force on the area of glass that has cracked. Make necessary correction before installing the new windshield.

2. New weatherstrip will be required if the old is damaged.

3. To install the windshield, remove all old sealer and cement from the original weatherstrip. Apply sealer in fence and glass groove part of weatherstrip. Apply a ⅜-inch [9.5-mm] bead of sealer completely across the cowl top panel where the windshield weatherstrip will rest.

4. Position weatherstrip lower section at the tab area, starting at corners and installing it over the tab. Work toward the center.

5. Install weatherstrip all the way around the opening. Seat it with hand force.

6. With an assistant, slide the upper edge of the glass into the channel of the weatherstrip (Figs. 26-18 and 26-19). Use a fiber tool to force the weatherstrip lip over the glass.

7. Seat the glass in the weatherstrip, pounding the glass with the palm of the hand, using an upward motion.

8. Insert a fiber tool between the weatherstrip and the glass at either corner. Slide the tool along the top, sides, and bottom of the glass, forcing the lip over the glass.

9. Using the fiber tool, force the weatherstrip locking tab into the locked position in the fence.

10. Water-test the seal. Install moldings and windshield-wiper blades.

≡ 26-12 REAR-WINDOW SERVICE

There are about 3000 different sizes and shapes of side and rear windows used in automobiles. Rear windows are installed in a variety of ways, similar to those used to install windshields. The removal and installation procedures are also similar. However, with rear windows, you may need vacuum cups as shown in Fig. 26-20. In some cars, you and an assistant can remove the rear window by working partly on the inside and partly on the outside.

Figure 26-21 shows a typical installation arrangement for rear windows. The installation procedures for windshields and rear windows are similar. These procedures were described in earlier sections.

However, one special design is different. This is the "frenched" back window (Fig. 26-20), in which the vinyl roof covering is carried to the glass and tucked under the molding. This is shown to the upper right in Fig. 26-20, which also shows the special procedures required to remove and replace the glass. With the vinyl pulled out from under the molding and taped back, the window can be removed. Then, when the window has been reinstalled, the ground-off putty knife is used to tuck the vinyl back in under the molding. A thin bead of clear adhesive is used to seal between the vinyl and the glass.

≡ 26-13 HEATED-REAR-WINDOW SERVICE

Some cars have a heated rear window (Fig. 26-22). These windows have a heating element embedded in the glass. The heating element is connected to wiring harnesses on the two sides of the window. On some cars, the window is supplied with high voltage from a special alternator. On other cars, the heating current is supplied from the 12-volt alternator.

— **CAUTION** —————————————

The engine must be off when you work on a rear window which has a heating element. The voltage is high enough to give you an extremely severe shock.

———————————————————

The only additional action required on the heated rear window is to disconnect the wiring from the window. If the same window is to be reinstalled, tape the leads to the glass so they will not be damaged.

≡ 26-14 SIDE-WINDOW SERVICE

These windows are fixed glass windows back of the rear door, above the quarter panel (Fig. 26-23). They are retained in place either by adhesive, such as butyl rubber tape, or by rubber channels. Their removal and installation are very similar to the procedures previously described for windshields and rear windows. Other installation methods using nuts, or brackets, also are used.

≡ 26-15 LIFT-GATE-WINDOW SERVICE

Many smaller cars have a lift gate with a window at the rear that serves as a third, or rear-opening, door. Figure 26-24 shows two versions and their installation methods. Refer to these illustrations if you are required to replace the glass.

≡ 26-16 QUARTER WINDOW FOR STATION WAGON

Figure 26-25 shows the installation of a quarter window on a station wagon. This installation requires spacers, sealers, and molding similar to that used in installing other stationary glass described above.

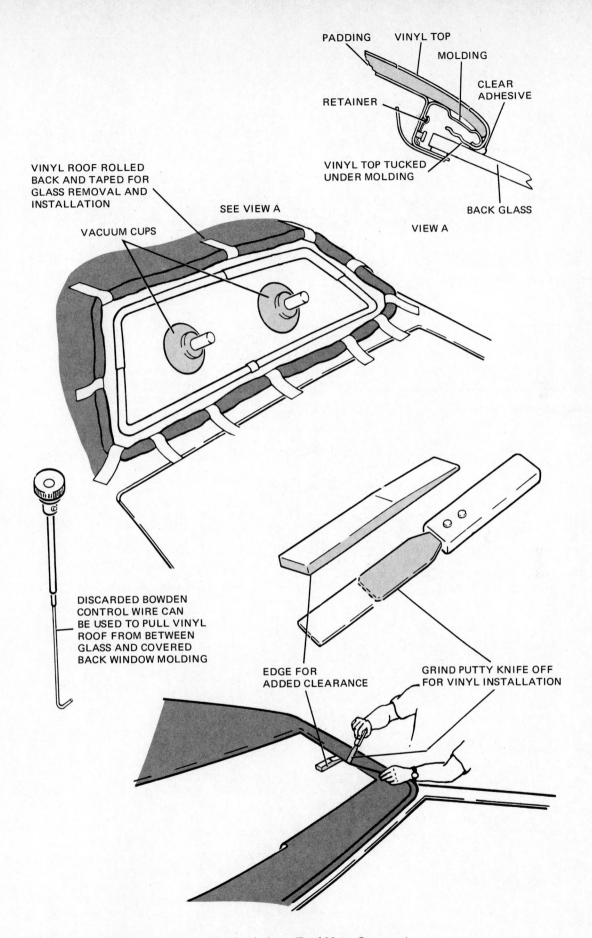

PADDING   VINYL TOP

MOLDING

CLEAR
ADHESIVE

RETAINER

VINYL TOP TUCKED
UNDER MOLDING

BACK GLASS

VIEW A

VINYL ROOF ROLLED
BACK AND TAPED FOR
GLASS REMOVAL AND
INSTALLATION

SEE VIEW A

VACUUM CUPS

DISCARDED BOWDEN
CONTROL WIRE CAN
BE USED TO PULL VINYL
ROOF FROM BETWEEN
GLASS AND COVERED
BACK WINDOW MOLDING

EDGE FOR
ADDED CLEARANCE

GRIND PUTTY KNIFE OFF
FOR VINYL INSTALLATION

Fig. 26-20 Servicing the frenched back window. *(Ford Motor Company)*

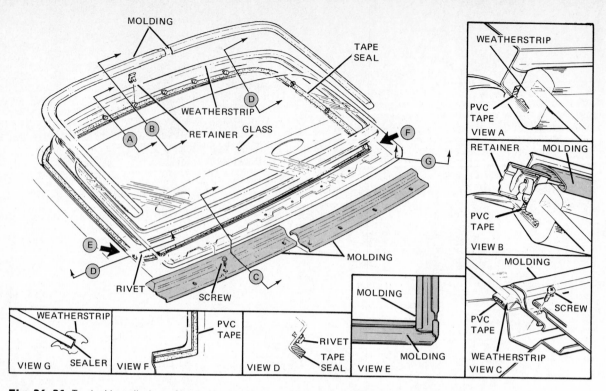

Fig. 26-21 Typical installation of back window and moldings. *(Ford Motor Company)*

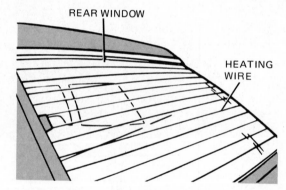

Fig. 26-22 A back glass in which the wires for the electric rear-window defroster are included. *(Ford Motor Company)*

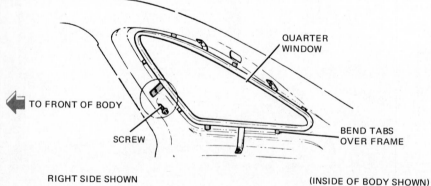

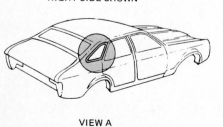

VIEW A

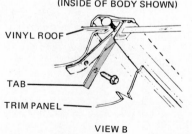

VIEW B

Fig. 26-23 A quarter window on a four-door sedan. *(Ford Motor Company)*

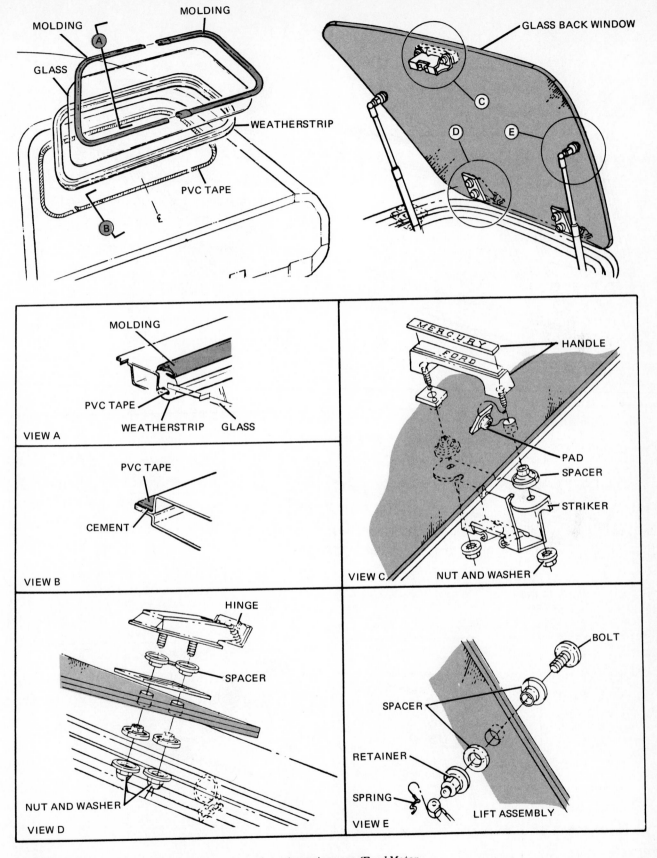

Fig. 26-24 Back window and exterior moldings for a three-door car. *(Ford Motor Company)*

MOLDING

MOLDING

MOLDING

A

GLASS

WEATHERSTRIP

PVC TAPE

B

GLASS BACK WINDOW

C

D

E

MOLDING

PVC TAPE

WEATHERSTRIP   GLASS

VIEW A

PVC TAPE

CEMENT

VIEW B

MERCURY

FORD

HANDLE

PAD

SPACER

STRIKER

VIEW C   NUT AND WASHER

HINGE

SPACER

NUT AND WASHER

VIEW D

BOLT

SPACER

RETAINER

SPRING

LIFT ASSEMBLY

VIEW E

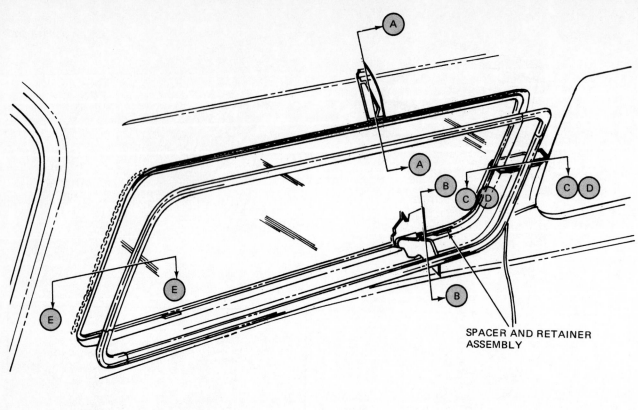

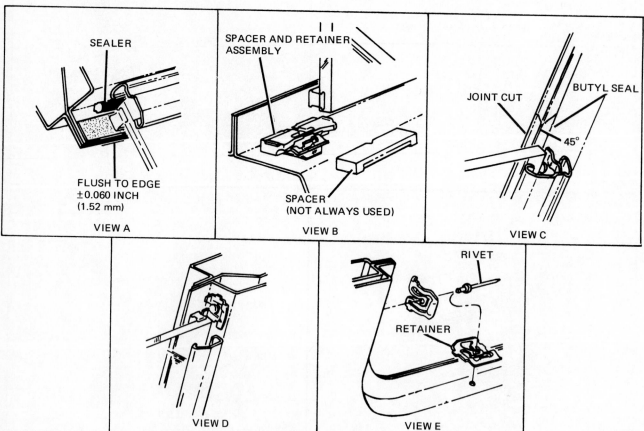

Fig. 26-25 Quarter window and molding installation on a station wagon. *(Ford Motor Company)*

REVIEW QUESTIONS

Select the *one* correct, best, or most probable answer to each question. You can find the answers in the section indicated at the end of each question.

1. An adhesive is   (≡26-2)
   a. plastic body filler
   b. caulking compound
   c. glue
   d. fiberglass

2. Two methods of windshield replacement are the (≡26-3)
   a. slow and quick methods
   b. plain-glass and tinted-glass methods
   c. short and extended methods
   d. dry and glue methods

3. Adhesive can be cut with   (≡26-5)
   a. music wire or a cutting knife
   b. a gas torch or soldering iron
   c. a knife or saw
   d. a drill or wire brush

4. The flange formed by the bent-down edge of the roof and the sheet metal welded to it is the   (≡26-3)
   a. drip channel
   b. core support
   c. pinchweld flange
   d. axle flange

5. A frenched back window has the vinyl roof   (≡26-12)
   a. cut off above the glass
   b. carried to the glass and tucked under the molding
   c. carried down the back of the car to the deck lid
   d. around the glass of a different color or texture than the rest of the roof

PART 8

AUTOMOTIVE SEATS AND INTERIOR TRIM

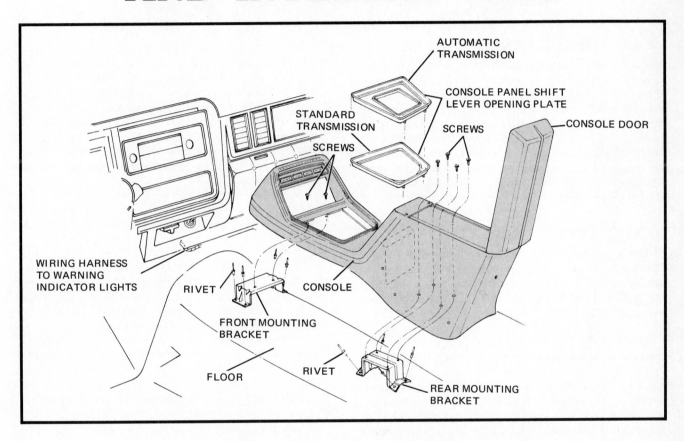

This part describes the various kinds of seats used in automotive vehicles and how to service them. In addition, you will learn about interior trim, including headliner, carpet, and trim panels. There are two chapters in Part 8 as follows:

Chapter 27 Automotive Seats
Chapter 28 Interior Trim

CHAPTER 27
AUTOMOTIVE SEATS

After studying this chapter, you should be able to:

1. Describe various types of seats and how they are constructed.

2. Explain what manual tracks are.

3. Discuss four-way and six-way power seats and how to check them.

≡ 27-1 OPERATION OF SEATS

Various kinds of seats are used in cars (Fig. 27-1).

Front seats have an arrangement which permits them to be moved forward or backward. This adjustment is made manually on some seats, by operating a release handle. On others, the adjustment is made electrically, by means of an electric motor. Electrically operated seats can also be raised or lowered. Four-way seats can be moved back and forth and up and down. Six-way seats have an additional control that changes the tilt of the seat.

≡ 27-2 TYPES OF SEAT

Figure 27-1 shows various kinds of automotive seats. These can be classified as standard or bench seats, and special seats. The greatest variety is in the different types of front seats and bucket seats. The various types are described below.

1. FRONT SEATS. All front seats (Fig. 27-1) except the bucket type are equipped with head restraints. The head restraints can be raised or lowered to suit the person using the seat. The purpose of the head restraints is to prevent neck backlash if the car is hit from the rear. Without a head restraint, when the car is struck from the rear, the head may be snapped back. This can cause severe neck injury from the backlash. With a properly adjusted head restraint, the back of the person's head hits the restraint. This prevents the head from being snapped back so far that it causes a neck injury.

All bench-type front seats used in two-door cars have hinged backs. This enables them to be folded forward, as shown in Fig. 2-35, so passengers can get into and out of the rear seat. The hinges have positive locks which prevent folding forward unless the control lever is operated. A typical latch and release mechanism is shown in Fig. 27-2.

On the full-width-bench seats, the bench can be moved forward or backward. This moves both seats together, so there is no individual choice of seat position. On the 60-40, 50-50, and 40-40 seats, the bench is in two parts and each seat can be individually controlled. The "60-40" means the passenger has 60 percent of the front-seat width and the driver has 40 percent. The "50-50" means the width is split evenly. The "40-40"

means that each seat takes 40 percent of the total width. The remaining 20 percent is taken up by a console in the center between the two seats.

Many front seats have reclining backs which can be tilted rearward about 30°, as shown in Fig. 27-3. The back is operated by lifting a lever and pushing back on the seat back. The back then reclines. To restore the back to an upright position, the weight is removed and the lever operated. The return spring then pushes the back upright again.

NOTE: Front-seat movement is manually controlled in some cars. In other cars, the movement is produced by electric motors, as explained later.

2. BUCKET SEATS. Bucket seats usually have integral head restraints that are part of the seat and are not adjustable. This type of seat is shown in Fig. 27-3. Bucket seats for two-door cars have hinged backs as for bench-type seats. The backs can be hinged forward to permit passengers to get into or out of the back seat. The exception is the swivel bucket seat, which can be swiveled, or turned, about 90° toward the door openings. This moves the back out of the way of anyone wanting to get into or out of the rear seat. The swivel bucket seat is normally locked in the forward position. Operating a lever releases the lock so the seat can be swiveled.

≡ 27-3 SEAT CONSTRUCTION

The seat and back cushions are of wire construction, padded with fibrous material or foam rubber (Fig. 27-4). The upholstery material is stretched over the padding and secured to the spring and frame with "clip rings" (Fig. 27-5). These are rings made of heavy wire with sharpened ends. The ends pierce the material and encircle a spring or the frame. Then the ring is pinched closed.

The cushions are shaped to provide comfortable seating and good support for the back. If springs sag, padding crushes down, or the upholstery is stained or damaged, repairs can be made. Cleaning of upholstery is covered later. Reupholstering seats is a specialized business not done in most body shops. Soft trim and upholstery work is usually performed by local specialty shops.

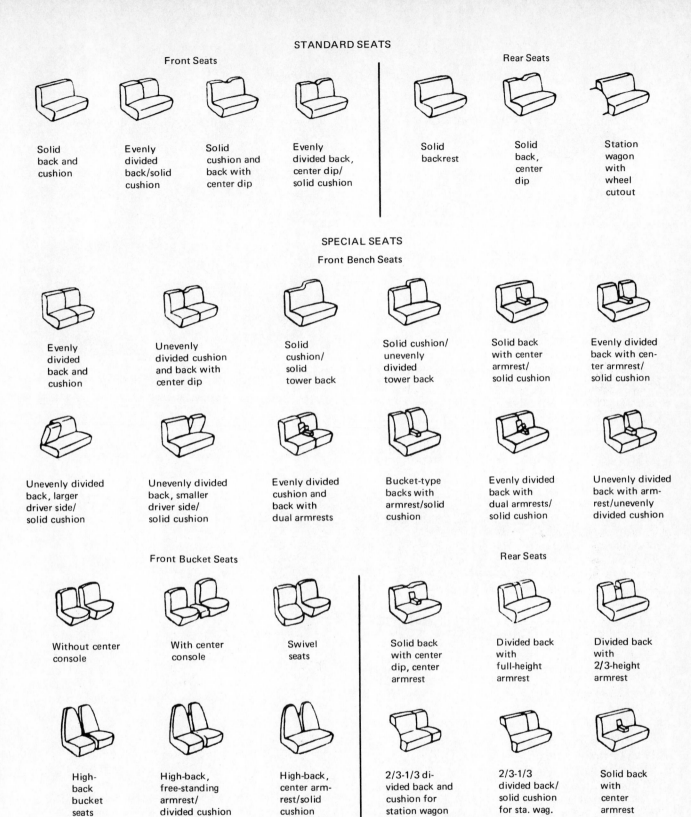

STANDARD SEATS

Front Seats

Solid back and cushion

Evenly divided back/solid cushion

Solid cushion and back with center dip

Evenly divided back, center dip/ solid cushion

Rear Seats

Solid backrest

Solid back, center dip

Station wagon with wheel cutout

SPECIAL SEATS

Front Bench Seats

Evenly divided back and cushion

Unevenly divided cushion and back with center dip

Solid cushion/ solid tower back

Solid cushion/ unevenly divided tower back

Solid back with center armrest/ solid cushion

Evenly divided back with center armrest/ solid cushion

Unevenly divided back, larger driver side/ solid cushion

Unevenly divided back, smaller driver side/ solid cushion

Evenly divided cushion and back with dual armrests

Bucket-type backs with armrest/solid cushion

Evenly divided back with dual armrests/ solid cushion

Unevenly divided back with armrest/unevenly divided cushion

Front Bucket Seats

Without center console

With center console

Swivel seats

High-back bucket seats

High-back, free-standing armrest/ divided cushion

High-back, center armrest/solid cushion

Rear Seats

Solid back with center dip, center armrest

Divided back with full-height armrest

Divided back with 2/3-height armrest

2/3-1/3 divided back and cushion for station wagon

2/3-1/3 divided back/ solid cushion for sta. wag.

Solid back with center armrest

Fig. 27-1 Types of seats.

≡ 27-4 MANUAL SEAT TRACKS

Manual seat tracks allow the front seats to be moved forward or backward when a release lever, or handle, is operated. There is one track on each side of the seat.

Figure 27-6 shows the arrangement for a full-bench seat. The arrangement for a split-bench seat is similar. Manually adjusted seats are attached to the floor pan with studs, nuts, and washers. The nuts or screws are removed from inside the vehicle on some cars and from

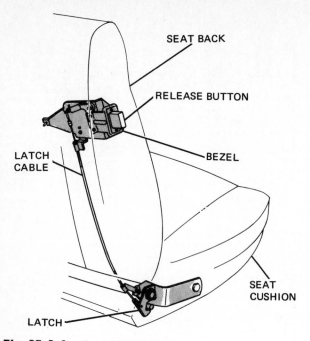

Fig. 27-2 Seat-back latch and release mechanism. (*Chrysler Corporation*)

Fig. 27-3 A reclining seat back. (*Chrysler Corporation*)

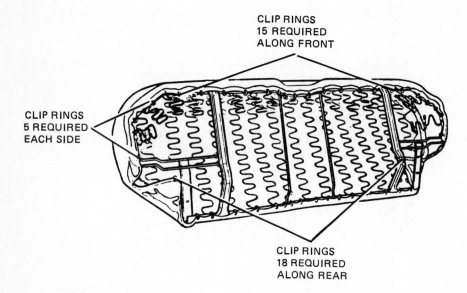

Fig. 27-4 Construction of a seat cushion. (*Ford Motor Company*)

Fig. 27-5 A clip ring, or "hog ring."

underneath on others. When they are removed, the seat can be taken out of the car and carried to a clean area where it can be worked on.

The track on which the seat rides may be level or may be inclined and also curved. These tracks are shown in Fig. 27-7, along with the seat action that each provides.

Mechanical seat tracks have an adjustment for the release mechanism. This adjustment coordinates the release for the two tracks. The adjustment affects only the track farthest away from the release handle or lever. Figure 27-8 shows one type of adjustment for a full-bench seat. If the right locking lever will not release, tighten the turnbuckle one turn at a time. Test the release each turn, until proper adjustment is reached. If the right side will not lock, loosen the turn-

buckle one turn at a time until the proper operation is obtained.

Figure 27-9 shows the adjustment on full-width seats used in many General Motors cars. Use a pick, awl, or small screwdriver to disengage the locking wire from the locking wire retainer. If the right (passenger side) adjuster does not lock, reposition the locking wire coil to loosen the tension. If the right adjuster does not unlock, increase the tension.

276

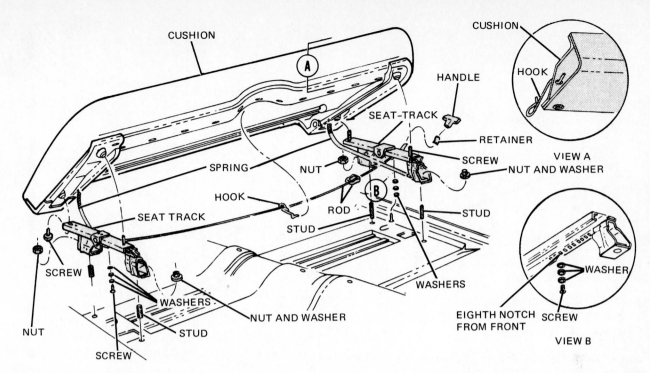

Fig. 27-6 Manual seat track for a full-bench seat. *(Ford Motor Company)*

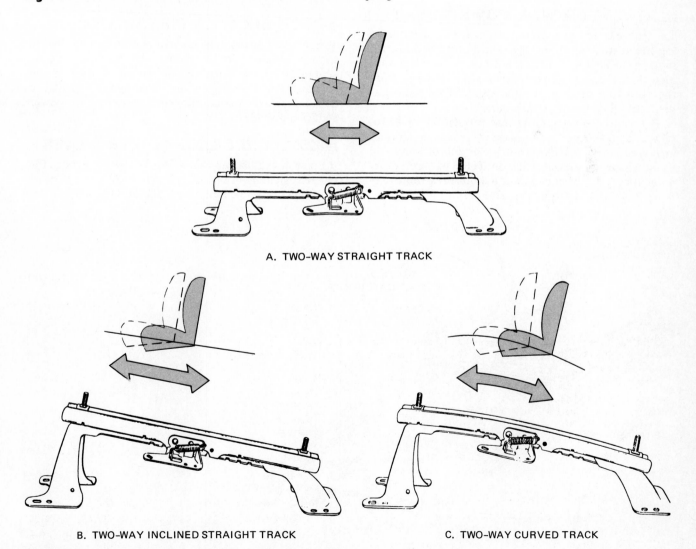

A. TWO-WAY STRAIGHT TRACK

B. TWO-WAY INCLINED STRAIGHT TRACK

C. TWO-WAY CURVED TRACK

Fig. 27-7 Types of seat tracks. *(Society of Automotive Engineers)*

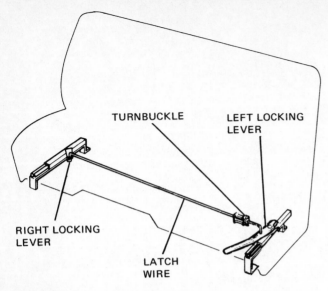

Fig. 27-8 Release-mechanism adjustment on a bench seat. (American Motors Corporation)

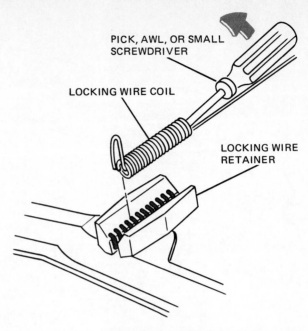

Fig. 27-9 Adjusting the locking wire on full-width seats used in General Motors cars. (© Fisher Body Division of General Motors Corporation)

If a seat is not level or at the right height, spacers can be added to or removed from under the tracks.

≡ 27-5 FOUR-WAY POWER SEAT

The four-way power seat has two motors, one for moving the seat forward and backward and the other for moving the seat up and down. To get to the track and motors, the cushion assembly must be removed from the operating mechanism and the operating mechanism detached from the floor pan.

Figure 27-10 shows the track assembly. It is removed from the car in the same way that the manual seat is removed: by taking out the attaching bolts and nuts. However, the electric connector to the motors must also be disconnected. The actions of the four-way power seat are shown in Fig. 27-11.

≡ 27-6 SIX-WAY POWER SEAT

The six-way power seat has three motors. One moves the seat forward and backward. The second moves the seat up and down. The third tilts the seat backward and forward. The three motors drive through cables. Figure 27-11 shows the various movements the six-way power seat can provide.

≡ 27-7 CHECKING POWER SEATS

If a power seat malfunctions, the trouble could be in the electric switches, wiring, motor, or transmission. In addition, the seat cushion or track could be loose. Also,

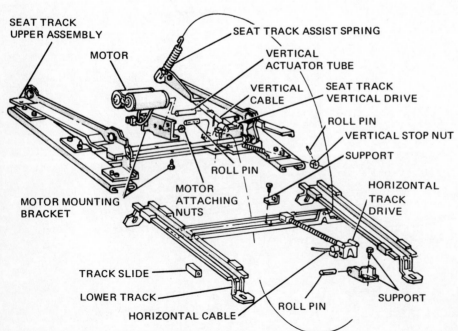

Fig. 27-10 Track assembly for a four-way power seat. (Ford Motor Company)

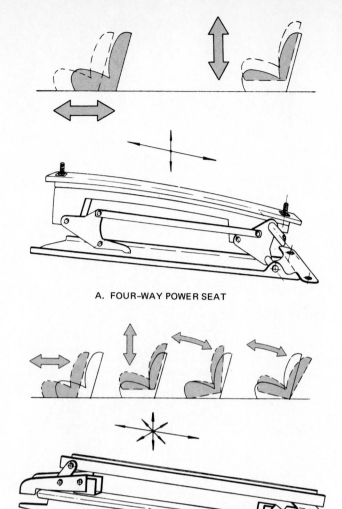

A. FOUR-WAY POWER SEAT

B. SIX-WAY POWER SEAT

Fig. 27-11 Actions of the four-way and six-way power seats. (*Society of Automotive Engineers*)

the carpet or some object under the seat may be interfering with its operation.

The type of trouble should give you some clue as to the cause. For example, if nothing happens when any of the switches is operated, the trouble probably is in the electrical system and either the circuit breaker, connectors, switch, or motor is at fault. If the power system operates in one mode but not another—for example, if it moves the seat forward and backward but not up and down—the problem could be electrical but it could also be a worn transmission.

When you have a complaint about power-seat operation, check out the electrical system first. If it is in good working order, suspect the transmission, loose drive cables, lack of lubrication, loose attaching bolts or nuts, or missing springs.

Each motor can be checked as follows. Disconnect the motor leads from the circuit. Connect the motor to the battery with jumper wires. The motor should run. Reverse the leads at the motor. It should run in the

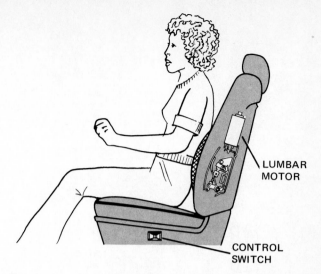

LUMBAR
MOTOR

CONTROL
SWITCH

Fig. 27-12 A power lumbar seat. The crosshatched area of the cushion shows the amount of movement. (*Ford Motor Company*)

opposite direction. If the motor runs satisfactorily, check the tracks and drive mechanisms for binding.

≡ 27-8 LUMBAR POWER SEAT

The lumbar seat provides a power adjustment of the contour of the driver's seat back (Fig. 27-12). It includes a reversible motor and a mechanical drive train to a metal plate behind the back of the seat. When the switch is operated, the motor moves the plate forward or backward to change the contour of the back. The range of adjustment is about 2 inches [51 mm].

Some seats have a manual lumbar-seat adjustment. A knob on the side of the seat is turned to make the adjustment.

≡ 27-9 SEAT-BACK LATCH

This is a latch which, when released, permits a front seat to be folded forward so that a passenger can enter the rear seat. All two-door cars with rear seats have such a latch on each front seat. Figure 27-13 shows details of various latches used on Ford-built cars. Latches for other cars are similar.

≡ 27-10 AUTOMATIC SEAT-BACK LATCH

Some cars are equipped with an arrangement which automatically releases both front-seat-back latches when either front door is opened. There is a switch in each front-door hinge pillar that operates when the door is opened. This connects a relay switch to the battery. The relay switch then closes, connecting two solenoids, one in the back of each seat, to the battery. The solenoids operate the releases so the latches are released and the seats can be folded forward. Figure 27-14 shows the arrangements for Ford and Mercury two-door cars.

≡ 27-11 RECLINING SEAT BACK

Some cars have passenger-side seats with backs that can be tilted backward (reclining back). Figure 27-15

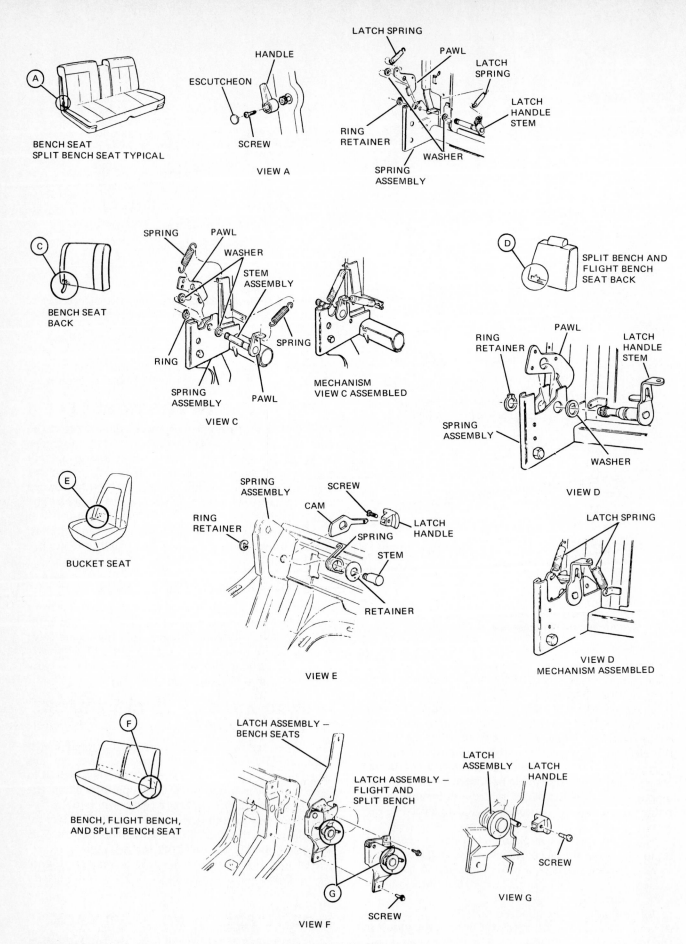

Fig. 27-13 Various types of seat-back latches. *(Ford Motor Company)*

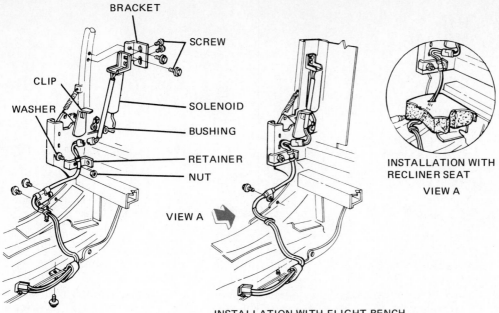

Fig. 27-14 Automatic seat-back latch mechanism. *(Ford Motor Company)*

BRACKET

SCREW

CLIP

WASHER

SOLENOID

BUSHING

RETAINER

NUT

VIEW A

INSTALLATION WITH BENCH SEAT

INSTALLATION WITH FLIGHT BENCH
AND SPLIT BENCH WITHOUT RECLINER

INSTALLATION WITH
RECLINER SEAT

VIEW A

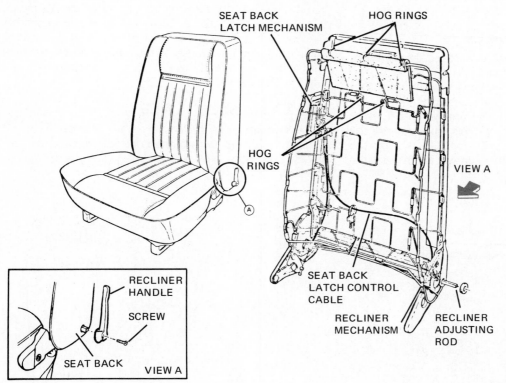

SEAT BACK
LATCH MECHANISM

HOG RINGS

HOG
RINGS

VIEW A

RECLINER
HANDLE

SCREW

SEAT BACK

VIEW A

SEAT BACK
LATCH CONTROL
CABLE

RECLINER
MECHANISM

RECLINER
ADJUSTING
ROD

Fig. 27-15 Reclining seat back, showing the passenger's seat. The recliner handle for the driver's seat is also inboard. *(Ford Motor Company)*

shows the arrangement used in some cars. Some models have a mechanical release lever. To operate it, turn the release handle and push back on the seat to get the desired tilt. Then release the lever, and the seat back will lock in that position.

Some cars are equipped with an electric motor which drives a tilt-back mechanism. When the switch is closed in the one direction, the motor runs in one direction, driving a screw that causes the seat back to move backward. When the switch is closed in the other direction, the motor runs in the opposite direction. This

brings the seat back upward toward an upright position.

≣ 27-12 HEAD RESTRAINTS

Head restraints are positioned back of the heads of the driver and passenger in the front seat. They consist of a pad set on one or two posts (Fig. 27-16). The pad should be adjusted in height so that it would center on the head of the driver or passenger. In case of a rear-end crash, the head restraint allows only a limited backward movement of the head. This prevents neck backlash, a

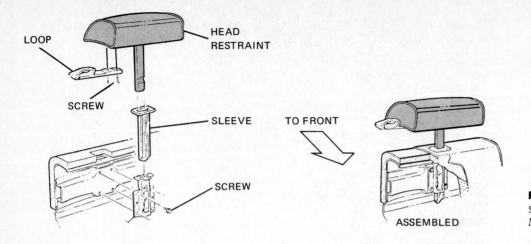

Fig. 27-16 Typical front-seat head restraint. *(Ford Motor Company)*

severe injury resulting from an unrestrained backward snapping of the head.

Some head restraints have a friction spring that allows the restraint to be moved up or down to the desired position. The spring holds the restraint in that position. It prevents the head restraint from being completely removed, however, without the use of a special tool to unlock the spring.

≡ 27-13 REAR SEATS

In most sedans, the rear seats are fixed. However, in station wagons and similar vehicles, the rear seat can fold down to provide additional space for hauling. Figure 27-17 shows typical rear-seat arrangements. In the type shown, the seat can be removed by applying knee force to the rear of the seat cushion. This unlocks the cushion so it can be removed. Then, to take off the back, remove the attaching screws at the bottom

brackets and lift the back up to disengage the wire hangers.

Many station wagons have fold-down rear seats. Figure 27-18 shows an arrangement which includes a folding second seat and filler panel, as well as a folding third seat and panel. The panels are used to level the floor. Then the load to be carried can be slid into place and removed with greater ease. Another arrangement is shown in Fig. 27-19. Two panels can be raised to uncover a stowage compartment that is beneath the floor of the station wagon. Several other arrangements have been used to utilize the rear of the station wagon in various ways.

≡ 27-14 SEAT TRIM

Seat trim includes the leather, fabric, or plastic covering the padding. Not all shops handle replacement of this covering. It is often called upholstery work and is

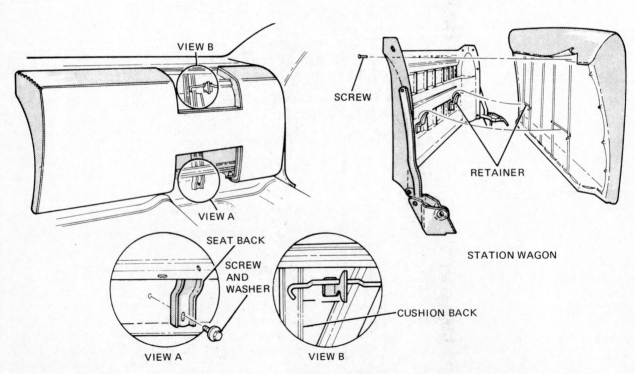

Fig. 27-17 Removing a conventional rear-seat back. *(Ford Motor Company)*

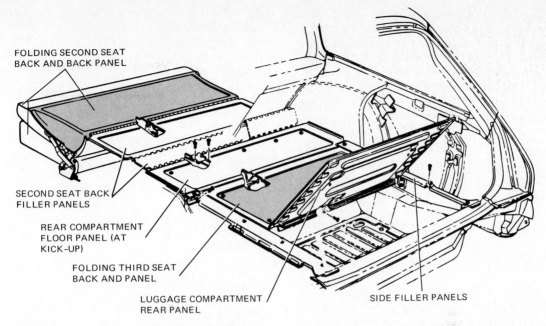

FOLDING SECOND SEAT
BACK AND BACK PANEL

SECOND SEAT BACK
FILLER PANELS

REAR COMPARTMENT
FLOOR PANEL (AT
KICK-UP)

FOLDING THIRD SEAT
BACK AND PANEL

LUGGAGE COMPARTMENT
REAR PANEL

SIDE FILLER PANELS

Fig. 27-18 Folding seats and load panels in a three-seat station wagon. (© *Fisher Body Division of General Motors Corporation*)

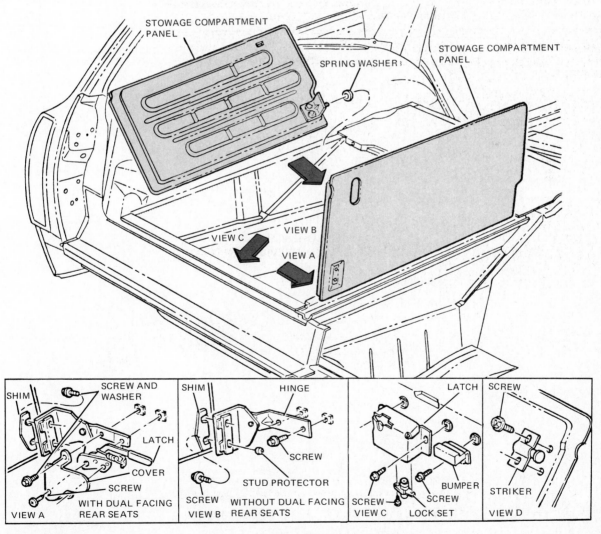

STOWAGE COMPARTMENT
PANEL

SPRING WASHER

STOWAGE COMPARTMENT
PANEL

VIEW C

VIEW B

VIEW A

SHIM

SCREW AND
WASHER

LATCH

COVER

SCREW

WITH DUAL FACING
REAR SEATS

VIEW A

SHIM

HINGE

SCREW

STUD PROTECTOR

SCREW
VIEW B

WITHOUT DUAL FACING
REAR SEATS

LATCH

SCREW

BUMPER

SCREW

SCREW
VIEW C

LOCK SET

SCREW

STRIKER

VIEW D

Fig. 27-19 Two panels, which can be raised, cover the stowage compartment beneath the rear floor of a station wagon. Several other arrangements have been used to utilize the rear of the station wagon in various ways. (*Ford Motor Company*)

performed by an upholstery or trim shop. The procedures used in typical trim work are described below.

As a first step, the seat or cushion should be removed from the car and taken to a clean area. Some upholstery work can be done without removing the seat, but it is usually better to work on a detached seat.

Seats and backs are of wire construction, padded with fibrous material or foam rubber (≡27-3). The upholstery cloth is stretched over the padding. It is then attached under the seat or back of the cushion to the

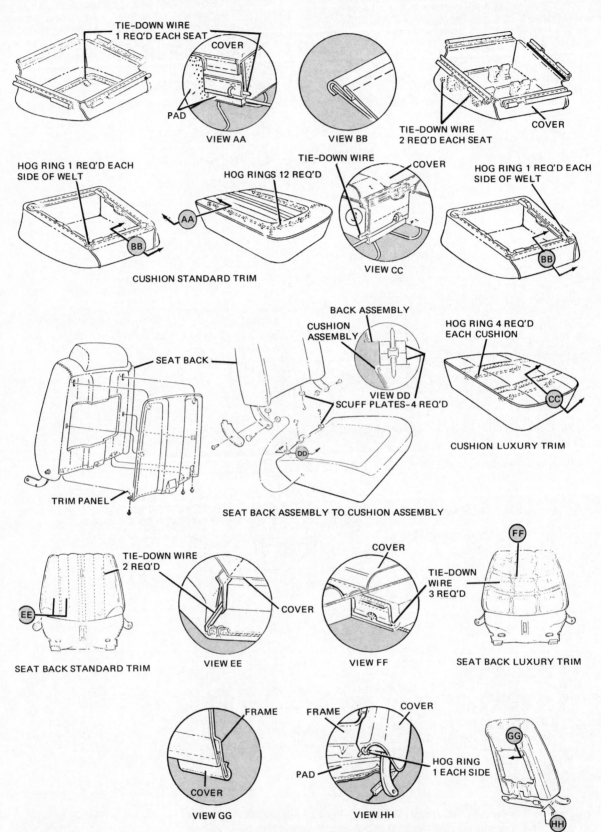

Fig. 27-20 Replacing the trim on the front seat. *(Ford Motor Company)*

frame or spring. The attachment uses wires and clip ("hog") rings. Typical installations are shown in Figs. 27-20 and 27-21. Some cars have plastic retainers to hold the fabric in place.

Whatever the attachment method, the old cover must be removed. Check the padding and, if it is not in good condition, replace it. When installing the new cover, be sure to align it properly and pull it straight so that it does not wrinkle. On some installations, cementing the fabric to the padding is recommended.

≡ 27-15 CENTER ARMRESTS

Some models have covers which can be removed by unzipping the zipper. Others use adhesive to secure the covering to the underlying pad.

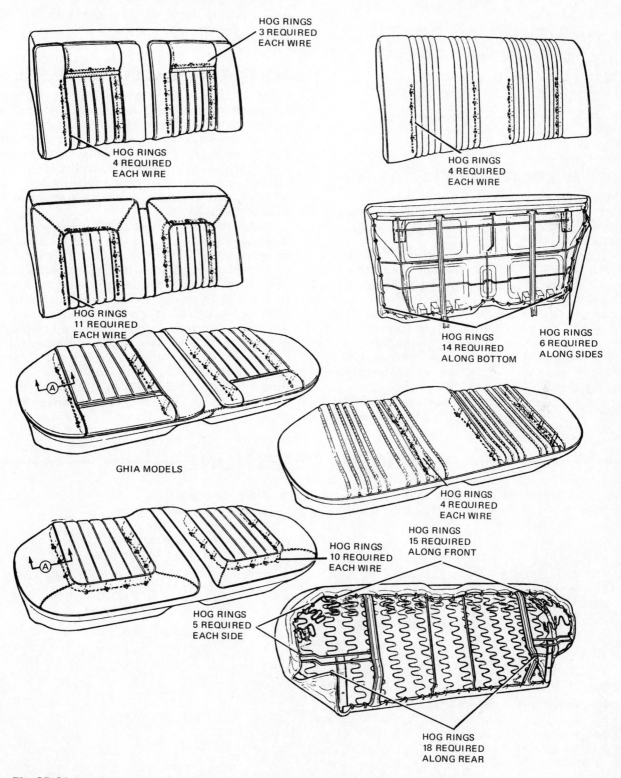

HOG RINGS
3 REQUIRED
EACH WIRE

HOG RINGS
4 REQUIRED
EACH WIRE

HOG RINGS
11 REQUIRED
EACH WIRE

GHIA MODELS

HOG RINGS
4 REQUIRED
EACH WIRE

HOG RINGS
14 REQUIRED
ALONG BOTTOM

HOG RINGS
6 REQUIRED
ALONG SIDES

HOG RINGS
4 REQUIRED
EACH WIRE

HOG RINGS
10 REQUIRED
EACH WIRE

HOG RINGS
15 REQUIRED
ALONG FRONT

HOG RINGS
5 REQUIRED
EACH SIDE

HOG RINGS
18 REQUIRED
ALONG REAR

Fig. 27-21 Installing a new cover on the rear-seat cushion and back. (*Ford Motor Company*)

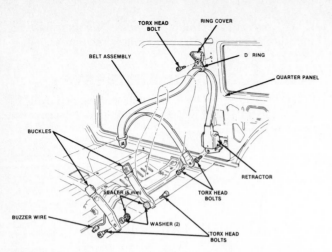

Fig. 27-22 Removal and installation of the passenger-side front-seat belt assembly. *(Ford Motor Company)*

≡ 27-16 CHECKING SEAT BELTS

The purpose and construction of seat-belt systems, which include lap and shoulder belts, are described in ≡ 2-20. Figure 2-37 shows a typical front seat-belt installation.

To check both front and rear seat belts, look for belt webbing that is frayed, split, or torn. Check that the belt buckles operate properly. Inspect the belt anchors. None should be loose, badly corroded, missing, or not fastened to the belt. The belt-mounting surfaces must not be badly deformed, damaged, or corroded. Also, check the operation of the seat-belt retractors.

Some shoulder belts have a retractor that can lock in various positions. This provides slack in the belt, which makes it more comfortable to wear.

To check the operation of the locking retractor, close the car door. Then extend the webbing from the retractor to a distance approximating the buckled position. Let the belt retract a minimum of 7 inches [178 mm]. Then extract the belt 1 to 3 inches [25 to 76 mm] and release it. The belt must return to the comfort-lock position previously set. Full retraction is a failure of the system. Extract the belt 7 inches [178 mm] and release it. The belt must fully retract without locking.

Any mounting surface defect must be properly repaired. Defects in the belts, buckles, anchors, and retractors require replacement of the affected parts (≡ 27-17).

≡ 27-17 REPLACING SEAT BELTS

Figure 27-22 shows how the passenger-side front-seat belt assembly is removed and installed. The retractor portions of the front-seat lap and shoulder belt for the outboard passenger and driver, and the buckle portion of the front-seat lap belt for the outboard passenger and driver, are available separately. All other belts are available only in complete sets. Be sure the belt sets are the same type. Never mix standard and deluxe belts on front or rear seats.

While installing new belts, keep sharp edges and damaging objects away from the new belts. Avoid bending or damaging any portion of the belt buckle or latch plate. Do not bleach or dye the belt webbing. If dirty, clean it with a mild soap and water solution. When installing a lap or shoulder-belt anchor bolt, start the bolt by hand to assure that the bolt is threaded straight. Do not attempt to repair lap or shoulder belt-retractor mechanisms or belt-retractor covers. Replace them.

Remove and install the belts, referring to the appropriate illustrations and procedures in the manufacturer's service manual. Then tighten all lap and shoulder-belt anchor bolts to the specified torque.

REVIEW QUESTIONS

Select the *one* correct, best, or most probable answer to each question. You can find the answers in the section indicated at the end of each question.

1. Seats are generally classed as   (≡27-2)
   a. soft or hard
   b. shifting or swinging
   c. adjustable or nonadjustable
   d. bench or bucket

2. Manual seat tracks allow the front seats to be moved
   a. forward or backward   (≡27-4)
   b. up or down
   c. right or left
   d. by an electric motor

3. Electrically operated power seats can move
   a. one way or two ways   (≡27-5 and 27-6)
   b. two ways or three ways
   c. one way or three ways
   d. four ways or six ways

4. The purpose of the head restraint is to   (≡27-12)
   a. unblock the driver's vision
   b. prevent neck backlash
   c. unblock entrance to the rear seats
   d. provide a headrest for sleeping

5. The material covering the padding of a seat is called the
   a. molding   (≡27-14)
   b. plastic
   c. seat trim
   d. watershield

CHAPTER 28
INTERIOR TRIM

After studying this chapter, you should be able to:

1. Service quarter trim panels.

2. Inspect and repair floor-pan insulators.

3. Explain how to repair damaged carpet.

4. Discuss the two types of headlining and explain how to service each.

5. Discuss interior care and maintenance.

≡ 28-1 SERVICING INTERIOR TRIM

Interior trim includes seat covering, quarter trim panels, trim panels on doors and front-seat backs, headliner, and carpet. It also includes interior molding. The removal and installation of door trim panels is described in Chap. 23.

≡ 28-2 QUARTER TRIM PANEL

This panel is shaped to fit over the quarter-panel interior. Figure 28-1 shows a typical installation of a quarter trim panel.

To remove a quarter trim panel, first take out the rear-seat cushion and back. Remove the window-regulator handle, if present. Then remove any screws, garnish-molding retaining screws, and the door-sill step-plate rear screw. Then unclip the trim-panel retaining clips and pull the trim panel from the quarter panel. Disconnect the power-window switch wires (if present). To reinstall the trim panel, reverse the procedure.

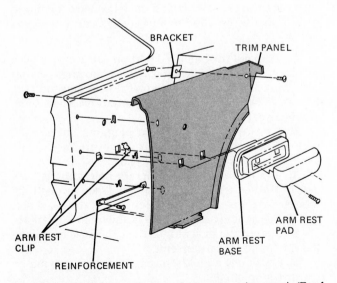

Fig. 28-1 Typical installation of a quarter trim panel. *(Ford Motor Company)*

≡ 28-3 QUARTER UPPER TRIM PANEL

This type of trim panel (Fig. 28-2) covers the upper quarter-panel area and includes the opening for any quarter, or opera, window. The quarter upper trim is attached by clips and screws in a manner similar to that used to attach the lower quarter trim panel (Fig. 28-2). General Motors calls this panel the quarter upper trim. Ford calls it the roof side trim panel. The panel is removed and installed in the same way as the quarter trim panel.

≡ 28-4 FLOOR-PAN INSULATORS

Floor-pan insulators are required on many cars because of catalytic converters in the exhaust system. Catalytic converters produce considerable heat, requiring some form of insulation in between the floor pan and the carpet. Figure 28-3 shows the typical installation of insulation in various cars produced by General Motors. Materials used for insulators include aluminum silica, resinated fiber, and fiberglass.

NOTE: When doing any carpet work or repairing any vehicle that has been damaged in an accident, any insulator that has been damaged or removed must be reinstalled. The proper material must be used, and it must be installed in the correct position.

Here are special points to observe when replacing a floor-pan insulator:

Use the original insulator as a template for cutting out the new insulator. The new material must be the type specified for that location in the vehicle. The new insulator must have the same shape as the old, and it must be installed in the same position. Do not enlarge any holes or cutouts in the insulator.

Electrical harness must be routed over the insulators, not under them. Do not use spray-on sound deadeners and trim adhesives on the floor pan in any area that is directly over the catalytic converter or muffler.

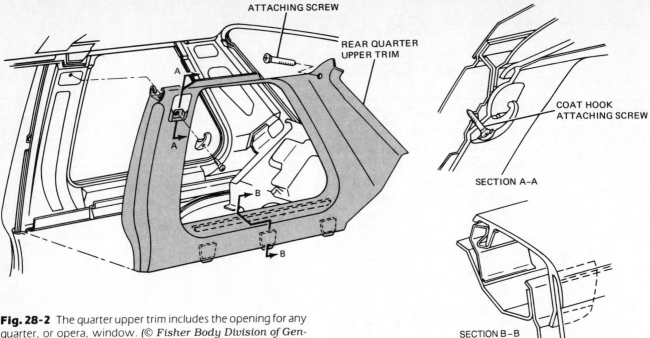

Fig. 28-2 The quarter upper trim includes the opening for any quarter, or opera, window. (© *Fisher Body Division of General Motors Corportion*)

ATTACHING SCREW

REAR QUARTER UPPER TRIM

COAT HOOK ATTACHING SCREW

SECTION A–A

SECTION B–B

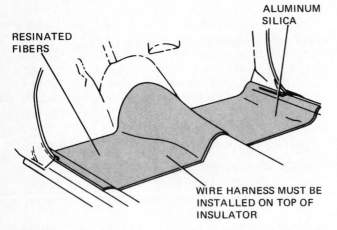

RESINATED FIBERS

ALUMINUM SILICA

WIRE HARNESS MUST BE INSTALLED ON TOP OF INSULATOR

Fig. 28-3 Front floor-pan insulator. (© *Fisher Body Division of General Motors Corporation*)

≡ 28-5 CARPET

The floor carpet for some cars comes in two pieces, one for the front and one for the rear. Other cars have a one-piece carpet molded to fit over any irregularities, such as the drive-line channel in the floor pan. To remove the old one-piece carpet and install a new carpet, everything in the way must be removed. This includes seats, console (if supplied), and seat belts. Also, the door-sill scuff plates will require removal. Two-piece carpets usually have cutouts that allow them to be removed and installed with the seats in place.

Some floors are covered with heavy rubber floor mats. These are replaced like sections of floor carpet. Another type of floor covering is carpet, with rubber mats in the heavy-wear areas.

Carpet with small cuts, tears, burns, or other minor damage often can be repaired by patching. This usually can be done without removing the carpet from the vehicle.

When the carpet has a straight cut or tear, it can be repaired without additional trimming around the damaged area. Here is the procedure to follow:

1. Remove all parts required to gain access to the back side of the carpet at the area to be repaired.

2. With the carpet supported from the front side, apply fast-tack adhesive to the back side of the carpet over the cut or torn area.

3. Place a piece of waterproof cloth-back tape over the cut or torn area. Heat the tape with a heat gun until the tape begins to soften. Then, while the repair area and tape are still warm, press the tape firmly in place with a flat tool. This will fuse the carpet backing to the tape.

4. Allow the repaired area to cool for about 5 minutes. Then install all previously removed parts.

If the carpet has a small hole or a burned or damaged area, it can be repaired by installing a carpet plug, as follows:

1. Trim out the damaged portion of the carpet with a razor-blade knife. The cut is made at an angle so that the trimmed-out area is larger on the back side than the top, as shown in Fig. 28-4. The cutout area should be symmetrical.

2. To get the material for a plug, cut out a small section of carpet from an obscure or covered area, such as from under a seat or the sill plate.

3. Lay the plug section under the hole with the back side of the section up. Using a pen, trace through the trimmed-out hole to obtain an outline of the exact size and shape of plug needed. This is shown in Fig. 28-4B.

4. Cut out the new plug to the exact size by following the line you marked on it.

5. Brush pile on both the carpet and plug to match the direction of pile.

6. Coat the back side of the carpet and the plug with fast-tack adhesive around the repair area, as shown in

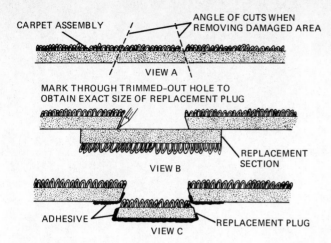

VIEW A

MARK THROUGH TRIMMED-OUT HOLE TO
OBTAIN EXACT SIZE OF REPLACEMENT PLUG

VIEW B

VIEW C

Fig. 28-4 Repairing small damage to the carpet by installing a plug. *(Cadillac Motor Car Division of General Motors Corporation)*

Fig. 28-4C. Place the plug into the trimmed-out hole. Tape it in place with waterproof cloth-back tape. Heat the tape with a heat gun until the tape begins to soften. Then, while the repaired area and tape are still warm, press the carpet firmly in place with a flat tool. This fuses the carpet backing to the tape.

7. Work carpet pile so that the plug blends into the adjacent carpet. Allow the repaired area to cool for about 5 minutes.

8. Then reinstall all previously removed parts.

≡ 28-6 FLOOR CONSOLE

The console is attached to floor brackets with screws, as shown in Fig. 28-5. To remove a console, take out the screws, disconnect any wiring, and the console is free.

≡ 28-7 SUN VISOR

The sun visor is attached by screws, as shown in Fig. 28-6, to roof brackets. Note how the center clip is attached to a bracket at the roof. Some sun visors have vanity mirrors, as shown in Fig. 28-6. Others have lighted vanity mirrors.

≡ 28-8 HEADLINING TYPES

Headlining is of two types: soft (cloth or vinyl-coated) and formed (molded). Typical installation procedures for the two are described in following sections. The methods of attachment of the two types are described below.

1. SOFT (CLOTH OR VINYL-COATED) HEADLINING. This headlining assembly is attached to the roof inner panel by concealed plastic retaining strips. The retaining strips are sewed to the headlining assembly and contain rectangular lugs that fit into T slots in the roof inner panel (Fig. 28-7). In addition, the headlining is cemented into place along the sides. Garnish molding or finishing lace also helps to hold the headlining in place. Garnish molding along the side roof rail is secured to a headlining retainer or to the side roof rail by clips located in the molding.

When finishing lace is used at the windshield and back window or rear body opening, the headlining is secured at these places with nonstaining adhesive. Removal and replacement of the cloth or vinyl headlining is covered in ≡28-9 and 28-10.

2. MOLDED (FORMED) HEADLINING. This headlining is made of molded hardboard covered with foam and cloth or vinyl facing. It may be of either the one-piece type or the two-piece type. Formed headlining is used in station wagons and utility vehicles. Removal

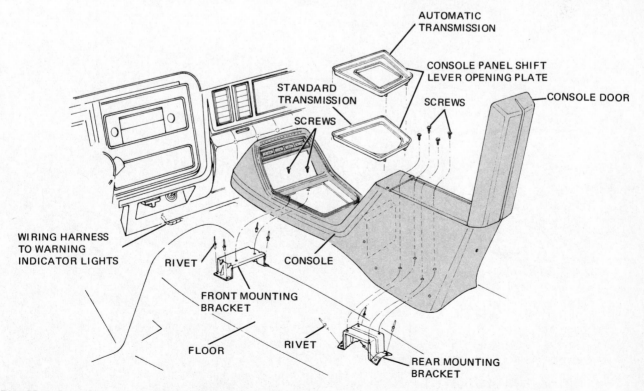

Fig. 28-5 Floor-console installation. *(Ford Motor Company)*

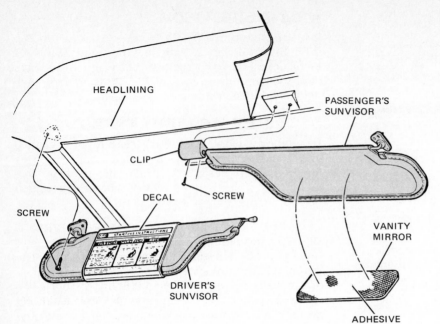

Fig. 28-6 Mounting of sun visors above the front seat. *(Ford Motor Company)*

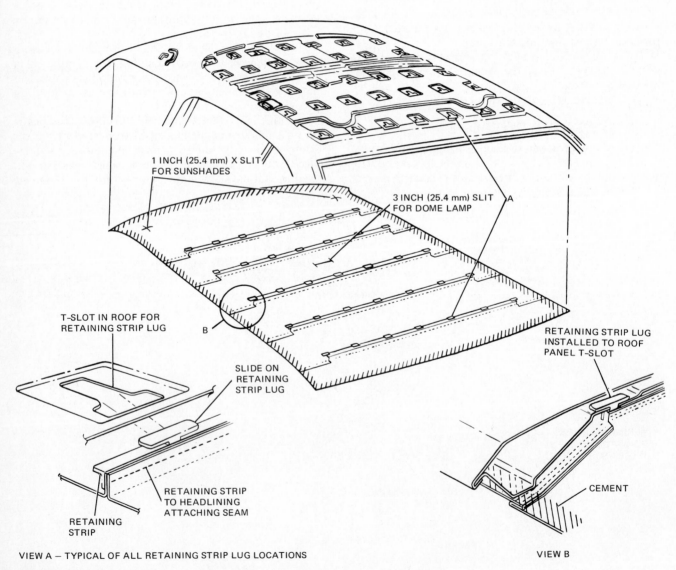

VIEW A – TYPICAL OF ALL RETAINING STRIP LUG LOCATIONS

VIEW B

Fig. 28-7 Headlining attached by lugs and T slots. *(© Fisher Body Division of General Motors Corporation)*

and installation of the formed headlining is covered in ≡28-11.

≡ 28-9 GENERAL MOTORS CLOTH-AND VINYL-COATED-HEADLINING SERVICE

The following procedure is for the removal and installation of cloth and vinyl-coated headlining in General Motors cars:

1. Cover the seat cushions and backs to protect them. Then remove all hardware and trim installed over the headlining. This could include the following:

    a. Garnish moldings and finishing lace around the windshield, along the sides, at vista vent (sun roof), and around back window

    b. Map lamp, dome lamp, and visor or sunshade supports

    c. Center-pillar upper trim assembly

    d. Rear-quarter and quarter upper trim panels

    e. Shoulder strap retainers

NOTE: Remove only those parts that will get in the way.

2. Detach the cemented edges of the headlining all around the edge of the headlining. If headlining is difficult to detach, apply heat with a heat gun to the cemented areas. If you are going to use the headlining again, use care to avoid tearing it. Also, gather or fold the assembly with retaining strips on the outside of the material to keep the headlining from getting dirty.

3. Start at the front and carefully detach the retaining strips by pulling toward the rear to detach the rectangular lugs from the T slots in the inner roof (Fig. 28-7). Fold the headlining as you detach it.

4. Before installing the headlining, check the retaining strips for cracked or broken rectangular lugs. Replace all damaged or missing lugs. If installing a new headlining on a car with a vista vent, or sun roof, you will have to cut out an opening in the headlining to fit around the roof opening. Cement the seams at the retaining strips next to the retaining lugs to prevent the stitching from coming out.

5. Lift the headlining into the car, and start at the back to engage the lugs in the T slots. Keep tension on the headlining as you work forward, inserting the lugs in the slots.

6. Cement the edges of the headlining, stretching and securing them in the following order: Stretch and apply the cemented edge at the windshield first. Then work the edge into place at the back window. Continue working forward on the sides until the headlining is secure all the way around.

NOTE: Be sure the headlining is well cemented and properly attached around the base of the seat-belt retractor assembly openings. Material inside the trim area can cause interference with the seat-belt retractor.

7. Reattach all hardware and parts that have been removed. You can locate the holes for the attaching screws by pressing the headlining up against the inner roof panel.

≡ 28-10 FORD CLOTH-HEADLINING SERVICE

The following is a typical headlining removal and installation procedure for Ford-built cars. Instead of employing rectangular lugs and T slots, Ford uses support rods that span the roof area from side to side, as shown in Fig. 28-8.

1. Remove all hardware and trim that would interfere with headlining removal. This includes sun visor and brackets, moldings, shoulder belts, and coat hooks. Then remove the rear-seat cushion and back and quarter-panel lower- and upper-panel trim assemblies.

2. Also remove the dome light and package tray.

3. Then take out the staples that fasten the headlining to the roof side retainer assemblies. Pull the headlining loose from all cemented areas.

4. Unhook the right and left retainers from the headlining rear support rod. Unhook all support rods from the holes in the left and right roof rails and remove the headlining from the car.

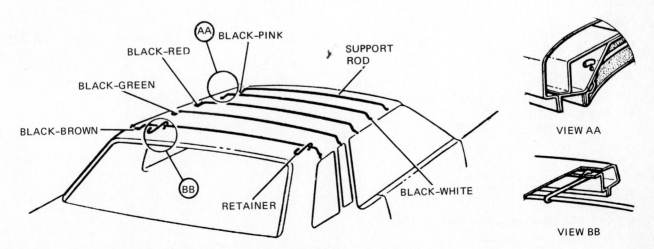

Fig. 28-8 *Headlining attached by support rods. (Ford Motor Company)*

5. Unwrap the new headlining and spread it out on a clean surface.

6. Trim the "listings" (pockets for the support rods) to the same length as on the old headlining.

7. Remove the support rods from the old headlining and install them in the same relative rod listings of the new headlining. Do not mix them up. They are color-coded at each end. This determines their positions in the roof, as shown in Fig. 28-8.

8. Position the headlining in the car. Start hooking the support rods into the holes in the roof rails. Insert the rods into the upper holes so as to provide the most headroom and wrinkle-free installation.

9. Hook the rear retainers to the rear support rods.

10. Staple the headlining to the retainer assemblies.

11. Cement the headlining into place and trim off the excess material.

12. Install all moldings, trim panels, hardware, seat back and cushion that were removed.

≡ 28-11 FORMED-HEADLINING SERVICE

This type of headlining is formed from molded hardboard covered with foam and cloth or vinyl facing. There are two kinds: the one-piece type used in sedans and the two-piece type used in station wagons.

To remove the headlining, first remove all hardware, moldings, and trim panels that would interfere. Then disengage the tabs or clips on each side of the headlining assembly. Move the assembly rearward enough to provide sufficient clearance to remove it. Take it out through the front-door opening.

On reassembly, be careful not to bend the headlining too much. This could crack it. If the new headlining does not have an insulator cemented to the upper surface, remove the insulator from the old assembly and cement it onto the new. Use only enough cement in spots to hold it in place during assembly.

Raise the headlining up into position, and engage the tabs or clips on each side of the headlining. Reinstall all hardware and other parts that were removed.

≡ 28-12 INTERIOR CARE AND MAINTENANCE

A well-kept interior adds to the appearance and value of the vehicle. Following are suggestions about cleaning the trim, seats, vinyl, and carpets:

1. Most stains can be removed from the interior trim while they are fresh and have not hardened and set into the fabric. The exception is mud or clay, which should be allowed to dry so that it can be brushed off. Remove the rear seat, and vacuum the interior thoroughly, including under the front seat.

2. Shampoo all vinyl interior surfaces, including headlining, door panels, instrument panel, package shelf, and carpeting or floor mat. Use a good grade of cleaner, following the directions on the label. Use a spot remover to remove obvious spots before shampooing.

3. There are special tints and dyes which can be used to restore interior trim to its original color. For example, there is an upholstery tint that can be added to the shampoo. Use a natural sponge when doing this job, because such a sponge can be rinsed out and used again. Other sponges may retain some of the tint.

4. Vinyl panels that are faded can be redyed. Wash the area with cleaner to remove all wax. Then mask it off and spray it with the proper color of paint. Damaged vinyl can be repaired as explained in Chap. 29.

5. If the package shelf needs attention, remove it. Wipe it down with a cloth saturated with lacquer thinner. Then spray-paint it.

REVIEW QUESTIONS

Select the *one* correct, best, or most probable answer to each question. You can find the answers in the section indicated at the end of each question.

1. You must remove the window-regulator handle to remove　　　　　　　　(≡28-2)
 a. a quarter trim panel
 b. a quarter upper trim panel
 c. the floor-pan insulator
 d. the carpet

2. Cars with catalytic converters must be equipped with
 a. floor carpet　　　　　　　　(≡28-4)
 b. floor-pan insulators
 c. vinyl seat covers
 d. solid headlining

3. A cigarette burn in a carpet can be repaired with a
 a. new carpet　　　　　　　　(≡28-5)
 b. rubber floor mat
 c. piece of matching tape
 d. carpet plug

4. Sun visors may have a　　　　　　　　(≡28-7)
 a. map case
 b. rearview mirror
 c. vanity mirror
 d. dome light

5. Two widely used types of headlining are　　(≡28-8)
 a. cut and sewn
 b. soft and formed
 c. riveted and stapled
 d. insulating and sound-deadening

PART 9

VINYL ROOFS, OVERLAYS, AND DECALS

This part explains how to make repairs to vinyl roofs and padded dashes, how to apply wood-grain overlays and decals, and how to replace a vinyl roof cover.

Vinyl is widely used today in cars. Many cars have grain-textured vinyl roof covers in various colors. Inside, the instrument panel and other interior surfaces are covered with vinyl. Vinyl is easily repaired if it is torn or damaged. Wood grain, used on many station wagons, is a thin vinyl film with an adhesive on the back.

There are two chapters in Part 9, as follows:

Chapter 29 Vinyl Repair and Roof Replacement
Chapter 30 Servicing Wood-Grain Overlays and Decals

CHAPTER 29
VINYL REPAIR AND ROOF REPLACEMENT

After studying this chapter, you should be able to:

1. Explain how to repair a damaged vinyl roof.

2. Explain how to repair a damaged padded dash.

3. Describe the removal and installation of a vinyl roof cover.

≡ 29-1 VINYL REPAIR PROCEDURE

When vinyl was first used in cars, damaged vinyl had to be replaced if the appearance of the car was to be restored. Now many types of damage can be repaired. Repairing is much less expensive and often requires less time than installing new vinyl material. The basic repair technique was made possible by the availability of *liquid vinyl.*

Liquid vinyl actually is a paste that can be used to fill small holes in vinyl material. Then, with the application of heat, the liquid vinyl cures, or hardens. In curing, the liquid vinyl fuses to the original material. Most vinyl has a grain or pattern in it. The original grain can be given to the patched area. This is done by using graining paper, or another piece of the original material, as a die to press against the liquid vinyl as it cures.

Liquid vinyl is available in a variety of colors, which can be mixed like paint to match the original color. Or, after the vinyl patch has cured, it can be painted to match the color of the original material.

To repair vinyl that is damaged, first trim back the damaged area until you leave only original material that is in good condition. New liquid vinyl is applied to the cutout area and heated with a heat gun. During this curing process, a piece of the original vinyl is used as a die and pressed onto the hot vinyl. The vinyl die has the same grain structure as the damaged vinyl. This gives the new vinyl a grain that blends in with the surrounding old vinyl. After the repair has dried, it is spray-painted with the same color paint to match the old vinyl.

≡ 29-2 MATERIALS FOR VINYL REPAIR

In addition to the liquid-vinyl patching compound, other materials needed to repair vinyl include vinyl dies, a heat gun (Fig. 29-1), a razor knife, a pallet knife, vinyl cleaner, scissors, and vinyl repair paint. For any specific repair job, the vinyl die used must match the surrounding grain. Also, the paint used must match. Figure 29-2 shows materials for a vinyl repair kit.

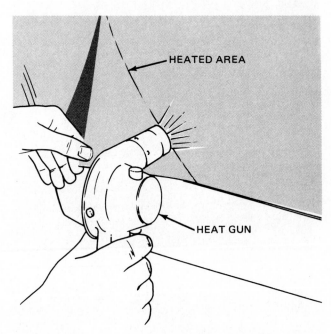

Fig. 29-1 A heat gun, used in vinyl repair. (*American Motors Corporation*)

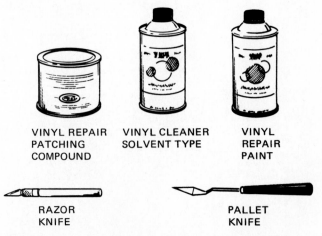

VINYL REPAIR PATCHING COMPOUND   VINYL CLEANER SOLVENT TYPE   VINYL REPAIR PAINT

RAZOR KNIFE   PALLET KNIFE

Fig. 29-2 Materials needed to repair vinyl. (© *Fisher Body Division of General Motors Corporation*)

≡ 29-3 PATCHING A VINYL ROOF

Figure 29-3 shows a vinyl roof which has a small hole rubbed in it. This is a new car, and the damage occurred during transportation of the car to the dealership. A retaining chain rubbed on the vinyl roof, causing the damage. Before repair started, the area was cleaned with vinyl cleaner (Fig. 29-2). Figure 29-4 shows the technician applying vinyl from a dispensing can to the damage. Figure 29-5 shows a pallet knife being used to smooth the vinyl into the hole. Figure 29-6 shows a heat gun being used to heat and cure the vinyl. Note that the technician is holding a vinyl die near the damaged area. When the vinyl is almost hard, the technician will press the die onto it. This imparts a grain to the vinyl. When the vinyl is cured, it is spray-painted. The resulting repair is almost impossible to detect.

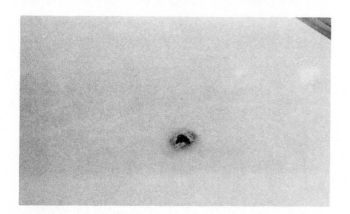

Fig. 29-3 A hole rubbed in the vinyl roof of a new car by a loose chain on the car carrier.

Fig. 29-4 Applying liquid vinyl to the damaged area with a dispensing can.

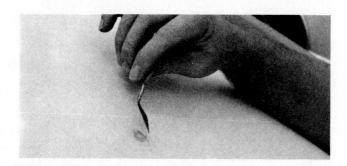

Fig. 29-5 Using a pallet knife to smooth the liquid vinyl into the hole.

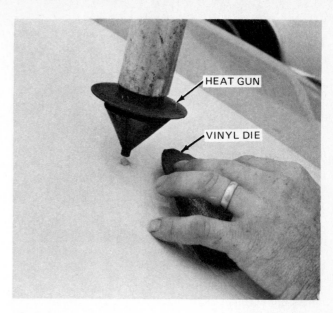

Fig. 29-6 Using a heat gun to heat and cure the liquid vinyl.

≡ 29-4 REPAIRING A PADDED DASH

Figure 29-7 shows the instrument panel of a car which has been damaged. There is a crack in the vinyl at one place. At another, the vinyl material is completely missing.

As a first step in the repair, the area was cleaned. Figure 29-8 shows the repair job in process. The tech-

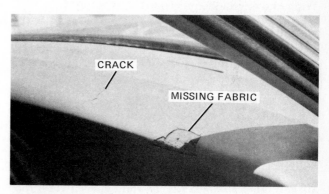

Fig. 29-7 A damaged padded dash.

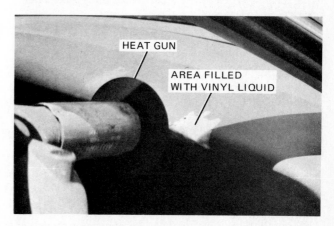

Fig. 29-8 Curing a vinyl patch in a padded dash.

Fig. 29-9 Graining a vinyl patch, using a graining die.

nician has filled the damaged area, which had material missing, with several thin coats of vinyl, smoothed in with a pallet knife. Each coat was heated to cure it. After the patched area is built up so that it is level with the surrounding vinyl, the technician uses a vinyl die to impress a grain on the vinyl (Fig. 29-9). Lastly, the technician spray-paints the patched area so that it matches the rest of the padded dash.

Larger damaged areas of vinyl can be repaired by applying patches of matching vinyl. These are cut out to approximately fit the damage. Then, after the edges of the damaged vinyl are trimmed, the patch is applied and cemented into place. Finally, the joint between the patch and original vinyl is filled with liquid vinyl. This is heat-treated, and then a vinyl die is used to grain the liquid vinyl. Then the area is painted.

≡ 29-5 TYPES OF VINYL ROOF COVER

Figure 25-15 shows various styles of vinyl roof covers. Vinyl roofs are installed primarily to enhance the appearance of the car. They usually are installed on new cars during assembly, although many are installed by dealers and trim and upholstery shops.

Not all vinyl roof covers are the style shown in Fig. 25-15A. For example, Fig. 25-15B shows a vinyl roof cover that is fitted over only the rear half of the roof. This style often is called a Landau top (≡25-9). There are two basic types of vinyl roof covers:

1. Vinyl-coated fabric
2. Vinyl-coated material with an integral pad

The vinyl roof covers are cemented either directly to the roof panel, to a plastic cap covering the roof panel, or to an additional foam pad between the cover and the roof panel. When the plastic cap or foam pad is used, the entire cap or pad is cemented to the roof panel. Then the roof cover is cemented to the cap or pad.

≡ 29-6 VINYL-ROOF INSTALLATIONS

The installation of a typical vinyl roof cover is shown in Fig. 29-10. On styles where the covers extend into the windshield and back-window openings, the cover is re-

tained in the opening by adhesive and one or more of the following:

1. Clips installed over weld-on studs (view A in Fig. 29-10)
2. Drive nails (views D and E in Fig. 29-10)
3. Reveal molding and finishing lace

On styles where the back-window reveal moldings are not exposed, the cover is retained in that area by one or more of the following:

1. Cement
2. Tabbed retainers
3. Finishing lace

Where the cover extends in and around drop moldings, or folds around the roof-panel flange, it is retained by one or more of the following:

1. Adhesive and drip scalp moldings

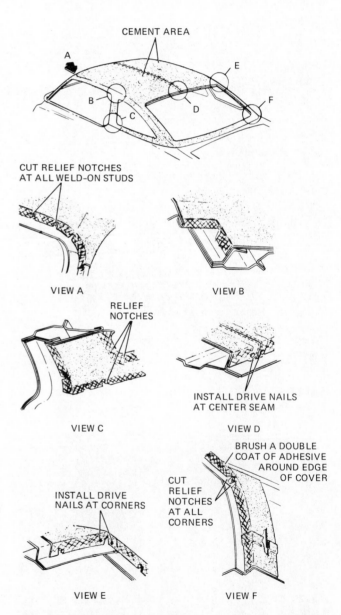

Fig. 29-10 Typical vinyl-roof-cover installation. (© *Fisher Body Division of General Motors Corporation*)

2. Weatherstrip retainers

3. Finish moldings

On styles with roof-panel moldings, the cover is retained under the moldings by adhesive and clips installed over weld-on studs.

≡ 29-7 PREPARING TO REMOVE THE VINYL ROOF

Two removal and installation methods are required for the two different installation designs. One method is required for vinyl-coated fabric. Another method is required when a foam pad is integral with the fabric.

Regardless of the type of roof cover and the method required to remove and install it, the following are removed:

1. Windshield and back-window reveal moldings (where present) except where the cover does not extend into the windshield or back-window openings.

2. Roof drip scalp moldings, weatherstrip retainers, or finish moldings (where cover extends into the drip moldings or folds around roof-panel flange).

3. Rear-quarter-belt reveal moldings and rear-end-belt reveal moldings.

4. The following items, if present:

   a. Roof-cover retainer-to-rear-body lock pillar

   b. Roof-extension-panel emblem, name plate assembly, or opera lights

   c. Roof-panel moldings and finishing trim lace

   d. Quarter-window reveal moldings

   e. Stationary quarter window (if required)

   f. Louver quarter stationary windows

   g. Sliding sun-roof panel (if cover for panel is being replaced)

   h. Louver in quarter sail area

   i. Vista-vent glass and weatherstrips

5. Reveal molding clips across the top and sides of the windshield, quarter, and back glass openings. On styles where fabric cover extends below the back window, remove the reveal molding clips along the bottom of the back window. Clean off excessive adhesive.

6. Vinyl on the center post, fastened with four rivets and retainers (on some styles). To remove the vinyl from the post, drill out the rivets and remove the retainers.

≡ 29-8 DIRECTLY CEMENTED VINYL-ROOF-COVER REMOVAL

This roof covering is directly cemented to the roof panel. The roof cover is removed as follows after all the preliminary work is done as outlined in the previous section:

1. Remove all drive nails around windshield and back window. On styles that do not have back-window and quarter-glass reveal moldings, carefully work cover from under covered retainer in those areas. Use a special reveal molding tool. Make sure that any tabs present on retainers around the back-window opening are not damaged.

NOTE: *When removing drive nails, protect the edge of the glass by applying several layers of cloth body*

Fig. 29-11 Using a hand-held heat lamp to loosen the edges of the vinyl roof.

tape. Drive nails can be removed by forcing a screwdriver under the nail heads. Then use diagonal cutters to twist them out. Don't enlarge the holes more than necessary.

2. Mask off areas of the roof panel not covered by the fabric. Mask the upper windshield, back window, roof opening around the sun roof, doors, and flat-painted areas such as the hood and trunk lid. This will protect them from the cement you will use in applying the new roof covering.

3. Apply heat with a hot-air gun to the edges of the roof cover to loosen them. A hand-held heat lamp can also be used, as shown in Fig. 29-11. Avoid excessive heat.

4. After loosening the edges of the cover all around, carefully remove the cover.

5. Examine the cemented surfaces on the roof panel. Wire-brush by hand all areas where excessive padding from the cover backing or adhesive buildup is evident. If any metal finishing has been done on the roof panel, paint the repaired area.

6. To avoid "show-through" bumps or unevenness when the new cover is applied, the roof panel must be reasonably smooth.

≡ 29-9 DIRECTLY CEMENTED VINYL-ROOF-COVER INSTALLATION

The recommended cement adhesive must be used to ensure a good job. General Motors recommends 3M Vinyl Trim Adhesive or the equivalent. The preferred application method is to spray it on with a compressed-air spray gun.

1. The new cover should be installed at room temperature. It is more difficult to get a smooth job when the car and cover are cold. Use fabric-roof-cover pliers (Fig. 29-12) to grasp and pull the fabric and remove wrinkles as the cover is applied.

NOTE: *Some fabrics cannot be pulled to any extent to correct a misalignment. Therefore, it is very important that, before cementing, the cover must be properly positioned on the roof. Mark the cover with reference lines so it will be properly centered, front to back and side to side.*

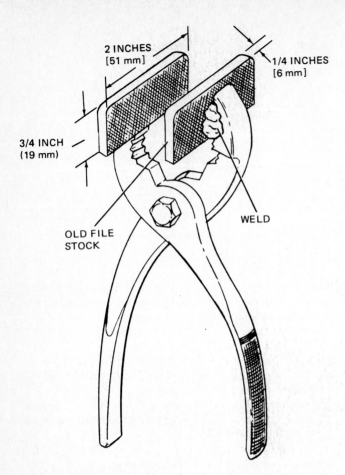

Fig. 29-12 How to make the special pliers needed for installing vinyl roof covers. (© *Fisher Body Division of General Motors Corporation*)

2 INCHES [51 mm]

1/4 INCHES [6 mm]

3/4 INCH (19 mm)

OLD FILE STOCK

WELD

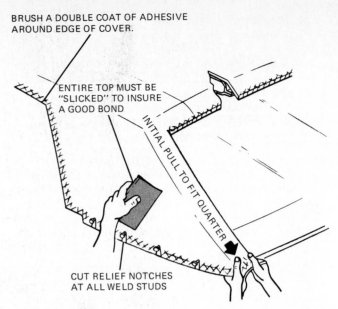

BRUSH A DOUBLE COAT OF ADHESIVE AROUND EDGE OF COVER.

ENTIRE TOP MUST BE "SLICKED" TO INSURE A GOOD BOND

INITIAL PULL TO FIT QUARTER

CUT RELIEF NOTCHES AT ALL WELD STUDS

Fig. 29-13 Cementing cover to upper quarter. (© *Fisher Body Division of General Motors Corporation*)

2. If the old roof cover was properly aligned, you may be able to use the seam marks on the roof (which can usually be seen) as reference points to align the new cover.

3. Mark the centerlines of the roof panel on the windshield and rear window with tape.

4. If no seam marks are available to help align the new cover, lay the cover on the roof. Fold it lengthwise at the center location. Mark the center at the front and rear of the cover.

5. With the cover folded lengthwise, brush on or spray on adhesive along the centerline of the cover and roof panel. Allow it to dry for 3 to 5 minutes, or until it becomes tacky. Do not use too much adhesive. This can cause the vinyl to come loose from its pad or underlining.

6. Make certain that the cover is free of wrinkles and properly aligned as you press it down into place. Do not pull too hard on the fabric to smooth it. Use pliers (Fig. 29-12) to help remove wrinkles. Pulling too hard can separate the backing from the vinyl and cause wrinkles or highlights (shiny areas from bumps or stretched vinyl). Use a plastic squeegee to "slick" down the cover as shown in Fig. 29-13.

7. Once the cover is centered and the center portion is cemented and slicked down, work away from the center on one side of the cover. Apply cement to the back of one side of the cover and to the adjacent roof

panel. Do not include the quarter upper area at this time.

8. Then, starting along the center area, slick down the roof covering. Have an assistant help you by pulling and holding the cover away from the roof panel until you actually get to the area you want to press and slick down. Make sure the cover goes down free of wrinkles.

9. If the roof has a multiple-piece "plastic cap," make sure the cover seams align with the plastic cap seams.

10. Repeat the operation on the other side.

11. On cars which have the vinyl running down the center pillars, cement these down next.

12. Now work on the quarter upper area as shown in Fig. 29-13. Apply cement to the cover and quarter upper area. Make the initial pull as shown to fit the quarter. Then slick it all down. If the vinyl extends below the back window, cement and apply the cover at this point.

13. Brush a double coat of adhesive on the edge of the cover to ensure good adhesion.

14. Figures 29-10 and 29-14 show how the vinyl is worked down around the sun-roof opening, up to roof-panel moldings, or up to halo moldings. Figure 29-10 also shows the use of nails to hold the center seam in place. The cover is notched out at all weld-on studs. This notching should be done with sharp scissors as the cover is being slicked down.

15. Finally, when the cover has been installed and is completely down all around, remove the protective masking from the car. Install all hardware and parts removed.

≡ 29-10 REPLACING VINYL ROOF COVERING WITH FOAM PAD

This roof covering has a foam pad under it. The vinyl fabric is removed from the foam pad in the same way as

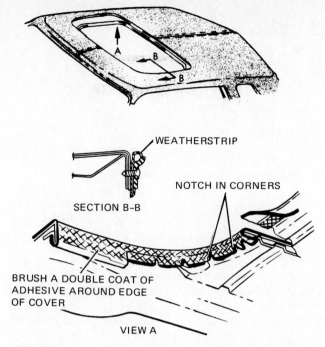

WEATHERSTRIP

SECTION B-B

NOTCH IN CORNERS

BRUSH A DOUBLE COAT OF
ADHESIVE AROUND EDGE
OF COVER

VIEW A

Fig. 29-14 Installing vinyl roof cover on a car with a sun roof.
(© *Fisher Body Division of General Motors Corporation*)

the directly cemented type is removed from the roof panel (≡29-8). First, all parts that would interfere should be removed. Then all areas that might be damaged should be masked with masking tape and paper. Then heat is applied around the edges to loosen the roof cover. Finally, the cover can be removed from the foam pad.

If the foam pad must be removed, it can be worked off with a putty knife or another flat-bladed tool.

The replacement procedure is as follows:

1. Check the roof panel for excessive pad material and adhesive. If metal repair and finishing have been necessary, the repaired area must be painted. It is not necessary to remove all old pad material and adhesive. However, the surface should be smooth enough so that when the new pad and cover are applied, there will be no apparent bumps or unevenness.

2. The pad is installed and cemented down onto the roof panel in the same way that the directly cemented vinyl roof covering is installed (Fig. 29-15). First, lay the pad on the roof panel, getting it accurately centered front to back and side to side. Then cement down the center area. After that, work from the center to one side, slicking down the pad. Then repeat the procedure for the other side.

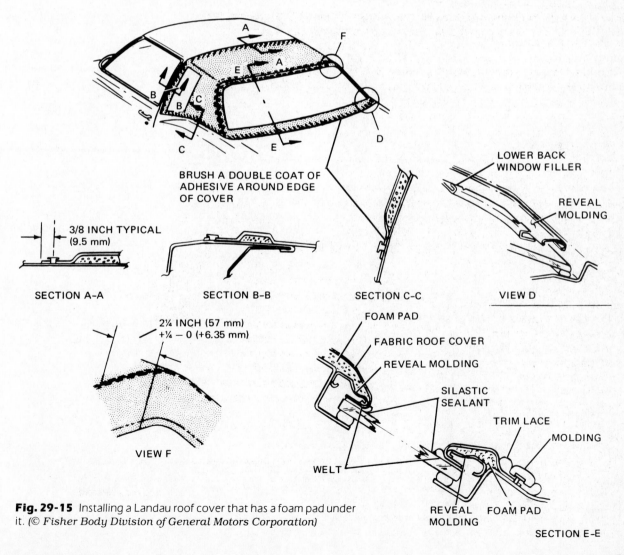

BRUSH A DOUBLE COAT OF
ADHESIVE AROUND EDGE
OF COVER

3/8 INCH TYPICAL
(9.5 mm)

SECTION A-A

SECTION B-B

SECTION C-C

LOWER BACK
WINDOW FILLER

REVEAL
MOLDING

VIEW D

2¼ INCH (57 mm)
+¼ – 0 (+6.35 mm)

VIEW F

FOAM PAD

FABRIC ROOF COVER

REVEAL MOLDING

SILASTIC
SEALANT

TRIM LACE

MOLDING

WELT

REVEAL
MOLDING

FOAM PAD

SECTION E-E

Fig. 29-15 Installing a Landau roof cover that has a foam pad under it. (© *Fisher Body Division of General Motors Corporation*)

NOTE: *Work accurately. If you cement the pad down in a misaligned position, you may have to cut out some of the pad and patch in the needed material.*

3. Be sure to slick down the pad to avoid bubbles or wrinkles as you work out from the center.

4. Trim off excessive padding. Be sure the padding is cemented down along all edges that have been trimmed.

5. The procedure of installing the vinyl roof covering over the foam pad is very similar to the procedure used to install the directly cemented vinyl roof covering (≡29-9). First, center the cover on the pad, front to back and side to side. Then cement down the center area, slicking it down to make sure it is smooth and without wrinkles and bubbles. Next, work one side down, moving away from the center, cementing and slicking the cover down. Then repeat the procedure for the other side. Finally, remove all masking tape and paper. Install all parts that were removed.

≡ 29-11 REMOVING WRINKLES FROM ROOF COVER

Fabric-roof-cover wrinkles that do not disappear after several days exposure to sunlight can be corrected as follows:

1. Use a household iron applied over a dampened shop cloth, as shown in Fig. 29-16. Set the iron for medium heat (cotton or lower). Continue to iron until the wrinkles are smoothed out or until it is obvious that this method is not going to work.

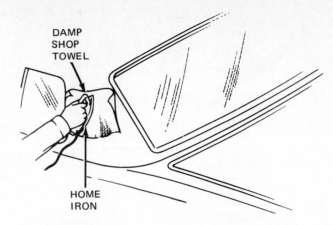

Fig. 29-16 Removing wrinkles from a vinyl top with a household iron. (© *Fisher Body Division of General Motors Corporation*)

2. The next step, if ironing does not work, is to remove the moldings next to the wrinkled area. Apply heat to the wrinkled area with a heat gun. At the same time, pull on the edge of the fabric to raise it from the roof panel.

NOTE: *Overheating the fabric—applying heat above 200°F [93.9°C]—may cause the vinyl to lose its grain, become shiny, or blister.*

3. Once the wrinkled area has been pulled clear of the roof panel, brush on adhesive. After the adhesive has become sticky, press the cover down into place. Slick it down to make sure the wrinkles do not reappear.

━━━━━ REVIEW QUESTIONS ━━━━━

Select the *one* correct, best, or most probable answer to each question. You can find the answers in the section indicated at the end of each question.

1. The material used to fill a hole in vinyl is (≡29-1)
   a. a repair kit
   b. liquid vinyl paste
   c. caulking compound
   d. vinyl cleaner

2. A heat gun is used in vinyl repair to (≡29-1)
   a. soften the liquid vinyl
   b. cure the liquid vinyl
   c. warm the technician's hands
   d. all of the above

3. The vinyl roof is held on the car with (≡29-6)
   a. adhesive cement
   b. finish moldings
   c. clips installed over weld-on studs
   d. all of the above

4. The vinyl on a padded dash has a large damaged area. Mechanic A says to repair it by applying a patch of matching vinyl cut out to approximately fit the damage. Mechanic B says to fill the joint between the patch and original vinyl with liquid vinyl. Who is right? (≡29-4)
   a. mechanic A
   b. mechanic B
   c. both A and B
   d. neither A nor B

5. Deep holes or long cuts in vinyl must be (≡29-4)
   a. filled with one thick layer
   b. sanded smooth before filling
   c. filled in several layers
   d. enlarged before they can be filled

CHAPTER 30
SERVICING WOOD-GRAIN OVERLAYS AND DECALS

After studying this chapter, you should be able to:

1. Explain how to repair small damage to wood-grain overlays.
2. Describe the removal and installation of a wood-grain overlay.
3. Discuss decal repair and installation.

≡ 30-1 WOOD-GRAIN OVERLAYS

Wood-grain overlays (or *transfers*) are used on the panels of some cars and station wagons. These overlays are usually made of vinyl material. Some wood-grain overlays are translucent (partly transparent). This allows some of the paint color underneath to show through.

Replacement wood-grain-overlay material is available in rolls of various sizes. Some cars also have stripes and decals. These are often decorative designs that enhance the appearance of the car.

≡ 30-2 WOOD-GRAIN-OVERLAY MATERIAL

Figure 30-1 shows a car that has wood-grain overlays on it. This material is made of vinyl with a wood-grain design. The vinyl has a pressure-sensitive adhesive back which is protected by paper backing in the roll. When the vinyl is to be applied, the paper backing is removed. The vinyl is applied to a previously prepared surface with a special wetting solution. Preparation of the surface, the wetting solution, and how to apply the vinyl are covered in following sections.

Fig. 30-1 A car that has wood-grain overlays along the sides. *(Chrysler Corporation)*

≡ 30-3 REPAIRING SMALL DAMAGE

Small nicks, bruises, or scratches in wood-grain overlays can be touched up with paint in much the same manner as painted surfaces. First, blend the paint to get the proper color. Then carefully touch up the damaged area.

Blisters or air bubbles can be removed by piercing with a sharp needle. Then work the trapped air out through the pinhole, and press the overlay firmly against the panel. You may have to heat the panel with a lamp or heat gun (Fig. 30-1) to soften the adhesive so the vinyl will stick. Heat may also be used to remove small wrinkles or bulges around the fuel-tank opening or other areas where the vinyl fits around a corner or opening.

≡ 30-4 MATERIALS REQUIRED TO REPLACE OVERLAYS

The following materials are required to remove and install overlays:

1. Wood-grain and stripe remover—3M or equivalent
2. Adhesive remover—3M or equivalent
3. Detergent such as Joy or Vel (Chrysler recommends a powdered detergent)
4. Wax-and-silicone remover—3M General Purpose Adhesive Cleaner or equivalent
5. Isopropyl alcohol (rubbing alcohol)
6. Squeegee 4 to 5 inches [102 to 127 mm] wide, of plastic or rubber
7. Water bucket and sponge
8. Sandpaper (360 to 400, wet-or-dry type)
9. Heat gun or lamp
10. Wiping rags or paper towels
11. Sharp razor knife
12. Scissors
13. Sharp needle
14. Grease pencil

≡ 30-5 WETTING SOLUTION

The wetting solution is required to shift the transfer into the proper position on the body panel. The solution is made by mixing the detergent (liquid or powder) with warm water. Do not use harsh detergents or soap.

≡ 30-6 REMOVING OLD OVERLAY

The temperature in the shop should be between 65° and 95°F [16° and 35°C]. Overlay material cannot be removed satisfactorily at temperatures below 65°F [16°C].

If the old overlay must be removed and new overlay installed, proceed with the removal as follows:

1. Clean the surface to be repaired and the adjacent panels and openings.

2. Remove overlay reveal moldings, door handles, lock assembly, side-marker lamps, and other parts that overlap the transfer.

3. Mask off the surrounding area so that paint or chrome will not be damaged by the chemicals used to remove the transfer.

4. Spray wood-grain remover on a flange area first. Then spray the entire overlay to be removed (Fig. 30-2). Move the spray can back and forth across the entire overlay smoothly to evenly apply the remover. Make sure the entire overlay is covered.

— CAUTION

Use the wood-grain remover only in a well-ventilated area. The vapors from this chemical are toxic (poisonous). Observe the safety cautions and warnings printed on the label. Note that wood-grain remover is for use on acrylic-enamel paint only.

5. Spray the entire panel again. This time move the can up and down.

6. Wait for 20 minutes for the remover to work.

7. Then start peeling the overlay off. Begin at a flange area. Start at one corner and peel the overlay away from the panel (Fig. 30-3). If you have any trouble peeling it off, use the squeegee (Fig. 30-4).

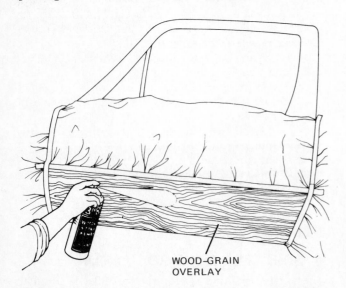

Fig. 30-2 Spraying wood-grain remover on the overlay. *(American Motors Corporation)*

WOOD-GRAIN OVERLAY

302

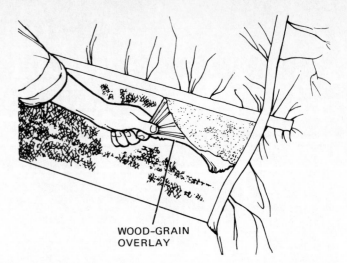

WOOD-GRAIN OVERLAY

Fig. 30-3 Peeling overlay from panel. *(American Motors Corporation)*

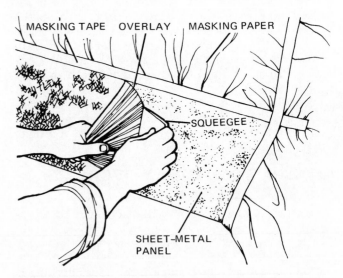

MASKING TAPE   OVERLAY   MASKING PAPER

SQUEEGEE

SHEET-METAL PANEL

Fig. 30-4 Using a squeegee to assist in removing the overlay. *(American Motors Corporation)*

8. Scrape all wood-grain remover from the panel. Then spray the panel with adhesive remover to remove any remaining adhesive. Use a slow spray application and apply the remover uniformly over the panel. The adhesive remover must be left on from 3 to 5 minutes.

9. After 5 minutes, squeegee the adhesive residue off (Fig. 30-5). If some adhesive is hard to remove, spray on more remover. Wait 2 minutes, and then use the squeegee again.

10. Remove the masking tape and paper.

11. Wash the panel with general-purpose adhesive cleaner. If any spots of adhesive remain on the panel, hard rubbing will remove it.

≡ 30-7 PREPARING SURFACE FOR OVERLAY APPLICATION

Sand all areas to be covered with the overlay, using 360 to 400 sandpaper soaked in water or mineral spirits (paint thinner). (American Motors and General Motors recommend dry sanding.) The area to be sanded should

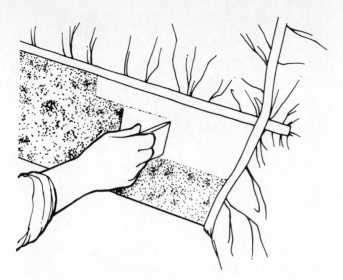

Fig. 30-5 Removing the adhesive residue from the panel. *(American Motors Corporation)*

be about ¼ inch [6 mm] larger than the size of the overlay, except where the overlay is turned at the door and other comparable openings.

Cars having overlays with no surround moldings should not be sanded beyond the area to be covered by the overlay. All metal and paint nibs (bumps) must be removed. The surface must be free of grease, oil, and other foreign materials. Wipe off the area with isopropyl alcohol or other solvent that will not damage the painted surfaces. Wipe dry with a clean, lint-free cloth. Use a clean cloth dampened with alcohol to wipe off

(tack off) the area that was sanded to remove all traces of dust.

NOTE: If a panel has been repaired, it must be repainted to match the surrounding paint on the car body. Then this paint must dry. If it is not dry, residual solvents in the paint can cause the overlay to blister the paint. It must be sanded in preparation for the application of the overlay, as explained above.

≡ 30-8 INSTALLING OVERLAY

After the area has dried, proceed as follows:

1. Position the overlay material, with paper backing still attached, on the panel surface. Mark the approximate outline of the overlay on the material with a grease pencil. Make sure that you allow enough excess material—½ inch [13 mm]—so it can be wrapped around edges. Use scissors to cut out the overlay. Make sure that you allow enough extra at the top and bottom. The material should extend halfway into the area to be covered by moldings (or to the molding studs, as shown in Fig. 30-6).

2. Lay the overlay on a clean, flat surface, protective paper up. Bend a corner of the overlay down to separate the paper backing from the overlay. Hold the overlap firmly to the flat surface and pull the paper backing from the overlay. Hold the overlay by the corners. Fingerprints on the vinyl backing can prevent proper adhesion.

NOTE: Always pull the paper backing from the overlay. If you pull the overlay from the paper, you will stretch and damage the overlay.

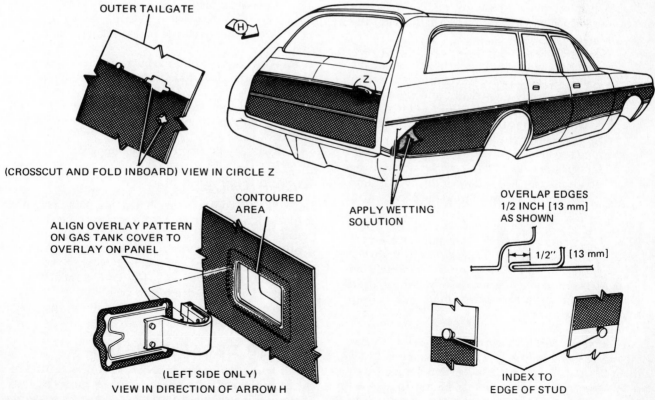

OUTER TAILGATE

(CROSSCUT AND FOLD INBOARD) VIEW IN CIRCLE Z

CONTOURED AREA

ALIGN OVERLAY PATTERN ON GAS TANK COVER TO OVERLAY ON PANEL

(LEFT SIDE ONLY)
VIEW IN DIRECTION OF ARROW H

APPLY WETTING SOLUTION

OVERLAP EDGES 1/2 INCH [13 mm] AS SHOWN

1/2" [13 mm]

INDEX TO EDGE OF STUD

Fig. 30-6 Installation of wood-grain overlay. *(Chrysler Corporation)*

Fig. 30-7 Working overlay down into area to be covered with molding.

Fig. 30-8 Squeegee from the center to the edges of the overlay. Note use of heat lamp.

3. Use a clean sponge and apply the wetting solution to the back of the overlay and to the panel surface. The wetting solution allows you to shift the overlay around on the panel so you can position it correctly.

4. Immediately apply the wetted overlay to the panel. Position it in the center of the area to be covered with at least ½ inch [13 mm] extending beyond the edges (Fig. 30-7). Apply wetting solution to the grain surface of the overlay so you can use the squeegee effectively.

5. Squeegee from the center to edges of the overlay (Fig. 30-8) with firm strokes to remove all air bubbles and wetting solution and to ensure bonding of overlay to the painted surface. On large overlays, the following steps will help:

    a. Squeegee a short, 3- to 6-inch [102- to 152-mm] horizontal section of the overlay at the center of the panel. Lift right or left side of overlay, position it straight and close to the panel, and squeegee toward the lifted edge. Avoid stretching the overlay at the lifted end. Squeegee from the middle with firm, overlapping strokes.

    b. Lift the upper area of the overlay down to the bonded area. Now squeegee the overlay into place, working upward from the bonded area at the center.

NOTE: If a wrinkle or bubble is trapped during the squeegee operation, stop at once. Carefully lift the affected section. Realign the section to the panel and work outward to remove the wrinkle. Don't worry if a few small air or solution bubbles are trapped. They can be removed later.

6. Notch the corner or curved edges of the overlay where necessary and trim off excessive material. Allow ½ inch [13 mm] of extra material beyond the edges so it can be wrapped around the flange areas. To activate the adhesive at the edges, wipe it with isopropyl alco-

hol. Then use a heat gun or lamp to warm the edges. Firmly press the edges into place with your fingertips, then a cloth, and finally a squeegee. Alternately warm the edge and press until good adhesion is obtained.

NOTE: Avoid excessive pulling or stretching at the ends of the overlay. You could tear the overlay.

7. Apply heat to the overlay at door-handle holes, side-marker lamps, and other depressions, using a heat gun. Press overlay uniformly into the depressions to get a good bond, as shown in Fig. 30-9. Note the use of a piece of plastic or metal scale placed from the edge of the overlay to the depression. This allows trapped air to escape when the overlay is pressed down into the depression.

8. With a sharp knife, cut out excessive overlay material from the door handle, side-marker lamp, and other areas.

9. Inspect the overlay, using a side light to detect any irregularities. Remove all air or moisture bubbles as already described.

10. Install all parts previously removed.

≣ 30-9 DECALS

Figure 30-10 shows a car that has a side decal and stripes. Figure 30-11 shows an intricate hood decal. Decals and stripes are made of tough, durable, weather-resistant solid vinyl. They have a pressure-sensitive back which is protected by a paper backing. The backing is removed when the decal is applied to the car body. The front face of the decal may be covered with an easy-release paper to protect it during storage and shipping.

≣ 30-10 DECAL REPAIRS

Decal damage such as nicks or scratches can be repaired in the same manner as vinyl overlays (≣30-3). The materials required to remove and replace decals

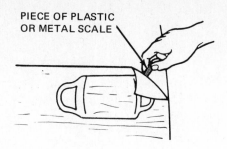

PIECE OF PLASTIC OR METAL SCALE

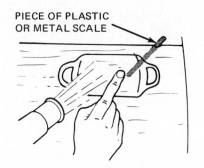

PIECE OF PLASTIC OR METAL SCALE

1. MAKE SURE THE DEPRESSION IS FREE OF MOISTURE.
2. HEAT SHEET METAL IN DOOR DEPRESSION AREA TO APPROXIMATELY 200°F [94°C] AND APPLY TRANSFER IN NORMAL MANNER.
3. WITH A PIECE OF PLASTIC OR METAL SCALE IN PLACE, ALLOW THE TRAPPED AIR TO ESCAPE, SO A VACUUM IS CREATED TO HOLD TRANSFER FIRMLY IN DEPRESSION (DO NOT PUNCH HOLES IN TRANSFER). SQUEEGEE THE TRANSFER FILM INTO PLACE AROUND THE HANDLE.
4. PRESS THE FILM SECURELY INTO THE SHALLOW DEPRESSIONS.
5. USING HOT AIR TO MAKE THE FILM PLIABLE, CAREFULLY PRESS THE FILM INTO THE DEEP DEPRESSION, EXHAUSTING THE TRAPPED AIR TOWARD THE PIECE OF PLASTIC. WITH THE AIR EXHAUSTED, REMOVE THE PLASTIC TOOL AND SMOOTH THE FILM.

Fig. 30-9 To stick permanently, the overlay must have a good bond. Work the overlay into any depression in the car body with your finger. (© *Fisher Body Division of General Motors Corporation*)

Fig. 30-10 A car with side decal and stripes. (*Chrysler Corporation*)

Fig. 30-11 An intricate hood decal. (*Pontiac Motor Division of General Motors Corporation*)

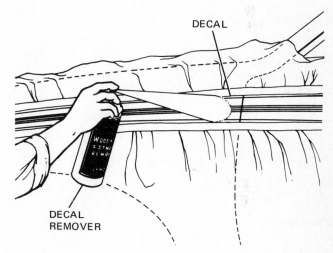

Fig. 30-12 To remove a decal, first spray it with remover. (*American Motors Corporation*)

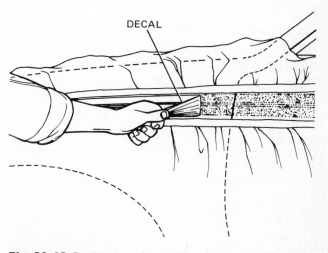

Fig. 30-13 Peeling decal from panel. (*American Motors Corporation*)

are the same as those used to remove and replace overlays (≡30-4). Also, the removal procedure is the same for removing decals and overlays. Figures 30-12 to 30-15 show the procedure for decals. Note the use of masking tape and paper, which must be very accurately placed to prevent damaging adjacent paint.

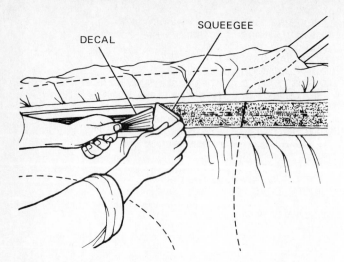

Fig. 30-14 Use a squeegee to assist in removing decal. *(American Motors Corporation)*

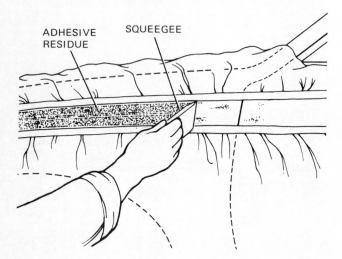

Fig. 30-15 Removing adhesive residue with a squeegee. *(American Motors Corporation)*

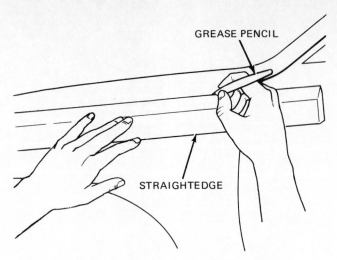

Fig. 30-16 Marking position of decal. *(American Motors Corporation)*

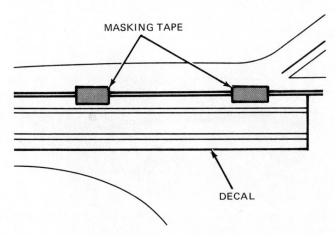

Fig. 30-17 Positioning the decal with masking tape. *(American Motors Corporation)*

≡ 30-11 INSTALLING DECALS

The preparation for installing a decal is the same as for installing an overlay except that a wetting solution may not be necessary (≡30-7). The following are special steps required for decals:

1. Before removing the backing paper, position the decal on the panel surface and mark the position with a grease pencil (Fig. 30-16). Make sure to leave ½ inch [13 mm] to be wrapped around the door and fender areas. Cut decal to approximate length.

2. Position the decal, with paper still on the back, on the panel. Secure the decal in place with small strips of masking tape (Fig. 30-17). Be sure the decal is aligned with decals on adjacent panels.

3. Lift the decal, using the masking tape as hinges (Fig. 30-18). Strip off about 6 inches [152 mm] of backing paper from one end (Fig. 30-19).

NOTE: *To avoid stretching the decal or getting it stuck on the panel in the wrong position, do not re-*move more than about 6 inches [152 mm] of paper at a time.

4. Fold the decal back into the aligned position. With firm strokes, squeegee the decal to the panel with one hand while removing the paper with the other (Fig. 30-20).

5. Wrap the end of the decal, where possible, around the corner or edge (Fig. 30-21) of the panel. Be careful not to trap air when you do this.

6. Remove the easy-release paper from the front of the decal (if used).

7. Inspect the decal for irregularities, using side light. Remove all air or moisture bubbles.

8. Reinstall all parts that were removed.

For large, intricately shaped decals, you may find it easier to use a wetting solution and treat the decal as the overlay was treated.

Some technicians will paint on stripes, rather than install decals. Painting on stripes requires careful masking.

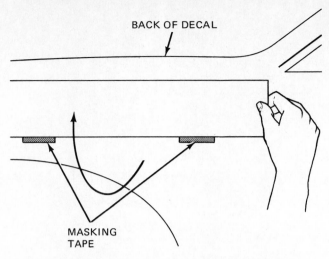

BACK OF DECAL

MASKING
TAPE

Fig. 30-18 Lifting the decal. *(American Motors Corporation)*

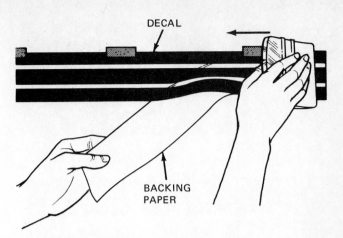

DECAL

BACKING
PAPER

Fig. 30-20 Installing decal with a squeegee. *(American Motors Corporation)*

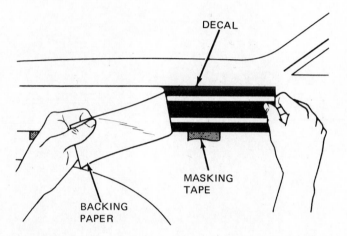

DECAL

MASKING
TAPE

BACKING
PAPER

Fig. 30-19 Removing backing paper from decal. *(American Motors Corporation)*

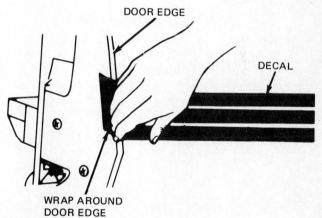

DOOR EDGE

DECAL

WRAP AROUND
DOOR EDGE

Fig. 30-21 Working the decal around the edge of the door. *(American Motors Corporation)*

REVIEW QUESTIONS

Select the *one* correct, best, or most probable answer to each question. You can find the answers in the section indicated at the end of each question.

1. Vinyl material that has a wood grain in it is called (≡30-2)
  a. a stripe
  b. a strip
  c. an overlay
  d. a decal

2. Small damage to a wood-grain overlay can be corrected with (≡30-3)
  a. touch-up paint
  b. masking tape
  c. cellophane tape
  d. a needle

3. Air bubbles in overlays can be removed with (≡30-3)
  a. a squeegee
  b. touch-up paint
  c. a needle and heat gun
  d. a detergent

4. A wetting solution is made by mixing warm water and
  a. glue (≡30-5)
  b. vinyl liquid
  c. detergent
  d. adhesive

5. Stripes may be put on with (≡30-11)
  a. sandpaper or wax
  b. decal or paint
  c. masking tape
  d. vinyl liquid

PART 10
PAINTING AND REFINISHING

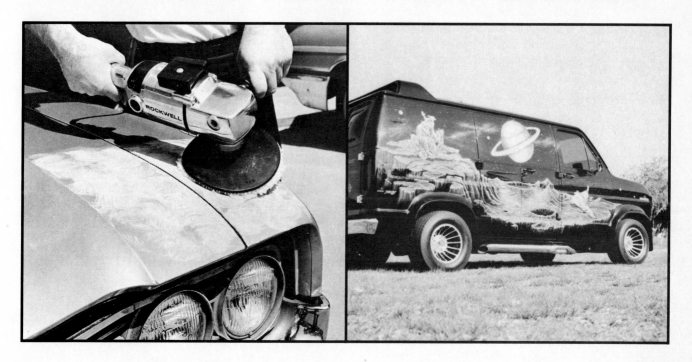

This part describes how to paint and refinish the car body and the interior and exterior parts attached to it. When a car body is to be painted, the surface must first be prepared as described in earlier chapters. Then the parts that are not to be painted must be masked, or covered with tape and paper. Finally, the paint is selected and the surface is primed and painted with a spray gun.

There are seven chapters in Part 10, as follows:

CHAPTER 31
PAINTING SUPPLIES AND EQUIPMENT

After studying this chapter, you should be able to:

1. Discuss safety in the paint shop and list the basic paint-shop safety cautions.

2. List the steps in painting a car body.

3. Describe the various shop supplies required in painting a car, including the tack rag, paint paddle, strainer, and masking tape and paper.

4. Explain why and how a car is properly masked before painting.

5. Explain the use of sandpaper and what *featheredging* means.

6. Describe the use of rubbing compound.

≡ 31-1 SAFETY IN THE PAINT SHOP

Almost all paint materials, including lacquers, enamels, varnishes, and solvents such as thinners and reducers, are potential fire hazards. These materials can catch fire easily. When they do catch fire, they burn violently and quickly get out of control. Vapors from thinners and other solvents can spread quickly through an enclosed area and become ignited by sparking motors, lighted cigarettes, welding torches, even the spark from turning off an electric switch. For this reason, the paint shop *must* have adequate ventilation.

The general safety rules for the shop were discussed in Chap. 3. Review these rules now by turning back to ≡3-10 and studying them again. In addition to these general shop safety rules, listed below are some of the special safety cautions you must follow in the paint shop.

1. Make sure the ventilation system is adequate and is working properly.

2. Make sure the No Smoking signs are prominently displayed and are being obeyed.

3. Make sure fire extinguishers are in good working order and are prominently displayed.

4. Do not drive a car into or out of the spray booth. Push it in or out by hand. A running engine can ignite any vapors in the paint booth.

5. Don't try to connect extra electrical equipment to a circuit by using three-way plugs. This can overload the circuit and cause sparking if something burns out.

6. Check all electrical equipment regularly. Make sure the ground wires are connected properly.

7. Keep the area clean. Do not allow rags and shop towels to accumulate in piles on the floor. They can ignite spontaneously and burst into flames. Make sure they are removed from the area periodically — at least once a day and especially before you go home in the evening. Dispose of them as you would oily rags — by putting them into the special container set aside for this purpose. The container should have an airtight lid, and it should be emptied frequently.

8. Always wear a respirator when in the paint shop. The fumes from the paint and other materials used in the paint shop are toxic (poisonous). They can cause a variety of diseases if inhaled over a period of time.

9. Always read the label on the container of paint or other material you are working with. If a respirator, rubber gloves, safety goggles, and protective clothing are recommended, put them on and wear them! Don't allow any unprotected person in the area. Fumes from some materials (and the materials themselves) must not be inhaled, ingested (swallowed) or allowed to touch your skin.

≡ 31-2 STEPS IN PAINTING A CAR BODY

The panel must be straightened and repaired, filled with plastic filler, and sanded. Then it is given additional treatment. Here are the various steps:

1. Sheet metal and frame are repaired and straightened by the methods covered in Part 3.

2. Sheet metal is filled with plastic filler (as covered in Part 4) and sanded down to contour.

3. Dust is wiped off. The car is washed and dried. All crevices where dust might collect are blown out with compressed air.

4. Repaired area is smoothed with fine sandpaper and blown clean.

5. Car is masked as explained in ≡31-7.

6. Repaired area is wiped down with clean paper towels and tack rag (≡31-4)

7. Bare metal is treated with metal conditioner (≡38-16) and conversion coating (≡38-17) to prevent rust and provide a slightly etched surface for good undercoat adhesion.

8. Primer coats are sprayed on.

9. Guide coat is sprayed on and wet-sanded (see ≡34-9) to remove any trace of sand scratches.

10. Repaired area is washed clean with water and remasked if necessary.

11. Chip-resistant plastisol material (if used) is sprayed on to specific lower areas of the body.

12. Final colorcoats are sprayed on.

13. Clearcoat (if used) is sprayed over colorcoats.

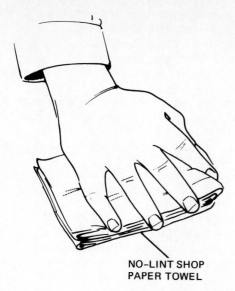

NO-LINT SHOP
PAPER TOWEL

Fig. 31-1 *Wiping the area to be painted with a clean towel.*

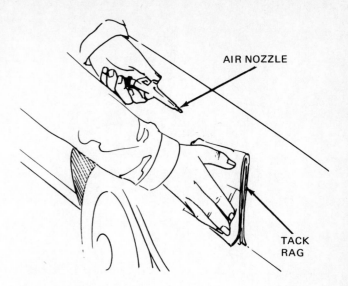

AIR NOZZLE

TACK
RAG

Fig. 31-2 *Wiping up lint and dust with a tack rag.*

These various steps are described in later chapters. The following sections discuss the painting materials, tools, and equipment not covered earlier in the book.

≡ 31-3 CLOTH AND PAPER TOWELS

The areas on the vehicle to be painted must be clean. Disposable paper towels are best for this purpose. Shop cloths, even if clean, can leave lint. No matter how well laundered, they can still contain foreign material that would ruin a paint job.

NOTE: The paper towels used for this purpose are not the type that come in a roll for home use. These are special no-lint shop paper towels.

Here are some hints on how to use paper or cloth towels:

1. Fold the towel into a pad. Refold it frequently so you will always be wiping with a clean section of the towel (Fig. 31-1).

2. When using cleaning solvent, wet the towel thoroughly.

3. Use a second dry towel to wipe away the solvent. Don't try to use the first towel, even if it feels dry.

4. Use plenty of towels. You must get the area to be painted clean and free of all traces of grease and oil.

NOTE: Don't touch the cleaned area with your fingers. Even if you have just washed your hands, you will leave traces of skin oil that will show up later in the paint job.

≡ 31-4 TACK RAG

The *tack rag* is a cheesecloth pad that has been soaked in a sticky, nondrying varnish. It is used to pick up lint, dust, and dirt. Just before the primer is applied, the repaired area is wiped off with a tack rag to make sure that the surface is clean (Fig. 31-2). The tiniest particles of dust will show up and spoil an otherwise good paint job.

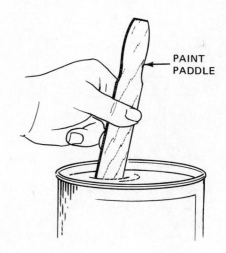

PAINT
PADDLE

Fig. 31-3 *Stirring paint with a paint paddle.*

≡ 31-5 PAINT PADDLE

The paint paddle is made of wood, plastic, or metal (Fig. 31-3). It is used to stir the paint in the container before the paint is poured into the spray gun. A good paint paddle should have sharp edges to get down into the corners of the container and stir up any pigment that has settled there. If the paint container has been thoroughly shaken by a paint shaker before opening (Fig. 6-16), it is not necessary to use a paint paddle. Nevertheless, it is good practice to stir the paint with the paddle after you open the container. You will need a paddle in any event to mix the paint with thinner, or reducer, as explained later.

≡ 31-6 STRAINER

Most paint strainers are funnel-shaped paper cones which are used to strain out any dirt, lumps, or scum in the paint as it is poured into the spray-gun cup (Fig. 31-4). Any foreign material in the spray gun will cause trouble. Impurities either will clog the gun so it throws an irregular pattern or will show up in the final paint

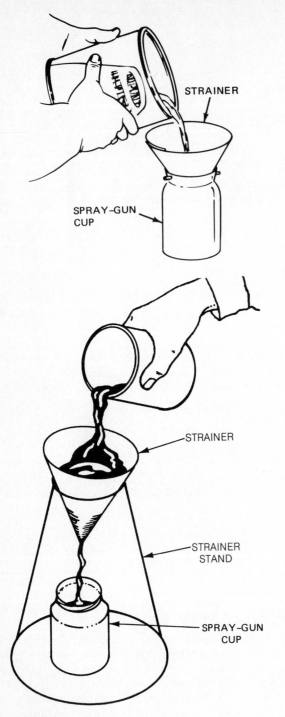

Fig. 31-4 Using a strainer to strain out any impurities in the paint. *(ATW)*

job as raised specks on the paint that will have to be removed. Strainers are made of mesh, fiber or wire, or disposable filter paper.

NOTE: *If you strain metallic paints through too fine a filter, you will remove the metal flakes in the paint.*

≡ 31-7 MASKING TAPE AND MASKING PAPER

When any material is sprayed on the car, some of the spray may hit surfaces that should be protected from it.

This unwanted spray is called *overspray.* Extra time and work are required to remove it. In the paint shop, surfaces that the spray should not hit are protected by *masking.* This is the procedure of applying special masking tape and masking paper to form a shield against unwanted spray.

Figure 31-5 shows a car completely masked and ready for painting. Masking has two purposes: First, it greatly reduces the time necessary to clean up the car after it is painted. Second, by catching any overspray, the masking tape and paper prevent primer and paint from getting on any surfaces other than those you intend to paint. This avoids hard-to-remove paint spray on adjacent glass and trim.

There is no special way that a car has to be masked. However, a good, fast masking requires the use of a masking stand (Fig. 31-6). This device dispenses various widths of paper with a strip of masking tape stuck to one edge. Special wheel covers that quickly slip over the complete wheel assembly are sometimes used. Some technicians tape newspaper (rather than masking paper) over the glass and wheels. However, newspaper must not be taped over a painted surface. The newspaper ink may dissolve and stain the paint. There are some water-soluble masking compounds available. These are brushed on, and then later washed off.

Masking tape should be applied to a clean, dry surface that is free of dust, dirt, and lubricants. On weatherstrip and rubber seals, apply a thin coat of clear lacquer with a cloth. Allow the lacquer to dry, and then apply the tape. Masking tape should not be stretched, except where you have to stretch it on curves. Position the tape, lay it down, and then press it in place with your fingers. Never apply masking tape to, or remove masking tape from, a cold car. The vehicle should be at room temperature of 60°F [16°C] or above for masking.

When masking large areas, use the widest masking paper that is available. Many shops use 15-inch [381-mm] masking paper for windows and windshields. Two widths of this paper usually will cover the windshield (Fig. 31-7). When applying masking paper to large areas, be sure that the top strip of paper (or apron) overlaps the bottom, as shown in Fig. 31-7. This prevents dust and water seepage through the layers of paper and onto the car.

Various widths of masking paper and masking tape are used to mask taillights and headlights and the areas around them (Fig. 31-8). Protection of these areas is important; overspray is very difficult to remove from some rear-light lenses. Paper that is 3 inches [76 mm] wide, called *three-inch paper,* is very handy for this type of masking. Six-inch [152-mm] paper also is used frequently. In general, the widest paper possible should be used, to keep down the cost of paper and labor to mask a car.

When spraying door jambs, sills, and pillars, be careful to prevent overspray from hitting the interior of the car. Too much masking paper spread about is wasteful. However, you must be sure that enough masking paper is used to protect all other areas, especially the interior of the car.

If you are spraying acrylic lacquer on a fender, hood, or trunk lid, use a double layer of masking paper. This will prevent dulling of the protected paint surface

Fig. 31-5 A car completely masked and ready for painting. *(3M Company)*

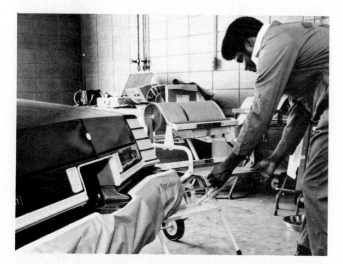

Fig. 31-6 Using a masking stand to dispense strips of masking paper with masking tape along one edge. *(3M Company)*

Fig. 31-7 Two widths of 15-inch [381-mm] masking paper usually will cover the windshield. *(3M Company)*

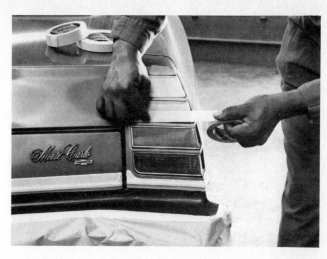

Fig. 31-8 Various widths of masking tape are used to cover the rear lights and the areas around them. *(3M Company)*

caused by solvent penetrating through the paper and contacting the paint.

Rubber and weatherstrip around doors, trunks, and windows often are coated with silicone lubricant. It is difficult to get masking tape to stick to coated rubber. To overcome this problem, apply a thin coat of clear lacquer to the rubber with a cloth or brush. Allow a few minutes for the lacquer to dry before applying the masking tape. The tape will stick more easily to the rubber. Also, the tape can be removed without tearing the rubber or transferring the adhesive. Do not use thinners or solvents to remove silicone from the rubber. Such materials can cause the adhesive from the tape to stick to the rubber.

When masking a car for a spot repair, reverse masking is often used. In this technique, the apron, or strip of paper, is folded back over the area to be protected. This exposes the adhesive side of the tape. The result is a less definite line and easier blending of the paint. The fold in the paper gives added protection against solvent and paint bleeding, a condition that occurs with acrylic paints.

Very narrow masking tape, usually ¼ inch [6 mm] wide, is used to mask letters and emblems (Fig. 31-9). This is usually less costly than removing the letters and emblems. Also, it eliminates the possibility of breaking the letters or emblems during removal and installation. Other masking tape widths, such as ½ inch [13 mm] and 1 inch [25 mm], can sometimes be used to quickly cover large emblems, molding, and trim (Fig. 31-10).

Remove the masking tape as soon as the paint is no longer sticky. To remove the tape, pull it at a 90° angle to the surface. This lessens the chances that the tape will pull paint from the body. The masking tape should be stored in a cool place, never on radiators, solvent cans, or in sunlight.

≡ 31-8 SANDPAPER

Sandpaper is available in many grit sizes, as explained in ≡6-5. The grit size refers to the coarseness or fineness of the cutting edge of the sandpaper. Each grit size has a number, and sandpaper is ordered by this grit

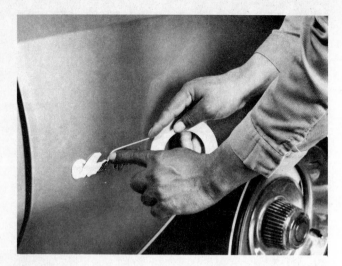

Fig. 31-9 Narrow masking tape, ¼ inch [6 mm] wide, is used to mask letters. *(3M Company)*

Fig. 31-10 Use ½-inch [13-mm] masking tape to cover body trim. *(3M Company)*

number. The greater the number, the finer the grit. A coarse sandpaper, such as 24 or 50, is used to remove old paint and prepare the metal surface for fine sanding. Fine sandpaper, such as 360 or 400, is used to featheredge (≡31-9) from painted areas into metal to be painted and to get rid of sand scratches from coarser sandpaper.

≡ 31-9 FEATHEREDGING

When a spot repair is being done, the old paint is *feathered* out into the bare metal. This means the paint is sanded so that it tapers off from full thickness to no thickness (Fig. 31-11). The thickness of the paint gradually slopes off into the bare metal. This is important, because the slightest ridge of paint would show up when the area is repainted. Featheredging is done with

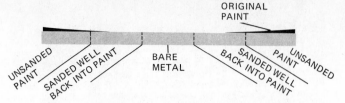

Fig. 31-11 Sectional view of featheredging. *(Rinshed-Mason Company)*

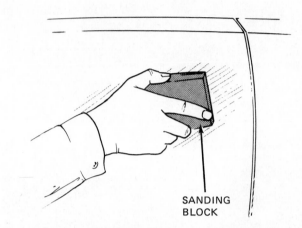

Fig. 31-12 Using a sanding block.

fine sandpaper (400 or finer). Then the surface is cleaned before painting, as explained later.

≡ 31-10 SANDING BLOCKS

When sanding flat surfaces by hand, always use a sanding block (Fig. 31-12). The block usually is made of plastic, or wood with a rubber face. By using the block, the sandpaper is applied to the surface evenly. If you try to sand by holding the sandpaper to the surface with your fingers or hand, a very uneven sanding job can result.

For curved surfaces, a sanding block backed with a sponge-rubber pad can be used. The sponge rubber adjusts to the shape of the curve. For reverse curves, use an abrasive tube (≡17-6), or a short length of radiator hose with sandpaper wrapped around it.

≡ 31-11 SPOT AND GLAZE PUTTY

After plastic body filler is applied and sanded (Chap. 17), small scratches and pinholes may be noticeable. These surface imperfections will be very obvious after the repaired surface is sprayed with primer. To repair these defects, a special type of putty is used.

In the paint shop, putty is a thick paste used to fill flaws in the surface that are not filled by the primer-surfacer (Fig. 31-13). Spot putty is for small pinholes, nicks, and other minor surface imperfections. Drying time for some spot putty is usually less than an hour. Always read and follow the safety cautions and directions on the tube or can.

Putty should not be used to fill deep gouges or dents. These require metal straightening and filling with plas-

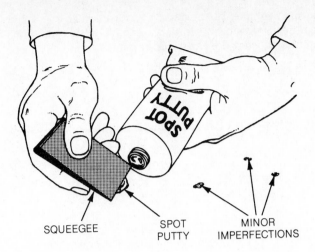

Fig. 31-13 Filling minor flaws in surface with spot putty. (ATW)

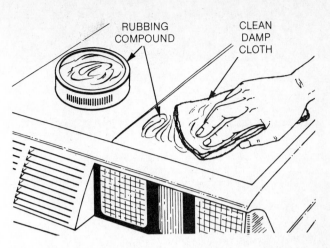

Fig. 31-14 Using hand rubbing compound on dried lacquer. (ATW)

tic body filler. Also, spot putty should not be applied directly to bare metal before priming. Poor adhesion would result.

NOTE: If a painter encounters deep imperfections in a panel, the car should be sent back to the body shop for proper repairing with plastic body filler. Putty or glazing compound should not be used.

≡ 31-12 RUBBING COMPOUND

After spraying the car (or a spot-repair area) with lacquer, the new finish will dry to a slightly dull, rough finish. To bring out the high gloss (shine) of the new finish, it must be rubbed out, or compounded, with *rubbing compound.* This is an abrasive paste (coarser than polishing compound) that smoothes the paint film. It can be applied by hand with a dampened rag, or with a power polisher.

Hand rubbing compound differs from machine compound. Hand rubbing compound contains fairly coarse pumice (a volcanic rock) grit, which requires little rubbing force to cut the paint. Therefore, hand rubbing compound is used mainly for small repairs. It is applied with a clean damp cloth (Fig. 31-14).

Machine compound contains fine particles of pumice, and is for use with a power polisher (Fig. 31-15). This compound is normally used for compounding large areas or entire vehicles.

NOTE: Hand rubbing compound must not be used with a power polisher. It would create so much friction and heat that you could burn through the finish to the primer. Then the area would have to be repainted again.

Compounding is also done to remove sand scratches and original paint around a repair area, and to prepare an area of acrylic lacquer or acrylic enamel which is to be spot-repaired with acrylic lacquer. (This is discussed later.) When compounding, do not push the buffing pad into the finish with too much force. Keep the polisher moving. If you let it stay in one spot too long, it will burn

or cut through the finish. To avoid cutting through styling edges, mask them with masking tape.

≡ 31-13 POLISH AND WAX

Today, the paint on new cars has more durability than ever before. But the finish needs care if it is to last. Paint deteriorates because of exposure to air, sunlight, and water. Polish and wax are applied over the finish to restore and protect it.

Polishing compound, or simply *polish,* is a fine abrasive paste for smoothing and polishing a paint film. Hand rubbing action, or the use of a power polisher (≡6-11), helps make the surface smooth and shiny. The slight abrasive action removes any road film or *chalking* of the finish. (Chalking makes the finish look dull. It is a paint problem described in Chap. 37.)

When there is no need to use even a mild abrasive on the finish, then either a liquid or paste wax should be

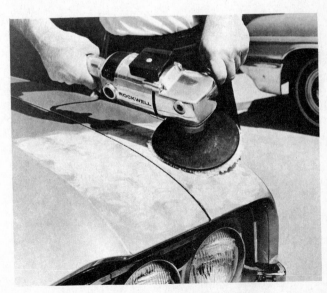

Fig. 31-15 Using machine rubbing compound and a polisher to compound a car repainted with lacquer. (*Rockwell International Corporation*)

used. Wax has no abrasive properties. When applied, it forms a thin protective film over the finish.

Wax is *hydrophobic*, which means that it tends to reject water. This characteristic is seen when water forms beads on the surface of a new car. To check if a car needs waxing, sprinkle water on it. If the water does not bead, then the car needs waxing.

REVIEW QUESTIONS

Select the *one* correct, best, or most probable answer to each question. You can find the correct answers in the section indicated at the end of each question.

1. Before painting, the purpose of treating bare metal with metal conditioner and conversion coating is to   (≡31-2)
   a. prevent rust
   b. provide good undercoat adhesion
   c. both a and b
   d. neither a nor b

2. A tack rag is used to   (≡31-4)
   a. polish the car
   b. dissolve the old paint
   c. pick up lint, dust, and dirt
   d. make the masking tape tacky

3. To remove masking tape after painting, you should   (≡31-7)
   a. pull the tape as soon as the paint is no longer sticky
   b. pull at a 90° angle to the surface
   c. both a and b
   d. neither a nor b

4. Feathering is used to prevent   (≡31-9)
   a. ripples in the paint
   b. a ridge line in the paint
   c. dirt in the paint
   d. scratch marks in the paint

5. A car that has been painted with lacquer has a dull, rough finish. Mechanic A says to sand the finish and spray the colorcoat again. Mechanic B says to rub out the finish with rubbing compound. Who is right?
   a. mechanic A
   b. mechanic B
   c. both A and B
   d. neither A nor B

CHAPTER 32
SPRAY GUNS

After studying this chapter, you should be able to:

1. Describe the operation of the suction-feed and the pressure-feed spray gun.
2. Explain how to clean a spray gun.
3. Describe how to use a spray gun.
4. Discuss various spray-gun problems and how to correct them.

≡ 32-1 TYPES OF SPRAY GUNS

A *spray gun* is a tool that uses compressed air to atomize paint and other sprayable materials. There are two types of spray gun: the suction-feed type and the pressure-feed type. Both types are described in following sections.

The purpose of the spray gun is to change liquid paint or other coating material into tiny droplets, or spray, and throw this spray uniformly onto the surface to be painted. The process of changing the liquid into fine droplets is called *atomization*.

Fig. 32-1 A suction-feed spray gun. *(The DeVilbiss Company)*

≡ 32-2 SUCTION-FEED SPRAY GUN

Figure 32-1 shows a suction-feed spray gun. In this gun, compressed air flows through a small opening around a fluid tip in the gun cap. This produces a slight vacuum which, in effect, "pulls" paint up from the cup. The paint flows up and out past the fluid tip. The stream of compressed air is also directed through the two side portholes of the cap (Fig. 32-1). Without any air flowing through the side portholes, the spray would be round (Fig. 32-2) and it would be hard to get an even layer of paint when spraying a panel, for example. With the air flowing through the two side portholes, the spray is reshaped, or fanned out, into an oval pattern (Fig. 32-3).

Figures 32-4 to 32-7 show the principle parts of the spray gun and how they work. The fan-adjustment screw (Fig. 32-4) changes the amount of air flowing through the two side portholes in the air cap. If this screw is backed off, more air flows and the oval spray pattern is elongated. If the fan adjustment screw is turned in, the pattern changes toward a rounder shape. The fluid-adjustment screw adjusts the amount of paint that flows out past the fluid needle. If this screw is backed out, more paint flows. If it is turned in, less paint flows. The two screws must be properly adjusted so that the right amount of paint flows and the right amount of air flows to produce the desired pattern. The adjustments are different for different paints and mixtures of paint and thinner. Also, adjustments vary according to the type of paint job (spot repair or complete car paint job).

Figure 32-5 shows the conditions with the air and fluid valves closed. Figure 32-6 shows the conditions with the trigger at the halfway point. The air valve is opened, allowing compressed air to flow out through the two side portholes in the air cap and also around the fluid tip. No paint can flow, because the fluid-needle valve is closed at the half-trigger position.

Figure 32-7 shows the conditions when the trigger is pulled all the way back, to the spraying position. This pulls the needle valve back so the paint can flow up from the cup and out past the paint of the needle valve. The compressed air breaks the paint up into tiny drop-

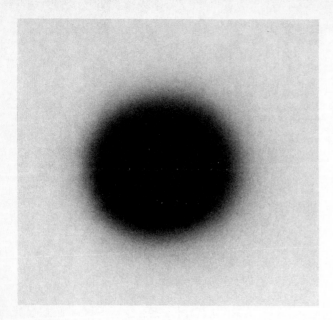

Fig. 32-2 When no air flows through the side portholes, the spray pattern is round.

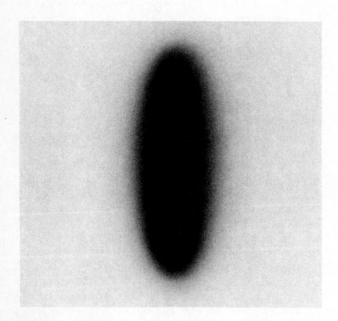

Fig. 32-3 Normal oval-shaped pattern from a spray gun.

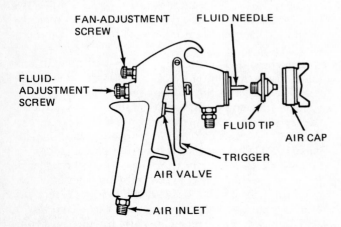

Fig. 32-4 Main parts of a spray gun. *(Ford Motor Company)*

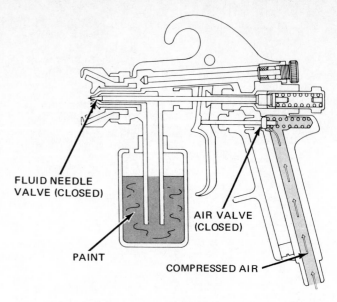

Fig. 32-5 Conditions in the spray gun with the air and fluid valves closed. *(Ford Motor Company)*

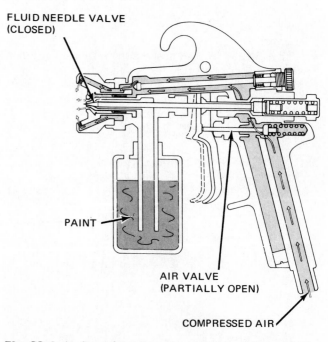

Fig. 32-6 Air flows from the side portholes and around the fluid tip at the half-trigger position. *(Ford Motor Company)*

lets (atomizes it) so the paint emerges as a fine spray. The compressed air from the two side portholes in the air cap shapes this into an oval pattern.

***NOTE:** There are three trigger positions: OFF, AIR ON, and AIR AND FLUID ON. Do not pull the trigger back only part way past the AIR ON position to partly open the fluid-needle valve. Always pull the trigger all the way back to fully open the needle valve.*

We mentioned previously that the vacuum formed by the compressed air flowing past the fluid tip "pulled" paint up from the cup. Actually, atmospheric pressure, acting on the paint in the cup, pushes the

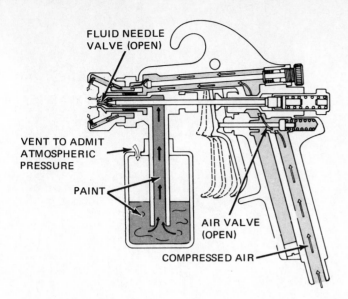

Fig. 32-7 Full-trigger position with air and fluid valves open. *(Ford Motor Company)*

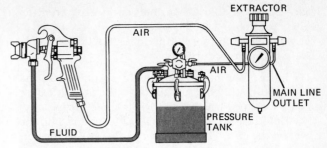

Fig. 32-8 A complete pressure-feed spray-gun system. *(Binks Manufacturing Company)*

paint up (Fig. 32-7). The vacuum at the fluid tip means there is less pressure at that point than atmospheric pressure. Therefore, the difference in pressure pushes the paint up and out past the needle-valve tip. The vent to admit atmospheric pressure to the cup is shown in Fig. 32-7.

☰ 32-3 PRESSURE-FEED SPRAY GUN

The pressure-feed spray gun (Fig. 32-8) is not often found in the typical auto paint shop, because it is less convenient for small jobs. This type of gun is more useful for big jobs, such as trucks, or for fleets where all vehicles are painted the same color. The pressure-feed spray gun uses a pressure tank, partly filled with paint and pressurized by the compressed-air system. This pressure forces the paint through a tube to the gun and out the fluid tip. A second tube sends compressed air into the gun and out the air openings in the fluid tip and air cap.

The advantages and disadvantages of the two types of spray guns are listed below:

SUCTION-FEED SPRAY GUN

Advantages	Disdvantages
Can handle small jobs	Gun, which includes cup, is heavier and harder to handle
Easy to change from one color or material to another	Limited control of spray pattern and rate of paint flow; harder to use around curves
Easy to clean	
Simple to operate and adjust	

PRESSURE-FEED SPRAY GUN

Advantages	Disdvantages
Can handle large amounts of paint and big jobs	Not suitable for small jobs requiring small amounts of paint
Provides constant flow of paint at uniform pressure	Frequent changes of color and material not practical
Will handle heavy materials such as spray-on vinyl	Difficult to clean
Lightweight and easy to handle	
Working angles of nozzle are unlimited	

☰ 32-4 CLEANING THE SPRAY GUN

The first priority in using a spray gun is keep it clean. If the gun is not clean and the air holes are blocked, strange spray patterns will emerge (Fig. 32-9). The top-heavy or bottom-heavy spray is due to clogged side portholes in the air cap. The crescent-shaped pattern is

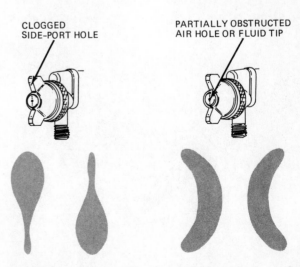

Fig. 32-9 Faulty spray patterns. *(Binks Manufacturing Company)*

caused by a partly blocked air hole or by an obstruction on the fluid tip.

Always clean the spray gun immediately after using it. Here is the procedure:

1. Loosen the cup from the gun (Fig. 32-10) and raise the gun, still holding the end of the fluid line over the cup. Unscrew the air cap two or three turns.

2. Hold a cloth over the air cap (Fig. 32-11). Pull the trigger on the gun. This forces any paint still in the gun back into the cup.

3. Empty the cup and rinse it out with solvent. Discard this solvent after the cup is clean, and add more solvent. Put the cup back on the gun and operate it to flush out all paint from the gun (Fig. 32-12).

4. Remove the air cap from the gun and soak it in solvent. Then dry it off with compressed air.

5. If the holes in the air cap become clogged, soak the cap in solvent. Then use a toothpick or a broom-straw to clean out the holes (Fig. 32-13). Never use a metal object such as a drill or wire to clean out the holes. This can enlarge the holes and completely destroy the proper spray pattern.

6. After the spray gun is cleaned, reassemble it in readiness for future use.

Fig. 32-12 Spraying solvent to flush all paint from the gun.

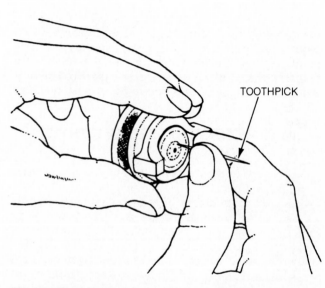

Fig. 32-13 Using a toothpick to clean the holes in the air cap.

TOOTHPICK

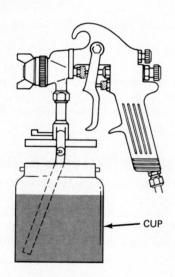

Fig. 32-10 To clean a spray gun, first remove the cup. (*Binks Manufacturing Company*)

CUP

Fig. 32-11 Hold a cloth over the air cap, and pull the trigger to force any paint in the gun back into the cup.

7. Lubricate the spray gun daily (preferably before using) with the lubricant recommended by the spray-gun manufacturer. A typical recommendation is to use light machine oil on the fluid-needle packing, air-valve packing, side-port-control packing, and the trigger pivot points (Fig. 32-14). Also, coat the needle-valve spring with petroleum jelly.

NOTE: *Never lubricate any part of the spray gun with a lubricant containing silicone. If silicone gets into a spray gun or hose, the silicone cannot be completely flushed out.*

≡ 32-5 CHECKING PAINT VISCOSITY

When using the spray gun, temperature is important — both the temperature of the paint and the temperature of the surface to be sprayed. If the temperature is

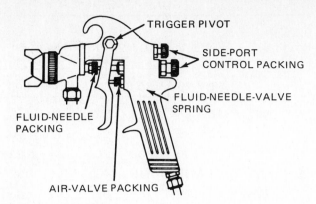

Fig. 32-14 Lubrication points for a spray gun. *(Binks Manufacturing Company)*

too low, the paint will go on sluggishly, dry slowly, and run. If the temperature is too high, the solvent may evaporate too fast. Then the paint will not smooth out, or flow, to provide a good job. The ideal temperature for spray painting is about 75°F [24°C].

Temperature also affects the paint *viscosity*. This is the resistance to flow, or thickness, of a liquid. The paint should be at room temperature. After mixing the paint, check the label for the recommended viscosity that the mixture should have when it is ready to spray. Paint viscosity is checked with a *viscosity cup* (Fig. 32-15). The cup holds a standard amount of paint, primer, or other material applied with the spray gun. A small hole in the bottom of the cup allows the liquid to run out. The length of time (in seconds) required for the cup to empty is the viscosity reading of the paint. Specifications are given by the paint manufacturers.

To use the cup, dip it into the paint until the cup is full (Fig. 32-15A). Raise the full cup out of the paint (Fig. 32-15B). As the cup clears the surface of the paint, begin timing the flow from the small hole in the bottom of the cup. Measure the time with a watch (preferably a stopwatch). Stop the watch when the stream of paint first breaks (as shown in Fig. 32-15C), and not when it stops completely. This will give you an accurate viscosity reading.

Figure 32-16 shows the ranges of recommended viscosities for spraying various kinds of finishes (as measured with a Du Pont M-50 viscosity cup). If the viscosity is within the recommended range, the paint is ready to spray. The paint can now be strained into the spray-gun cup. If the viscosity is not correct, the paint mixture must be further thinned, or thickened by adding unthinned paint.

≡ 32-6 SETTING THE AIR PRESSURE

The paint, solvent, and other additives should be properly mixed, agitated, strained, and poured into the spray-gun cup (≡31-6). Then attach the cup to the gun and connect the air hose to the gun. Open the air-outlet valve leading to the air hose, if necessary. Adjust the regulator valve on the air transformer or on the gun to the recommended air pressure for the material to be sprayed.

The recommended air pressure varies with the kind of paint and the type of repair. Typical spray pressures recommended *at the gun* are shown in Fig. 32-17. Notice that spraying enamel requires more air pressure than spraying lacquer. Also, more air pressure is needed for spraying an acrylic (both enamel and lacquer) on a complete vehicle than for making a spot repair. (The various kinds of paint are described in Chap. 33.)

When the air pressure is adjusted at the air transformer, the pressure at the gun will be the same *as long as no air is flowing*. However, as soon as the gun is triggered, the pressure at the gun will be somewhat less. This pressure loss is caused by the friction of the compressed air as it passes through the transformer, the hose, and the hose couplings.

The actual pressure at the gun varies, depending primarily on the length and diameter of the hose. For example, a 25-foot [7.6-m], ¼-inch [6-mm] hose will cause a lower pressure at the gun than a 10-foot [3-m], ⁵⁄₁₆-inch [8-mm] hose. This is why the air pressure should be measured at the gun, if possible. Some spray guns have an air-pressure indicator, similar to a tire-pressure gauge, built into the handle.

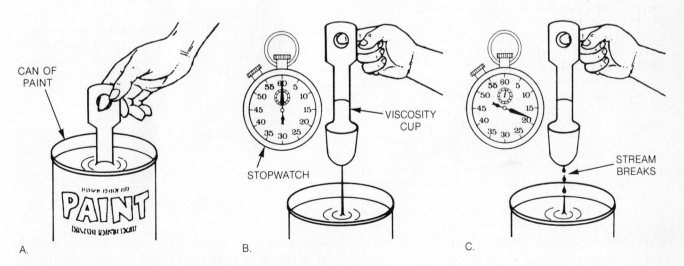

Fig. 32-15 Checking paint viscosity with a viscosity cup. *(Du Pont)*

Kind of Paint	Recommended Viscosity, Seconds
Acrylic lacquer	18–22
Acrylic enamel	18–21
Alkyd enamel	20–23
Polyurethane enamel	18–22
Flexible finish	16–20

Fig. 32-16 Ranges of recommended viscosities for spraying various kinds of finishes. *(Du Pont)*

Kind of Paint	Recommended Air Pressure at the Gun, psi	
	Spot Repair	Panel/Overall
Acrylic lacquer	20–35	40–45
Acrylic enamel	30–40	50–65
Alkyd enamel	50–60	50–60
Polyurethane enamel (nonmetallic)	50	50
Polyurethane enamel (metallic)	65	65
Flexible finish	35	35

Fig. 32-17 Typical spray pressures recommended at the gun. *(Du Pont)*

NOTE: The size of a hose is its internal diameter. This determines the volume of air or other fluid that can flow through.

If you do not have a gauge to measure the pressure at the gun, then you can use a chart to approximate it. Figure 32-18 shows the estimated air pressures at the gun for various lengths of ¼-inch and ⁵⁄₁₆-inch hose. These are based on readings at the transformer. Each quick coupling (snap connector) between the transformer and the gun reduces the pressure at the gun by an additional 1 psi. Also, the pressures given in Fig. 32-18 are approximate, and are for new hose. Old hose may further increase the pressure drop.

The most accurate method of checking air pressure at the gun is with an air-pressure gauge attached to the gun (Fig. 32-19). Painting-equipment manufacturers make small gauges with a built-in regulator which can be adjusted to set the desired pressure at the gun. This device is called an *air controller*. By increasing the pressure at the transformer, triggering the gun, and adjusting the regulator, the pressure at the gun can be accurately set.

Pressure Reading, lb, at the Transformer	Pressure at the Gun for Various Hose Lengths					
	5 ft	10 ft	15 ft	20 ft	25 ft	50 ft
¼ inch Hose						
30	26	24	23	22	21	9
40	34	32	31	29	27	16
50	43	40	38	36	34	22
60	51	48	46	43	41	29
70	59	56	53	51	48	36
80	68	64	61	58	55	43
90	76	71	68	65	61	51
⁵⁄₁₆ inch Hose						
30	29	28½	28	27½	27	23
40	38	37	37	37	36	32
50	47	48	46	46	45	40
60	57	56	55	55	54	49
70	66	65	64	63	63	57
80	75	74	73	72	71	66
90	84	83	82	81	80	74

Fig. 32-18 Estimated air pressures at the gun for various lengths of hose. *(Du Pont)*

GUN PRESSURE GAUGE

AIR CONTROLLER

Fig. 32-19 An air-pressure gauge, or air controller, attached to the gun. *(ATW)*

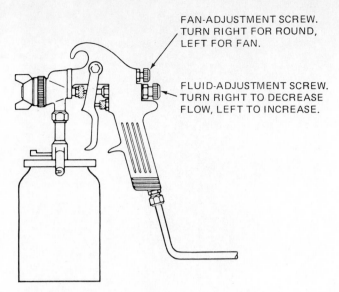

FAN-ADJUSTMENT SCREW.
TURN RIGHT FOR ROUND,
LEFT FOR FAN.

FLUID-ADJUSTMENT SCREW.
TURN RIGHT TO DECREASE
FLOW, LEFT TO INCREASE.

Fig. 32-20 *Air and fluid adjustments at the gun. (ATW)*

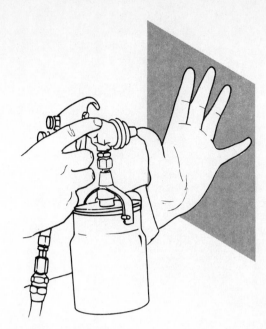

Fig. 32-21 *Measuring the correct distance for spray painting.*

≡ 32-7 THREE BASIC SPRAY-GUN ADJUSTMENTS

To obtain the proper coating of the sprayed material, three basic adjustments must be made to the spray gun. These are:

1. Set the pressure at the gun. This may be done before filling the cup with paint and attaching it to the gun. The procedure was described in ≡32-6. If an initial adjustment is needed, set the air pressure to 50 psi [345 kPa] at the gun.

2. Set the fan-adjustment (air) screw for the size of the job (wide open for complete panels, less open for spot repairs). For an initial adjustment of maximum size, turn the fan-adjustment screw counterclockwise until it stops (Fig. 32-20). This positions the air valve wide open. When the screw is all the way in, it will take 1½ to 2 turns to fully open the air valve.

3. Set the fluid-adjustment (paint) screw to fill the fan. For an initial adjustment of maximum size, back out the fluid-adjustment screw to the wide-open position (Fig. 32-20). This is when the first thread on the screw is visible. Although the screw can be turned counterclockwise several more turns, this does not allow more fluid to flow.

≡ 32-8 USING THE SPRAY GUN

After properly preparing the paint and pouring it into the spray-gun cup, you are ready to begin using the spray gun. Proceed as follows:

1. Set the air pressure at the gun, following the procedures in ≡32-6.

2. Turn the fan-adjustment screw fully open (≡32-7).

3. Turn the fluid-adjustment screw fully open (≡32-7). One thread of the screw should be visible.

4. Hold the spray gun about 8 inches [200 mm] from a test panel. A quick way to measure the correct distance is to stretch your fingers and touch the surface with your little finger and the tip of the spray gun with

your thumb (Fig. 32-21). This puts the gun at the proper distance from the surface.

5. Pull the trigger all the way back and quickly release it. Now examine the size and shape of the pattern. A normal spray pattern is shown in Fig. 32-3. It should be about 8 to 10 inches [200 to 250 mm] high, and about 2 to 3 inches [50 to 75 mm] wide. If no air is flowing through the side portholes, the pattern will be round (Fig. 32-2). Patterns caused by low or high air pressure are shown in Fig. 32-22. Adjust the air pressure at the gun until the proper pattern shape is obtained. If the pattern is too small (from top to bottom), turn the fan-adjustment screw counterclockwise (open) to get the proper pattern height.

6. Examine the texture of the spray pattern (Fig. 32-23). If it is a rough, dry, or thin coating without luster, the air pressure or the gun needs adjusting. Either decrease the air pressure at the gun by 5 psi [35 kPa] or turn the fluid-adjustment screw slightly open to increase the amount of paint being applied. If the pattern is too wet with a heavy coating that sags, ripples, or has orange peel, the air pressure is too low. Increase the air pressure at the gun by 5 psi [35 kPa]. Continue shooting test patterns and making adjustments until the desired pattern is obtained.

7. Be sure the gun is held the proper distance from the surface when spraying (Fig. 32-21). Hold the gun 6 to 8 inches [150 to 200 mm] from the surface for spraying lacquer. For spraying enamels, the gun should be held 8 to 10 inches [200 to 250 mm] away. If the distance is too short, the high velocity of the spraying air tends to ripple the wet film. If the distance is too great, too much of the thinner will evaporate on the way to the work. This can result in orange peel, or a dry film.

8. Hold the gun level with and at right angles (Fig. 32-24) to the panel. Keep your wrist stiff, and use your arm and shoulder to move the spray gun across the surface to be painted. Keep the gun pointing vertically at the surface. Before you actually squeeze the trigger,

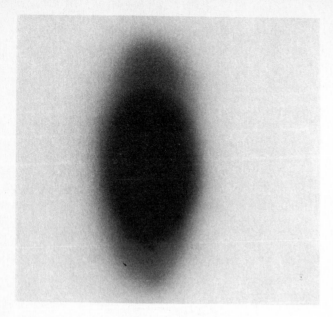

A. LOW AIR PRESSURE   B. HIGH AIR PRESSURE

Fig. 32-22 Spray patterns with low and high air pressure.

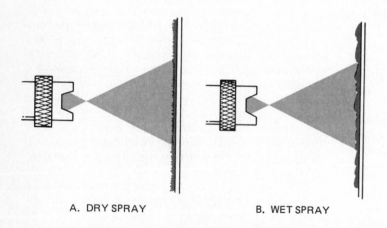

A. DRY SPRAY   B. WET SPRAY

Fig. 32-23 Improper texture of the spray pattern indicates further adjustments are necessary. *(Ditzler Automotive Finishes Division of PPG Industries, Inc.)*

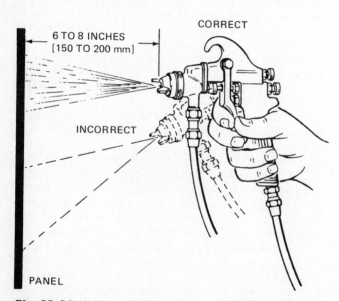

CORRECT

6 TO 8 INCHES [150 TO 200 mm]

INCORRECT

PANEL

Fig. 32-24 Hold the spray gun level with and perpendicular to the panel. *(Binks Manufacturing Company)*

practice moving the gun in steady, sweeping strokes, across the panel you are about to paint.

NOTE: We assume the panel has been properly prepared for painting and the car has been properly masked.

9. To apply the paint, aim the gun nozzle at the top of the panel and several inches to one side. Figure 32-25 shows how the spray pattern is positioned at the top of the panel. Some of the paint will spray onto the masking paper, but that is what the paper is there for. It is important to get the center part of the spray pattern, where the most paint is being applied, to cover the top of the panel.

10. Now, with the gun aimed at the top of the panel and to one side, pull the trigger. At the same time, start the gun moving sideways across the panel. Move the gun smoothly, at a constant speed of about 1 foot [0.3 m] per second. Keep the gun at the same distance from and aimed vertically at the panel (Fig. 32-26). Never stop

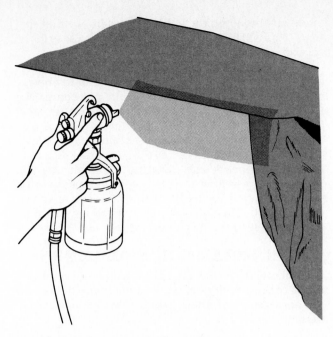

Fig. 32-25 Starting to apply the paint.

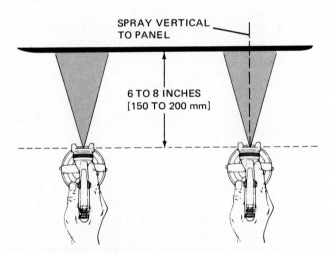

Fig. 32-26 Keep the spray gun at the same distance from and aimed vertically at the panel. *(Ford Motor Company)*

the motion of the gun across the panel. The gun must be moved with uniform speed. If you move the gun too fast, the film will be too thin. If you move it too slowly, too much paint will get on the surface. Then the paint will sag or run.

11. As you reach the end of the first pass across the panel, release the trigger just enough to close the fluid-needle valve and stop the flow of paint. The air valve remains open. This action, known as *triggering,* prevents paint buildup at the edge of the panel, reduces paint waste caused by overspray, and makes the job easier. Relaxing your hand muscles at the end of each pass reduces muscle fatigue so you can do a better and more accurate job.

12. As you move the gun out past the end of the panel, shift the aim downward one-half of the height of the spray pattern. Aim at the bottom of the previous pass. Now, on the second pass, the upper half of the

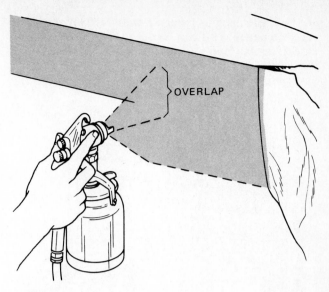

Fig. 32-27 How to overlap the spray pattern.

pattern that is sprayed on will overlap the lower half of the spray pattern of the previous pass (Fig. 32-27).

13. In making the second pass, if the first pass was from right to left, the second pass must be from left to right. Just before the gun moves onto the panel, trigger it. Keep the gun moving across the panel at a steady speed, holding the gun perpendicular to the panel and at the correct distance from it. Aiming the gun at the bottom of the previous pass will give a 50 percent overlap. This is the ideal overlap for a good paint job.

14. Continue to move the gun back and forth in a series of passes until the complete panel is covered with paint.

15. If you have a panel to paint that is longer than about 3 feet [1 m], handle the job by spraying it in overlapping sections (Fig. 32-28). Divide the panel into two or three equal widths. Handle the first section as though it were a complete panel. As quickly as you finish the first section, move to the second section, overlapping the passes, as shown in Fig. 32-28. Then paint the third section. Properly done, the completed paint job will reveal no signs of the overlap. The secret here is that as you near the inner end of the first strokes, let up

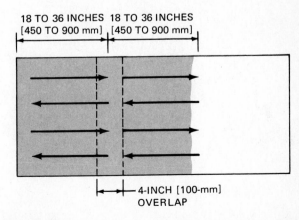

Fig. 32-28 Spray a long panel in overlapping sections. *(Binks Manufacturing Company)*

on the trigger (just as though it were actually the other edge of a panel). This causes the last part of the pass to fade off into nothing. Now, as soon as the first section of the panel is painted, move on to the second section. The first pass there should start at the point where the "fade-off" began on the adjacent pass (in the first section). This will fill in the fade-off area as the pass in the second section starts.

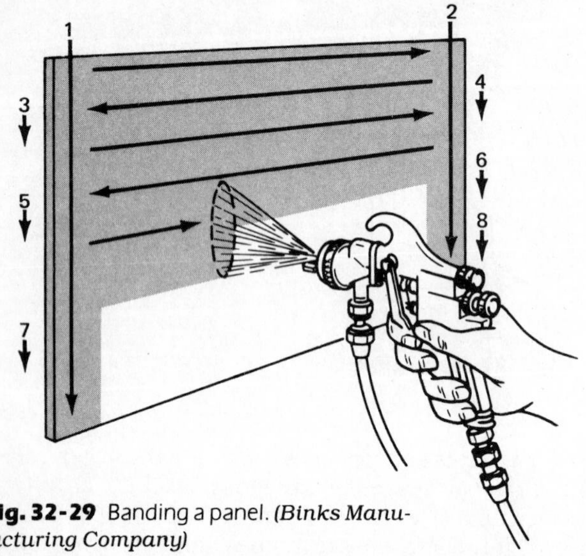

16. Banding is used on panels to ensure good coverage at the start and end of the passes and to prevent overspraying. Figure 32-29 shows the procedure. The first two passes are vertical at the two sides of the panel (1 and 2 in Fig. 32-29). Then the panel is covered with horizontal, overlapping strokes, as shown at 3 to 8.

17. An exception to holding the gun perpendicular to the panel surface is when spotting in a small area on a panel. Then you may start and end each pass with a sweeping motion angling away from the work as shown in Fig. 32-30. This fades the paint off on the two sides and helps blend the new paint into the old.

≡ 32-9 SPRAY-GUN PROBLEMS

Several problems can cause paint trouble if everything is not done correctly. Here are common problems with the spray gun and their possible causes and corrections:

1. Spray-gun spitting. If the spray gun suddenly starts to spit, or produce a fluttering spray pattern, the cause could be air leakage into the fluid or blockage of the airflow. Check for the following conditions:

   a. The level of paint in the cup may be low, allowing air to leak into the fluid line (Fig. 32-31A).

   b. The spray gun may have been tilted (Fig. 32-31B), allowing air to enter the fluid line.

   c. The spray gun may have been tilted with the cup full, causing the paint to block the air vent (Fig. 32-31C). When this happens, air cannot enter. Therefore, the paint will not be pushed up to the fluid-needle valve by atmospheric pressure.

   d. Other causes could be a loose or cracked fluid tube, a loose cup lid, dry packing in the gun or a loose fluid-needle-packing nut, material too thick to flow freely, or material not properly strained and containing particles that clog the fluid-needle valve.

Fig. 32-29 Banding a panel. (*Binks Manufacturing Company*)

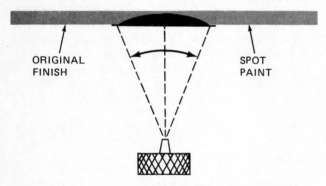

Fig. 32-30 The spray gun may be swung in a slight arc when making a spot repair.

ORIGINAL FINISH

SPOT PAINT

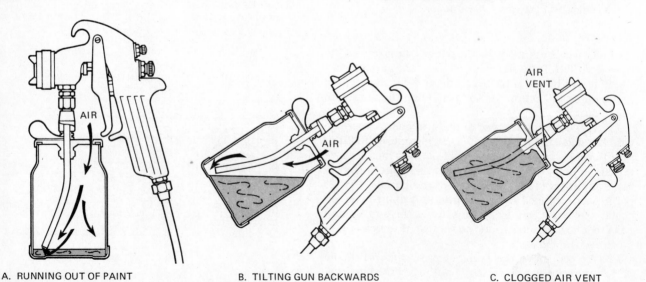

A. RUNNING OUT OF PAINT   B. TILTING GUN BACKWARDS   C. CLOGGED AIR VENT

AIR VENT

AIR

AIR

Fig. 32-31 Spray-gun problems. (*Ford Motor Company*)

2. Thin coat that is rough, dry, and has no luster (Fig. 32-23A). This can be caused by any of the following:

   a. Fluid-adjustment screw not opening enough to feed sufficient paint

   b. Gun held too far from panel

   c. Paint too thin

   d. Too much air

   e. Gun moved too fast across panel

   f. Not enough overlap of the various passes

3. Heavy coat with sags, ripples, or orange peel (Fig. 32-23B). Orange-peel finish is a finish that is rough, like the peel of an orange. Orange peel, sags, or ripples can be caused by any of the following:

   a. Dirty air nozzle

   b. Gun held too close to panel

   c. Paint too thin or too thick

   d. Low air pressure

   e. Stroke too slow

   f. Too much overlap

Faulty spray patterns caused by a gun that needs cleaning are described in ≡32-4 and illustrated in Fig. 32-9. Faulty paint jobs and their causes are described and illustrated in Chap. 36. Several conditions not related to the spray gun or how it is used can cause paint problems. These are also discussed in Chap. 36.

≡ 32-10 TOUCH-UP GUN

The spray guns described so far in this chapter are "production" guns. They are used by the automotive painter for production work in the shop. These jobs range from spraying a spot repair to complete vehicle refinishing. However, there are many jobs that are too small to be handled easily by the production gun. These

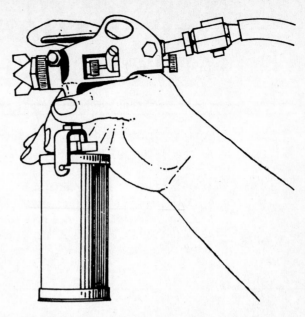

Fig. 32-32 A touch-up gun is often used for touch-up, spotting, shading, and custom painting.

jobs are ideal for the *touch-up gun* (Fig. 32-32). This is a small spray gun that is often used for touch-up, spotting, shading, and custom painting (Chap. 37).

The touch-up gun has the same general construction as the production gun, and operates in the same way. However, the paint cup is smaller, holding a pint or less of paint. The trigger is usually "overhead," and operated by the index finger. The smaller size and lighter weight make the touch-up gun very handy for small jobs.

REVIEW QUESTIONS

Select the *one* correct, best, or most probable answer to each question. You can find the answers in the section indicated at the end of each question.

1. The spray gun operates on   (≡32-2)
   a. vacuum
   b. water pressure
   c. hydraulic pressure
   d. compressed air

2. In the half-trigger position   (≡32-2)
   a. no air flows
   b. only paint flows
   c. a small amount of paint flows
   d. no paint flows

3. The three trigger positions are   (≡32-2)
   a. off, air on, air and fluid on
   b. air on, fluid on, air and fluid on
   c. off, air on, fluid on
   d. air off, fluid on, air and fluid on

4. The ideal temperature for spray painting is   (≡32-5)
   a. any temperature above freezing
   b. about 75°F [24°C]
   c. 32°F [0°C]
   d. 212°F [100°C]

5. When spraying enamels, hold the gun away from the panel about   (≡32-8)
   a. 6 to 8 inches [150 to 200 mm]
   b. 2 to 3 inches [50 to 75 mm]
   c. 8 to 10 inches [200 to 250 mm]
   d. 3 feet [1 m]

CHAPTER 33
AUTOMOTIVE BODY PAINTS

After studying this chapter, you should be able to:

1. Describe the three basic ingredients in paint.
2. Explain the difference between enamel and lacquer.
3. Describe the different types of enamel.
4. Compare acrylic lacquer and acrylic enamel.
5. Explain how metallic paint is made so it produces a metallic color.
6. Discuss metal conditioners and their purpose.
7. Explain the purpose of primer, primer-surfacer, and primer-sealer.
8. Discuss the guide coat and what it is used for.

≡ 33-1 AUTOMOTIVE PAINTS

A great variety of body paints have been used on cars in the past, including numerous kinds of enamels and lacquers. Today, however, the original finishes on new cars produced in the United States are of two types: acrylic enamel and acrylic lacquer. The word "acrylic" pertains to a type of chemical—a liquid plastic—used in the manufacture of enamel or lacquer.

≡ 33-2 MR. FORD'S "BLACK"

Cars produced early in this century were usually painted black. Henry Ford was supposed to have said he would supply cars in any color—"so long as they're black." The reason for this was that in those days it was difficult enough to get one color right—black—without having to be concerned with other colors. It took up to a month to paint a car in the early days. The paint was applied with a brush. After each coat dried, it was hand-sanded and rubbed and then repainted. Several coats were applied. The final coat was then waxed. This lengthy procedure for painting the bodies was a real bottleneck to fast production.

In the early 1920s Du Pont came out with a product that changed all this: Duco (for *DU* Pont *CO*mpany). This was a synthetic lacquer. It could be applied with a spray gun and dried in a few hours. Duco could be made in many colors, so colors other than black became popular. Still later, other types of lacquer and enamel appeared. By 1959, General Motors was using a form of acrylic lacquer on all its cars. This type of finish is used on GM cars today. American Motors Corporation, Chrysler Corporation, and Ford Motor Company used baking enamel before about 1955, but in the early 1960s switched to acrylic enamel, similar to the enamel used by these companies today.

Research continues on paints for automotive bodies, and improvements appear from time to time. Many factories now paint cars with a new type of enamel, called *water-based* acrylic. This enamel is said to have superior wearing qualities and holds its color longer (does not fade or streak). However, it does require some special care if a spot repair is required.

There is one aspect of developing new paints that the paint chemists and engineers must keep in mind. Any new paint must be repairable with the equipment and skills available in the field. Therefore, you need not worry that the cars produced next year or the year after will have new paint jobs that require some new kind of equipment or painting procedures. In spite of the great variety of paints that have been used on cars in the past, the same general repair and painting procedures have not changed. Different materials are used on enamel and lacquer, but the general procedures are still the same.

≡ 33-3 PAINT INGREDIENTS

All paints, regardless of the type or who manufactures them, have three basic ingredients:

1. Pigment
2. Binder
3. Vehicle

Following sections describe each of these in detail.

≡ 33-4 PIGMENTS

Pigments give the paint its color. They come in all sorts of colors, from white to black. If you saw a white pigment all by itself, you'd say it looks like talcum powder. Pigments are finely ground powder. The materials from which the pigment is ground determine its color and the color of the paint job on the car.

The so-called glamour paints—the paints with a metallic sheen—have tiny chips of metal, such as aluminum, mixed in with the pigment. These chips are shiny and impart an iridescent, or sparkling, appearance to the paint.

≡ 33-5 BINDER

The binder does what its name implies. It binds the pigment together and to the surfaces of the car body. By itself, the binder looks like syrup for pancakes. Adding the pigment gives the binder its color. Many different kinds of binders have been used, with many different chemical formulas. The binder in general use today is the liquid plastic called *acrylic*. There are different kinds of acrylic. One is used in acrylic enamel, another in acrylic lacquer. These two paints are described later.

☰ 33-6 VEHICLE

A binder mixed with pigment would be too heavy to spray. It must be thinned out. The chemical used to thin the mixture is called the *vehicle*. Adding the vehicle to the binder-and-pigment mix results in a paint thin enough to be sprayed. The vehicle is highly volatile, so it evaporates very easily. Actually, part of the vehicle evaporates from the paint on the way from the gun to the surface being painted. The rest of the vehicle, once it carries the paint to the surface and flows it out to a smooth surface, also evaporates. At that point, the vehicle has done its job.

There are two kinds of vehicle, one for enamel and another for lacquer:

1. LACQUER VEHICLE. This vehicle is called a *thinner*. It has the correct chemical composition to work with the other chemicals in the paint—the acrylic and pigment.

2. ENAMEL VEHICLE. This vehicle is called a *reducer*. It has the correct chemical composition to work with the other chemicals in the paint—the acrylic and pigment.

Note that, while both are *vehicles*, the lacquer vehicle is called a *thinner* while the enamel vehicle is called a *reducer*. The reason for this difference in name is to guard against using the wrong vehicle. A lacquer vehicle (a thinner) will not work with enamel. Nor will an enamel vehicle (a reducer) work with lacquer.

NOTE: There are several varieties of thinners and reducers, differing in the speed with which they evaporate. You should always choose the slowest-drying thinner or reducer that you can safely handle without sags or runs. This ensures a smooth surface.

Some universal vehicles are available which the manufacturers claim can be used with either lacquer or enamel. The advantage of these is that the paint shop using a universal vehicle has one less chemical to stock. However, many painting technicians say they get the best results with vehicles designed specifically for the enamel or lacquer they are using.

☰ 33-7 DIFFERENCE BETWEEN ENAMEL AND LACQUER

Acrylic enamel and acrylic lacquer are different in chemical composition, in the vehicle used to thin them, and in the way they are applied and finished. However, their similarities are much greater than their differences.

The main difference between lacquer and enamel, as far as the paint technician is concerned, is what happens to the paint after it is sprayed onto the car body. With lacquer, the paint dries as the vehicle (thinner) evaporates to form the final paint coat. With enamel, the paint also dries as the vehicle (reducer) evaporates to form the paint coat. However, the enamel

Fig. 33-1 Car body being spray-painted by hand on the assembly line. *(©Fisher Body Division of General Motors Corporation)*

Fig 33-2 Car body being spray-painted by robots on the assembly line. *(Buick Motor Division of General Motors Corporation)*

binder, having a different chemical composition, gradually oxidizes over a period of weeks to produce the final hard finish. This difference requires the paint technician to handle the two jobs—acrylic lacquer finishing and acrylic enamel finishing—in different ways.

☰ 33-8 LACQUER

The first synthetic lacquer, Duco, was brought out by Du Pont. Later developments continually improved lacquer, up to the presently used acrylic lacquer. At the automotive assembly plant, the lacquer is sprayed on by a painter (Fig. 33-1) or by robots (Fig. 33-2). Then, before any glass, rubber, or plastic is attached, the body is baked at high temperature (Fig. 33-3). This makes the lacquer flow out smoothly to produce a high-luster shine.

In the body shop, such high temperatures cannot be used. The heat would damage the rubber and plastic attached to the body panels. Also, the heat could damage the glass and interior trim. Therefore, another method of obtaining a high gloss is required.

To achieve the high gloss that is so desirable, the lacquer finish must be "rubbed out." This process is called *compounding*. After the lacquer has dried sufficiently, a technician applies the "compound" either by

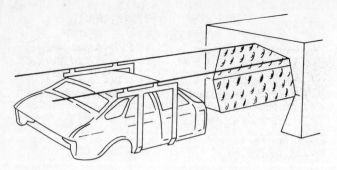

Fig. 33-3 After painting, the car body is baked to dry the paint. (©Fisher Body Division of General Motors Corporation)

hand or with a power polisher (sometimes called a *wheel*). The compound is a paste with a very fine abrasive material in it. When compound is rubbed on, it removes any surface irregularities, so the final finish is smooth and glossy. After the lacquer has had time to cure or dry completely (a time of up to 3 months' duration), the lacquer should be waxed. Compounding is described in ≡31-12.

Because some of the lacquer is removed during compounding, and also because the lacquer coats go on more thinly than enamel, four or more lacquer coats are required. (Enamel requires only two or three coats, at most.) Differences in using lacquer and enamel are described in ≡33-7.

≡ 33-9 ENAMEL

Acrylic enamel sets up (the paint film forms) by both evaportion of the vehicle (reducer) and by oxidation of the binder. Three of the major companies manufacturing automobiles in the United States have been using acrylic enamel in recent years. These are American Motors Corporation, Chrysler Corporation, and Ford Motor Company. However, General Motors uses acrylic lacquer on its cars.

Enamels are baked at high temperatures on the car bodies at the assembly plant. Such high temperatures cannot be used in the body shop. However, the enamels supplied to body shops today are properly compounded to flow out smoothly if properly mixed with reducer and properly sprayed onto the car body. Acrylic enamels are slow drying as compared with acrylic lacquers. However, they dry to a high gloss, if properly used, and do not require compounding. In fact, because it takes up to a month for the binder in the acrylic enamel to oxidize, the enamel should not be rubbed or polished during that time. It is fairly soft at first, gradually hardening as it oxidizes.

≡ 33-10 POLYURETHANE ENAMEL

Polyurethane enamel uses a special plastic binder which sets up chemically when an activator is added to the paint. The paint materials come in two containers. One is a regular paint can which contains the mix of pigment, binder, and vehicle. The other is a small container which holds an activating chemical. Just before the enamel is to be used, the two are mixed and then poured into the spray-gun cup. No thinner or reducer is

required. The activator causes the binder to set up chemically to form a hard, smooth finish.

NOTE: *This paint, with the activator mixed in, may set up, or jell, in the spray gun within a short time—in as little as 2 hours if the temperature is high. Therefore, the spray gun must be cleaned immediately after it is used to spray polyurethane enamel.*

≡ 33-11 WATER-BASED ACRYLIC ENAMEL

In recent years, some vehicles have been finished at the factory with water-based enamel. The solvent used is water instead of a chemical vehicle. Use of this type of paint cuts atmospheric pollution. During the baking process following the application of the paint, only water evaporates, not a chemical thinner or reducer. However, the process uses more energy because it takes more heat to cure the paint after it is applied. The paint is repaired in the usual manner, with one exception. The finish must be sanded and a sealer applied before the repair paint is sprayed on. You cannot do a spot-repair job on water-based enamel. Instead, you must repair the complete panel, out to its nearest definition lines. The procedure for repairing water-based acrylic paint is described in ≡35-5.

≡ 33-12 BASECOAT/CLEARCOAT FINISH

A two-step paint process is used on some selected-model cars. The finish is made up of two coats of a highly pigmented enamel, followed by two coats of clear acrylic. This provides a brighter, more reflective surface which has a high luster. Tests with a special light-reflective meter show that this finish has almost the same reflective ability as a mirror. This finish also has greater resistance to discoloration or spotting from industrial fallout. In addition, minor scratches that do not penetrate to the colorcoats can be buffed out of the clear acrylic surface.

≡ 33-13 URETHANE PAINT FOR FLEXIBLE BODY PARTS

Urethane is a type of plastic that is flexible, like rubber. Several body parts are made of urethane in modern cars, including the bumpers. Ordinary lacquer or enamel will not work very well on these parts. Lacquer and enamel do not form a sufficiently flexible film. Special urethane paint is required for such parts. Also, there are special urethane additives that can be mixed with lacquer or enamel to give the resulting paint film sufficient flexibility. You must follow the directions on the container to achieve the results necessary.

≡ 33-14 CHASSIS PAINT

Chassis parts are painted with flat black enamel. This protects them against rust. New chassis parts that come from the factory are painted. If the paint on chassis parts has been damaged, either by an accident or by the metal-straightening procedure, the parts should be repainted. Any place the paint film has been broken should be sanded clean and repainted.

≡ 33-15 TRUNK PAINT

This type of paint produces a spatter appearance when sprayed on. It is not a single color, but contains small droplets of a second color, which show up in the finished job as specks of a different color. This provides a pleasing finish without the necessity of careful preparation of the panels that form the trunk. However, many paint technicians prefer to use the same color in the trunk as for the body. Normally, the trunk is painted only when a complete body paint job is being done.

≡ 33-16 COMPARING ACRYLIC LACQUER AND ACRYLIC ENAMEL

Some shops prefer lacquer over enamel. Other shops prefer enamel. There are advantages and disadvantages to each. Some of these are described below.

Lacquer is fast drying. It can be used over old lacquer and enamel. Small nicks such as on door edges can be touched up with a small brush dipped in lacquer of the correct color. Disadvantages are that lacquer requires more coats (four or five) and needs polishing to bring out the high gloss. Also, it will not hide small imperfections, such as sand scratches or chips, as well as enamel.

Enamel covers better with fewer coats (two or three) and needs no compounding to bring out the gloss. It covers well and can hide small surface imperfections. Disadvantages are that it is slower drying, which means the paint booth must be more dust-free. An enamel job may come out less glossy with some orange peel.

Enamel also is considered to be more sensitive to spraying techniques. The air pressure used, the adjustments of the spray gun, and the distance the gun is held from the surface must all be more carefully controlled when spraying enamel. This is the reason that, in many body shops, the new paint technician is started out spraying lacquer. When this is mastered, the technician can then move on to spraying enamel.

≡ 33-17 METALLIC PAINT

Metallic paints (sometimes called the "glamour" paints) contain a large number of tiny metallic chips, usually of aluminum, which impart a metallic sheen to the finish. They reflect the light that hits the surface, to give the surface a sparkling appearance. Figure 33-4 shows this effect. The light strikes the entire surface uniformly at the same angle. But since the chips are oriented in all directions, the light rays are reflected at all angles from the surface. This gives the surface an iridescent, or sparkling, appearance.

When metallic paint requires repair, a special problem comes up for the paint technician. The final appearance of the repair job will depend on matching the new paint color correctly with the old, and also on the way the new paint is sprayed onto the surface.

If the new paint goes on comparatively dry, the metallic chips will be scattered throughout the paint film as shown in Fig. 33-4. The metallic chips do not have time to sink down, because the paint is almost dry when it hits the surface. If the paint is sprayed on wet, the wetness of the film gives the metallic chips enough time to settle to the bottom of the film (Fig. 33-4A). Now,

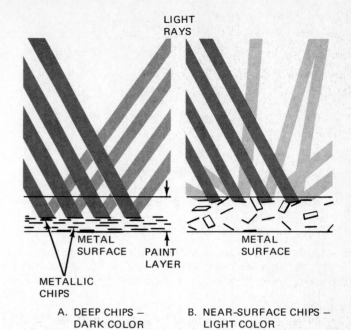

Fig. 33-4 Left, metallic flakes deep in the paint create a dark metallic color. Right, flakes near the surface create a light metallic color.

when light hits the paint, it will be reflected basically in one direction. The paint is duller and darker. It has lost its iridescence.

The paint technician must control the variables during spraying to get the same orientation of the metallic chips in the new paint as the old paint had. The following must be properly controlled:

1. Amount and type of thinner used
2. Adjustment of the paint flow from the gun
3. Adjustment of the airflow to get the proper dispersion of paint
4. Distance of the gun from the surface
5. Speed of the stroke — how fast the gun is carried across the panel
6. Time between coats

For example, if more thinner is used, the paint will still be wet when it hits the surface. The same result can be achieved by holding the gun closer to the surface or moving the gun more slowly across the surface. Also, if less time elapses between coats, the thinner will not have time to evaporate, or to "flash-off."

The technique of spraying metallic paint is described later.

≡ 33-18 BUYING PAINT

Larger paint shops blend their own paints. They do this for two reasons. One is the cost. It is cheaper to buy the basic ingredients (premixed binder and vehicle, and tints to color the paint) than to buy the paint readymixed. Second, if a particular color is needed, blending in the shop eliminates the wait for delivery from a supplier.

However, most shops buy their paint from an automotive-paint supplier ready-mixed to match the old

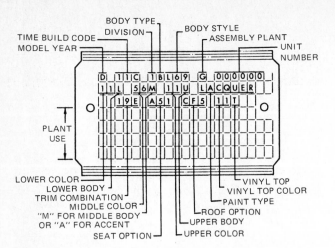

Fig. 33-5 Body number, or identification, plate showing the numbers and letters identifying the type and color of paint. *(©Fisher Body Division of General Motors Corporation)*

paint, or if the customer wants something different, the new color the customer selects. The new paint must be properly matched with the old. All cars carry a body number plate (Fig. 33-5). It has the numbers and letters identifying the type and color of paint used on the car body. Figure 33-6 shows the location of the identification plates on 1984 cars made in the United States.

The average paint shop has two choices. It can buy a can of factory-mixed paint (Fig. 33-7) or a can of custom-mixed paint (Fig. 33-8). The factory-mixed paint is packaged at the paint factory. However, this paint is not the same as the paint used in the assembly plant to paint the car body. The paint applied to the car body at the assembly plant is baked on. Therefore, the paint has a special formulation which permits it to be finished that way. The paint used in the body shop is applied and dried differently. Therefore, it has a different formulation. But the factory-mixed paint from your supplier will look the same as the paint applied at the assembly plant.

When repairing the paint on a late-model car, many painters prefer to use the factory-mixed paint. However, this is not always possible. After several years, the paint manufacturers discontinue their color coverage for older cars. Then you may have to use a custom-mixed paint. This may be helpful to you in matching faded old paint. Also, an older car may have already been repainted. With either condition, you would not know the paint number to use in ordering custom-mixed paint.

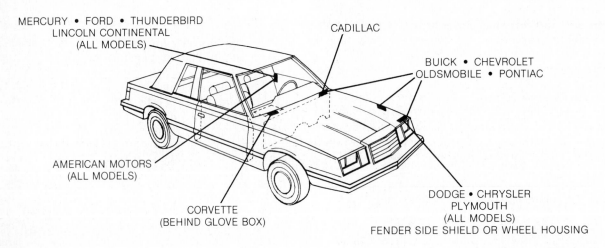

Fig. 33-6 Location of plate containing paint number. *(Ditzler Automotive Finishes Division of PPG Industries, Inc.)*

Fig. 33-7 A can of factory-mixed paint.

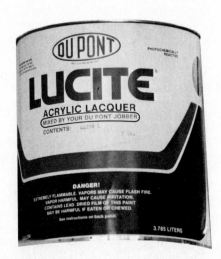

Fig. 33-8 A can of custom-mixed paint.

NOTE: When buying paint, specify one brand of materials (color, thinner, reducer, primer, sealer, additives, etc.). Mixing brands may cause paint problems and void any product warranty. Different brands of similar products may be chemically incompatible.

One way to match an unknown color is to use the color-chip book. This book, updated annually, is maintained in almost all body and paint shops. A typical page from a color-chip book is shown in Fig. 33-9. Compare the chips in the book with the car paint until you find a color that matches the car paint. Wetting the car surface and the chip will help you more accurately make the match. The surface of the car you are trying to match should be clean.

When you find the chip that matches, note its code number so you can order the color paint you need. Sometimes you will be unable to find a chip that matches. This is possible if the owner had an unusual blend of colors used in the previous paint job. If you are not mixing your own paint, either drive the car to your paint supplier or take off some small part as a color sample and send it to the shop. With the actual paint sample to see, your paint supplier can make a blend that will accurately match the old paint. This may take a while, because several tints might be required. Every time a paint sample is prepared, it should be sprayed on a panel and then dried. The paint color changes as it

Fig. 33-10 The layers in the finish of a completely painted surface.

dries. After finding the matching paint, prepare the car body for painting. Then apply the paint correctly to obtain the desired color match.

Chapters 34 and 35 describe how to prepare the surface for painting, typical paint repair jobs, and complete paint jobs.

≡ 33-19 UNDERCOATS

Acrylic lacquer and acrylic enamel, among other paints, will not stick on metal, old paint, or plastic filler. After the surface is prepared for painting, it must first receive an undercoat. The paint is then sprayed onto the undercoat. Therefore, the finish consists of at least two layers: an undercoat and a topcoat (Fig. 33-10). When you do a paint repair job or a complete repaint job, you will always spray on an undercoat before you put on the finish or topcoat.

Three different types of undercoats are used in automotive body painting. These are primer (≡33-20), primer-surfacer (≡33-21), and primer-sealer (≡33-22). However, before any type of undercoat is applied to metal, the surface must be properly prepared. The steps in surface preparation are described in Chap. 34.

≡ 33-20 PRIMER

Primers are a special type of undercoat material. They prevent rusting and corrosion. They also help bond the topcoat to bare metal. However, straight primers are not often used in the auto body paint shop. The reason is that a primer, by itself, does not fill and cover sand scratches and other slight imperfections in the surface to be painted.

NOTE: Before applying a primer to plastic body filler, check that the primer is recommended for this use. Some primers and paints do not work well with plastic body filler.

≡ 33-21 PRIMER-SURFACER

The primer-surfacer is, in effect, a primer to which has been added a surfacing material. This prepares the surface so the paint will stick. It also prevents rust and corrosion from forming on the bare metal. In addition, the surfacer material in the primer-surfacer fills in small scratches, nicks, and other minor surface imperfections.

The type of primer-surfacer that is used depends on the type of topcoat and also the type of surface to be painted. The usual recommendation is to use a lacquer primer-surfacer if the topcoat is to be lacquered. For an enamel topcoat, an enamel primer-surfacer should be used. Some companies put out an all-purpose primer-surfacer which can be used with either enamel or lac-

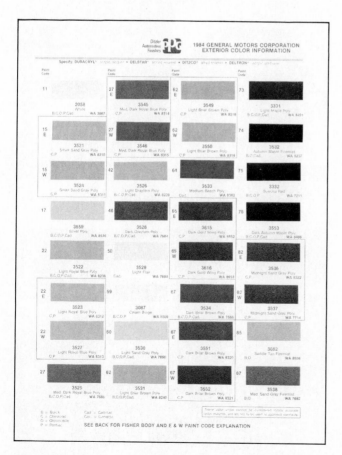

Fig. 33-9 A typical page from a color-chip book. (*Ditzler Automotive Finishes Division of PPG Industries, Inc.*)

quer. In addition, there are special primer-surfacers for aluminum and for galvanized steel surfaces.

Primer-surfacers are made in several colors. You would normally use a dark primer-surfacer if the topcoat is to be a dark paint. You would normally use a light primer-surfacer if the topcoat is to be a light paint. The color of the last coat of primer-surfacer should match, as nearly as possible, the color of the topcoat to be applied. Some jobs may require several coats of primer-surfacer.

≡ 33-22 PRIMER-SEALER

Primer-sealer provides a sealing film between the primer-surfacer and the topcoats. Sealers are desirable for some jobs and are not used for others. For example, if you apply enamel over lacquer, use a sealer first. This prevents the lacquer from bleeding through the enamel and giving the topcoats a spotty appearance. Also, if enamel primer-surfacer was used and the topcoat is to be lacquer, then a sealer should be applied before the lacquer topcoat is sprayed on.

If you apply lacquer over enamel, sealer is also recommended (Fig. 33-11). However, if you apply enamel over enamel, or lacquer over lacquer, a sealer is not generally required. But, if there are sand scratches present and they are not wet-sanded away (using a guide coat as described later), then a sealer often is used. It tends to prevent the sand scratches from showing through the topcoats. The reason is that the sealer prevents the thinner from getting to the undercoat covering the scratches. If thinner gets to the undercoat, it causes the primer-surfacer embedded in the scratches to swell. Since this undercoat is thicker than the undercoat on the surrounding unscratched surface, it swells more and will show through the topcoats.

Whether you use a sealer or not depends on the type and quality of the job you are doing. However, if you are building up the undercoat from bare metal, the sealer is applied last. For example, you may decide to use a primer. Then, to fill in the sand scratches, you use primer-surfacer. Finally, the primer-sealer is applied over the primer-surfacer to obtain the best possible color holdout (Fig. 33-12).

≡ 33-23 GUIDE COAT

At many body paint shops, a guide coat is sprayed on after the primer-surfacer coats have been applied. The purpose of the guide coat is to help the painter detect and eliminate sand scratches. If the primer-surfacer that has been applied is a dark color, then the guide coat should be a light color. If the primer-surfacer is a light color, then the guide coat should be dark. The pur-

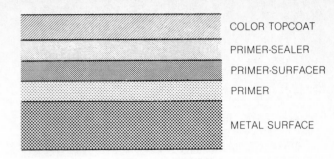

Fig. 33-12 To obtain the best possible color holdout, primer-sealer is applied over the primer-surfacer. Then the color topcoat is applied. (ATW)

pose is to provide contrast which will show up any imperfections in the surface.

The guide coat is a light mist coat. After it has flashed off, the surface is wet-sanded with a very fine sandpaper (400, for example). This sands off the guide coat. If there are any sand scratches, they will show up during the sanding, because traces of the guide coat will lie in these scratches. When scratches show up, sanding is continued until they are sanded out.

Figure 33-13 shows the paint technician wet-sanding a car hood that has had a guide coat sprayed on it. Note the rough, misty appearance of the surfaces

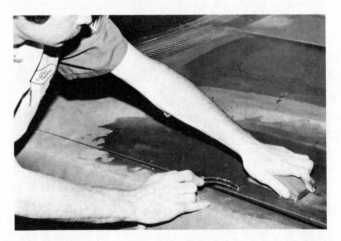

Fig. 33-13 Wet-sanding the guide coat from a car hood.

Fig. 33-14 An area that has had the guide coat sanded off, and is now ready for painting.

Fig. 33-11 When a surface painted with enamel is to be covered with lacquer, a sealer must be used between the two different paints. (Du Pont)

around the area being sanded. This is due to the guide coat, which goes on almost dry. Figure 33-14 is a close-up of an area that has been sanded to remove the guide coat. It is very smooth and ready to take the topcoat.

≡ 33-24 PAINT ADDITIVES

Many conditions may cause a painter to use an *additive* in the paint. When mixed with the paint, a very small amount of additive may make a great difference in how the paint acts. For example, additives can be used to speed up drying and improve gloss. Other additives slow drying. And others may lower the gloss.

Some additives perform several jobs, such as eliminate wrinkling, provide faster through-cure, and improve chemical resistance.

Additives that speed up curing and improve gloss are often called *hardeners*. Additives that are slow drying are called *retarders*. Additives that lower gloss are called *flatteners*. One of the most widely used paint additives is *fisheye eliminator*. When a small amount of fisheye eliminator is added to acrylic lacquer, the additive eliminates the effects of silicone contamination. Fisheye eliminator can also be added to acrylic enamel, if hardeners are not added.

─── REVIEW QUESTIONS ───

Select the *one* correct, best, or most probable answer to each question. You can find the answers in the section indicated at the end of each question.

1. General Motors cars are painted with   (≡33-2)
   a. acrylic enamel
   b. acrylic lacquer
   c. Duco
   d. reducer

2. Chrysler and Ford cars are painted with   (≡33-2)
   a. polyurethane enamel
   b. acrylic lacquer
   c. pigment
   d. acrylic enamel

3. The three basic ingredients of automotive body paints are   (≡33-3)
   a. metal chips, enamel, and reducer
   b. reducer, thinner, and compound
   c. pigment, binder, and vehicle
   d. vehicle, reducer, and enamel

4. At the assembly plant, lacquer is sprayed on and then the car is   (≡33-8)
   a. sandblasted
   b. baked at high temperature
   c. rubbed out with compound
   d. stored for 3 weeks to dry

5. A paint that requires addition of a chemical activator is
   a. polyurethane   (≡33-10)
   b. acrylic enamel
   c. acrylic lacquer
   d. Duco

CHAPTER 34
PREPARING THE SURFACE FOR PAINTING

After studying this chapter, you should be able to:

1. Describe the three basic types of paint job.
2. Explain how to prepare the surface for painting.
3. Discuss wet sanding and its purpose.
4. Explain how to determine the type of paint on the vehicle.
5. Describe the procedure of repainting a body panel.
6. Explain how to completely repaint a vehicle.

≡ 34-1 SURFACE PREPARATION

The surface requiring painting must be properly prepared so that it will take the undercoats and topcoats. Unless the surface is properly prepared, the paint job will be a failure. The auto paint shop handles vehicles that have been repaired in the body shop and also vehicles that need only paint work. Some paint jobs involve painting a panel or spot-painting only part of a panel. Other vehicles require complete repainting. In addition to handling on-vehicle paint jobs, the paint technicians may also paint detached parts. For example, a new fender might be painted before it is installed on a car. Or a detached door might have a new skin (outer panel) installed. It might be more convenient for the new panel to be painted before the door is reinstalled on the car.

≡ 34-2 TYPES OF PAINT JOB

There are three basic types of paint job. These are spot repair, panel repair, and complete repainting. In the spot-repair job, only the immediate area around the damage is repainted, not a complete panel. Figure 34-1 shows the preparation for a spot-repair job. Note that only the area around the panel has been masked. The painting will be confined to the small area arrowed in Fig. 34-1. To make this type of repair, the painter must be skilled in blending new paint into old. Further, the paint color must match accurately. Otherwise, the repair would show as a spot of different color on the panel.

In the panel-repair job, a complete panel is painted. A panel is defined as a surface which has a stopping point at the top, bottom, front, and rear. For example, Fig. 34-2 shows a right-fender paint job, masked in readiness for the undercoats and topcoats. The stopping places (where the masking is applied) are called *definition lines*. At the top, the definition line is the line where the upper trim is attached. At the front, the definition line is where the front end of the fender stops. At the bottom, the definition line is the line where the lower trim is attached. At the rear, the definition line is where the fender ends. Note that, at this point, the masking paper is tucked into the joint between the fender and the front of the door.

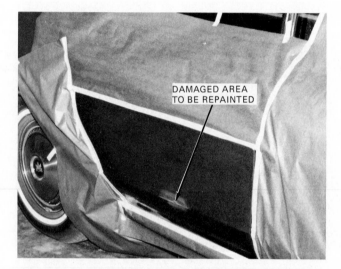

DAMAGED AREA TO BE REPAINTED

Fig. 34-1 Preparing to paint a spot repair.

AREA TO BE PAINTED

Fig. 34-2 Preparing a panel for repair.

It is easier to paint a panel than to make a spot repair. The entire panel between the definition lines is painted uniformly. You don't have to be particularly careful about the stopping points where you trigger the spray gun. (These are important in a spot-repair job.)

In the complete repainting job, you do the complete vehicle. In many shops, this includes painting the trunk area, door jambs, and other interior surfaces that were originally painted.

≡ 34-3 STEPS IN SURFACE PREPARATION

Before surface preparation for painting can begin, any metal damage must be straightened and filled. Then you are ready to prepare the surface for painting. Several steps are required. The actual procedure varies with the kind of paint repair job, and also with the type of paint already on the vehicle. The steps in surface preparation are listed below. Each step is described in detail in following sections.

1. Blow the dust off, including the dust between joints.

2. Wash the car. Dry it completely.

3. Clean the area to be repaired, using a wax-and-silicone remover to remove all traces of wax, tar, and polish.

4. Examine the type of damage and the condition of the paint. On some jobs, you will grind off the paint and featheredge out to good paint surrounding the damage. On other jobs, you will remove all the paint from the panel and paint the complete panel instead of making a spot paint repair. A third procedure would be to treat the old paint as necessary, and then spray the new paint over it. These alternatives are described later.

5. Reclean the area to be repainted with wax-and-silicone remover.

6. Clean the metal with a metal conditioner. This dissolves any rust or corrosion, and also slightly etches the metal.

7. Apply a suitable metal treatment, or conversion coating, to the surface to help prevent rust and to provide maximum adhesion of the primer.

≡ 34-4 DUSTING OFF THE VEHICLE

Use the air hose to blow the dust off the car. Blow into all joints and crevices to remove any dust that might have accumulated. This includes the joints between the hood and surrounding metal, the trunk lid and surrounding metal, and the joints around the doors. Unless this is done, some of the dust in these joints could blow out while you are spray-painting the car and could get on the wet paint. You would then have an extra paint repair job to do.

≡ 34-5 WASHING THE CAR

Use a mild detergent and water to wash off the car, or at least the area you must repair (Fig. 34-3). Washing removes all dust and dirt on the paint that compressed air will not remove. Also, getting all the dust off gives you a clear view of the paint color. Then, if you have to match paint chips from the paint book, you can make a more accurate match. Also, when masking, the tape will stick better to the clean surface.

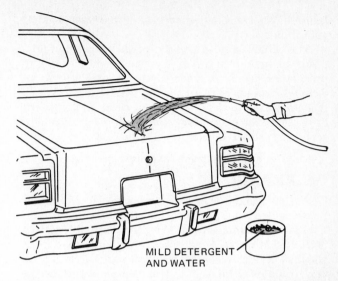

MILD DETERGENT AND WATER

Fig. 34-3 Wash the car with a solution of mild detergent and water.

≡ 34-6 USING A PRECLEANING SOLVENT (WAX-AND-GREASE REMOVER)

Clean the area to be repaired with precleaning solvent (Fig. 34-4). Use new, clean shop towels, or special paint-shop towels. Do not use cloths that have been laundered, because they may still have traces of grease or other materials. These could wipe onto the car surface and cause a paint failure.

The precleaning solution must be used regardless of whether or not the paint is to be ground off. If the painted area is sanded down before the wax or polish is removed, some of this material could be ground into the metal. Wherever there is a trace of grease, wax, or polish on the metal, the undercoat will not adhere. As a result, you would end up with a defective paint job. Even touching the cleaned surface with your fingers can leave oil on the surface which will cause a paint

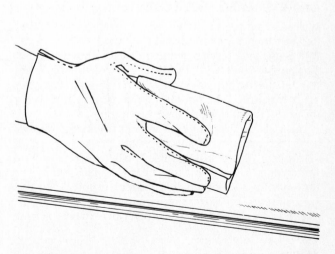

Fig. 34-4 Remove all remaining contaminants from the paint by cleaning it with a precleaning solution.

failure. This can happen even after you have washed your hands.

The proper way to use the precleaner is to fold a clean shop cloth in a pad (Fig. 34-4) and wet it with precleaner. Then rub the cloth on the area to be cleaned, rubbing hard enough to loosen the wax or polish. Immediately take a dry shop cloth and wipe the area. Repeat as necesssary to make sure the area to be repaired is clean. Use plenty of shop cloths.

≡ 34-7 DECIDING ON THE TYPE OF REPAIR

If you have taken the preceding steps, you probably have decided what has to be done to the damaged area. If it is a small damaged area in a panel, probably all that is needed is a spot-repair job. If the damage is larger, you may decide to repaint the whole panel. In this case, you would examine the undamaged paint and decide whether it should be removed or whether you can paint on top of it. Following sections discuss each of these possibilities.

≡ 34-8 PREPARING FOR A SPOT REPAIR

If only a small area of paint is damaged and the rest of the paint on the panel looks good, you will probably decide to do a spot repair (Fig. 34-1). The damage might have been caused when a stone was thrown by the car wheels or perhaps when a door of another car hit the panel in a parking lot. Since there is no metal damage, all that is necessary to prepare the damaged area is to sand it, featheredging out into the good paint.

If the damage is minor, wet-sand it lightly, removing only the topcoat around the damage (wet sanding is described in ≡34-9). Featheredge out into the good paint. Featheredging takes a special touch to get it right. Don't sand *out* into the good paint. Start the sanding strokes on the good paint and carry them into the damaged area. Sand *into* the damaged area. Try not to cut through the undercoat. If you do, you will have to treat the bare metal with metal conditioner, followed by a conversion coating. Then you will have to coat the bare spot with primer-surfacer.

≡ 34-9 WET SANDING

Wet sanding requires the use of very fine sandpaper (400 or finer, for example) and plenty of water. Figure 33-13 shows a painter wet-sanding the hood of a car. The purpose of wet sanding is to remove sand scratches left by the earlier use of a coarser sandpaper. Also, slightly scuffing the remaining old paint or undercoat improves the adhesion of the new paint.

In wet sanding, the water continuously washes away the products of sanding that could cause other scratches. Wet sanding is used on bare metal and on undercoats to smooth them before application of the topcoats. Wet sanding is used after the guide coat has been sprayed on (Figs. 33-13 and 33-14). Use 400-grit paper for wet-sanding primer-surfacer when acrylic lacquer is to be the topcoat.

NOTE: Different painters recommend different grades of sandpaper for final wet sanding, depending

on the type of topcoat to be applied. For enamel, they recommend 320 paper. For lacquer, some recommend 400 paper. Other painters believe that the paper for wet sanding cannot be too fine. They recommend 600-grit paper.

≡ 34-10 DETERMINING TYPE OF OLD PAINT

Before selecting the type of paint you will use to make the spot repair, you must determine what the old finish is. Also, you must select the right color of new paint to match the old.

If the vehicle has not been repainted, you can check the body identification plate (Figs. 33-5 and 33-6) to determine the code numbers and letters identifying the type and color of paint used originally. If the vehicle has been repainted and you cannot identify the type of paint used, there is another method of determining whether the old paint is lacquer or enamel. A container of special compound supplied by the paint manufacturer is required for the test. Put a little of the compound on a shop cloth and rub a small area of the old paint with it. If the paint is lacquer, it will dissolve and come off on the cloth. Enamel will not dissolve.

Another test can be made using lacquer thinner. When rubbed on the old paint, lacquer thinner will dissolve nitrocellulose lacquer very quickly and acrylic lacquer with hard rubbing. However, lacquer thinner does not dissolve alkyd enamel, acrylic enamel, or polyurethane finishes.

After you have determined the type and color of paint, you can mix it or order it from your paint supplier. The paint supplier will then deliver the paint, either factory-mixed or custom-mixed.

≡ 34-11 REMOVING OLD PAINT

If the damage to the panel has been extensive, then the whole panel should be repainted. If the sheet metal has been straightened or patched, there will be areas which have been filled with plastic body filler. However, some parts of the panel still may have the original paint on them. This paint can be removed so that you start with the bare metal and refinish the complete panel. Or you can featheredge into this paint. Either way, you will paint the complete panel.

There are three methods that can be used to remove unwanted old paint. These are:

1. Sandblasting
2. Chemically stripping
3. Grinding and sanding

Each of these methods is described below.

≡ 34-12 SANDBLASTING

Sandblasting is seldom used in the auto body shop. It is used on trucks and industrial equipment with large areas of rust to remove. It can also be used in areas that cannot be reached with a sander or grinder. However, sandblasting will easily damage plastic panels beyond repair. In addition, all chrome, glass, and plastic must be double-masked for protection.

☰ 34-13 USING PAINT STRIPPER

Old paint can be removed by using a liquid chemical paint remover which strips off the paint. The *paint stripper* is brushed on and allowed to stand for a short time. The paint bubbles, and then it is scraped off with a putty knife (Fig. 34-5) or washed off with water.

Many painters prefer to remove paint by sanding and grinding, instead of using paint stripper. Sanding and grinding is usually more convenient and less messy. For example, paint stripper will soften any plastic body filler, which will then have to be replaced. Also, the use of paint stripper requires protective clothing, including safety goggles, respirator, cap, coveralls, and industrial rubber gloves.

— CAUTION

Always wear full-body protective clothing when using paint stripper. You must keep paint stripper and its fumes off your skin, out of your eyes, and out of your lungs.

When using paint stripper, you must know the type of surface you are stripping. Paint stripper may attack plastic, glass, previous repairs, and adhesives. Therefore, always follow the safety cautions and directions on the label of the container.

☰ 34-14 GRINDING AND SANDING

The most common method of removing old paint and rust is by grinding and sanding. After the sanding job is finished with an orbital sander using a fine grade of sandpaper, the area to be painted should be wet-sanded and featheredged (☰34-9). When power-sanding or hand-sanding, mask off adjacent panels to protect them from accidental damage (Fig. 34-6).

☰ 34-15 METAL-TREATMENT PROCESS

After the old paint has been removed, and wet sanding has been completed, the panel should be washed off with water and dried. Then the area to be repainted should be cleaned with a wax-and-grease remover (☰34-6). After this, steel, aluminum, and galvanized panels must receive a two-step treatment (Fig. 34-7). The exposed surface must be treated with a *metal cleaner*, or *conditioner*, and then washed with a *metal treatment* or *conversion coating*. These steps are described in the following sections.

☰ 34-16 METAL CLEANER, OR CONDITIONER

Bare metal should be given a two-step treatment and then primed as soon as possible. The less time that bare metal is exposed, the less likely that the surface will begin to rust or become contaminated. Metal cleaner, or conditioners, provides a chemically clean surface. It dissolves any microscopic rust or corrosion which might have started. It also slightly etches the metal, for better adhesion of the undercoat. The etching provides more surface area for the undercoat to grip when it is sprayed on. The undercoat cannot grip a very smooth

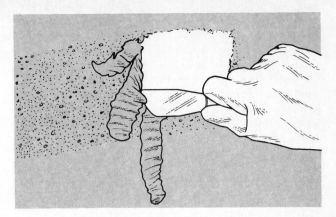
Fig. 34-5 Removing old paint that has been treated with paint stripper.

Fig. 34-6 When sanding, mask off adjacent panels to protect them from accidental damage.

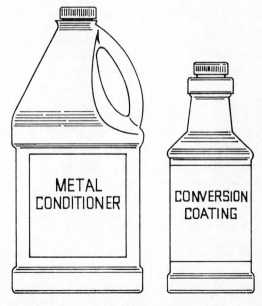
Fig. 34-7 Before applying primer, a bare metal surface must be treated with a metal cleaner, or conditioner, and then washed with a metal treatment or conversion coating.

surface as tightly as a rougher, etched surface. Always use metal conditioner on a bare metal panel *after* plastic body filler has been applied.

Mix the metal conditioner with water in a plastic bucket, following the directions on the container. Then apply the solution to the surface with a cloth or sponge. Use a stiff brush or steel wool, if you can see any rust. Then, while the surface is still wet, wipe it dry with clean cloths.

— CAUTION —————————————

Always wear rubber gloves and goggles when working with metal conditioner. It is an acid that could damage your eyes and attack your skin if safety precautions are not followed. Always read and follow the safety instructions printed on the container label.

≡ 34-17 CONVERSION COATING

After a metal panel is cleaned with metal cleaner, or conditioner (≡34-16), a metal treatment or conversion coating should be applied. Like metal conditioner, the conversion coating is also a liquid chemical. When applied over the metal conditioner, the conversion coating performs two jobs. First, it chemically coats (or reacts with) the metal surface to provide the proper paint-binding surface for primer and primer-surfacer. Second, the conversion coating acts to inhibit the formation of rust and corrosion.

To use the conversion coating, follow the directions on the label. Pour the amount needed into a plastic container. Using an abrasive pad, apply the conversion coating to the metal surface. No diluting or mixing of the conversion coating may be required.

Allow the conversion coating to remain on the surface for 2 to 5 minutes. Work on only a small area so that the solution can be wiped on and rinsed off before it dries. (If the surface dries before rinsing, recoat it.) Then rinse off the surface with cold water, or wipe the surface with a damp sponge or cloth rinsed in clean water. Then, using more clean cloths, wipe the surface dry, or allow it to air dry. Now the surface is ready for spraying with primer or primer-surfacer.

The conversion coating may cause the metal surface to turn color. This is a normal condition. It is the finish to which the undercoat should be applied. Steel may turn gray. Galvanized steel and zinc may turn dark gray. Aluminum may turn a gold color.

NOTE: Different types of conversion coating are available, depending on the type of metal surface to be treated. Steel and iron, galvanized steel and zinc, and aluminum are types of metals for which a special conversion coating is required.

— CAUTION —————————————

Always follow the safety cautions on the container. Wear safety goggles or eye protection when working with or around any liquid chemical. Adequate ventilation is also necessary.

≡ 34-18 APPLYING THE UNDERCOATS

After the panel has been washed with water and dried, it should be wiped off with a tack rag. Then the panel should be masked out. The glass and metal surfaces around the area to be refinished should be covered with masking tape and paper (≡31-7). Then the panel is ready for undercoating and painting.

Apply primer-surfacer to any bare metal or areas where the original paint and primer have been sanded thin. Allow the primer-surfacer coats to dry. If you see any small nicks or scratches that the primer-surfacer has not filled, fill them with spot putty. Wet-sand the panel again, with special attention to the areas where primer-surfacer has been applied. A guide coat, applied before this final sanding, will help locate any sand scratches that should be sanded out (≡33-23).

≡ 34-19 PREPARING A DETACHED PANEL

Replacement panels from the manufacturer—such as fenders, door skins, quarter panels, hoods, and trunk lids—are given a coating at the factory. This protects them from rust and corrosion. However, the coating is not always primer. If not, the paint colorcoat cannot be applied until after primer is applied. Do not remove the factory coating, but check it carefully for imperfections. These must be sanded (and treated as described earlier) before the complete panel is sprayed with primer. Paint sprayed directly onto the factory coating will not adhere properly.

In deciding how to prepare a detached panel, first note the method to be used to attach the panel. If the panel is to be bolted into place (like a door, for example), then the best procedure usually is to treat and paint the panel off the car (Fig. 34-8). If the panel is to be spot-welded into place, it should be installed on the vehicle first and then painted. Spot welding will probably create some sheet-metal damage. This must be repaired before the paint job.

There is one refinement here that is recommended but not always performed. This is drilling holes in the panel for the trim. Fenders, for example, usually come without trim holes drilled. If these holes are drilled before the fender is painted, the bare metal exposed by the drilling will also be painted. Otherwise, the bare metal provides a starting point for rust.

The painting of the detached panel proceeds in the same manner as the repainting of a panel on the car. The entire panel should be wet-sanded with 360 or 400 sandpaper. The panel should be washed off with water and dried. Any spots which are sanded down to bare metal should be treated with metal conditioner and conversion coating. Then the panel should be cleaned with a wax-and-grease remover. Primer-surfacer should be applied to any bare spots or areas where the original primer has been sanded almost to the metal. If there are small imperfections such as nicks, they should be filled with spot or glaze putty.

After the primer-surfacer coats have dried, wet-sand the panel. One recommendation is to use 320 sandpaper if the topcoat is to be enamel, 400 sandpaper if the topcoat is to be lacquer. Reclean with a wax-and-

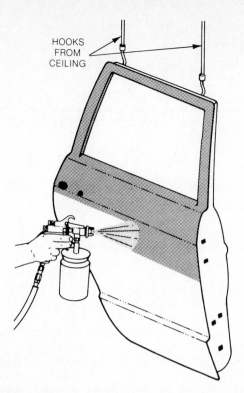

HOOKS FROM CEILING

Fig. 34-8 If a panel is to be bolted into place, treat and paint the panel off the car. *(ATW)*

grease remover. After the panel has dried, wipe it with a tack cloth. It is now ready for the topcoat.

NOTE: *Plastic components do not require any special chemical treatment, such as the metal conditioner and conversion coating required by metals. However, certain plastics do require special paints and finishes.*

≡ 34-20 PREPARING A VEHICLE FOR COMPLETE REPAINTING

Sometimes the owner of a car which has been in a collision will want a complete repaint job. There are also other reasons for a complete repaint job: The owner may want a different color. The original paint on the car may have begun to deteriorate, so it looks bad. There may be rust spots which the owner wants repaired, so an extensive repair and complete repaint job are in order. At any rate, assume that the car comes to the paint shop after all repairs on the body panels have been made. All trim is removed.

The next step is a careful examination of the original paint to determine its condition. If it is in good condition, it can serve as a base for the new paint. If it is in poor condition, then it will have to be removed either by grinding and sanding or by the use of a paint stripper.

One method of checking the adhesion of the paint to the metal is to sand through the paint in one spot. Then featheredge from the bare metal out to the original paint. Examine the featheredge. If the thin edge of the paint does not flake off, it is binding well to the metal. Make this check in several places, especially along the lower edges of the doors, rocker panels, and quarter panels. These are places where rust frequently begins. Sometimes the lower edge of a panel starts to rust from the inside. Rust may be well advanced before it shows through the paint. Sanding through the paint in any spot where rust has started will usually show up the damage. If there are rusted areas, they should be patched as described previously.

The preparation of the body for repainting is basically the same as the preparation of a panel for repainting, as covered in previous sections. The major difference is that there is more surface to work on. However, the steps in the process are the same. Wherever bare metal is exposed, use a metal conditioner, conversion coating, and then a primer-surfacer as previously described.

─── REVIEW QUESTIONS ───

Select the *one* correct, best, or most probable answer to each question. You can find the answers in the section indicated at the end of each question.

1. The three basic types of paint job are (≡34-2)
   a. spot repair, panel repair, and complete repainting
   b. enamel, lacquer, and metal flake
   c. precleaning, metal conditioning, and sealing
   d. car, truck, and van painting

2. The chemical used to remove any trace of wax and polish is called (≡34-3)
   a. metal conditioner
   b. sealer
   c. primer
   d. precleaning solvent

3. Wet sanding requires the use of (≡34-9)
   a. very fine sandpaper
   b. very coarse sandpaper
   c. a wire brush
   d. plenty of oil

4. Old paint can be removed by grinding and sanding, or with (≡34-11)
   a. paint sealer
   b. putty knife
   c. paint stripper
   d. primer-surfacer

5. Mechanic A says the main job of metal conditioner is to dissolve rust. Mechanic B says the main job of the conversion coating is to promote adhesion. Who is right? (≡34-16 and 34-17)
   a. mechanic A
   b. mechanic B
   c. both A and B
   d. neither A nor B

CHAPTER 35
TYPICAL PAINT JOBS

After studying this chapter, you should be able to:

1. Explain how to do a spot repair.
2. Describe the procedure for painting a panel.
3. Discuss how to repaint a complete vehicle.
4. Explain how to use metallic paint.
5. Describe how to apply a clearcoat.

≡ 35-1 DOING A SPOT REPAIR

Figure 35-1 shows the paint technician pointing to a small nick in the paint of a door. This probably was caused when the door was hit by the door of another car. As a first step in this minor repair job, the immediate area is sanded. Figure 35-2 shows the technician feeling the featheredging from the bare metal to the original good paint. This minor repair job does not require all the steps listed in ≡34-8, which covers preparing an area for a spot repair. With the minor job shown in Fig. 35-1, wet sanding is not always needed. However, metal conditioner and conversion coating should be used on bare metal, followed by primer-surfacer. Then the technician uses the spray gun to colorcoat the area being repaired, feathering the paint out on both sides of the repair. The paint used matches the color of the original and is of the same type as the original. If the paint is lacquer, it is compounded after it has dried.

≡ 35-2 PAINTING A PANEL

The various steps required to prepare a body panel for painting are described in ≡34-19. After these steps have been taken, the car is masked to protect sur-rounding metal and glass from the spray. Then the proper paint of the proper color is sprayed onto the panel.

Wait long enough between coats for the paint to flash off (for the thinner or reducer to largely evaporate). If you don't wait long enough, the paint could sag or run. If you wait too long, the new coat will not blend properly with the old. It is often a matter of judgment how long to wait, and this judgment comes from experience.

You can test the paint after you have sprayed on a coat and waited for a few minutes. Touch the masking tape adjacent to a sprayed area. If the paint is still slippery, wait longer. If the paint is tacky or sticky, but not wet, it is time to spray on another coat.

If lacquer is applied, it will require compounding after it has dried. Enamel should not be compounded or polished for a month after it has been put on.

≡ 35-3 THE COMPLETE REPAINTING JOB

Repainting a complete vehicle requires a plan. You must know where you will start, where you go from

Fig. 35-1 A small nick in the paint.   **Fig. 35-2** Feeling the featheredge.

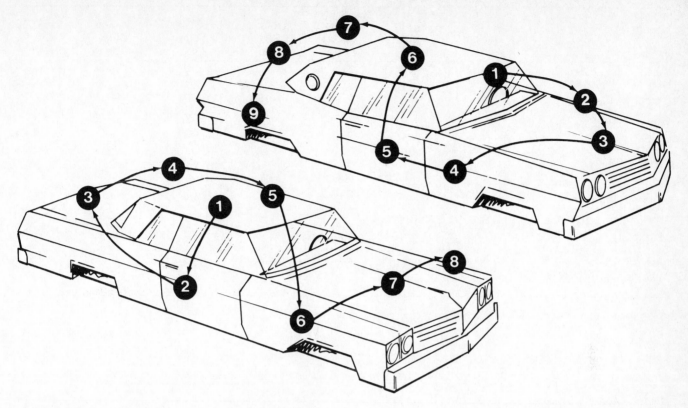

Fig. 35-3 *Spraying sequences for the complete paint job.*

there, and the sequence in which the body panels will be painted. Figure 35-3 shows two sequences. Whatever sequence you select, follow it carefully. By the time you have circled the car once, the paint where you started should be flashed off, so you can start again with the second coat.

Before starting on the main sequence, paint the hidden edges such as the door jambs, trunk-lid edges, and hood edges. Use low air pressure to spray these to prevent overspray. Weatherstripping and the car interior should be adequately masked to prevent paint from getting to the wrong places. Leave the doors, trunk lid, and hood slightly ajar to permit them to dry without sticking.

Most painters prefer to do half the roof to start with and then come back to the other half after they have partly circled the car. Whatever the sequence used, the plan should minimize the blending required on a panel between coats. You should try to paint complete panels with each coat and not do half a panel later.

≡ 35-4 SPRAYING METALLIC PAINT

Metallic paint is described in ≡33-17. The way the paint is sprayed on determines how light or dark the paint will be, and also how iridescent, or sparkling, the paint will appear (Fig. 33-4). If you must match the original paint, you must not only match the color of the pigment but you must also spray the paint on correctly. This means careful attention to the amount of thinner used, the adjustment of the spray gun, and the manner in which you handle the gun.

The first step is getting a can of the right paint. Usually this would be a can of factory-mixed paint of the proper code number or letters. The code is found on the body identification plate (≡33-18). Before spraying, the paint can must be agitated on a shaker for at least 10 minutes to make sure the pigment and metallic particles are well mixed. After the can is opened, the paint should be stirred with a paint paddle to make certain it is thoroughly mixed. Then add the proper amount of thinner or reducer as recommended on the can.

NOTE: Straining metallic paint through an excessively fine strainer can remove metallic flakes. This will change the appearance of the paint.

Next spray a test panel and allow it to dry. Wash a small area of the original paint on the car and polish it, if necessary, to remove any chalk and bring up the gloss. A low-gloss finish will reflect the light differently from a high-gloss finish and this changes the appearance.

Now compare the test panel with the original finish. If the color on the test panel is too light (dry), make one or more of the following adjustments to darken the metallic color:

1. Open the fluid adjustment on the spray gun.

2. Decrease the fan pattern on the spray gun by adjusting the fan-adjustment screw.

3. Decrease the air pressure to the gun.

4. Slow down the speed with which you move the spray gun across the panel.

5. Decrease the distance between the gun and the work.

6. Use a thinner or reducer that evaporates more slowly.

7. Decrease the time between coats.

Fresh Color	If Too Dark Add:	If Too Light Add:	If Too Green Add:	If Too Red Add:	If Too Yellow Add:	If Too Blue Add:	If Too Gray Add:
Gray metallic	E	L	F	H	K	F	—
Blue metallic	E	K	G	H	—	H	K
Green metallic	E	H	K	H	K	J	H
Red	D	F	—	—	F	D	—
Maroon metallic	E	G	—	B	G	C	—
Yellow	A	J	A&C	H	—	—	—
Ivory or white	A	—	C	H	A&K	—	A
Tan or brown metallic	E	B	G	B	G	—	—
Pastel blue	A	K	G&A	H&A	—	H&A	K
Pastel green	A	H	K&A	H&A	K	J	H
Pastel tan or brown	A	B	G	B	G&A	—	—

Fig. 35-4 Shading chart for acrylic enamel and acrylic lacquer. *(Ford Motor Company)*

If the color on the test panel is too dark (wet), make one or more of the following adjustments to lighten the metallic color:

1. Close the fluid adjustment on the spray gun.
2. Increase the fan pattern of the gun.
3. Increase the air pressure to the gun.
4. Speed up the spray stroke. Move the gun across the panel more rapidly.
5. Increase the distance between the gun and the work.
6. Use a thinner or reducer that evaporates more rapidly.
7. Increase the time between coats.

If you cannot get a good match after taking the steps listed above, the original finish may have changed color. This can result from exposure to weather over a period of time. Then you can use special tints to change the color of the new paint. If the paint is enamel, be sure to use an enamel tinting color. If the paint is lacquer, use a lacquer tinting color. Figure 35-4 is a shading chart for acrylic enamel and acrylic lacquer. Figure 35-5 lists the tint-color-code letters and their colors.

Your paint supplier might do a quicker and more accurate job of tinting the paint to match the old finish. To get the match, drive the car or send a chip from the car to the supplier.

☰ 35-5 REPAIRING WATER-BASED ACRYLIC ENAMEL

Some cars are painted with a water-based acrylic enamel. The body identification plate identifies this type of paint in the paint code number. This paint is repairable with acrylic lacquer in the usual manner. However, you must sand the finish and apply sealer over the enamel before the lacquer is sprayed on. This means that spot repairs are not possible. If a paint re-

Code	Color
A	White
B	Gold
C	Indo orange
D	Moly orange
E	Aluminum
F	Mono red
G	Indo maroon
H	Green toner
J	Yellow green toner
K	Blue toner
L	Black

Fig. 35-5 Tint color-code letters for acrylic-enamel and acrylic-lacquer shading chart in Fig. 35-4. *(Ford Motor Company)*

pair must be made, the complete panel, to the nearest definition lines, must be painted.

The procedure recommended is to clean the complete panel with precleaning solvent. Then wet-sand the finish with 400 sandpaper, and wash and dry the car. Apply the sealer recommended by the manufacturer. Paint the panel with acrylic lacquer in the usual manner. After the lacquer has dried, compound it.

☰ 35-6 REPAIRING A CLEARCOAT

Many new cars are factory-finished using a two-step process to obtain the final finish. This process is called *basecoat/clearcoat*, or *colorcoat/clearcoat*. The topcoat is applied normally over the undercoats. Then ad-

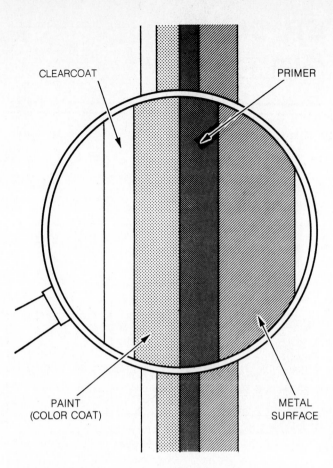

CLEARCOAT

PRIMER

PAINT
(COLOR COAT)

METAL
SURFACE

ditional clearcoats are sprayed over the topcoat (Fig. 35-6). Follow the manufacturer's instructions as to when and how much clear to apply. The result will be a deep, lustrous, glossy finish.

Making a clearcoat paint repair is the same as repairing other painted surfaces. First, determine that the vehicle has a clearcoat by checking the paint code number on the body identification plate. If the finish has a clearcoat, inspect the problem to determine if the defect is in the clearcoat itself, or under the clearcoat and in the paint. If the damage or sanding goes through the clearcoat, then the panel will require refinishing to the nearest definition lines. Minor scratches and nicks in the clearcoat can be sanded and buffed out the same way as on a painted surface without a clearcoat.

When spraying a clearcoat, apply only the recommended number of coats. For example, Ford recommends two coats on some cars. Too many clearcoats can alter the color and later cause cracking and other problems, in addition to wasting material.

Fig. 35-6 Many new cars now have an additional clearcoat sprayed over the topcoat while it is still wet. *(Chrysler Corporation)*

REVIEW QUESTIONS

Select the *one* correct, best, or most probable answer to each question. You can find the answers in the section indicated at the end of each question.

1. When the thinner or reducer has largely evaporated, the paint is said to (≡35-2)
   a. have dried
   b. still be wet
   c. have flashed off
   d. turned chalky

2. The type of paint that requires compounding after it dries is (≡35-2)
   a. lacquer
   b. enamel
   c. pigment
   d. binder

3. Straining metallic paint through a fine strainer may
   a. improve the finish (≡35-4)
   b. prevent the paint from drying normally
   c. break up the metal flakes
   d. remove metal flakes from the paint

4. A water-based acrylic-enamel finish can be repaired by spraying with sealer and then applying a topcoat of
   a. acrylic enamel (≡35-5)
   b. acrylic lacquer
   c. clearcoat
   d. polyurethane enamel

5. A car with colorcoat/clearcoat has been scraped, with bare metal showing on a door panel. Painter A says a spot repair can be made on the damaged area. Painter B says use two coats of acrylic lacquer to repair the paint, instead of using a clearcoat. Who is right? (≡35-6)
   a. painter A
   b. painter B
   c. both A and B
   d. neither A nor B

CHAPTER 36

PAINT PROBLEMS

After studying this chapter, you should be able to:

1. Name and identify the most common types of paint problems.

2. Explain the possible causes of each type of paint problem.

3. Discuss the prevention of each paint problem.

4. Describe how to repair each type of paint problem.

≡ 36-1 POSSIBLE PAINT PROBLEMS

There are many different troubles that might occur with a paint job. Some of these troubles are caused by using the wrong materials, or by using the right materials in the wrong way. Some come from improper preparation of the surface for painting. Whatever the cause, this chapter describes paint troubles and their causes. In addition, it explains the things to do to prevent or correct the troubles that are discussed. For convenience of locating specific troubles, the conditions are described in alphabetical order, starting with ≡36-2, Bleeding. The following paint problems are covered in this chapter:

- Bleeding (≡36-2)
- Blisters, Bubbles, Pop-ups (≡36-3)
- Blushing (≡36-4)
- Chalking, Dulling (≡36-5)
- Chipping (≡36-6)
- Color Mismatch, Mottle (≡36-7)
- Cracking, Checking (≡36-8)
- Craters, Fisheyes (≡36-9)
- Dirt in Paint (≡36-10)
- Foreign Material on Surface (≡36-11)
- Industrial Fallout (≡36-12)
- Lifting (≡36-13)
- Metal-Finishing Marks and Sand Scratches (≡36-14)
- Molding Installation Damage or Rust (≡36-15)
- Orange Peel (≡36-16)
- Overspray (≡36-17)
- Peeling (≡36-18)
- Poor Drying, Hardness (≡36-19)
- Rusting (≡36-20)
- Sags, Runs (≡36-21)
- Scratches (≡36-22)
- Sealer, Deadener under Paint (≡36-23)
- Stains, Tarnish, Fading (≡36-24)
- Thin Paint, No Paint (≡36-25)
- Water Spotting (≡36-26)
- Wrinkling (≡36-27)

≡ 36-2 BLEEDING

Bleeding is the result of colored soluble hues or pigments in the old finish, or undercoat, which dissolve in the solvents of the refinish paint, causing it to go off color. This is usually a problem only when a color

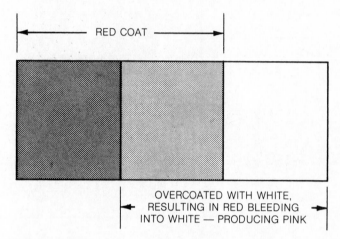

Fig. 36-1 Bleeding paint. *(Rinshed-Mason Company)*

change is involved in repainting. It also usually occurs only with maroon or red original finishes (Fig. 36-1).

CAUSE

Bleeding is caused by the solubility of the dyes or pigments used in previous paint applications. There is nothing you can do to change the solubility of an old paint coat. However, a few precautions can be used to reduce bleeding problems.

PREVENTION

1. Before repainting over a color suspected of being a bleeder, spray a small area with the new color. Bleeding will generally appear in a few minutes if the old finish is a bleeder. If it is a bleeder, either remove the old finish or use a "bleeder sealer" before applying the finish coats.

2. When using refinish materials which are known to be bleeders, never allow overspray to fall on any other vehicles. Also, thoroughly clean your equipment after spraying a bleeder to avoid contaminating subsequent colors.

REPAIR

The best way to repair a bleeding paint job is to remove the paint and refinish. Mild cases of bleeding can often be corrected by spraying a bleeder sealer followed by additional finish coats.

≡ 36-3 BLISTERS, BUBBLES, POP-UPS

Blistering is the formation of many small eruptions in the finish and may occur between the metal and the undercoats or between the undercoats and the enamel topcoat. Blisters usually follow one of two distribution patterns: usually they are either uniformly distributed over a comparatively large area or concentrated in a localized area in the shape of a water spot or drip streak. Sometimes they are so small that they are difficult to identify without using a magnifying glass. On other cars, blisters may be confused with dirt. To verify the condition, prick the suspected area with a sharp point, and note whether a void (hole) or water exists. If so, blistering is confirmed. As the problem progresses, it may be accompanied by peeling if the eruption flakes off and by rusting if the blister extends down to the metal. Figure 36-2 shows blisters near the rear edge of a door.

A pit has the appearance of a void in the base metal or undercoat that is not filled or covered with paint. "Pop-up" is the term applied to a problem in the paint film around a pit. It results from the formation of a bubble in wet paint over the pit. If the bubble does not break, it is called a pop-up. If the bubble does break while the paint is still wet, a craterlike ring is formed.

The causes, prevention, and repair of blisters, bubbles, and pop-ups are indicated below.

CAUSES

1. Moisture or contamination on the surface such as water, oil, grease, tar, or silicone
2. Moisture in the spray lines
3. Rust under the surface
4. Not enough drying time of undercoat

PREVENTION

1. Clean the surface thoroughly. Use a metal conditioner on bare metal. Use wax-and-silicone remover on old finishes. Keep bare hands off bare metal and primed surface.
2. Make sure all the water is wiped off the surface after wet sanding.
3. Drain air compressors, transformers, and lines daily.
4. Make sure the undercoat is dry before applying either more undercoat or topcoats. Failure to do this can trap solvents under the film and cause blisters.

REPAIR

The only way to repair a blistered finish is to remove the blisters to their full depth and repaint.

Pop-ups found in factory finishes sometimes can be repaired by sanding, polishing, and buffing.

If the pop-up is so large that it cannot be removed by light sanding, polishing, and buffing, it will be necessary to fill the defect with air-dry lacquer applied with a fine-tipped brush.

An excess of lacquer should be applied to completely fill the void after drying (drying time can be accelerated by using a heat gun). After the lacquer is dry, lightly sand it to level it out to the depth of the original surface.

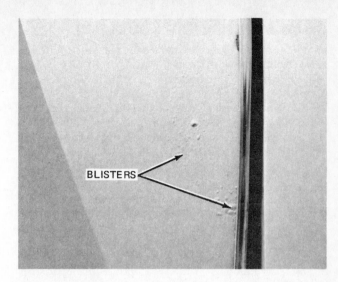

Fig. 36-2 Bubbles, blisters, and pop-ups.

Then polish and buff. In extreme cases, it may be necessary to remove the blemish and repaint.

≡ 36-4 BLUSHING

This condition occurs during or after acrylic lacquer is applied in hot, humid weather. Some of the fast-drying thinner evaporates rapidly. This lowers the surface temperature, causing the moisture in the air to condense in and on the paint film. This gives the finish a dull, hazy, or cloudy look (Fig. 36-3).

CAUSES

1. Moisture droplets trapped in the wet paint film
2. Excessive air pressure at the gun
3. Too fast a thinner

PREVENTION

1. In hot, humid weather, try to paint early in the morning.
2. Reduce air pressure to minimize cooling effect of the spray.
3. Use a slow-evaporating thinner that is suitable for the temperature and humidity.

REPAIR

Add 1 to 2 ounces of retarder to each quart of thinned or reduced color. Then apply a final coat.

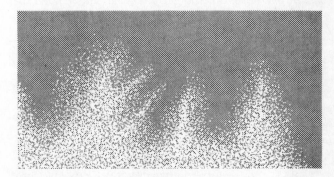

Fig. 36-3 Blushing paint. (Ditzler Automotive Finishes Division of PPG Industries, Inc.)

≡ 36-5 CHALKING, DULLING

This condition may be called poor gloss or no luster. The terms describe a paint durability problem which may show up in extended service (6 to 24 months). Chalking or dulling is usually confined to the horizontal surfaces of the vehicle such as the hood, tops of fenders, roof, tops of quarter panels, and deck lid. Chalking is the presence of loose, nonadherent pigment on the finish. Dulling is a loss of luster (Fig. 36-4).

CAUSES

1. Dry spray resulting from improper spray techniques (high air pressure, low paint flow, wide air fan, gun distance too great, etc.), poor reducing solvent (evaporation too fast, low solvency, etc.), or an excessive amount of reducer or thinner.

2. Poor holdout of undercoat and resulting absorption of topcoats, which may also be accompanied by sand scratches showing excessively.

3. Dry overspray falling on incompletely masked surfaces adjacent to the one being repainted.

4. Application of paint to a surface contaminated with wax, oil, grease, soap, etc.

5. Use of abrasives which are too coarse when sanding the undercoat.

6. Application of topcoat to a heavily chalked or checked finish without adequate sanding.

7. Applying material from a can which had been previously opened and used but which had been improperly mixed. The remaining material would have an excess of pigment in proportion to the vehicle remaining and therefore would have low gloss.

8. Mixing improper additives, such as flatting agents, with the finishes.

9. Applying topcoat to primer, primer-surfacer, or spot or glaze putty which is not sufficiently dried.

10. Insufficient topcoat film thickness.

PREVENTION

1. Use spray techniques and reducing solvents which will provide a wet film and good flow-out.

2. Use undercoats (primer, primer-surfacer, sealer, and putties) which are formulated for the particular refinishing material employed—lacquer or enamel. Also use all materials from the same source of manufacture. Using a sealer coat is good insurance against poor holdout.

3. Carefully mask adjacent surfaces. If refinish paint overspray should get on old finish, remove the overspray before it dries with enamel reducer or lacquer thinner.

4. Thoroughly clean all surfaces to be painted, using a wax-and-silicone remover.

5. Use fine abrasive, such as 400 grit, in all final sanding of the old finish or undercoats before applying refinish coats.

6. Completely sand off all old chalked or checked original finish.

7. Always be sure that all materials are completely mixed in the original package before using.

8. Do not use unknown additives. Use only those recommended by the manufacturer.

Fig. 36-4 Chalking and dull paint. *(Ford Motor Company)*

9. Be sure undercoats have been sufficiently air- or force-dried in line with supplier's recommendations before applying finish coats.

10. Always apply sufficient undercoat and topcoat to provide a full, glossy finish. Low film thickness of either can lead to a dull coating.

REPAIR

Poor gloss encountered in original finishes or refinishing can usually be improved by polishing with a fine compound and buffing. However, the polishing and buffing should take place only after the finish has become thoroughly dry and hard. If this does not produce the desired gloss, refinishing will be necessary.

≡ 36-6 CHIPPING

This condition may also be called stone bruise. The problem represents damage resulting from the impact of a sharp object which removes some of the finish. It may be caused from such things as road gravel, misaligned door, deck lid, tailgate or hood edges, or a sharp tool striking a painted surface. If the impact is light, only the topcoat will be removed and the red or gray primer will show. If the impact is severe, the entire finish will be removed, exposing bare metal, and early rusting will result (Fig. 36-5).

REPAIR

If the chipping is minor and confined to an edge or isolated location, it can be repaired by brush touch-up. If the chipping is centrally located in a highly visible area, it must be repaired by repainting.

≡ 36-7 COLOR MISMATCH, MOTTLE

This condition may also be called off-color, wrong color, streaked, flooding, or blotchy. "Color mismatch" is the term applied to the appearance of adjacent areas that

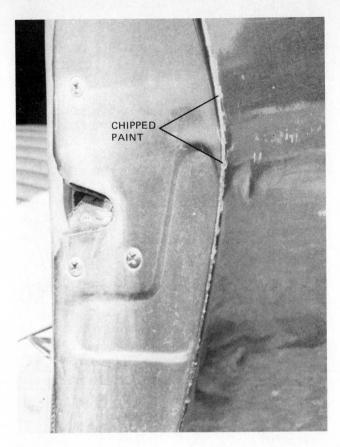

Fig. 36-5 Chipped paint.

Fig. 36-6 Mottled paint. *(Ford Motor Company)*

do not match. Mismatch of two different panels can result under the following conditions:

1. If the panels were painted with two different batches of topcoat which were two different shades

2. If the color of the undercoat shows through on one panel

3. In the case of metallic colors, if the adjacent panels were not sprayed with the same degree of wetness

The terms "mottled," "flooding," and "streaking" are applied to metallic colors and describe the appearance of light and dark areas within a panel (Fig. 36-6). These differences depend on the wetness or dryness of the coating during application.

CAUSES

1. Improper spraying techniques
2. Refinish color not thoroughly agitated
3. Insufficient hiding
4. Applying the topcoat to a cold surface or in a cold room
5. Failure to use a mist coat on metallics
6. Using a solvent that evaporates too slowly

PREVENTIONS

1. Use good spraying techniques. Keep the gun a constant distance from the work, trigger the gun at the end of each stroke, and avoid "toeing" and "heeling"

the gun. Spray a test panel to check color match before you apply color to the vehicle.

2. Thoroughly agitate topcoat materials before application. Failure to do this causes uneven pigment dispersion in the paint and results in mottling or off color.

3. Apply the required number of topcoats. Insufficient hiding is almost always caused by films that are too thin.

4. Never spray on a cold surface or in a cold room.

5. Spray a mist coat over metallic colors to obtain color uniformity.

6. Use solvents that are compatible with your shop conditions. Use of a slow-drying solvent where a regular-drying solvent would do can cause pigment particles to drift to uneven layers in the paint film.

REPAIR

In some cases of off color in metallics, a light area can be corrected by polishing and buffing, as this will tend to darken the appearance. If polishing and buffing does not correct the mismatch condition, the off-color area must be repainted.

≡ 36-8 CRACKING, CHECKING

This condition may also be called crazing, crow's-foot checking, spider-webbing, cobwebbing, alligatoring, hairline cracks, cold cracking. The terms "cracking" and "checking" describe durability problems which show up with extended service of 6 to 24 months after exposure to the weather. They are fractures in the paint film resulting from shrinkage which is caused by oxidation or extreme cold.

"Cracking" is the term applied to a fracture which extends down through the paint film to the surface painted. It may be accompanied by curling of the edges of the fracture and peeling, also rusting if the finish peels off bare metal. Cracking is often observed in ex-

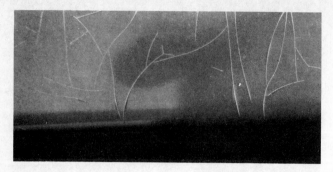

Fig. 36-7 Cracked paint.

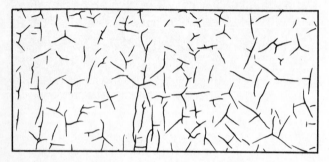

Fig. 36-8 Checked paint. *(Ford Motor Company)*

cessively thick films (10 mils or more) which have been exposed to a low temperature (Fig. 36-7).

"Checking" is the term applied to the fractures if they occur only on the surface of the topcoat and do not extend down through the film. It may be observed in combination with chalking or dulling (Fig. 36-8).

CAUSES

1. Application of a new finish over an old finish which has already checked

2. Application of a new finish over a surface which is too soft or undercured

3. Application of a new finish over an undercoat that is either too thick or not dry

4. Insufficient stirring or mixing

5. Improper thinners, for example, using a lacquer thinner in an enamel

6. Application of extremely thick finish coats

7. Adding unproven additives, such as gloss improvers, with the color coat

8. Addition of excessive amounts of clear lacquer or enamel to a color

PREVENTION

1. Check the old finish carefully with a magnifying glass. If the old film shows any sign of checking, remove it completely.

2. Apply undercoats in medium-thin coats, allowing plenty of time for each coat to flash off.

3. Make sure each coat is thoroughly dry before applying the next coat.

4. Stir all materials thoroughly. Thinned materials settle faster. So occasionally agitate the material while it is in the spray cup.

5. Always use the solvents recommended by the paint manufacturer. Don't intermix solvents from one company with materials from another.

6. Don't apply the paint too thick.

7. Don't add anything to refinishing materials that is not specifically recommended by the manufacturer.

8. Don't shoot several coats of clear enamel over the colorcoat. Clear enamel has a tendency to check on prolonged exposure to sunlight or sudden changes in temperature.

REPAIR

Checking or cracking found in any type of paint film can be repaired only by stripping off the defective film and repainting.

≡ 36-9 CRATERS, FISHEYES

This condition may also be known as crawling or poor wetting. Craters or fisheyes are surface conditions caused by paint flowing away from a contaminated spot before it dries. The contamination may be water, oil, grease, silicone, wax, soap, or detergent. It may affect a small localized area or extend over a complete panel. The contamination may exist on the surface before paint is applied, it may fall into the film while paint is being applied, or it may fall on the wet paint after the last coat has been applied (Figs. 36-9 and 36-10).

CAUSES

1. Silicone containing wax not completely removed from original paint surface

2. Oil or grease not cleaned from surface before repainting

3. Oil or water from air compressor sprayed into finish

4. Airborne dirt containing silicone falling into wet paint

5. Residue from dirty or contaminated shop towels remaining on surface before application of paint

PREVENTION

1. Clean the surface of the original finish thoroughly by using silicone-and-wax remover.

2. Use disposable paper towels for all cleanup operations.

3. Drain air compressors, air-line pressure regulators, and blow-off air lines daily.

4. Confine topcoat painting to a spray booth supplied with clean tempered air.

5. Use *fisheye eliminator*, following the manufacturer's instructions.

REPAIR

Shallow craters in the original finish may be removed by sanding, polishing, and buffing. If the crater is deep or if the cratering is extensive, it will be necessary to sand out the defect and repaint the affected panel.

≡ 36-10 DIRT IN PAINT

This is also called foreign material, contamination, hair, lint, sand, grit, trash, etc. It is due to a foreign body under or in the finish. It is covered by paint so that it has the same color as the topcoat but becomes objectionable because it protrudes above the finished surface (Fig. 36-11).

Fig. 36-9 Craters in paint. *(Ford Motor Company)*

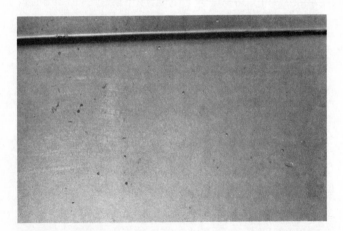

Fig. 36-10 Fisheyes in paint.

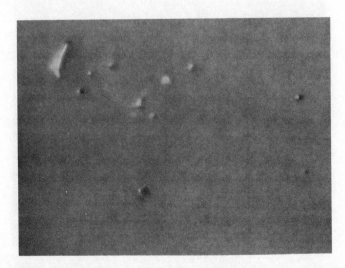

Fig. 36-11 Dirt in paint. *(Chrysler Corporation)*

CAUSES

1. Improper surface preparation techniques
2. Dirty spray booth
3. Dirty air lines or spray guns
4. Improper solvent, adding the paint to the solvent, or adding the solvent to the paint too quickly
5. Spraying in an open room
6. Dirty car or clothing
7. Improper straining of or not straining the paint

PREVENTION

1. Thoroughly clean the surface being painted. Wash the vehicle with warm water and a mild detergent. Rinse, and then apply wax-and-silicone remover. Make sure to blow out all cracks and body joints while the car is outside the spray booth. Once the vehicle is in the spray booth, always tack it off thoroughly with new tack rags immediately before the application of paint.

2. Make sure the spray area is clean. Wetting down the booth, frequently changing the air filters in the booth, and never sanding in the booth will help ensure jobs that are free from dirt.

3. Always use clean equipment. Dirty air regulators, air lines, and spray guns are frequently the cause of dirt in paint.

4. Always use the type and amount of solvent recommended by the paint manufacturer. Also, be careful how you mix the paint and the solvent. Adding the paint to the solvent or adding the solvent to the paint too quickly can result in "kick-out," which looks like dirt in the paint.

5. Never spray any paint in an open area where other work is being done. Confine spraying operations to the spray booth.

6. Make sure the car being painted is thoroughly blown off before it enters the spray booth. Seal the door jambs and edges with a thin wet coat of paint before painting the surface. Always wear clean, lint-free clothing and a cap to prevent dirt, oil, lint, hair, dandruff, etc., from falling on a freshly painted surface.

7. Always strain the reduced material through a fine strainer. Some recommendations are to strain the material a second time through the same strainer.

REPAIR

In most cases, dirt found in original factory finishes can be repaired by polishing and buffing.

Dirt found in enamel paint sprayed by refinishers will usually have to be sanded out and repainted because of the long cure time required for refinishing enamels. Dirt found in acrylic lacquer used for refinishing can usually be removed by sanding and polishing.

≡ 36-11 FOREIGN MATERIAL ON SURFACE

This is also called fluid drippings, organic fallout, trim cement, glue. The term describes contamination on the paint film surface which is difficult to remove and which may have damaged the paint. It applies to such foreign materials as chemical sprays like insecticides and weed killers, alkaline water spots, brake fluid, oil, grease, road tar, and dead insects. If any of these are left on the finish, under certain conditions they will cause permanent damage.

All these substances can cause dulling, discoloration, pitting, crazing, and finally disintegration of the paint at the points of contact.

CAUSES

All the materials will seriously damage paint on horizontal surfaces, especially during hot, dry weather. Frequent heavy rainfall will either dilute or wash off these chemical substances and possibly prevent or greatly restrict the severity of paint damage. On the other hand, the cycling of hot sun and dew formation serves to extract and concentrate the destructive chemicals so as to accelerate the damage to the paint film (Fig. 36-12).

PREVENTION

1. In the more seriously affected areas, it is recommended that all vehicles be washed and inspected on arrival. Vehicles that are kept in outside storage should be inspected weekly and washed as required to remove all contaminants. This should aid considerably in preventing severe spotting that cannot be removed by ordinary polishing.

2. There are conditions, however, where insect control is not feasible during long intervals of storage. In such places, it would be far better to apply an approved protective wax coating on the cleaned cars as they are received. There are many protective wax products now being offered for this purpose. Several have been found to be most effective in reducing paint spotting by insects. The coating itself is not damaging to the paint. This coating should be applied as a medium wet continuous coat on horizontal surfaces with ordinary paint spray equipment in a sheltered area. A light film thickness is sufficient. (Heavier coats should be avoided as they are more difficult to remove). Cars so protected can remain in outside storage for as long as 90 days. Longer intervals are not recommended because of increasing trouble in removing the coating. Many solvent detergent cleaners are available for washing off wax coatings so that one technician can usually clean a car in about 20 minutes. This type of protection is much less expensive than paint repairs.

3. Another approach to the insect problem is by special illumination at the storage lot. Many lots are equipped with ordinary white incandescent lights or floodlights. These all emit enough blue light to attract most insects. For the same reason, most blue cars attract insects more than cars of other colors. Actually, red lights would be least attractive to bugs. But because of the many objections to this color, a yellow or an orange-yellow light is generally recommended. None of these colored lights are insect-repellent and only those high in blue content are capable of attracting insects. Therefore, a blue light at some distance from the stored cars might serve as a decoy, causing the insects to detour around the lot.

REPAIR

In many cases, this contamination can be removed by washing the vehicle, using a mild detergent, and damage will not result. If, after washing, some contamination remains, it can usually be removed by a combination of sanding, hand or machine polishing, and buffing. In extreme cases, the damage will have penetrated the topcoat, and repainting will be required.

≡ 36-12 INDUSTRIAL FALLOUT

Industrial fallout is the result of particles being exhausted into the air by the various processes of heavy industry. Examples are fly ash, foundry dust, and soot.

Iron-based fallout particles, such as foundry dust, appear to the eye as tiny rust-colored dots on the paint film. They cause the surface to feel rough to the touch. Some of the particles have excellent adhesion and are difficult to remove (Fig. 36-13).

PREVENTION

1. Wash the car regularly.
2. Use a wax protective coating.
3. Use covers.

REPAIR

A procedure that has proven effective in the removal of industrial fallout follows on p. 353:

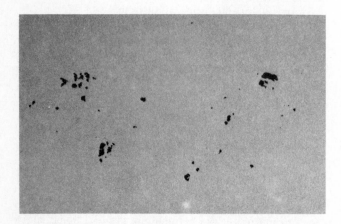

Fig. 36-12 Foreign material on surface of paint.

Fig. 36-13 Industrial fallout in paint. (*Chrysler Corporation*)

1. First, wash the car with a body-wash detergent compound to remove any loose soil. Rinse well and examine the painted surfaces for iron-base fallout particles. If there is a significant quantity of fallout not removed by ordinary washing, the following oxalic treatment should then be used. All cracks, ledges, and grooves where fallout has accumulated should be cleaned by wiping or by air blow-off.

2. Apply industrial fallout remover (oxalic acid-water solution) liberally to all affected surfaces of the vehicle with a large sponge. Use a broad wiping stroke, and keep the work completely wet for about 15 minutes or until you can no longer feel any surface roughness or even isolated gritty particles with bare or gloved fingertips. If this is not done thoroughly, rust staining may soon develop. The surface must be kept wet, since a dry acid residue is not active in loosening fallout. Be sure that the entire acid cleaning procedure is performed in a sheltered area so that the body will be kept as cool as possible. This will prevent rapid evaporation of water and consequent surface drying. *Do not work in the sun.* Even a strong breeze makes it difficult to keep the job wet over a large area.

3. Rinse the area with clear water. This must be done thoroughly to prevent possible corrosion. No traces of acid should be left on any surface. Bright trim parts, particularly anodized aluminum and stainless steel, may be stained by prolonged contact with the cleaning solution. Even painted areas can be spotted by prolonged exposure. It is also important to keep the oxalic acid cleaner solution from leaking inboard, because some fabrics might be bleached or discolored by it.

If the fallout is not completely removed or is deeply embedded in the paint film, cleaning with the acid-detergent mixture must be repeated. This may be aided by using a fine nylon bristle type of scrub brush. Be sure that the light scrubbing required does not scratch the paint. Rubbing the work with a mixture of equal parts of oxalic-acid cleaner and body polish, using a piece of heavy towel, is also sometimes helpful. Then, thoroughly rinse with water.

Small black spots may remain after the oxalic cleaning has removed all iron-based fallout. These deposits might be asphaltic or overspray from certain air-dry paints used in the engine compartment during assembly operations. They can usually be removed by rubbing vigorously with a cloth saturated with wax-and-silicone remover.

≡ 36-13 LIFTING

This is also called puckering, swelling, raising. Lifting describes the effect of a refinish paint on a previously applied paint coating in which the original coat will separate from the surface to which it was applied. It is usually caused by the solvents in the refinish paint which have attacked the original finish, causing it to swell and lose adhesion in a distorted pattern. This is a common occurrence when lacquer is sprayed over an undercured enamel. Lifting may also occur when air-dry enamels have been recoated within a critical time range without the use of a recoating sealer (Fig. 36-14).

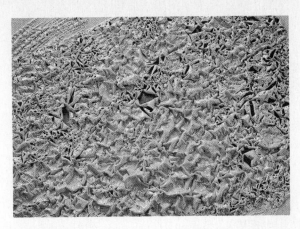

Fig. 36-14 Paint that is lifting. *(Du Pont)*

CAUSES

1. Use of lacquer over undercured enamel
2. Use of lacquer thinner or "hot" solvents in reducing refinish enamels
3. Application of a color over an incompletely cured or incompatible undercoat
4. Application of a second coat of enamel over first enamel coat which has become partially cured (oxidized)

PREVENTION

1. Do not use lacquer thinner in enamels.
2. Do not recoat air-dried enamel with lacquer.
3. Use undercoats which are compatible with the topcoat used. A primer-surfacer designed for use with enamel will not necessarily work with lacquer colorcoats.
4. Don't apply colorcoats over undercoats which are not completely dry and hard.
5. Always apply a recoating sealer when recoating an air-dry enamel surface that has cured between 4 and 72 hours.

REPAIR

Remove the lifted film and repaint.

≡ 36-14 METAL-FINISHING MARKS AND SAND SCRATCHES

Metal-finishing marks are the result of poor surface preparation techniques. Usually they are caused by gouging metal with coarse grinder disks or files. Sometimes they are caused by the use of too coarse a grit of sandpaper on undercoats. These marks were not removed in the final metal-finish operation or were not properly filled and surfaced with putty (Fig. 36-15).

CAUSES

1. Improper metal-finishing techniques
2. Too thin a coating of primer-surfacer
3. Failure to use putty when required
4. Failure to allow primer-surfacer or putty to dry long enough before sanding
5. Cross sanding
6. Poor sanding techniques

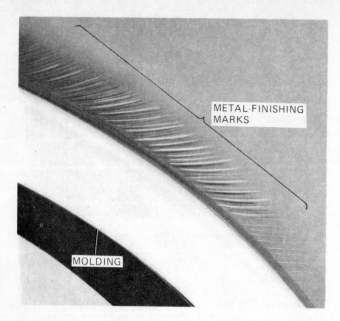

Fig. 36-15 Metal-finishing marks in paint. *(Ford Motor Company)*

7. Use of too coarse a sandpaper
8. Use of poor or improper topcoat solvents

PREVENTION

1. Always finish off a stripping or metal-finishing operation with a fine-grit abrasive (No. 80 or finer).

2. Apply a coating of primer-surfacer, but not too heavily. Very heavy applications of primer-surfacer often lead to sand scratches.

3. Use glaze putty to fill surface variations that primer-surfacer won't fill. Don't try to fill deep scratches with heavy applications of primer-surfacer. Apply the putty in thin layers.

4. Allow both primer-surfacer and putty to flash off before applying succeeding coats. Failure to do this results in crusting, a defect which eventually makes sand scratches show up more.

5. Use good sanding techniques. The best sanding jobs usually come from wet-sanding operations. If you do use dry sandpaper, tap it frequently to remove the sanding sludge. Never cross-sand. Use a sanding block, never your fingers.

6. Use the proper grit of sandpaper. Try to finish all sanding operations with No. 400 grit paper or finer.

7. Use the solvent recommended by the topcoat manufacturer. Poor solvents usually lead to sand-scratch swelling.

REPAIR

Metal-finishing marks and sand scratches found on original factory finishes can usually be repaired by a combination of sanding, polishing, and buffing. In some extreme cases, the surface may have to be repainted.

The long cure time of refinishing enamels prevents polishing and buffing from being used on newly painted surfaces. Most cases of metal-finishing marks or sand scratches found on refinished cars will have to be repaired by repainting.

☰ 36-15 MOLDING INSTALLATION DAMAGE OR RUST

This describes a specific kind of scratching or chipping of the paint finish adjacent to, or underneath, bright moldings, or ornaments. This damage occurs during the installation process. The rust may not be apparent until after outdoor weathering has caused rust to form at the edges or rust stain to bleed out from underneath (Fig. 36-16).

REPAIR

Repair of this problem requires removing the molding or ornament, removing the rust, and repainting the affected area.

☰ 36-16 ORANGE PEEL

"Orange peel" is a term which indicates the uneven appearance of a paint film which has not flowed out to a smooth, glossy surface (Fig. 36-17).

CAUSES

1. Wrong solvent or improper reduction
2. Poor gun techniques
3. Improper air pressure

PREVENTION

1. Always reduce the paint with the amount and type of solvent specified by the paint manufacturer. Poor-quality solvents, fast-evaporating solvents, and underreduction are common causes of orange peel.

2. Use good gun techniques. Apply topcoats in wet coats, holding the gun 6 to 10 inches [150 to 250 mm] from the surface, keeping the gun at right angles to the area being painted.

3. Use the proper air pressure. Too high an air pressure causes a dry spray and prevents the paint from flowing out. Too low an air pressure causes poor atomization. Poor flow-out and atomization both result in orange peel.

REPAIR

Orange peel found in any painted surface can usually be repaired by a combination of sanding, polishing, and buffing as long as the film is completely cured. In some extreme cases, it may be necessary to sand out the orange peel and repaint.

☰ 36-17 OVERSPRAY

"Overspray" is a term used to describe the appearance of small particles of paint of a contrasting color on the surface of the car. It is usually caused by poor masking or sloppy gun technique (Fig. 36-18).

CAUSES

1. Sloppy gun technique
2. Improper masking
3. Spraying onto a car near the car being painted

PREVENTION

1. Make sure adjacent surfaces are adequately covered with tape and masking paper before spraying.

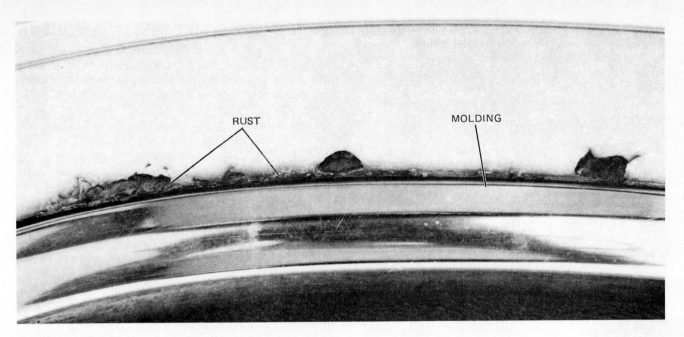

Fig. 36-16 Damage or rust from molding installation.

Fig. 36-17 Paint that has orange peel.

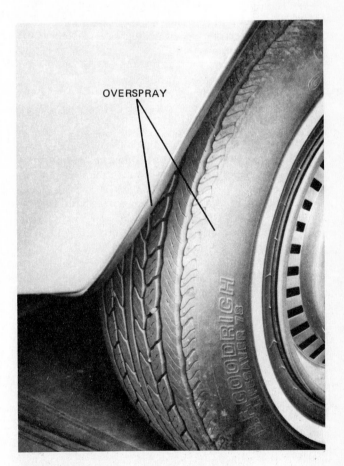

Fig. 36-18 Overspray of paint.

2. Make sure all your masking tape and paper are properly stuck down.

3. Trigger the gun at the end of each stroke. Don't use such an excess of air pressure that you start to remove the masking tape.

4. Always spray in the spray booth. Keep the spray-booth doors closed and other cars out of the booth while you are spraying.

5. Don't blow paint all over the booth while making a spot repair.

REPAIR

Overspray found on original factory finishes can usually be repaired by wiping the surface with a good solvent. In some extreme cases, a combination of sanding, polishing, and buffing may have to be used.

Overspray caused by refinish operations over a factory finish usually can also be repaired by wiping the surface with a good solvent. However, if the overspray has aged and is insoluble in solvent, it will have to be compounded off.

Overspray caused by refinish operations over a refinished surface can sometimes be repaired by wiping the surface with a good solvent. If the solvent does not take all of the overspray off, it will probably have to be stripped off. (The long cure time of refinish enamels usually prevents a sanding and polishing operation.)

≡ 36-18 PEELING

This is also known as scaling or flaking. "Peeling" is the term applied to the separation of a paint film from the surface to which it has been applied. It includes peeling of the finish coats from the primer, separation of topcoat films (enamel from enamel or striping lacquer from enamel), or peeling of the finish from the metal, which may be accompanied by rusting (Fig. 36-19).

CAUSES

1. Presence of any foreign material such as wax, silicone, or oil on the surface before painting

2. Improper or no use of metal conditioner and conversion coating on bare metal

3. Too high an air pressure on the undercoat

4. Use of the wrong undercoat; for example, using an enamel undercoat under lacquer

5. Insufficient sanding

6. Applying additional coats of primer-surfacer before preceding coats are thoroughly dry

7. Using cheap solvent

8. Surface material or solvents, too hot or too cold

PREVENTION

1. Remove all dirt, wax, and grease before sanding.

2. Use a metal conditioner and conversion coating on bare metal.

3. Thoroughly sand all surfaces where paint is to be applied.

4. Follow manufacturer's directions for thinning, applying, drying, and recoating.

5. Prime bare metal areas as soon as possible to prevent rusting.

6. Keep surface, paint, and thinners at room temperature.

REPAIR

Remove all of the paint having poor adhesion, and re-paint as required.

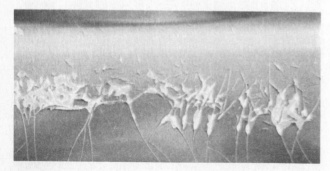

Fig. 36-19 Peeling paint.

≡ 36-19 POOR DRYING, HARDNESS

This condition is also called softness, tackiness, slow drying. The drying of a paint film goes through several stages, or degrees of hardness, in progressing from a liquid to a solid coating. These may be described as follows:

- STAGE 1. *Dust-free* is the point at which dust or lint settling on the surface will not become embedded but can be wiped or blown off.
- STAGE 2. *Tack-free* is the point at which light finger pressure will not leave a print and the surface will no longer feel sticky.
- STAGE 3. *Dry to handle* is the point at which the painted part may be moved or handled without damaging the fresh paint. It is also the point at which taping and recoating can be accomplished.
- STAGE 4. *Hard dry* is the point at which optimum hardness is reached and the finish may be compounded, wheel-polished, buffed, waxed, washed, or otherwise treated.

The term "poor drying" or "hardness" can therefore apply to the result obtained at any of these four stages. In addition, the result obtained is related to the type of material used. For example, nitrocellulose and acrylic lacquers will dry harder, faster than enamels. Acrylic enamels will dry dust-free and tack-free faster than alkyd enamels. Differences in drying rate sometimes occur between colors with the same general type of formulation.

"Poor drying," then, describes the occurrence of softness in a film when experience indicates that it should be harder.

CAUSES

1. Use of slow-reducing solvents

2. Use of excess amounts of retarders or other additives

3. Excessive film thickness

4. Painting over oil, grease, or other contamination

5. Oil in compressed air

6. Poor ventilation

7. Excess humidity in atmosphere

8. Low temperature—atmosphere, paint, solvent, or part

9. Dryer left out (if required by type of formulation)

10. Wet undercoat

PREVENTION

1. Do not use excessive slow-reducing solvents or retarder. Use only as required in hot, dry weather in order to obtain flow-out.

2. Use only the additives prescribed by your paint supplier.

3. Avoid excessive undercoat and colorcoat film thickness by following the recommendation of the supplier regarding the amount and kind of reducing solvent used and the number of coats to be applied.

4. Clean surfaces to be painted with wax-and-silicone remover.

5. Drain compressor and air lines frequently to prevent buildup of oil or water. Use a trap on all air lines used for blow-off or spray operations.

6. Spraying and drying of paint should be done only in a well-ventilated area.

7. Excess atmospheric humidity will retard drying. This can be partly compensated for through the use of faster solvents and higher air pressure. Further drying can be accelerated by the use of heat.

8. Maintain temperature in spray booth and drying room above 70°F [21°C]. Also, the temperature of the paint materials and solvents used should be at least 70°F [21°C]. The surface of the car to be painted should be at room temperature. Cars brought in from the outside in cold weather should be allowed to reach room temperature before painting. Steam, hot water, or hot air can be used to warm the surface if necessary.

9. Certain types of material require the addition of dryers if hardness is to be obtained with room-temperature air drying. Be sure the necessary dryers are added before attempting to use one of these types.

10. Make sure that the undercoats have thoroughly dried before applying colorcoats.

REPAIR

Air-dry the soft film for 24 hours or force-dry for ½ hour under radiant heat. If, after this, the film has still not reached sufficient hardness, it will be necessary to remove and repaint the defective area.

≡ 36-20 RUSTING

This may also be called corroding, rust stain, or rust bleed. This condition is the result of weathering (oxidation) of exposed or insufficiently protected or prepared metal. Either the metal was not painted, the metal was not painted enough, or the paint was applied over a rusted surface or was removed, with rusting the result. Accordingly, rusting may be the secondary effect of a primary problem, such as thin paint, chipping, scratching, or peeling (Fig. 36-20).

CAUSES

1. Exterior damage to the paint film
2. Insufficient film thickness or incomplete coverage
3. Applying paint to a metal which contains rust not completely removed
4. Painting over metal touched by bare hands, or metal contaminated by chemical deposits from sanding water

PREVENTION

1. Apply the recommended number of coats to get adequate thickness.
2. Apply paint carefully to ensure complete coverage.
3. Thoroughly prepare metal for painting by sanding to remove all traces of rust from the surface.
4. Always use a metal conditioner and conversion coating on bare metal.
5. Don't touch bare metal with your hands after the metal conditioner is applied. Apply primer-surfacer within 30 minutes of the metal conditioner application.

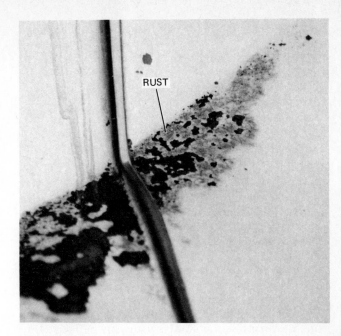

Fig. 36-20 Metal rusting under paint.

REPAIR

Remove the affected paint film down to the metal, and remove the rust. Then apply metal conditioner and conversion coating, and repaint.

≡ 36-21 SAGS, RUNS

This condition may also be called drips, blobs, tears, curtains. All these terms describe a condition resulting from the application of an excessive amount of paint to a localized area. Then the paint flows downward and accumulates in objectionable thickness (Fig. 36-21).

CAUSES

1. Spraying over a surface contaminated with wax, oil, grease, or silicone

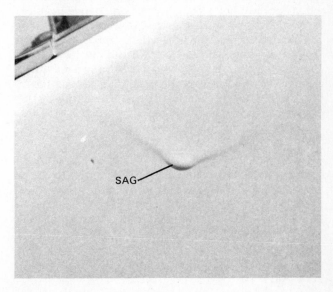

Fig. 36-21 Sag in paint.

2. Solvent, material, surface, or spray booth too cold

3. Using too much or too little solvent or a solvent that dries too slowly

4. "Piling on" coats by recoating before preceding coats have flashed off

5. Using too low an air pressure

6. Improper spray-gun adjustment

7. Improper spray-gun technique

PREVENTION

1. Thoroughly clean the surface to be painted. Use a wax-and-silicone remover before applying paint to a previously painted surface.

2. Keep the surface, solvents, and material at room temperature. Delay spraying in a spray booth until the booth has reached normal room temperature.

3. Make sure the paint is properly reduced following the paint manufacturer's recommendations. Runs can be caused by overreduction and use of a solvent which evaporates too slowly. Sags can be caused by underreduction, which results in "piling on" in heavy coats.

4. Allow preceding coats to flash off before applying the next coat. Failure to do this can cause sags.

5. Make sure sufficient air pressure is used. Low air pressure can cause sags, because the paint will not properly atomize.

6. Properly adjust the fluid and fan controls on the spray gun. Too narrow a fan with too much paint will cause sags.

7. Keep the gun at the proper distance from the work. Holding the gun too close piles on the paint and invites sags. Also, avoid using a jerky spray stroke and moving the gun too slowly.

REPAIR

Sags found in original nonmetallic finishes can usually be corrected by cutting off the excess paint with a knife or razor blade followed by sanding, polishing, and buffing to remove the excess paint. Sags in metallic colors, when they are not accompanied by a change in color, can be repaired in the same way. However, when there is a change in color, the area will have to be repainted.

Runs or sags caused by refinishers in local paint shops will usually have to be sanded off or washed off (if the paint is still wet) and then repainted. Sometimes a sag that is still wet can be removed by picking up the excess paint with a wet finger or by flowing it off the panel by spraying it with solvent.

≡ 36-22 SCRATCHES

These may also be called marred paint. The term "scratch" describes the appearance of the finish when it has been damaged by the penetration of a sharp object. The result is a permanent scar or tear in the film which, in extreme cases, penetrates to the bare metal and may be accompanied by rusting (Fig. 36-22).

REPAIR

If the scratch is in but not through the topcoat and the topcoat is thoroughly cured, the finish can usually be

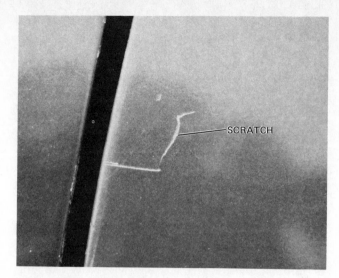

Fig. 36-22 Scratches or marred paint.

repaired by polishing and buffing. If the scratch is through the topcoat, but not through the undercoat, and is in an inconspicuous location, the finish can be repaired by brush touch-up. If the scratch has penetrated to the metal and the metal has rusted or corroded, the scratch must be removed and the area repainted.

≡ 36-23 SEALER, DEADENER UNDER PAINT

This condition is also caused by oil, grease, or other contamination. These terms describe specific types of dirt under paint resulting from poor repaint cleanup operations. Proper identification can therefore assist in the initiation of proper corrective action. Since these are usually substantial "gobs" of contamination, their removal will probably result in exposing primer or bare metal.

REPAIR

Remove the contamination and repaint.

≡ 36-24 STAINS, TARNISH, FADING

This condition may also be called off-color spots, discolored spots, bleeding. The terms "stains" and "off-color or discolored spots" describe the result of surface contamination which has affected the color of the finish. The term "fading" describes a change in color from the original, resulting from exposure to weathering in service.

Most of the comments listed above under ≡36-11, Foreign Material on Surface, and ≡36-12, Industrial Fallout, apply to stains and off-color spots. Many times, these off-color spots are caused by acid containing industrial fallout or by battery acid.

Fading of the finish in extended service (6 to 24 months) represents a color change occurring in the paint pigment on exposure to sunlight (Fig. 36-23).

REPAIR

Off-color spots or stains on the surface can often be removed by sanding, polishing, and buffing. If the con-

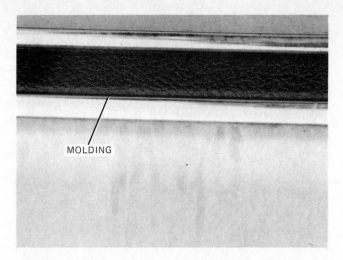

Fig. 36-23 *Stained, tarnished, and faded paint.*

tamination has penetrated the topcoat and is not removed by polishing, repainting will be necessary.

Faded areas require repainting to restore the color.

≡ 36-25 THIN PAINT, NO PAINT

This condition may also be called skips, holidays, primer shows, no primer under topcoat.

The term "thin paint" describes a condition in which an insufficient amount of paint has been applied or an excessive amount has been removed by abrasion or erosion (Fig. 36-24). The result is that either bare metal is exposed (in which case rusting may be evident) or primer shows through the finish coats, causing an off-color condition.

CAUSES

1. Incomplete coverage
2. Insufficient film thickness
3. Abnormal polishing of colorcoat
4. Wrong color undercoat
5. Improper or overreduced materials

PREVENTION

1. Use care when applying paint to be sure all surfaces are coated.
2. Use normal coating thicknesses.
3. Be careful not to overcompound or overpolish, especially on edges and corners where it is very easy to remove the color.
4. Use undercoats similar in color to the color of the topcoat being applied.
5. Follow the recommendations of the paint manufacturer regarding the amount and type of solvent used for reduction and the number of coats required.

REPAIR

Thin paint must be repaired by repainting.

≡ 36-26 WATER SPOTTING

Water spotting is usually caused by exposing the surface of a paint film (that has not dried sufficiently) to snow, rain, or dew. The effect of this water is magnified

Fig. 36-24 *Thin paint. (Ford Motor Company)*

if the droplets are dried by sunlight. The damage may appear either as a roughening of the surface of the paint or as a circular, whitish water residue embedded in the surface (Fig. 36-25).

CAUSES

1. Allowing rain, snow, or dew to get on the surface or washing the surface before it is thoroughly dry
2. Applying excessively thick coats or using any techniques that cause poor drying

PREVENTION

1. Allow freshly painted vehicles sufficient air-dry or force-dry time before exposing them to the elements.
2. Use materials that have maximum resistance to water spotting.
3. See also preventions listed in ≡36-19, Poor Drying, Hardness.

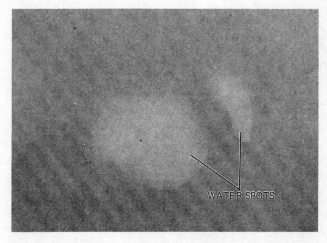

Fig. 36-25 *Water spotting in paint. (Ford Motor Company)*

REPAIR

Minor water spotting may be removed by polishing and buffing after the finish has been allowed to harden. Severe water spotting requires sanding and repainting to correct.

≡ 36-27 WRINKLING

Wrinkling is seldom encountered in today's original finishes. However, it does occur in thick air-dry finishes as the result of uneven drying between the top surface and undersurface of the finish-coat material (Fig. 36-26).

CAUSES

1. Too heavy a coat or coats of paint; rapid drying of the top surface of the film while the film underneath remains soft

2. Force drying of enamels without using a baking additive to retard surface setup

3. Use of lacquer thinner in enamel, which may cause wrinkling or lifting of the original finish or the primer-surfacer

4. Exposing enamel to sunlight before it is thoroughly dry

5. Any technique or condition that would produce sags or slow drying

6. Abnormally hot and humid weather

PREVENTION

1. Don't spray enamel too thick. Avoid piling on.

2. If you force-dry enamels, make sure you add a baking converter to the paint if it is recommended by the paint manufacturer.

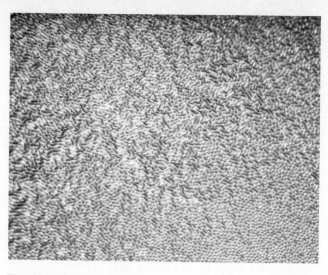

Fig. 36-26 Wrinkled paint.

3. Use the solvent recommended by the paint manufacturer.

4. Try to keep the spray booth and car at normal temperature.

5. Avoid spray-gun techniques that cause very heavy applications of paint (for example, holding the gun very close to the work and moving the gun very slowly).

6. Keep the car out of the sunshine until it has thoroughly dried.

REPAIR

The only way to repair a wrinkled surface is to remove the wrinkled film and to repaint.

REVIEW QUESTIONS

Select the *one* correct, best, or most probable answer to each question. You can find the answers in the section indicated at the end of each question.

1. The condition most likely to cause blushing is   (≡36-4)
   a. spraying on a cold surface
   b. using too much retarder
   c. low air pressure
   d. cold, dry weather

2. Checking may be caused by   (≡36-8)
   a. insufficient drying time between coats
   b. application of extremely thick coats
   c. addition of excessive clear to a color
   d. all of the above

3. As a paint film dries, the surface develops orange peel. Painter A says the cause could be improper reduction or high air pressure. Painter B says the surface can probably be repaired with rubbing compound and then buffing. Who is right?   (≡36-16)
   a. painter A
   b. painter B
   c. both A and B
   d. neither A nor B

4. Wrinkling may occur when spraying   (≡36-27)
   a. lacquer over a wet topcoat of lacquer
   b. enamel over a wet topcoat of enamel
   c. a light color over a dark color
   d. lacquer over enamel

5. Fisheyes in a new paint job should be repaired with
   a. spot putty   (≡36-9)
   b. glazing putty
   c. plastic filler
   d. sanding and refinishing

CHAPTER 37
CUSTOM PAINTING

After studying this chapter, and with proper instruction and equipment, you should be able to:

1. Prepare the surface for a custom paint job.
2. Use the airbrush and touch-up gun.
3. Make flames, ribbons, fish scales, fans, lace, and other special effects.
4. Use spray mask, frisket paper, and stencils to produce various special effects.
5. Protect a custom paint job.
6. Plan and execute a landscape, mural, or other piece of art.

≡ 37-1 CUSTOM-PAINTING RULES

Custom painting of automotive vehicles is very popular with many people, especially van owners. As with many specialties, it is based on a thorough knowledge of the fundamentals. Before you try custom painting, be sure you know how to refinish cars. This was covered in earlier chapters.

There are some fundamental rules for doing a custom paint job. The first rule is to know exactly what you want on the vehicle. Stripes? Flames? Names? Figures? Animals? Landscapes? Anything is possible. But when you are getting your start in custom painting, don't try to tackle something too ambitious at first.

≡ 37-2 TECHNIQUE AND ARTISTRY

If you can do a spot paint repair (and get it right the first time), you can probably do an adequate job of painting flames, simple murals, or landscapes. All it takes is the equipment and a steady hand. But it requires experience to do the more complex decorations — monsters, beautiful women, moonscapes — that you see on some vehicles. Start simple, and work toward the more complicated gradually as your skill develops. Then you will be able to successfully execute the more advanced decorations.

Work out your decorations on paper first, keeping in mind the effect that you want to achieve. What looks good on one vehicle may not be appropriate for another. The design must fit the vehicle. The following sections describe the equipment you need and how to use it to achieve the effect you want.

≡ 37-3 EQUIPMENT NEEDED

Chapter 31 covers painting supplies and equipment for refinishing automotive vehicles. Chapter 32 covers the use and care of spray guns. Chapter 34 covers the preparation of the surface for painting.

Everything in those three chapters applies to custom-painting work. You must know about masking, surface preparation, and how to use the spray gun. Custom painting is a refinement of these basic techniques.

Special equipment needed to do custom painting, in addition to those items described in Chaps. 31, 32, and 34, includes:

1. Airbrush, which is a special type of small spray gun
2. Touch-up gun (described briefly in ≡32-10), which is a medium-size spray gun
3. Special air supply to the airbrush or the touch-up gun
4. Spray mask, a viscous liquid that is applied with a spray gun and turns into a transparent, rubbery film
5. Narrow masking tape, ¼, ⅛, and 1/16 inch wide
6. Stripes, which are narrow films of various colors, backed with peel-off paper
7. Dagger brushes and special pens
8. Masking paper, frisket paper, cardboard to make stencils
9. Lacquer or acrylic lacquer, plus any special-effect material such as sequin flakes which produce a glittering effect

Each of these is described below.

≡ 37-4 AIRBRUSH

In operation, the airbrush (Fig. 37-1) is similar to the standard spray gun. However, the airbrush is much smaller. It can be adjusted to produce a varying spray width, from 1½ inch down to a fine line. The typical airbrush has three interchangeable tips. The tip with the smallest opening can be used for extra-fine detailing. Its spray width can vary from a pencil-line thickness up to 1 inch. The medium tip sprays 1/16- to 1¼-inch patterns. The tip with the largest opening sprays a pattern from ⅛ to 1½ inches.

The airbrush has a cup or jar to contain the paint, ink, dye, or watercolor to be applied. The airbrush can be adjusted to provide varying amounts of the liquid being applied. Depressing the trigger admits air to the airbrush. As the air flows through, it picks up the liquid from the jar or cup. The air and liquid mix to form the spray.

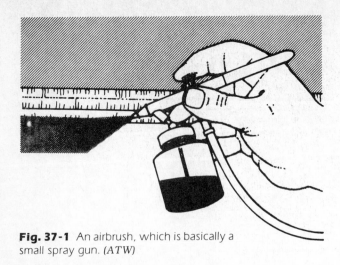

Fig. 37-1 An airbrush, which is basically a small spray gun. *(ATW)*

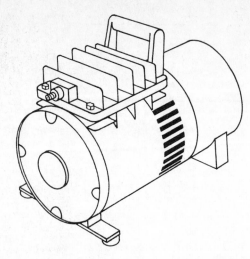

Fig. 37-2 A small air compressor, which supplies air to the airbrush.

☰ 37-5 TOUCH-UP GUN

The touch-up gun (Fig. 32-32) is smaller than a production spray gun but larger than an airbrush. However, the touch-up-gun container holds more liquid than the airbrush container. The touch-up gun is used in areas that are too small for a production spray gun and too large for the airbrush. This includes door-jamb painting, corners, and large areas of a mural being painted on a door, hood, trunk lid, or side panel.

The touch-up gun can handle details almost as fine as the airbrush. Then the gun can be adjusted to deliver a wide fan pattern, such as needed for spraying a protective coating over a large mural.

☰ 37-6 AIR FOR AIRBRUSH OR TOUCH-UP GUN

There are five methods for supplying air to the airbrush or touch-up gun:

1. THE SHOP COMPRESSED-AIR SYSTEM. If the shop compressed-air system supplies clean, moisture-free air, it can be used. A pressure regulator is required to reduce the pressure to the value required for the airbrush or touch-up gun.

2. A SPECIAL COMPRESSOR. Where many custom-painting jobs are done, shops may have a special compressor used exclusively for this work (Fig. 37-2).

3. A TANK OF COMPRESSED CARBON-DIOXIDE (CO_2) GAS. This is the source that many commercial artists use. The tank is available in various sizes to suit the artists' needs. It is equipped with a pressure regulator so the pressure can be adjusted as required. Although the CO_2 gas is not "air," it serves the same purpose as the air from a compressor. Carbon dioxide is a harmless gas when used with adequate ventilation.

4. CANS OF PROPELLANT. These cans contain a gas or liquid under pressure (Fig. 37-3). The cans have a limited capacity. Therefore, they are not recommended for use with anything larger than the airbrush. But they are very handy for small custom jobs or touch-up work.

5. A SPARE TIRE. The air from a spare tire can be used with a special spare-tire adapter (Fig. 37-4). The adapter is attached to the tire valve to tap the compressed air in the tire. The tire must be mounted on the wheel, and inflated to its safe maximum pressure.

Fig. 37-3 Cans of propellant for small airbrush jobs. *(Badger Air-Brush Company)*

☰ 37-7 SPRAY MASK

Spray mask is a thick liquid that is applied straight from the can to the surface to be custom painted. It dries to a transparent, rubbery film. The surface should first be prepared ("prepped") as explained in Chap. 34. This will leave the surface ready to accept the paint or ink when the spray mask is cut away.

After the spray mask has dried, the area to be painted is removed. First, draw the outline of the pattern you want with a felt-tip marker, chalk, crayon, or grease pencil. Then carefully cut along the marked lines with a razor blade or an X-Acto knife. Peel off the spray-mask film from the area to be painted. Then paint the exposed area.

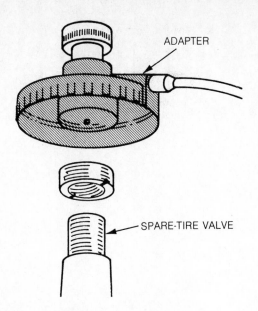

Fig. 37-4 Spare-tire adapter for using the tire air supply for the airbrush. *(Badger Air-Brush Company)*

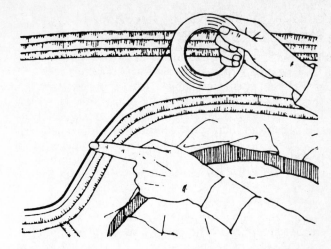

Fig. 37-5 Applying narrow masking tape to make curves. *(Ditzler Automotive Finishes Division of PPG Industries, Inc.)*

The procedure can be repeated. For example, you might paint the exposed area a light blue to represent the sky. Then spray additional spray mask on and cut out smaller areas where you could paint in birds, airplanes, or anything else.

≡ 37-8 NARROW MASKING TAPE

To make intricate patterns with curves, narrow ⅛- and ¹⁄₁₆-inch masking tape is used to outline the pattern. Wider tape cannot be used because it will not form the curves properly.

To use narrow tape, first prepare the area and then paint it with the desired background color. After it has dried, use the narrow masking tape to apply the outline. It takes practice to use the narrow tape. It is easy enough to apply the tape in a straight line. But for curves, you need a steady hand and a feeling for the way you want the final job to look. Figure 37-5 shows the procedure. Hold the roll of tape in one hand, keeping the tape pulled tight. With a finger of the other hand, guide the tape onto the surface.

Next, use wider masking tape and masking paper to mask the area outside the area you want to paint. The paint job can then proceed. After the area is painted, peel off the tape and paper, and you have the finished design.

≡ 37-9 STRIPES

Stripes may be painted on. But many stripes are films backed with adhesive, with a peel-off back. They are applied in the same way as the overlays and decals described in Chap. 30.

≡ 37-10 PINSTRIPING BRUSHES AND DRAFTING PENS

Pinstriping brushes (Fig. 37-6) are small paintbrushes that are shaped to a sharp tip. The bristles hold a considerable amount of paint. They can be used for *pinstriping*—the drawing of a very thin uniform line.

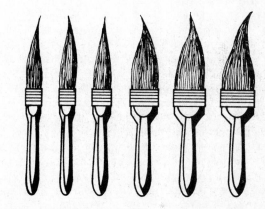

Fig. 37-6 Pinstriping brushes.

Also, with practice, the brushes can be used to draw curved lines.

The fingers of the hand holding the brush are used to slide along the surface and maintain the correct brush-to-surface distance. This prevents any up-and-down movement which would vary the stripe width. To make curved lines, the brush is pivoted by rotating the hand on the little finger. Practice the technique on an old body panel until you can draw straight lines and curves of various sizes.

Some types of drafting pens (Fig. 37-7) can be used to draw fine lines. The pens can be used either freehand or with a straightedge. You will need practice to learn how to use drafting pens.

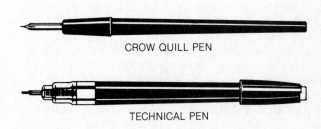

CROW QUILL PEN

TECHNICAL PEN

Fig. 37-7 Types of drafting pens used in custom painting.

≡ 37-11 MASKING PAPER, FRISKET PAPER, AND STENCILS

The use of masking paper was described in Chap. 31. The masking paper is applied with masking tape.

Frisket paper is available in art-supply stores. It is a thin paper with adhesive on one side, protected with a backing sheet of paper. It is used by drawing a design on the paper and then cutting out the area to be painted. The resulting pattern is applied to the body panel after peeling off the backing paper. Very intricate designs can be worked onto the body panel by using frisket paper.

For example, suppose you were painting a halloween pumpkin on a car panel (Fig. 37-8). After roughing in the pumpkin on the panel, you want to show the mouth, nose, and eyes in bright yellow (Fig. 37-9). Cut out these features from a sheet of frisket paper. Then peel off the backing paper and apply the frisket paper to the panel. Next, spray-paint the exposed areas (mouth, nose, and eyes) with the bright yellow paint you have selected.

To be sure you get the proper registration so that the eyes, nose, and mouth appear in the correct places, apply the frisket paper using the same technique as in putting decals on a car (Figs. 30-16 to 30-19). First, position the frisket paper properly and secure it at the top with two short strips of masking tape. When you are satisfied that the position is correct, lift up the frisket paper and peel off the backing paper. Then lower the frisket paper into place. After spray-painting the exposed area, peel the frisket paper from the panel.

The stencil is used in a similar way. It can be cut from clean cardboard or art board, available in art-supply stores. The cardboard must be cut cleanly, with no rough edges. Any sort of design can be cut out, from narrow lines to wide areas. Then the stencil is temporarily taped to the surface to be painted. It must be taped down tightly so there is no gap between it and the panel surface. Any slight gap could allow the paint to blow under. This would create an irregular line.

≡ 37-12 PAINT FOR CUSTOM PAINTING

A great variety of paint is available for automotive refinishing (Chap. 33). Acrylic lacquer is usually the preferred paint for custom work. It can be tinted to produce hundreds of colors. In addition, several types of metal flakes or tiny beads can be mixed with the paint to produce a brilliant finish. Metallic paint is described in ≡33-17.

≡ 37-13 CUSTOM PAINT JOBS

If you wandered through an art museum, you would see hundreds of paintings by different artists. The subject matter could range from landscapes or seascapes to portraits of people, animals, still life, and fantasies. A custom paint job can vary just as widely. Therefore, in getting started in custom painting, you must first decide what you would like on the vehicle. Then you must decide if all or part of the job is too complicated for you. If so, get help, and learn how it is done. Then practice. As your skills develop, you will be able to successfully complete more advanced custom-painting projects.

Fig. 37-8 A pumpkin.

Fig. 37-9 A frisket with openings for the eyes, nose, and mouth cut out.

Various custom paint jobs are described in following sections. These include:

1. Flames
2. Fish scales
3. Ribbons
4. Fans
5. Lace
6. Freak drops
7. Murals

≡ 37-14 SURFACE PREPARATION

Proper surface preparation is very important to the success of any custom paint job. If the surface has been stripped down to bare metal, it will have to be treated with metal conditioner and conversion coating (Chap.

34). Then the undercoats (≡34-18) and topcoats will have to be applied (Chap. 35).

If the old paint is in good condition so the custom work can be applied to it, wash the surface with a wax-and-grease remover. Wet-sand the area to be custom painted with 400-grit paper to roughen the surface so the sealer will adhere. Wipe the surface with a clean rag. Then use a tack rag to remove any trace of dust.

Mask off the area to be custom painted. Apply two coats of clear sealer over the area. This will prevent the solvents in the custom-job paint from penetrating to the base paint. After the sealer has dried, the surface is ready for the custom work.

≡ 37-15 PROTECTING THE CUSTOM PAINT JOB

After you have completed a custom paint job, it must be protected. This is done by applying two coats of clear sealer. Then, after 60 days, you can wet-sand the area with 600-grit paper, and compound and wax it.

≡ 37-16 FLAMES

Flames of various designs have always been popular (Fig. 37-10). Outline the pattern selected with narrow masking tape (Fig. 37-5). Then mask off the surrounding area with wider masking tape and masking paper. Spray the area with the color of paint desired. After the paint has dried sufficiently, apply two coats of clear sealer.

A refining touch can be added with the airbrush before the sealer is applied. Airbrush along the edges of the flames with a different color paint to emphasize the flame color. For example, you could add a light fog of yellow along the edges to emphasize the basic red of the flame. Or you could outline the flame in black to set it off

Fig. 37-10 Flames have always been a popular design in custom painting. *(Chevrolet Motor Division of General Motors Corporation)*

from the background of the car panel. Outlining can also be done with a pinstriping brush.

≡ 37-17 FISH SCALES

To apply fish scales, first the surface is prepared and then the area to be painted is masked off. Fish scaling requires you to make a special mask. Make the mask by applying adhesive-backed circles to a 3 × 5 index card, or to a larger piece of card stock (Fig. 37-11). The circles are available in various sizes from stationery stores and art-supply stores.

Measure the diameter of the circles. Then draw a line parallel to the edge of the card. The distance from the line to the edge of the card should be the same as one-half the diameter of the circle. Then apply the circles to the card so that exactly one-half the circle extends past the edge. Turn the card over and apply more circles to exactly cover the exposed adhesive backing on the first row of circles. Now the mask is ready to use.

Hold the mask in the first position, with the top edge of the circles almost touching the masking tape. Fog the area with an airbrush. Do not try to achieve solid coverage of the area. You want a shaded effect that darkens into the next layer of circles (Fig. 37-11). After airbrushing the first row, move the mask up one half-circle. Fog in the area just under the circles on the mask to make them darker than the adjacent areas.

≡ 37-18 RIBBONS

Ribbons are another very popular design used in custom painting. To make a ribbon, first prepare the background as previously described. Then draw in the outline of the ribbon with eyebrow pencil (Fig. 37-12A).

Next, prepare to paint the first section of ribbon. A ribbon has both shaded and solid color in it (Fig. 37-12B). On the front of the ribbon, the color fades from almost solid to light. Use masking tape and paper to mask out all around the area you will paint. Then apply the paint. After it dries, repeat the procedure on the other parts of the ribbon that are facing the front. When these are done, paint the back sides of the ribbon. These are darker, and may be solid color (Fig. 37-12C). Then remove all masking tape and paper. Wash off the pencil lines.

≡ 37-19 FANS

Fans are often basic designs which can be very effective. Figure 37-13 shows the procedure. First, prepare the surface as described earlier. Then use a 3 × 5 index

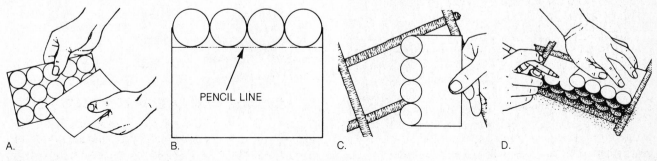

PENCIL LINE

A. B. C. D.

Fig. 37-11 Preparing and using the mask to paint fish scales. *(ATW)*

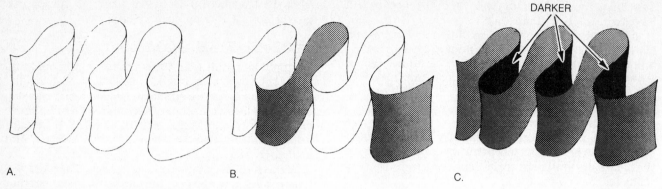

A.   B.   C.

DARKER

Fig. 37-12 Steps in making ribbons. *(Metalflake, Inc.)*

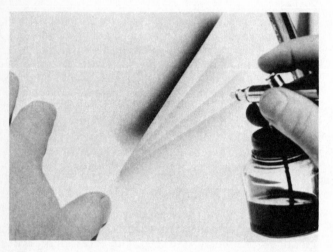

Fig. 37-13 To make a fan, use a piece of straight-edged cardboard as a guide. *(Badger Air-Brush Company)*

card, or a piece of cardboard, to define the lower edge and fog along it. Keep the distances uniform as you swing the card down. Have the edges pointing to a common center to create the fan effect. A variation of this design is to use a corner of the card, as shown in Fig. 37-14.

Fig. 37-14 Using the corner of an index card to make another fan design. *(Badger Air-Brush Company)*

≡ 37-20 LACE

Lace painting is a form of stencil painting in which a piece of lace material serves as the stencil. Lace is available in many patterns. Tape the lace to the previously prepared surface. Make sure that it is pulled tight so that there are no wrinkles and it is tight against the surface. Then airbrush the lace and the surface underneath. Be careful not to saturate the lace. The paint should be fogged on in several thin coats. Allow each cost to dry before applying the next coat.

≡ 37-21 FREAK DROPS

Freak drops (Fig. 37-15) are simple to make, although the results are somewhat unpredictable. A freak drop is

Fig. 37-15 Freak drops. The size and shape of the drops depend on how close the airbrush is held to the surface and how long the paint is applied. *(Metalflake, Inc.)*

Fig. 37-16 Murals painted on vans by an expert custom painter. *(Badger Air-Brush Company)*

made by reducing the paint to a waterlike consistency by adding thinner. Then the airbrush is held about 2 inches [50 mm] away from the surface. Give the airbrush a short, full burst while pointed at one spot. The size and shape of the drop depends on how much paint is deposited and the effect of the airstream. A short burst gives a larger center with short legs. A longer burst makes the legs longer. Excessively long bursts will run excessively.

≡ 37-22 MURALS

Murals are advanced-design art that require experience in handling the airbrush, pinstriping brushes, and pens (Fig. 37-16). Basically, however, they are done by the various techniques described in this chapter. Each design is built up, bit by bit, using masking, frisket paper, stencils, and spray mask. Some designs are available that allow you to paint murals by numbers.

REVIEW QUESTIONS

Select the *one* correct, best, or most probable answer to each question. You can find the answers in the section indicated at the end of each question.

1. Three types of tools that use air to apply paint are the
   a. air gun, air hose, and airbrush   (≡37-3)
   b. airbrush, touch-up gun, and spray mask
   c. airbrush, air gun, and air tool
   d. airbrush, touch-up gun, and spray gun

2. Air for the airbrush or the touch-up gun can be supplied by the shop compressed-air system or   (≡37-6)
   a. a spare tire or tank of CO_2 gas
   b. a tank of propane
   c. the engine intake manifold
   d. a bicycle-tire pump

3. Spray mask is a   (≡37-7)
   a. tinted paint that can be peeled off
   b. liquid that dries to a transparent, rubbery film
   c. type of frisket paper
   d. kind of stencil

4. To protect the finished job, you should   (≡37-15)
   a. apply a coat of spray mask
   b. apply two coats of clear sealer
   c. sand the surface and then polish it
   d. remove the topcoats and sealer

5. Frisket paper is a   (≡37-11)
   a. form of masking tape available in rolls
   b. form of masking paper available in rolls
   c. thin adhesive-backed paper protected by a backing paper
   d. type of stencil

PART 11
ESTIMATING

A written estimate is used by body and paint technicians as a "roadmap" to guide them through the repair of damaged vehicles. It is the job of the estimator to prepare this roadmap, which is properly called the **written estimate**, or simply the **estimate**.

There are many things to consider in preparing an accurate estimate. This means that the estimator must be a person who knows automotive construction and repair procedures. This part describes some of the things the estimator must check and do to prepare the estimate.

There is one chapter in Part 11:

Chapter 38 Estimating Collision and Paint Damage

CHAPTER 38

ESTIMATING COLLISION AND PAINT DAMAGE

After studying this chapter, you should be able to:

1. Explain the duties of the estimator.

2. Discuss the inspection of air-conditioning systems.

3. Explain how to inspect and test energy-absorbing bumpers.

4. Prepare a written estimate.

≡ 38-1 DUTIES OF THE ESTIMATOR

The job of the body-shop estimator is to keep a steady flow of work coming into the shop. The duties of the estimator and the importance of this job to successful body-shop operations are described in ≡1-5. If the estimator makes mistakes and cannot accurately estimate how much repair jobs will cost, the body shop can be in serious financial trouble.

A person who is an estimator must have many skills. The major task is writing the estimate. Then, when approved by whoever is to pay the bill and accepted by the body shop, the written estimate becomes the roadmap to be followed by the body and paint technicians in restoring the vehicle. Preparation of the written estimate is covered later in ≡38-4 to 38-8.

In addition to estimating, the estimator usually is the only contact the car owner has with the body shop. This means that the estimator must be good at customer relations. Also, the estimator must work with the adjuster for the insurance company on many jobs. This requires skill at negotiating, flexibility, and an accurate knowledge of both parts and labor costs.

The insurance adjuster makes a separate estimate and compares it with the body-shop estimate. If the estimates are comparable, the body shop is given the go-ahead to do the repair job. Sometimes the insurance adjuster simply examines the damaged car with the estimator and does not make a detailed estimate.

≡ 38-2 FREQUENCY OF COLLISIONS

There are about 160 million cars, trucks, and buses operating on the streets and highways throughout the United States. Statistics indicate that there are about 17 million major and minor collisions each year. In other words, cars are damaged at a rate exceeding one car every other second of every hour each day!

Before most of these damaged cars are repaired, an estimate of the cost of repair is prepared. Then a decision is made as to whether the vehicle is economically repairable. This is a problem that arises frequently in major collisions and roll-overs. It is not often a problem when only one fender or panel must be repaired. However, written estimates usually are not prepared on a car that is obviously totaled. For example, a large tree falling on a car and crushing it probably will total the car (Fig. 38-1).

≡ 38-3 AFTER THE DAMAGE

After a minor collision, the car may still be drivable. If so, the owner drives the car to the body shop, where the estimator inspects the damage and prepares the written estimate. After a major collision, the car usually is towed away. It may be taken directly to the body shop or to a local storage lot designated by the police or the insurance company. Sometimes it takes a tow truck to move a wrecked car. In this case, the estimator travels to the car to inspect it so the estimate can be prepared. After the decision is made as to which body shop will do the repair job, arrangements are made for towing the car to that body shop.

≡ 38-4 INSPECTING THE DAMAGE

The first thing the estimator does when a damaged car is driven in or brought in by a wrecker (Fig. 38-2) is to inspect the car and decide what work is required, how many hours it will take, and what parts are needed and how much they will cost. In some cases, the car is so badly damaged it is not worth repairing. Such a car is called a *total*.

If the car is worth repairing, the estimator fills out a written estimate form such as shown in Fig. 38-3. On the form, the left columns list operations such as replacing parts, straightening panels, refinishing, and so on. The labor column lists the hours of labor required for each operation. The next column lists the costs of new or salvaged parts that are needed. The right column lists the costs of certain jobs that may be sublet. Sublet jobs are those that will be done by another shop. They may include such operations as straightening and rechroming a bumper, aligning the front wheels, adjusting headlights, and checking the charging or ignition system.

When you inspect a vehicle for damage, the first question to answer is about the whole car. *Is the vehicle repairable?* If so, then you must ask another question about each damaged part. *How is this part to be repaired?* It may be replaced with a new one, straightened and refinished, or replaced with a used part from a

Fig. 38-1 A written estimate is not always needed when the damage has obviously totaled the car.

Fig. 38-2 A written estimate is prepared on cars brought to the body shop by a wrecker.

salvaged vehicle. Sometimes a lack of parts availability helps answer the question for you.

To inspect damage, begin by standing directly in front of it. Carefully note each crushed part. Then work through the damaged area, analyzing each damaged part in terms of *"What's wrong?"* and *"How can it be fixed?"* Your biggest concern is that you see all of the damage. Many types of collision damage are not readily visible. For example, a car that has been struck hard on the side may have frame and drive-shaft damage. Also, the impact may have broken the engine mounts. To check for this type of damage, have the car placed on safety stands so you can get under the vehicle to make a

UNISET ☒ THE REYNOLDS AND REYNOLDS COMPANY · CELINA, OHIO ☒ UNISET
BUSINESS FORMS / ACCOUNTING SYSTEMS / EDP SERVICES

RAY W. REYNOLDS COMPANY
2619 HEMSTEAD BLVD. TELEPHONE 224-2678
HOMETOWN, STATE 19787

BODY AND FENDER REPAIRS • EXPERT REFINISHING

NAME _____   DATE _____
ADDRESS _____   PHONE _____
    DATE WANTED _____

YEAR-MODEL-COLOR	MAKE OF CAR	BODY TYPE	LICENSE NO.	SERIAL NO.	MOTOR NO.	MILEAGE

REPAIR	REPLACE		LABOR	PARTS AND MATERIALS	SUBLET WORK

TOTALS

LABOR	
PARTS AND MATERIALS	
SUBLET WORK	
TAX	
GRAND TOTAL	

THIS ESTIMATE IS BASED ON OUR INSPECTION AND DOES NOT COVER ADDITIONAL PARTS OR LABOR WHICH MAY BE REQUIRED AFTER THE WORK HAS BEEN STARTED. AFTER THE WORK HAS STARTED, WORN OR DAMAGED PARTS WHICH ARE NOT EVIDENT ON FIRST INSPECTION MAY BE DISCOVERED. NATURALLY THIS ESTIMATE CANNOT COVER SUCH CONTINGENCIES. PARTS PRICES SUBJECT TO CHANGE WITHOUT NOTICE. THIS ESTIMATE IS FOR IMMEDIATE ACCEPTANCE.

THIS WORK AUTHORIZED BY _____

ESTIMATE SHEET AND REPAIR ORDER

FORM 5A-87   THE REYNOLDS & REYNOLDS CO., CELINA, OHIO   LITHO IN U.S.A.

Fig. 38-3 Form used to prepare an estimate. *(The Reynolds & Reynolds Company)*

thorough inspection. Detecting and correcting structural damage are covered in Chaps. 15 and 16.

A front-end collision also can cause damage that you can easily overlook. For example, a punctured air-conditioner condenser and engine radiator will have to be repaired or replaced. In addition, the air-conditioning system will have to be recharged with refrigerant, and the radiator will have to be refilled with antifreeze. Both of these chemicals are expensive. You must be sure to include their costs in preparing the estimate.

There are many types of hidden damage that only experience will teach you to find. When estimating any vehicle repair, always check for hidden damage.

≡ 38-5 THE ESTIMATING PROCEDURE

Start the estimating procedure on the outside of the vehicle in front of the damage. On the estimate form, list each damaged panel or major part, along with all other parts attached to it that also are damaged. Start outside the vehicle and work inward with your inspection until there is no more damage to be repaired.

When you finish inspecting each panel or major part, carefully take a second look at it. Make sure that you have included any emblems or moldings that must be replaced or reinstalled on the new panel. Next, carefully inspect all adjacent parts for damage and proper alignment. Check all doors, hood, and trunk lid for proper operation and locking, if any of these could have been affected by the collision. Check the bumpers and grill for damage, and all lights and the brakes for proper operation.

If the collision could have caused bent wheels or steering or suspension damage or affected front-end or rear-wheel alignment, then these items must be checked. By following the steps discussed above as you prepare the estimate, you will have written on the estimate form a complete list of all the damaged parts.

≡ 38-6 CHECKING FOR AIR-CONDITIONER DAMAGE

Figure 38-4 shows the location of the air-conditioning components in a car. If a car has been in a collision, the air-conditioner system should be inspected as soon as possible. If the system has been opened by the impact, it should be repaired without delay. Leaving an air-conditioner system exposed to the atmosphere allows air, moisture, and dirt to enter. The longer the exposure, the greater the amount of air, moisture, and dirt that get in. Therefore, the greater the damage to the system.

You can often tell at a glance when components are damaged beyond repair or the whole system is useless. The inspection procedure recommended by Chevrolet follows. Note that the procedure is merely a general guide. Details of air-conditioner service are covered in *Automotive Air Conditioning*, another book in the McGraw-Hill *Automotive Technology Series*.

1. Remove the drive belt. Cut it off if necessary.

2. Look at the various components of the system—condenser, evaporator, VIR unit, compressor, mounting brackets, connecting lines, and controls—to determine if any have been damaged. The condenser, being in front of the engine radiator, is the most vulnerable and most apt to be damaged in a front-end collision.

NOTE: *No repairs of any kind, including soldering, welding, or brazing, should be attempted on the condenser. If the vapor passages are bent or damaged in any way or if the fins are mashed together, discard the condenser and install a new one.*

3. Inspect the VIR unit for cracks and other damage. If it appears to be intact, clean it with a suitable cleaner. Dry it thoroughly. Replace the desiccant bag.

4. If the evaporator shows any signs of damage, replace it.

5. Check the control system, connecting wires, vacuum hoses, and vacuum motors for damage. Install new parts as necessary.

6. Check all connecting lines and flexible hoses for damage. Inspect them along their full length. Make sure all connections are in good condition. Replace any lines or hoses that are damaged in any way.

7. Check the clutch pulley for proper operation.

8. Check the compressor (Fig. 38-4) for damage.

9. Install the charging station, and discharge the refrigerant system.

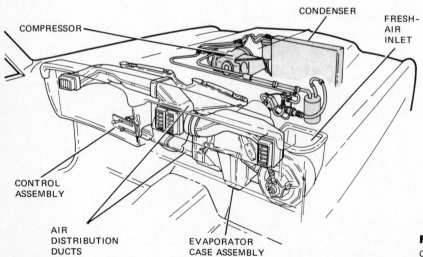

COMPRESSOR

CONDENSER

FRESH-AIR INLET

CONTROL ASSEMBLY

AIR DISTRIBUTION DUCTS

EVAPORATOR CASE ASSEMBLY

Fig. 38-4 Location of the air-conditioning components in the car. *(Ford Motor Company)*

10. Remove the compressor from the engine. Unscrew the oil test fitting, and pour the oil into a clean glass container. Examine the oil for dirt, water, metal particles, etc. If any of these are present, discard the compressor and the desiccant bag in the VIR unit. Flush the other system components with liquid refrigerant.

11. If the compressor oil is clean and free of any harmful substance, discard it. Put the same amount of new, fresh oil into the compressor.

NOTE: If system components have been flushed, replace the full charge of oil. If not, add no more new oil than you poured out.

12. Use a can or supply tank of refrigerant to charge the compressor. Use the leak detector to check the compressor for leaks. If it has no leaks, reinstall it.

13. Evacuate the system. Put some refrigerant into the system, and leak-test it.

14. If the system passes the leak test, recharge it.

≡ 38-7 INSPECTING ENERGY-ABSORBING BUMPERS

Energy-absorbing bumpers are required by law. Such bumpers will withstand collisions at low speed without damage to the bumper or vehicle. Most energy-absorbing bumpers are designed to assume their original position after the collision. There are several types, for both the front and rear of the vehicle.

Checking energy-absorbing bumpers, both on and off the car, is described and illustrated in Chap. 12. How to remove bumpers and safely dispose of a scrapped energy absorber are also discussed in Chap. 12.

— CAUTION

Some energy absorbers are filled with gas at high pressure. They can explode if heat is applied to them. Under no condition should heat be applied, as, for example, to repair the unit by welding.

≡ 38-8 DETERMINING COST OF REPAIR

Now that you know what parts are damaged on a car, you must figure out how much it will cost to restore the car to its precollision condition. Usually, in a commercial body shop, you will find the prices of parts to be replaced in the *Motor Crash Estimating Guide*, the *Glenn Mitchell Collision Estimator*, or other source. Any of these publications, if up to date, will provide you with parts prices and the estimated labor time to replace them. However, the labor times listed in these manuals are only guides. Many conditions, such as cutting away the crushed sheet metal, may require the labor time for any job to be increased.

──────── REVIEW QUESTIONS ────────

Select the *one* correct, best, or most probable answer to each question. You can find the answers in the section indicated at the end of each question.

1. The person in the body shop who usually deals with the customer is the   (≡38-1)
  a. body technician
  b. estimator
  c. paint technician
  d. wrecker driver

2. When a car is obviously totaled, you do not always need to   (≡38-4)
  a. prepare a detailed written estimate
  b. tow the car away
  c. attempt to repair the car
  d. order paint for the car

3. When inspecting a damaged car, the first question to answer is,   (≡38-4)
  a. How much does the damaged panel cost?
  b. Is the car repairable?
  c. Can the car be towed?
  d. How much paint time is required?

4. When a car has been in a front-end collision, you should check for   (≡38-4)
  a. transmission damage
  b. rear-end damage
  c. damage to the headliner
  d. damage to the air conditioner

5. The estimator usually completes the written estimate by using   (≡38-8)
  a. manufacturers' parts catalogs
  b. a collision estimating guide
  c. manufacturers' time-labor standards
  d. none of the above

GLOSSARY

A/C Abbreviation for air conditioning.

abrasive A substance used for cutting, grinding, lapping, or polishing metals.

accessories Devices not considered essential to the operation of a vehicle, such as the radio, car heater, and electric window lifts.

acetylene One of the two gases used in brazing, welding, and cutting.

acrylic A clear chemical compound used in lacquer and enamel paint binder. Gives paint durability, and helps retain the original color and gloss.

adhesion Ability of a substance to stick to a surface.

adhesive A substance that causes two surfaces to stick together.

adjust To bring the parts of a component or system to the specified relationship, dimension, or pressure.

adjustments Necessary or desired changes in clearances, fit, or settings.

adsorb To collect in a very thin layer on another surface.

aerosol spray Small metal container that sprays paint in a mist.

aiming screws Horizontal and vertical self-locking adjusting screws, used to aim a headlight and retain it in position.

air bags A passive restraint system consisting of balloon-type passenger-safety devices that inflate automatically on vehicle impact.

air compressor A mechanical device used to compress air from normal atmospheric pressure to the pressures required to operate various air-operated equipment.

air conditioning An accessory system that conditions passenger-compartment air by cleaning, cooling, and drying it.

air dry Allowing a finish, such as paint, to harden completely under normal atmospheric conditions.

air filter A screen that traps any dust and dirt particles in the air flowing through.

air line A hose, pipe, or tube through which air passes.

air pressure Atmospheric pressure; also the pressure produced by an air pump or by compression of air in a cylinder.

air pump Any device for compressing air.

air suspension A suspension system that uses contained air, such as in air bags, for vehicle springing.

air transformer A device used to reduce and control the pressure of air coming from the air compressor. Transformers also contain filters which clean the air as it passes through.

alignment The act of lining up, the state of being in a true line.

alkyd A chemical compound used in paint binder.

alloy A mixture of two or more metals.

ambient temperature The temperature of the air surrounding the car.

antifreeze A chemical, usually ethylene glycol, that is added to the engine coolant to raise the coolant boiling temperature and lower its freezing temperature.

atomization The spraying of a liquid through a nozzle so that the liquid is broken into a very fine mist.

automatic level control A suspension system which compensates for variations in load in the rear of the car; positions the rear at a predesigned level regardless of load.

axle A cross bar supporting a vehicle and on which one or more wheels turn.

back light The back window, usually located in the roof panel.

base coat The coat of paint over which final coats will be applied.

base metal The metal to be welded or cut.

battery An electrochemical device for storing energy in chemical form so that it can be released as electricity; a group of electric cells connected together.

battery acid The electrolyte used in a battery, a mixture of sulfuric acid and water.

battery charging Restoration of chemical energy to a battery by supplying a measured flow of electric current to it over a specified period of time.

bead weld A type of weld made by one pass of the electrode or rod.

belt tension Tightness of a drive belt.

bevel angle The angle of bevel on the prepared edge of a part to be welded.

binder One of the substances in paint which acts as a glue to bond the pigment particles together and to the painted surface to form a paint film.

bleeding An old color which comes through and colors a fresh topcoat of paint.

blistering Small bubbles that form in a paint film.

Bloc-Chek A tester that is inserted in the radiator filler neck of a running engine to detect the leakage of exhaust gas into the cooling system.

blushing A topcoat with a milky or misty appearance.

body On a vehicle, the self-contained unit that provides enclosures for the passengers, engine, and luggage.

body hardware Includes the door handles, window cranks, and other appearance and functional parts, both inside and outside of the body.

body lock pillar The body pillar that contains the lock striker plate; usually part of the center pillar or rear quarter assembly.

body mounting Putting a car body onto a car chassis. Also, the placing of rubber cushions along the chassis to soak up noise and vibration.

body panels Sheets of metal or plastic which are fastened together to form the car body.

body side molding The principal trim molding used around the exterior of the body, approximately horizontal to the ground.

body spoon   Hand tool used in bodywork.

body trim   Material used to upholster and line the interior of the body and rear luggage compartment.

brake lines   The tubes or hoses connecting the master cylinder to the wheel cylinders, or calipers, in a hydraulic brake system.

brazing   A welding process in which the filler metal is a nonferrous metal or alloy whose melting point is higher than 800°F [427°C] but lower than that of the metals or alloys to be joined.

bronzing   The formation of a metallic-appearing haze on a paint film.

buckles   Distortion of body panel due to impact.

build   The depth or thickness of the paint film deposited, measured in mils (thousandths of an inch).

bulb   An assembly which contains a source of light, normally used in a lamp.

burr   A feather edge of metal left on a part being cut with a file or other cutting tool.

butt joint   A welded joint between two abutting parts lying in approximately the same plane.

cables   Stranded conductors, usually covered with insulating material, used for connections between electrical devices.

calibrate   To check or correct the initial setting of a test instrument.

carburizing flame   A gas flame having the property of introducing carbon into the metal heated.

catalytic converter   A mufflerlike device for use in an exhaust system; it converts harmful exhaust gases into harmless gases by promoting a chemical reaction between a catalyst and the pollutants.

caulking compound   A sealing substance used to close cracks.

Celsius   A thermometer scale on which water boils at 100° and freezes at 0°. The formula °C = 5/9 (°F − 32) converts Fahrenheit readings to Celsius. Formerly called centigrade.

CENTARI   DuPont's name for acrylic enamel; introduced in 1969.

center pillar   A box-type construction used on four-door bodies. The center pillar forms the front-door body lock pillar and the rear-door body hinge pillar.

centigrade   *See* Celsius.

centimeter (cm)   A unit of linear measure in the metric system; equal to approximately 0.390 inch.

chalking   The presence of loose, powdery pigment which is no longer held to the surface by the binder. Finish looks dull.

change of state   Transformation of a substance from solid to liquid, from liquid to vapor, or vice versa.

charcoal canister   A container filled with activated charcoal, used to trap gasoline vapor from the fuel tank and carburetor while the engine is off.

chassis   The assembly of mechanisms that makes up the major operating part of the vehicle; usually assumed to include everything except the car body.

check   To verify that a component, system, or measurement complies with specifications.

check (paint)   A break on the surface of the topcoat caused by shrinkage, due to oxidation or extreme cold.

check valve   A valve that opens to permit the passage of air or fluid in one direction only, or operates to prevent some undesirable action.

chemical instability   An undesirable condition caused by the presence of contaminants in a refrigeration system. Refrigerants are stable chemicals, but in contact with contaminants they may break down into harmful chemicals.

chemical reaction   The formation of one or more new substances when two or more substances are brought together.

chipping   Damage resulting from the impact of a sharp object, such as a stone, which removes some of the finish. Also called stone bruise.

circuit   The complete path of an electric current, including the current source. When the path is continuous, the circuit is closed and current flows. When the path is broken, the circuit is open and no current flows. Also used to refer to fluid paths, as in refrigerant and hydraulic systems.

clear   A finish having no pigments (color) or transparent pigments only.

clear coat   A clear finish sprayed over the color coat.

clearance   The space between two moving parts, or between a moving and a stationary part.

coach joint   Pinchweld joint on the exterior surface of the body.

coalescence   Fusion or flowing together, as atomized paint droplets.

coat: double   Two single coats of paint, one followed by the other with little or no flash time between each coat.

coat: single   A coat produced by two passes of the spray gun, one pass overlapping the other by 50 percent.

cold   The absence of heat. An object is considered cold to the touch if its temperature is less than body temperature of 98.6°F [37°C].

collapsible steering column   An energy-absorbing steering column designed to collapse if the driver is thrown into it by a severe collision.

compartment shelf panel   The horizontal panel located between the rear seat-back and the back window.

compatibility   The ability of two or more materials to work with each other. Oil and water are not compatible.

compounding   *See* Polishing.

compressor   The pump in an air-conditioning system that compresses refrigerant vapor to increase its pressure and temperature.

condensate   Water that is removed from air. It forms on the exterior surface of the air-conditioner evaporator.

condensation   A change of state during which a gas turns to liquid, usually because of temperature or pressure changes. Also, moisture from the air, deposited on a cool surface.

condenser   In an air-conditioning system, the radiatorlike heat exchanger in which refrigerant vapor loses heat and returns to the liquid state.

conductor Any material or substance that allows current or heat to flow easily.

cone The conical part of a gas flame that is next to the original orifice of the tip.

contaminants (air-conditioning) Anything other than refrigerant and refrigerant oil in a refrigerator system; includes rust, dirt, moisture, and air.

contaminants (painting) Anything on the surface to be painted that might harm the finish. Examples are polishes, waxes, dirt, tree sap, and tar.

conversion coating A chemical applied to a metal surface after the metal conditioner to improve the adhesion of the finish to be applied.

convex fillet weld A fillet weld having a convex face.

coolant The liquid mixture of about 50 percent antifreeze and 50 percent water used to carry heat out of the engine.

core In a radiator, a number of coolant passages surrounded by fins through which air flows to carry away heat.

corrosion A chemical reaction which results in deterioration of a metal. Rust is an example of corrosion.

coverage The surface area a given amount of paint will cover.

cracking A break in the paint film which extends down to the metal surface or undercoat.

craters Holes in the paint film caused by paint flowing away from contaminated spots before it dries.

crazing A breakdown of the finish in the form of small cracks in all directions. Similar to crow's-feet.

crease line A line on the body caused by a crease or break in the body surface.

cubic centimeter (cu cm, cm³, or cc) A unit of volume in the metric system; equal to approximately 0.061 cubic inch.

curb weight The weight of an empty vehicle without payload or driver but including fuel, coolant, oil, and all items of standard equipment.

curing The complete or final drying stage in which the paint reaches its full strength owing to solvent evaporation and chemical change.

cutting attachment A device that is attached to a welding torch to convert it to a cutting torch.

cutting tip A torch tip especially adapted for cutting.

cylinder A portable container used for storage of a compressed gas.

dash panel A panel in the body front-end assembly forming the front vertical plane of the body.

defroster The part of the car heater system designed to melt frost or ice on the inside or outside of the windshield; includes the required ductwork.

degree Part of a circle. One degree is 1/360 of a complete circle.

deposited metal Metal that has been added by a welding process.

desiccant A drying agent. In an air conditioner, desiccant is placed in the receiver-dehydrator to remove moisture from the refrigerant.

detent A small depression in a shaft, rail, or rod into which a pawl or ball drops when the shaft, rail, or rod is moved; this provides a locking effect.

device A mechanism, tool, or other piece of equipment designed to serve a special purpose or perform a special function.

diagnosis A procedure followed in locating the cause of a malfunction.

diaphragm A thin dividing sheet or partition which separates an area into compartments.

dimmer switch A two-position switch which is operated by the driver to select the high or low headlight beam.

direct damage Damage occurring at the point of impact.

directional signal A device on the car that flashes lights to indicate the direction in which the driver intends to turn.

dirt in paint Foreign material under or in a paint finish.

disassemble To take apart.

discharge To depressurize; to crack a valve to allow refrigerant to escape from an air conditioner; to bleed.

discharge air Conditioned air leaving the refrigeration unit of an air conditioner.

discharge line In an air conditioner, the tube that connects the compressor outlet and the condenser inlet. High-pressure refrigerant vapor flows through the line.

discharge pressure In an air conditioner, the pressure of refrigerant being discharged from the compressor; also called the high pressure.

dolly blocks Blocks of metal, variously shaped and contoured, used to straighten body panels and fenders. The dolly block is held on one side of the panel while the other side is struck with a special hammer.

dowel A metal pin attached to one object which, when inserted into a hole in another object, ensures proper alignment.

drier A catalyst added to paint to speed up the curing or drying time.

drip molding A channel molding over the door and quarter openings to drain the water from the roof away from the openings.

drive shaft An assembly of one or two universal joints and slip joints connected to a heavy metal tube; used to transmit power from the transmission to the differential. Also called the propeller shaft.

drop light A portable light, with a long electric cord, used in the shop to illuminate the immediate work area.

drop-center wheel The conventional passenger-car wheel, which has a space (drop) in the center for one bead to fit into while the other bead is being lifted over the rim flange.

dry-spray A small amount of paint in relation to the spray-gun air pressure, resulting in a light, thin dry film of paint.

DUCO DuPont's name for nitrocellulose lacquer, the original modern automotive finish developed first by DuPont in 1924.

duct A tube or channel used to convey air or liquid from one point to another.

DULUX Dupont's name for alkyd enamel; introduced first by DuPont in 1928.

durability Length of life of a paint film.

eccentric An offset section of a shaft used to convert rotary to reciprocating motion. Also called a cam.

electric system In the automobile, the system that electrically cranks the engine for starting; furnishes high-voltage sparks to the engine cylinders to fire the compressed air-fuel charges; lights the lights; and powers the heater motor, radio, and other accessories. Consists, in part, of the starting motor, wiring, battery alternator, regulator, ignition distributor, and ignition coil.

electrolyte The mixture of sulfuric acid and water used in lead-acid storage batteries. The acid enters into chemical reaction with active material in the plates to produce voltage and current.

enamel A type of finish which dries or cures through evaporation of solvents and through a chemical change called oxidation.

epoxy A plastic compound that can be used to repair some types of cracks in metal.

ethylene glycol Chemical name of a widely used type of permanent antifreeze.

evacuate To use a vacuum pump to pump any air and moisture out of an air-conditioner refrigerant system; required whenever any component in the refrigerant system has been removed and replaced.

evaporation To change from a liquid to a gas. In painting, the process during which the solvent in paint changes to a gas and evaporates.

evaporator The heat exchanger in an air conditioner in which refrigerant changes from a liquid to a gas (evaporates), taking heat from the surrounding air as it does so.

exhaust pipe The pipe connecting the exhaust manifold with the muffler.

expansion tank A tank at the top of an automobile radiator which provides room for heated coolant to expand and to give off any air that may be trapped in the coolant. Also, a similar tank used in some fuel tanks to prevent fuel from spilling out of the tank through expansion.

fading A change in color from the original, usually resulting from exposure to weathering during use.

fan The bladed device on the front of the engine that rotates to draw cooling air through the radiator, or around the engine cylinders; an air blower such as the heater fan and the A/C blower.

fanning Use of pressurized air through spray gun or dusting gun to speed up the drying time of a finish. Not a recommended procedure.

fatigue failure A type of metal failure resulting from repeated stress which finally alters the character of the metal so that it cracks.

featheredge A tapered paint edge from base metal to topcoat.

filler metal Metal to be added in making a weld.

filter A device through which air, gases, or liquids are passed to remove impurities.

finish A protective or decorative coating; to apply such a coating.

fisheyes *See* Craters.

flash The first stage of drying during which some of the solvents evaporate, dulling the paint from a very high gloss.

flasher An automatic-reset circuit breaker used in the directional-signal and hazard-warning circuits.

floor pan The main stamping in the underbody assembly; forms the floor of the body in the passenger compartment.

flow The ability of the droplets of paint sprayed to merge or melt together to form a smooth film. Also called flow-out.

fluid Any liquid or gas.

flush In an air conditioner, to wash out the refrigerant passages with refrigerant to remove contaminants; in a brake system, to wash out the hydraulic system and the master cylinder and wheel cylinders, or calipers, with clean brake fluid to remove any dirt or impurities in the system.

flux A fusible material or gas used to dissolve and prevent the formation of oxides, nitrides, or other undesirable inclusions formed in welding.

fog coat A coat of regularly reduced enamel or lacquer, sprayed at slightly higher pressure and greater distance with the gun set for reduced fluid flow.

force dry Accelerated drying of finishes by means of heat or air.

foreign material on surface Contamination, such as oil, grease, road tar, insecticides, on the paint film surface. This condition is often difficult to remove and may damage the paint.

frame The assembly of metal structural parts and channel sections that supports the car engine and body and is supported by the wheels.

frame gauges Gauges hung from the car frame to check its alignment.

Freon-12 Refrigerant used in automobile air conditioners. Also known as Refrigerant-12 and R-12.

friction The resistance to motion between two bodies in contact with each other.

front body hinge pillar A structural member on which the front door is hung.

fuel gauge A gauge that indicates the amount of fuel in the fuel tank.

fuel line The pipe or tubes through which fuel flows from the fuel tank to the carburetor.

fuel tank The storage tank for fuel on the vehicle.

fuse A device designed to open an electric circuit when the current is excessive, to protect equipment in the circuit. An open, or "blown," fuse must be replaced after the circuit problem is corrected.

fuse block A boxlike unit that holds the fuses to the various electric circuits in an automobile.

fusible link A type of fuse in which a special wire melts to open the circuit when the current is excessive. An open, or "blown," fusible link must be replaced after the circuit problem is corrected.

fusion Melting; conversion from the solid to the liquid state.

fusion welding A group of processes in which metals

are welded together by bringing them to the molten state at the surface to be joined; with or without the addition of mechanical pressure or force.

gas pocket   A cavity in a weld caused by gas inclusion.

gas welding   A nonpressure (fusion) welding process in which the welding heat is obtained from a gas flame.

gasket   A layer of material, such as cork or metal or both, placed between two surfaces to provide a tight seal between them.

gasket cement   A liquid adhesive material, or sealer, used to install gaskets; in some applications, a layer of gasket cement is used as a gasket.

gauge set   One or more instruments attached to a manifold (a pipe fitted with several outlets for connecting pipes) and used for measuring pressures in the air conditioner.

gloss   The shininess of a paint film, caused by the paint's ability to reflect light.

goggles   Special safety glasses worn over the eyes to protect them from flying chips, dirt, dust, spraying refrigerant, and splashing liquids.

grit   A measure of the size of the abrasive particles on abrasive disks or sandpaper.

grommet   A device, usually made of hard rubber or plastic, used to encircle or support a part.

ground-return system   Common system of electric wiring in which the chassis and frame of a vehicle are used as part of the electric return circuit to the battery or alternator; also known as the single-wire system.

gutter   A trough following the contour of a body opening which provides a water drain and also aids in sealing the opening.

GVW   Abbreviation for gross vehicle weight; the total weight of a vehicle, including the body, payload, fuel, driver, etc.

hammer-off-dolly   Method of using hammer and dolly in which the hammer taps around the area where dolly is being held.

hammer-on-dolly   Method of using hammer and dolly in which the hammer taps on the area where dolly is being held.

hardness   That quality which gives a dry paint film resistance to surface damage or deformation.

hardtop   Auto body style with rigid roof and convertible-type doors.

hazard-warning system   Also called the emergency signal system; a driver-controlled system of flashing front and rear lights, used to warn approaching motorists when a car has made an emergency stop.

headlights   Lights at the front of a vehicle; designed to illuminate the road ahead of the vehicle.

headlining   Interior trim which covers the underside of the roof panel.

heater core   A small radiator, mounted under the dash, through which hot coolant circulates. When heat is needed in the passenger compartment, a fan is turned on to circulate air through the hot core.

Heli-Coil   A thread insert used when original threads are worn or damaged. The insert is installed in a re-tapped hole to reduce the thread size to the original size.

hem flange   A finished edge for a metal assembly, such as a door assembly. It is formed by folding the outer panel over the inner panel.

hiding   The degree to which a paint obscures the surface to which it is applied. Also called hiding ability.

high-pressure lines   The lines from the air-conditioner compressor outlet to the thermostatic-expansion valve or orifice tube inlet that carry high-pressure refrigerant. The two longest high-pressure lines are the discharge and liquid lines.

hold-out   Ability of the surface to keep topcoat from sinking in.

hood   The part of the car body that fits over and protects the engine.

hub   The center part of a wheel.

humidity   Amount of moisture in the air. Relative humidity is the ratio of the amount of moisture present to the greatest amount possible at the given temperature.

hydraulic brakes   A braking system that uses hydraulic pressure to force the brake shoes against the brake drums, or rotors, as the brake pedal is depressed.

hydraulic pressure   Pressure exerted through the medium of a liquid.

hydraulics   The use of a liquid under pressure to transfer force or motion, or to increase an applied force.

hydrometer   A device used to measure specific gravity. In automotive servicing, a device used to measure the specific gravity of battery electrolyte to determine the state of the battery charge; also a device used to measure the specific gravity of coolant to determine its freezing temperature.

idler arm   In the steering system, a link that supports the tie rod and transmits steering motion to both wheels through the tie-rod ends.

independent front suspension   The front-suspension system in which each front wheel is independently supported by a spring.

indicator   A device used to make some condition known by use of a light or a dial and pointer; for example, the temperature indicator or oil-pressure indicator.

indirect damage   Damage occurring away from the point of impact.

industrial fallout   A condition caused by particles being blown into the air by the various processes of heavy industry and then being deposited on a vehicle's surface. The particles often cause rust- or off-color spots in the finish which require repair.

inertia   Property of an object that causes it to resist any change in its speed or the direction of its travel.

inspect   To examine a component or system for correct surface, condition, or function.

install   The installation of any part, accessory, option, or kit which has not previously been part of, or attached to the vehicle.

instrument panel An interior body panel carrying such components as the instrument cluster, glove compartment, and radio speaker grille.

insulation Material that stops the travel of electricity (electrical insulation) or heat (heat insulation).

insulator A poor conductor of electricity or of heat.

integral Built into, as part of the whole.

interchangeability The manufacture of similar parts to close tolerance so that any one of the parts can be substituted for another in a device, and the part will fit and operate properly; the basis of mass production.

kerf The space from which the metal has been removed by a cutting process.

kilogram (kg) In the metric system, a unit of weight and mass; approximately equal to 2.2 pounds.

kilometer (km) In the metric system, a unit of linear measure equal to 0.621 mile.

kinetic energy The energy of motion; the energy stored in a moving body through its momentum; for example, the kinetic energy stored in a rotating flywheel.

kingpin In older cars and trucks, the steel pin on which the steering knuckle pivots; attaches the steering knuckle to the knuckle support or axle.

knuckle A steering knuckle; a front-suspension part that acts as a hinge to support a front wheel and permits it to be turned to steer the car. The knuckle pivots on ball joints or, in older cars, on kingpins.

knurl A series of ridges, formed on the outer surface of a material.

lacquer A type of paint that dries or cures through evaporation of solvents only, without chemical reaction. In a lacquer, the binder is made up of solid particles.

lamb's-wool bonnet A round pad of lamb's wool used for final polishing.

laminated Made up of several thin sheets or layers.

lamp A divisible assembly that provides a light; contains a bulb or other light source and sometimes a lens and reflector.

lap joint A welded joint in which two overlapped parts are connected by means of fillet, plug, slot, spot, projection, or seam welds.

leak detector Any device used to locate an opening where refrigerant may escape from an air conditioner. Common types are flame, electronic, dye, and soap bubbles.

lifting A condition in which a refinish paint is applied over a paint coating, causing the original coat to separate from the surface to which it was applied.

light A gas-filled bulb enclosing a wire that flows brightly when an electric current passes through it; a lamp. Also, any visible radiant energy.

linkage-type power steering A type of power steering in which the power-steering units (power cylinder and control valve) are part of the steering linkage; frequently a bolt-on type of unit.

liquid line In an air conditioner, hose that connects the receiver-dehydrator outlet and the thermostatic-expansion valve or orifice tube inlet. High-pressure liquid refrigerant flows through the line.

liter (L) In the metric system, a measure of volume; approximately equal to 0.26 gallons (U.S.) or about 61 cubic inches. Used as a metric measure of engine-cylinder displacement; 33.8 fluid ounces.

low-pressure line *See* Suction line.

low-pressure vapor line *See* Suction line.

lower beam A headlight beam intended to illuminate the road ahead of the vehicle when meeting or following another vehicle.

LUCITE DuPont's name for acrylic lacquer; introduced in 1956.

machining The process of using a machine to remove metal from a metal part.

mag wheel Name given to many types of styled-chrome, aluminum, offset, or wide-rim wheel.

Magna-Flux A process in which an electromagnet and a special magnetic powder are used to detect cracks in iron and steel which might otherwise be invisible to the naked eye.

make A distinctive name applied to a group of vehicles produced by one manufacturer; may be further subdivided into car lines, body types, etc.

malfunction Improper or incorrect operation.

manifold gauge set A high-pressure and a low-pressure gauge mounted together as a set, used for checking pressures in the air-conditioning system.

manufacturer Any person, firm, or corporation engaged in the production or assembly of motor vehicles or other products.

masking Covering of areas not to be painted.

mass production The manufacture of interchangeable parts and similar products in large quantities.

master cylinder The liquid-filled cylinder in the hydraulic braking system or clutch where hydraulic pressure is developed when the driver depresses a foot pedal.

matter Anything that has weight and occupies space.

measuring The act of determining the size, capacity, or quantity of an object.

mechanism A system of interrelated parts that make up a working assembly.

member Any essential part of a machine or assembly.

metal conditioner An acid-type cleaner that removes rust and corrosion from bare metal and etches it for better adhesion. Also forms a film which inhibits further corrosion.

metal-finishing marks (sand scratches) The result of poor surface preparation techniques, such as gouging by coarse grinder disks or files, poor sanding, or the use of too coarse a sandpaper. These marks were not removed in the metal-finish operation or properly filled and surfaced with putty glaze.

metallic paints Lacquers or enamels in which small metal flakes (usually aluminum) are added to the color pigment to give a metallic effect.

meter (m) A unit of linear measure in the metric system, equal to 39.37 inches. Also, the name given to any test instrument that measures a property of substance passing through it, as an ammeter measures electric current. Also, any device that measures and controls the flow of a substance passing through it.

millimeter (mm) In the metric system, a unit of linear measure, approximately equal to 0.039 inch.

mineral spirits A petroleum product commonly called paint thinner which may be used as a lubricant for wet sanding.

mist coat A coat of rich, slow evaporating thinner with little or no color added.

model year The production period for new motor vehicles or new engines, designated by the calendar year in which the period ends.

modification An alteration; a change from the original.

moisture Humidity, dampness, wetness, or very small drops of water.

mold A hollow form into which molten metal or plastic is poured and allowed to harden.

molding clips Clips that hold metal trim to a panel.

molecule The smallest particle into which a substance can be divided and still retain the properties of the substance.

motor A device that converts electric energy into mechanical energy; for example, the starting motor.

motor vehicle A vehicle propelled by other than muscle power, usually mounted on rubber tires, which does not run on rails or tracks.

mottling A painting problem with metallics in which the coat is so wet that the metal flakes float together to form a spotty or dappled effect.

mph Abbreviation for miles per hour, a unit of speed.

muffler In the engine exhaust system, a device through which the exhaust gases must pass and which reduces the exhaust noise. In an air-conditioning system, a device to minimize pumping sounds from the compressor.

neoprene A synthetic rubber that is not affected by chemicals harmful to natural rubber.

neutral In a transmission, the setting in which all gears are disengaged and the output shaft is disconnected from the drive wheels.

neutral flame A gas flame wherein the portion used is neither oxidizing nor carburizing.

neutral-start switch A switch wired into the ignition switch to prevent engine cranking unless the transmission shift lever is in NEUTRAL.

NHTSA Abbreviation for National Highway Traffic Safety Administration.

noble metals Metals (such as gold, silver, platinum, and palladium) which do not readily oxidize or enter into other chemical reactions, but do promote reactions between other substances. Platinum and palladium are used as catalysts in catalytic converters.

normal surface of metal The general contour of the part excluding any local deformations.

nut A removable fastener used with a bolt to lock pieces together; made by threading a hole through the center of a piece of metal which has been shaped to a standard size.

O ring A type of sealing ring, made of a special rubberlike material; in use, the O ring is compressed into a groove to provide the sealing action.

odometer The meter that indicates the total distance a vehicle has traveled, in miles or kilometers; usually located in the speedometer.

oil pan The detachable lower part of the engine, made of plastic or sheet metal, which encloses the crankcase and acts as an oil reservoir.

oil-pressure indicator A gauge that indicates to the driver that there is adequate oil pressure in the engine lubricating system.

one-wire system On automobiles, use of the car body, engine, and frame as a path for the grounded side of the electric circuits; eliminates the need for a second wire as a return path to the battery or alternator.

open circuit In an electric circuit, a break or opening which prevents the passage of current.

orange peel A rough texture in the paint resembling the skin of an orange, caused by failure of the sprayed paint film to flow out smoothly.

original finish The finish applied to the vehicle at time of manufacture.

overflow Spilling of the excess of a substance; also, to run or spill over the sides of a container, usually because of overfilling.

overflow tank *See* Expansion tank.

overhaul To completely disassemble a unit, clean and inspect all parts, reassemble it with the original or new parts, and make all adjustments necessary for proper operation.

overheat To heat excessively; also, to become excessively hot.

overlap Protrusion of weld metal at the toe of a weld beyond the limits of fusion.

overspray Droplets of paint from a spray gun which fall on areas where they are not wanted.

oxidation The combining of a material with oxygen; rusting is slow oxidation, and combustion is rapid oxidation. A chemical reaction, between the oxygen in the air and a substance in the paint, during which oxygen is absorbed from the air by the paint.

oxidizing flames A gas flame with excess oxygen having an oxidizing effect on weld area.

oxy-acetylene welding A gas-welding process wherein the welding heat is obtained from the combustion of oxygen and acetylene.

oxygen (O) A colorless, tasteless, odorless, gaseous element which makes up about 21 percent of air. Capable of combining rapidly with all elements except the inert gases in the oxidation process called burning. Combines very slowly with many metals in the oxidation process called rusting.

oxygen cutting A process of severing ferrous metals by means of the chemical action of oxygen on elements in the base metal at high temperatures.

paint remover A chemical which reacts with the old finish to lift it from a base surface or which breaks down an old finish by liquefying it. The old finish can then be easily wiped off. Also called paint stripper.

parking brake Mechanically operated brake that is independent of the foot-operated service brakes on the vehicle; set when the vehicle is parked.

particle A very small piece of metal, dirt, or other impurity.

pass The weld metal deposited by one general progression along the axis of a weld.

passenger car Any four-wheeled motor vehicle manufactured primarily for use on streets and highways and carrying 10 passengers or fewer.

pawl An arm, pivoted so that its free end can fit into a detent, slot, or groove at certain times to hold a part stationary.

peeling The separation of a paint film from the surface to which it has been applied.

peen To mushroom or spread the end of a pin or rivet.

penetration The penetration, or depth of fusion, of a weld is the distance from the original surface of the base metal to that point at which fusion ceases.

pick hammer A metal-working hammer with a flat face on one side of the head and a point on the other side.

pigment Finely ground particles in the paint which give it its color, durability, and hiding ability.

pilot shaft A shaft that is used to align parts and that is removed before final installation of the parts; a dummy shaft.

pinchweld Two metal flanges pointing in the same direction and spot-welded together.

pinholing Tiny holes that form in the topcoat or undercoat.

pivot A pin or shaft upon which another part rests or turns.

plastic gasket compound A plastic paste which can be squeezed out of a tube to make a gasket in any shape.

pneumatic tool A power tool driven by compressed air.

polisher A portable electric or air-driven motor used with various pads and bonnets to polish a paint film; usually operates at 1700 to 1900 rpm.

polishing Rubbing action using a fine abrasive compound, which helps make a surface smooth and lustrous.

polishing compound Fine abrasive paste for smoothing and polishing a paint film.

polishing pad A round tufted cotton pad made to fit a polisher.

poor drying (hardness) Softness in a paint film when it should be harder.

porosity The presence of gas pockets or inclusions in a weld.

postheating Heat applied after welding or cutting operations.

power brakes A brake system that uses vacuum and atmospheric pressure to provide most of the force required for braking.

power cylinder An operating cylinder which produces the power to actuate a mechanism. Both power brakes and power-steering units contain power cylinders.

power plant The engine or power source of a vehicle.

power steering A steering system that uses hydraulic pressure (from a pump) to multiply the driver's steering force.

power tool A tool whose power source is not muscle power; a tool powered by air or electricity.

power train The mechanisms that carry the rotary motion developed in the engine to the car wheels; includes the clutch, transmission, drive shaft, differential, and axles.

PR Abbreviation for ply rating; a measure of the strength of a tire, based on the strength of a single ply of designated construction.

preheating Heat applied before welding or cutting operations.

press fit A fit (between two parts) so tight that one part has to be pressed into the other, usually with an arbor press or hydraulic press.

pressure Force per unit area, or force divided by area. Usually measured in pounds per square inch (psi) and kilopascals (kPa).

pressure bleeder A piece of shop equipment that uses air pressure to force brake fluid into the brake system for bleeding.

pressure cap A radiator cap, with valves, which causes the cooling system to operate under pressure at a somewhat higher and more efficient temperature.

pressure regulator A device which operates to prevent excessive pressure from developing.

pressure-relief valve A valve in the line that opens to relieve excessive pressures.

pressure-sensing line In an air conditioner, a line that prevents the compressor suction pressure from dropping below a predetermined pressure. It opens the thermostatic expansion valve, allowing liquid refrigerant to flood the evaporator.

pressure tester An instrument that clamps in the radiator filler neck; used to pressure-test the cooling system for leaks.

pressurize To apply more than atmospheric pressure to a gas or liquid.

preventive maintenance The systematic inspection of a vehicle to detect and correct failures, either before they occur or before they develop into major defects. A procedure for economically maintaining a vehicle in a satisfactory and dependable operating condition.

primer A base or undercoat next to the metal or substrate which improves adhesion of the topcoat.

primer-surfacer A primer with solids in it to promote adhesion of the topcoat and fill minor surface imperfections to provide a smooth level surface.

printed circuit An electric circuit made by applying a conductive material to an insulating board in a pattern that provides current paths between components mounted on or connected to the board.

prussian blue A blue pigment; in solution, useful in determining the area of contact between two surfaces.

psi Abbreviation for pounds per square inch; a unit of pressure.

psig Abbreviation for pounds per square inch of gauge pressure.

puller Generally, a shop tool used to separate two

closely fitted parts without damage. Often contains a screw, or several screws, which can be turned to gradually apply force.

pulley A metal wheel with a V-shaped groove around the rim; drives, or is driven by, a belt.

pump A device that transfers gas or liquid from one place to another.

punch A hand-held tool that is struck with a hammer to drive one piece of metal from inside another.

purge To remove, evacuate, or empty trapped substances from a space. In an air conditioner, to remove moisture and air from the refrigerant system by flushing with nitrogen or refrigerant.

putty A thick material used to fill flaws in the panel surface that are too large to be filled by primer-surfacer.

quarter panel A major panel forming the rear corner sections of the body. The front edge of the panel forms the rear body lock piller.

quick charger A battery charger that produces a high charging current and substantially charges, or boosts, a battery in a short time.

R&I Remove a part or assembly from a vehicle to facilitate other work and reinstall the same part or assembly on the vehicle. Includes alignment that can be done by shifting the part or assembly.

R&R Remove a part or assembly from a vehicle; transfer bolted, riveted, or clipped-on parts to new part; and install part or assembly on the vehicle. Includes alignment or adjustment that can be done by shifting the part or assembly.

radiator In the cooling system, the device that removes heat from coolant passing through it; takes hot coolant from the engine and returns the coolant to the engine at a lower temperature.

radiator pressure cap *See* Pressure cap.

ratio Proportion; the relative amounts of two or more substances in a mixture. Usually expressed as a numerical relationship, as in 2 : 1.

reamer A round metal-cutting tool with a series of sharp cutting edges; enlarges a hole when turned in it.

rear compartment lid A door, made up of an inner and outer panel, located over the rear luggage compartment.

rear compartment pan That part of the underbody forming the floor in the luggage compartment.

rear end panel A body panel running across the rearmost part of the body immediately under the rear compartment opening.

rear quarter window The rearmost side window located in the rear quarter panel. Not used in all body styles.

rear seat pan A part of the underbody assembly located under the rear seat.

reassembly Putting the parts of a device back together.

recapping A form of tire repair in which a cap of new tread material is placed on the old casing and cemented or vulcanized into place.

reciprocating motion Motion of an object between two limiting positions; motion in a straight line back and forth or up and down.

reducer A solvent used to reduce or dilute enamels.

refrigerant A substance used to transfer heat in an air conditioner through a cycle of evaporation and condensation.

relative humidity The actual moisture content of the air, as a percentage of the total moisture that the air can hold at a given temperature.

relay An electrical device that opens or closes a circuit or circuits in response to a voltage signal.

relief valve A valve that opens when a preset pressure is reached. This relieves or prevents excessive pressures.

remove and install (R&I) The removal of a part and the reinstallation of the same part in its original position, and any inspection, adjustment, cleaning, and lubrication operations which may be required.

remove and reinstall (R&R) To perform a series of servicing procedures on an original part or assembly; includes removal, inspection, lubrication, all necessary adjustments, and reinstallation.

replace To remove a used part or assembly and install a new part or assembly in its place; includes cleaning, lubricating, and adjusting as required.

respirator A breathing mask used to filter particles out of the air being breathed.

retarder A very slow-drying solvent that slows paint drying time by reducing the rate of solvent evaporation. An additive; opposite of drier.

return spring A "pull-back" spring, often used in brake systems.

rivet A semipermanent fastener used to hold two pieces together.

rocker panel The inner panel and outer panel which form a box located at the outer edge of the floor pan, immediately below the doors. It extends from the front body hinge pillar to the rear body lock pillar.

roof panel The body upper closure.

roof rail A box consisting of an inner and outer panel. It extends from the front end frame to the rear quarter side panel forming the upper line of the door body openings.

rotary The motion of a part that continually rotates or turns.

rpm Abbreviation for revolutions per minute, a measure of rotational speed.

rubbing compound An abrasive paste (coarser than polishing compound) that smoothes the paint film.

ruler A graduated straightedge used for measuring distances, usually up to 1 foot.

runout Wobble.

rust A condition resulting from weathering (oxidation) of exposed or insufficiently protected or prepared metal.

rust inhibiting Slows down rusting or oxidation of metals.

SAE Abbreviation for Society of Automative Engineers.

safety Freedom from injury or danger.

safety rim A wheel rim with a hump on the inner edge of the ledge on which the tire bead rides. The hump helps hold the tire on the rim in case of a blowout.

safety stand A pinned or locked device placed under a car to support its weight after the car has been raised with a floor jack or lift. Also called a car stand or jack stand.

sags A paint film that drips or runs because of applying too much paint.

sander A power tool designed to sand finishes. May be powered by electricity or air and can be straight-line reciprocal, orbital, or rotary-type.

sanding A scrubbing action using an abrasive material to remove defects, smooth surfaces to be painted, and improve adhesion of paint coats.

sanding block A hard, flexible block to provide a smooth backing for hand sanding.

sanding sludge Particles of paint which have been loosened during sanding and mixed with water or mineral spirits to form a mudlike substance.

sand-scratch swelling Swelling in sandscratches in the old finish caused by solvents in the topcoat being applied.

sand-scratches Metal-finish marks or scratches, usually caused by poor surface-preparation techniques.

Schrader valve A spring-loaded valve through which a connection can be made to a refrigeration system; also used in tires.

scratched The appearance of the finish when it has been damaged by the penetration of a sharp object.

screens Pieces of fine-mesh metal fabric; used to prevent solid particles from circulating through any liquid or vapor system and damaging vital moving parts. In an air conditioner, screens are located in the receiver-dehydrator, thermostatic expansion valve or orifice tube, and compressor.

screw A metal fastener with threads that can be turned into a threaded hole, usually with a screwdriver. There are many different types and sizes of screws.

screwdriver A hand tool used to loosen or tighten screws.

seal A material shaped around a part, used to close off a compartment.

sealed-beam headlight A headlight that contains the filament, reflector, and lens in a single sealed unit.

sealer An intercoat between the topcoat and primer-surfacer or old topcoat. Promotes adhesion and helps prevent sand-scratch swelling.

sealer under paint Types of dirt under paint resulting from poor prepaint cleanup operations.

seat The surface upon which another part rests, as a valve seat.

seat adjuster A device that permits forward and backward (and sometimes upward and downward) movement of the front seat of a vehicle.

self-locking screw A screw that locks itself in place, without the use of a separate nut or lock washer.

self-tapping screw A screw that cuts its own threads as it is turned into an unthreaded hole.

service manual A book published annually by each vehicle manufacturer, listing the specifications and service procedures for each make and model of vehicle. Also called a shop manual.

setscrew A type of metal fastener that holds a collar or gear on a shaft when its point is turned down into the shaft.

settling The tendency of solids (pigment and binder) in a paint to drop to the bottom of the container.

shackle The swinging support by which one end of a leaf spring is attached to the car frame.

sheet metal Parts that are not integral with the body, such as bumpers, grille, hood, front fenders, and gravel guards.

shift lever The lever used to change gears in a transmission.

shim A slotted strip of metal used to make small front-end alignment on many cars; also used to make small corrections in the position of body sheet metal and other parts.

shimmy Rapid oscillation. In wheel shimmy, for example, the front wheel turns in and out alternately and rapidly; this causes the front end of the car to oscillate, or shimmy.

shock absorber A device placed at each vehicle wheel to regulate spring rebounds and compression.

shop layout The locations of aisles, work areas, machine tools, etc., in a shop.

shrink fit A tight fit of one part into another, achieved by heating or cooling one part and then assembling it to the other part. A heated part will shrink on cooling to provide the tight fit; a cooled part will expand on warming to provide the tight fit.

shroud A hood placed around an engine fan to improve fan action.

sight glass In a car air conditioner, a viewing glass or window set in the refrigerant line, usually in the top of the receiver-dehydrator; the sight glass allows a visual check of the refrigerant passing from the receiver to the evaporator.

silicone An ingredient in waxes and polishes which makes them smooth and slippery to the touch. The primary cause of fisheyes in refinish coatings if not removed.

silicone and wax remover A chemical solution used to remove grease, tar, and wax from a paint during surface preparation.

skinning Formation of a film on the top of the liquid in a container of paint. Also the formation of a film on heavy or thick topcoats before the solvents in the underlayer of the topcoat have evaporated.

socket wrench A wrench that fits entirely over or around the head of a bolt.

soldering Joining pieces of metal with solder, flux, and heat.

solids The percentage, on a weight basis, of solid material in a paint after the solvents have evaporated.

solvent A chemical liquid that dissolves, dilutes, or liquefies another liquid or solid. Reducers, thinners, and cleaners are solvents.

solvent popping Bubbles which form in a paint film.

solvent tank In the shop, a tank of cleaning fluid, in which most parts are brushed and washed clean.

specific gravity The weight per unit volume of a substance as compared with the weight per unit volume of water.

specifications Information provided by the manufacturer that describes each automotive system and its components, operation, and clearances. Also, the service procedures that must be followed for a system to operate properly.

specs Short for specifications.

speed The rate of motion; for vehicles, measured in miles per hour or kilometers per hour.

speedometer An instrument that indicates vehicle speed; usually driven from the transmission.

spray booth A room which provides the proper lighting and ventilation required to properly spray paint.

spray gun A tool which uses air pressure to atomize paint.

spring A device that changes shape under stress or force, but returns to its original shape when the stress or force is removed; the component of the automotive suspension system that absorbs road shocks by flexing and twisting.

sprung weight That part of the car which is supported on springs (includes the engine, frame, and body).

squeak A high-pitched noise of short duration.

squeal A continuous, high-pitched, low-volume noise.

squeegee A flexible rubber or plastic block used to wipe off wet-sanded areas and apply putty.

stabilizer bar An interconnecting shaft between the two lower suspension arms; reduces body roll on turns.

stains The result of surface contamination which has affected the color of the finish.

steam cleaner A machine used for cleaning large parts with a spray of steam, often mixed with soap.

steering-and-ignition lock A device that locks the ignition switch in the OFF position and locks the steering wheel so it cannot be turned.

steering gear That part of the steering system that is located at the lower end of the steering shaft; carries the rotary motion of the steering wheel to the car wheels for steering.

steering knuckle The front-wheel spindle which is supported by upper and lower ball joints and by the wheel; the part on which a front wheel is mounted and which is turned for steering.

steering system The mechanism that enables the driver to turn the wheels for changing the direction of vehicle movement.

steering wheel The wheel, at the top of the steering shaft, which is used by the driver to guide, or steer, the car.

stepped thickness gauge A feeler gauge which has a thin tip, of a known dimension and is thicker along the rest of the gauge; a "go–no-go" feeler gauge.

stoplight switch The switch that turns the stoplights on and off as the brakes are applied and released.

stoplights Lights at the rear of a vehicle which indicate that the brakes are being applied to slow or stop the vehicle.

storage battery A device that changes chemical energy into electrical energy; that part of the electric system which acts as a reservoir for electric energy, storing it in chemical form.

strainer A fine screen used to filter out undesirable particles in paint before spraying.

streamlining The shaping of a car body or truck cab so that it minimizes air resistance and can be moved through the air with less energy.

stripper *See* Paint remover.

strut A bar that connects the lower control arm to the car frame; used when the lower control arm is of the type that is attached to the frame at only one point. Also called a brake reaction rod.

stud A headless bolt that is threaded on both ends.

stud extractor A special tool used to remove a broken stud or bolt.

substrate The surface of the material to be painted. May be an old finish or an unpainted surface.

suction line In an air conditioner, the tube that connects the evaporator outlet and the compressor inlet. Low-pressure refrigerant vapor flows through this line.

suction throttling valve In an air conditioner, a valve located between the evaporator and the compressor; controls the temperature of the air flowing from the evaporator, to prevent freezing of moisture on the evaporator.

suspension The system of springs and other parts which supports the upper part of a vehicle on its axles and wheels.

suspension arm In the front suspension, one of the arms pivoted on the frame at one end, and on the steering-knuckle support at the other end.

sway bar *See* Stabilizer bar.

switch A device that opens and closes an electric circuit.

tachometer A device for measuring engine speed, or revolutions per minute.

tack rag A cloth saturated with diluted varnish to make it sticky so it will pick up dust and dirt particles.

taillights Steady-burning low-intensity lights used on the rear of a vehicle.

tank unit The part of the fuel-indicating system that is mounted in the fuel tank.

tap A tool used for cutting threads in a hole.

temperature The measure of heat intensity or concentration, in degrees. Temperature is not a measure of heat quantity.

temperature gauge A gauge that indicates to the driver the temperature of the coolant in the engine cooling system.

temperature indicator *See* Temperature gauge.

temperature-sending unit A device in contact with the engine coolant whose electrical resistance changes as the coolant temperature increases or decreases; these changes control the movement of the indicator needle of the temperature gauge.

template A gauge or pattern, commonly a thin metal plate or board, used as a guide to establish the form of the work to be done.

thermal   Of or pertaining to heat.

thermometer   An instrument which measures heat intensity (temperature) by the thermal expansion of a liquid.

thermostat   A device for the automatic regulation of temperature; usually contains a temperature-sensitive element that expands or contracts to open or close off the flow of air, gas, or liquid.

thin paint   A condition in which not enough paint has been applied or an excessive amount has been removed by abrasion or erosion.

thinner   A solvent used to thin or dilute lacquers.

thread chaser   A device similar to a die that is used to clean threads.

threaded insert   A threaded coil that is used to restore the original thread size to a hole with damaged threads; the hole is drilled oversize and tapped, and the insert is threaded into the tapped hole.

tie rods   In the steering system, the rods that link the pitman arm to the steering-knuckle arms; small steel components that connect the front wheels to the steering mechanism.

tilt steering wheel   A type of steering wheel that can be tilted at various angles, through a flex joint in the steering shaft.

tire   The casing-and-tread assembly (with or without a tube) that is mounted on a car wheel to provide pneumatically cushioned contact and traction with the road.

topcoats   The final layers of paint material such as lacquers or enamels used to give the vehicle color and resistance to corrosion.

torque   Turning or twisting force; usually measured in pound-feet or newton-meters. Also, a turning force such as that required to tighten a connection.

torque wrench   A wrench that indicates the amount of torque being applied.

touch-up paint   A pastelike topcoat that comes in a tube. Used for touching up minor surface damage.

tracking   Rear wheels following directly behind (in the tracks of) the front wheels.

tramp   Up-and-down motion (hopping) of the front wheels at higher speeds, due to unbalanced wheels or excessive wheel runout. Also called high-speed shimmy.

transmission   An assembly of gears that provides the different gear ratios, as well as neutral and reverse, through which engine power is transmitted to the differential to rotate the drive wheels.

tread   That part of the tire that contacts the road. It is the thickest part of the tire, and is cut with grooves to provide traction for driving and stopping.

trim   Any part that is attached to the body after it is painted. Usually, divided into hard trim, such as moldings, and soft trim, such as upholstery.

trim finishing molding   A decorative molding used on the interior trim of the doors and quarters.

trouble diagnosis   The detective work necessary to find the cause of a trouble.

turn signal   *See* Directional signal.

turn under   The portion of the body surface below the widest part of the body that sweeps down and toward the center line of the body.

twist drill   A conventional drill bit.

two-tone   Two different colors on a paint job; to apply two colors on the same paint job.

U bolt   An iron rod with threads on both ends bent into the shape of a U and fitted with a nut at each end.

under-dash unit   The hang-on type air-conditioning system installed under the dash, usually after the vehicle leaves the factory. Air outlets are in the evaporator case, and the system normally uses only recirculated air. The discharge air temperature is controlled by a cycling thermostatic expansion switch or a suction throttling valve.

underbody assembly   A welded assembly of metal stampings consisting mainly of a floor pan, rear seat pan, and rear compartment pan. It forms the body closure next to the chassis.

undercoats   Layers of paint material such as primer-surfacer, putty glaze, and sealer used to provide a smooth base for the topcoats. They help the topcoat stick to the surface and prevent rust and corrosion.

unit   An assembly or device that can perform its function only if it is not further divided into its components.

unitized construction   A type of automotive construction in which the frame and body parts are welded together to form a single unit.

universal joint   In the power train, a jointed connection in the drive shaft that permits the driving angle to change.

unsprung weight   The weight of that part of the car which is not supported on springs; for example, the wheels and tires.

upper beam   A headlight beam intended primarily for distant illumination; not for use when meeting or following other vehicles.

vacuum   Negative gauge pressure, or a pressure less than atmospheric pressure. Vacuum can be measured in psi, but is usually measured in inches or millimeters or mercury (Hg); a reading of 30 inches [762 mm] Hg would indicate a perfect vacuum.

vacuum motor   A small motor, powered by intake-manifold vacuum; used for jobs such as raising and lowering headlight doors.

vacuum pump   A mechanical device used to evacuate the refrigerant system of an air conditioner.

vacuum switch   A switch that closes or opens its contacts in response to changing vacuum conditions.

valve   A device that can be opened or closed to allow or stop the flow of a liquid or gas.

vapor   A gas; any substance in the gaseous state, as distinguished from the liquid or solid state.

vaporization   A change of state from liquid to vapor or gas, by evaporation or boiling; a general term including both evaporation and boiling.

vehicle   All of a paint except the pigment. This includes solvents, diluents, resins, gums, driers, etc.

vehicle identification number (VIN)   The number assigned to each vehicle by its manufacturer, primarily for registration and identification purposes.

vent An opening through which air can leave an enclosed chamber.

ventilation The circulating of fresh air through any space, to replace impure air.

vibration A rapid back-and-forth motion; an oscillation.

VIN Abbreviation for vehicle identification number.

vinyl tape A plastic type which has a pressure-sensitive adhesive and which is used as an accent stripe.

viscous Thick; tending to resist flowing.

vise A gripping device; used to hold a part steady while it is being worked on.

volatile Evaporating readily. For example, Refrigerant-12 is volatile (evaporates quickly) at room temperature.

volatility A measure of the ease with which a liquid evaporates; has a direct relationship to the flammability of a fuel.

water spotting Damage caused by exposing to snow, rain, or dew a new paint film that has not completely dried. Appears as a rough area in the paint or as a circular, whitish water residue embedded in the surface.

weight distribution The percentage of a vehicle's total weight that rests on each axle.

weld A localized consolidation of metals by a welding process.

weld metal The metal resulting from the fusion of the base metal or the base metal and the filler metal.

welding The process of joining pieces of metal by fusing them together with heat.

welding procedure The detailed methods and practices involved in the production of a welded structure.

welding rod Filler metal, in wire or rod form, used in the welding process.

welding tip A gas-torch tip especially adapted for welding.

welding torch A device used in gas welding for mixing and controlling the gases.

wet spots Areas where the paint fails to dry and adhere uniformly; generally caused by grease spots, finger marks, etc.

wheel alignment A series of tests and adjustments to ensure that wheels and tires are properly positioned on the vehicle.

wheel tramp Tendency for a wheel to move up and down so it repeatedly bears down hard, or "tramps" on the road. Sometimes called high-speed shimmy.

wheelbase The distance between the center lines of the front and rear axles. For trucks with tandem rear axles, the rear center line is considered to be midway between the two rear axles.

wheelhouse An inner body housing over the rear wheel.

window regulator A device for opening and closing a window; usually operated by a crank.

windshield pillar The structural member joining the shroud assembly to the roof panel and defining the sides of the windshield opening.

windshield wiper A mechanism which moves a rubber blade back and forth to wipe the windshield; operated electrically.

wire thickness gauge A set of round wires of known diameters; used to check clearances between electrical contacts.

wiring harness A group of individually insulated wires, wrapped together to form a neat, easily installed bundle.

work The changing of the position of an object against an opposing force; measured in foot-pounds, meter-kilograms, or joules. The product of a force and the distance through which it acts.

wrench A tool designed for tightening and loosening nuts and bolts.

wrinkling Skinning of a thick or heavy coat of paint before the underpart of the film has properly dried, resulting in wrinkling.

■

Occupational Safety and Health
    Administration (OSHA), 25
Oil-can damage, 126, 132
Oil cooler, transmission, 123–
    124
Orange peel in paint, 354
Orbital sander, 63
OSHA (Occupational Safety and
    Health Administration), 25
Overcorrection in body
    straightening, 169
Overlays, wood-grain (see
    Wood-grain overlays)
Oxyacetylene (gas) welding
    equipment, use of, 82–87
    [See also Welding,
        oxyacetylene (gas)]
Oxygen cylinder, 83

■

Paint jobs, typical, 342–345
Paint paddle, 311
Paint shaker, 65
Paint spray gun (see Spray
    guns)
Paint strainer, 311–312
Paint stripper, 339
Paint viscosity, checking, 320–
    321
Painting, 310–316
    of car body, steps in, 310–311
    custom, 361–367
        designs in, 365–367
        equipment for, 361–364
        surface preparation for,
            364–365
    materials for, 311–315
    preparing surface for, 336–341
        for complete repainting, 341
        for custom painting, 364–
            365
        dusting off surface, 337
        paint stripping, 339
        removing old paint, 338–339
        sandblasting, 338
        for spot repair, 338
        steps in, 337
        using precleaning solvent,
            337–338
        washing, 337
        wet sanding, 338
    safety precautions in, 301
Painting problems, 346–360
    bleeding, 346
    blistering, 347
    blushing, 347
    bubbles, 347
    chalking, 348
    checking, 349–350
    chipping, 348
    cracking, 349–350
    craters, 350
    dirt in paint, 350–351
    fisheyes, 350
    industrial fallout, 352–353

Painting problems (Cont.)
    lifting, 353
    mottle, 348–349
    orange peel, 354
    overspray, 354–356
    peeling, 356
    pop-ups, 347
    runs, 357–358
    rust, 354, 357
    sags, 357–358
    skips, 359
    stains, 358–359
    water spotting, 359–360
    wrinkles, 360
Paints, automotive, 328–335
    acrylic, 329–331, 344
    additives, 335
    binder, 328–329
    buying, 331–333
    for chassis, 330
    enamel, 329, 330
    lacquer, 329–330
    metallic, 331, 343–344
    pigments, 328
    for trunk, 331
    urethane, 330
    vehicle, 329
Panel, body (see Body panels)
Panelspotter, 112–113
Paper towels for paint jobs, 311
Patching a panel, 144–146
Peeling of paint, 356
Perimeter frame, 148
Pick-and-file method, 140
Pigment, paint, 328
Pinstriping brushes, 363
Pitch, thread, 34
Plastic automotive parts, 190–
    197
    repairing, 191–194
    types of, identifying, 190
Plastic body filler (see Body
    filler, plastic)
Plastic body panels, 17–18
Plastic welding (see Welding,
    plastic)
Pliers, 48–49
Pneumatic tools (see Air tools)
Polish, 315–316
Polisher, power, 93
Polyester resin, 183
Polypropylene plastic, 190
Polyurethane enamel, 330
Pop rivets, 40–41
Pop-ups in paint, 347
Power-driven equipment, use of,
    30
Power jack, hydraulic, 76
Power polisher, 93
Power tools, electric, 60–65
    (See also specific tools, for
        example: Drill; Sander)
Press, hydraulic, 76
Press-fit, 33
Pressure-feed spray gun, 319
Prevailing-torque fasteners, 38–
    39
Primer, 333
Primer-sealer, 334

Primer-surfacer, 333–334
Pry bars, 53, 137
Pull rods, 51, 133–135
Pull tabs, 133–135
Pullback, 132
Pulling equipment, safety
    cautions in use of, 161
Punches, 56
Putty, spot and glaze, 314–315

■

Quarter window, 226
Quenching, 143–144
Quick coupler for air tools, 66–
    67

■

Radiator, cooling-system, 123–
    124
Ragtop, 19
Ram:
    hydraulic, 135
    spread, 137–138
Ratchet, air, 69
Rear-window service, 266
Reciprocating sander, 62–63,
    176
Regulator for oxyacetylene
    welding, 84–85
Resin, 190
Respirator, 26
    for fiberglass work, 184
Ribbon design, 365
Rivets, 40–41
Roofs, special, 250–256
    sun, 22, 252–256
    vinyl (see Vinyl roof)
Rubbing compound, 315
Running a bead, 105

■

Safety in the shop, 25–31
Safety rules, 29–30
Safety stands, 29–30
Sag:
    correcting, 163–164
        in unitized bodies, 166
    frame, 154–157
Sandblasting, 338
Sander, 62–63, 68, 175–176
    air, 68
    belt, 63
    cautions in use of, 63
    disk, 175–176
    orbital, 63
    power, 62
    reciprocating, 62–63, 176
Sanding block, 314
Sandpaper:
    grit, 180
    for paint job, 313–314
Scrapers, 57
Screw threads, 34–38

1/00   3   9/99
12/01   5   4/01
5/04   (9)   3/04
12/06   12   2/06
9/15 (24) 8/12 LCT
7/17 (25) 2/7